# Strategies for Sustainable Territorial Development

Anna D'Auria
*University of Naples L'Orientale, Italy*

Javier Sanchez-Rivas Garcia
*Universidad de Sevilla, Spain*

IGI Global
Scientific Publishing
Publishing Tomorrow's Research Today

Vice President of Editorial — Melissa Wagner
Managing Editor of Acquisitions — Mikaela Felty
Managing Editor of Book Development — Jocelynn Hessler
Production Manager — Mike Brehm
Cover Design — Phillip Shickler

Published in the United States of America by
IGI Global Scientific Publishing
701 East Chocolate Avenue
Hershey, PA, 17033, USA
Tel: 717-533-8845
Fax: 717-533-8661
Website: https://www.igi-global.com E-mail: cust@igi-global.com



Library of Congress Cataloging-in-Publication Data

Library of Congress Cataloging-in-Publication Data

Names: D'Auria, Anna, DATE- editor. | Sánchez-Rivas García, Javier, editor.
Title: Strategies for sustainable territorial development / edited by Anna D'Auria, Javier Sánchez-Rivas García.
Description: Hershey, PA : IGI Global Scientific Publishing, [2025] | Includes bibliographical references and index. | Summary: "This volume aims to contribute to raising awareness about the importance of local resources as a lever for sustainable development, which can support the territory both in terms of economic growth and social progress"-- Provided by publisher.
Identifiers: LCCN 2024055452 (print) | LCCN 2024055453 (ebook) | ISBN 9798369370810 (hardcover) | ISBN 9798369370827 (paperback) | ISBN 9798369370834 (ebook)
Subjects: LCSH: Sustainable development.
Classification: LCC HC79.E5 S768155 2025 (print) | LCC HC79.E5 (ebook) | DDC 338.9/27--dc23/eng/20250115
LC record available at https://lccn.loc.gov/2024055452
LC ebook record available at https://lccn.loc.gov/2024055453

British Cataloguing in Publication Data
A Cataloguing in Publication record for this book is available from the British Library.

# Table of Contents

# Detailed Table of Contents

attractive brand image. Additionally, the findings from this chapter are anticipated to contribute to the scientific community and, fundamentally, to the local authorities of Tabuaço, facilitating the implementation of effective marketing and communication strategies for the town's economic and tourism development. This chapter provides insights into territorial marketing and regional development. Finally, avenues for future research will be proposed.



The impact of the European Structural and Investment Funds (ESIF) on regional economic development in the member states of the European Union is attracting increasing attention. Despite numerous studies, there is no consensus on the effects of ESIF on economic growth and regional cohesion. The study aims to contribute to this debate by examining the effects of ESIF on regional economic development in Bulgaria for the period 2007-2023. The methods used are descriptive, comparative, correlation and regression analysis. The results show that all six NUTS-2 regions are converging with the EU-27 average in terms of key development indicators, but regional disparities persist, as more developed regions absorb larger amounts of EU funding. ESIF have a positive effect on regional GDP, employment, gross fixed capital formation and household income, but do not demonstrate a significant impact on labor productivity and the percentage of people living at risk of poverty. The results are useful for policy makers to determine appropriate organizational and financial interventions.



Social capital in tourism is a key factor for sustainable territorial development. This, in turn, is related to other factors, such as environmental, economic and social factors. There are several methodologies for its measurement, such as Stakeholder Theory and the examination of interactions and relationships, known as Social Network Analysis (SNA), which are analysed in this chapter through their application in Ecuadorian cities as research context. Through these methodologies It has been possible to determine that there are different types of actors with attributes of power, legitimacy and urgency, the formation of networks or groups of actors that can also lead to greater or lesser participation and collaboration in a tourism destination.

Using Bushbuckridge Local Municipality as a case study, the study investigates how identifying cultural heritage tourism opportunities can unlock tourism activities that contribute to sustainable economic development. CHT is presented as a vehicle that can be utilised by the municipality and Bushbuckridge Local Economic Development Forum Management Committee (BLEDFMC) within the municipality to mitigate poverty alleviation and socio-economic development, thus addressing sustainable development. A qualitative desk study with a triangulation design was adopted for this study. Key findings revealed that a capacitated BLEDFMC is vital in leading and monitoring the process of identifying assets and opportunities, including linking these assets with key attractions in the area, supported by the municipality. It will also aim to address the primary needs of the communities and ensure fair benefits sharing in its true sense. This research advocates for a capacitated BLEDFMC that recognises the role of research, and local community participation, including the Gap analysis model.



Gastronomic tourism has grown significantly in recent years, acquiring interesting relevance due to its potential for enhancing endogenous resources in the destinations where it develops, which stimulates the local economy and promotes sustainable development. Based on the results of a survey conducted with 421 international gastronomic tourists, this chapter demonstrates that the expectations and level of satisfaction of gastronomic tourists with the experiences they enjoy during their trip influence their willingness to purchase (or recommend) a quality-certified gastronomic product, as well as their average daily expenditure during their stay at the destination. The results obtained are relevant for appraising the role of gastronomic tourism as a sustainable territorial development strategy.



Urban vitality is key to preserving and revitalizing heritage spaces, ensuring the history, culture, and identity of a place remain vibrant while promoting social integration and economic growth. The Andador 20 de Noviembre in Zapopan, Jalisco, Mexico, exemplifies this as a central axis of the city's historical and cultural life, offering a hub for social interaction through its commercial, gastronomic, and cultural activities. The Pilgrimage of Zapopan, a UNESCO-recognized event, further enhances this vitality by attracting millions and boosting the local economy. The interplay between the urban vitality of Andador 20 de Noviembre and the pilgrimage underscores the necessity of keeping such heritage spaces active. These places serve not only as historical witnesses but also as catalysts for social, cultural, and economic development. The study highlights the importance of preserving and promoting these spaces as dynamic centers of urban life, enriching the experiences of both inhabitants and visitors.

The study demonstrates, through empirical research on the development regions in Romania, that the average monthly income per household can be an element for evaluating the attractiveness of the regions for an adult, especially a young person, who is looking for a suitable job or an area in which to settle down and build a future. We considered factors that might be correlated with economic development in the region (GDP/place at the regional level, population occupancy rate, investments, turnover of active companies, tourist accommodation capacity, the employed population with higher education in the region). We built simple and multiple linear regression models, with data series from 2007-2019, obtained by processing data from the Statistical Yearbook of Romania (2008-2020). We concluded that all these factors are correlated with the size of the average monthly income indicator on a regional household. The results were interpreted and explained.



Low Carbon Tourism has elicited significant academic interest in recent years due its important role in the promotion of environmentally responsible destinations. The appearance of different climate problems, such as the generalised increase in temperatures, droughts or rising sea levels, has challenged the current economic model, with tourism being of the main economic actors responsible for this situation. The main objective of this article is to identify the lines of research related to Low Carbon Tourism through the application of mapping techniques. The content analysis performed, by applying the VOSviewer tool for the 2010-2024 period, allows the identification of four relevant lines of research: Sustainable Development in Tourism; Relationship between Carbon Footprint and Tourism; Effects of Climate Change in Tourism and Low Carbon Tourism in China; with Sustainable Development in Tourism; and Effects of Climate Change on Tourism being the lines with the greatest academic impact and relevance in the final years of the period that is the subject of this study.



This chapter aims to explore the impact of AI and its generative version on the sustainable development of Cultural Heritage. Narrowly, generative AI is the first technological innovation capable of producing creative work through textual or vocal input. Therefore, this is both an innovative opportunity for museums

vernacular architecture may provide. This paper will focus on important vernacular architecture styles of India and Central Asia.

# Preface

In response to growing global challenges, sustainable territorial development, which integrates economic, social, and environmental dimensions, is increasingly recognized as a key focus for governments, businesses, and communities globally, aiming for balanced and resilient development. This volume, *Strategies for Sustainable Territorial Development*, seeks to provide a comprehensive framework for understanding and addressing these challenges. In detail, by presenting a broad spectrum of innovative, diverse, and evidence-based strategies, the book serves as both a guide and a reference for regions striving toward sustainability. It draws upon the contributions of esteemed scholars and practitioners from various corners of the globe, offering an extensive exploration of sustainable development from a territorial perspective. In also analyse both the successes and the obstacles encountered in real-world applications, providing valuable insights into the dynamic and evolving landscape of sustainable territorial development.

Each chapter presents unique aspects of sustainability, from the role of corporate social responsibility (CSR) in fostering local community development, to the integration of renewable energy solutions in agricultural practices, and the exploration of cultural heritage as a driver for tourism and regional growth. Whether discussing collective impact strategies, energy innovations in agriculture, or the economic potential of low-carbon tourism, this collection of contributions serves as a valuable resource for policymakers, academics, and practitioners involved in sustainable territorial development.

Despite the diversity of topics, a common thread unites the chapters: the belief that territorial development is most effective when it is inclusive, flexible, and built upon collaboration. In addition, as emerges in the following description, the combination of theoretical analysis with concrete case studies, providing readers with a nuanced understanding of regional development complexities and showcasing successful initiatives, ensures that the book contributes not only to academic discourse but also to practical efforts aimed at implementing sustainable practices in the real world.

The first chapter, *The Collective Impact Approach for Sustainable Territorial Development*, written by Anna D'Auria and Alessandra De Chiara, delves into the Collective Impact (CI) framework as a means to promote sustainable territorial development. The authors explore how structured collaboration among various stakeholders—such as governments, businesses, non-profits, and local communities—can lead to meaningful, long-term development. Through detailed case studies, the chapter illustrates how the five key elements of CI—common agenda, shared measurement systems, mutually reinforcing activities, continuous communication, and backbone support—have successfully contributed to sustainability. It also addresses the challenges of power imbalances, rigidity, and inclusivity, offering practical recommendations for improving flexibility and equity within the CI framework.

The chapter entitled *Community-Based Corporate Social Responsibility in Businesses: Strategies and Initiatives*, by Pratap Mandal, examines the role of businesses in enhancing community well-being through CSR initiatives. This chapter emphasizes the importance of integrating community-focused CSR into business strategies to promote sustainable growth. By exploring various CSR models, including corporate philanthropy and services aimed at low-income communities, Mandal highlights the potential of businesses to drive societal benefits while improving their long-term success and reputation.

In *An Energy Perspective on the Role of Olive Groves in Sustainable Development in Andalusia*, Jesús Marquina, María Pablo-Romero, and Javier Sanchez-Rivas explore the potential of olive groves in Andalusia as a renewable energy source. The authors discuss the use of olive by-products for energy production and analyze the impact of public policies on these efforts. They highlight the challenges of waste collection and transportation costs, and the broader implications of energy policy changes, including the deregulation of renewable energy premiums in 2012, for regional sustainability.

The chapter by Vicente Fruet-Cardozo, José Valverde-Roda, Lorena Caridad-López del Río, and Rosario Brito-Guerrero, *Sustainable Development and Foreign Trade: Evaluating Macro-economic Indicators in the MENA Region*, provides a macroeconomic analysis of how foreign trade, particularly hydrocarbon exports, influences GDP per capita in the MENA region. This study emphasizes the growing importance of renewable energy and the need to diversify income sources to ensure sustainable growth in a region heavily dependent on fossil fuels.

In *Territorial Marketing and Region Development: An Exploratory Approach in Tabuaço (Portugal)*, Mariana Taveira Gouveia and Bruno Sousa examine the role of territorial branding in regional development. Using Tabuaço, Portugal, as a case study, they demonstrate how an attractive and recognizable regional brand can enhance tourism and economic development. The chapter concludes with practical recommendations for local authorities and suggestions for future research on the subject.

The chapter entitled *The Impact of European Structural and Investment Funds on Regional Economic Development: The Case of Bulgaria*, by Desislava Stoilova, explores how EU funds have influenced regional development in Bulgaria between 2007 and 2023. Stoilova investigates the effectiveness of these funds in promoting economic growth, highlighting regional disparities and the varying impact on different sectors of the economy.

In *Social Capital in Tourism as a Key Factor of Sustainable Territorial Development: A Network Approach*, Diana López-Molina and Juan Pulido-Fernández explore how social capital in tourism destinations influences collaboration and sustainable development. They apply methodologies such as Social Network Analysis (SNA) and Stakeholder Theory to Ecuadorian cities, offering insights into how tourism networks can foster sustainable development through collective engagement and resource sharing.

In *Unlocking Tourism Activities Through the Identification of Cultural Heritage: Tourism Opportunities for Sustainable Economic Development*, by Lombuso Shabalala, the author focuses on the importance of identifying cultural heritage tourism opportunities in the Bushbuckridge Local Municipality. Shabalala advocates for community involvement in leveraging cultural assets for tourism development, ensuring that the benefits are equitably shared and contribute to long-term sustainability.

In *The Role of Gastronomic Tourism as a Sustainable Territorial Development Strategy*, Cristina Barzallo-Neira and Juan Ignacio Pulido Fernández assess the growing significance of gastronomic tourism in local economies. Their study, based on surveys of 421 international tourists, demonstrates how culinary tourism can serve as a sustainable development tool, enhancing local economies and preserving regional identities.

Rogelio Martínez Cárdenas and Francisco Partida Hoy's chapter, *Urban Vitality and Sustainability of Heritage Manifestations: Interdisciplinary Analysis of the Andador 20 de Noviembre and the Pilgrimage of Zapopan, Jalisco*, investigates how heritage sites contribute to urban vitality and economic growth. They explore the role of these sites in promoting social integration and community interaction, emphasizing the importance of preserving cultural heritage for both cultural sustainability and urban development.

In *Sustainable Development and the Attractiveness of Development Regions*, Mihai Botezatu, Alexandru Tabuca, and Iuliu Ivanescu explore how regional factors like income, GDP, and employment opportunities influence the attractiveness of development regions in Romania. Their study uses regression analysis to show how these factors impact decisions regarding settlement and investment, offering valuable insights for policymakers seeking to enhance regional development.

The chapter *Low Carbon Tourism: A Content Analysis With Mapping Technique* by Jesús Pérez Gálvez, Jaime Orts Cardador, and Elena Carvajal Trujillo uses content analysis and mapping techniques to explore the concept of low-carbon tourism. They identify key research areas such as carbon footprints and the environmental impacts of tourism, highlighting the growing academic interest in reducing tourism's environmental footprint.

Marco Tregua and Davide Bizjak, in *Re-Thinking the Cultural Heritage Sustainability in the AI Era: From Virtualization to Authenticity*, discuss the intersection of artificial intelligence and cultural heritage. They examine how AI can enhance the visitor experience while challenging the authenticity and preservation of cultural sites. The chapter provides case studies and recommendations for balancing technological innovation with cultural integrity.

Maria Bogren, Anna Sörensson, Charlotta Faith-Ell, Marta Lindvert, and Anna-Maria Jansson explore the role of industrial parks in rural Europe in *Industrial Parks in Europe: Challenges for Sustainable Rural Territorial Development*. They examine the challenges and opportunities industrial parks present, particularly in light of the EU's Green Deal, and highlight the importance of communication and infrastructure in fostering sustainable development in rural areas.

Finally, in *Vernacular Architecture: A Climate Change Mitigation and Adaptation Strategy*, Jayati Talapatra discusses how traditional building practices, adapted to local climates, can mitigate and adapt to climate change. The chapter presents examples from India and Central Asia, demonstrating how vernacular architecture offers sustainable solutions to infrastructure challenges.

In conclusion, the book aims at stimulating new ideas and fostering dialogue among scholars, policymakers, and practitioners committed to building sustainable futures for communities across the globe. The diverse contributions in this volume reflect the interdisciplinary nature of sustainable territorial development, with each chapter demonstrating the importance of integrating environmental, economic, and social dimensions into cohesive and actionable strategies. Ultimately, *Strategies for Sustainable Territorial Development* serves not only as a call to action but also as a reference point for continued research and implementation of sustainable practices. Through collaboration, innovation, and persistence, we can achieve the sustainable world we aspire to create.

**Anna D'Auria**
*University of Naples L'Orientale, Italy*

# Section 1
# Sustainable Development and Resources Management

# Chapter 1
# The Collective Impact Approach for the Sustainable Territorial Development

**Anna D'Auria**
*University of Naples L'Orientale, Italy*

**Alessandra De Chiara**
*University of Naples L'Orientale, Italy*

## ABSTRACT

*The chapter analyses the application of the Collective Impact (CI) approach to sustainable territorial development, focusing on structured collaboration among diverse stakeholders to address complex social, economic, and environmental challenges. The CI framework emphasizes five key elements: a common agenda, shared measurement systems, mutually reinforcing activities, continuous communication, and backbone support. Through case studies, the study demonstrates how the CI approach has been successfully used to promote sustainable development goals, fostering collaboration between governments, businesses, non-profits, and local communities. While the CI model offers a structured approach for addressing territorial development, the paper also highlights potential challenges, including power imbalances, rigidity, and the need for greater inclusivity. Recommendations for improving flexibility, equity, and adaptability in applying the CI model to territorial development are provided, aiming to enhance its effectiveness in fostering sustainable and equitable growth.*

## INTRODUCTION

Scholars, organizations, and practitioners now frequently debate sustainable territorial development (Bryden et al., 2012; Rodríguez-Pose, 2013; Duarte et al., 2020). Aligned with the Sustainable Development Goals of the 2030 Agenda and based on the sustainable development principles it was created with, the strategy seeks the integrated and holistic development of the regions, trying to maintain an equilibrium between environmental, economic, and social aspects (Medeiros, 2021; Popovic et al., 2021; Demeterova, 2023). This strategy aims to establish unified areas where social justice, environmental sustainability, and economic growth coexist. While tackling issues like urbanization, climate change,

DOI: 10.4018/979-8-3693-7081-0.ch001

and socioeconomic inequality, it places a strong emphasis on long-term land-use planning, effective local resource management, social inclusion, and economic diversification (Maier, 2012; Semenescu, 2014; Demeterova, 2023).

The collective impact approach presents a convincing viewpoint in this area of research. To accomplish long-term goals and common visions for territorial development, it encourages organized cooperation amongst important stakeholders, including institutions, governmental bodies, non-profits, corporations, and communities (Szarleta, 2017; Walzer et al., 2018; Brown, 2019). A shared agenda, mutually reinforcing activities, shared assessment systems, and ongoing communication are all essential components of this strategy (Raderstrong and Boyea-Robinson, 2018; Weaver, 2018). The collective impact strategy, in contrast to standalone impact strategies, emphasizes the value of collaboration and coordinated efforts across several sectors, promoting a more cohesive and successful route towards sustainable development.

The collective effect approach and sustainable territorial development should be integrated, according to recent studies and institutional and policy actions. For example, a number of scholars consider this strategy to be a useful instrument for accomplishing the 2030 Agenda's Sustainable Development Goals (LeSage et al., 2021; Jano Reiss et al., 2022). Zhang et al. (2018) point out that governments and businesses alike gain from the collective impact strategy, especially when voluntary agreements are used. They contend that these agreements act as an additional tool for policy, allowing for substantial cost reductions and aggressive resource-efficiency goals (Zhang et al., 2018, p. 296). In a similar vein, De Chiara (2015) emphasizes the strategic importance of creating networks to control the effects of environmental harm. Meanwhile, Chiodo et al. (2019) propose an analytical and monitoring model for collaborative processes rooted in the collective impact approach, aiming to support and enhance tourism development in rural areas.

Building on these discoveries, the purpose of this study is to assess the efficacy of the collective impact method with an emphasis on stakeholder participation and cooperative procedures. To reach significant conclusions, the writers look at sample case studies and evaluate institutional and political initiatives. Along with specific advice for businesses, especially those operating locally, the research also offers useful legislative and managerial implications.

## OVERVIEW ON THE COLLECTIVE IMPACT APPROACH

A structured framework for promoting significant social change was developed by the Collective Impact (CI) approach (Kania and Kramer, 2011). CI stresses the significance of methodical, coordinated actions among multiple stakeholders, including governments, corporations, and charitable organizations, in contrast to traditional collaboration, which frequently entails dispersed efforts and unofficial agreements. Fundamentally, the strategy is based on the notion that complicated societal issues cannot be resolved by a single organization. Rather, these issues necessitate a team effort, in which individuals and associations cooperate on a common goal, underpinned by a structure for continuous cooperation (Kania and Kramer, 2011).

Scholars and practitioners in a variety of sectors, including community development, education, healthcare, and environmental protection, have taken a keen interest in CI in recent years (Roseland, 2000; Hart, 2013; O'Neill, 2020; Mandayam et al., 2023). The focus on establishing clear partnerships, coordinating efforts around common objectives, and guaranteeing steady progress through transparent communication, accountability frameworks, and ongoing monitoring distinguishes CI from other collaborative approaches (De Chiara, 2017; De Moor, 2018; Fox et al., 2023).

Each of the five fundamental components that make up the Collective Impact (CI) model is thought to be necessary for its success. The first is the common agenda, which highlights how important it is for everyone involved in a CI project to have a common knowledge of the issue and a consistent plan for resolving it. "Broad cross-sector coordination [...] a commitment by a group of important actors from different sectors to a common agenda for solving a specific social problem" is necessary for "large-scale social change," as Kania and Kramer (2011) emphasize (p. 36). Without this common goal, stakeholders may pursue divergent objectives or approaches, which could cause efforts to become dispersed or ineffective.

Shared measurement systems, which guarantee that everyone tracks progress uniformly, make up the second component. Companies can use these systems to evaluate their contributions and make sure they are in line with the initiative's overarching objectives (Judelsohn et al., 2022; Panjwani et al., 2023). CI projects can accomplish quantifiable and transparent progress, encourage participant accountability, and generate learning and course correction opportunities by employing consistent measurements (LeChasseur, 2018).

The concept that participants in a CI initiative can take various actions as long as those actions complement and support the initiative's overall goals is reflected in the third element, mutually reinforcing activities (De Chiara, 2015). Each stakeholder in this framework contributes special resources that can be used as levers for shared growth plans, increasing the group's overall influence. All activities must be coordinated and supportive of one another in order to accomplish this.

Building trust, encouraging alignment, and facilitating collaboration all depend on the fourth component, which is continuous communication (Walzer and Weaver, 2018; Linderman, 2019). All participants will remain linked, updated on developments, and prepared to handle obstacles or misalignments as they appear if there is constant and open communication. Without consistent communication, miscommunications or conflicting priorities may cause collaboration to fail.

Backbone support, the fifth and last component, is a specialized group or organization in charge of managing and enabling the entire project (Easterling, 2013; Walzer and Weaver, 2018; Brown and Moore, 2019). By exercising leadership, organizing events, handling logistics, and maintaining everyone's attention and alignment, this establishment plays a crucial function. Large-scale and long-term social change is facilitated by the CI strategy, which provides an organized framework for effective collaboration across various associations and stakeholders. The following table summarizes the five fundamental components that make up the Collective Impact (CI) model (Table 1).

*Table 1. Five conditions of collective success*

| Category | Description |
|---|---|
| Common Agenda | All participants share a unified vision of change, including a common understanding of the problem and a joint approach to solving it through agreed-upon actions. |
| Shared Measurement | Consistent data collection and measurement across all participants ensure efforts remain aligned, and stakeholders hold each other accountable. |
| Mutually Reinforcing Activities | Participants' activities are differentiated but coordinated through a mutually reinforcing plan of action, ensuring that each effort supports the broader goals. |

continued on following page

*Table 1. Continued*

| Category | Description |
|---|---|
| Continuous Communication | Open and consistent communication among all stakeholders builds trust, ensures alignment with shared objectives, and fosters a sense of common motivation. |
| Backbone Support | A dedicated organization (or organizations) with specialized staff skills is required to serve as the backbone of the initiative, coordinating participating organizations and agencies to maintain focus and alignment. |

Source: De Chiara, A. (2015). From stakeholder engagement to the collective-impact approach for sustainability paths in complex problems. Sinergie Italian Journal of Management, 33(Jan-Apr), 57-91, p. 80.

The StriveTogether initiative in Cincinnati and Northern Kentucky is a particularly pertinent example of how the Collective Impact (CI) framework can lead to notable improvements in educational outcomes. From a practical perspective, the CI approach has been successfully applied across various sectors, demonstrating its flexibility and effectiveness in tackling complex social issues. Education, health, and environmental protection are among the most notable examples (O'Day and Smith, 2016).

In order to improve student accomplishment from early infancy through postsecondary education, this program brought together local school districts, corporations, government agencies, and community organizations. StriveTogether was able to produce quantifiable increases in important educational measures, such high school graduation rates and college enrolment, by uniting disparate stakeholders behind a shared vision and using data to monitor progress. This initiative's success has led to its spread to several American cities, demonstrating the CI model's scalability in the educational field (Hanley-brown et al., 2012).

The Collective Impact (CI) approach has been successfully applied in the health sector to address difficult public health issues like childhood obesity. One notable example is the Shape Up Somerville Initiative in Massachusetts, which used the CI framework to unite community organizations, local schools, healthcare providers, and city authorities in a concerted effort to lower the rates of children obesity (Folta et al., 2013). The initiative's mutually reinforcing activities, shared assessment methods, and organized collaboration were key factors in its success. For example, municipal planners created walkable neighborhoods and schools promoted healthier meals—all of which helped achieve a common objective. Progress could be monitored over time and efforts stayed in line thanks to the use of a common measurement system (De Chiara, 2015; Panjwani et al., 2023).

The Great Lakes Restoration Initiative is one example of how the CI approach has been used in the environmental protection field (Tyner and Boyer, 2020; Alsip et al., 2021). In order to address ecological degradation in the Great Lakes region, this effort brought together a wide range of stakeholders, including community organizations, nonprofits, and several governmental levels. Significant advancements in pollution control, habitat restoration, and water quality were made possible by this cooperative effort.

## THE COLLECTIVE IMPACT APPROACH AND THE NETWORK APPROACH

The Network approach should be taken into consideration when talking about cooperation as a lever for sustainable territorial development (Frey et al., 2019). The Network approach and the Collective Impact (CI) approach both stress how crucial cooperation and interdependency are when dealing with complicated issues. But their structure and aim are different. The Network approach places a higher priority on the relationships and information and resource flows between participants, whereas the CI approach depends on a coordinated system with established relationships among stakeholders. Notwithstanding these variations, both strategies emphasize the necessity of a cooperative system. Strong ties between network nodes and centralized coordination—like a backbone organization in the CI model—are essential in both models. Each strategy offers resources to maximize stakeholder relationships, but they do it in different ways.

When applied to territorial development, the CI approach and the Network approach offer contrasting methods for organizing and driving collaboration. Each has its own strengths and limitations, making them suitable for different contexts and challenges.

When tackling complicated, multi-stakeholder issues at the territorial or regional level, such infrastructure development, social inclusion, or economic growth, these distinctions are particularly important. Fundamentally, the Collective Impact (CI) approach is based on a highly organized and synchronized framework that is constructed around the five previously mentioned essential components. This entails uniting many stakeholders, such as local governments, corporations, nonprofits, and community organizations, around a common goal for the development of the area in the framework of territorial development. The coordination of these initiatives is managed by a backbone organization, which is frequently an impartial or external institution. This establishment makes sure that every participant's actions are in line with the overall objectives. A CI project for territorial development, for instance, can have specific, quantifiable goals like lowering unemployment rates or expanding access to reasonably priced housing. Then, through carefully thought-out, complementary actions, all stakeholders would collaborate to accomplish these goals.

But the Network approach is far more adaptable and decentralized (Brito and Correia, 2012). Instead of a strict, predetermined goal, networks thrive on natural, informal collaboration among stakeholders who gather around certain initiatives or shared interests (Manser et al., 2016). Applying the Network approach to territorial development could entail a dynamic grouping of local actors, including individuals, civic organizations, small enterprises, and regional authorities, working together on different projects as needed. There might not be a single coordinating body, in contrast to the CI model. When there exist reciprocal advantages, participants can engage with others while pursuing their own objectives or interests. Stakeholders in a network typically work alone or in small groups rather than together towards a common goal, occasionally cooperating on projects that align with their priorities.

The way these two strategies handle alignment and coordination is one of the main distinctions in territorial growth. The backbone organization in the Collective Impact (CI) model is crucial in making sure that every action is strategically coordinated to further the predetermined development objectives. The CI strategy, for example, would guarantee that government associations, housing developers, neighborhood companies, and community organizations collaborate on urban revitalization projects, whether they be enhancing infrastructure, offering social services, or generating employment possibilities.

It's crucial to remember that various stakeholders frequently have different—and perhaps conflicting—goals. However, by establishing a more comprehensive, common objective that takes into account personal motivations, the CI strategy makes it possible for these disparate actors to unite. By facilitating interaction, communication, and teamwork, the backbone organization turns possible conflicts into cooperative endeavors.

Every action in the Collective Impact (CI) approach is planned and carried out with the group's objective in mind, and advancement is monitored using a common measuring system. Because all activities are intended to support and forward the common goals, this centralized coordination promotes increased efficiency and accountability. To guarantee alignment with the overall objectives, stakeholders in a territorial development project, for instance, could track indicators like housing availability, economic growth, or infrastructure advancements (Johansen et al., 2018; Clifford and Barnes). Because of this transparency, each participant's contributions may be evaluated in relation to the predetermined goals, establishing a clear framework for accountability and facilitating necessary revisions.

The Network approach, on the other hand, gives players more freedom. In the context of territorial development, this could entail local governments, corporations, and community organizations pursuing their own plans or initiatives while collaborating when possibilities present themselves (Torre and Wallet, 2015). A local company and a community organization, for example, might work together to create a new public area, while another group concentrates on social services in the same vicinity. Though they might have similar goals or chances for collaboration, these projects aren't always in line with one cohesive vision for the area.

Because stakeholders can use their resources and experience in a variety of ways, this flexible coordination promotes flexibility and creativity. But it can also result in fragmentation, as initiatives lack unity and don't have the cumulative effect required for extensive territorial expansion.

Accountability is frequently less codified in the Network approach (Håkansson et al., 2010). Usually, each stakeholder or group monitors its own development according to its own objectives, which might not necessarily coincide with the territory's overarching aims. For instance, one group may focus on economic effect through job creation, while another may gauge success by the quantity of public parks created. It can be difficult to make sure that these separate initiatives support a more comprehensive, coherent territorial development strategy in the absence of a common assessment mechanism.

Greater flexibility is made possible by this lack of official accountability, but it can also make it more difficult to evaluate the overall effectiveness of network-based collaborations. Because stakeholders are free to try new things and pursue different strategies depending on their own resources and areas of expertise, networks may quickly adjust to changing conditions and promote creative solutions.

Last but not least, the Collective Impact (CI) strategy has come under fire for possibly consolidating power inside the main organization or bigger, more well-resourced companies when it comes to inclusivity and power relations. Smaller stakeholders may be eclipsed by these powerful entities throughout decision-making processes (Bradbrook, 2018). This could imply that in territorial development, big businesses or local governments have more power to define the agenda, while marginalized or smaller community organizations find it difficult to be heard. Even though CI's formal structure encourages efficiency, it occasionally leaves out smaller stakeholders or grassroots associations, which restricts their involvement.

Conversely, the Network approach frequently encourages greater inclusivity and participation from a wide range of stakeholders due to its less hierarchical and more open structure. This could result in a wider range of viewpoints and efforts in territorial development, with smaller associations, local groups, and community people actively influencing projects and priorities. However, formal responsibility and coordination are sacrificed for this inclusivity, which occasionally lessens the network's overall influence.

In conclusion, the Collective Impact (CI) strategy provides a highly associated and organized framework that unites all stakeholders around a common goal when used in territorial development. The Network approach, on the other hand, offers a flexible and decentralized model that promotes increased independence and creativity. Each strategy has advantages and disadvantages of its own, and the decision between them is based on the particular objectives and circumstances of the territorial development project.

The Network strategy is frequently more appropriate for encouraging widespread engagement and innovation at the local level, even when the CI approach can produce more targeted and quantifiable results. Both models provide distinct advantages, and by being aware of their distinctions, stakeholders can select the approach that best suits their requirements.

## THE COLLECTIVE IMPACT APPROACH AND SUSTAINABLE TERRITORIAL DEVELOPMENT

One effective strategy for addressing difficult social and environmental issues, such as sustainable territorial development, is the Collective Impact (CI) approach. The CI strategy, which is well-known for its organized cooperation amongst various stakeholders, fits in perfectly with the complex ideas of sustainability. The CI framework offers a coordinated approach to addressing important concerns including social fairness, economic growth, and environmental protection—all of which are fundamental components of sustainable territorial development—by bringing together governments, corporations, non-profit organizations, community associations, and citizens.

Fostering balanced and equitable growth—meeting present demands without jeopardizing the potential of future generations to thrive—is the main objective of sustainable territorial development (Monaco, 2024). "A process of managing a collection (portfolio) of assets aimed at preserving and expanding people's opportunities" is how World Bank experts define sustainable development (Voronkova et al., 2019, p. 663). This calls for long-term planning that incorporates social well-being, economic dynamism, and environmental preservation within a certain geographic area. With its focus on cross-sector cooperation and common aims, the Collective Impact (CI) method offers a useful framework for the various players attempting to accomplish these goals (De Chiara, 2015; De Toni et al., 2021).

The CI approach's capacity to establish a common agenda among all stakeholders is one of its main advantages in sustainable territorial development. Issues of territorial sustainability are frequently complicated and include conflicting interests; for instance, environmental preservation initiatives may not align with the objectives of economic growth. By motivating stakeholders to come together around common objectives, including lowering carbon emissions, advancing equitable economic opportunities, or safeguarding natural resources, the CI model aids in bringing these disparate viewpoints into alignment.

Furthermore, as was already indicated, the CI approach highlights the significance of shared measuring methods, which are essential for sustainability initiatives. For example, preserving biodiversity, reducing pollution, increasing the use of renewable energy, or improving social outcomes like housing and education are all examples of key indicators that can be used to manage a territory's sustainable development. All parties involved can measure progress in a consistent and transparent manner by utilizing the same set of indicators. This helps the territory stay on track towards its sustainability targets by ensuring accountability and enabling strategy modifications (Pope et al., 2013).

Another crucial component of the Collective Impact (CI) strategy that supports sustainable territorial development is the function of the backbone organisation. A sustainability council, a non-profit consortium, or a regional planning body could serve as the main company in this situation (De Chiara, 2015). For instance, the backbone organization of a sustainable development project to safeguard a regional watershed would make sure that laws, community conservation initiatives, and business practices all function in unison to preserve biodiversity, water quality, and local livelihoods.

The CI strategy helps avoid fragmentation and guarantees that the combined effort accomplishes more than what individual activities might do on their own by offering this crucial coordination. For sustainable territorial development to make significant and long-lasting progress, this synergy is essential.

The Collective Impact (CI) approach's emphasis on mutually reinforcing activities is another important advantage for sustainable territorial development (De Chiara, 2015). In sustainability projects, several stakeholders in a region frequently play different roles, but when their efforts are well-coordinated, they can work in tandem. For instance, governments may modernize their infrastructure for renewable energy, local businesses could invest in green technologies, and non-profit associations could concentrate on educating communities about sustainable practices and increasing public awareness. These initiatives are linked together and strategically coordinated by the CI framework, which guarantees that the actions of every stakeholder support those of the others. More significant and comprehensive progress towards sustainability results from this combination.

However, there are drawbacks to using the CI approach for sustainable territorial development, especially when it comes to inclusion and coordination dynamics. Local communities, which are frequently severely impacted by territorial changes, may be excluded from decision-making processes when larger organizations or governmental agencies control them. Although CI seeks to promote widespread cooperation, it needs to be properly controlled to guarantee that every stakeholder has a say and significant influence in determining the agenda for sustainable development.

Furthermore, long-term dedication and flexibility are necessary for territorial growth that is sustainable in the environmental, social, and economic domains. According to Kani et al. (2014), the Collective Impact (CI) method offers a structured framework, but it must also be adaptable to changing social, economic, and environmental circumstances. For example, the effects of climate change may compel a reassessment of territorial priorities, requiring adjustments to plans or objectives. This is addressed by CI's continuous communication component, which keeps stakeholders informed and involved and permits prompt adjustments in response to emerging opportunities or obstacles. The design and implementation of plans for sustainable territorial development are also influenced by the CI approach. It encourages a very organized and systematic approach to intervention, in which every activity is in line with the agreed agenda and evaluated using the same metrics. This guarantees that initiatives stay coordinated and focused, resulting in significant advancements towards sustainability objectives.

Some criticisms of the Collective Impact (CI) approach in sustainable territorial development are revealed when reading the literature on the subject. Its propensity to ignore unofficial or emerging actors is one noteworthy critique (Kania and Kramer, 2011; Weaver, 2019). Stakeholders are frequently pre-defined in the CI model according to their roles in advancing the shared agenda and accomplishing objectives (Kolleck, 2019; Virtanen et al., 2021). However, community groups and informal networks often play a crucial role in promoting sustainability from the ground up in territorial development. These informal actors operate outside of traditional frameworks but have a considerable impact on sustainable results; the CI method, with its emphasis on formal partnerships and organized roles, may not fully engage or utilize their potential. For instance, traditional ecological practices and knowledge (Huntington, 2000; McGregor, 2004; Das et al., 2021) may be crucial for resource management and sustainability in rural areas. However, because of the CI model's rigidity, these unofficial groupings may not easily fit into predetermined tactics, which could result in their marginalization or removal from decision-making processes. In the end, this lack of inclusivity can restrict the efficacy and equity of sustainable development initiatives by producing policies that do not fully account for the diversity of stakeholders or the complexity of the region's socio-ecological systems.

In summary, the Collective Impact (CI) approach offers a useful framework for promoting systemic change, but when it comes to sustainable territorial development, its rigidity and dependence on predetermined sets of actors can present difficulties. Flexibility and adaptability are crucial in areas where dynamic situations necessitate constant adjustments, yet they may be limited by the regimented nature of CI. Furthermore, the hierarchical structure of CI stakeholders may lead to disparities and the exclusion of smaller groups, whose involvement is frequently essential to attaining long-term results.

More flexibility in the classification and engagement of stakeholders, more inclusive participation from diverse groups, and a move towards adaptive governance—which permits strategies to change in response to the territory's evolving needs—are all necessary to improve the efficacy of CI in sustainable territorial development.

The CI technique has developed further to overcome these constraints. In order to better manage the complexity of social challenges, recent modifications have an emphasis on implementing systems thinking, integrating adaptive leadership, and enhancing fairness and inclusion throughout CI projects. It is noteworthy that there is a growing concern in making sure marginalized communities are meaningfully integrated. CI efforts can better address the needs of people most impacted by social and environmental issues by involving these groups as equal partners in decision-making processes.

In addition, forms of adaptive leadership can help achieve greater flexibility and responsiveness in the face of uncertainty. This allows Collective Impact (CI) approach initiatives to remain agile, making it easier to adjust strategies as new information emerges or conditions change (Turner et al., 2012).

## PRACTICAL APPLICATIONS OF THE COLLECTIVE IMPACT APPROACH

For the sake of completeness, the following pages will present examples of the application of the Collective Impact (CI) approach.

In order to demonstrate the versatility of the CI strategy in various territorial situations, the authors have specifically chosen three case studies: Trentino-Alto Adige (Italy), Calgary (Canada), and Appalachia (USA). These illustrations provide a thorough examination of how the CI model works in a range of situations and problems by encompassing a variety of geographic, economic, and social contexts.

Each case study represents a fundamental pillar of sustainable territorial development: economic revitalization, social inclusion, and environmental sustainability. With its emphasis on regional economic recovery, the Appalachian instance illustrates how CI helps faltering economies by coordinating job training and educational programs. The Calgary case demonstrates how CI encourages cooperation between the housing, healthcare, and educational sectors to create long-term solutions for social issues, particularly juvenile homelessness. Last but not least, the Trentino-Alto Adige scenario highlights how CI enables the combination of sustainable tourism, environmental conservation, and rural development, illuminating the relationship between environmental and economic sustainability. The following table summarizes the key elements of the case studies (Table 2)

*Table 2. Different forms of adaptability of the CI model*

| Case Study | Category | Key Challenges Addressed |
|---|---|---|
| Appalachia (USA) | Regional Economic Revitalization | Economic stagnation, high unemployment, lack of education access |
| Calgary (Canada) | Social Inclusion & Housing | Youth homelessness, lack of social services, mental health issues |
| Trentino-Alto Adige (Italy) | Environmental & Economic Sustainability | Rural depopulation, sustainable tourism, environmental conservation |

Authors' elaboration

By selecting these three examples, the authors ensure a broad representation of territorial development challenges while showcasing the Collective Impact (CI) approach and its versatility in addressing complex, multi-stakeholder issues. These cases offer practical insights into both the strengths and limitations of CI, making them valuable references for policymakers and practitioners looking to implement similar strategies in other regions.

## THE COLLECTIVE IMPACT APPROACH IN THE APPALACHIAN REGION OF THE UNITED STATES

Appalachia in the United States is the subject of the first illustrative example (Millesen, 2015; Karmann et al., 2022; Kieffer and Socolof, 2024). Although this area is renowned for its varied natural riches and rich cultural legacy, it has had severe economic and social difficulties in recent decades (Feser, 2014; Holtkamp and Weaver, 2018). The region's development has been hampered by enduring problems like high unemployment, poverty, and educational inequalities.

The Collective Impact (CI) method was established by a coalition of stakeholders as a means of promoting sustainable territorial development in response to these issues. The use of the CI model in Appalachia is examined in this case study, which includes information on the projects carried out, the involvement of stakeholders, the results obtained, and the most important lessons discovered.

The Appalachian area, which stretches from southern New York to northern Alabama, has long been dependent on manufacturing and coal mining. However, economic stagnation and high levels of poverty have resulted from the decline of these industries, which has been made worse by environmental degradation and restricted access to healthcare and education. In the early 2010s, local actors, including administrations, nonprofits, educational institutions, and community groups, realized how urgently a concerted response was needed and started collaborating. Their objective was to coordinate efforts and promote sustainable social and economic development by putting the Collective Impact concept into practice.

Creating a common agenda among all parties involved was the first stage in putting the strategy into practice. This was accomplished by holding a number of community forums where local leaders and citizens shared their hopes and concerns for the area. The coalition determined important priorities based on these talks, such as raising educational attainment, increasing economic possibilities, and advancing the health and well-being of the community. These principles served as the cornerstone of the group's agenda and directed growth tactics.

The Appalachian Community Action Network (ACAN) was created as a backbone organization to coordinate initiatives. This association was essential in helping stakeholders collaborate, handling data gathering to monitor progress, setting up meetings, and offering logistical support. Accountability was guaranteed by the backbone organization, which also maintained everyone's alignment with the shared goal. In order to evaluate progress towards agreed objectives, the Network also collaborated with stakeholders to create common measuring tools.

In fields like health outcomes, economic development, and education, key performance indicators (KPIs) were developed. Metrics including access to healthcare services, employment placement rates, and graduation rates were among the KPIs, for instance. Stakeholders could assess the success of their projects and decide on future courses of action based on data by monitoring these indicators.

The coalition encouraged stakeholders to engage in mutually reinforcing activities because it understood that each actor had distinct resources and strengths. In order to provide job training programs that were suited to the economic demands of the area, educational institutions worked with nearby companies. Community health-focused nonprofits that provide resources for substance misuse prevention and mental health services. This cooperative strategy made sure that every effort supported the others, which helped the project succeed as a whole.

A key factor in the Collective Impact (CI) approach's effectiveness was effective communication (Fletcher, 2023). A digital platform was developed to allow participants to share resources, best practices, and success stories, and regular meetings and updates promoted information sharing among stakeholders (Floress et al., 2018). In addition to fostering a sense of community, this constant communication made sure that everyone involved was updated on the status of the shared goal.

Numerous benefits resulted from the Appalachian region's adoption of the Collective Impact (CI) strategy (Millesen, 2015; Kania et al., 2014). Participating school districts saw a 15% rise in graduation rates over a three-year period, and new job training initiatives helped graduates find work. Additionally, the availability of competent individuals trained through joint projects led to a 20% increase in hiring reported by local businesses. In order to encourage entrepreneurship, small business incubators were also founded, offering local startups tools and assistance. Additionally, when community health efforts increased mental health services and drug misuse programs, access to healthcare services improved, resulting in notable improvements in the general well-being of the community (The Appalachian Regional Commission).

The example of the Appalachian region offers several important lessons regarding the application of the Collective Impact (CI) approach in territorial development. Firstly, the role of the local community proved to be highly significant; involving residents in planning strategies ensured that the common agenda reflected local needs and priorities, fostering a sense of unity and belonging.

Flexibility and adaptability emerged as critical success factors, as noted in the literature. Although the CI model offers a structured framework, stakeholders understood that it was important to remain flexible in the face of changing circumstances, and regular evaluations allowed them to modify their strategies in response to new opportunities and needs. Additionally, establishing a backbone organization as an impartial facilitator helped to fortify relationships among diverse groups, facilitating more effective collaboration. Finally, data-driven decision-making was crucial, as shared measurement systems offered a clear framework for evaluating progress and making well-informed decisions on resource allocation and strategy adjustments.

Lastly, maintaining stakeholder motivation and engagement throughout the process required constant communication. All participants were kept in line with the group's goals by frequent updates and open communication.

To sum up, the implementation of the Collective Impact (CI) approach in the Appalachian region is a compelling illustration of how teamwork can tackle intricate problems in sustainable territorial development. Through the establishment of a shared agenda, coordination via a backbone organization, and the promotion of mutually reinforcing activities, stakeholders made substantial strides in addressing social and economic issues. Even though there are still obstacles to overcome, this initiative's achievements show that the CI approach is a practical means of advancing sustainable development in comparable situations.

## THE COLLECTIVE IMPACT APPROACH TO REDUCE YOUTH HOMELESSNESS IN CALGARY

The second example looks at how the Collective Impact (CI) approach was used in Calgary, Alberta (Calgary Homeless Foundation, 2021) to reduce youth homelessness. About 2,000 young people in Calgary experience homelessness or unstable housing annually, contributing to the city's growing crisis in the early 2000s (Cooper, 2006). The causes were varied, including family conflicts, substance abuse, mental health challenges, and a lack of social and economic opportunities.

The problem continued in spite of the efforts of a large number of community organizations, government institutions, and nonprofits. Without a coordinated, comprehensive approach, these groups frequently worked in silos, addressing just specific aspects of the issue. The fact that no one association could handle such a complicated and multidimensional problem by itself grew more and more clear.

In response, based on the ideas of Collective Impact, the Calgary Plan to End Youth Homelessness was introduced in 2011 (Calgary Youth Sector Refresh Steering Committee, 2017). By bringing together a variety of associations, each of which contributed their skills while working towards a shared objective, this program sought to eliminate teenage homelessness. Social services, healthcare organizations, educational institutions, and companies were among the stakeholders who united under a common goal to address the problem holistically.

The initiative's main goal was to decrease teenage homelessness by tackling its underlying causes and establishing long-term social reintegration paths. In order to secure long-lasting solutions, this strategy went beyond simply offering temporary accommodation and instead concentrated on more fundamental problems like unstable families, a shortage of affordable homes, and long-term support networks.

The alliance established a shared measuring system in order to accomplish the initiative's primary objective and in accordance with the Collective Impact (CI) methodology. This required gathering information on important metrics, like the percentage of young people who obtained stable housing, the decline in the number of youths seeking housing, the success rates of social reintegration programs, and the availability of support services like counselling and medical treatment.

Through activities that reinforced one another, the stakeholders in the project coordinated their efforts. For example, schools and educational institutions provided tutoring and mentoring programs, while housing organizations concentrated on offering both short-term and long-term housing. The youth's physical and emotional health needs were attended to by healthcare professionals. A far higher overall impact was achieved as a result of these concerted efforts, which made sure that each organization's operations supported and enhanced the others.

An important factor in the initiative's success was communication. The actors got together on a regular basis to talk about their progress, share their triumphs and setbacks, and make necessary strategy adjustments. By keeping everyone focused on the same objective and fostering confidence amongst the organizations, this constant communication enabled the project to change as needed.

The Collective Impact (CI) strategy produced noteworthy outcomes. Early progress in tackling the issue was demonstrated by the 20% reduction in the number of young people residing in shelters throughout the first five years of the program. More young people were able to get long-term housing through the program, which resulted in a notable improvement in housing stability. In actuality, there was a 30% increase in access to long-term housing options. Furthermore, there was a noticeable improvement in the youths' social and mental health. Relapse rates for substance usage were reduced by 15% for many of the youth who took part in the program. In general, their integration into Calgary's social and economic fabric improved.

The improvement in cooperation and trust amongst the participating organizations was one of the initiative's most significant results. Through regular collaboration, success sharing, and learning from setbacks, the organizations strengthened their bonds and became more open to potential partnerships on other social issues. By ensuring that the several organizations collaborated effectively and remained focused on the common objectives, the backbone organization was important in maintaining the initiative's direction.

Lastly, communication and trust were also crucial. The project was able to adjust to obstacles and maintain consensus thanks to the frequent sharing of information and updates. Last but not least, a clear, consistent method of monitoring development using common measurement tools made sure that all the organizations were aiming for the same goals and permitted continuous assessment and development.

## THE COLLECTIVE IMPACT (CI) APPROACH IN THE TERRITORIAL DEVELOPMENT OF THE TRENTINO-ALTO ADIGE REGION IN ITALY

The final case study examines the application of the Collective Impact (CI) approach to territorial development in the Trentino-Alto Adige region of Italy.

The Trentino-Alto Adige region is well known for its breathtaking scenery, rich cultural legacy, and prosperous economy. Concerns about environmental sustainability and rural population reduction are two major issues facing the region. The region is facing environmental challenges and demographic decline, which necessitate sustainable land use methods, notwithstanding its economic growth, especially in tourism and agriculture. After realizing these difficulties, local governments, corporations, community organizations, and regional authorities started looking into cooperative ways to improve territorial development.

In 2015, the Autonomous Province of Trento, in partnership with various stakeholders, launched the "Sustainable Trentino" project to promote sustainable development practices across the region (Provincia Autonoma di Trento Assessorato alle Infrastrutture e all'Ambiente, 2018) through the application of the Collective Impact (CI) approach.

Establishing a shared agenda among the various stakeholder categories was the initial stage, just like in the scenarios that were previously given. Residents, companies, non-governmental organizations, and government representatives participated in a number of seminars and public discussions to accomplish this. Together, the participants' identification of important priorities—such as fostering environmental sustainability, protecting cultural heritage, and enhancing local economies—created a common vision that reflected the region's goals.

The Trentino Innovation and Development Agency (Trentino Sviluppo: Impresa, Innovazione e Marketing Territoriale, Agenzia della Provincia Autonoma di Trento dedicated to favoring the sustainable development of the Trentino system) was founded as the backbone organization to promote this shared goal. The Agency was crucial in managing data gathering, setting up training sessions, and facilitating stakeholder participation. This made sure that every effort was in line with the group's objectives and that advancement was openly monitored.

The creation of shared measuring methods was another crucial element of the Collective Impact (CI) methodology. In order to evaluate the success of different programs, the Agency worked with stakeholders to develop key performance indicators (KPIs). These metrics assessed social inclusion, environmental impact, and economic progress. KPIs were created, for example, to track gains in environmental quality, the amount of community involvement in local decision-making, and the development of jobs in sustainable industries.

Regarding the many roles played by the participants, local governments worked with academic institutions to create vocational training programs that gave locals the skills they needed for new industries like sustainable tourism and renewable energy. While local companies were urged to embrace eco-friendly methods, NGOs concentrated on community development projects to improve social inclusion. This all-encompassing strategy made sure that every project supported the others and advanced the Sustainable Trentino project's overarching goals.

Furthermore, the CI initiative's success depended heavily on efficient communication. Collaboration and information exchange were made easier by frequent meetings, newsletters, and an online platform. Among stakeholders, this constant communication and information sharing aided in fostering trust.

Trentino-Alto Adige experienced notable benefits from the application of the Collective Impact (CI) strategy. The neighborhood saw significant progress in a number of categories during the course of three years. Vocational training programs helped to enhance employment in ecotourism and renewable energy, which in turn led to a significant increase in job creation in sustainable sectors. Numerous local companies started implementing eco-friendly operations and green technology as part of their sustainable practices.

Initiatives for social inclusion also promoted increased community involvement. Residents' greater sense of ownership and responsibility is reflected in their increased participation in municipal decision-making processes. Coordinated conservation efforts resulted in improved biodiversity and lower carbon emissions, according to statistics on environmental indicators (Provincia Autonoma di Trento Assessorato alle infrastrutture e all'ambiente, 2018).

To sum up, the Trentino-Alto Adige case provides important information about how well the Collective Impact (CI) strategy works for territorial development. For example, adaptability and flexibility have been identified as critical success factors. In actuality, the CI methodology enabled stakeholders to modify their plans in response to continuing assessments and input from the community. One could argue that this adaptability is essential for dealing with emerging possibilities and difficulties.

While obstacles remain, the positive outcomes of the Sustainable Trentino case highlight the CI model's potential as a viable framework for fostering sustainable development in similar contexts throughout Europe, especially due to its focus on the importance of collaboration, community engagement, and adaptability in achieving sustainable territorial development.

## DISCUSSION

This study has examined how the Collective Impact (CI) approach can be applied to sustainable territorial development, where collaboration between many different stakeholders is essential for tackling complex environmental, social, and economic challenges (Kania and Kramer, 2011). The illustrative examples show that the CI model can effectively coordinate efforts among various groups, favoring the achievement of common goals.

More precisely, the five essential components of the Collective Impact (CI) framework—a shared agenda, mutually reinforcing activities, continuous communication, a backbone organization, and shared measurement systems—can be used to analyze the three case studies, which demonstrate the use of the CI approach in various contexts.

Local players in the Appalachian area of the United States, such as administrators, nonprofits, and educational institutions, realized that addressing enduring social and economic issues required a concerted effort. The first stage was to create a shared agenda, which was accomplished through community meetings that determined objectives like healthcare, economic development, and education. Key performance metrics, such as job placement and graduation rates, were used to track progress through the development of a shared measurement system. Numerous actors participated in actions that reinforced one another, such as organizations growing healthcare programs and corporations and schools working together on job training programs. Regular meetings and a digital platform that made resource sharing and coordination easier allowed for constant communication. The foundational organization that ensured accountability and strategic alignment was the Appalachian Community Action Network (ACAN). As evidence of the effectiveness of concerted action, these initiatives produced observable gains, such as a 15% increase in graduation rates and a 20% increase in local hiring.

In Calgary, Canada, the Collective Impact (CI) model was implemented to address youth homelessness through the "Calgary Plan to End Youth Homelessness." Stakeholders from social services, healthcare, education, and nonprofits agreed on a common agenda that focused on addressing the root causes of youth homelessness, such as family instability and a lack of affordable housing, rather than simply providing shelter. A shared measurement system was developed to track key indicators, including shelter usage, reintegration success, and housing stability. Different organizations engaged in mutually reinforcing activities, with housing services providing accommodations, schools offering mentorship programs, and healthcare providers addressing mental health needs. Continuous communication was integral to the success of the initiative, with regular meetings and strategy adjustments fostering trust and collaboration. A backbone organization was tasked with coordinating efforts and ensuring that all actors remained aligned with the initiative's goals. Over the course of five years, the number of homeless youth in shelters decreased by 20%, while stable housing placements increased by 30%, accompanied by notable improvements in mental health and social well-being.

In Trentino-Alto Adige, Italy, the Collective Impact (CI) framework was applied to address demographic decline and environmental sustainability through the "Sustainable Trentino" project. A common agenda was established through workshops and public consultations, which identified priorities such as economic development, cultural preservation, and environmental sustainability. The Trentino Innovation and Development Agency facilitated a shared measurement system using key performance indicators related to job creation, environmental conservation, and community engagement. Various stakeholders engaged in mutually reinforcing activities, with local governments and educational institutions developing vocational training programs, NGOs focusing on community initiatives, and businesses adopting sustainable practices. Continuous communication was maintained through online platforms, newsletters, and regular stakeholder meetings. The backbone organization, Trentino Sviluppo, played a vital role in coordinating activities, organizing training sessions, and ensuring transparency. Over three years, the region saw increased employment in sustainable industries, greater community involvement in decision-making, and improved environmental indicators, demonstrating the effectiveness of the CI approach in fostering sustainable territorial development.

Across all three cases, the five key elements of the Collective Impact framework played a crucial role in achieving meaningful change. Establishing a common agenda enabled diverse stakeholders to align their efforts toward shared goals. Implementing shared measurement systems ensured accountability and supported data-driven decision-making. Engaging in mutually reinforcing activities allowed organizations to leverage their strengths, creating synergies for greater impact. Maintaining continuous communication fostered trust and kept all participants engaged, while a backbone organization provided strategic coordination and oversight. In conclusion, these cases demonstrate that the CI model is an effective tool for addressing complex social, economic, and environmental challenges, promoting sustainable development, and strengthening community resilience.

## CONCLUSIONS

The CI approach offers a strong framework for overseeing sustainable territorial development projects, as demonstrated by case studies and literature. Aligning stakeholders—from governments to community organizations—around a single vision of sustainability has proven to be facilitated by crucial components including a shared agenda and measuring mechanisms. By planning events, maintaining communication, and holding participants accountable, the backbone organization was important in keeping everyone on course.

Case studies from areas like as Canada, Trentino-Alto Adige, and Appalachia show how the CI model may be modified to fit many situations, each of which has its own particular set of difficulties. For instance, in Trentino-Alto Adige, CI helped strike a balance between environmental sustainability and economic development, while in Appalachia, it improved employment and educational prospects. These achievements demonstrate that CI can significantly alter territorial development when used appropriately.

For policymakers and regional planners, this holds particular significance. The CI approach's capacity to bring together stakeholders from multiple sectors—such as government, industry, and civil society—makes it a useful tool for solving the multi-layered difficulties of sustainable territorial development. Furthermore, shared measurement methods enable constant monitoring and modifications, ensuring that programs may evolve as needed.

In conclusion, this study's findings show how important it is to have more robust institutional frameworks in order to promote sustainable business practices and improve corporate social responsibility. It emphasizes how crucial legislators are to establishing a regulatory framework that balances economic and environmental concerns and encourages sustainable business. Companies are urged to incorporate sustainability into their main plans in order to increase their resilience and long-term competitiveness. The report also highlights the value of training and education initiatives that raise awareness and develop sustainability-related skills. Promoting innovation and sustainable development requires cooperation between the public and commercial sectors. Last but not least, the results indicate that financial support systems and incentives ought to be modified to motivate companies to embrace socially and ecologically conscious operations.

Despite the positive outcomes observed, the CI approach is not without weaknesses. One major issue is the potential for power imbalances. In many cases, larger organizations or government bodies may dominate the decision-making process, pushing smaller or marginalized groups—such as local communities—out of the conversation. This can lead to unequal representation, which is particularly problematic in territorial development projects, where the contribution of those directly impacted is crucial. Additionally, while the CI framework is effective in creating alignment, its structured nature can make it too rigid for the fast-changing conditions often found in territorial development (Kania and Kramer, 2011; Weaver, 2019). Because of the CI model's focus on predetermined goals and responsibilities, sustainability projects may not be able to quickly adjust to changes in the environment, economic, or social landscape. Because of this, it may be difficult to modify plans in response to fresh possibilities or obstacles (Turner et al., 2012).

The CI approach's emphasis on quantitative measures is another drawback (Kania and Kramer, 2013). Although these shared measurement systems aid in ensuring transparency and accountability (Pope et al., 2013), they frequently give preference to easily quantifiable outcomes, such as job numbers or emissions reductions, over more intricate, difficult-to-quantify outcomes, like biodiversity preservation or community well-being. This may lead to the neglect of certain facets of territorial sustainability (Kania and Kramer, 2011; Weaver, 2019).

Future studies should concentrate on improving the Collective Impact model's adaptability to the intricacies of territorial sustainability in order to overcome these problems. CI projects may become more adaptable and responsive by including adaptive leadership and systems thinking, enabling frequent modifications in response to changing territorial needs (Turner et al., 2012). Furthermore, CI programs should focus more on equity and inclusivity (Maier, 2012; Semenescu, 2014; Demeterova, 2023). Local communities, particularly under-represented ones, must play a major role in determining the objectives and tactics of territorial development initiatives. It may be possible to guarantee that all parties concerned participate in and contribute to the decision-making process by moving towards more participatory government.

To sum up, the Collective Impact approach is a useful instrument for encouraging cooperation and structural change in sustainable territorial development, but it must adapt to meet its present issues. CI can continue to assist various stakeholders in collaborating to produce more equitable and sustainable territorial outcomes by emphasizing flexibility and inclusivity.

## REFERENCES


Alsip, P. J., Hartig, J. H., Krantzberg, G., Williams, K. C., & Wondolleck, J. (2021). Evolving institutional arrangements for use of an ecosystem approach in restoring Great Lakes Areas of Concern. *Sustainability, 13*(3), 1532. DOI: 10.3390/su13031532 PMID: 34676112

Bradbrook, C. (2018). Theoretical foundations for CI applications. In *Using collective impact to bring community change* (pp. 17–38). Routledge. DOI: 10.4324/9781315545073-2

Brito, C., & Correia, R. (2012). Regions as Networks: Towards a Conceptual Framework of Territorial Dynamics. In *International Trade from Economic and Policy Perspective* (p. 17). IntechOpen.

Brown, M., & Moore, T. L. (2019). Addressing complex public problems through coalition-based approaches: Collective impact and the CEP competencies. *The International Journal of Research on Service-Learning and Community Engagement, 7*(1). Advance online publication. DOI: 10.37333/001c.11491

Brown, M. E., Rizzuto, T., & Singh, P. (2019). Strategic compatibility, collaboration and collective impact for community change. *Leadership and Organization Development Journal, 40*(4), 421–434. DOI: 10.1108/LODJ-05-2018-0180

Bryden, J. M., Efstratoglou, S., Ferenczi, T., Johnson, T., Knickel, K., Refsgaard, K., & Thomson, K. J. (2012). Multifunctionality, sustainable territorial development and rural policies in Europe: Some concluding reflections. In *Towards Sustainable Rural Regions in Europe* (pp. 302–320). Routledge. DOI: 10.4324/9780203831403

Calgary Homeless Foundation. (2021). Guiding the Fight Against Homelessness. *Focus (San Francisco, Calif.), 2025*, •••. https://www.calgaryhomeless.com/discover-learn/our-approach/plans/

Calgary Youth Sector Refresh Steering Committee. (2017). Calgary Plan to Prevent and End Youth Homelessness–2017 Refresh. *Available at:*http://homelesshub. ca/sites/default/files/Youth_Plan_Refresh_2017. pdf

Clifford, J., & Barnes, K. (2022). Why and what to measure? The justification for social impact measurement. *Social impact measurement for a sustainable future: The power of aesthetics and practical implications*, 49-73.

Cooper, M. (2006). *Demographic trends and implications for the city of Calgary*. Calgary, Alberta: Canadian Policy Research Networks. Corporation for Ohio Appalachian Development (COAD), available at: https://coadinc.org/

Das, A., Gujre, N., Devi, R. J., & Mitra, S. (2021). A review on traditional ecological knowledge and its role in natural resources management: North East India, a cultural paradise. *Environmental Management*, •••, 1–22. PMID: 34791537

De Chiara, A. (2015). From stakeholder engagement to the collective-impact approach for sustainability paths in complex problems. *Sinergie Italian Journal of Management, 33*(Jan-Apr), 57–91.

De Chiara, A. (2017). Collective Impact Approach: A "Tool" for Managing Complex Problems and Business Clusters Sustainability. *Metropolitan Universities, 28*(4), 101–114. DOI: 10.18060/21739

De Moor, A. (2018). A community network ontology for participatory collaboration mapping: Towards collective impact. *Information (Basel)*, *9*(7), 151. DOI: 10.3390/info9070151

De Toni, A., Vizzarri, M., Di Febbraro, M., Lasserre, B., Noguera, J., & Di Martino, P. (2021). Aligning Inner Peripheries with rural development in Italy: Territorial evidence to support policy contextualization. *Land Use Policy*, *100*, 104899. DOI: 10.1016/j.landusepol.2020.104899

Demeterova, B. (2023). Urban and Regional Planning for Territorial Cohesion. In *Public Policies for Territorial Cohesion* (pp. 129–143). Springer International Publishing. DOI: 10.1007/978-3-031-26228-9_7

Duarte, A., Braga, V., Marques, C., & Sá, A. A. (2020). Geotourism and territorial development: A systematic literature review and research agenda. *Geoheritage*, *12*(3), 65. DOI: 10.1007/s12371-020-00478-z

Easterling, D. (2013). Getting to collective impact: How funders can contribute over the life course of the work. *The Foundation Review*, *5*(2), 7. DOI: 10.9707/1944-5660.1157

Fletcher, R. A., Long, R. E., & Schumann, W. (Eds.). (2023). *Engaging Appalachia: A Guidebook for Building Capacity and Sustainability*. University Press of Kentucky. DOI: 10.2307/j.ctv3596zs0

Floress, K., Connolly, S., Halvorsen, K. E., Egan, A., Schuler, T., Hill, A., DeSenze, P., Fenimore, S., & Karriker, K. (2018). Implementing landscape scale conservation across organizational boundaries: Lessons from the central Appalachian region, United States. *Environmental Management*, *62*(5), 845–857. DOI: 10.1007/s00267-018-1081-y PMID: 30046845

Folta, S. C., Kuder, J. F., Goldberg, J. P., Hyatt, R. R., Must, A., Naumova, E. N., Nelson, M. E., & Economos, C. D. (2013). Changes in diet and physical activity resulting from the Shape Up Somerville community intervention. *BMC Pediatrics*, *13*(1), 1–9. DOI: 10.1186/1471-2431-13-157 PMID: 24093936

Fox, A., Mwangi, C. G., Pachucki, M., Wells, R., Dasgupta, B., Thoma, H., Dunton, S., & Kimball, E. (2023). Rethinking Backbones in Collective Impact: Examining a Broadening STEM Participation Program as a Feminist Matrix Organization. *Innovative Higher Education*, *48*(5), 925–947. DOI: 10.1007/s10755-023-09660-x

Hanleybrown, F., Kania, J., & Kramer, M. (2012). *Channeling change: Making collective impact work*. FSG.

Hart, R. A. (2013). *Children's participation: The theory and practice of involving young citizens in community development and environmental care*. Routledge. DOI: 10.4324/9781315070728

Huntington, H. P. (2000). Using traditional ecological knowledge in science: Methods and applications. *Ecological Applications*, *10*(5), 1270–1274. DOI: 10.1890/1051-0761(2000)010[1270:UTEKIS]2.0.CO;2

Jano Reiss, M., Rotem, A., Gridinger, O., Tzur, Y., Reichman, G., Berenbaum, R., & Tziraki, C. (2022). Health and wellbeing (SDG3) in urban design and spatial planning–a retrospective roadmap towards the collective impact model. *Cities & Health*, *6*(5), 993–1003. DOI: 10.1080/23748834.2022.2147469

Johansen, P. H., Ejrnæs, R., Kronvang, B., Olsen, J. V., Præstholm, S., & Schou, J. S. (2018). Pursuing collective impact: A novel indicator-based approach to assessment of shared measurements when planning for multifunctional land consolidation. *Land Use Policy*, *73*, 102–114. DOI: 10.1016/j.landusepol.2018.01.040

Judelsohn, A., Hoey, L., Shapiro, L. F., & Colasanti, K. (2022). Incorporating shared measurement in social change initiatives: Benefits, challenges, and lessons learned. *Community Development Journal: An International Forum*, *57*(3), 533–551. DOI: 10.1093/cdj/bsab009

Kania, J., Hanleybrown, F., Juster, J. S., Edmondson, J., Hecht, B., Bartczak, L., & White, E. (2014). Collective insights on collective impact. *Stanford Social Innovation Review*, *12*(4), 1–24.

Kania, J., Hanleybrown, F., Juster, J. S., Edmondson, J., Hecht, B., Bartczak, L., & White, E. (2014). Collective insights on collective impact. *Stanford Social Innovation Review*, *12*(4), 1–24.

Kania, J., & Kramer, M. (2011). *Collective impact.* FSG.

Karmann, M., Martinez, Z., Meier-Dörnberg, J., & Santos, V. (2022). An assessment of FSC certification solutions for smallholders and community-managed forests. In *Routledge Handbook of Community Forestry* (pp. 237–255). Routledge. DOI: 10.4324/9780367488710-19

Kieffer, E. L., & Socolof, J. (2024). *Rural Arts Management*. Taylor & Francis. DOI: 10.4324/9781003365853

Kolleck, N. (2019). The power of third sector organizations in public education. *Journal of Educational Administration*, *57*(4), 411–425. DOI: 10.1108/JEA-08-2018-0142

LeChasseur, K. (2018). Re-examining power and privilege in collective impact. In *Collective Impact and Community Development Issues* (pp. 70–85). Routledge. DOI: 10.4324/9781315112916-6

LeSage, T., Timur, A., & Pawlicki, D. (2021). A case study on the use of the SDGs with a collective impact initiative in Southwest Florida. The foundation review, 13(4), 6.

Linderman, A. (2019). Systemic Collective Impact and Rapid City's Ongoing Success Story. *Interdisciplinary Journal of Partnership Studies*, *6*(2), 5–5. DOI: 10.24926/ijps.v6i2.2206

Maier, K. (2012). The pursuit of balanced territorial development: The realities and complexities of the cohesion agenda. In Territorial Development, Cohesion and Spatial Planning (pp. 266-290). Routledge.

Mandayam, G., Nandan, M., & Bowen, E. (2023). Convergence of community social work practice, collective impact, and design thinking: What, why, and how? *Journal of Social Work : JSW*, *23*(5), 916–938. DOI: 10.1177/14680173231166112

Manser, K., Hillebrand, B., Woolthuis, R. K., Ziggers, G. W., Driessen, P. H., & Bloemer, J. (2016). An activities-based approach to network management: An explorative study. *Industrial Marketing Management*, *55*, 187–199. DOI: 10.1016/j.indmarman.2015.10.004

McGregor, D. (2004). Traditional ecological knowledge and sustainable development: Towards coexistence. *In the way of development: Indigenous peoples, life projects and globalization*, 72-91.

Medeiros, E. (2021). The territorial dimension of the united nations sustainable development goals. *Area*, *53*(2), 292–302. DOI: 10.1111/area.12681

Millesen, J. (2015). Understanding collective impact in a rural funding collaborative: Collective grantmaking in Appalachian Ohio. *The Foundation Review*, *7*(4), 12. DOI: 10.9707/1944-5660.1271

Monaco, S. (2024). Introduction: Integrating Territorial Identity into SDGs. In *Identity, Territories, and Sustainability: Challenges and Opportunities for Achieving the UN Sustainable Development Goals* (pp. 1-14). Emerald Publishing Limited.

O'Day, J. A., & Smith, M. S. (2016). Equality and Quality in US Education: Systemic Problems, Systemic Solutions. Policy Brief. *Education Policy Center at American Institutes for Research.*

O'Neill, M. (2020). Increasing community engagement in collective impact approaches to advance social change. *Community Development (Columbus, Ohio)*, *51*(1), 17–35. DOI: 10.1080/15575330.2020.1714684

Panjwani, S., Graves-Boswell, T., Garney, W. R., Muraleetharan, D., Spadine, M., & Flores, S. (2023). Evaluating collective impact initiatives: A systematic scoping review. *The American Journal of Evaluation*, *44*(3), 406–423. DOI: 10.1177/10982140221130266

Popovic, S. G., Dobricic, M., & Savic, S. V. (2021). Challenges of sustainable spatial development in the light of new international perspectives-The case of Montenegro. *Land Use Policy*, *105*, 105438.

Provincia Autonoma di Trento Assessorato alle infrastruture e all'ambiente (2018), Trentino sostenibile verso l'Agenda [Autonomous Province of Trento Department of Infrastructure and Environment (2018), Sustainable Trentino towards the Agenda] 2030, available at: https://www.mase.gov.it/sites/default/files/archivio/allegati/CReIAMO_PA/L2WP1/peer_learning_visit/8_Cattani_Progetto_CPA_L2WP1_Workshop_13giugno.pdf

Raderstrong, J., & Boyea-Robinson, T. (2018). The why and how of working with communities through collective impact. In *Collective Impact and Community Development Issues* (pp. 26–38). Routledge.

Rodríguez-Pose, A. (2013). Do institutions matter for regional development? *Regional Studies*, *47*(7), 1034–1047. DOI: 10.1080/00343404.2012.748978

Roseland, M. (2000). Sustainable community development: Integrating environmental, economic, and social objectives. *Progress in Planning*, *54*(2), 73–132. DOI: 10.1016/S0305-9006(00)00003-9

Semenescu, G. (2014). From Local Urban Development to Cooperation and Territorial Cohesion. Annals Constantin Brancusi U. Targu Jiu, Letters & Soc. Sci. Series, 100.

Szarleta, E. (2017). Capacity building for social innovation: A collective impact approach. *Metropolitan Universities*, *28*(4), 81–100. DOI: 10.18060/21744

The Appalachian Regional Commission (ARC). available at: https://www.arc.gov/

Torre, A., & Wallet, F. (2015). Towards new paths for regional and territorial development in rural areas. *European Planning Studies*, *23*(4), 650–677. DOI: 10.1080/09654313.2014.945812

Turner, S., Merchant, K., Kania, J., & Martin, E. (2012). Understanding the value of backbone organizations in collective impact. *Stanford Social Innovation Review*, •••, 1.

Tyner, E. H., & Boyer, T. A. (2020). Applying best-worst scaling to rank ecosystem and economic benefits of restoration and conservation in the Great Lakes. *Journal of Environmental Management*, *255*, 109888. DOI: 10.1016/j.jenvman.2019.109888 PMID: 31790870

Virtanen, P., Ristikari, T., & Niemelä, M. (2021). Collective Impact Partnership and Backbone Organizations as Enablers of Children's Well-Being. *Partnerships for the Goals*, 183-196.

Voronkova, O. Y., Yankovskaya, V., Kovaleva, I., Epishkin, I., Iusupova, I., & Berdova, Y. (2019). Sustainable territorial development based on the effective use of resource potential. *Entrepreneurship and Sustainability Issues*, *7*(1), 662–673. DOI: 10.9770/jesi.2019.7.1(47)

Walzer, N., & Weaver, L. (2018). Changing roles and practices in collective impact usage. In *Using collective impact to bring community change* (pp. 1–15). Routledge. DOI: 10.4324/9781315545073-1

Walzer, N., Weaver, L., & McGuire, C. (2018). Collective impact approaches and community development issues. In *Collective Impact and Community Development Issues* (pp. 1–11). Routledge. DOI: 10.4324/9781315112916-1

Weaver, L. (2019). *The Journey of Collective Impact: Contributions to the Field from Tamarack Institute*. FriesenPress.

Weaver, L., & Cabaj, M. (2018). Collective impact 3.0: Extending the collective impact vision for community change 1. Using collective impact to bring community change, 97-112.

Zhang, M., Cui, Y., ter Avest, E., & van Dijk, M. P. (2018). Adoption of voluntary approach: Can voluntary approach generate collective impacts for China achieving ambitious energy efficiency targets? *Energy & Environment*, *29*(2), 281–299. DOI: 10.1177/0958305X17744491

# Chapter 2
# Community-Based Corporate Social Responsibility in Businesses:
## Strategies and Initiatives

**Pratap Chandra Mandal**
https://orcid.org/0000-0002-0300-4002
*Indian Institute of Management, Shillong, India*

## ABSTRACT

*It is imperative for businesses to be socially responsible towards the community which they serve. The objective of the study is to analyze the various aspects of community-based corporate social responsibility for businesses. The methodology adopted is a conceptual analysis of the various aspects and the strategies and initiatives adopted by various companies towards serving the community. They require focusing on corporate social responsibility in the workplace, corporate philanthropy, services to low-income communities, cause marketing, and social marketing. Strategies and initiatives adopted by companies are discussed. Academicians may suggest effective models for community-based corporate social responsibility for businesses to adopt. Businesses and practitioners will realize the importance of corporate social responsibility and incorporate community-based corporate social responsibility in their activities. All these will help companies to create a positive impression and to achieve business excellence in the long run.*

## 1. INTRODUCTION

Companies will be able to achieve healthy growth in the long term when they engage in many marketing activities and satisfy a broad set of constituents and objectives (Wang, Sua, & Dolar, 2024). Companies should not only focus on the selfish motive of generating revenues and profits for themselves. They require considering the societal impact of their actions (Dörr & Lautermann, 2024). Companies focus on corporate social responsibility which has become a priority in the present-day business scenario. Corporate social responsibility is ingrained in the business models of companies (Das, Taneja, & Arora, 2021). For example, some organizations, like Tata Trust from India, fully embrace the vision of social

DOI: 10.4018/979-8-3693-7081-0.ch002

responsibility (Chatterjee, 2016). A company will be successful when it focuses on effective relationship marketing, integrated marketing, internal marketing, and performance marketing (Keller & Kotler, 2015). Companies should consider the societal impact of their marketing activities and should examine the key dimension of corporate social responsibility (Pfajfar, Shoham, Małecka, & Zalaznik, 2022).

Companies focus on the *triple bottom line* – people (social component), planet (sustainability component), and profit (monetary component) (Liute & De Giacomo, 2022). Triple bottom line indicates that the responsibility of a company lies with stakeholders and all entities which are directly or indirectly influenced by the actions of the company. These responsibilities do not lie only with the shareholders who actually own the firm (Farooq, Fu, Liu, & Hao, 2021). The stakeholders may include, in addition to the shareholders, company employees, customers, and the society at large. Companies engage in corporate social responsibility in three broad domains which include community, sustainability, and market profit (Idowu & Kasum, 2016).

Community is an important aspect when companies think of corporate social responsibility. Companies are a part of the community in which they operate and function. So, it is imperative that companies focus on the community to achieve success in the long term.

The discussions indicate that companies should be aware about their responsibilities not only towards their customers but also towards the community and the society at large. Although the topic is important and relevant, researchers have not focused on the important aspect of community-based corporate social responsibility. The study aims to address this research gap.

The objective of the study is to analyze the various aspects of corporate social responsibilities of companies towards communities. It is important for companies to be sensitive about their responsibilities towards the community.

The methodology adopted is a conceptual analysis of the various aspects of community-based corporate social responsibilities of companies. Research studies which are published in reputed academic journals on the topic are analyzed. Case studies of different companies which have a focus on corporate social responsibility, are analyzed. Primary data is not collected and empirical analysis is not done.

The novelty and the contributions of the study lie in the fact that a conceptual analysis of the various aspects of community-based corporate social responsibility for businesses is conducted. Based on the analysis, academicians may suggest models of corporate social responsibility and establish the importance of community-based corporate social responsibility for businesses. Companies and practitioners will be sensitized about corporate social responsibility for communities. They will be motivated to serve the communities if they are not already doing so. All these will help companies to build a positive perception in the minds on the communities which they serve and the society at large.

The study is structured as follows:

The discussions start with a focus on the roles of corporate social responsibility for businesses. Community-based corporate social responsibility is discussed while highlighting the various aspects of corporate social responsibility in the workplace, corporate philanthropy, services to low-income communities, cause marketing, and social marketing respectively. The various initiatives adopted by Gokaldas Exports, Fairtrade, McDonald's, Naandi Foundation, Dawn, PRODUCT (RED), Plaeto, and World Wildlife Fund are discussed. The salient points of the study are discussed. Theoretical implications and managerial implications of the study are highlighted. Limitations of the study and avenues of future research are highlighted.

## 2. ROLES OF CORPORATE SOCIAL RESPONSIBILITY FOR BUSINESSES

Effective business activities should be matched by a strong sense of ethics, values, and social responsibility (Grbac & Lončarić, 2009). According to the PwC Global CEO Survey conducted in 2016, 64 percent of CEOs believe that "corporate social responsibility is core to their businesses rather than just an adjunct stand-alone program" (Kotek, Schoenberg, & Schwand, 2018). Those companies which adopt a more active and strategic role in corporate social responsibility, are successful in the long run. Such activities are thought to benefit not only customers, employees, the community, and the environment, but also shareholders (Shen, Au, & Li, 2020).

A variety of reasons motivates companies to engage in prosocial activities and invest in corporate social responsibility. Many companies believe that creating societal benefits is a key element of the corporate culture and the value system of the company (Hiller, 2013). Again, many consumers favor those companies which they feel are concerned about the society and which exhibit civic virtues. So, companies focus on corporate social responsibility to differentiate themselves from other companies which are not serious about corporate social responsibility (Wang, 2021). Some companies do it at the insistence of their collaborators who prefer to deal with companies that care about creating value for the society. Again, many companies do it so that potential criticisms are offset and they are able to deal with marketing crises more effectively (Magrizos & Harris, 2023). Some companies engage in corporate social responsibility to increase employee loyalty and to create investor goodwill (Stojanovic, Milosevic, Arsic, Urosevic, & Mihajlovic, 2020).

Companies are most admired and are most successful when they abide by the high standards of business and marketing conduct. Such conduct satisfies the interests of both customers and companies (James, 2013). For example, Procter & Gamble (P&G) has made *brand purpose* a key component of its marketing strategies. P&G has launched a number of initiatives and award-wining programs which support various causes. These programs include *Touch of Comfort* by Downy fabric softener, *Loads of Hope* by Tide laundry detergent, and *Mean Stinks* by Secret deodorant (Chipp & Maphalala, 2019). Stonyfield Farm is also another company which has put socially responsible marketing at the center of all its activities (Hoeffler, Bloom, & Keller, 2010).

Companies which conduct socially responsible marketing adopt a three-pronged approach which includes the community, the environment, and the marketplace (Özturan & Grinstein, 2022). Social justice advocates and environmentalists suggest a broader definition of bottom line into public consciousness. They introduce societal and environmental benefits as key components of a company's bottom line (Hervani, Sarkis, & Helms, 2017).

## 3. COMMUNITY-BASED CORPORATE SOCIAL RESPONSIBILITY

Marketers require satisfying a broad set of constituents and objectives to achieve healthy growth in the long term (Jones, Comfort, & Hillier, 2006). One major objective of a company is to create value for the community in which it operates. Companies operate in several domains to fulfill their responsibilities towards the community. These domains include improvement of the workplace, engagement in corporate philanthropy, support for low-income communities, support for cause marketing, and engagement in social marketing (Breeze & Wiepking, 2020). Different types of community-based corporate social responsibility are discussed in the following sections.

## 3.1. Corporate Social Responsibility in the Workplace

Companies should create an environment in the workplace where employees are treated in a fair and ethical manner which is consistent with the societal norms (Sánchez-Torné, Morán-Álvarez, & Pérez-López, 2020). Companies are able to implement corporate social responsibility in the workplace when they focus on a number of domains which include fair compensation, work-life balance, diversity, safe and healthy working environment, and employee development (Marôco, Nogueira, Gonçalves, & Marques, 2022).

- *Fair Compensation:* Fair compensation ensures that wages are consistent with the industry norms. The wages should also be sufficient to meet basic living requirements (Uche & Khalid, 2023).
- *Work-life Balance*: Employees should be free to allocate their time to other aspects of lives which include family, personal interests, socializing, and leisure activities (Diamantis & Puhr, 2022).
- *Diversity:* Companies should encourage and promote diversity in the work environment. They should avoid artificial barriers or distinctions based on factors such as culture, religion, ethnicity, and race (Starostka-Patyk, Tomski, & Zawada, 2015).
- *Safe and Healthy Working Environment:* Companies should foster a work environment that protects employees against violence in workplace and work-related illnesses (Al Doghan & Zakariya, 2022).
- *Employee Development:* Companies should invest in employee development. They should invest resources in training and in advancement of employees (Zientara, Kujawski, & Bohdanowicz-Godfrey, 2015).

Companies are able to reap benefits by investing in corporate social responsibility (Fordham, Robinson, & Blackwell, 2017). Bob Stiller, founder of Green Mountain Coffee Roasters (renamed as Keurig Green Mountain in 2014 and Keurig Dr. Pepper in 2018), has said that "people are motivated and more willing to go the extra mile to make the company successful when there's a higher good associated with it" (Fuhrman, 2009). Employees are motivated when they feel that the company is dedicated towards the principles of corporate social responsibility and adopt initiatives towards fulfilling such responsibilities. In such cases, chances are higher that employees are more likely to do so themselves. This, in turn, helps in building and developing closer relationships among employees because of shared goals and a greater sense of identity with the company. It becomes easier for companies which are committed to socially responsible causes, to recruit, to motivate, and to retain key employees. This is because for many employees, the social responsibility component is as important as the financial compensation.

The management of a company cannot implement workplace corporate social responsibility programs single-handedly. The programs must reflect the requirements and preferences of employees. It should be ensured that the employees are on board and are engaged in the efforts of the company in improving the workplace environment. Companies should create a great corporate culture that reflects societal values. Such values can pay off for companies that stand behind their corporate social responsibility initiatives. Gokaldas Exports is one company which has implemented workplace corporate social responsibility programs successfully (Merk, 2014).

Companies should treat employees in a fair and ethical manner. This is more important for businesses that operate in international locations with labor laws that differ from those in the United States (Berger-Walliser & Scott, 2018). Companies which truly embrace the principles of corporate social responsibility apply the same principles to their global subsidiaries and business partners as to their home-based operations. Fairtrade is an organization which helps companies find socially responsible business partners in developing countries and ensures that they follow sustainable business practices (Bradley & Botchway, 2018).

## 3.2. Corporate Philanthropy

Companies and businesses, at present, focus on corporate philanthropy. Firms believe that corporate social responsibility in the form of cause marketing and employee volunteerism programs are not just the *right thing* but also the *smart thing* to do (Gardberg, Zyglidopoulos, Symeou, & Schepers, 2019).

Many companies focus on corporate social responsibility and assign a prominent role to it. Such companies include The Body Shop, Working Assets, Newman's Own, and Smith & Hawken. Newman's Own is late actor Paul Newman's homemade salad dressing venture. The company has grown into a huge business that includes pasta sauce, salsa, popcorn, and lemonade. The products are now sold in more than 15 overseas markets (Loutskina, Yemen, Mead, Loutskina, & Yemen, 2024). The company donates all its profits and royalties after tax, which amount to more than $400 million, to thousands of educational and charitable programs worldwide, including the Hole in the Wall Gang camps that Newman created for children with serious illnesses (Quarter, Mook, & Armstrong, 2017).

The trend of corporate giving is on a rise. This raises the question of the ultimate impact of corporate philanthropy on the market performance of a company. Researchers argue that corporate giving can have a positive impact in various domains. These domains include enhancing company image, enhancing customer loyalty, and enhancing perceived product performance (Saha, Ranjan, Pappu, & Akhlaghpour, 2023).

Studies reveal that consumers favor those companies which are engaged in corporate philanthropy (Han, Kim, & Nam, 2020). Consumers view such companies as warmer, more compassionate, more ethical, more likable and trustworthy, and less blameworthy in the midst of corporate crises. Research also reveals that the reputation of a company for social responsibility tends to enhance customer loyalty, increase customer satisfaction, decrease consumer price sensitivity, and increase their brand commitment (Pérez, & Rodríguez del Bosque, 2015). Socially responsible behavior of companies is likely to increase product sales by motivating consumers to reward a company for its prosocial behavior and giving consumers the opportunity to attain moral satisfaction from the *warm glow of giving* (Chernev & Blair, 2015).

Corporate social responsibility has a positive impact of social goodwill on company image and consumer loyalty. Research also suggests that the positive effect of corporate social responsibility can extend to perceptions of the performance of the products of companies (Barauskaite & Streimikiene, 2021). The products of those companies which are engaged in charitable giving are likely to be perceived as having higher levels of performance (Chen & Huang, 2018). All these indicate that companies are more successful when they focus on corporate social responsibility.

Companies may face dilemmas when they practice corporate philanthropy. Companies like Bank of America, Walmart, DuPont, and Merck have each donated more than $100 million to charities annually (English, 2024). However, in many instances, good deeds may be overlooked. Consumers may resent the company if it is seen as exploitative or fails to live up to a *good guy* image. Critics worry that cause marketing or consumption philanthropy may replace virtuous actions with less thoughtful consumer buying, reduce emphasis on real solutions, or divert attention from the fact that markets themselves pose many social problems (English, 2024).

## 3.3. Services to Low-Income Communities

Many companies provide services to communities with low incomes. The bottom of the pyramid (BOP) is a socio-economic concept used in reference to the largest but poorest group of the world's population. Such groups live on less than $2.50 a day (Prahalad, 2005). It is important to address the needs of the world's poorest citizens. This is emphasized by business writer C.K. Prahlad who believed that much innovation can come from developments in emerging markets such as China and India (Prahalad, 2012). Firms operating in such markets should be able to do more with less. Such firms focus on innovation to serve the communities in such markets.

Companies should do proper planning and execution to satisfy the individuals at the bottom of the pyramid. Each individual in such markets has low income with low purchasing power parity. However, collectively, such individuals may be worth several trillion dollars. Conventional wisdom says a *low-price, low-margin, and high-volume* business model is the key to successfully appealing to lower-income consumers in developing markets (Singh, Bakshi, & Mishra, 2015). Many companies like Hindustan Unilever with Wheel detergent in India have successfully implemented such strategies. However, many other companies have struggled. Procter & Gamble (P&G) launched its Pur water-purification product in India. However, the product was not a success in the Indian market. Finally, P&G transitioned the brand to a philanthropic venture (White, 2009).

The approach discussed above may work in highly complex product categories such as medical care (Abreu, David, & Crowther, 2005). For example, in Bangalore, Narayana Hrudayalaya Hospital charges a flat fee of $1500 for heart bypass surgery. The same surgery may cost 50 times as much in the United States. The hospital is able to reduce its cost because of low labor, operating expenses, and an assembly-line view of care (Cappelli, Singh, Singh, & Useem, 2010). The approach generates results for the hospital. The mortality rates for the hospital are half those of U.S. hospitals. Hundreds of infants are operated on for free. It also offers catastrophic health insurance profitably to more than 2.5 million poor individuals for 11 cents a month (Bajaj, 2018). Similarly, ITC introduced its e-Choupal initiative which uses the power of the internet to empower more than 4 million farmers. The initiative allows farmers to improve farm productivity, replenish natural resources, and provide efficient market access (Venugopal & Agrawal, 2023). Fab India and Big Basket create market linkages which aim to improve income generation opportunities for traditional artists, craftsmen, and marginal farmers (Singh et al., 2015). Naandi Foundation introduced Araku Coffee project which is supported by eminent business leaders. The project aims at improving the lives and livelihoods of the tribal communities of Araku Valley in Andhra Pradesh. All these have helped Araku Coffee to establish itself as a premium global coffee brand (Chavan, Gowan, & Vogeley, 2023).

Companies may be benefited by serving low-income communities in higher-income markets. Companies have the opportunity of transferring the innovations done in developing markets to developed markets. This is termed as reverse innovation. Reverse innovation adopts successful solutions which are developed to meet the needs and constraints of a developing market, to create an inexpensive product that can be introduced as a cheaper alternative in developed markets (Dudaklı, Felekoğlu, & Baykasoğlu, 2022). Public policy benefits may be included in reverse innovation. Reverse innovation may result in successful development of ultra low-cost transportation, renewable energy, clean water, micro-finance, affordable health care, and low-cost housing. All these innovations may help the companies in transforming industries (Malik, 2017).

Nestlé is a company which invests in reverse innovation. Reverse innovation helped Nestlé to re-position its low-fat Maggi brand dried noodles which is a popular, low-priced meal in rural Pakistan and India. The repositioning allowed Nestlé to launch the brand as a budget-friendly healthy food in Australia and New Zealand (Pedroza, 2020). Harman International is a U.S-based company known for its high-end dashboard audio systems developed by German engineers. The company applied reverse innovation to develop a radically simpler and cheaper way to create products for the emerging markets of China and India. The company is also applying the innovation to its product development centers in the West (Govindarajan & Ramamurti, 2018). The company sells a number of products across various price ranges. The company is also focusing on innovation to develop infotainment systems for motorbikes which is a popular form of transportation in emerging markets and around the world (Govindarajan & Euchner, 2012).

Companies focus on serving a growing middle class in many emerging markets. Many firms assemble product portfolios to tap into different income segments. Danone is a French food company which markets high-end healthy products like Dannon yogurt, Evian water, and Bledina baby food. At the same time, the company also sells lower-priced products. These products are targeted towards consumers with *dollar-a-day* food budgets. In Indonesia, the average daily per-capita income is about US $10. For such markets, the company sells Milkaut which is a neutral ph milk beverage with a six-month shelf life. At present, the majority of sales for Danone is generated from emerging markets (Pandey & Yadav, 2020).

Companies do not compromise with quality, functionality, and brand image when they sell products with low prices. Again, consumers with low income may not be the individuals who are looking for the cheapest option. Although they may be limited by budgetary constraints, many of them aspire to buy premium products and brands.

Companies are able to reap substantial benefits from developing markets if they develop their marketing strategies for such markets properly. For example, Nokia sent marketing, sales, and engineering staff from its entry-level phone group to spend a week in the homes of individuals in rural China, Thailand, and Kenya. The staff observed how the individuals in such markets used their phones. Based on the feedback, Nokia was able to develop phones with the right functionalities and at rock-bottom prices. All these also helped Nokia to retain market share and leadership in some parts of Africa and Asia despite being surpassed by other brands in various parts of the developed world (Arora, 2015).

## 3.4. Cause Marketing

Many companies blend corporate social responsibility initiatives with marketing activities. Cause marketing links the contributions of a firm toward a designated cause to the engagement of customers directly or indirectly in revenue-producing transactions with the firm (Smith & Alcorn, 1991). For example, a company may decide to donate a percentage of the revenues or profits earned from sales to charity. Procter & Gamble applies cause marketing for its dishwashing liquid, Dawn (Newmeyer, Obeng, & Hulland, 2020).

A successful cause marketing program may have several benefits. The program can improve social welfare, create differentiated brand positioning, build strong consumer bonds, enhance the public image of the company, create a reservoir of goodwill, boost internal morale, drive sales, galvanize employees, and increase the market value of the firm (Ballings, McCullough, & Bharadwaj, 2018). A strong and unique bond may be formed between the consumers and the firm that transcends normal marketplace transactions. One study revealed that 90 percent U.S. consumers have a more positive image of, are more loyal to, and have more trust in a company that supports a cause. The study also found that 54 percent of consumers have purchased a product because it was associated with a cause (Pandey & Bajpai, 2024). Goldman Sachs started *10000 Women (GS10K) program* in 2008. The program funds initiatives for facilitating women entrepreneurs with business and management education, mentoring and networking, and access to capital (Lartey, 2020). The program is offered in partnership with top business schools and on Coursera's online platform. Women entrepreneurs receive assistance in growing and scaling up their ventures. Goldman Sachs is able to reach to more than 100000 women entrepreneurs in more than 200 countries. The program contributes to the overall development of the global economy through stronger communities, empowered and enabled by women entrepreneurs through education, opportunities and access to capital to grow their businesses (Lartey, 2020). Goldman Sachs developed partnership with the N.S. Raghavan Center for Entrepreneurial Learning (NSRCEL) in India at Indian Institute of Management Bangalore to educate over 1600 women entrepreneurs in three years (Lartey, 2020).

Companies are benefited when they associate their brands with relevant social causes. Companies are able to build brand awareness, enhance brand image, strengthen brand credibility, evoke an emotional response to the brand, create a sense of brand community, and elicit brand engagement (Kim, Cheong, & Lim, 2015). Companies can target those individuals who are particularly socially minded and who use social media to learn about cause activities and engage with companies that support them.

Cause-related marketing may backfire if companies are not able to handle it carefully. Consumers may question the linkages between the product and the cause. They may also view the firm as self-serving and exploitative. So, many companies adopt a soft-sell approach to cause marketing (Kuo, Lin, & Liu, 2022). Consumers suspect companies when they think that a company is inconsistent or when they feel that a company is not sufficiently responsible for its behavior (Sabri, 2018).

Companies make a number of decisions while designing and implementing a cause marketing program. They decide on which causes to choose and how to brand the cause program. Experts believe that the impact of cause programs is less when the company is involved in a number of causes. Many companies focus on one or a few main causes to simplify execution and to maximize impact.

Limiting support to a single cause may not always result in a transfer of positive feelings from the cause to the firm (De Vries & Duque, 2018). Companies sponsor a number of popular causes. For example, the corporate partners of Susan G. Komen for the Cure include American Airlines, Walgreens, Samsung, Merck, Georgia Pacific, Ford, Dell, and American Express (Handel, 2012). So, a brand may be overlooked in a number of symbolic pink ribbons. PRODUCT (RED) is a cause marketing program. It has been able to avoid the potential drawback of multiple sponsors by directly incorporating the symbolic aspect of the cause into the product itself (Gao, 2020).

Companies choose those causes which align with their corporate or brand image and matter to their employees and shareholders (Kim et al., 2015). For example, Give the Gift of Sight is a social cause program initiated by LensCrafters. LensCrafters is a family of charitable vision-care programs providing free vision screenings, eye examinations, and glasses to millions of needy individuals in North America and developing countries around the world. The company rebranded OneSight after the company was purchased by the Italian firm Luxottica (Kim et al., 2015). Luxottica pays most of the overhead. Consequently, more than 90 percent of all donations go directly to fund programming (Kim et al., 2015). Animal Crackers from Barnum is another brand which launched a campaign to raise awareness of endangered species and to help protect the Asian tiger. The brand issues special-edition packaging and collaborates with World Wildlife Fund. Based on all these, the Nabisco brand saw a *healthy lift in sales*

(Kuo & Rice, 2015). Plaeto is a startup which has a strong focus on sustainability. It differentiates its brand while building a new business in the competitive footwear industry (Barman, 2021).

## 3.5. Social Marketing

Philip Kotler and Gerald Zaltman introduced social marketing as a distinct marketing discipline in the early 1970s (Kotler & Zaltman, 1971). The aim of both social marketing and cause marketing is to provide benefits to the community in which the company operates. Cause marketing aligns its business activities to support a cause. However, social marketing aims to *further* a cause. Examples of social marketing may be *say no to drugs* and *exercise more and eat better* (Lancendorfer & Reece, 2010). Cause marketing is usually done by for-profit organizations. On the other hand, social marketing is typically done by non-profit or government organizations and is not directly related to a particular business activity (Partnerships & Andreasen, 2009).

Social marketing aims to influence behavioral change for a social good. It applies a systematic marketing planning process which involves some audience segment which is well-defined. Initially, the focus of social marketing was the issues of tobacco, family planning, and HIV/AIDS. At present, social marketing involves a number of activities which aim to improve public health, prevent injuries, protect the environment, contribute to communities, and enhance financial well-being (Truong, 2014). There are more than 2000 practitioners around the world working mainly in non-profit organizations for the advancement of social good. Again, social marketing is not the same as social media marketing. Social media marketing describes how to use social media in marketing campaigns (Evans, Bratton, & McKee, 2021).

Organizations in the United States focus on social marketing. Government agencies which are involved in social marketing include the U.S. Environmental Protection Agency, the Department of Transportation, the Department of Health and Human Services, and the Centers for Disease Control and Prevention (Gordon, Russell-Bennett, & Lefebvre, 2016). There are many non-profit organizations which are engaged in social marketing. These include the American Cancer Society, the United Way, and the American Red Cross (Lee, 2020).

It is imperative for organizations to choose the right goal or objective of the social marketing program judiciously. For example, organizations need to decide whether a family-planning campaign should focus on abstinence or on birth control. They should also decide whether a campaign to fight air pollution should focus on ride sharing or on mass transit. Social marketing applies a number of tactics to achieve its goals. However, the planning process follows many of the same steps as those used for traditional products and services. World Wildlife Fund is one organization that has accomplished its goals through the application of modern marketing practices (White, 2018).

It is complex for organizations to implement and to execute social marketing programs. Such programs may take time and may require phased stages or actions. For example, to reduce the prevalence of smoking, aiming individuals may require multiple activities. Such activities include release of cancer reports, labeling of cigarettes as harmful, bans on cigarette advertising, education about the effects of secondhand smoke, bans on smoking in restaurants and planes, increased taxes on cigarettes to pay for anti-smoking campaigns, lawsuits filed by states against tobacco companies (Truong, 2017).

The discussions done above indicate that it is difficult to develop and implement a successful social media campaign. Consequently, organizations should design the campaigns in a systematic and disciplined manner. They should have a clearly defined goal, a well-structured strategy, meaningful tactics that translate the strategy into a reality, a viable implementation plan, and a process for evaluating the effectiveness and success of the program. Social marketing programs are often implemented by non-profit organizations. However, non-profit organizations can benefit from the same strategic marketing approach that for-profit companies use. The aim of both for-profit and non-profit organizations is to create market value. However, for-profit organizations define value in monetary terms and non-profit organizations define it in terms of benefiting the society.

Social marketing is related to brand activism for companies (Moorman, 2020). Brand activism entails a company taking a stand on an important social, economic, environmental, or political issue. The issue may sometimes be controversial. Brand activism is associated with a focus on societal issues that customers and employees care about. Brand activism does not focus on issues that concern the bottom line for a company. Brand activism is an important form of social marketing because it involves a company taking a prominent and early position on a divisive issue that has important societal implications.

Nike decided to prominently feature former San Francisco 49 ers quarterback, Colin Kaepernick. He was the front man of an NFL player movement to kneel during performance of the U.S. national anthem in protest of police killings of Black Americans. This was featured in an advertisement campaign celebrating the 30$^{th}$ anniversary of its motto *Just Do It* (Brown, Brison, & Bennett, 2020). The tagline of Nike's campaign was *Believe in something. Even if it means sacrificing everything.* The tagline took a clear stance in support of the values espoused by Kaepernick's actions. The campaign resulted in some customers embracing the actions of the brand and others boycotting Nike products (Schartel Dunn & Nisbett, 2023).

## 4. INITIATIVES BY COMPANIES

Various companies are sensitive about their responsibilities towards the community. They adopt strategies and initiatives to fulfill such responsibilities.

### 4.1. Initiatives by Gokaldas Exports

Gokaldas Exports is a leading exporter of apparel. The company supplies over 30 million pieces of garments annually to giant global fashion brands and retail chains. The retail chains include GAP, H&M, Marks and Spencer, Banana Republic, Puma, Adidas, JC Penny, Walmart, and Carrefour. The retail chains sell to over 50 countries through their outlets (Dash & Shetty, 2012). The company focuses on processes which are people-centric. It empowers its 25000 women employees who constitute 75 percent of its total workforce. The goal of the company is to make its women employees self-reliant. Towards achieving this goal, the company offers continuous engagement through training workshops on financial management, health, hygiene, communication, and well-being. Programs related to rural development, healthcare, education, environmental sustainability, and gender equality are organized. Such programs contribute to the active development of communities around more than 20 factories of the company. The company also organizes programs on adult literacy, vocational training, and credit through self-help groups (Dash & Shetty, 2012). All such programs create an engaged workforce while contributing to community development.

## 4.2. Initiatives by Fairtrade

The Fairtrade Foundation aims to empower producers in developing countries, advance social fairness, and enhance environmental standards (Hughes, 2015). The focus of the foundation is sustainable development. It advocates for better trading conditions for small producers and workers in developing countries. The primary focus of Fairtrade is on commodities which are frequently exported to developed countries. Such commodities include home goods, gold, flowers, chocolate, fruits, sugar, wine, cocos, and coffee. An important aspect of the fair-trade movement is that buyers of Fairtrade goods pay the producers a social premium. The premium goes toward sustainability and socio-economic development. The core principles of Fairtrade include (1) *income sustainability,* meaning that earnings should fulfill basic household needs regardless of volatile market prices; (2) *empowerment*, meaning that producers have the ability to make decisions based on their own interests; (3) *individual and community well-being*, meaning that producers can decide how to invest the Fairtrade premium based on their own and the needs of the community; and (4) *environmental stewardship*, meaning that sustainable practices are used in order to protect natural resources (Hughes, 2015).

## 4.3. Initiatives by McDonald's

McDonald's has a strong focus on children, family, health, and well-being. It has four major programs (Powell & Piggin, 2021). *Ronald McDonald Houses* operate in 35 countries and regions. It offers more than 8000 rooms each night to families that need support while their children are in the hospital. This results in a savings of a total of $657 million annually in hotel costs for the families (Cosquer & Jousselme, 2023). *Ronald McDonald Family Rooms* operate in 23 countries. The rooms furnish more than 4000 families each day with a place to rest and regroup at the hospital next to their sick children. *Ronald McDonald Care Mobiles* operate in nine countries. More than 50 care mobiles provide neighborhood on-site medical care for children (Rubin & Franck, 2017). Again, *Ronald McDonald House Charities* has awarded more than $100 million in funding through its Global Grants Program. The funding allows non-profit organizations to extend their reach and to impact health and well-being of children worldwide (Powell & Piggin, 2021).

## 4.4. Initiatives by Naandi Foundation

Naandi Foundation is a leading public service organization which is committed to the socio-economic development of the backward and poor sections of society (Dick, 2015). The foundation was established in 1998 by renowned scientist, entrepreneur, and philanthropist, Dr. K. Anji Reddy who was also the Founder Chairman of Dr. Reddy's Laboratories. He was supported by corporate leaders, Anand Mahindra and Kris Gopalakrishnan (Menon & Guha, 2021). The foundation runs several community-based projects in partnership with government, corporate houses, and with national and international NGOs. The main objective is to support the underprivileged communities. The foundation conducts a number of education programs. The programs include many successful initiatives for primary schools, educating the girl child (Nanhi Kali), and mid-day meal programs offering nutritious lunch to school kids, skill development for youth, among others. The foundation works extensively with the tribal communities to increase their livelihoods. One of the most successful projects is the development of a global coffee brand *Araku Coffee*. The project is aimed at creating sustainable livelihoods for the tribal farmers of the

Araku Valley in Andhra Pradesh (Ramamurthy & Srivastava, 2021). The project has become synonymous for the sustainable development of tribal communities. After the project was implemented, more than two decades back, Araku Valley has experienced visible transformation and upliftment in terms of education, hygiene, health care, employability as well as empowerment of women. The foundation has a mission to serve the society. It has touched the lives of more than seven million underprivileged individuals spread across 17 states of India (Menon & Guha, 2021).

## 4.5. Initiatives by Dawn

Dawn is a top dishwashing liquid marketed by Procter & Gamble in the United States. The liquid has an unusual side benefit. It can clean birds which are caught in oil spills. The U.S. Fish and Wildlife Service called Dawn as "the only bird-cleaning agent that is recommended because it removes oil from feathers; is non-toxic; and does not leave a residue" (Helm, Carter, Ford, Fry, Moreno, Sanpera, & Tseng, 2014). A catastrophic BP oil spill happened in 2010. After the oil spill, Procter & Gamble came to the rescue. It donated thousands of coded bottles of Dawn. It also donated $1 to Gulf wildlife causes for each code activated by customers. The initiative resulted in $500000 (Jue, 2019). The company donated more than 50000 bottles of Dawn to help rescue and release 75000 animals which are affected by oil pollution. In 2018, Dawn marked the 40th anniversary of its legacy wildlife campaign by partnering with Kate Mara, actress and wildlife activist. The initiative tried to educate consumers on how Dawn has helped organizations save an extraordinary number of birds and marine animals (Jue, 2019). The Golden Duck Contest was also organized by Dawn. The contest allowed consumers who purchase a 40th Anniversary Bottle of Dawn Dish Soap, a chance to have a behind-the-scenes look at these wildlife-saving efforts (Helm et al., 2014).

## 4.6. Initiatives by PRODUCT (RED)

PRODUCT (RED) had a highly publicized launch in 2006. The launch was championed by U2 singer and activist Bono and by Bobby Shriver, co-founder of DATA (Debt, AIDS, Trade in Africa). The aim of the launch was to raise awareness and money for the Global Fund to Fight AIDS, Tuberculosis, and Malaria. The brand teamed with some of the world's most iconic brands which included Armani sunglasses, Apple iPhones, Gap T-shirts, Converse sneakers, and American Express cards to produce (RED)-branded products (Gallant, 2013). More than 50 percent of the profits from sales of these products go to the Global Fund. The objective is to help women and children affected by HIV/AIDS in Africa. Each company that becomes PRODUCT (RED) places its logo in the *embrace* signified by the parentheses and is *elevated to the power of red*. Many well-known brands support the cause. These brands include Starbucks, Microsoft, Montblanc, Coca-Cola, Amazon, and Bank of America. The brand has generated more than $500 million for the Global Fund and to support HIV/AIDS grants. The grants help countries which include Ghana, Kenya, Lesotho, Rwanda, South Africa, Swaziland, Tanzania, and Zambia. One hundred percent of that money is put to work on the ground and no overhead is taken (Gallant, 2013).

## 4.7. Initiatives by Plaeto

Plaeto is a direct-to-consumer (D2C) foot-health focused brand which offers *shoes for growing feet* of Indian children. The brand was launched by Ravi Kallayil, Sara Kilgore, and Pavan Kareti in 2021 (BW Online Bureau, 2021). Plaeto is committed towards protecting the foot health of children while caring for Mother Earth. The fundamental value of Plaeto is *accessible sustainability*. It delivers the value by creating high performing, affordable, durable, and sustainable shoes. One pair of its shoes has a carbon footprint of 6.5 kilograms carbon-dioxide. This is among the lowest in the global footwear industry (Barman, 2021). The brand applies disruptive design principles which include minimizing weight and materials, choosing lower carbon impact materials, and making locally and sustainable packaging. Low-energy manufacturing helps the brand to achieve a carbon footprint that is around 50 percent lower than an average athletic shoe. The shoes are durable. So, consumers need to purchase lesser number of shoes. This reduces carbon impact. Plaeto has developed key industry partnerships which help the brand create circularity in its process and materials for the product (Barman, 2021). The company has design, manufacturing, and engineering teams from India, U.S., and Italy. The teams develop proprietary design elements that deliver on the brand purpose of safeguarding the health of Indian children's feet. At present, the company aims to shift to recycled plastic, renewable plastic, renewable energy manufacturing, and an end-of-life plan to keep shoes out of landfills (BW Online Bureau, 2021). Innovative product engineering and local sourcing allow Plaeto to lower the *time to market*. Plaeto responds to market trends in a more responsive manner. It avoids the problem of over-production and waste which is the issue with every footwear and apparel brand. The long-term goal of Plaeto is net-zero carbon footprint. The brand has adopted a *Made in India* and *Made for India* approach. The approach helps Plaeto to contribute to economic, societal, and environmental development (BW Online Bureau, 2021).

## 4.8. Initiatives by World Wildlife Fund

The World Wildlife Fund (WWF) is the leading conservation organization in the world. It works in more than 100 countries and is supported by more than one million members in the United States and more than five million globally (Hardin, 2016). The organization has limited funds to promote itself. Consequently, it relies primarily on direct marketing to solicit contributions. The organization sends about 36 million pieces of eco-friendly mail in the United States every year. This helps the organization to generate 65 percent of its membership revenue. The organization is active on Facebook, Instagram, and Twitter. It has created partnerships with a number of firms. The firms include Royal Caribbean Cruises, Disney, Gap, and Avon. It also organizes joint marketing programs with its partners. For example, Coca-Cola donated $2 million for a campaign to help create safe areas for polar bears in Canada and other Arctic regions (Hardin, 2016). WWF also addresses important wildlife issues. It organized a multimedia anti-poaching campaign that used billboards, print advertisements, online posters, and public service announcements with the tagline *Stop Wildlife Crime – It's Dead Serious* (Minton, 2020). WWF also offers cause marketing opportunities to for-profit companies. For example, it joined hands with Bank of America to offer World Wildlife Fund Visa credit card (Pownall, 2015).

## 5. DISCUSSIONS

Companies are admired when they abide by high standards of business and marketing guidelines. The guidelines are formed based on the interests of individuals rather than the interests of the companies. Companies require pursuing a triple bottom line for raising the level of socially responsible marketing. It focuses on the community and the environment, in addition to corporate profits.

Marketers cannot achieve socially responsible growth unless they invest in resources to create value for the community in which they operate. Marketers can offer community-based corporate social responsibility across several domains. These domains include improving the workplace, engaging in corporate philanthropy, supporting low-income communities, fostering cause marketing, and engaging in social marketing. The salient points of all these aspects are discussed in the study. These aspects have both positive and negative impact on the community and the society. Companies and businesses should focus on the positive impact of these aspects and should aim to eliminate the negative impact of the aspects. Based on these, companies will be sensitive towards performing their social responsibilities and will appreciate their corporate social responsibilities and formulate their strategies and initiatives accordingly. It will also increase the accountability of companies and businesses towards the communities and the society in which they function. The discussions emphasize that companies and businesses will not be successful in the long run unless they understand and internalize the issues of the community and the society at large. They should address such issues. The study has both theoretical implications and managerial implications.

### 5.1. Theoretical Implications

Academicians may study and analyze the various aspects of community-based corporate social responsibility and its importance in the modern-day business scenario. They may analyze and suggest areas where marketers may provide services to the communities in which they operate. They may develop models of corporate social responsibility and establish their connections with the community. This will help marketers to realize and appreciate the importance of community-based corporate social responsibility.

### 5.2. Managerial Implications

Companies require creating value not only for their customers and themselves, but also for the community in which they operate. The discussions will sensitize companies about the importance of community-based corporate social responsibility and the various ways in which they can serve the community. Many companies already have a strong focus on corporate social responsibility towards the community. The discussions will motivate companies to serve their communities, if they are not already doing so. Companies will be sensitive and accountable in their responsibilities towards the communities and the society. Companies will achieve growth in the long run only when they grow with the communities which they serve. Practicing managers will appreciate all these and incorporate community-based social responsibilities in all their strategies and initiatives.

## 6. CONCLUSIONS

Various aspects of community-based corporate social responsibility are discussed in the study. Companies do community-based corporate social responsibility across various domains – corporate social responsibility in the workplace, corporate philanthropy, services to low-income communities, cause marketing, and social marketing. All these domains and aspects contribute and lead to the sensitivity of corporate social responsibility in the community.

### 6.1. Limitations

The study conducted a conceptual analysis about various aspects of community-based corporate social responsibility adopted by companies. Primary data is not collected and empirical analysis is not performed. Also, the study focused on conducting an analysis of mainly the markets in the United States with examples from the United States and India. The study did not perform an analysis of other markets. The study did not develop any model for companies and businesses. A model may help companies and businesses to understand and appreciate their responsibilities and accountability better and serve the community accordingly.

### 6.2. Avenues of Future Research

Researchers may conduct an in-depth analysis about the importance of community-based corporate social responsibility for companies and businesses. They may develop models which emphasize the importance of community-based corporate social responsibility. They may collect primary data not only from the markets in the United States but also from other markets and conduct empirical analysis. Based on the analysis, they may suggest strategies and initiatives which companies and businesses may adopt to serve the communities in which they operate.

## REFERENCES


Abreu, R., David, F., & Crowther, D. (2005). Corporate social responsibility is urgently needed in health care. *Social Responsibility Journal*, *1*(3/4), 225–240. DOI: 10.1108/eb045813

Al Doghan, M. A., & Zakariya, A. (2022). Developing positive health behavior among employees: Exploring role of green work environment in healthcare sector. *AgBioForum*, *24*(3), 84–96.

Arora, S. (2015). Micromax Informatics Ltd: Marketing strategy for emerging markets. *Emerald Emerging Markets Case Studies*, *5*(5), 1–22. DOI: 10.1108/EEMCS-06-2014-0158

Bajaj, H. (2018). Corporate Governance: At the Crossroads? *Governance and Governed: Multi-Country Perspectives on State. Social Development*, •••, 189–205.

Ballings, M., McCullough, H., & Bharadwaj, N. (2018). Cause marketing and customer profitability. *Journal of the Academy of Marketing Science*, *46*(2), 234–251. DOI: 10.1007/s11747-017-0571-4

Barauskaite, G., & Streimikiene, D. (2021). Corporate social responsibility and financial performance of companies: The puzzle of concepts, definitions and assessment methods. *Corporate Social Responsibility and Environmental Management*, *28*(1), 278–287. DOI: 10.1002/csr.2048

Barman, A. (2021). "New playbook: Is Plaeto out to disrupt kids' sneaker market dominated by Bata, Nike and Campus?", Economic Times (12th November 2021), Accessed on 23rd December 2021 from, https://economictimes.indiatimes.com

Berger-Walliser, G., & Scott, I. (2018). Redefining corporate social responsibility in an era of globalization and regulatory hardening. *American Business Law Journal*, *55*(1), 167–218. DOI: 10.1111/ablj.12119

Bradley, O. J., & Botchway, G. O. (2018). Communicating corporate social responsibility (CSR) in the coffee industry: An examination of indicators disclosed. *Sustainability Accounting. Management and Policy Journal*, *9*(2), 139–164.

Breeze, B., & Wiepking, P. (2020). Different drivers: Exploring employee involvement in corporate philanthropy. *Journal of Business Ethics*, *165*(3), 453–467. DOI: 10.1007/s10551-018-4093-x

Brown, S., Brison, N., & Bennett, G. (2020). Corporate Social Marketing: An analysis of consumer response to Nike's campaign featuring Colin Kaepernick. *Global Sport Business Journal*, *8*(1), 33–50.

BW Online Bureau. (2021). 'Plaeto To Power Untapped Indian Market for Kids' Footwear', Business World, December 3, http://www.businessworld.in Accessed on December 22, 2021.

Cappelli, P., Singh, H., Singh, J., & Useem, M. (2010). The India way: Lessons for the US. *The Academy of Management Perspectives*, *24*(2), 6–24. DOI: 10.5465/amp.24.2.6

Chatterjee, S. R. (2016). Corporate social responsibility in India: From traditional ethos to contemporary transitions. *Key Initiatives in Corporate Social Responsibility: Global Dimension of CSR in Corporate Entities*, 303-323.

Chavan, M., Gowan, S., & Vogeley, J. (2023). Collaborative corporate social responsibility praxis: Case studies from India. *Social Responsibility Journal*, *19*(2), 229–248. DOI: 10.1108/SRJ-06-2021-0216

Chen, X., & Huang, R. (2018). The impact of diverse corporate social responsibility practices on consumer product evaluations. *Journal of Product and Brand Management*, *27*(6), 701–715. DOI: 10.1108/JPBM-01-2017-1390

Chernev, A., & Blair, S. (2015). Doing well by doing good: The benevolent halo of corporate social responsibility. *The Journal of Consumer Research*, *41*(6), 1412–1425. DOI: 10.1086/680089

Chipp, K., & Maphalala, J. (2019). When elephants fight: South African washing powder wars. *Emerald Emerging Markets Case Studies*, *9*(1), 1–24. DOI: 10.1108/EEMCS-02-2018-0031

Cosquer, M., & Jousselme, C. (2023). The experience of parents in Ronald McDonald houses in France. *Archives de Pédiatrie*, *30*(4), 219–225. DOI: 10.1016/j.arcped.2023.02.004 PMID: 36990937

Das, J. K., Taneja, S., & Arora, H. (Eds.). (2021). *Corporate social responsibility and sustainable development: Strategies, practices and business models*. Taylor & Francis. DOI: 10.4324/9780429295997

Dash, M., & Shetty, R. (2012). The Impact of Global Recession on the Foreign Exchange Exposure of Indian Readymade Apparel Manufacturing Companies. *Asian Journal of Research in Business Economics and Management*, *2*(5), 169–177.

De Vries, E. L., & Duque, L. C. (2018). Small but sincere: How firm size and gratitude determine the effectiveness of cause marketing campaigns. *Journal of Retailing*, *94*(4), 352–363. DOI: 10.1016/j.jretai.2018.08.002

Diamantis, D., & Puhr, R. (2022). Corporate social responsibility and work–life balance provisions for employee quality of life in hospitality and tourism settings. *Worldwide Hospitality and Tourism Themes*, *14*(3), 207–209. DOI: 10.1108/WHATT-02-2022-0026

Dick, W. (2015). Naandi Foundation: Delivering High Quality Elementary Education in India. In *Experiencing Innovation in Asia: Cases in Business Model Development* (pp. 27-44).

Dörr, S., & Lautermann, C. (2024). Beyond direct stakeholders: The extensive scope of Societal Corporate Digital Responsibility (CDR). *Organizational Dynamics*, *53*(2), 101057. DOI: 10.1016/j.orgdyn.2024.101057

Dudaklı, N., Felekoğlu, B., & Baykasoğlu, A. (2022). Building blocks of the reverse innovation process. *Innovation (Abingdon)*, *35*(2), 196–223. DOI: 10.1080/13511610.2021.1925527

English, W. (2024). Can Welfare Economics Justify Corporate Philanthropy? Proposing the Philanthropy Multiplier as a Metric for Evaluating Corporate Philanthropic Expenditures. *Business Ethics Quarterly*, *34*(3), 440–470. DOI: 10.1017/beq.2023.2

Evans, D., Bratton, S., & McKee, J. (2021). *Social Media Marketing*. AG Printing & Publishing.

Farooq, Q., Fu, P., Liu, X., & Hao, Y. (2021). Basics of macro to microlevel corporate social responsibility and advancement in triple bottom line theory. *Corporate Social Responsibility and Environmental Management*, *28*(3), 969–979. DOI: 10.1002/csr.2069

Fordham, A. E., Robinson, G. M., & Blackwell, B. D. (2017). Corporate social responsibility in resource companies–Opportunities for developing positive benefits and lasting legacies. *Resources Policy*, *52*, 366–376. DOI: 10.1016/j.resourpol.2017.04.009

Fuhrman, E. (2009). Green mountain coffee roasters gives a one-two punch; Single-cup brewers fuel specialty coffee success. *Beverage Industry*, *100*(3), 29–35.

Gallant, L. (2013). Product (RED): The case against consumerism as a form of aid. *Te Canadian Undergraduate Journal of Development Studies*, *X*(I), 22.

Gao, F. (2020). Cause marketing: Product pricing, design, and distribution. *Manufacturing & Service Operations Management*, *22*(4), 775–791. DOI: 10.1287/msom.2019.0772

Gardberg, N. A., Zyglidopoulos, S. C., Symeou, P. C., & Schepers, D. H. (2019). The impact of corporate philanthropy on reputation for corporate social performance. *Business & Society*, *58*(6), 1177–1208. DOI: 10.1177/0007650317694856

Gordon, R., Russell-Bennett, R., & Lefebvre, R. C. (2016). Social marketing: The state of play and brokering the way forward. *Journal of Marketing Management*, *32*(11-12), 1059–1082. DOI: 10.1080/0267257X.2016.1199156

Govindarajan, V., & Euchner, J. (2012). Reverse innovation. *Research Technology Management*, *55*(6), 13–17. DOI: 10.5437/08956308X5506003

Govindarajan, V., & Ramamurti, R. (2018). *Reverse innovation in health care: How to make value-based delivery work*. Harvard Business Press.

Grbac, B., & Lončarić, D. (2009). Ethics, social responsibility and business performance in a transition economy. *EuroMed Journal of Business*, *4*(2), 143–158. DOI: 10.1108/14502190910976501

Han, C. M., Kim, K. A., & Nam, H. (2020). Can corporate philanthropy change consumers' perceptions of Japanese multinationals and reduce animosity toward them? *Asia Pacific Journal of Marketing and Logistics*, *32*(1), 65–85. DOI: 10.1108/APJML-09-2018-0383

Handel, K. (2012). *Planned Bullyhood: The Truth Behind the Headlines about the Planned Parenthood Funding Battle with Susan G. Komen for the Cure*. Simon and Schuster.

Hardin, R. (2016). Collective contradictions of corporate environmental conservation. *The Anthropology of Corporate Social Responsibility*, 179-198.

Helm, R. C., Carter, H. R., Ford, R. G., Fry, D. M., Moreno, R. L., Sanpera, C., & Tseng, F. S. (2014). Overview of efforts to document and reduce impacts of oil spills on seabirds. *Handbook of Oil Spill Science and Technology*, 429-453.

Hervani, A. A., Sarkis, J., & Helms, M. M. (2017). Environmental goods valuations for social sustainability: A conceptual framework. *Technological Forecasting and Social Change*, *125*, 137–153. DOI: 10.1016/j.techfore.2017.07.015

Hiller, J. S. (2013). The benefit corporation and corporate social responsibility. *Journal of Business Ethics*, *118*(2), 287–301. DOI: 10.1007/s10551-012-1580-3

Hoeffler, S., Bloom, P. N., & Keller, K. L. (2010). Understanding stakeholder responses to corporate citizenship initiatives: Managerial guidelines and research directions. *Journal of Public Policy & Marketing*, *29*(1), 78–88. DOI: 10.1509/jppm.29.1.78

Hughes, A. (2015). Retailers, corporate ethics and fair trade. In *Handbook of research on fair trade* (pp. 298–315). Edward Elgar Publishing. DOI: 10.4337/9781783474622.00027

Idowu, S. O., & Kasum, A. S. (2016). *People, Planet and Profit: Socio-Economic Perspectives of CSR*. Routledge. DOI: 10.4324/9781315599915

James, M. L. (2013). Sustainability and integrated reporting: Opportunities and strategies for small and midsize companies. *The Entrepreneurial Executive*, *18*, 17.

Jones, P., Comfort, D., & Hillier, D. (2006). Healthy eating and the UK's major food retailers: A case study in corporate social responsibility. *British Food Journal*, *108*(10), 838–848. DOI: 10.1108/00070700610702091

Jue, M. (2019). Fluid Cuts: The Anti-visual Logic of Surfactants after Deepwater Horizon. *Configurations*, *27*(4), 525–544. DOI: 10.1353/con.2019.0034

Keller, K. L., & Kotler, P. (2015). Holistic marketing: a broad, integrated perspective to marketing management. In *Does marketing need reform?: Fresh Perspectives on the Future* (pp. 308-313). Routledge.

Kim, K., Cheong, Y., & Lim, J. S. (2015). Choosing the right message for the right cause in social cause advertising: Type of social cause message, perceived company–cause fit and the persuasiveness of communication. *International Journal of Advertising*, *34*(3), 473–494. DOI: 10.1080/02650487.2015.1006081

Kotek, K., Schoenberg, A. M., & Schwand, C. (2018). CSR behavior: Between altruism and profit maximization. *Innovation Management and Corporate Social Responsibility: Social Responsibility as Competitive Advantage*, 159-169.

Kotler, P., & Zaltman, G. (1971). Social marketing: An approach to planned social change. *Journal of Marketing*, *35*(3), 3–12. DOI: 10.1177/002224297103500302 PMID: 12276120

Kuo, A., & Rice, D. H. (2015). The impact of perceptual congruence on the effectiveness of cause-related marketing campaigns. *Journal of Consumer Psychology*, *25*(1), 78–88. DOI: 10.1016/j.jcps.2014.06.002

Kuo, Y. F., Lin, C. S., & Liu, L. T. (2022). The effects of framing messages and cause-related marketing on backing intentions in reward-based crowdfunding. *Journal of Retailing and Consumer Services*, *64*, 102799. DOI: 10.1016/j.jretconser.2021.102799

Lancendorfer, K. M., & Reece, B. B. (2010). Can you market God? A case study of the 'God Speaks' social marketing campaign. *International Journal of Nonprofit and Voluntary Sector Marketing*, *15*(4), 324–338. DOI: 10.1002/nvsm.401

Lartey, F. M. (2020). Ethical Challenges of Complex Products: Case of Goldman Sachs and the Synthetic Collateralized Debt Obligations. *International Business Research*, *13*(6), 115–115. DOI: 10.5539/ibr.v13n6p115

Lee, N. R. (2020). The future of social marketing: Let's get it in orbit by 2025! *Social Marketing Quarterly*, *26*(1), 3–13. DOI: 10.1177/1524500419889141

Liute, A., & De Giacomo, M. R. (2022). The environmental performance of UK-based B Corp companies: An analysis based on the triple bottom line approach. *Business Strategy and the Environment, 31*(3), 810–827. DOI: 10.1002/bse.2919

Loutskina, E., Yemen, G., Mead, J., Loutskina, E., & Yemen, G. (2024). Impact Makers (A): The Newman's Own of Management Consulting. *Darden Business Publishing Cases*, 1-25.

Magrizos, S., & Harris, L. C. (2023). Crisis induced CSR innovation: CSR implementation in B2B firms before and after COVID-19. *Industrial Marketing Management, 115*, 44–56. DOI: 10.1016/j.indmarman.2023.09.009

Malik, O. R. (2017). When Davids start becoming Goliaths: Unique capabilities of emerging-market multinational enterprises and how they foster growth in developed markets? *International Journal of Technology Management, 74*(1-4), 45–69. DOI: 10.1504/IJTM.2017.083594

Marôco, A. L., Nogueira, F., Gonçalves, S. P., & Marques, I. C. (2022). Work-family interface in the context of social responsibility: A systematic literature review. *Sustainability (Basel), 14*(5), 3091. DOI: 10.3390/su14053091

Menon, M., & Guha, S. (2021). Role of Corporate in Promoting Social Enterprises. In *In Search of Business Models in Social Entrepreneurship: Concepts and Cases* (pp. 119–148). Springer Singapore. DOI: 10.1007/978-981-16-0390-7_6

Merk, J. (2014). The rise of tier 1 firms in the global garment industry: Challenges for labour rights advocates. *Oxford Development Studies, 42*(2), 259–277. DOI: 10.1080/13600818.2014.908177

Minton, E. A. (2020). Reducing crimes against wildlife through promoting animal–human continuity beliefs: The role of consumers' religiosity. *Psychology and Marketing, 37*(12), 1731–1742. DOI: 10.1002/mar.21415

Moorman, C. (2020). Commentary: Brand activism in a political world. *Journal of Public Policy & Marketing, 39*(4), 388–392. DOI: 10.1177/0743915620945260

Newmeyer, C. E., Obeng, E., & Hulland, J. (2020). Joining forces for doing good: Getting the international cause-alliance right. *International Marketing Review, 37*(5), 829–839. DOI: 10.1108/IMR-04-2019-0122

Özturan, P., & Grinstein, A. (2022). Can the marketing department benefit from socially responsible marketing activities? The role of legitimacy and customers' interest in social responsibility. *European Journal of Marketing, 56*(2), 400–441. DOI: 10.1108/EJM-09-2020-0670

Pandey, P., & Yadav, R. (2020). Danone India: The challenges of expanding into an emerging market. *South Asian Journal of Business and Management Cases, 9*(2), 189–197. DOI: 10.1177/2277977920911904

Pandey, P. K., & Bajpai, N. (2024). Mapping the research pattern of cause-related marketing: A bibliometric analysis of publications during 2000-2020. *Journal of Nonprofit & Public Sector Marketing, 36*(3), 271–298. DOI: 10.1080/10495142.2022.2133066

Partnerships, S., & Andreasen, A. R. (2009). Cross-Sector Marketing Alliances. *Nonprofits & Business*, 155.

Pedroza, L. (2020). *Lean Brands: Catch Customers, Drive Growth, and Stand Out in All Markets*. Red Wheel/Weiser.

Pérez, A., & Rodríguez del Bosque, I. (2015). Corporate social responsibility and customer loyalty: Exploring the role of identification, satisfaction and type of company. *Journal of Services Marketing, 29*(1), 15–25. DOI: 10.1108/JSM-10-2013-0272

Pfajfar, G., Shoham, A., Małecka, A., & Zalaznik, M. (2022). Value of corporate social responsibility for multiple stakeholders and social impact–Relationship marketing perspective. *Journal of Business Research, 143*, 46–61. DOI: 10.1016/j.jbusres.2022.01.051

Powell, D., & Piggin, J. (2021). Teaching young people about health?. *Critical Pedagogies in Physical Education, Physical Activity and Health.*

Pownall, C. (2015). Social and Environmental Threats. In *Managing Online Reputation: How to Protect Your Company on Social Media* (pp. 37–51). Palgrave Macmillan UK.

Prahalad, C. K. (2005). *The Fortune at the Bottom of the Pyramid*. Financial Times/Prentice Hall.

Prahalad, C. K. (2012). Bottom of the pyramid as a source of breakthrough innovations. *Journal of Product Innovation Management, 29*(1), 6–12. DOI: 10.1111/j.1540-5885.2011.00874.x

Quarter, J., Mook, L., & Armstrong, A. (2017). *Understanding the social economy: A Canadian perspective*. University of Toronto Press.

Ramamurthy, V. S., & Srivastava, D. K. (2021). A Multidimensional Approach to Sustainable Rural Development. *Science and Culture, 87*(9-10), 351–360. DOI: 10.36094/sc.v87.2021.A_Multidimensional_Approach_to_Sustainable.Ramamurthy.351

Rubin, N., & Franck, L. (2017). The role of Ronald McDonald House Charities® in keeping families close. *Pediatric Nursing, 43*(4), 202.

Sabri, O. (2018). The detrimental effect of cause-related marketing parodies. *Journal of Business Ethics, 151*(2), 517–537. DOI: 10.1007/s10551-016-3232-5

Saha, S., Ranjan, K. R., Pappu, R., & Akhlaghpour, S. (2023). Corporate giving and its impact on consumer evaluations: A meta-analysis. *Journal of Business Research, 158*, 113656. DOI: 10.1016/j.jbusres.2023.113656

Sánchez-Torné, I., Morán-Álvarez, J. C., & Pérez-López, J. A. (2020). The importance of corporate social responsibility in achieving high corporate reputation. *Corporate Social Responsibility and Environmental Management, 27*(6), 2692–2700. DOI: 10.1002/csr.1993

Schartel Dunn, S., & Nisbett, G. S. (2023). When celebrity endorsements collide with social activism: Exploring athlete celebrity endorsements, social issues and brand perception. *International Journal of Sports Marketing & Sponsorship, 24*(3), 558–569. DOI: 10.1108/IJSMS-01-2023-0010

Shen, N., Au, K., & Li, W. (2020). Strategic alignment of intangible assets: The role of corporate social responsibility. *Asia Pacific Journal of Management, 37*(4), 1119–1139. DOI: 10.1007/s10490-019-09681-1

Singh, R., Bakshi, M., & Mishra, P. (2015). Corporate social responsibility: Linking bottom of the pyramid to market development? *Journal of Business Ethics*, *131*(2), 361–373. DOI: 10.1007/s10551-014-2283-8

Smith, S. M., & Alcorn, D. S. (1991). Cause marketing: A new direction in the marketing of corporate responsibility. *Journal of Consumer Marketing*, *8*(3), 19–35. DOI: 10.1108/07363769110035054

Starostka-Patyk, M., Tomski, P., & Zawada, M. (2015). Diversity management as a part of corporate social responsibility policy. *Procedia Computer Science*, *65*, 1038–1045. DOI: 10.1016/j.procs.2015.09.055

Stojanovic, A., Milosevic, I., Arsic, S., Urosevic, S., & Mihajlovic, I. (2020). Corporate social responsibility as a determinant of employee loyalty and business performance. *Journal of Competitiveness*, *12*(2), 149–166. DOI: 10.7441/joc.2020.02.09

Truong, V. D. (2014). Social marketing: A systematic review of research 1998–2012. *Social Marketing Quarterly*, *20*(1), 15–34. DOI: 10.1177/1524500413517666

Truong, V. D. (2017). Government-led macro-social marketing programs in Vietnam: Outcomes, challenges, and implications. *Journal of Macromarketing*, *37*(4), 409–425. DOI: 10.1177/0276146716660833

Uche, C., & Khalid, S. (2023). The effect of organised hypocrisy: Compensation committees and fair compensation in the Ghanaian mining industry. *Critical Perspectives on Accounting*, *95*, 102509. DOI: 10.1016/j.cpa.2022.102509

Venugopal, P., & Agrawal, D. (2023). Can corporate social responsibility make business sense? framework based on itc e-choupal. In *Strategic Corporate Responsibility and Green Management: Perspectives and Issues in Emerging Economies* (pp. 69-81). Emerald Publishing Limited.

Wang, C. (2021). Monopoly with corporate social responsibility, product differentiation, and environmental R&D: Implications for economic, environmental, and social sustainability. *Journal of Cleaner Production*, *287*, 125433. DOI: 10.1016/j.jclepro.2020.125433

Wang, H., Sua, L. S., & Dolar, B. (2024). CAMELS-DEA in assessing the role of major factors in achieving higher efficiency levels: Evidence from Turkish banks. *Applied Economics*, •••, 1–18. DOI: 10.1080/00036846.2024.2339186

White, L. A. (2018). Social marketing in the Caribbean: Philosophy, programs, projects, and pedagogy. *Social Marketing Quarterly*, *24*(1), 35–44. DOI: 10.1177/1524500417752311

White, P. (2009). Building a sustainability strategy into the business. *Corporate Governance (Bradford)*, *9*(4), 386–394. DOI: 10.1108/14720700910984936

Zientara, P., Kujawski, L., & Bohdanowicz-Godfrey, P. (2015). Corporate social responsibility and employee attitudes: Evidence from a study of Polish hotel employees. *Journal of Sustainable Tourism*, *23*(6), 859–880. DOI: 10.1080/09669582.2015.1019511

# Chapter 3
# An Energy Perspective on the Role of Olive Groves in Sustainable Development in Andalusia

**Jesús Marquina**
https://orcid.org/0000-0003-3331-2011
*Escuela Universitaria de Osuna, Spain*

**María Pablo-Romero**
*Universidad de Sevilla, Spain*

**Javier Sanchez-Rivas**
*Universidad de Sevilla, Spain*

## ABSTRACT

*This chapter examines the significance of the olive grove and its agro-industrial sector in advancing sustainable development through enhanced production and the utilisation of renewable energy. To this end, the chapter assesses the various by-products for the generation of electrical and thermal energy in the region, analyzes the impact of the public policies adopted for its promotion, and identifies the primary obstacles it has faced and continues to face in improving its energy capacities. Furthermore, the analysis considers the potential impact of this development on the region from an energy, territorial, and sustainable development perspective. The findings indicate that the primary challenges historically encountered by the biomass industry pertain to the elevated costs associated with waste collection, transportation, and labor. Similarly, the regulatory changes introduced in 2012, which abolished the premium system for renewable energy sources, also represented a significant challenge for the continued deployment of such technologies.*

DOI: 10.4018/979-8-3693-7081-0.ch003

## 1. INTRODUCTION

In Andalusia, olive groves constitute a significant portion of the region's cultivated land, often reaching a monoculture character in a considerable portion of the territory. This is exemplified by the province of Jaén (Sánchez-Martínez et al., 2015). In 2023, olive groves constituted a cultivated area of 1.68 million hectares in the Andalusia region, representing 60% and 30% of the area occupied by this crop in Spain and the European Union (EU), respectively (Ministerio de Agricultura, Pesca y Alimentación, 2023).

Consequently, Andalusia has a substantial agro-industrial sector centered around this crop. In 2023, the region had 865 oil mills (48% of the national total), 222 table olive industry (45% of the national total), and 45 olive pomace extractors (71% of the national total). Furthermore, the region is responsible for the majority of existing facilities at the national level. It is the primary producer of Spanish olive oil, with an average production of 1.03 million tons over the past five seasons, and the primary producer of Spanish table olives, with an average production of 462,853 tons over the past five seasons (Consejería de Agricultura, Pesca, Agua y Desarrollo Rural de la Junta de Andalucía, 2023). (Consejería de Agricultura, Pesca, Agua y Desarrollo Rural de la Junta de Andalucía, 2023).

In addition to the agro-industrial products derived from the olive grove, a range of by-products with high energy content are also generated (Berbel et al., 2018; Romero-García et al., 2016; Rodríguez et al., 2008). In this regard, the by-products derived from pruning (branch and wood) and the agro-industrial process, including olive pomace, extracted pomace, olive stones, and leaves from olives for milling, are particularly noteworthy (Agencia Andaluza de la Energía, 2020). These by-products can be employed in the generation of electrical and thermal energy, thereby offering an alternative to the use of fossil energy in a region where the latter represents 78% of primary energy and is a significant source of polluting emissions (Román-Collado et al., 2021). Consequently, the utilisation of olive by-products can diminish the necessity for polluting energy sources and facilitate the sustainable development of the region.

The scientific community has shown considerable interest in recent years in the potential of using by-products from the olive sector as an alternative energy source, as opposed to fossil fuels. This is evidenced by research into the potential of these by-products for energy use, as exemplified by the studies conducted by Marquina et al. (2021a), Algieri et al. (2019), Alatzas et al. (2019), and Dounavis (2019). Most of these studies concentrate on Mediterranean countries where olive trees are widely cultivated, such as Andalusia.

Nevertheless, despite the scientific interest generated and the fact that successive Andalusian governments have promoted the use of renewable energies through the implementation of energy plans (see Consejería de Medio Ambiente y Ordenación del Territorio de la Junta de Andalucía, 1994; Consejería de Empleo y Desarrollo Tecnológico de la Junta de Andalucía, 2003; Consejería de Innovación, Ciencia y Empresa de la Junta de Andalucía, 2007; Consejería de Empleo, Empresa y Comercio de la Junta de Andalucía, 2013), the use of olive biomass remains insufficient. Consequently, approximately 70% of the potential for utilizing olive biomass for electric and thermal energy generation remains untapped (Marquina et al., 2021a). Nevertheless, if olive residues were fully utilized, an average of 3.9 million tons of biomass could be obtained per year, as opposed to the current 2 million tons (Marquina et al., 2021a). This biomass would generate 84% and 65% more electrical and thermal energy, respectively (Marquina et al., 2021a).

The increase of biomass is a crucial step towards achieving the ambitious objectives set out in the Andalusian Energy Strategy 2030, specifically in regard to the expansion and utilisation of renewable energies (Consejería de Industria, Energía y Minas, 2022). Furthermore, it is notable that the development of total biomass in Andalusia has not reached the same level as that of other renewable energies. In terms of installed renewable electricity capacity, Andalusia ranks fifth, with 274.0 MW in 2022. This is compared to 3,535.5 MW for wind, 4,703.0 MW for photovoltaic, and 997.4 MW for thermosolar (Agencia Andaluza de la Energía, 2024a). Similarly, although the installed capacity for thermal uses is relatively higher (1,816.8 MW in 2022), biomass represents only 3.3% of the total installed renewable capacity in the region (Agencia Andaluza de la Energía, 2024a). Therefore, greater utilization of olive grove biomass would facilitate more effective attainment of the energy targets established by Europe, Spain, and Andalusia. Furthermore, it would provide a valuable opportunity to establish an economic model based on the bioeconomy and circular economy, thereby contributing to sustainable development (Marquina et al., 2021b).

This chapter examines the significance of the olive grove and its associated agroindustrial sector in advancing sustainable development through enhanced production and the utilisation of renewable energies that are compatible with the surrounding territory. In the initial section of this chapter, an evaluation of the various by-products that can be employed for the generation of electric and thermal energy within the region is presented. Secondly, the chapter examines the impact of the public policies that have been implemented to promote this sector. Thirdly, the chapter identifies the principal obstacles that olive biomass has encountered and continues to face in order to enhance its energy capabilities. In conclusion, the potential impact of this development on the region is examined from the perspectives of energy, territorial development, and sustainable development. The study enables an evaluation of the significance of this energy crop for the region in terms of enhanced sustainability and energy efficiency. The analysis is based on three fundamental pillars: a review of previous literature, an analysis of statistical data, and an examination of the measures implemented and in force by public administrations.

## 2. LITERATURE REVIEW

The scientific community has recently focused its attention on the potential of olive by-products as a source of energy, given their role as an alternative energy source that can contribute to the sustainable development of the region.

A significant number of these studies have concentrated on the Andalusia region, given the considerable potential of the olive grove and its agroindustrial sector. An illustrative example is the study conducted by García-Maraver et al. (2012). This study examines the considerable potential of olive biomass in Andalusia and the numerous benefits it offers. These include its abundance and renewability, its capacity to reduce $CO_2$ emissions into the atmosphere, and its role as an energy alternative that can reduce the reliance on imported fossil fuels. In this regard, Marquina et al. (2021a) calculate that if the potential of olive biomass were fully exploited, approximately 4 million tons of biomass could be obtained annually for energy purposes, as opposed to the 2 million tons currently obtained. Consequently, olive biomass represents a valuable energy alternative for the Andalusia region, offering potential for both climate change mitigation and enhanced energy efficiency. This is corroborated by the findings of Torrus-Castillo et al. (2023), which indicate that the majority of olive groves in Andalusia are contributing to climate change mitigation. However, the authors highlight that the potential for further improvement can be achieved through the implementation of management practices that promote nature-based processes and facilitate the greater utilization of olive by-products.

The provinces of Almería, Jaén, and Córdoba are the most significant contributors to olive biomass production in the region, largely due to the prevalence of olive residues (Attard et al., 2020). In light of the aforementioned relevance of these provinces, a number of studies have been conducted with a particular focus on them. An illustrative example is the study conducted by Ossorio-Aravena et al. (2022), which underscores the economic and environmental impact of increased utilization of this organic matter in the province of Jaén. Similarly, Cardoza et al. (2021) concentrates its research on olive biomass in the provinces of Córdoba, Seville, and Jaén. In this research study, the authors perform an analysis to determine the optimal location for olive biorefineries, considering suitable areas of low environmental fragility and high availability of olive biomass, which would reduce transportation costs. In this sense, it should be noted that the high costs derived from transportation and labor, together with the regulations approved in Spain since 2012, have been an obstacle to the development of the biomass energy sector in the region of Andalusia (Marquina et al. 2021b). However, despite the obstacles faced by this energy sector, the economic value of olive biomass is sufficient to cover the value chain involved in the energy use of this organic matter (Marquina et al. 2021a).

Other authors have concentrated their efforts on determining the potential biomass yield of olive groves in comparison to other agricultural products. In this regard, Rosúa et al. (2012) underscore the significance of olive groves in terms of biomass production when compared to other crops, including vines, fruit trees, and poplars. The authors conclude that olive grove biomass would be capable of meeting approximately 52% of the energy needs for heating homes in this region, which serves to validate the potential of biomass as an alternative energy source to the intensively exploited fossil fuels. Furthermore, this approach could be applied in many other regions with similar Andalusian crops. Similarly, Menéndez et al. (2018) demonstrate the significance of this crop in Spain, particularly in Andalusia, in comparison to vineyards, another crop with the largest occupied area. The authors ascertain that the biomass derived from olive groves is four times greater than that of the latter crop, with Andalusia representing the region with the highest production and utilization of biomass from olive groves. However, the potential for its application is even more extensive. Consequently, the olive grove exhibits a multitude of varieties that collectively yield considerable biomass on an annual basis. Velázquez-Martí et al. (2011) quantify the residual biomass obtained per olive tree, considering the diverse varieties of this crop and the variables of pruning frequency (annual or biennial) and tree age.

Therefore, the energetic value of firewood and branches for energy production is high, which has been analyzed in several research works. Soltero et al. 2020 propose a novel methodology to determine the potential value of firewood to be used as biomass in the form of pellets for thermal use. The authors argue that if agricultural and energy sustainability policies favoring this model were adopted, this region would produce 160,000 tons of pellets per year, and 266,500 tons per year if it were extended to all of Spain, representing a potential supply of 70% of the current total consumption of pellets. Extending the model to other Mediterranean countries, such as Greece and Italy, would mean an additional 124,000 and 144,000 tons of pellets per year, respectively.

In addition, other authors have directed their attention to the agro-industrial olive oil processing sector. Contreras et al. (2020) have determined that oil represents, on average, only 20% of the weight of olives. Accordingly, the remainder of the average weight is attributed to by-products that are suitable for energy utilization. These by-products include those obtained in the olive oil production process, among which are the pits, leaves, and pomace. Additionally, the extracted pomace is a notable by-product, derived from the filtering of the pomace to produce olive pomace oil.

Conversely, it is imperative to underscore a salient benefit of biomass as an energy source: its independence from battery storage facilities. This independence is a notable advantage over other renewable energy sources, such as solar power, which are often constrained by the necessity of on-site battery storage (Kumar et al. 2021).

In summary, an increased production of olive biomass could assist in addressing challenges such as emigration, demographic shifts, and unemployment, as previously analyzed by Koch (2023) in his research work.

## 3. THE MAIN OLIVE BY-PRODUCTS

Andalusia is the region in Spain with the largest area under olive cultivation (60% of the national total), exhibiting a significant disparity in comparison to the rest of the regions (Ministerio de Agricultura, Pesca y Alimentación, 2023). In 2023, the region encompassed 1.68 hectares of cultivated olive groves, with Castile-La Mancha and Extremadura following at 0.45 and 0.30 hectares, respectively (Ministerio de Agricultura, Pesca y Alimentación, 2023). Consequently, Andalusia occupies the foremost position in the national ranking for both olive oil and table olive production, in addition to the production of biomass derived from its by-products (Cardoza et al., 2021). However, despite the positive impact of these extensions of olive grove cultivation on biomass production, further expansion of the area under olive cultivation may result in a significant loss of biodiversity, particularly in areas where olive groves are monocultures. This phenomenon has the potential to impact food security in the region (Suarez et al., 2023).

*Figure 1. Distribution of the area under olive cultivation in Spain (units: number of hectares)*

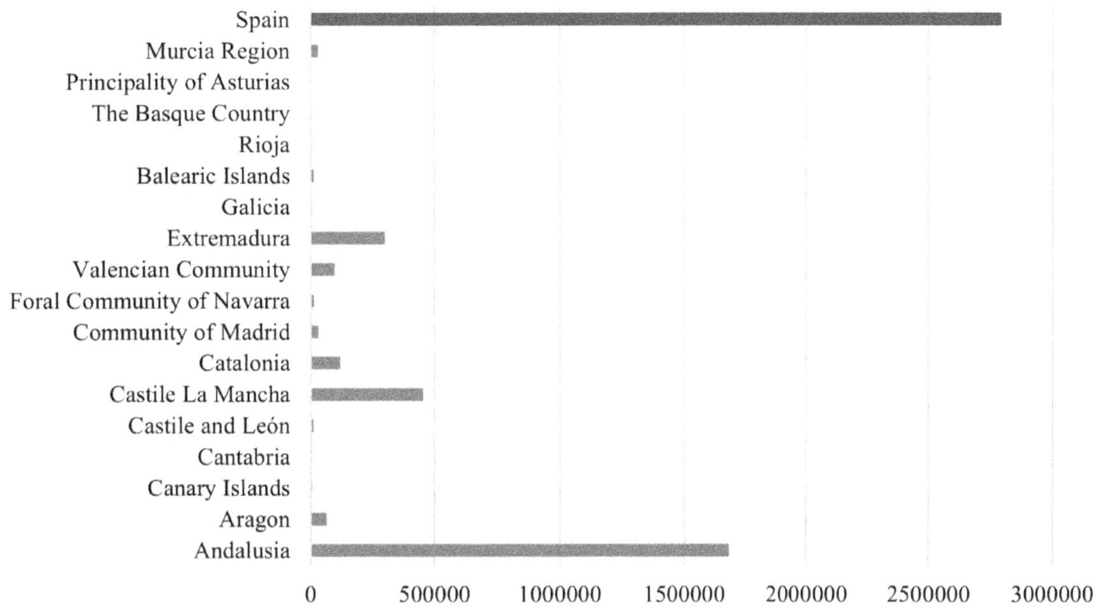


*Source: Ministerio de Agricultura, Pesca y Alimentación (2023) and own elaboration.*

The olive industry in Andalusia is characterised by a diversity of olive varieties, which can be classified according to their distinctive characteristics. Consequently, a variety of olive tree species yield olives of diverse varieties, including Hojiblanca, Arbequina, Manzanilla, Gordales, and numerous others (Ministerio de Agricultura, Pesca y Alimentación, 2024). These characteristics indicate that the olives are intended for use in the production of olive oil (olive mills), the production of table olives, or that they can be used for dual purposes (Ministerio de Agricultura, Pesca y Alimentación, 2024). Consequently, the pruning of olive groves is carried out on an annual or biennial basis, depending on the aforementioned characteristics (Rodríguez-Lizana et al., 2023). In particular, groves dedicated to the production of table olives are pruned annually, whereas those intended for oil mills are pruned biennially (Agencia Andaluza de la Energía, 2020). The pruning process generates two distinct by-products: branches and wood, which possess a considerable energy value (García Martín et al., 2020). Consequently, in their research, Marquina et al. (2021a) categorize the two types of olive groves and establish a mass balance of the by-products obtained. The aforementioned mass balances are illustrated in Figures 2 and 3, which follow. Figure 2 illustrates the potential yield in tonnes that could be obtained from table olive groves if all the residues generated from the pruning process were utilized.

*Figure 2. Mass balance of the harvesting process of branches and wood from table olives*

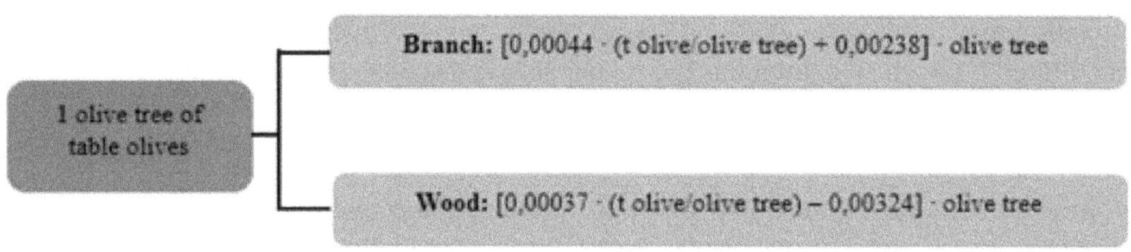


*Source: Marquina et al. (2021a) and own elaboration.*

Figure 3 illustrates the quantity of waste generated by the olive mill and olive grove.

*Figure 3. Mass balance of the process of collecting branches and wood from the olive mill*

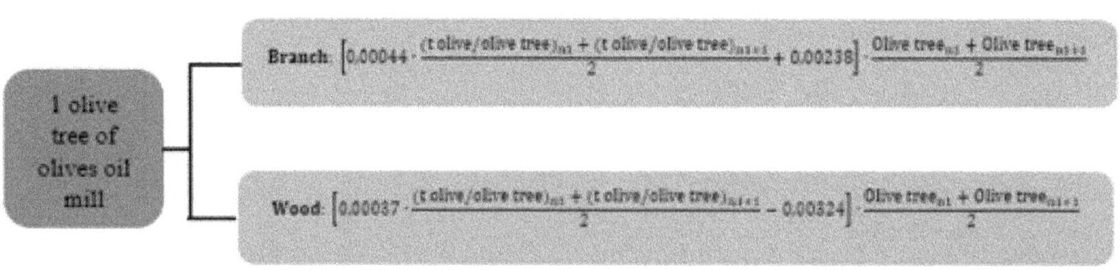


*Source: Marquina et al. (2021a) and own elaboration.*

The findings of the Marquina et al. (2021a) study indicate that among the by-products derived from pruning, the branch represents the largest annual yield. In particular, the average yield from table olive groves and olive oil mills is approximately 3 million tons per year. In terms of wood, it constitutes approximately 31% of the total by-products derived from olive pruning. The mean annual yield is estimated to be approximately one million tons.

In addition, the agro-industrial sector generates by-products from the production of olive oil, olive pomace oil, and table olives. Figure 4 illustrates that the production of olive oil in the oil mill generates leaf and olive pomace residues with a high energy content. In particular, the processing of one ton of olives into extra virgin olive oil results in the production of 8% of leaves from olives for milling and approximately 85% of olive pomace. Nevertheless, a portion of the olive pomace is utilized for the production of olive pomace oil subsequent to its passage through the olive pomace extractor. Additionally, the production of olive pomace oil generates by-products that can be utilized for energy generation. Such by-products include olive stones and extracted pomace. The aforementioned by-products account for 11.5% and 27%, respectively.

*Figure 4. Mass balance of the olive oil and olive pomace oil production process*

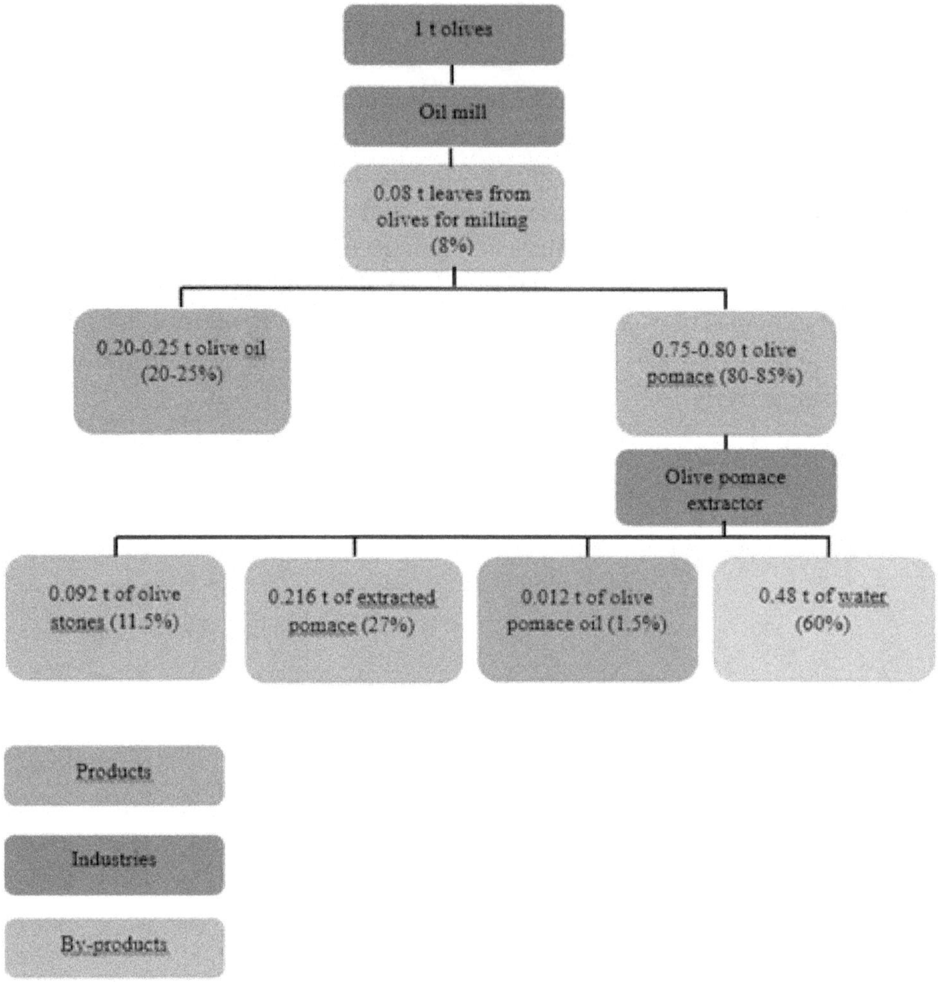


*Source: Agencia Andaluza de la Energía (2020) and own elaboration.*

Conversely, the production of table olives also yields by-products derived from olive stones. In this instance, the aforementioned olive stones are pitted for the purpose of marketing them as a final product. As illustrated in Figure 5, approximately 15% of the olives are processed into stones for further use.

*Figure 5. Mass balance of the table olive production process*

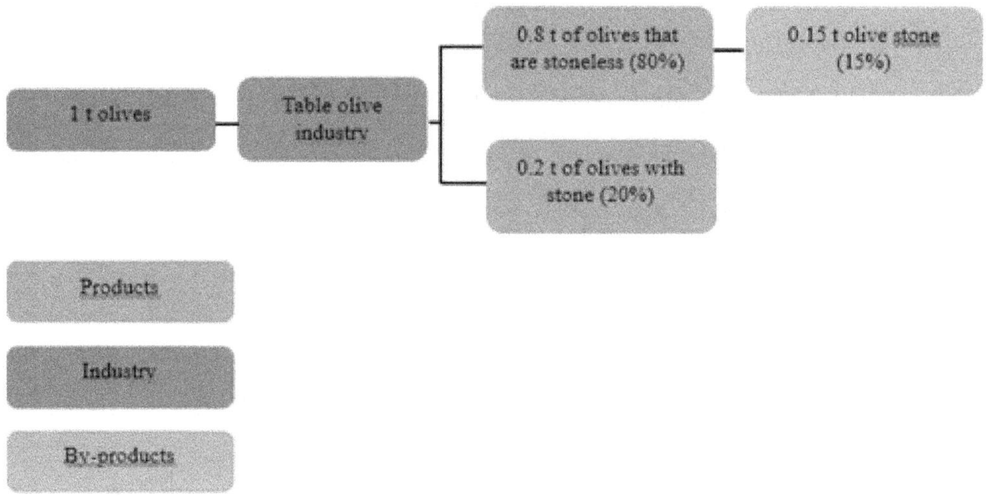


*Source: Agencia Andaluza de la Energía (2020) and own elaboration.*

As illustrated in Figures 4 and 5, the olive mill is the primary contributor of by-products to the energy sector within the olive industry. As indicated in the study conducted by Marquina et al. (2021a), the industry in question is capable of procuring approximately 1.5 million tons of by-products on an annual basis. Conversely, the authors posit that olive pomace extractors could produce an average of just over half a million tons per year, while renderers could obtain an average of only approximately 50,000 tons per year.

In conclusion, the agro-industrial sector of olive oil, olive pomace oil, and table olives has the potential to produce approximately 2 million tons of by-products annually if fully exploited (Marquina et al., 2021a).

## 4. MEASURES APPROVED TO PROMOTE THE USE OF BIOMASS FROM OLIVE GROVES

In recent years, the Andalusian government has implemented a series of energy plans, regulations, and incentives with the objective of promoting the consumption of renewable energy sources, thereby reducing the reliance on fossil fuels. The overarching objective of these regulatory frameworks is to reduce $CO_2$ emissions into the atmosphere and combat climate change.

In terms of planning, the Andalusian region has implemented five energy plans since 1995, as illustrated in Figure 3. All five plans exhibit a commitment to enhancing energy efficiency and expanding the utilization of renewable energy sources, even beyond the requirements set forth at the national and EU levels. To illustrate, the PLEAN 2003-2006 plan aims to meet at least 15% of the region's total primary energy demand by 2010, representing a three percentage point increase over the European target for that same year (12%). Biomass plays a significant role in each of the energy plans, particularly in olive cultivation. Figure 6 illustrates the principal elements.

*Figure 6. Relevant aspects of biomass within the different plans aimed at promoting the use of renewable energies in Andalusia*

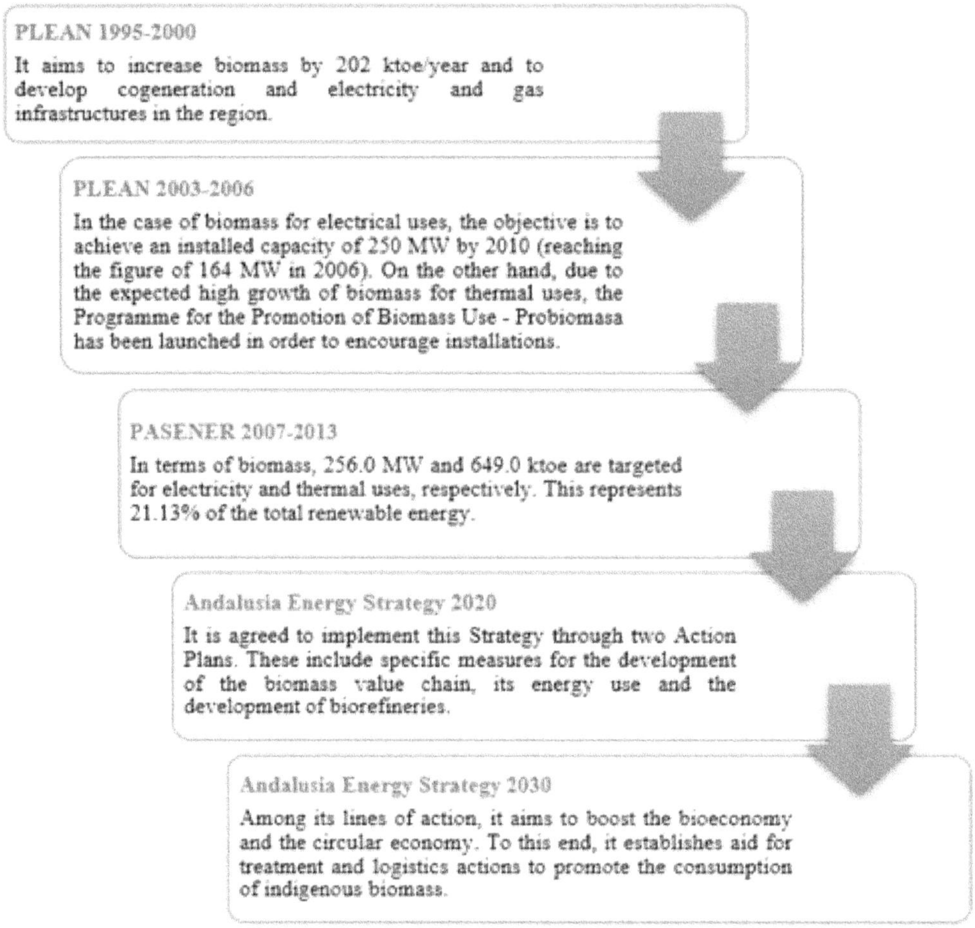


*Source: Junta de Andalucía (Consejería de Medio Ambiente y Ordenación del Territorio de la Junta de Andalucía, 1994; Consejería de Empleo y Desarrollo Tecnológico de la Junta de Andalucía, 2003; Consejería de Innovación, Ciencia y Empresa de la Junta de Andalucía, 2007; Consejería de Empleo, Empresa y Comercio de la Junta de Andalucía, 2013; Consejería de Industria, Energía y Minas de la Junta de Andalucía, 2022) and own elaboration.*

The implementation of these plans has prompted a transformation in the regional energy model. Consequently, there has been an uptick in the consumption of clean energy. At the present time, energy sources such as solar, wind, and biomass comprise approximately 40% of the installed electricity capacity (Agencia Andaluza de la Energía, 2024a). This figure represents approximately 41% of the electricity consumed by the Andalusian population.

In addition to these plans, other strategies have been formulated and are being implemented concurrently with the objective of achieving the desired outcomes. These include the Regional Strategy for Climate Change, approved in 2002, and the Andalusian Strategy for Sustainable Development. In 2004, the Andalusian government approved the "Agenda 21 for Andalusia." These were established with the objective of reducing greenhouse gas emissions. In order to achieve this objective, the following measures are being implemented: the promotion of renewable energy sources, the reduction of energy dependency, the encouragement of energy savings, the development of energy efficiency tools, and the promotion of energy-efficient housing construction (BOJA, 2002; Consejería de Medio Ambiente, 2004).

Similarly, the Andalusian Climate Action Plan (2007-2012-Mitigation Program) was approved in 2007, and the Andalusian Climate Change Adaptation Program was approved in 2010. These documents delineate the principal measures for adapting to climate change in the energy sector, the advancement of renewable energy, and the promotion and encouragement of energy conservation and efficiency (Consejería de Medio Ambiente, 2007 and 2010). Similarly, in September 2018, the Andalusian Circular Bioeconomy Strategy was approved with the objective of contributing to the sustainable growth and development of Andalusia. In order to achieve this objective, the strategy aims to encourage the production of renewable biological resources and processes, including olive biomass. In this way, the strategy represents an economic model based on the production and use of renewable biomass resources and their sustainable and efficient transformation into bioproducts, bioenergy, and services for society (Consejería de Agricultura, Pesca y Desarrollo Rural de la Junta de Andalucía, 2018).

In light of the pivotal role that olive cultivation plays in Andalusia's agricultural landscape, the sector has also demonstrated a proclivity towards utilising olive biomass. An illustrative example is the Strategic Plan for Andalusian Agroindustry 2020[1], which encompasses nine strategic lines of action pertaining to climate change. The objective is to encourage initiatives that enhance productivity and yield superior outcomes while reducing resource consumption, particularly of water, energy, and raw materials. This is to be achieved by employing alternative resources with less polluting impacts, such as waste, discharges, and emissions (Consejería de Agricultura, Pesca y Desarrollo Rural de la Junta de Andalucía, 2017).

From a legislative standpoint, the primary regulations pertaining to olive biomass in Andalusia can be classified according to the sector of activity they regulate, as illustrated in Figure 7.

*Figure 7. Main regulations in the energy and agricultural sector in Andalusia*

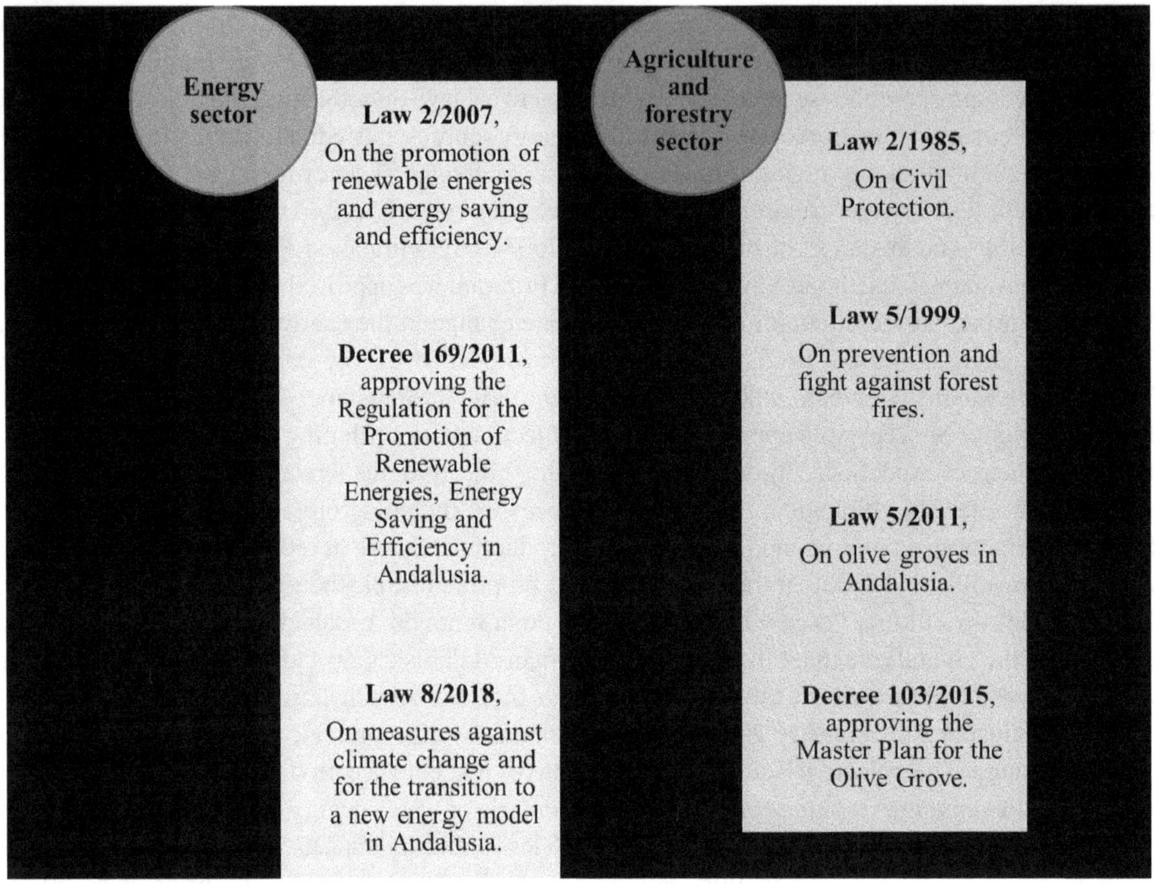


*Source: BOJA (2007; 2011a; 2018; 1999; 2011b; 2015), BOE (1985) and own elaboration.*

It is important to note that there is no specific legislation regulating olive biomass in Andalusia. In matters pertaining to energy, the pertinent legislation is Law 2/2007, which aims to establish the primacy of the use of renewable energies over other energy sources (BOJA, 2007). The aforementioned legislation comprises a series of measures designed to encourage the utilization of renewable energy sources. In regard to the measures for the promotion and use of biomass, Article 17 of this law establishes the commitment of the Andalusian Regional Government to regulate the use of biomass as an energy source and to develop promotional measures, the procedure for the recovery of biomass resources, and to carry out programs for the promotion of energy crops.

Subsequently, Decree 169/2011 provides further elaboration on the provisions of Law 2/2007. Henceforth, the Andalusian Energy Certificate shall be regarded as a document attesting to compliance with energy requirements for buildings and industries. Moreover, it sets forth a series of obligations, including the implementation of energy efficiency and cost-saving measures that are profitable in the short term, the use of renewable energies for thermal energy demand, and the implementation of an energy management system for large consumers (BOJA, 2011a).

In consideration of the considerable importance ascribed to the Andalusian olive grove, the regional government enacted a dedicated legislative measure pertaining to this specific agricultural product. Although it is not the sole focus, it is nevertheless a significant factor conducive to its advancement. Consequently, in 2011, Law 5/2011 on olive groves in Andalusia came into force. The objective of this legislation is to establish a regulatory framework for the maintenance and enhancement of olive cultivation in Andalusia, the sustainable development of its territories, and the advancement of the quality and promotion of its products. In order to achieve this objective, the aforementioned law (BOJA, 2011b) proposes the promotion of the biomass sector. Similarly, in accordance with the stipulations set forth in this legislation, Decree 103/2015 (Master Plan for the Olive Grove) was enacted in 2015. The plan outlines the specific strategies for olive biomass (BOJA, 2015):

- It is recommended that actions be promoted with the objective of achieving improvements in energy savings and efficiency in the olive grove industries.
- The objective is to reduce the volume of emissions and effluents generated by the olive industry.
- It is also recommended that new technologies be incorporated for the purification of waste from olive-derived industries.
- It is also important to consider the value of by-products obtained from olive industries and to encourage measures for their reuse and/or commercialization.
- The objective is to enhance the utilisation of renewable energies in olive industries, thereby achieving greater energy self-sufficiency.

In light of the aforementioned considerations, the Master Plan for the Olive Grove presents a valuable opportunity to advance the utilization of biomass energy in olive-growing regions, thereby contributing to the 2020 Strategy and the 2014-2020 Rural Development Programme.

Similarly, the Spanish legislation, namely Law 5/1999 of 29 June on the prevention and fight against forest fires and Law 2/1985 of 21 January on civil protection, encourages the utilisation of olive pruning waste for the generation of energy from biomass. Similarly, Law 8/2018 establishes a series of measures aimed at reducing greenhouse gas emissions into the atmosphere. In order to achieve this, the proposal is to transition towards an energy model based on renewable energies. In this regard, the objective of this legislation is to facilitate citizen involvement and to promote educational, research, developmental, and innovative activities (BOJA, 2018).

Conversely, at the municipal level, numerous Andalusian cities and towns have collectively ratified the Covenant of Mayors. This has further facilitated the utilization of renewable energies, particularly olive biomass, in Andalusia. The 548 participating municipalities (representing over 40% of the Spanish municipalities) have pledged to reduce their $CO_2$ emissions at the municipal level. In this manner, the objective is to fulfill the objectives established by the European Union (Consejería de Medio Ambiente y Ordenación del Territorio de la Junta de Andalucía, 2018). Those who have signed the Covenant are required to present an Action Plan for Climate and Sustainable Energy (PACES). The plan delineates the principal actions to be undertaken. Furthermore, the potential of biomass as a renewable energy source is emphasised, given its significant potential in the region (Ayuntamiento de Sevilla, 2016). In summary, olive groves constitute a significant energy alternative for the implementation of the various renewable energy projects that have been established.

Ultimately, the primary instruments utilized by the Andalusian government to encourage the utilization of renewable energies, with a particular emphasis on olive biomass, are subsidies for investment in equipment and installations that employ these energy sources. Since 2003, the Andalusian Energy Agency has been responsible for the administration of the subsidies. In the case of biomass, it should be noted that in 2006 the Andalusian Society for the Energetic Valorization of Biomass was established with the objective of developing technologies that promote the energetic use of biomass as a means of wealth creation in the agricultural and forestry sectors. This mixed public-private company represents a pioneering initiative in Europe (Europa Press, 2006).

The most significant measures undertaken in Andalusia to advance the utilization of renewable energies, particularly olive biomass, are illustrated in Figure 8. The most recent measures are presented here, although other forms of incentives for the promotion of renewable energies and energy efficiency in different economic sectors and households have existed previously.

*Figure 8. Most recent economic incentives*

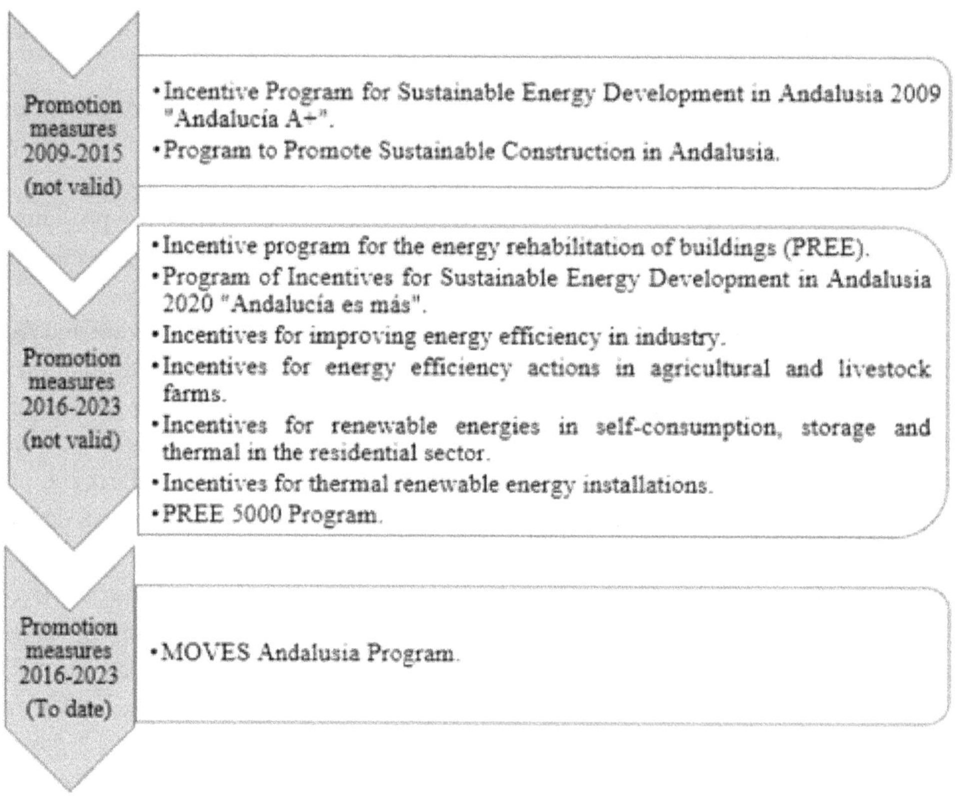


*Source: Agencia Andaluza de la Energía (2024b) and own elaboration.*

Over the course of the initial promotional phase, which spanned from 2009 to 2015, a total of 22,949 biomass projects were initiated. These projects have received incentives amounting to 61 million euros. The majority of these projects (19,979) pertain to thermal biomass, with the remainder falling under the umbrella of biomass logistics and treatment. Furthermore, since the implementation of the Programme for the Promotion of Sustainable Construction in Andalusia in April 2014 until May 31, 2016, 2,910 thermal biomass projects (including cookers, wood-burning fireplaces, and boilers) have been supported with an incentive exceeding 15 million euros. This results in an associated investment of 23 million euros (FFE, 2016).

As a consequence of these initiatives, there has been a discernible increase in the number of thermal biomass installations in the residential and services sectors. Accordingly, data provided by the Andalusian Energy Agency indicates that in 2015, biomass consumption in the residential sector surpassed that of the industrial sector for the first time, with a consumption rate of nearly 40% compared to 26% in the latter (Consejería de Empleo, Empresa y Comercio de la Junta de Andalucía, 2013). The principal olive by-products play a pivotal role in this growth, as they are the most prominent figures in the biomass sector as a whole (Agencia Andaluza de la Energía, 2020).

Subsequently, in order to continue promoting the use of renewable energies in the region, a series of incentive programs were initiated between the years 2016 and 2023. The objective of these programs is to provide support for sustainable construction, smart grids, and sustainable small and medium-sized enterprises (SMEs). Moreover, the objective is to encourage energy efficiency in both industrial and agricultural contexts. Furthermore, incentives have been introduced with the objective of promoting self-consumption and storage, particularly within the residential sector. In this manner, the various lines of action concentrate on the development of systems designed to enhance biomass logistics and its utilisation as a source of energy in a range of economic sectors, as well as in residential settings.

The third line of the Incentive Program for the Promotion of Electric Mobility (MOVES Andalusia) has been in effect since September 20, 2021. The budget of this program, financed by the European Union through the Next Generation EU funds, amounts to over 99.6 million euros. The objective is to encourage the adoption of electric mobility, with a particular focus on the purchase of electric vehicles and the deployment of charging infrastructure for these vehicles. This final measure indirectly impacts the olive biomass sector.

## 5. MAIN OBSTACLES FACED BY OLIVE BIOMASS FOR ITS ENERGY USE

The primary impediments to the utilization of olive biomass in Andalusia can be categorized into three distinct groups, as illustrated in Figure 6.

*Figure 9. Main obstacles facing olive biomass in Andalusia*

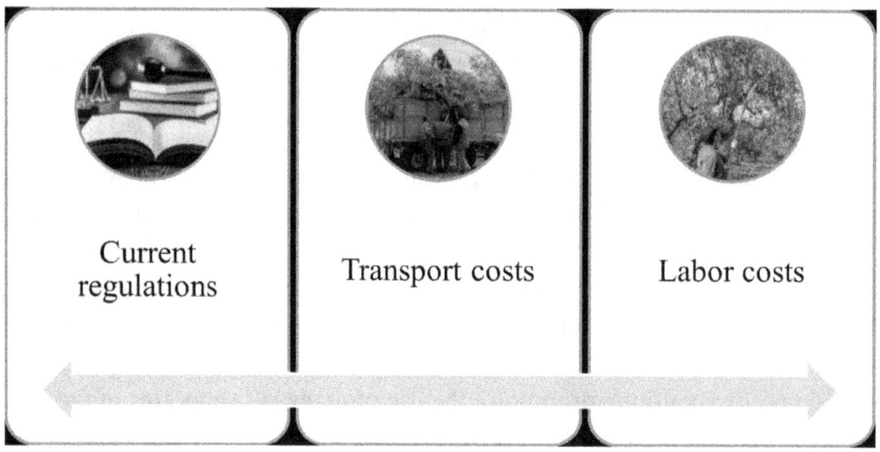


*Source: Own elaboration.*

Firstly, at the regulatory level, it should be noted that the implementation of energy plans, laws, and promotional measures to encourage the use of olive biomass for thermal and electrical uses in Andalusia has been insufficient. Despite the extensive acreage devoted to olive cultivation in Andalusia (representing 60% of the national total and 30% of the European total), the development of this energy source has only reached 274.0 MW of installed electrical capacity in 2022 and 1,816.8 MW of installed thermal capacity in the same year (Agencia Andaluza de la Energía, 2024a). Indeed, the enactment of Royal Decree-Law 1/2012 and Royal Decree-Law 2/2013 constituted a significant impediment to the advancement of olive biomass. From that point forward, the system of premiums, which had constituted a substantial advantage for these energy sources, was effectively terminated (BOE, 2012; BOE, 2013). From that moment on, the regulatory framework constituted a setback not only in the development of olive biomass for energy use, but also represented an obstacle to the commitment to greater sustainable development and thus contributed to the failure to achieve the objectives set by Europe in terms of energy and sustainability.

Conversely, the olive biomass sector is also confronted with a number of significant challenges, which have historically resulted in a comparatively limited utilization of this resource for energy-related applications. This is exemplified by the considerable expenses associated with waste collection, including transportation and labor costs (Andalusian Energy Agency, 2020). The paucity of incentives for this activity has constituted a significant barrier to the utilisation of these by-products, given that the associated costs do not offer an acceptable return on investment.

## 6. THE IMPACT OF OLIVE BIOMASS ON REGIONAL ANDALUSIAN ENERGY AND SUSTAINABILITY

By-products resulting from olive cultivation and the associated agroindustrial sector can be utilized for the generation of thermal and electrical energy (García-Maraver et al. 2012). As stated by Marquina et al. (2021a), the abundance of by-products suitable for electrical use outweighs that of by-products suitable for thermal use. However, the results for the period 2004-2016 indicate that the average potential electrical power with full utilization would have been 826.2 MW, capable of generating 5,370.2 GWh per year. Regarding the average thermal power, the potential with full utilization would have been 2,372.9 MW, generating 8,779.9 GWh per year.

The potential outcomes presented by Marquina et al. (2021a) can be contrasted with the actual data observed in the Andalusian region. Table 1 presents two sets of data: the first on installed power and energy generated in Andalusia in 2016 from olive biomass, and the second on the power and energy that Andalusia could have generated on average if olive biomass had been fully exploited. It can be observed that both for electrical and thermal uses, the potential value is clearly higher than that which was observed in 2016.

*Table 1. Actual data and potential results of olive grove biomass in Andalusia.*

| | **Actual data (2016)** | | **Potential resuls (average 2004-2016)** | |
|---|---|---|---|---|
| | **Installed capacity MW** | **Energy generation GWh** | **Installed capacity MW** | **Energy generation GWh** |
| Electrical Uses | 158,6 | 1.030,9 | 826,2 | 5.370,2 |
| Thermal uses | 1.279,2 | 4.733,1 | 2.372,9 | 8.779,9 |

Source: Agencia Andaluza de la Energía (2024a) and own elaboration.

In 2016, the installed power for electrical uses was 158.6 MW, with energy generation equaling 1,030.9 GWh. However, the results of the potential analysis indicate that these figures could be significantly higher, reaching 826.2 MW and 5,370.2 GWh, respectively. In contrast, the installed capacity for thermal power production in 2016 was 1,279.2 MW, with an energy generation of 4,733.1 GWh. The potential yield is nearly double the figures, amounting to 2,372.9 MW and 8,779.9 GWh, respectively. The complete utilization of olive biomass for both applications would result in a significant increase in installed power and electricity generation. In this context, the incorporation of biomass from olive groves would lead to an 83.9% increase in electric power and a 64.9% increase in thermal power, with a proportional increase in the generation of both applications.

Similarly, the results obtained for each of the uses should be highlighted, demonstrating the considerable potential of thermal uses in comparison to electrical uses. This is evidenced by the fact that thermal uses account for 62% of the total generation between the two uses.

In summary, the full utilization of olive grove biomass would result in the generation of 5,370.2 GWh of electrical energy, which would be approximately four times the total energy generated from biomass in Andalusia in 2016 (1,484.8 GWh). This would also represent 40.6% of the total renewable electricity. Similarly, the full utilization of olive grove biomass would result in the generation of 8,779.9 GWh of thermal energy, which would be approximately 10% greater than the energy generated from biomass in 2016 (7,975.9 GWh). This would represent 98.6% of the total renewable thermal energy.

## 7. CONCLUSIONS AND POLICY IMPLICATIONS

In Andalusia, the olive grove has a vast cultivated area (1.68 million hectares in 2023), representing 60% of the total area occupied by this crop in Spain and 30% of the EU. This characteristic indicates that Andalusia has considerable potential for the utilization of olive biomass for energy purposes. Consequently, an increased deployment of olive biomass for thermal and electrical applications would represent a valuable opportunity for the advancement of the energy transition and the establishment of a more robust bioeconomy and circular economy model. Furthermore, the greater utilization of olive biomass would contribute to the mitigation of climate change, enhance environmental quality, and tend to reduce the consumption of fossil fuels.

Despite the approval and implementation of various legislative measures, plans, and incentives at the national and regional levels, the development of olive biomass has not reached the desired level. Consequently, while olive grove biomass has increased for electrical and thermal uses in Andalusia since 2005, reaching the objectives of PASENER 2007-2013, this progress has been impeded by the enactment of various regulations approved from 2012 onwards. In this regard, Royal Decree-Law 1/2012 and Royal Decree-Law 2/2013 have had a detrimental impact on the advancement of olive biomass. From this point forward, the premium system, which had been a significant advantage for these energy sources, has been terminated.

This sector also has other barriers (such as transportation and labor costs in the case of olive pruning) that have not yet been corrected. Incentives are still scarce, and it is not profitable for farmers to collect them for later use. This is due to the low remuneration, which does not even cover the harvesting costs. In addition, there is a lack of information on the possibilities of using this organic matter.

Regarding the promotion of biomass electricity, the regulations have not been able to correct the existing difference between this energy source and the other renewable energies. The need to acquire the fuel (biomass from olive groves) requires sufficient remuneration to make the high investments profitable, which makes it less competitive than wind or photovoltaic. As a result, in Andalusia, biomass for electrical use has only reached 274.0 MW of installed capacity. This is a rather scarce development given its high potential.

In order to correct this situation, it would be necessary to organize specific electricity auctions for biomass power plants, with adequate remuneration to ensure the profitability of the projects. Similarly, to promote olive biomass, it would be necessary to establish specific measures aimed at this sector to promote environmental practices among farmers that make it possible to obtain biomass. These measures would include those aimed at training and advising farmers, subsidies for investments in machinery and the promotion of agricultural service companies specialized in the extraction of olive biomass.

However, with regard to biomass for thermal use, it seems that regulations such as the incorporation of renewable energies in buildings (mandatory in the Technical Building Code) or national and regional subsidy programs for this technology have favored its development, making it one of the most widely used in the residential sector. In any case, the implementation of the aforementioned regional policies would further boost its use.

From this study it is concluded that olive by-products and their agro-industrial sector can contribute to the growth of alternative energy products to fossil fuels, especially in Mediterranean countries, among which Spain and therefore the region of Andalusia. Thus, the use of these by-products for energy purposes is considered an essential element in reducing $CO_2$ emissions and combating climate change. Likewise, a greater use of these by-products would allow a more intensive implementation of the economic model of bioeconomy and circular economy proposed by the EU. Thus, it should be noted that there is a high underutilization of olive residues for energy purposes. Specifically, when comparing the potential data with the actual data, referring to the year 2016, a wastage of almost 70% of the by-products generated can be observed. In short, the full energy use of these wastes would account for 56% of total biomass electricity generation and 30% of total biomass thermal generation. It would also account for 6% of renewable electricity generation and 27% of renewable thermal generation. It would therefore contribute to the achievement of national and regional renewable energy targets.

The valorization of the entire olive biomass would require the adoption of different measures. On the one hand, agricultural policies could establish systems of subsidies and regulatory obligations. This would provide incentives for agricultural operations that reduce the environmental impact of the sector. On the other hand, it is proposed that energy policy should provide greater support through various incentive programs. For example, the importance of biomass electricity could be highlighted as a manageable energy source compared to other renewable energies (wind or photovoltaic), since it is an energy source that does not directly depend on variable factors such as wind or sun. This characteristic provides greater operational security to the electricity system, without the need for new investments in storage infrastructure as in the case of wind or solar photovoltaic energy.

In the same sense, it would be necessary to establish specific auction systems for this biomass in order to start up new generation plants. With regard to thermal energy, it is essential to develop district air conditioning systems in Spain and Andalusia, as well as large industrial plants. All of this by taking advantage of existing European funds (such as ERDF or NextGenerationEU funds) and creating a regulatory framework that promotes the use of biomass as opposed to fossil fuels. The NextGenerationEU funds have great potential, since they can promote incentive programs for biomass installations, logistics systems and the Strategic Projects for Economic Recovery and Transformation (PERTE), created by the Spanish government to promote the economy. In this sense, the configuration of a PERTE tractor project related to the development of biomass technology would be desirable and, above all, an opportunity for the primary and energy sector. Finally, social and rural policies could promote the importance that the use of this biomass offers to reduce the depopulation of rural areas.

Finally, in parallel with these agricultural, energy and social policies, it would be necessary to add other measures aimed at solving the main obstacles faced by this sector. It would be advisable to establish incentive programs aimed at reducing the costs of transporting and collecting waste, thus establishing a certain profitability for entrepreneurs in the sector.

In conclusion, a greater use of this organic material would make it possible for Spain and Andalusia to meet the objectives set out in the energy plans, reducing energy dependence and $CO_2$ emissions into the atmosphere, thus contributing to sustainable development.

## REFERENCES


Agencia Andaluza de la Energía. *La Bioenergía en Andalucía.* 2020. Available online: https://www.agenciaandaluzadelaenergia.es/sites/default/files/Documentos/3_2_0068_20_LA_BIOENERGIA_EN_ANDALUCIA.PDF. Accessed on 4 July 2024.

Agencia Andaluza de la Energía. *INFO-ENERGÍA.* 2024a. Available online: https://www.agenciaandaluzadelaenergia.es/info-web/loginController. Accessed on 4 July 2024.

Agencia Andaluza de la Energía. *Ayudas a la financiación.* 2024b. Available online: https://www.agenciaandaluzadelaenergia.es/es/todos-los-programas. Accessed on 17 September 2024.

Attard, J., McMahon, H., Doody, P., Belfrage, J., Clark, C., Ugarte, J. A., Pérez-Camacho, M. N., Cuenca Martín, M. S., Giráldez Morales, A. J., & Gaffey, J. (2020). Mapping and Analysis of Biomass Supply Chains in Andalusia and the Republic of Ireland. *Sustainability (Basel), 12*(11), 4595. DOI: 10.3390/su12114595

Ayuntamiento de Sevilla. *Plan de Acción por el Clima y la Energía Sostenible (PACES).* 2016. Available online: https://www.sevilla.org/servicios/economia/agencia-energia-sostenibilidad/documentos/paces-2016-aprobado.pdf. Accessed on 14 September 2024.

Berbel, J., & Posadillo, A. (2018). Review and analysis of alternatives for the valorisation of agro-industrial olive oil by-products. *Sustainability (Basel), 10*(1), 237. DOI: 10.3390/su10010237

Cardoza, D., Romero, I., Martínez, T., Ruíz, E., Gallego, F. J., López-Linares, J. C., Manzanares, P., & Castro, E. (2021). Location of Biorefineries Based on Olive-Derived Biomass in Andalusia, Spain. *Energies, 14*(11), 3052. DOI: 10.3390/en14113052

Consejería de Empleo y Desarrollo Tecnológico de la Junta de Andalucía. *Plan Energético de Andalucía 2003-2006.* 2003. Available online: https://www.agenciaandaluzadelaenergia.es/sites/default/files/1129906106388_plean2003-20061.pdf. Accessed on 4 July 2024.

Consejería de Industria. Energía y Minas. *Estrategia Energética de Andalucía 2030.* 2022. Available online: https://www.agenciaandaluzadelaenergia.es/sites/default/files/Documentos/Planificaci%C3%B3n/estrategia_energetica_andalucia_2030-8_junio_2022_def.pdf. Accessed on 4 July 2024.

Consejería de Medio Ambiente. *Estrategia Andaluza de Desarrollo Sostenible: Agenda 21 Andalucía.* 2004. Available online: https://www.famp.es/export/sites/famp/.galleries/documentos-consejo-andaluz-gobiernos-locales/DOC-AGENDA-21.pdf. Accessed on 14 September 2024.

Consejería de Medio Ambiente. *Plan Andaluz de Acción por el Clima.* 2007. Available online: https://www.juntadeandalucia.es/medioambiente/portal/documents/20151/1009070/plan_accion_clima_mitigacion.pdf/bfcd49a4-1220-f59e-b5a6-6d221b3ee8f9. Accessed on 14 September 2024.

Consejería de Medio Ambiente. *Programa Andaluz de Adaptación al Cambio Climático.* 2010. Available online: https://www.juntadeandalucia.es/export/drupaljda/programa_adaptacion_clima.pdf. Accessed on 14 September 2024.

Consejería de Medio Ambiente y Ordenación del Territorio de la Junta de Andalucía. *Medio Ambiente en Andalucía. Informe 1994*. 1994. Available online: http://www.juntadeandalucia.es/medioambiente/portal_web/ima/1994/ima94_ret.pdf. Accessed on 4 July 2024.

Consejería de Medio Ambiente y Ordenación del Territorio de la Junta de Andalucía. *Actuaciones de la Junta de Andalucía en cambio climático/COP21*. 2018. Available online: https://www.juntadeandalucia.es/medioambiente/site/portalweb/menuitem.30d4b35a97db5c61716f2b105510e1ca/?vgnextoid=355466afc1141510VgnVCM2000000624e50aRCRD&vgnextchannel=4c770f000a421510VgnVCM2000000624e50aRCRD&vgnextfmt=portalwebSinMenu. Accessed on 14 September 2024.

Contreras, M. M., Romero, I., Moya, M., & Castro, E. (2020). Olive-derived biomass as a renewable source of value-added products. *Process Biochemistry (Barking, London, England)*, *97*, 43–56. DOI: 10.1016/j.procbio.2020.06.013

de Agricultura, C. Pesca y Desarrollo Rural de la Junta de Andalucía. *Plan Estratégico para la Agroindustria de Andalucía Horizonte 2020*. 2017. Available online: https://www.juntadeandalucia.es/export/drupaljda/Propuesta_Plan_Agroindustria_Andaluza_Horizonte_2020_2017_11_30.pdf. Accessed on 14 September 2021.

de Agricultura, C. Pesca y Desarrollo Rural de la Junta de Andalucía. *Estrategia Andaluza de Bioeconomía Circular*. 2018. Available online: https://www.juntadeandalucia.es/export/drupaljda/Estrategia_Andaluza_Bioeconomia_Circular_EABC_18.09.2018.pdf. Accessed on 14 September 2024.

de Agricultura, C., Pesca, A., & de la Junta de Andalucía, D. R. *Aforo de la producción de olivar en Andalucía – Campaña 2023/2024*. 2023. Available online: https://www.juntadeandalucia.es/sites/default/files/inline-files/2023/10/Estimacion_ACEITE_MESA_2023_24.pdf. Accessed on 4 July 2024.

de Empleo, C. Empresa y Comercio de la Junta de Andalucía. *Estrategia Energética de Andalucía 2020*. 2013. Available online: https://www.agenciaandaluzadelaenergia.es/EEA/files/assets/basic-html/index.html#1. Accessed on 4 July 2024.

de Innovación, C. Ciencia y Empresa de la Junta de Andalucía. *Plan Andaluz de Sostenibilidad Energética 2007-2013*. 2007. Available online: https://www.agenciaandaluzadelaenergia.es/sites/default/files/2_pasener_2007-2013_documento_completo.pdf. Accessed on 4 July 2024.

Europa Press. *Junta y Gobierno constituyen la Sociedad Andaluza para la Valorización de la biomasa "pionera en Europa"*. 2006. Available online: https://www.europapress.es/andalucia/innova-00232/noticia-innova-junta-gobierno-constituyen-sociedad-andaluza-valorizacion-biomasa-pionera-europa-20061101160415.html. Accessed on 14 September 2024.

Fundación para la Eficiencia Energética (FEE). *Crece en Andalucía el consumo de biomasa en el sector residencial*. 2016. Available online: https://www.eseficiencia.es/2016/09/07/crece-en-andalucia-el-consumo-de-biomasa-en-el-sector-residencial. Accessed on 14 September 2024.

García-Maraver, A., Zamorano, M., Ramos-Ridao, A., & Díaz, L. F. Analysis of olive grove residual biomass potential for electric and thermal energy generation in Andalusia (Spain). Renewable and Sustainable Energy Reviews, 2012, 16(1), 745-751.

García Martín, J. F., Cuevas, M., Feng, C. H., Álvarez Mateos, P., Torres García, M., & Sánchez, S. (2020). Energetic Valorisation of Olive Biomass: Olive-Tree Pruning, Olive Stones and Pomaces. *Processes (Basel, Switzerland)*, *8*(5), 511. DOI: 10.3390/pr8050511

Koch, P. (2023). Where limits to growth are tangible: The olive sector in Jaén and its bioeconomic future. *Sustainability Science*, *18*(2), 661–674. DOI: 10.1007/s11625-022-01236-6

Kumar, A., & Verma, A. (2021). Optimal techno-economic sizing of a solar-biomass-battery hybrid system for off-setting dependency on diesel generators for microgrid facilities. *Journal of Energy Storage*, *36*, 102251. DOI: 10.1016/j.est.2021.102251

Marquina, J., Colinet, M. J., & Pablo-Romero, M. D. P. (2021a). The economic value of olive sector biomass for thermal and electrical uses in Andalusia (Spain). *Renewable & Sustainable Energy Reviews*, *148*, 111278. DOI: 10.1016/j.rser.2021.111278

Marquina, J., Colinet, M. J., & Pablo-Romero, M. D. P. (2021b). Measures to Promote Olive Grove Biomass in Spain and Andalusia: An Opportunity for Economic Recovery against COVID-19. *Sustainability (Basel)*, *13*(20), 11318. DOI: 10.3390/su132011318

Menéndez, J. A., Fernández-Tresguerres, L. G., Villanueva, S. F., Durán, M., Montes-Morán, M. A., & Arenillas, A. (2018). *Report on the availability of Biomass Sources in Spain: vineyards and olive groves*. Digital CSIC.

Ministerio de Agricultura. Pesca y Alimentación. *Encuesta sobre Superficies y Rendimientos de Cultivos (ESYRCE)*. 2023. Available online: https://www.mapa.gob.es/es/estadistica/temas/estadisticas-agrarias/agricultura/esyrce/default.aspx. Accessed on 4 July 2024.

Ministerio de Agricultura. Pesca y Alimentación. *Material vegetal*. 2024. Available online: https://www.mapa.gob.es/app/MaterialVegetal/fichaMaterialVegetal.aspx?idFicha=6. Accessed on 10 September 2024.

Ossorio-Aravena, J. C., Rodríguez-Segura, F. J., Frolova, M., Terrados-Cepeda, J., & Muñoz-Cerón, J. (2022). How much solar PV, wind and biomass energy could be implemented in short-term? A multi-criteria GIS-based approach applied to the province of Jaén, Spain. *Journal of Cleaner Production*, *366*, 132920. DOI: 10.1016/j.jclepro.2022.132920

Rodríguez, G., Lama, A., Rodríguez, R., Jiménez, A., Guillén, R., & Férnandez-Bolaños, J. (2008). Olive stones an attractive source of bioactive and valuable compunds. *Bioresource Technology*, *99*(13), 5261–5269. DOI: 10.1016/j.biortech.2007.11.027 PMID: 18160280

Rodríguez-Lizana, A., Ramos, A., Pereira, M. J., Soares, A., & Castro Ribeiro, M. (2023). Assessment of the Spatial Variability and Uncertainty of Shreddable Pruning Biomass in an Olive Grove Based on Canopy Volume and Tree Projected Area. *Agronomy (Basel)*, *13*(17), 1697. DOI: 10.3390/agronomy13071697

Román-Collado, R., & Colinet, M. J. (2021). Energy efficiency's key role in explaining the performance of energy consumption in Andalusia (Spain). *Environmental Science and Pollution Research International*, *28*(16), 20188–20208. DOI: 10.1007/s11356-020-11829-2 PMID: 33410050

Romero-García, J. M., Sánchez, A., Rendón-Acosta, G., Martínez-Patiño, J. C., Ruiz, E., Magaña, G., & Castro, E. (2016). An olive tree pruning biorefinery for co-producing high value-added bioproducts and biofuels: Economic and energy efficiency analysis. *BioEnergy Research*, *9*(4), 1086–1070. DOI: 10.1007/s12155-016-9786-3

Rosúa, J. M., & Pasadas, M. Biomass potential in Andalusia, from grapevines, olives, fruit trees and poplar, for providing heating in homes. Renewable and Sustainable Energy Reviews, 2012, 16(6), 4190-4195.

Sánchez-Martínez, J. D., & Paniza Cabrera, A. (2015). The olive monoculture in the south of Spain. *Eruopean Journal of Geography*, *6*(3), 16–29.

Soltero, V. M., Román, L., Peralta, M. E., & Chacartegui, R. (2020). Sustainable biomass pellets using trunk wood from olive groves at the end of their life cycle. *Energy Reports*, *6*, 2627–2640. DOI: 10.1016/j.egyr.2020.09.017

Suarez, A., & Gwozdz, W. (2023). On the relation between monocultures and ecosystem services in the Global South: A review. *Biological Conservation*, *278*, 109870. DOI: 10.1016/j.biocon.2022.109870

Torrús-Castillo. Calero, J.; García-Ruíz, R. Does olive cultivation sequester carbon?: Carbon balance along a C input gradient. Agriculture, Ecosystems & Environment, 2023, 358, 108707.

Velázquez-Martí, B., Fernández-González, E., López-Cortés, I., & Salazar-Hernández, D. M. (2011). Quantification of the residual biomass obtained from pruning of trees in Mediterranean olive groves. *Biomass and Bioenergy*, *35*(7), 3208–3217. DOI: 10.1016/j.biombioe.2011.04.042

# APPENDIX

*Table 2.*

| Strategic Plan for Andalusian Agroindustry 2020 | |
|---|---|
| **Strategic lines** | **Description** |
| Efficiency and size | The objective is to generate an extensive, diversified, robust, and sustainable business fabric comprised of larger, more competitive, innovative, and secure companies. |
| Promotion of differentiated quality products and market niches. | It is imperative to prioritize the promotion of quality and differentiation in the domain of agroindustrial production. This objective should be pursued by means of a systematic exploration and exploitation of specific market niches. |
| Balance, cooperation and transparency of the agri-food chain | The objective of this study is to enhance the functioning, structuring, cooperation, and transparency of the food chain. This will be achieved by increasing the efficiency and competitiveness of the Andalusian agri-food sector. Additionally, the imbalance in commercial relations between the different links in the value chain will be reduced. |
| Commercial Quality, Guarantee and Consumer Orientation | In order to ensure the safety and well-being of consumers, while concurrently addressing the evolving demands of a dynamic market, it is imperative to implement a multifaceted approach. This objective necessitates the dissemination of information to consumers regarding the attributes of the products, in addition to fostering awareness about the appropriate utilization of food. |
| Internationalization of the Andalusian agri-food industry | Increasing the degree of internationalization of Andalusian agroindustries, in order to contribute to the economic development of the region. The aim is to promote the international marketing of Andalusian agroindustry in order to expand, diversify and consolidate markets beyond our borders. |
| Promoting the integral sustainability of the agri-food industry | The promotion of the integral sustainability of the Andalusian agri-food ecosystem is of paramount importance, as is the improvement of the competitiveness of the companies that comprise it. It is imperative to acknowledge that integral sustainability encompasses three dimensions: environmental respect, the social aspects of production, and the economic profitability of productive activity. |
| Product and process innovation and knowledge transfer | The following measures should be taken to strengthen innovation in Andalusian agribusiness and the bioeconomy:<br>-The incorporation of knowledge that allows the introduction of innovations demanded by the market through technology transfer, cooperation, and knowledge transfer.<br>- The detection of opportunities.<br>- The use of big data in decision making. |
| Governance | In order to achieve a unified strategic direction, it is imperative that all Andalusian administrations, institutions, and organizations involved in the drafting, implementation, monitoring, and evaluation of the Plan act in a coordinated manner. This collaborative effort is essential for the collective defense of the interests of the Andalusian agroindust |
| Imposed Agribusiness 4.0. | The introduction of digital technologies in the agri-food sector is imperative for companies to establish a smart agribusiness. A smart agribusiness is defined as one that is capable of generating benefits at the process, product, and business model levels. |

Source: Consejería de Agricultura, Pesca y Desarrollo Rural de la Junta de Andalucía, 2017 and own elaboration.

# Chapter 4
# Sustainable Development and Foreign Trade:
## Evaluating Macro-Economic Indicators in the MENA Region

**Vicente Fruet-Cardozo**
*University of Córdoba, Spain*

**José Valverde-Roda**
*University of Almería, Spain*

**Lorena Caridad López del Río**
*University of Sevilla, Spain*

**Rosario Brito-Guerrero**
*University of Córdoba, Spain*

## ABSTRACT

*This study examines the impact of foreign trade on GDP per capita in North African and Southwest Asian (MENA) countries, which predominantly rely on hydrocarbon exports. While current reserves are projected to last for decades, the pressing need for sustainable development necessitates exploring alternative financing options that promote environmental stewardship and social equity. The analysis utilizes a dataset of 840 data points spanning from 2009 to 2020, sourced from credible official entities and international organizations. Employing the Structural Equation Model (SEM) in the Path Analysis modality, this research estimates multi-equation regression models to clarify the variability of endogenous variables. The findings substantiate the study's hypotheses, validated through key indicators such as CMIN, DF, p, FMIN, CFI, and RMSEA. Notably, MENA countries are increasingly concerned about the global shift toward renewable energy, highlighting the urgent need to diversify their income streams beyond traditional hydrocarbon exports to foster sustainable development.*

DOI: 10.4018/979-8-3693-7081-0.ch004

## INTRODUCTION

The primary objective of this article is to investigate the influence of specific macroeconomic variables on various economic indicators, particularly GDP per capita, in ten selected countries within the Middle East and North Africa (MENA) region. As of December 2021, the countries analyzed had a combined population of approximately 458.19 million people living in an expansive area of 8,898.3 million km$^2$. Furthermore, the region's GDP was reported at $2,253.02 billion (World Bank, 2021a and 2021b), underscoring the economic relevance of this diverse and complex region. Understanding these dynamics is critical not only for economic growth but also for promoting sustainable development in a region characterized by significant challenges.

*Figure 1. Table showing main macroeconomic data for MENA countries. Year 2021*

| Mena Countries | Area Thousand Km$^2$ | Population Million | GDP Billion $ | GDP per Cap. |
|---|---|---|---|---|
| Morocco | 446.6 | 37.10 | 142.87 | 3,795.4 |
| Algeria | 2,382.0 | 44.18 | 163.04 | 3,690.6 |
| Tunisia | 163.6 | 12.26 | 46.69 | 3,807.1 |
| Lybia | 1,759.5 | 6.74 | 42.82 | 6,357.2 |
| Egypt | 1,002.0 | 109.26 | 414.14 | 3,698.8 |
| Jordan | 89.3 | 11.15 | 45.74 | 4,103.3 |
| Syria | 185.2 | 21.30 | 11.08 1) | 533,4 |
| Iraq | 438.3 | 43.50 | 207.89 | 4,775.4 |
| Iran | 1,648.2 | 87.90 | 359.71 | 4,091.1 |
| Türkiye | 783.6 | 84.80 | 819.04 | 9,661.2 |
| TOTAL | **8,898.3** | **458.19** | **2,253.02** | |

*1) Year 2020*

Source: own elaboration based on data from the World Bank (2021b).

This study encompasses a 12-year period, from 2009 to 2020, a time frame strategically chosen to assess the effects of the financial crisis that began in 2007 on the GDP per capita of the MENA region. Analyzing the impact of this crisis is crucial, especially given the region's susceptibility to external economic shocks and its implications for sustainable development. The financial crisis highlighted the vulnerabilities in many MENA economies, emphasizing the need for diversification and resilience to enhance long-term economic stability and sustainable growth. The first group of the MENA countries is conformed by AMU (Arab Maghreb Union) region, that includes the following five countries: Morocco, Algeria, Tunisia, Libya, and Egypt, whose recent peculiarity has been the so-called "Arab Spring", which has turned some countries into quasi-failed states. This is the case of Libya, where for 12 years, peace has not yet been known, due to its continuous civil war (Apuuli, 2021). This region was conquered by the Muslims in the second half of the seventh century (Franco, 2001 This economic reliance poses substantial risks, particularly in the context of climate change and the global shift towards sustainable energy sources. Furthermore, ongoing political disputes hinder the consolidation of modern democratic states and impede efforts to promote sustainable governance and economic development. The second group of MENA countries is made up of what is identified as the Middle East, corresponding to one of the most belligerent areas in the world. They are Jordan, Syria, Iraq, Iran, and Türkiye.

Apocada del Hoyo (2016) attributes many of the conflicts in this area, to the creation of the State of Israel. It was proclaimed by the United Nations Assembly in 1948 (Ricardo & Göttig, 2015) and had a rapid recognition from 33 countries, among which were all the allies of World War II, led by the United States (US). The wars undertaken, in addition to their political and economic causes, also have religious edges. In this regard, with periods of intermediate peace, from the first Arab-Israeli war in 1948 to date, there have been more than 70 years of armed conflict between the Arab world and the Israelis, turning the region into a tinderbox (Cocchini, 2021). Likewise, in the eighties, Iran and Iraq maintained a warlike confrontation that lasted eight years. In this context, between the 1990s and the early 2000s, the so-called "Gulf Wars" took place between Iraq and coalitions of Western armies led by the US. Likewise, as of 2011, Syria survives during a bloody conflict where political, economic, and religious interests intermingle (Alvarez & Ossorio, 2019). This context poses significant challenges to sustainable development, as ongoing instability hampers economic growth and exacerbates social inequalities. Figure 1 shows the map of the MENA countries analyzed.

*Figure 2. The Maghreb and the Middle East*

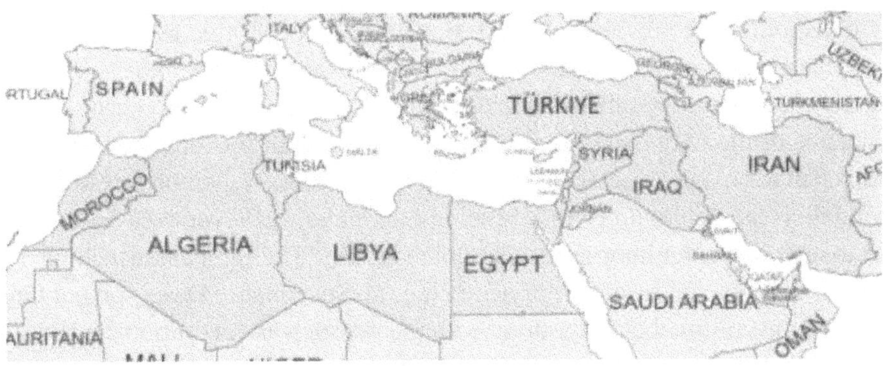


Source: own elaboration using the software of https://www.mapchart.net

To analyze the behavior of these economies, GDP per capita serves as a crucial indicator. Since 1990, the United Nations Development Program (UNDP) has introduced the Human Development Index (HDI), which combines economic and social metrics to assess overall development (Sánchez, 2016). However, this study prioritizes GDP per capita as the main focus, examining its relationship with various macroeconomic variables. Understanding these relationships is essential for identifying pathways toward sustainable economic growth in the region.

Out of the ten countries analyzed, six are predominantly monoproducers and monoexporters of two key energy resources—oil and gas—that are not renewable. This heavy reliance on non-renewable energy sources, coupled with an unstable political environment, has left these countries trailing in terms of global competitiveness. In contrast, Egypt, Türkiye, Iran, and Morocco exhibit slightly more diversified economies, suggesting a greater potential for sustainable development through economic diversification and resilience building.

The choice of these countries for this research is influenced by Spain's historical and ongoing contributions to their development. Geographical proximity and substantial immigration, particularly from the Maghreb, have also shaped this decision. Spain has maintained a significant investment presence in both Morocco and Algeria, contributing to economic ties and development initiatives. Algeria, in particular, has been a major supplier of gas to Spain until the onset of the Ukrainian War, which has altered energy dynamics in the region (Government of Spain, 2021).

The chapter is structured as follows. After the introduction, it continuous with the literature review, provides context and supporting evidence for the research. The methodology section outlines the research methods employed, including the use of Path Analysis, a variant of Structural Equation Modeling (SEM). This approach aims to confirm causal associations among directly observable data, operating under the assumption of linear relationships, though extensions for non-linear situations exist. Following the methodology, the results obtained from the analysis are presented. Finally, the discussion and conclusions highlight the implications of the findings for sustainable development in the MENA region, emphasizing the need for integrated policies that address economic, social, and environmental dimensions.

## Literature Review

The following is a literature review which begins with the economic aspects. This section aims to provide a comprehensive foundation for the study by analyzing current academic contributions, identifying gaps, and situating the research within the broader scholarly discourse. Bouyghrissi et al., (2022) study the high dependence of the MENA countries on fossil fuels, both for local consumption and exports, which makes this fact the main cause of environmental issues. The transition toward sustainable energy sources is essential, as the depletion of fossil fuel reserves and the adverse environmental impacts necessitate a shift to renewables for long-term economic viability. The fight against climate change and the reduction of CO2 emissions are essential for achieving the Sustainable Development Goals. Saboori et al. (2024) shows that institutional quality, along with factors such as corruption control and government effectiveness, significantly impacts the reduction of emissions. Promoting green economic growth and increasing investment in renewable energy are key to achieving this goal. Wani et al. (2024) explores the relationship between economic development, GDP, and environmental degradation using the Environmental Kuznets Curve (EKC) hypothesis, focusing on CO2 emissions in the MENA region. It shows negative relationship between FDI and CO2 emissions, and a positive link between trade openness and CO2 emissions, suggesting MENA countries should adopt green energy to mitigate the environmental impact of non-renewable energy. Ji et al. (2022) state that, the Gregory–Hansen test for cointegration, reveals a permanent equilibrium relation among sustainable economic growth, and exports and imports. They demonstrate that exports can stimulate GDP growth, yet emphasize the importance of diversifying trade to include sustainable products, thereby aligning economic objectives with environmental sustainability. Mawejje & Odhiambo, (2022) affirm the positive relationship of the fiscal deficit with the negative current account balance, the decrease of the GDP per capita and also with the increase of the interest rate. These findings suggest that economic mismanagement can hinder progress toward sustainability, making it imperative for MENA countries to adopt sound fiscal policies that support sustainable development. Semosa & Kanayo, (2021), reveal a negative relationship between unemployment and inflation rates, indicating that economic stability is crucial for sustainable development. Policies aimed at reducing unemployment should therefore consider environmental impacts, ensuring that job creation aligns with sustainable practices. Michail, (2021) discusses how devaluation of local currencies in developing countries negatively affects local economies and long-term growth. This points to the need for stable currencies and economic policies that foster sustainability and encourage foreign investment in renewable energy sectors. Ibrahiem & Hanafy, (2021) study North African countries, showing that regulating carbon dioxide emissions, increasing international trade openness, and promoting foreign direct investment can drive economic development. This underscores the necessity of integrating environmental regulations into economic policies to promote sustainability. Němečková et al., (2021) highlight Russia's return to Africa due to current geopolitical strategies, particularly focusing on countries like Egypt and Algeria, which engage in significant trade with Russia. This shift in geopolitical dynamics calls for a reevaluation of trade relationships, emphasizing the need for sustainable practices in economic partnerships. Likewise, Shoori et al., (2021) analyze Russia's influence in Western Asia, particularly as a major arms supplier, which raises concerns regarding military expenditures at the expense of sustainable development initiatives. MENA countries must balance security needs with sustainable economic growth to enhance regional stability.. Kujawa, (2021) primarily focuses on Türkiye, identifying it as a strategic tool to expand NATO influence. As nations navigate complex geopolitical landscapes, there is a growing recognition of the need for sustainable diplomacy that fosters cooperation over conflict. Alizadeh, M., (2020) underscores the significance of justice within Islamic economic principles. Economic justice is intertwined with sustainability, as equitable resource distribution is essential for long-term development. Understanding the intersection of economic and social justice can provide insights into developing more sustainable economic frameworks. According to Thabit et al. (2020) population growth, urbanization, and lifestyle changes have increased waste generation in the MENA region, where waste management systems remain underdeveloped. While developed countries have advanced in waste-to-energy solutions, the region could benefit from implementing waste incineration plants, addressing economic challenges. A simulated model demonstrates that such plants could generate electricity and potable water while reducing waste treatment costs. The cost of treating municipal solid waste is estimated at around US$39 per ton over 30 years. Dutta, (2015) and Ricoy, (2005) argue that economic development is a circular, cumulative, and endogenous process. This perspective reinforces the importance of sustainable foreign trade practices, as they play a crucial role in facilitating structural transformation and enhancing overall welfare. Arranz & Martin, (2009) note that migrants' remittances significantly influence socioeconomic growth in Morocco, constituting 9% of GDP. The recognition of remittances as a source of economic stability reinforces the argument for sustainable practices that enhance the productivity of migrant communities, thereby contributing to sustainable development. Sghaier (2021) confirms the positive correlation between remittances and economic growth, suggesting that policies aimed at supporting migrant communities can lead to more sustainable economic outcomes.

Regarding the sociopolitical matters, it is worth highlighting the analysis of Robins et al., (2022). They study how the 2011 Tunisian revolution went from claiming generic socioeconomic and political aspects towards a specific proposal to repair the large marginal areas of society. The inclusion of social justice in governance is crucial for sustainable development. Groizard, J. et al., (2022), investigate the effects of the Arab Spring, noting the significant impact on the tourism sector, which is vital for many MENA economies. The adverse effects on international travel underscore the need for sustainable tourism practices that enhance resilience in the face of political instability. The Mena region tourism industry, bolstered by air transport, contributes significantly to GDP and employment. However, this growth has led to notable environmental impacts. Onifade & Haouas (2023) examines the relationship between tourism, air transportation, and emissions, considering factors like globalization, income, and energy use across five key countries. Results show that while air transport boosts tourism, it also contributes to environmental degradation, highlighting the need for policies to address these impacts. Other authors underline the great negative impact that the political upheavals had on international travel, which resulted in a sharp reduction in tourist demand for two years in Egypt, Tunisia, and Türkiye. This is the case of Fourie, J. et al., (2020) who, in their study on the impact of terrorism on tourism, demonstrate that tourists prefer to travel to countries with higher security levels, highlighting the interconnection between sociopolitical stability and sustainable tourism development. Colombo & Soler, (2021) analyze one of the most important aspects of the Middle East that concerns the numerous and strategic changes in geopolitical matters. In this regard, it is worth noting the growing influence of the Gulf States, in their attempt to achieve greater global significance, despite the well-known alliances and rivalries in the region. Postema, (2021) illustrates the challenges posed by ongoing political instability, civil wars, and economic crises in the region. These factors impede progress toward sustainable development, necessitating comprehensive strategies that promote peace and stability. Völlers et al., (2021) discuss the difficulties faced by Türkiye in attracting foreign direct investment since 2013, primarily due to its authoritarian governance style. A shift toward more democratic and transparent governance could foster a more conducive environment for sustainable investment. Hernando de Larramendi (2019) examines the complex rivalries within the MENA region, particularly between Morocco and Algeria. Understanding these dynamics is crucial for establishing collaborative approaches to sustainable development and regional stability. For their part, Bassil, C. et al., (2019) use Lebanon, Türkiye, and Israel as case studies to demonstrate the impact of terrorism on tourism demand. The findings suggest that enhancing security and stability is vital for promoting sustainable tourism development in the region. A study carried out by Artetxe, (2016), points out the challenges faced by countries on the southern and eastern shores of the Mediterranean due to political conflicts and instability. These issues highlight the urgent need for comprehensive strategies that promote sustainable development and regional cooperation. Within the sociopolitical matters, it is important to mention the illiteracy situation in the region. For instance, the studies of Abu-Fadil, M. et al., (2016) and Cohen & Jaïdi (2006) underlines the urgent need to end this issue. This problem affects, from an economic point of view, the labor market. Also, from the perspective of political instability, it is significant to note radical movements that take advantage of this fact, recruiting young illiterate men and women. In addition, even when countries like Morocco, for example, submit to the harsh conditions to access the "Structural Adjustment Loans" from the World Bank and the IMF, no notable progress has been observed in the illiteracy rate. In fact, in 2018, in Morocco, this rate was still around 31.5% (Ministry of National Education, Morocco, 2014).

In the following sentences, the literature reviews that support the statistical model applied in this research are presented. In relation to the identifiability of a multi-equation model, Caridad, (2016) affirms that the Path Analysis method is a way of specifying the representation of a multiequational model. Bollen & Hoyle, (2012) propose the use of SEM to study different social science sectors. Elosua, (2011) recommends a particular SEM to analyze the preferences between the dimensions of the quality of life of the elderly. Badri & Alshare, (2008) design a Path Analysis model to measure the business value of the government. Badri et al., (2000) also apply Path Analysis to investigate the effects of the environment on the choice of operating strategy. Bentler & Yuan, (1999) state that the normalized, CFI, and non-normalized, NFI, fit indices are usually used as complements to chi-square statistics. Bagozzi & Heatherton, (1994) suggest a SEM in order to represent personality behaviours at four different levels of abstraction. Browne & Cudeck, (1993) consider two types of errors involved in the fit of a model: the first configures the approximation error, while the second is related to the global error associated with the fit of the model.

## RESEARCH METHODS

### SEM. Path Analysis

SEM is an extension of the General Linear Model, and Path Analysis is a particular case of SEM. It focuses on describing the relationships among all the variables selected for the research, and not just, for example, the relationship between GDPs per capita and exports. Path Analysis is used with observable numerical variables and, besides the specification of a model, it can be used to disaggregate the correlation coefficients among the variables in several parts to represent the direct, indirect, and non-causal effects (Caridad, 2016). The so-called observable variables are identified and classified as follows: (i) Exogenous variables, which affect other variables, but are not affected by any of them. (ii) Endogenous variables, which are impacted by other variables, and can also be causal of other endogenous variables. They are also affected by error variables, which represent the non-explained part of the endogenous variables (Garson, 2008).

### Data

In the first stage of model specification, the original matrix included seven observable variables of the ten countries studied, from 2009 to 2020; that is, a matrix of 840 data, for a period of 12 years. The variables were GDP per capita, External debt, Fiscal deficit, Exports, Imports, Unemployment rate and Currency quote (World Bank, 2021a). SPSS and AMOS software were used to model the variables.

In the second phase - the estimation stage - of the seven original variables, all of them were selected, which presented a better fit in table 2. Therefore, the 840 original cases have been validated.

*Figure 3. Table showing selected variables*

| Acronyms | Variables | Type of variables |
|---|---|---|
| X1 | GDP per capita | Exogenous |
| X2 | External debt | |
| X3 | Fiscal deficit | |
| Y1 | Imports | Endogenous |
| Y2 | Exports | |
| Y3 | Currency quote | |
| Y4 | Unemployment rate | |

Note: The seven selected variables are those used in the SEM.
Source: own elaboration.

## HYPOTHESES

From the perspective of the literature review set out above, the research of Ji et al. (2022) give rise to the first hypothesis related to the increase in foreign trade and its relationship with GDP per capita. What is mentioned by Semosa & Kanayo (2021), on the one hand, and by Michail, (2021) on the other, support the second hypothesis that concerns the devaluation of the currency price and its negative effect on GDP per capita. The statement by Mawejje & Odhiambo (2022) supports the third hypothesis, which mentions that a permanent increase in the fiscal deficit has a negative impact on GDP per capita. Below are presented the three hypotheses:

$H_1$: The increase in foreign trade positively influences the GDP per capita of the MENA countries.
$H_2$: The devaluation of the value of the MENA countries' currencies negatively affects the GDP per capita of the countries.
$H_3$: The permanent increase in the fiscal deficit has a negative impact on the GDP per capita of the MENA countries.

## CALCULATION

This section presents the practical development of the research concentrated on the graph designed with AMOS. This software performs a control (although not complete) of the identifiability of the model, as a previous step to the estimation. Although, other programs do not introduce this sort of control. The graph results from the relationships among the variables selected and mentioned in the previous section.

## MODEL ESTIMATION

To homogenize them, the 840 data of the mentioned variables were converted to percentages and tabulated in a matrix treated with SPSS. The typology of the estimated model is in figure 2, where the causal relations are represented with a unidirectional arrow, while the interdependences are shown with a double arrow. The structural coefficients are presented in tables 4, 5, and 6. The proposed model allows the testing of the hypotheses through statistical tests to assess the causal relations. Figure 2 shows the exogenous and endogenous variables of the designed model.

The exogenous variables include the Imports, Exports, Currency quote, and Unemployment rate. On the other hand, the three endogenous variables are: GDP per capita, Fiscal deficit, and External debt.

*Figure 4. Path analysis model to test the four research hypotheses*

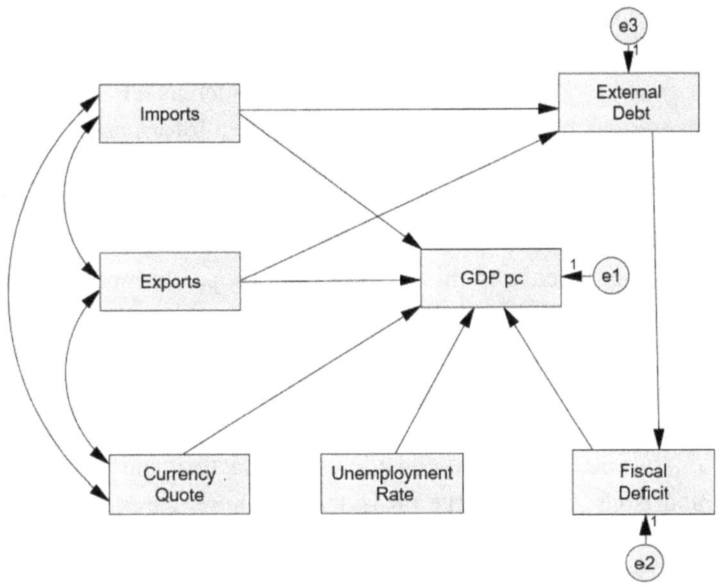


Source: own elaboration using the AMOS software.

## RESULTS

The model presents an adequate goodness of fit, and all its parameters are significant. Regarding the global significance of the model and different fit criteria, the following has been recommended by Browne & Cudeck, (1993): the likelihood ratio statistic, CMIN, with a fairly large *p*-value, corresponding to an adequate global fit, and several measures such as the Minimum Discrepancy Function (FMIN), the Comparative Fit Index (CFI), and the Root Mean Square Error (RMSEA), that is an index based on the covariance matrix estimated with the model.

## Global Test for the Model. Chi-Square (CMIN)

The chi-square ($\chi^2$) goodness-of-fit test is one of the most widely used nonparametric tests to determine the discrepancy between an observed dataset and an expected dataset. This test and its *p*-value *(p)* are the only goodness-of-fit tests associated with significance testing. The result obtained with the log-likelihood statistic is $G^2$ or *CMIN* (in AMOS terminology) = 10.2, corresponding to a chi-square distribution with 10 degrees of freedom. Also, its *p*-value $(p = 0.42)$ leads to the acceptance of the model, and it is higher than any reasonable level of significance $(\alpha = 0.05, 0.10$, and even more than 0.20). The proposed model can be accepted, and it will be used to test the research hypotheses (Caridad, 2016).

## Goodness of Fit Indexes

Fit indexes in the SEM are structured in different groups. Some can be labelled as discrepancy indexes, as are the statistics CMIN, or FMIN, and the residual-based measures as the RMSEA. Other ratios compare to the proposed model with the observed data, such as CFI. Other groups are related to Information Theory measures, such as the Akaike or the Bayesian Information Criteria. Other measures treat problems associated with at non-centrality indexes. Some of these measures are presented for the proposed model, as well as an interval of possible values corresponding to the independence model as the worse possible limit, and also for the saturated model, that is, a best possible model with no degrees of freedom (Caridad, 2016). In the case of this research, the proposed model indexes are, in all cases, near the optimum value corresponding to the saturated model.

- The Minimum Value of Discrepancy Function (FMIN) is the value of the discrepancy function obtained by fitting a model to the moments of the population, instead of the moments of the sample. The value of $FMIN = 0.086$, is also considered satisfactory and near its optimum value.
- The Baseline Comparisons. Comparative Fit Index (CFI) compares the discrepancy between the covariance matrix predicted by the model and the observed covariance matrix, with the discrepancy between the covariance matrix of the null model and the observed covariance matrix. This serves to assess the degree of loss that occurs when changing the model to the independence model. The values of this index vary between 0 and 1. Conventionally, the value of CFI should be greater than 0.90 indicating that at least 90% of the covariance in the data can be reproduced by the model. Therefore, the CFI = 0.99, and it is excellent.
- The Root Mean Square Error of Approximation (RMSEA) is a measure of goodness of fit for statistical models, where the goal is for the model to have an approximate or close fit to the data, rather than an exact fit, which is often not practical for large populations. Values below 0.05 indicate a good fit of the model. Therefore, the RMSEA = 0.014 also indicates a very good fit of the model.

In the table 3, a summary of all the results obtained and discussed above are presented. The goodness of fit measures of the proposed model are close to their optimum possible values stated in the saturated model, separated from the independence model.

*Figure 5. Table showing goodness of fit measures and likelihood ratio test*

| Statistics | Proposed model | Saturated model | Independence model |
|---|---|---|---|
| *CMIN* ($G^2$) | 10.2 | 0 | 260.797 |
| *FMIN* | 0.086 | 0 | 2.19 |
| *CFI* | 0.99 | 1 | 0 |
| *RMSEA* | 0.014 | 0 | 0.31 |

Note: The default model is the proposed; the saturated model is for a perfect fit with no degrees of freedom, and the independence model corresponds to a set of uncorrelated variables.
Source: own elaboration.

## Regression Weights, Covariances, and Variances

It can be mentioned that, in general terms, all the observed results - the coefficients of regression (table 4), the estimated covariances (table 5) and the estimated variances (table 6) - are significant in all cases. These confirm and indicate an adequate fit of the model to the observed data. All its $p$-values, for the individual tests on the coefficients are very small (below 0.001), leading to and including the proposed causal links, that is, to the acceptance of the research hypothesis.

*Figure 6. Table showing regression coefficients of the model and the corresponding z-tests (C.R.)*

| Variables | | | Estimate | S.E. | C.R. | $p$ |
|---|---|---|---|---|---|---|
| External Debt | □ | Imports | 1.154 | 0.489 | 2.361 | 0.018 |
| External Debt | □ | Exports | -0.996 | 0.362 | -2.750 | 0.006 |
| Fiscal Deficit | □ | External Debt | 0.284 | 0.107 | 2.670 | 0.008 |
| GDP pc | □ | Fiscal Deficit | -0.049 | 0.011 | -4.432 | <0.001 |
| GDP pc | □ | Unemployment Rate | 0.295 | 0.117 | 2.525 | 0.012 |
| GDP pc | □ | Currency Quote | -0.028 | 0.012 | -2.225 | 0.026 |
| GDP pc | □ | Imports | 0.243 | 0.074 | 3.274 | <0.001 |
| GDP pc | □ | Exports | 0.362 | 0.054 | 6.719 | <0.001 |

Note: The estimated coefficients are all significant with the z-tests, supporting the global acceptance of the model and the research hypothesis.
Source: own elaboration.

*Figure 7. Table showing covariances*

| Variables | | | Estimate | S.E. | $p$ |
|---|---|---|---|---|---|
| Imports | ↔ | Exports | 0.154 | 0.024 | <0.001 |
| Exports | ↔ | Currency Quote | -0.293 | 0.088 | <0.001 |
| Imports | ↔ | Currency Quote | -0.251 | 0.066 | <0.001 |

Note: All the estimated covariances are significant with the z-tests; most with $p$-values under 0.001.
Source: own elaboration.

*Figure 8. Table showing variances*

| Variables | Estimate | S.E. | *p* |
|---|---|---|---|
| Imports | 0.157 | 0.020 | <0.001 |
| Exports | 0.286 | 0.037 | <0.001 |
| Unemployment Rate | 0.029 | 0.004 | <0.001 |
| Currency Quote | 2.924 | 0.379 | <0.001 |
| e3 | 2.116 | 0.274 | <0.001 |
| e2 | 3.047 | 0.395 | <0.001 |
| e1 | 0.046 | 0.006 | <0.001 |

Note: All the estimated variances are significant with the z-tests; most with p-values under 0.001.
Source: own elaboration.

## Comments Regarding the Contrast on Hypotheses

As a corollary to this section, it is worth mentioning that, although the evolution tends to be different in each country, which is obvious, it is considered that the results of the standardized coefficients of the model confirm all three hypotheses proposed.

Therefore, despite the great financial crisis that started in 2007, a favorable behaviour of the endogenous variables "Imports" and "Exports" positively affect the exogenous variable "GDP per capita", with which $H_1$ is contrasted. Likewise, the effect of an increase of the endogenous variable "Currency exchange rate" - the foreign currency - on the exogenous "GDP per capita" is negative, which confirms $H_2$. And regarding $H_3$, the model also presents the negative effect of a rise in the endogenous variable "Fiscal deficit" on the exogenous "GDP per capita".

## DISCUSSIONS

The foreign trade dynamics of countries are influenced by a multitude of factors, especially within the MENA (Middle East and North Africa) region. This area is particularly notable for its economic dependence on the export of petroleum derivatives, making the understanding of macroeconomic variables crucial for assessing the health and stability of these economies. The improvements in transportation infrastructure, highlighted by Njoya & Ragab, (2022), play a vital role in enhancing trade efficiency. Enhanced transport means not only facilitate faster movement of goods but also reduce logistical costs, thereby making exports more competitive. Countries such as Morocco, Algeria, Egypt, Jordan, and Türkiye exemplify this trend, showing a positive correlation between infrastructure development and economic expansion (Abdullah, N. et al., 2015). Despite these developments, it is essential to acknowledge the underlying geopolitical tensions that can hinder economic cooperation. For instance, the historical animosities between Morocco and Algeria, stemming from conflicts like the Sand War in 1963, have created an environment of distrust and limited collaboration in trade (Torres, 2013). Such political tensions not only disrupt bilateral trade relations but can also deter foreign investment, as potential investors may view instability as a risk factor.

Moreover, the question of economic justice is particularly relevant in the MENA context. Alizadeh (2020) emphasizes the significance of justice—both economic and distributive—as foundational principles in Islamic economics. However, in practice, the reality often diverges significantly from these ideals. In many of the analyzed countries, disparities in wealth and opportunity persist, resulting in economic marginalization for significant portions of the population (Acar & Dogruel, 2012). This situation raises questions about the effectiveness of current economic policies and the need for more equitable distribution mechanisms that could foster inclusive growth.

From a broader sustainability perspective, addressing climate change and reducing CO2 emissions are essential for achieving the Sustainable Development Goals. Saboori et al. (2024) demonstrate that institutional quality, along with factors like corruption control and government effectiveness, plays a significant role in reducing emissions. Strengthening governance structures in MENA countries is therefore key to mitigating environmental degradation. Furthermore, Wani et al. (2024) explore the relationship between economic development, GDP, and environmental degradation through the Environmental Kuznets Curve (EKC) hypothesis. Their study highlights a negative relationship between foreign direct investment (FDI) and CO2 emissions, and a positive correlation between trade openness and emissions. This suggests that transitioning to green energy solutions is vital for mitigating the environmental impact of non-renewable energy sources in the MENA region.

The appropriation of labor from developing nations by more prosperous countries presents another critical issue. The analysis by Hickel et al. (2022) points to a systemic exploitation where labor resources from MENA countries are utilized to fuel the economies of developed nations. This situation not only stifles local economic development but also perpetuates a cycle of dependency that can hinder long-term growth prospects. Addressing this issue requires a concerted effort to enhance labor rights and promote fair trade practices that prioritize the welfare of local workers. The MENA region also faces significant challenges in waste management, with rapid population growth, urbanization, and changes in lifestyle leading to increased waste generation. Thabit et al. (2020) argue that adopting waste-to-energy solutions, such as waste incineration plants, could address these challenges by generating electricity and potable water, while reducing waste treatment costs. The estimated cost of treating municipal solid waste over 30 years is US$39 per ton, offering both environmental benefits and contributions to sustainable development.

Furthermore, the MENA region's tourism industry, supported by air transport, contributes substantially to GDP and employment, but it also causes considerable environmental degradation. Onifade & Haouas (2023) examine the relationship between tourism, air transportation, and emissions, highlighting that while air transport drives tourism, it also exacerbates environmental harm. Their findings emphasize the need for policies aimed at addressing the environmental impacts of the aviation sector in the region.

In addition, the COVID-19 pandemic has compounded existing challenges faced by the MENA countries, leading to severe economic disruptions. The impact of the pandemic must be quantified comprehensively, taking into account its effects on foreign trade, international monetary reserves, unemployment rates, and currency depreciation (Babshetti et al., 2022). The pandemic's influence on global supply chains further exacerbates vulnerabilities in economies that are heavily reliant on a narrow range of exports, thereby highlighting the urgency for diversification.

Political instability remains a significant macroeconomic cost in the MENA region. The work of Novta & Pugacheva (2021) provides compelling evidence that a decade of conflict can lead to a substantial 28% reduction in GDP per capita. This statistic underscores the far-reaching implications of prolonged instability, which can curtail private consumption by nearly 25%, exports by 58%, and imports by 34%. The intricate relationship between conflict and economic performance suggests that addressing political grievances and establishing a stable governance framework is paramount for fostering economic resilience. The authors also highlight that to mitigate the adverse effects of conflict on GDP, it is critical to monitor pre-conflict GDP forecasts from the IMF's World Economic Outlook, emphasizing the need for proactive economic planning in politically sensitive regions.

Finally, the importance of social stability and governance cannot be overstated. In countries where political instability is rampant, economic growth is often stunted due to a lack of investor confidence and the diversion of resources towards security measures rather than development. Future research could explore the correlation between governance indicators—such as transparency, accountability, and political stability—and macroeconomic performance, shedding light on potential pathways for improving economic conditions in the MENA region.

## CONCLUSION

The empirical analysis conducted in this study supports the three proposed hypotheses effectively, demonstrating that specific macroeconomic variables significantly influence GDP per capita in the selected MENA countries. Despite the substantial financial turbulence initiated in 2007, the results of the estimated Structural Equation Model (SEM) reveal crucial insights into the economic dynamics of the region. However, a central theme emerging from the analysis is the pressing issue of political instability, which remains a critical factor influencing economic outcomes. Future research endeavors should consider political instability as a latent variable, as its ramifications on economic performance are profound and multifaceted.

The heterogeneity of the data across the ten MENA countries presents a limitation in this study; however, this diversity also enriches the analysis by highlighting different responses to similar macroeconomic challenges. While the current study focused on global macroeconomic indicators, it is essential to consider the unique socio-economic contexts of each country. This nuanced approach can lead to a more comprehensive understanding of the factors driving economic performance and resilience across the MENA region.

A significant advantage for these countries lies in their abundant natural resources, particularly oil and gas, which are strategic commodities that underlie approximately 60% of global economic activity (Cerezo et al., 2022). This reliance on hydrocarbons provides a substantial revenue stream, but it also creates vulnerabilities. As the global energy landscape shifts toward renewable alternatives, MENA countries must contemplate the future of their economies. The critical question arises: how will these nations adapt when their primary export commodities face competition from renewable energy substitutes? This reflection is not merely hypothetical; it signals an urgent need for strategic planning and diversification. To ensure long-term sustainability, MENA countries must urgently pursue viable alternatives to diversify their export revenues. This includes investing in sectors such as renewable energy, technology, agriculture, and tourism. Policymakers should focus on creating an environment conducive to innovation and entrepreneurship, which can foster economic diversification and resilience against external shocks.

Moreover, future lines of research should aim to explore not only endogenous and exogenous variables but also additional latent factors that could influence economic performance. Critical aspects such as literacy rates, the role of women in society, and the levels of religious and ethnic tolerance are fundamental dimensions that warrant attention. These factors are integral to understanding the socio-economic landscape and could have profound implications for policy formulation and implementation.

In conclusion, the MENA region stands at a crossroads. While it possesses significant advantages in terms of natural resources and strategic geopolitical positioning, it also faces substantial challenges related to political instability, economic dependency on hydrocarbons, and social inequities. Addressing these issues through informed research and inclusive policy frameworks will be essential for fostering sustainable development and improving the quality of life for the populations within these countries. The journey toward resilience and diversification is complex, but it is imperative for securing a prosperous future in an increasingly uncertain global environment.

## ACKNOWLEDGEMENTS

The authors would like to thank Dr. Alan Smith (Adviser on Natural Resource Management, Bonn, Germany) for his scientific recommendations.

## REFERENCES

Abdullah, N., Hussin, A., & Hadi, M. (2015). The determinants of trade and trade direction of Arab Maghreb Union. *Journal of Economic Cooperation and Development*, *36*(3), 123–148.

Abu-Fadil, M., Torrent, J., & Grizzle, A. (2016). Opportunities for media and information literacy in the Middle East and North Africa. *The International Clearinghouse on Children, Youth & Media at Nordicom*, University of Gothemburg. (pp. 55-115).

Acar, S., & Dogruel, F. (2012). Sources of inequality in selected MENA countries. *Structural Change and Economic Dynamics*, *23*(3), 276–285. DOI: 10.1016/j.strueco.2012.03.004

Alizadeh, M. (2020). Analysis of economic convergence of Islamic Justice in selected Islamic Countries. *Journal of Economic Structures*, *9*(1), 24. Advance online publication. DOI: 10.1186/s40008-020-00191-8

Alvarez, I., & Ossorio, A. (2019). Spain, Israel and Palestine. History of encounters and disagreements. *Hispania*, *79*(261), 221–248. DOI: 10.3989/hispania.2019.008

Apocada del Hoyo, M. (2016). Middle East and the great powers. International Relations and the Cold War, 1945-1948. Retrieved from https://dialnet.unirioja.es/servlet/dctes?codigo=155576

Apuuli, K. (2021). The competing mediations in the post-Qaddafi Libyan political crisis. *International Negotiation*, *8*(1), 1–31. DOI: 10.1163/15718069-bja10019

Arranz, M., & Martín, J. (2009). The factors of socio-economic development and territorial of Morocco: The contribution of the remittances from migrants. *Annales de Géographie*, *29*(2), 9–35.

Artetxe, A. (2016). The European Union and Spain in their relationship with the Maghreb: The cases of Morocco and Algeria. Retrieved from http://hdl.handle.net/10810/18490

Babshetti, V., Singh, J., & Yaragol, P. (2022). The impact of COVID-19 on the socio-economic indicators of the selected Asian countries. *India Quarterly*, *78*(1), 28–46. DOI: 10.1177/09749284211068162

Badri, M., & Alshare, K. (2008). A path analytic model and measurement of the business value of e-government: An international perspective. *International Journal of Information Management*, *28*(6), 524–535. DOI: 10.1016/j.ijinfomgt.2006.10.004

Badri, M., Davis, D. & Davis, D. (2000). Operations strategy, environmental uncertainty, and performance: a path analytic model of industries in developing countries. *Omega, 28(2):155-173.* doi: 00041-9.DOI: 10.1016/S03050483(99)

Bagozzi, R., & Heatherton, T. (1994). A general approach to representing multifaceted personality construct: Application to state self-esteem? *Structural Equation Modeling*, *1*(1), 35–67. DOI: 10.1080/10705519409539961

Bassil, C., Saleh, A., & Anwar, S. (2019). Terrorism and tourism demand: A case study of Lebanon, Türkiye and Israel. *Current Issues in Tourism*, *22*(1), 50–70. DOI: 10.1080/13683500.2017.1397609

Bentler, P., & Yuan, K. (1999). Structural Equation Modeling with Small Samples: Test Statistics. *Multivariate Behavioral Research*, *34*(2), 181–197. DOI: 10.1207/S15327906Mb340203 PMID: 26753935

Bollen, K., & Hoyle, R. (2012). Latent Variables in Structural Equation Modeling. In Hoyle, R. H. (Ed.), *Handbook of Structural Equation Modeling* (Vol. 1, pp. 56–67). The Guilford Press., DOI: 10.1177/0049124189017003004

Bouyghrissi, S., Murshed, M., Jindal, A., Berjaoui, A., Mahmood, H., & Khanniba, M. (2022). The importance of facilitating renewable energy transition for Abating CO2 emissions in Morocco. *Environmental Science and Pollution Research International*, *29*(14), 20752–20767. DOI: 10.1007/s11356-021-17179-x PMID: 34741744

Browne, M., & Cudeck, R. (1993). *Alternative ways of assessing model fit.* In S. Publication (Ed.), Testing structural equation model (pp. 136-162). Bollen, K.A. & Long, J.S. DOI: 10.1177/0049124192021002005

Caridad, J. (2016). *Path Analysis. Structural models with AMOS.* (pp. 47-72). EDF, S.L.

Cerezo, J., & Fruet, V. (2022). *Spanish and International Economy* (pp. 60-86). EDF, S.L.

Cocchini, A. (2021). A decade of war in Syria: Current situation and possible outcomes. *UNISCI*, *2021*(57), 149–183. DOI: 10.31439/UNISCI-124

Cohen, S. & Jaïdi, L. (2013). *Morocco: Globalization and its consequences.* Routledge. DOI: 10.4324/9781315810904

Colombo, S., & Soler, E. (2021). Europe and the 'New' Middle East: Geopolitical shifts and strategic choices. *Journal of Balkan & Near Eastern Studies*, *23*(3), 403–422. DOI: 10.1080/19448953.2021.1888246

Dutta, D. (2015). Adam Smith theory of development in Economics (Main Features). Retrieved from http://www.economicsdiscussion.net/econo mics-2/adam-smith-theory-of-development-in-economics-main-features/4514

Elosua, P. (2011). Subjective values of quality-of-life dimensions in elderly people. A SEM preference model approach. *Social Indicators Research*, *104*(3), 427–437. DOI: 10.1007/s11205-010-9752-y

Fourie, J., Rossello, J., & Santana, M. (2020). Fatal attraction: How security threats hurt tourism. *Journal of Travel Research*, *59*(2), 209–219. DOI: 10.1177/0047287519826208

Franco, F. (2001). The Muslim conquest of the Maghreb and Al-Andalus according to the Mozarabic chronicles. Retrieved from http://hdl.handle.net/10045/25131

Garson, D. (2008). Path Analysis with structural equation model. *In Path Analysis* (pp.1- 21). Academia. Accelerating the world's research.

Government of Spain. Ministry of Foreign Affairs, European Union and Cooperation (2021). Maghreb and Middle East. Retrieved from https://www.exteriores.gob.es/es/PoliticaExterior/Paginas/MagrebOrienteProximo.asp

Groizard, J., Mohanad, I., & Santana, M. (2022). Political upheavals, tourism flight, and spillovers: The case of the Arab Spring. *Journal of Travel Research, 61*(4), 921–939. DOI: 10.1177/00472875211002652

Hernando de Larramendi, M. (2019). Doomed regionalism in a eedrawn Maghreb? The changing shape of the rivalry between Algeria and Morocco in the post-2011 era. *Journal of North African Studies, 24*(3), 506–531. DOI: 10.1080/13629387.2018.1454657

Hickel, J., Dorninger, C., Wieland, H., & Suwandi, I. (2022). Imperialist Appropriation in the World Economy: Drain from the Global South through Unequal Exchange, 1990–2015. *Global Environmental Change, 73*, 102467. DOI: 10.1016/j.gloenvcha.2022.102467

Ibrahiem, D., & Hanafy, S. (2021). Do energy security and environmental quality contribute to Renewable Energy? The Role of Trade Openness and Energy Use in North African Countries. *Renewable Energy, 179*, 667–678. DOI: 10.1016/j.renene.2021.07.019

Ji, X., Dong, F., Zheng, C., & Bu, N. (2022). The influences of international trade on sustainable economic growth: An economic policy perspective. *Sustainability (Basel), 14*(5), 1–15. DOI: 10.3390/su14052781

Kujawa, K. (2021). Turkish-Russian Cooperation: Implications for NATO. *Journal of International Students, 14*(2), 194–207. DOI: 10.14254/2071-8330.2021/14-2/13

Lopez, R. (2015). *Fight against antisemitism and promotion of religious tolerance in Argentina. The creation of the State of Israel*. Democratic Bridge Program of CADAL.

Mawejje, J., & Odhiambo, N. (2022). The determinants and cyclicality of fiscal policy: Empirical evidence from East Africa. *Inter Economics, 169*, 55–70. DOI: 10.1016/j.inteco.2021.12.001

Meneses, R. (2022). The tension between Morocco and Algeria: A stoked historic rivalry for Western Sahara and the 'gas war'. *CEIPAZ, 2021-2022*, 157–170.

Michail, N. (2021). The impact of conflict on the exchange rate of developing economies. *Review of Development Economics, 25*(2), 916–930. DOI: 10.1111/rode.12749

Ministry of National Education. Morocco (2014). Statistics of education indicators. Retrieved from https://www.men.gov.ma/Fr/Pages/Indices-sysp%C3%A9dag.aspx

Němečková, T., Melnikovová, L., & Piskunova, N. (2021). Russia's return to Africa: A comparative study of Egypt, Algeria, and Morocco. *The Journal of Modern African Studies, 59*(3), 367–390. DOI: 10.1017/S0022278X21000070

Njoya, E., & Ragab, A. (2022). Economic impacts of public air transport investment: A case study of Egypt. *Sustainability (Basel), 14*(5), 2651. DOI: 10.3390/su14052651

Novta, N., & Pugacheva, E. (2021). The macroeconomic costs of conflict. *Journal of Macroeconomics, 68*, 103286. Advance online publication. DOI: 10.1016/j.jmacro.2021.103286

Onifade, S. T., & Haouas, I. (2023). Assessing environmental sustainability in top Middle East travel destinations: Insights on the multifaceted roles of air transport amidst other energy indicators. *Environmental Science and Pollution Research International*, *30*(45), 101911–101926. DOI: 10.1007/s11356-023-29183-4 PMID: 37653199

Postema, J. (2021). *The Middle East: U.S. policy, foreign assistance and key issues*. Nova Science Publishers, Inc., Retrieved from https://pesquisa.bvsalud.org/global-literature-on-novel-coronavirus-2019-ncov/resource/pt/covidwho-1469274

Ricoy, C. (2005). Adam Smith's theory of economic growth. *Economy and Development*, *138*(1), 11–47.

Robins, S., Gready, P., Aloui, A., Andrieu, K., Hamza, H., & Ferchichi, W. (2022). Transitional justice from the margins: Collective reparations and Tunisia's Truth and Dignity Commission. *Political Geography*, *94*, 102565. Advance online publication. DOI: 10.1016/j.polgeo.2021.102565

Saboori, B., Mahdavian, S. M., & Radmehr, R. (2024). Assessing the environmental impact of institutional quality at aggregate and disaggregate levels: The role of renewable and non-renewable energy consumption and trade in MENA countries. *Sustainable Environment*, *10*(1), 2426833. Advance online publication. DOI: 10.1080/27658511.2024.2426833

Sánchez, J. (2016). Human Development Index (HDI). Retrieved from https://economipedia.com/definiciones/indice-desarrollo-humano.html

Semosa, P., & Kanayo, O. (2021). Is there a nexus between inflation, exchange rate and unemployment in South Africa: An econometric analysis? *Montenegrin Journal of Economics*, *17*(1), 45–58. DOI: 10.14254/1800-5845/2021.17-1.3

Sghaier, I. (2021). Remittances and economic growth in MENA Countries: The role of financial development. *Economic Alternatives*, *2021*(1), 43–59. DOI: 10.37075/EA.2021.1.03

Shoori, M., Bijan, A., & Ejazi, E. (2021). Security implications of Russian arms exports to West Asian countries (Iran, Egypt, Syria, and Iraq). *Central Eurasia Studies*, *14*(2), 25–46. DOI: 10.22059/jcep.2022.320197.449990

Tamburini, F. (2021). The COVID-19 outbreak in North Africa: A legal analysis. *Journal of Asian and African Studies*, *56*(7), 1738–1754. DOI: 10.1177/0021909620983586 PMID: 38603075

Thabit, Q., Nassour, A., & Nelles, M. (2020). Potentiality of Waste-to-Energy Sector Coupling in the MENA Region: Jordan as a Case Study. *Energies 2020, Vol. 13, Page 2786, 13(11),* 2786. DOI: 10.3390/en13112786

Torres, A. (2013). US diplomacy and the North African 'War of the Sands' (1963). *Journal of North African Studies*, *18*(2), 324–348. DOI: 10.1080/13629387.2013.767041

Völlers, P., Yavan, N., & Franz, M. (2021). The reaction of foreign firms to institutional changes: The case of German Direct Investment in Türkiye. *Applied Geography (Sevenoaks, England)*, *134*, 102503. Advance online publication. DOI: 10.1016/j.apgeog.2021.102503

Wani, M. J. G., Alamir, I. A., Ghazwani, M., Ahmed, I., Alkaraan, F., & Khan, M. A. (2024). Asymmetric Effect of Green Energy and Economic Growth on the Environmental Deterioration and the Environmental Kuznets Curve Validation in MENA Countries. *International Journal of Finance & Economics*, ijfe.3079. Advance online publication. DOI: 10.1002/ijfe.3079

World Bank. (2021a). Economic data of Middle East and North Africa (MENA) countries. Retrieved from https://data.worldbank.org/region/middle-east-and-north-africa

World Bank. (2021b). Country data of Middle East and North Africa (MENA). Retrieved from https://data.worldbank.org/country/

# Chapter 5
# Territorial Marketing and Region Development:
## An Exploratory Approach in Tabuaço (Portugal)

**Mariana Taveira Gouveia**
*Polytechnic University of Cávado and Ave (IPCA), Portugal*

**Bruno Barbosa Sousa**
https://orcid.org/0000-0002-8588-2422
*Polytechnic University of Cávado and Ave (IPCA), Portugal & Applied Management Research Unit (UNIAG), Portugal & Centro de Investigação, Desenvolvimento e Inovação em Turismo (CiTUR), Portugal*

## ABSTRACT

*This chapter seeks to elucidate the significance of territorial branding for the municipality of Tabuaço and to determine whether visitors are more inclined towards tourist destinations with a recognizable and attractive brand image. Additionally, the findings from this chapter are anticipated to contribute to the scientific community and, fundamentally, to the local authorities of Tabuaço, facilitating the implementation of effective marketing and communication strategies for the town's economic and tourism development. This chapter provides insights into territorial marketing and regional development. Finally, avenues for future research will be proposed.*

## INTRODUCTION

Territorial marketing emerges from the interactions among various stakeholders and the communication established within the territory with its interacting publics. Some authors segment audiences based on their relationship with the place and its population, categorizing them into internal and external customers. Internal customers include local residents, employees, and companies, with the primary objective of territorial marketing being to meet their needs (Sousa and Rocha, 2019). External customers, on the other hand, are non-residents, such as visitors and companies not present in the location, where the aim of territorial marketing is to attract them. The perspectives of visitors on tourist destinations are

DOI: 10.4018/979-8-3693-7081-0.ch005

continually evolving, and nowadays, individuals choose destinations not only for leisure but also for study or work. In this case, the perception of the territory influences decision-making and it is necessary that the destinations themselves offer tangible and intangible benefits, transmitting messages about identity, lifestyle and status (Morgan et al., 2004; Pike, 2005). The perception that a consumer holds of a particular territory must be positive and can be shaped through marketing and communication techniques tailored to the specificities of the territories. Given that territories possess unique characteristics, the process of adapting and adopting these techniques can be complex and challenging, necessitating a more meticulous and personalized approach (Cardoso, 2016). One of the primary objectives of destinations is to attract the maximum number of visitors, residents, and investments to secure the resources necessary for their growth and to create a positive development cycle (Priporas et al., 2020). In summary, territorial marketing is a powerful tool for fostering local development and enhancing the well-being of the community. One of the primary challenges of city marketing in the future will be effectively integrating the concept of smart cities (Sharifi et al., 2024). To this end, territorial branding aids in promoting the destination to achieve this goal, in addition to fostering urban development and gaining a competitive advantage (Beck & Ferasso, 2022). Consequently, this chapter aims to serve as a crucial tool for supporting territorial management in the specific context of Tabuaço. From an interdisciplinary perspective, this chapter provides insights into territorial marketing and regional and local development.

## TERRITORIAL MARKETING

Territorial marketing, also known as city marketing, place marketing or urban marketing, presents different concepts, interrelated and with similar characteristics (Vuignier, 2017; Sousa & Rocha, 2019; Dash, 2024). This instrument plays a fundamental role in place management, contributing to the achievement of established objectives and enhancing a destination's competitiveness (Kavaratzis & Ashworth, 2008). Roseta et al. (2020) further assert that territorial marketing is a process through which regional activities optimize economic and social efficiency sustainably, thereby making the destination appealing to its target audiences. Given the importance of territorial marketing for regional development, it is crucial to comprehend this tool. Beyond satisfying residents, investors, and companies, it necessitates strategic planning to ensure the development and management of the destination, thereby strengthening its competitive advantages and creating opportunities for the locale (Carvalho, 2019). Additionally, territorial marketing results from the interactions among various stakeholders and the communication established within the territory with its interacting publics (Barros & Gama, 2009). Valdani and Ancarani (2001) segment audiences based on their relationship with the place and its population, categorizing them into internal and external customers. Internal customers include local residents, employees, and companies, with the primary objective of territorial marketing being to meet their needs (Lindström & Vanhala, 2013). External customers, on the other hand, are non-residents, such as visitors and companies not present in the location, where the aim of territorial marketing is to attract them.

As a management technique, territorial marketing aids in market analysis, identifying opportunities that benefit communities and regions. It defines market and communication strategies to publicize the image and identity of the place and prepares for potential market changes and needs, thereby enhancing competitive advantages and strengthening the territory's market positioning (Kavaratzis and Ashworth, 2008; Carvalho, 2019). Thus, territorial marketing extends beyond mere promotion and advertising; it is also a tool for identifying problems, proposing solutions, analyzing, planning, implementing, and controlling the outcomes of the measures outlined (Carvalho, 2019). Moreover, this tool promotes the export of products and services, stimulates tourism, and attracts new investments or businesses. In addition to fostering territorial development at various levels, it ensures that residents remain content and satisfied with living in the area (Lages, 2017).

Kotler et al. (1993) argue that to achieve an effective long-term solution, it is essential to implement four marketing factors: adequate infrastructure and service provision; the construction of new attractions to sustain business and attract new investments and people; clear communication of the territory's qualities through a strong communication plan; and obtaining support from residents, leaders, and institutions to transform the community into a welcoming place for new businesses and visitors. Territorial marketing, through strategic and well-structured planning, promotes the territory, develops the destination sustainably and inclusively, enriches its identity, gains recognition, and maximizes notoriety. This is feasible only if the objectives consider the demands and needs of all stakeholders involved (D'Auria et al., 2018; Grein & Dallabrida, 2020).

Given the increasing competition between territories, it is necessary to differentiate destinations and acquire a competitive advantage. Unlike products and services, tourist destinations gain a competitive edge through their ability to attract new businesses, investments, visitors, or companies (Valdani & Ancarani, 2001). To achieve this, territories must be perceived as providers of goods and services or promoters of local products and values, managed according to outlined marketing strategies to satisfy the interests of all stakeholders and enhance attractiveness (Cardoso, 2016). Segmentation is a crucial task in territorial marketing as it enables the implementation of more effective strategies and informed decisions about the main target audiences (Lages et al., 2018). Destinations must understand the needs of their diverse audiences, analyze and interact with them to avoid economic stagnation or, in the worst-case scenario, decline (Almeida, 2004). Therefore, orienting strategies towards internal customers is fundamental for the strategic management of destinations, as the satisfaction of residents and companies will influence the territory's success and may prevent their abandonment (Rodrígues, 2003).

A territory must be cognizant of the strategic planning required to achieve objectives and create value. To attain these results, it is necessary to understand the external environment; comprehend the needs, desires, and behaviors of all stakeholders; construct a realistic perspective of the destination's aspirations and develop a strategic plan based on that perspective; effectively communicate its characteristics and benefits through a positive image; garner the support of the population, leaders, and institutions by managing common interests to attract new investments and companies; and evaluate the progress of each stage of the action plan (Kotler et al., 1993; Rainisto, 2003).

According to Kotler et al. (1993), there are four activities within the scope of Place Marketing: creating the community's mix of characteristics and services; implementing incentives for current and future investors and users of goods and services; offering the place's products and services efficiently and accessibly; and promoting the place's values and image to make future users aware of its advantages.

Differentiation is a crucial aspect of building positive territorial brands, requiring continuous and consistent effort (Lages et al., 2018). Alongside this, the creation of location-appropriate marketing strategies and the ability to attract new investments, companies, and visitors are essential factors for obtaining a competitive advantage (Kotler et al., 1993).

Therefore, it is vital for territories to clearly and precisely define their image and values to develop a more effective relationship with external customers (Correia and Brito, 2011). This is one of the fundamental principles of territorial marketing, which faces the demanding challenge of maintaining the territory's identity and characteristics. This challenge helps avoid potential mischaracterizations often associated with overly aggressive marketing strategies (Lages et al., 2018). In summary, destinations must identify the values that will reinforce their positioning and identity, which, once defined, are disseminated to create a coherent image of the territory among stakeholders (Correia & Brito, 2011).

Therefore, city marketing is a tool that allows you to get the attention of tourists and communicate to external markets, through the choice of attractive images, through which they are disseminated through different media (Hospers, 2009). Following Hospers' (2009) approach, territorial marketing professionals do not necessarily need to create a completely personalized and interactive experience, but rather ensure that the experience offered matches the images used to publicize and promote the destination. It is crucial to know how to communicate coherently and clearly. In territorial marketing, communication is the key instrument to achieve the success of the defined objectives, attract external customers and, consequently, develop the territory at different levels, since communication, for Pinto (2016), is essentially informing, publicizing and influence behaviors and attitudes.

Each destination must create a coherent story about itself and identify its target audiences, in order to develop appropriate communication, through messages and communication tools adapted to each target audience (Kotler and Keller, 2006). However, it is crucial that the city, destination or region maintains its identity and is cohesive in all forms of communication, even if it has different stakeholders and target audiences that require different objectives and communication strategies suited to them (Poço, 2017). The participatory approach and community involvement (population, associations, local public and private agents, among other stakeholders) are important for urban strategic planning and contribute positively to the construction of the destination's image. This image must be communicated effectively, promoting common interests (Alas, 2017).

According to Pinto (2016), communication must be based on the context of the marketing mix, composed of its four variables: Product, Price, Promotion and Place, since that communication allows you to inform, publicize and promote existing products and services, the associated costs and prices, the method of distribution and also inform how and when they are available. The ability to communicate a message is essential, especially during the value proposition development process. In other words, knowing how to effectively transmit the message is important, both in the act of direct communication, and also in the construction of the value proposition (Rizzi and Dioli, 2010). To know how to communicate, it is necessary to know the different communication tools in order to achieve the defined objectives in an effective and efficient way. Therefore, the following figure represents the most common communication channels (Peterson, 2020; Martins, 2024)

## TERRITORIAL BRANDING

Regarding branding strategies, it is crucial to understand what constitutes a brand and analyze its significance for the development of marketing and communication strategies. When a consumer identifies with a particular brand, it implies that they share the same values, beliefs, emotions, or behaviors stimulated by the brand, thereby creating a relationship between them (Kotler and Gertner, 2004). If this relationship enables the brand to be remembered or recognized by the consumer compared to other brands in the market offering similar products or services, it is referred to as brand notoriety. Alongside this notoriety, a positive and favorable perception dictates the brand's success (Ferreira, 2022). Brand value, also known as brand equity, pertains to the power and affirmation of a brand in the market. Brand equity is linked to consumer choice and the brand's ability to win their preference and loyalty. A brand with strong brand equity is more likely to be chosen by consumers when making a decision, even if other products offer similar characteristics. This demonstrates the influence and power a brand exerts over the consumer's purchasing decision and the positive outcomes it can achieve, such as financial success and notoriety (Kotler and Armstrong, 2011; Huynh et al., 2021; Jazan et al., 2022; Alves et al., 2022). Therefore, brand equity is based on four main factors: perceived quality, recognition, brand associations, and loyalty (Blain et al., 2005). These factors influence decision-making and help strengthen the brand, attracting more customers and protecting it from competition. Consequently, the territorial brand gains a strong competitive advantage (Cheung et al., 2021; Ferreira & Coelho, 2020).

For Kavaratzis and Ashworth (2006), a territorial brand, to become quality, cannot be reduced to isolated elements with an attractive slogan or logo. Instead, a more comprehensive approach is needed, which takes into account three key elements: identity, image and positioning. This approach is important to build a unique brand capable of generating value for the place it represents. According to Beck and Ferasso (2022), the territorial brand is a reflection of the values, beliefs, culture, behaviors and personality of its residents and, therefore, its management should not be designed just to communicate a simple image of the place (Alves et al., 2022; Eshuis & Ripoll González, 2025).

Lages, Sousa and Azevedo (2018), state that creating a good value proposition for the brand is no longer enough. It is necessary to communicate it correctly and effectively, in order to reach the consumer and be recognized by them as a benefit to themselves. In other words, the message to be transmitted must create an emotional impression, which allows you to establish connections with the target audience. It is these connections that influence decision making and lead the consumer to choose that brand over another.

Furthermore, it is important to take into account that territorial brands cover different types of consumers – tourists, residents or investors – as they are made up of different characteristics, goods and services, which satisfy different needs, desires and interests. Therefore, brand, strategic and communication planning must be carefully adapted to meet all expectations created by each market segment. Highlighting the strengths of the territory that are most relevant and attractive to each group is essential, as it guarantees a positive response and maximizes the positive impact of the brand (Pike, 2017).

The creation of a territorial brand is crucial for differentiating and enhancing the value of a territory in an increasingly competitive market. Consequently, companies must develop effective branding strategies to distinguish themselves from competitors (Cham et al., 2021). The same necessity applies to destinations, as competition between territories intensifies. Understanding the importance of a brand for territories is essential for their success, as it is through the brand that emotional connections with consumers are established. In the context of territorial branding, identity forms the core of the brand. This identity comprises a set of characteristics and associations that enable the territory to be identified and differentiated in the market. In other words, brand identity reflects how those responsible for the destination perceive themselves, encompassing elements such as vision, culture, and positioning. By integrating these components, the territory creates a unique brand identity capable of forming relationships with consumers, establishing a genuine and consistent image, and aligning the perceived image with the projected image (You & Hon, 2021; Yang et al., 2022):

The creation of a unique and differentiating identity is essential for a territory's success. This implies that the territorial brand, composed of specific characteristics, attributes, and values of the territory, must explore and value its tangible resources (infrastructure and natural resources) and intangible resources (culture, history, language, and lifestyle). Thus, the brand serves as a means of expressing the territory's identity, attracting the interest and support of all stakeholders involved (Ginesta and San Eugenio, 2020). Kapferer developed a theoretical model for brand management, aimed at assisting in their development and understanding. This model, titled the Brand Identity Prism, emerged after the author realized that brands are not merely logos or slogans but also a set of elements with different dimensions that give rise to brand identity and make it more complex. Through the Brand Identity Prism, it is possible to visualize and perceive the six facets of the brand: physical, personality, relationship, culture, reflection, and self-image (Kapferer, 1992). The Brand Identity Prism is divided into six parts:

- Physical: Represents the specificities and qualities of the brand, composed of tangible and visible characteristics (design, logo, products, or services, among others). Kapferer (1992, p.43) also adds that "the physical is the basis of the brand" and is the first step towards creating a brand. During the process of defining the physical appearance of the brand, it is important to consider the following questions: What is it specifically? What does it look like? What does it do?
- Personality: Represents the brand's personality traits and appears when it begins to communicate. This means that the way the brand advertises and promotes its products or services demonstrates the type of individual it would be if it were a human being. The author states that "a brand has a personality," and it is through this that one may or may not identify with the brand (Kapferer, 1992, p.44).
- Culture: A set of values and symbols that fuel the brand's inspiration. It is through these principles that the product or service is created. Each brand must have its own culture, and its products or services must be a concrete representation of that culture and a means of communication. This aspect is essential, as it significantly impacts differentiation and is at the heart of the brand.
- Relationship: Mainly related to services but equally important in products, as brands establish relationships with their consumers and stakeholders. The way the brand communicates, interacts, or engages with the target audience is part of this facet and should be equally valued.
- Reflection: Represents the image, values, and meanings that the brand evokes in the consumer. In other words, reflection represents the set of feelings that the consumer wants to experience when using the brand, serving as the external mirror of the target audience.
- Self-image: The internal mirror of the target audience, representing consumers who use the brand to express their own identity.

In summary, the creation of a territorial identity based on its characteristics, values, and attributes allows visitors to feel connected with the brand. This means that the way the brand communicates will influence consumer emotions, attitudes, and behaviors. Therefore, understanding what consumers feel or think about the brand is crucial to deciphering the path to follow, in order to develop efficient and beneficial communication and marketing strategies for the tourist destination, in addition to satisfying the needs and desires of the consumer.

## DESTINATION IMAGE

The image of a destination is considered, by some authors, as the main criterion when choosing a place to travel, as it influences the visitor's behavior and decision. It is through this that consumers seek information and opinions from other tourists. On the other hand, the visitor's experience has a high importance in their satisfaction with the tourist destination, since it is through experiences that consumers are able to make emotional associations and, thus, reinforce the positioning of the territorial brand (Loureiro and Kaufmann 2012; Drennan et al., 2015).

The more positive the image of the territory, the more visitors it can attract and, consequently, the greater its development will be. This means that the perceptions that visitors have of the destination can influence the tourist growth of the place, attracting new investment and resources for tourist and economic activity (Prayag, 2010). To achieve this, it is necessary to promote memorable tourist experiences, through campaigns that highlight the destination's natural beauty and best settings. By exploring these sensory attributes, it is possible to create positive emotions and increase visitor engagement with the destination. These two elements are crucial for visitor behavior, as they tend to pay more attention to relevant information about the tourist experience when planning their trip (Santos et al., 2022).

Media and information sources are equally important to create interest in potential visitors, however they must be diversified, as they have a positive impact on the way tourists understand and analyze the image of a tourist destination. This means, the more varied and accessible information is available, the greater the probability of forming a favorable image of the territory. To this end, those responsible for the destination's image must actively promote it in different media, such as social networks, website, advertising, tourism magazines, among others, through promotional campaigns, interactive content or other communication methods. This allows the potential visitor to make a more informed and clear choice, as they have access to detailed information about the services, attractions, activities or infrastructure offered by the destination (Baloglu & McCleary, 1999; Zhang et al., 2014). That said, territorial marketing management must analyze the image perceived by the market and the target audience, as this image will influence the decision when choosing a tourist destination. This means that it is necessary to analyze feedback from everyone who has contact with the destination, be they visitors, residents, digital influencers, journalists, among others. The visitor's decision about which tourist destination to choose for their trip is influenced by the image of the place, the information available, in different media and by recommendations from other visitors. Therefore, marketing and communication strategies are crucial to arouse the interest of potential visitors. Since behavior, when making a decision, varies depending on the image of the territory on the market, it is important to constantly analyze whether the projected image coincides with the perceived image, so as not to compromise tourism and the development of the territory.

## RESEARCH PROCESS AND TABUAÇO CONTEXT

Regarding research process, this chapter seeks to elucidate the significance of territorial branding for the municipality of Tabuaço and to determine whether visitors are more inclined towards tourist destinations with a recognizable and attractive brand image. Additionally, the findings from this chapter are anticipated to contribute to the scientific community and, fundamentally, to the local authorities of Tabuaço, facilitating the implementation of effective marketing and communication strategies for the town's economic and tourism development. In this sense, an initial diagnosis and greater understanding of the context of the study is presented, with the aim of presenting preliminary insights into the importance that territorial marketing can represent in the regional and local development of certain specific destinations. The Municipality of Tabuaço is located in the North of Portugal, belonging to the district of Viseu. It is located in the Douro sub-region and is known for its wines and the region's characteristic landscapes. Its geographical area covers a territorial area of around 134 km$^2$, spread across 17 parishes. Tabuaço is positioned in a strategic region – in the heart of the Douro – which gives it a privileged position for tourist and economic development, in addition to becoming an attractive destination for tourists and investors. According to Rodrigues et al. (2021), he population residing in Tabuaço was around 5,008 inhabitants, 2,378 men and 2,630 women. Distributed by age groups, 447 residents between 0 and 14 years old, 2,918 between 15 and 64 years old and 1,647 inhabitants over 65 years old. It is an aging population, since the aging rate is high, that is, for every 100 young people there are 369 elderly people. Regarding economic activity, in 2021, the activity rate of the active population of Tabuaço was 39.2%, the employment rate was around 36.3% and the unemployment rate was 7.6%. On the other hand, in 2022 Tabuaço had 831 active companies distributed across different sectors of economic activity. The Tabuaço brand has undergone some improvements over the years, in order to become a more consolidated and recognized brand in the market. Recently, the City Council, together with marketing and communication professionals, developed the region's new identity, with a new logo and a new slogan: "Tabuaço, more than D'ouro".

## PRELIMINARY INSIGHTS

The slogan reflects the idea that Tabuaço is more than the Douro and the vineyard landscapes, it is also the Beira landscape, the heritage, endogenous products, traditions and culture. The objective is to convey the message that Tabuaço has a lot in one place and that there is still a lot of richness to explore. Tabuaço, like other municipalities in the Douro region, is a land of wines, olive oil, gastronomy, nature and traditions. However, Tabuaço communicates the Rijomax watch and the Legends and Myths as differentiating elements. In this way, these characteristics shape what Tabuaço's identity is.

To communicate, the municipality uses traditional communication strategies such as billboards on national roads and highways and flyers spread across strategic points in the region. Furthermore, in order to reach all audiences and consolidate its presence in the market, the municipality has a modernized website and maintains its presence on social media, frequently publishing recent news and events. Regarding Tabuaço's tourist activity, the region has increasingly become an attractive tourist destination for tourists and visitors (national and international) looking for authentic experiences in places rich in natural and cultural heritage.

Tabuaço is a destination that attracts different types of tourism, from classic wine tourism to sports, cultural, archaeological tourism, among others. Visitors range from all ages and range from families to friends, couples or individuals. One of the markets with the most weight in the municipality's tourist activity are tourists who travel in motorhomes, therefore there is a specific park for this activity. The famous Douro farms are highly sought after by wine lovers or curious people looking to find out more about production, especially Port Wine. The river also attracts some bathers or sport fishermen looking to enjoy the waters of the Douro River. Furthermore, the region has an activity, called the "Douro Passport", which promotes the various municipalities of the Douro and requires tourists to go to the municipality to collect the stamp. This activity essentially attracts families who come to spend the weekend in the region. There is also sports tourism, with outdoor activities such as hiking, climbing and water sports. Finally, there is a more recent niche market: archaeological tourism. The municipality has an archaeological map that is being worked on, where new antiquities have recently been discovered in the surrounding villages. Regarding tourist attractions, Tabuaço offers a variety of activities and attractive tourist attractions. As a way of providing support, the municipality has the Interactive Tourism Store, where it is possible to obtain information about activities and events taking place in the region, in addition to clarifying any doubts visitors may have about points of interest in Tabuaço, where to eat, where to sleep, between others. There are three local museums: the Abel Botelho Museum, the Museu do Imaginário Duriense (MIDU) and the Rijomax Museum, where the purpose of the museum is to showcase the region's stories, legends and myths, the art that is built here and the traditions. Furthermore, one of the experiences that the municipality offers is the Rota dos Miradouros, which consists of visiting the 14 viewpoints spread across the region and enjoying the beautiful landscapes of the Douro.

When it comes to heritage, Tabuaço has a rich historical and architectural heritage, which can be seen in the town of Tabuaço and the villages around it. The best-known and most peculiar monuments are the Monastery of São Pedro das Águias, the Marian Sanctuary of Nossa Senhora do Saboroso and the Igreja Matriz de Barcos. On the other hand, our archaeological heritage has gained some notoriety, especially at this time, since discoveries of rare pieces from antiquity are being made. In this case, Citânia de Longa stands out, also known as the Castle of the Moors, classified by IPPAR (Instituto Português Património Arqueológico) as a Property of Public Interest. Crafts and art are very present in the region as there are still products dedicated to producing unique pieces with different materials such as wood, granite, glass, among others. These products can be seen and sold in museums or among artisans.

## FINAL CONSIDERATIONS

The projected image of the tourist destination must convey positive emotions such as happiness, well-being or a memorable experience. The role of destination managers, in addition to creating, developing and maintaining a favorable image of the destination, is to constantly evaluate whether the projected image meets the perceived image and whether there is any influence, on the part of the projected image, on visitor behavior (Kim, 2014; Han and Hyun, 2015; Afshardoost and Eshaghi, 2020). Satisfactory behaviors tend to promote greater loyalty and, consequently, recommendation and return practices. In other words, if the visitor's expectations are exceeded, the probability of him returning and recommending the tourist destination is high (Sousa and Simões, 2018). Communication can and should be adjusted according to the needs and preferences of your target audience, seeking to increase recognition and establish an emotional relationship with them. Thus, managers, when adapting strategies and resources, satisfy the expectations of those involved, boosting the development of the destination and its competitiveness in the market (Lopes, 2011; Rodrigues et al., 2023). The word -of- mouth. It is an equally important and powerful marketing tool, which consumers consider highly reliable, as there is generally no financial interest associated with it. Before purchasing a product, service or even a trip, consumers use the opinions of other consumers to obtain feedback and help them make a purchasing decision. When word -of- mouth is positive, it means that consumers are satisfied with the brand or feel an emotional connection with it (Rodrigues et al., 2023).

Territorial marketing is crucial for local development as it enhances the attractiveness and competitiveness of a region. By strategically promoting the unique assets and strengths of a territory, such as its cultural heritage (D'Auria et al., 2021), natural resources, and economic opportunities, territorial marketing can attract investment, tourism, and skilled labor. This influx of resources and talent can stimulate economic growth, create jobs, and improve the overall quality of life for residents. Moreover, territorial marketing fosters a sense of identity and pride among the local community (Bouizgar et al., 2025). By highlighting the distinctive characteristics and achievements of a region, it can strengthen social cohesion and community engagement. Residents are more likely to participate in local initiatives and support local businesses when they feel a strong connection to their territory. This collective effort can lead to more sustainable and inclusive development, as the community works together to achieve common goals. Finally, territorial marketing plays a vital role in addressing challenges such as depopulation and economic decline. By effectively communicating the benefits and opportunities available in a region, it can counteract negative perceptions and attract new residents and businesses. This revitalization can lead to a more dynamic and resilient local economy, capable of adapting to changing circumstances and seizing new opportunities. In summary, territorial marketing is a powerful tool for fostering local development and enhancing the well-being of the community. One of the primary challenges of city marketing in the future will be effectively integrating the concept of smart cities (Sharifi *et al.*, 2024). As urban areas increasingly adopt advanced technologies to enhance infrastructure, services, and overall quality of life, city marketing must evolve to highlight these innovations. This involves not only promoting the technological advancements themselves but also demonstrating their tangible benefits to residents, businesses, and visitors. Ensuring that the narrative around smart cities is inclusive and accessible is crucial, as it must resonate with diverse audiences and address potential concerns about privacy, security, and the digital divide (Wolniak & Stecuła, 2024).

Another significant challenge is maintaining a balance between technological progress and sustainability. Smart cities aim to optimize resource use and reduce environmental impact, but city marketing must carefully navigate the potential trade-offs. It is essential to communicate how smart city initiatives contribute to long-term sustainability goals while also enhancing economic growth and social well-being (Kolotouchkina et al., 2024). Additionally, city marketing must address the potential for technological obsolescence and ensure that the city's brand remains relevant and adaptable in the face of rapid technological change. By effectively managing these challenges, city marketing can play a pivotal role in shaping the future of urban development and fostering resilient, vibrant communities (Dash, 2024).

Destinations must know how to identify the values that will reinforce their positioning and identity, which, once defined, is disseminated in order to create an image of that same territory among stakeholders. In this sense, the Tabuaço brand has undergone some improvements over the years, in order to become a more consolidated and recognized brand in the market. Recently, the City Council, together with marketing and communication professionals, developed the region's new identity, with a new logo and a new slogan: "Tabuaço, more than D'ouro". To this end, territorial branding helps promote the destination in order to achieve this objective, in addition to promoting urban development and acquiring a competitive advantage.

## REFERENCES


Academy of Marketing Science (AMS) World Marketing Congress (WMC), Vol. 617, Springer, .DOI: 10.1007/978-3-030-02568-7_165

Afshardoost, M., & Eshaghi, M. S. (2020). Destination image and tourist behavioral intentions: A meta-analysis. *Tourism Management, 81*, 104154. DOI: 10.1016/j.tourman.2020.104154

Aghazadeh, H., Beheshti Jazan Abadi, E., & Zandi, F. (2022). Branding advantage of agri-food companies in competitive export markets: A resource-based theory. *British Food Journal, 124*(7), 2039–2060. DOI: 10.1108/BFJ-08-2021-0952

Almeida, C. C. (2004). Cities Marketing. Management And Development, (12), 9-45. Retrieved from https://doi.org/DOI: 10.7559/gestaoedesenvolvimento.2004.104

Azevedo, A. (2009). Are you proud to live here? – A residents oriented place marketing audit (attachment, self-esteem and identity). In *38th European Marketing Academy Conference* (pp. 26-29).

Baloglu, S., & McCleary, K. W. (1999). A model of destination image formation. *Annals of Tourism Research, 26*(4), 868–897. DOI: 10.1016/S0160-7383(99)00030-4

Barros, C., & Gama, R. (2009). Territorial marketing as an instrument for valuing rural spaces: An application in the Schist Villages network. *Caderno de Geografia, 28*(29), 93–106.

Beck, D. F., & Ferasso, M. (2022). Image of cities as a tool for urban governance in Mercosur: contributions of city and urban branding. ReMark - Brazilian Marketing Magazine, 21(1), 9–28. DOI: 10.5585/remark.v21i1.19354

Björner, E., & Aronsson, L. (2022). Decentralized place branding through multiple authors and narratives: The collective branding of a small town in Sweden. *Journal of Marketing Management, 38*(13-14), 1587–1612. DOI: 10.1080/0267257X.2022.2043415

Blain, C., Levy, S. E., & Ritchie, J. R. B. (2005). Destination Branding: Insights and Practices from Destination Management Organizations. *Journal of Travel Research, 43*(4), 328–338. DOI: 10.1177/0047287505274646

Bouizgar, M., Aarabe, M., Khizzou, N. B., Alla, L., & Benjelloun, A. (2025). Smart Territorial Marketing and Promotion of Customer Engagement Towards the Territorial Brand: A Systematic Review of Literature. *Sustainable and Intelligent Territorial Marketing and Entrepreneurship*, 129-158.

Braun, E. (2008, October 30). City Marketing: Towards an Integrated Approach (No. EPS-2008-142-ORG). ERIM Ph.D. Series Research in Management. Erasmus Research Institute of Management. Retrieved from http://hdl.handle.net/1765/13694

Cham, T., Lim, Y., & Sigala, M. (2021). Marketing and social influences, hospital branding, and medical tourists' behavioral intention: Before- and after-service consumption perspective. *International Journal of Tourism Research*. Advance online publication. DOI: 10.1002/jtr.2489

Chan, C., Berger, J., & Van Boven, L. (2012). Identifiable but Not Identical: Combining Social Identity and Uniqueness Motives in Choice. *The Journal of Consumer Research*, *39*(3), 561–573. DOI: 10.1086/664804

Cheung, M. L., Pires, G., Rosenberger, P. J.III, Leung, W. K. S., & Chang, M. K. (2021). The role of social media elements in driving co-creation and engagement. *Asia Pacific Journal of Marketing and Logistics*, *33*(10), 1994–2018. DOI: 10.1108/APJML-03-2020-0176

Correia, R., & Brito, C. (2011). The importance of marketing for tourism development: The case of Montalegre. Tourism and Development Magazine. ISSN 1645-9261. 16, p. 127-143

D'Auria, A., Russo Spena, T., & Bifulco, F. (2021). Proximity marketing and context-information awareness. In *Digital Transformation in the Cultural Heritage Sector: Challenges to Marketing in the New Digital Era* (pp. 161–180). Springer International Publishing. DOI: 10.1007/978-3-030-63376-9_8

D'Auria, A., Tregua, M., & Vallejo-Martos, M. C. (2018). Modern conceptions of cities as smart and sustainable and their commonalities. *Sustainability (Basel)*, *10*(8), 2642. DOI: 10.3390/su10082642

Dallabrida, V., Tomporoski, A., & Sakr, M. (2016). From territorial marketing to territory branding: Theoretical concepts, analyzes and prospects for the Planalto Norte Catarinense. *Interactions (Campo Grande)*, *17*. Advance online publication. DOI: 10.20435/1984-042X-2016-v.17-n.4(10)

Dash, A. (2024). Smart mobility in smart cities: transforming the experiences of citizens into the future of smart cities. *Transforming Government: People. Process and Policy*, *18*(2), 287–302.

De Noni, I., Orsi, L., & Zanderighi, L. (2014). Attributes of Milan influencing city brand attractiveness. *Journal of Destination Marketing & Management*, *3*(4), 218–226. DOI: 10.1016/j.jdmm.2014.06.001

Drennan, J., Bianchi, C., Cacho-Elizondo, S., Louriero, S., Guibert, N., & Proud, W. (2015). Examining the role of wine brand love on brand loyalty: A multi-country comparison. *International Journal of Hospitality Management*, *49*, 47–55. DOI: 10.1016/j.ijhm.2015.04.012

Eshuis, J., & Ripoll González, L. (2025). Conceptualising place branding in three approaches: Towards a new definition of place brands as embodied experiences. *Journal of Place Management and Development*, *18*(1), 61–79. DOI: 10.1108/JPMD-11-2023-0109

Ferreira, J., & Coelho, A. (2020). Dynamic capabilities, innovation and branding capabilities and their impact on competitive advantage and SME's performance in Portugal: The moderating effects of entrepreneurial orientation. *International Journal of Innovation Science*, *12*(3), 255–286. DOI: 10.1108/IJIS-10-2018-0108

Ginesta, X., & San Eugenio, J. (2020). Rethinking Place Branding From a Political Perspective: Urban Governance, Public Diplomacy, and Sustainable Policy Making. *The American Behavioral Scientist*, •••, 1–18. DOI: 10.1177/0002764220975066

Gouveia, M., Aragonez, T., & Saur-Amaral, I. (2015). The Image of the Central Region: The Perspective of its Residents. *Tourism & Management Studies*, *11*(2), 93–102. DOI: 10.18089/tms.2015.11212

Han, H., & Hyun, S. S. (2015). Customer retention in the medical tourism industry: Impact of quality, satisfaction, trust, and price reasonableness. *Tourism Management*, *46*, 20–29. DOI: 10.1016/j.tourman.2014.06.003

Hanlan, J., Fuller, D., & Wilde, S. (2006). Destination Decision Making: The Need for a Strategic Planning and Management Approach. *Tourism and Hospitality Planning & Development*, *3*(3), 209–221. DOI: 10.1080/14790530601132385

Hospers, G.-J. (2009). Lynch, Urry and city marketing: Taking advantage of the city as a built and graphic image. *Place Branding and Public Diplomacy*, *5*(3), 226–233. DOI: 10.1057/pb.2009.10

Huynh, H. T. N., Trieu, H. D. X., Van Nguyen, P., Tran, T. G., & Lam, L. N. H. (2021). Explaining Brand Equity in the Information Technology Sector in Vietnam. *Administrative Sciences*, *11*(128), 1–25. DOI: 10.3390/admsci11040128

Insch, A., & Florek, M. (2010). Marketing cities: Controversies, contradictions and consequences - A special issue of the Journal of Town and City Management. *Journal Of Town & City Management*, *1*(3), 233–238.

Io, M.-U., & Wan, P. Y. K. (2017). Relationships between Tourism Experiences and Place Attachment in the Context of Casino Resorts. *Journal of Quality Assurance in Hospitality & Tourism*, *19*(1), 45–65. DOI: 10.1080/1528008X.2017.1314801

Kavaratzis, M. (2004). From city marketing to city branding: Towards a theoretical framework for developing city brands. *Place Branding*, *1*(1), 58–73. DOI: 10.1057/palgrave.pb.5990005

Kavaratzis, M., & Ashworth, G. (2006). City branding: An effective assertion of identity or a transient marketing trick? *Place Branding and Public Diplomacy*, *2*(3), 183–194. DOI: 10.1057/palgrave.pb.5990056

Kavaratzis, M., & Ashworth, G. (2008). Place marketing: How did we get here and where are we going? *Journal of Place Management and Development*, *1*(2), 150–165. DOI: 10.1108/17538330810889989

Kim, J.-H. (2014). The antecedents of memorable tourism experiences: The development of a scale to measure the destination attributes associated with memorable experiences. *Tourism Management*, *44*, 34–45. DOI: 10.1016/j.tourman.2014.02.007

Kolotouchkina, O., Ripoll González, L., & Belabas, W. (2024). Smart cities, digital inequalities, and the challenge of Inclusion. *Smart Cities*, *7*(6), 3355–3370. DOI: 10.3390/smartcities7060130

Kotler, P., & Gertner, D. (2002). Country as brand, product, and beyond: A place marketing and brand management perspective. *Journal of Brand Management*, *9*(4), 249–261. DOI: 10.1057/palgrave.bm.2540076

Kotler, P., & Gertner, D. (2011). A place marketing and place branding perspective revisited. Destination Brands, 33–53. DOI: 10.1016/B978-0-08-096930-5.10003-5

Kotler, P., Haider, D. H., & Rein, I. (1993). *Marketing Places: Attracting Investment, Industry, and Tourism to Cities, States and Nations*. Free Press.

Lages, R., Sousa, B., & Azevedo, A. (2018). Positioning and image in tourist destination marketing contexts: Case study applied to the city of Braga. *European Journal of Applied Business Management*, (Special Issue), 15–32.

Laimer, P. (2010). Basic Concepts and Definitions: Travel and Tourism (Domestic and International). In Paper on Regional Workshop for the CIS Countries on Tourism Statistics: Challenges and Good Practices. UNWTO/UNSD WS Moldova (Vol. 29).

Lindström, S., & Vanhala, S. (2013). Performance in local government HRM: The role of external customers. *Baltic Journal of Management*, *8*(3), 252–268. DOI: 10.1108/BJOM-10-2012-0094

Loureiro, S. M. C., & Kaufmann, H. R. (2012). Explaining Love of Wine Brands. *Journal of Promotion Management*, *18*(3), 329–343. DOI: 10.1080/10496491.2012.696460

Ma, W., de Jong, M., Hoppe, T., & de Bruijne, M. (2021). From city promotion via city marketing to city branding: Examining urban strategies in 23 Chinese cities. *Cities (London, England)*, *116*, 103269. DOI: 10.1016/j.cities.2021.103269

Pike, S. (2005). Tourism destination branding complexity. *Journal of Product and Brand Management*, *14*(4), 258–259. DOI: 10.1108/10610420510609267

Pike, S. (2017). Destination positioning and temporality: Tracking relative strengths and weaknesses over time. *Journal of Hospitality and Tourism Management*, *31*, 126–133. DOI: 10.1016/j.jhtm.2016.11.005

Poço, TB (2017). City brand management and the effect on place connection: a case study on the Viana do Castelo brand. [Master's Dissertation in Service Management, Faculty of Economics, University of Porto].

Prayag, G. (2010). Images as Pull Factors of a Tourist Destination: A Factor-Cluster Segmentation Analysis. *Tourism Analysis*, *15*(2), 213–226. DOI: 10.3727/108354210X12724863327768

Priporas, C. V., Stylos, N., & Kamenidou, I. E. (2020). City image, city brand personality and generation Z residents' life satisfaction under economic crisis: Predictors of city-related social media engagement. *Journal of Business Research*, *119*, 453–463. DOI: 10.1016/j.jbusres.2019.05.019

Qu, H., Kim, L. H., & Im, H. H. (2011). A model of destination branding: Integrating the concepts of the branding and destination image. *Tourism Management*, *32*(3), 465–476. DOI: 10.1016/j.tourman.2010.03.014

Rainisto, S. (2003) Success factors of place marketing: a study of place marketing practices in Northern Europe and the United States. Retrieved from https://urn.fi/urn:nbn:fi:tkk-000746

Rizzi, P., & Dioli, I. (2010). Strategic planning, place marketing and city branding: The Italian case. *Journal Of Town & City Management*, *1*(3), 300–317.

Rodrigues, A., Reis, J., Pinto, F., & Lucas, D. (2021). Mass movement risk in a Portuguese municipality: Tabuaço case study. *Proceedings of the Institution of Civil Engineers-Forensic Engineering*, *173*(3), 65–73. DOI: 10.1680/jfoen.20.00018

Rodrigues, D., Sousa, B., Gomes, S., Oliveira, J., & Lopes, E. (2023). Exploring consumer behavior and brand management in the automotive sector: Insights from a digital and territorial perspective. *Administrative Sciences, 13*(2), 36. DOI: 10.3390/admsci13020036

Roseta, P., Sousa, B. B., & Roseta, L. (2020). Determiners in the consumer's purchase decision process in ecotourism contexts: A Portuguese case study. *Geosciences, 10*(6), 224. DOI: 10.3390/geosciences10060224

Santos, V., Ramos, P., Sousa, B., Almeida, N. and Valeri, M. (2022), "Factors influencing touristic consumer behavior", Journal of Organizational Change Management, Vol. 35 No. 3, pp . 409-429. DOI: 10.1108/JOCM-02-2021-0032

Sertakova, E., Koptseva, N., Kolesnik, M., Libakova, N., Luzan, V., & Sergeeva, N. (2016). Brand-management of Siberian cities: Krasnoyarsk as a case study. *International Review of Management and Marketing*, *6*(S5), 185–191.

Sharifi, A., Allam, Z., Bibri, S. E., & Khavarian-Garmsir, A. R. (2024). Smart cities and sustainable development goals (SDGs): A systematic literature review of co-benefits and trade-offs. *Cities (London, England)*, *146*, 104659. DOI: 10.1016/j.cities.2023.104659

Sousa, B., & Rocha, A. T. (2019). The role of attachment in public management and place marketing contexts: A case study applied to Vila de Montalegre (Portugal). *International Journal of Public Sector Performance Management*, *5*(2), 189–205. DOI: 10.1504/IJPSPM.2019.099094

Sousa, B., & Simões, C. (2018). "An approach on place attachment, involvement and behavioral intentions in Iberian marketing contexts: the case of Galicia-North Portugal Euroregion: an abstract", in Rossi, P. and Krey, N. (Eds), Finding New Ways to Engage and Satisfy Global Customers, Proceedings of the 2018

Udir Mišič, K., & Podnar, K. (2018). Perception of city management, fellow residents, and Perceived External Prestige (PEP) as antecedents of city affective commitment - The city marketing perspective. *Cities (London, England)*. Advance online publication. DOI: 10.1016/j.cities.2018.04.016

Valdani, E., & Ancari, F. (2001). Marketing Places. A Resource-Based Approach and Empirical Evidence from the European Experience. SDA Bocconi, Research Division Working Paper, 01/55.

Vinerean, A. (2013). Consumer behavior in tourism and the influencing factors of the decision making process. *Revista Economica*, *65*(2), 186–198.

Vuignier, R. (2017). Place branding & place marketing 1976–2016: A multidisciplinary literature review. *International Review on Public and Nonprofit Marketing*, *14*(4), 447–473. DOI: 10.1007/s12208-017-0181-3

Wolniak, R., & Stecuła, K. (2024). Artificial Intelligence in Smart Cities—Applications, Barriers, and Future Directions: A Review. *Smart Cities*, *7*(3), 1346–1389. DOI: 10.3390/smartcities7030057

Yang, F. F., Li, X., & Choe, Y. (2022). What constitutes a favorable destination brand portfolio? Through the lens of coherence. *Tourism Management*, *90*, 104480. DOI: 10.1016/j.tourman.2021.104480

You, L., & Hon, L. C. (2021). Testing the effects of reputation, value congruence and brand identity on word-of-mouth intentions. *Journal of Communication Management (London)*, *25*(2), 160–181. DOI: 10.1108/JCOM-10-2020-0119

Zenker, S., Braun, E., & Petersen, S. (2017). Branding the destination versus the place: The effects of brand complexity and identification for residents and visitors. *Tourism Management*, *58*, 15–27. DOI: 10.1016/j.tourman.2016.10.008

Zenker, S., & Jacobsen, B. P. (2015). *Inter-Regional Place Branding. Best Practices, Challenges and Solutions*. Springer International Publishing. DOI: 10.1007/978-3-319-15329-2

Zhang, H., Fu, X., Cai, L. A., & Lu, L. (2014). Destination image and tourist loyalty: A meta-analysis. *Tourism Management*, *40*, 213–223. DOI: 10.1016/j.tourman.2013.06.006

## KEY TERMS AND DEFINITIONS

**Place Branding:** A cornerstone of territorial marketing, is the strategic process of creating a distinct and memorable identity for a specific geographical area.

**Place Marketing:** A general term that includes the work of many government and non- government organizations . What it comes down to is promoting economic development, by gading people to spend time and money in a specific location . That location can be anything from a small business district, to an entire country.

**Regional Development:** A broad category of policies aimed at reducing regional disparities within an economy or across economies.

**Territorial Marketing:** A strategy which aims to guide the action of the actors of a territory, to improve its placement at national and international level, through the identification and strengthening of its " personality ", as a set of tangible and intangible factors, and an effective " communication " policy .

# Chapter 6
# The Impact of European Structural and Investment Funds on Regional Economic Development:
## The Case of Bulgaria

**Desislava Stoilova**
https://orcid.org/0000-0001-6034-4225
*South-West University "Neofit Rilski", Bulgaria*

## ABSTRACT

*The impact of the European Structural and Investment Funds (ESIF) on regional economic development in the member states of the European Union is attracting increasing attention. Despite numerous studies, there is no consensus on the effects of ESIF on economic growth and regional cohesion. The study aims to contribute to this debate by examining the effects of ESIF on regional economic development in Bulgaria for the period 2007-2023. The methods used are descriptive, comparative, correlation and regression analysis. The results show that all six NUTS-2 regions are converging with the EU-27 average in terms of key development indicators, but regional disparities persist, as more developed regions absorb larger amounts of EU funding. ESIF have a positive effect on regional GDP, employment, gross fixed capital formation and household income, but do not demonstrate a significant impact on labor productivity and the percentage of people living at risk of poverty. The results are useful for policy makers to determine appropriate organizational and financial interventions.*

## INTRODUCTION

Bulgaria is a unitary state with 6.5 million population and 111 000 sq. km territory, situated on the Balkan Peninsula in the Southeast Europe. According to the World Bank classifications, Bulgaria has an emerging market economy in the upper middle-income range, where the private sector accounts for more than 80% of GDP (World Bank, 2024). Service sector has been the main engine of economic growth in the last two decades, contributing on average to 71.3% of the gross value added, while industry

DOI: 10.4018/979-8-3693-7081-0.ch006

and agriculture contribute respectively to 23.6% and 5.1% of the gross value added (National Statistical Institute of the Republic of Bulgaria - NSI, 2024).

The most important factor shaping the economic and social development of Bulgaria in the last fifteen years is the accession to the European Union (EU) in 2007. As the leading supranational organization, the EU has a profound political, economic, social and cultural impact across the European continent, benefitting both member and non-member states. The European Union promotes and maintains unprecedented levels of integration, cooperation and stability, shaping the future of Europe through its values and policies. The EU plays a central role in maintaining peace in Europe, especially after the devastations of the world wars. It contributes to conflict resolution in regions such as the Balkans and fosters political stability. The economic impact stems from the single market, which allows the free movement of goods, services, people and capital, thus stimulating economic growth and increasing competitiveness. The introduction of the euro as a common currency facilitates trade and economic integration between Eurozone countries, while stabilizing monetary policy. From a social and cultural perspective, EU citizens enjoy the right to live, work, and study in any member state, promoting cultural exchange and integration. Moreover, the European Union supports policies on human rights and equality, influencing societal standards across Europe.

After joining the EU, Bulgaria gained access to significant financial resources through the European Structural and Investment Funds (e.g., European Regional Development Fund, European Social Fund, European Agricultural Fund for Rural Development, European Maritime and Fisheries Fund, and Cohesion Fund), which are aimed at reducing regional disparities, promoting economic growth and enhancing competitiveness in the member states. EU funds have several directions of impact on regional economic development. First of all, these funds provide financing for critical infrastructure projects such as transportation, energy, and broadband networks. Improved infrastructure improves regional connectivity and reduces logistical costs, thereby attracting businesses and investments. By supporting entrepreneurship and innovation, EU funds stimulate job creation in economically disadvantaged regions. Also, EU funds are used for training programs, start-up incubators and workforce development initiatives. The EU places a strong emphasis on research and innovation as drivers of economic growth. Funds are allocated for research and development projects, technology transfer, and collaboration between universities and businesses. EU funds are often targeted at SMEs, which play a vital role in regional economies. Support for SMEs includes grants, loans, and consultancy services to help these businesses grow and create jobs. In addition, EU funds aim to improve the competitiveness of regions by supporting business clusters, industry networks and skills development. This helps regions specialize in areas where they have a comparative advantage.

Usually, the EU grants are intended to co-finance projects (on programs, priority axes, major areas and actions) in a proportion of up to 85%, being supplemented by allocations from national budgets and private contributions from beneficiaries. It is specific to the EU budget that it is set for 7-year periods. In Bulgaria, the total country budget (EU and national funding) was 11.4 billion EUR for the budgetary period 2007-2013, 11.9 billion EUR for the budgetary period 2014-2020 and 12.9 billion EUR for the budgetary period 2021-2027, which represented, on a yearly basis, around 3-4% of the GDP. On average, for the period 2007-2023, European funds finance 9% of total budget expenditure and around 80% of public investments (Ministry of Finance of the Republic of Bulgaria, 2024).

Supported by EU funds, Bulgaria's GDP per capita increased from 41% to 59% of the EU-27 average over the period 2007-2023 (Eurostat, 2024; NSI, 2024). At the same time, the economic development of Bulgaria demonstrates clearly expressed territorial disparities. According to the Common Classification of Territorial Units for Statistics (NUTS), defined by Regulation 1059/2003 of the European Parliament, Bulgaria has six regions at the NUTS-2 level, namely North-West Region, North-Central Region, North-East Region, South-East Region, South-West Region and South-Central Region. The main driver of economic growth over the past fifteen years has been the South-West region, which created 45.6% of Bulgaria's GDP in 2007. During the analyzed period its importance is constantly increasing, with regional GDP reaching 51.5% of national GDP in 2023. The differences between the other five regions are smaller, as they create between 7.1% and 13.6% of national GDP in 2023 (NSI, 2024). Obviously, regional disparities in Bulgaria persist and the impact of EU funds varies significantly between regions.

At the same time, there is a lack of comprehensive studies on the impact of EU funds on the economic and social development of Bulgarian regions. There are several authors who deal with the topic, such as Vasilev et al. (2011), Ganev and Simeonova-Ganeva (2012), Durova (2018, 2022) and Todorov et al. (2018), but their research efforts focus on the effects of EU funding on the national economy. In a series of annual reports, the Ministry of Finance of the Republic of Bulgaria also provides assessments of the macroeconomic effects of the implementation of the programs financed by the EU funds in Bulgaria, but does not reveal the impact on the regional economic development (Ministry of Finance, 2022). This study is intended to fill the gap by providing an analysis of the impact of European funding on key regional development indicators determining the economic development and prosperity of Bulgarian regions.

Keeping in mind these assumptions, the purpose of the study is to examine the impact of European Structural and Investment Funds (ESIF) on regional economic development in Bulgaria for the period 2007 – 2023. The hypothesis tested in the study is that EU funds have a positive effect on regional economic development through a positive impact on regional GDP, employment, household income and gross fixed capital formation. It is also expected to be found that financial support through EU-funded projects leads to increased labor productivity and a reduction in the percentage of the population living at risk of poverty. The study is structured in six main sections. After this brief introduction, the second section provides a literature review. The third section describes the methodological framework and data used in the study. The fourth section presents the main results and discusses our findings in the broader context of the evidence provided by previous research on the subject. The fifth section draws solutions, recommendations and policy implications. The last section concludes.

## BACKGROUND

The impact of European Structural and Investment Funds (ESIF) on regional economic development in the member states of the European Union (EU) is attracting increasing attention in the academic community. Numerous studies have assessed the effects of EU funds on economic growth and regional convergence, but despite the relatively large number of papers, no consensus has yet been reached on the actual impact and overall effectiveness of European funding.

Many authors claim that EU funds have a significant positive impact on regional economic growth. For example, a recent study by Vukašina et al. (2022) investigates the impact of the ESIF in 12 new EU member states in the period 2008–2016 and finds positive effects on regional GDP per capita. This is further confirmed by Fidrmuc et al. (2023) who use both ordinary least squares (OLS) and two-stage least squares (2SLS) and conclude that European funds have a significant positive effect on regional economic growth in the EU. Kisiała and Stępiński (2024) report similar results. They apply spatial econometrics methods and conclude that during the years 2007–2015 EU funds have positively affected economic growth in line with a process of reducing economic disparities between EU regions. Gagliardi and Percoco (2017) also argue that European cohesion funds have positively contributed to generating economic growth in the most disadvantaged regions during the programming period 2000–2006. Maynou et al. (2016) use a spatio-temporal econometric model and report that EU funds have contributed positively to the growth of regional GDP per capita in the Eurozone countries over the period 1990–2010.

Confirmation of the positive impact of EU funds on regional economic growth is provided by Žáček et al. (2019), who apply regression techniques on panel data for the regions of the Czech Republic for the period 2004-2015. Lolos (2009) argues that EU structural funds have positive effects on regional growth in Greece over the period 1990-2005. Piętak (2021) applies fixed effects estimator and generalized method of moments (GMM) to panel data for 16 Polish regions covering the period 2004-2016 and states that EU funds have a positive impact on regional economic growth. Di Cataldo and Monastiriotis (2020) examine how EU funds have contributed to regional economic growth in the United Kingdom from 1994 to 2013 and document significant and robust effects, particularly in less developed regions. These concepts are further confirmed by a recent study by Bachtrögler-Unger et al. (2024), who assess the local impact of EU regional policy funding on economic activity in the member states during the 2007–2013 programming period and highlight the positive links between European funding and economic growth at the regional and municipal level.

However, there are authors who report that the impact of EU funds on regional economic growth is not so clear, and in some cases is negligible or even negative. For example, Bouayad-Agha et al. (2013) apply an econometric model to a dataset of 143 NUTS-1 and NUTS-2 regions from 14 EU member states covering the period 1980-2005 and reveal that the total financing provided by the structural funds has no direct effect on regional GDP per capita growth rates. Similar results are reported by Mohl and Hagen (2010), who analyze the effects of EU structural funds in 126 NUTS-1 and NUTS-2 regions for the years 2000-2006 and conclude that the total amount of funding has no significant positive impact on the economic growth rates of EU regions. A study by Dumciuviene et al. (2015) shows that the correlation between the main economic indicators (including GDP per capita) and EU funds is not significant for the period 2000-2013 in the EU-28, suggesting an inefficient use of European financial resources.

Regarding economic convergence between European regions, there are several studies that show evidence of the positive impact of EU funds. For example, Fagerberg and Verspagen (1996) find a reduction of disparities of GDP per capita across 70 European regions in six of the EU members in the post-war period. Loddo (2006) argues that poorer regions in Italy have caught up with the richer regions over the period 1994-2004, so EU funds have a positive and significant impact on regional convergence. Beugelsdijk and Eijffinger (2005) conclude that EU structural funds contributed to fewer interregional disparities in the EU-15 countries over the period 1995-2001. Kyriacou and Roca-Sagalés (2012) find that structural and cohesion funds have reduced disparities between European regions in the years 1995-2006. In the same direction are the findings of Von Ehrlich (2024), who examines the effects of EU regional policy and provides empirical evidence that EU funding appears to have moderately mitigated regional disparities over the last thirty years.

At the same time, a number of authors are more skeptical about the efficacy of EU funds in promoting regional convergence. For example, Terrasi (1999) analyzes the regional GDP per capita in Italy during the period 1953-1993 and finds that the period of strong convergence is limited to the years 1960-1975, followed by a long-term trend of divergence. Cappelen et al. (2003) report that EU regional support has a significant positive impact on the growth of European regions in the 1990s, but the economic effects of absorbed financial resources are much stronger in more developed areas. This is further confirmed by the work of Dumciuviene et al. (2015) who find that more developed EU regions with higher GDP per capita and intensive capital formation absorb larger amounts of European funding, thereby exacerbating regional disparities. This conclusion is supported by Sotiriou and Tsiapa (2015), who explore the effect of EU structural funds on regional economic growth in Greece for the period 1994–2006 and argue that although financial support is directed towards less developed regions, the most advanced regions appear to benefit more from the EU funding.

Similar findings are reported by Schwab (2024), who highlights the intense debates regarding the fundamental objectives of European cohesion policy and the effectiveness of the strategies and measures implemented to promote regional development. He concludes that all European regions have made economic advances and have achieved economic prosperity since the advent of the single market in 1993 and the disparities within Europe have been eroded, but far from equally. Currently, the most prosperous regions, which are predominantly urban, are concentrated in the core of Europe, while many eastern and southern rural regions are experiencing stagnation and still lag behind the EU average in terms of their economic, social and territorial development. Diemer et al. (2022) use various indicators to analyze the economic performance, productivity and employment of European regions and conclude that despite regional policy and respective funding southern regions appear to be stagnant, caught in a "development trap". Authors argue that such regions face structural challenges in restoring previous dynamics and improving the prosperity of their inhabitants, thus generating social, economic and political risks not only at the national level, but also for the EU as a whole. This is recognized in the most recent reports on economic, social and territorial cohesion (European Commission, 2022, 2024a), which identify a number of less developed and middle-income regions that have suffered from economic stagnation or relative economic decline over the last 15 to 20 years, facing prolonged periods of low productivity and rising unemployment.

In addition, a review by Spilioti and Anastasiou (2024) analyzes findings from 11 studies on the effectiveness of ESIF in promoting economic growth and reducing regional disparities. The results reveal the nuanced efficiency of the EU funds in reducing regional disparities and highlight the need for more targeted fund allocation. A study by Antunes et al. (2020) points in the same direction. The authors apply a spatial econometric approach to a sample of 96 European regions for the period 1995 - 2009 and confirm the existence of convergence between regions, but do not detect the presence of positive impacts from the structural funds.

In the same line is the work of Mogila et al. (2022), who argue that EU cohesion policy fails to reduce disparities within the regions of the Czech Republic, Poland and Slovakia in the long run. This is confirmed by Dall'erba and Le Gallo (2008), who find that EU structural funds have no impact on the convergence process between 145 European regions for the years 1989-1999. Boldrin and Canova (2001) also state that there is no clear sign that regional policies financed by the EU funds actually reduce the large income disparities across the regions of the EU-15.

Rodríguez-Pose and Novak (2013) evaluate the effect of structural funds on the growth of regional GDP per capita in the EU during the programming periods 1994-1999 and 2000-2006 and conclude that investment financed by the EU funds tends to yield higher returns in better-off countries and wealthier regions within countries. Kersan-Škabić and Tijanić (2017) analyze a sample of 186 developed regions and 86 less developed regions and conclude that the absorption of EU funds is conditionally affected by regional economic development.

Although the majority of scientific efforts seem to focus mainly on the impact of European funds on regional GDP growth as a key development indicator, there are several studies that examine the effects of EU funding on other economic indicators, such as employment, gross fixed capital formation, household income, labor productivity and people living at risk of poverty. As expected, their findings point in different directions. For example, Pinho et al. (2015) report positive effects of EU support on income in a group of 137 European regions over the period 1995-2009. A recent study by Lang et al. (2022) also shows a positive impact of EU funds on household income, but argues that cohesion policy actually increases the incomes of wealthy households, while hardly affecting low-income households in supported regions, thus widening income inequality across European regions. These findings are consistent with the results of the standard income convergence analysis carried out by Marzinotto (2012), which confirms that while regions in the EU converge, regional income disparities within member states are increasing.

Several studies estimate the impact of EU funding on gross fixed capital formation through its effects on investment spending. Staehr and Urke (2022) reveal that ESIF have a positive short-term and long-term impact on public investment in the EU countries over the period 2000 – 2018. In the same line are the findings of Mohl (2016), who concludes that EU-funded projects stimulate investment spending. On the opposite side are the conclusions of Cantos et al. (2020), who argue that financial assistance provided under the EU regional policy did not have the expected positive impact on regional public investment in Spain over the period 1994 - 2014. Del Bo and Sirtori (2016) even estimate that EU funds had a displacement effect on the national and regional public investment in Italy during the period 1996 – 2010. A study by Becker et al. (2013) highlights interregional disparities and argues that only about a third of European regions, those with sufficient human capital and quality institutions are able to successfully convert transfers into faster growth in income and investment.

Most studies on the topic claim that EU funding has a positive impact on regional employment and labor productivity. For example, Giua (2017) performs an assessment of the effect of the EU regional policy in Italian regions and finds a positive impact on employment levels. This is further confirmed by a recent study by Destefanis and Rehman (2023), who find that ESIF have significant effect on employment across NUTS-2 European regions for the years 2000-2016. Ferraro et al. (2023) argue that funding provided under the EU cohesion policy in Estonia has a positive effect on labor productivity and employment over the period 2014–2018. At the same time, Bachtrögler et al. (2020) analyze the impact of the cohesion policy in seven European countries for the period 2007–2013 and find evidence that EU support promotes employment rather than productivity. This is confirmed by Dumciuviene et al. (2015) who find no significant relationship between structural funds and real labor productivity in the EU for the period 2000-2014. In contrast to these findings, Nemethova et al. (2019) evaluate the effectiveness of EU regional policy in less developed regions in Slovakia applying panel data fixed estimator on the base of Cobb-Douglas production function and find positive and significant impact on labor productivity, but point out that the effect disappears one year after subsidy allocation.

According to the estimates of Ilie et al. (2024) there is an inverse relationship between the development funds absorbed and the percentage of people living at risk of poverty and social exclusion in rural regions of the European Union for the period 2000 – 2022. This is considered evidence of the effectiveness of EU funds in supporting rural development and reducing poverty levels. Sompolska-Rzechuła and Kurdyś-Kujawska (2022) also conclude that poverty levels in EU countries decreased over the period 2010 – 2019 thanks to support from EU funds. However, they note that residents of the regions in Scandinavia and Western Europe are less affected by poverty than the population of Eastern and Southern European regions. On the opposite side are the conclusions of a EURACTIV report (2010). Authors argue that

EU-funded projects are designed to distribute huge subsidies, which can be a powerful weapon in the fight against poverty, but in fact have little real effect in solving such social problems in Hungary. This is further confirmed by Farrell (2021), who examines the impact of the European Social Fund on combating poverty in the period 2014 – 2020 and finds that the effects are nuanced and vary significantly across EU member states. The author concludes that in almost all countries and regions, much greater efforts are needed to target EU funding towards people living in poverty and social exclusion.

## METHODOLOGY AND DATA

This study uses descriptive and comparative analysis as well as correlation and regression analysis on panel data to examine the impact of ESIF on regional economic development in Bulgaria. Our empirical investigation follows the common approach applied in some of the researches on this topic. The conventional simple specification tries to explain how the main economic development indicators of a given region are impacted by the financing provided by the EU funds, so the regression equation has the following general structure (Equation 1):

$$y_{it} = b_0 + b_1 y_{it-1} + b_2 X_{it} + b_3 X_{it-1} + b_4 X_{it-2} + \varepsilon_{it} \tag{1}$$

Six specifications of the regression equation were created to investigate the effects of ESIF on key indicators of regional economic development. In this regard, the dependent variable ($y_{it}$) in the different specifications of the regression equation is respectively gross domestic product (GDP), employment (EMPL), gross fixed capital formation (GFCF), income of households (INC), people at risk of poverty (POV) and real labor productivity (LAB_PROD). The independent variables $X_{it}$, $X_{it-1}$ and $X_{it-2}$ are the amounts of grants provided by the EU funds and absorbed by the regions for the respective year (t) as well as with one- and two-year lags.

Thus, the variables included in the regression analysis are as follows:

- **GDPit:** gross domestic product of region i in year t (euro per inhabitant)
- **EMPLit:** employment in region i in year t (percentage of population aged from 15 to 64 years)
- **GFCFit:** gross fixed capital formation of region i in year t (million euro)
- **INCit:** income of households of region i in year t (euro per inhabitant)
- **POVit:** people at risk of poverty in region i in year t (percentage of population)
- **LAB_PRODit:** real labor productivity per person in region i in year t (percentage change on previous period)
- **EUFit:** financing provided by the ESIF in region i in year t (euro)

The parameters of the regression equation are $b_0$, $b_1$, $b_2$, $b_3$ and $b_4$. The symbol of $\varepsilon_{it}$ marks the error term. The robust least squares (RLS) method is used to estimate the parameters of the regression model. RLS estimations are reported in Table 1. Correlation coefficients between the main variables of the regression model are calculated and presented in the correlation matrix (Table 2). Hypotheses for bilateral causal relations are tested using the Pairwise Granger Causality Test (Table 3).

The study sample includes all six NUTS-2 regions in Bulgaria, namely North-West Region (NW), North-Central Region (NC), North-East Region (NE), South-East Region (SE), South-West Region (SW) and South-Central Region (SC). The analysis is focused on NUTS-2 regions, as they are considered core regions for the implementation of EU regional policies.

To conduct the empirical analysis, we use three main sources of data. Information on the dependent variables (regional GDP, employment, income, gross fixed capital formation, people at risk of poverty and real labor productivity) is extracted from the annual regional data provided by the European Commission in the Eurostat database (Eurostat, 2024) and the National Statistical Institute of the Republic of Bulgaria (NSI, 2024). Information on ESIF absorption in the Bulgarian regions is drawn from two databases created and maintained by the Bulgarian government, namely Unified Management Information System for the EU Structural Instruments in Bulgaria 2007-2013 (UMIS) and Information System for Management and Monitoring of EU Funds in Bulgaria 2014-2020 (UMIS 2020).

## RESULTS AND DISCUSSION

### Analysis of Regional Economic Development in Bulgaria

Since its accession to the European Union (EU) in 2007, Bulgaria and its NUTS-2 regions have gradually approached the average level of economic development in the EU, as measured by key indicators, such as GDP per capita, employment rate, gross fixed capital formation, household income, and people-at-risk-of-poverty rate. For the period 2007-2023, Bulgaria's GDP per capita increased from 41% to 59% of the EU-27 average (Figure 1). At the same time, the economic development of Bulgaria demonstrates clearly expressed territorial disparities. The main driver of economic growth over the past fifteen years has been the South-West Region, which created 45.6% of Bulgaria's GDP in 2007. During the analyzed period its importance is constantly increasing, with regional GDP reaching 51.5% of national GDP in 2023. The differences between the other five regions are smaller, as they create between 7.1% and 13.6% of national GDP in 2023 (NSI, 2024).

*Figure 1. GDP per capita by NUTS-2 Regions*

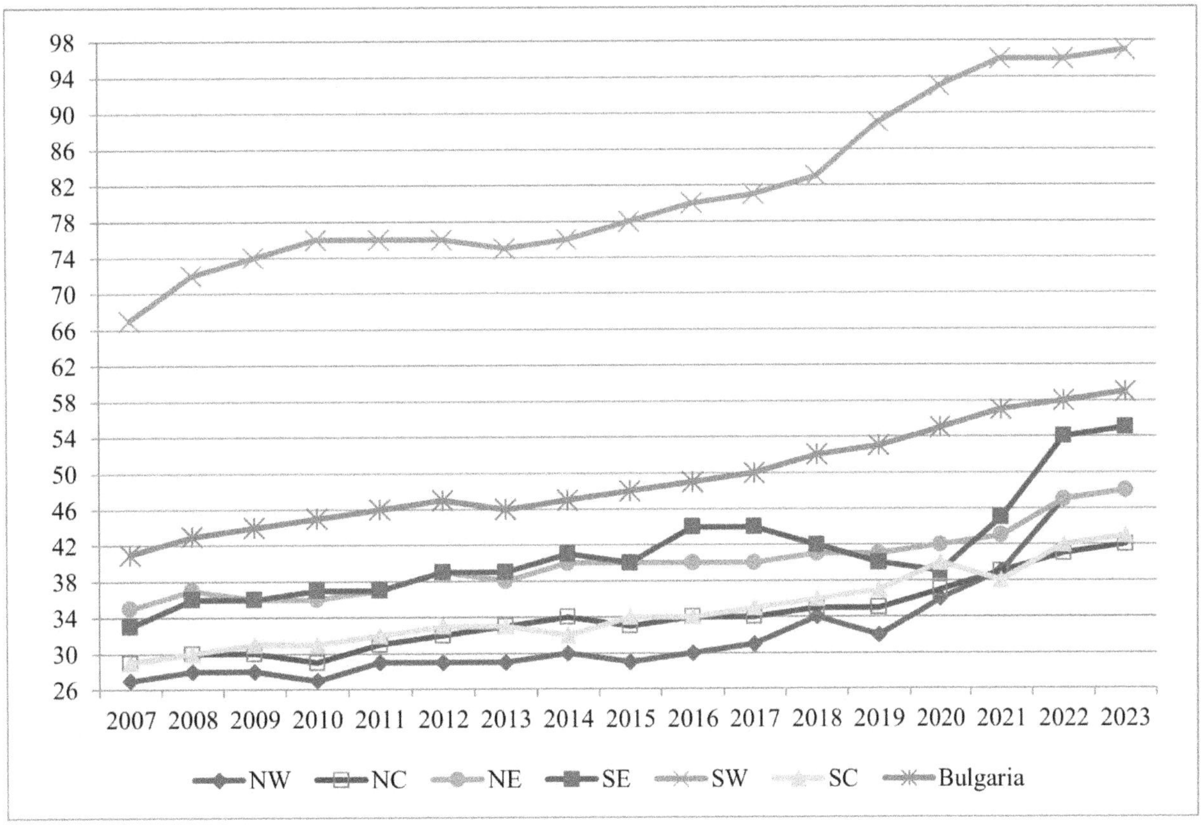


*Sources: Eurostat (2024); NSI (2024)*

The main factor for the faster development of the South-West Region is the capital city Sofia, which concentrates a significant part of the national economy. After the EU accession, the economic development of the South-West Region accelerated and the regional GDP per capita increased significantly from 67% (2007) to 97% (2023) of the EU-27 average (Figure 1). At the same time, the North-West, North-Central and South-Central regions reported a modest increase in this indicator from 27-29% to 42-43% of the EU-27 average. The situation is similar in the North-East and South-East regions, where GDP per capita increased slightly from 33-35% to 48-50% of the EU-27 average.

*Figure 2. Employment rate by NUTS-2 Regions*

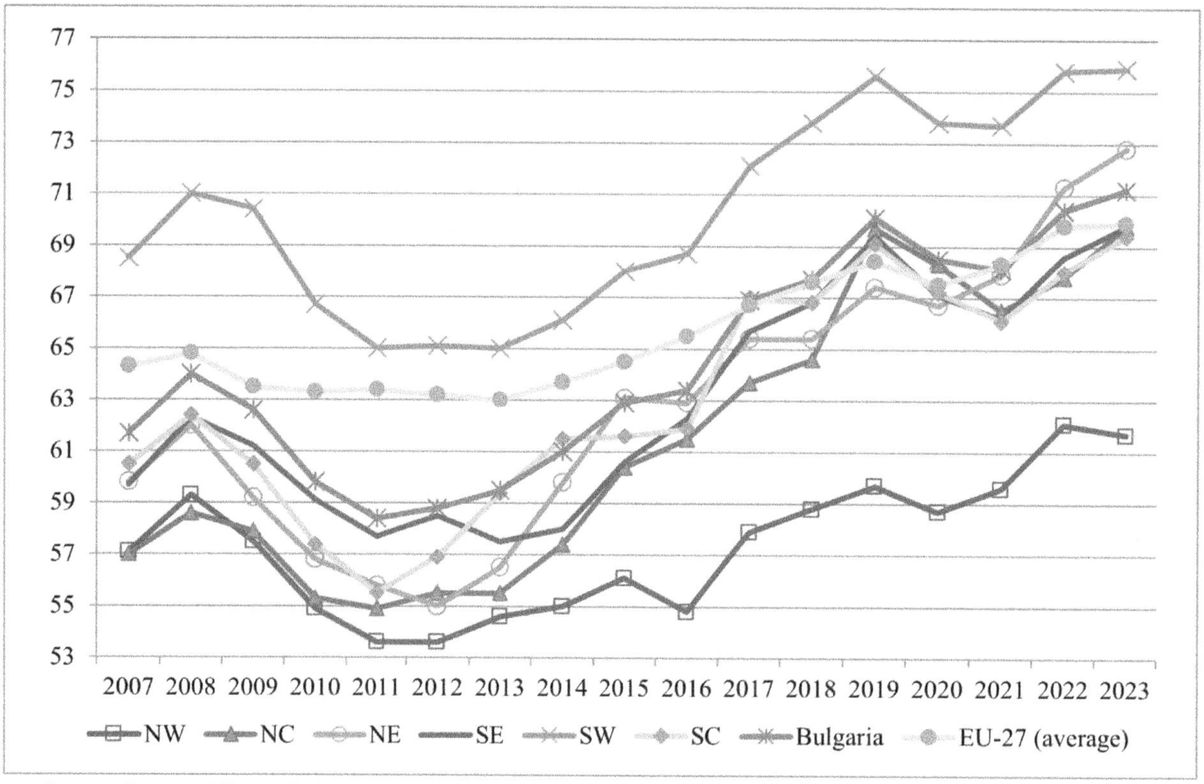


*Sources: Eurostat (2024); NSI (2024)*

The employment rate demonstrates cyclical dynamics for the period 2007-2023 (Figure 2). The overall growth trend was interrupted by the economic and financial crisis in 2008-2010, as well as the global crisis related to the COVID-19 pandemic in 2020-2021. As expected, South-West Region is the leader in terms of employment rate, which ranges between 65% and 76% during the analyzed period and is ahead of the EU-27 average (63%-70%). Four of the regions report employment rates around the country's average (58%-70%). The North-West Region lags behind with an employment rate between 53% and 62% for the analyzed period.

*Figure 3. Income of households (per capita) by NUTS-2 Regions*

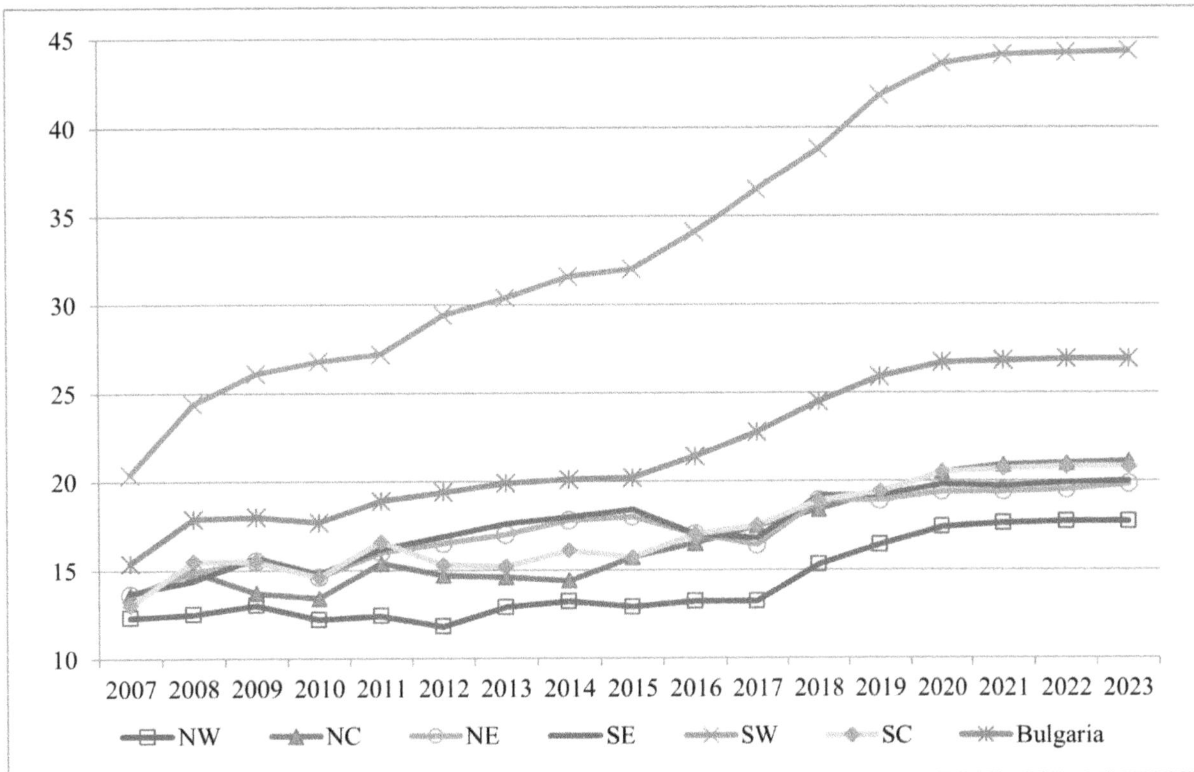


*Sources: Eurostat (2024); NSI (2024)*

The difference between the regional income levels is even more significant (Figure 3). The value of the indicator "primary income per inhabitant" in the South-West Region has more than doubled during the period 2007-2023 and is already more than twice as high as the values reported by the other regions. However, household income per capita in Bulgaria's NUTS-2 regions is quite low, reaching only 44.3% of the EU-27 average in the South-West region at the end of the period. The other five regions report a modest increase in per capita income, from 13% (2007) to 17-22% (2023) of the EU-27 average.

The indicator "people at risk of poverty" does not appear to be significantly affected by EU accession (Figure 4). There is not substantial reduction of the population living at risk of poverty, on the contrary, in most regions (e.g. North-West, South-Central, South-East, and South-West regions) at-risk-of-poverty rate has increased over the period 2007-2023. However, there is a visible difference between the levels of this indicator in the South-West Region and the other NUTS-2 regions. At the end of the analyzed period, the population at risk of poverty in five of the Bulgarian regions varies between 20.0% (North-East Region) and 31.8% (North-West Region), while the value of this indicator in the South-West Region does not exceed 15.5%.

*Figure 4. People living at risk of poverty by NUTS-2 Regions*

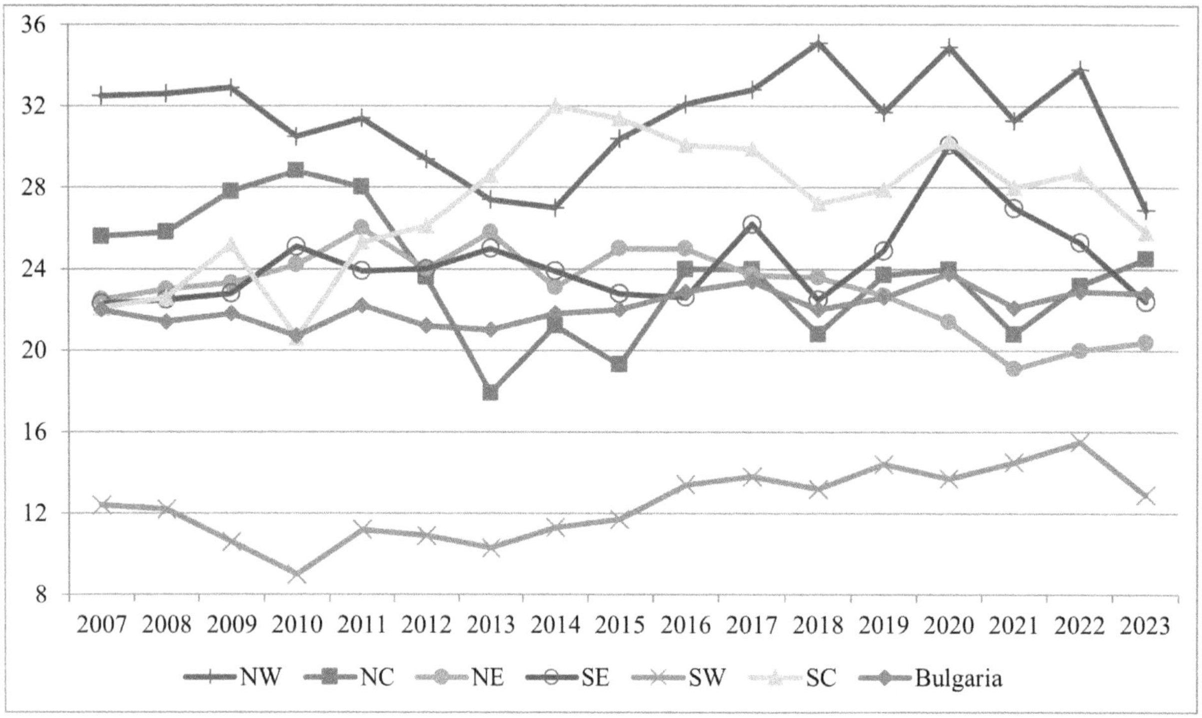


*Sources: Eurostat (2024); NSI (2024)*

Obviously, the comparative analysis finds evidence in favor of the gradual convergence of the Bulgarian regions with the EU-27 average in terms of GDP, employment and income. At the same time, regional disparities in Bulgaria persist and the impact of financial resources provided by the EU structural and investment funds varies significantly between regions. One of the factors that increase the differences in regional economic development is the uneven participation of the NUTS-2 regions in the absorption of European funds during the last two programming periods 2007-2013 and 2014-2020 (Figure 5).

*Figure 5. Distribution of EU Funds in Bulgaria by NUTS-2 Regions*

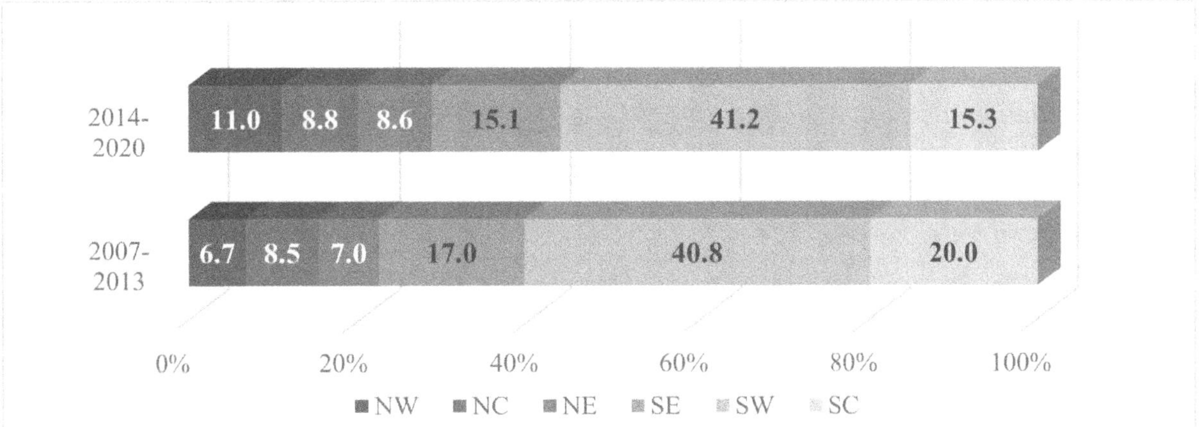


*Sources: Unified Management Information System for the EU Structural Instruments in Bulgaria 2007-2013 – UMIS (2024) and Information System for Management and Monitoring of EU Funds in Bulgaria 2014-2020 - UMIS 2020 (2024)*

Differences in regional economic development seem to cause disparities in the absorption of EU funds, thereby further increasing disparities in regional economic development. As can be seen, the financial resources absorbed by the beneficiaries in the South-West Region during the programming period 2007-2013 represent 40.8% of the total available funds under the EU funding programs in Bulgaria. Beneficiaries in the South-Central and South-East regions received 20.0% and 17.0% of the total grant amount respectively. At the same time, regions lagging behind in their economic development in North Bulgaria absorbed an extremely low share of the allocated funds. The North-West region, which has always been one of the poorest regions in the European Union, has absorbed only 6.7% of the total financial resources available to Bulgaria. The results for the programming period 2014-2020 are similar. The South-West Region absorbed the bulk (41.2%) of the European funding and the remaining 58.8% was distributed between the other five regions.

The analysis of the process of absorption of EU funds in Bulgaria during the first programming period (2007-2013) after the accession shows that both the managing authorities (ministries and agencies) and the potential beneficiaries (enterprises, municipalities, educational and research institutions, public agencies, NGOs, etc.) demonstrate low administrative capacity and unpreparedness to absorb European funding at the beginning of the period. Cumulatively, during the first three years of the period (2007-2009), no more than 23.1% of the planned budget was contracted and only 2.6% of the funds were paid to the beneficiaries (Figure 6).

*Figure 6. EU Funds Absorption Progress for Bulgaria*

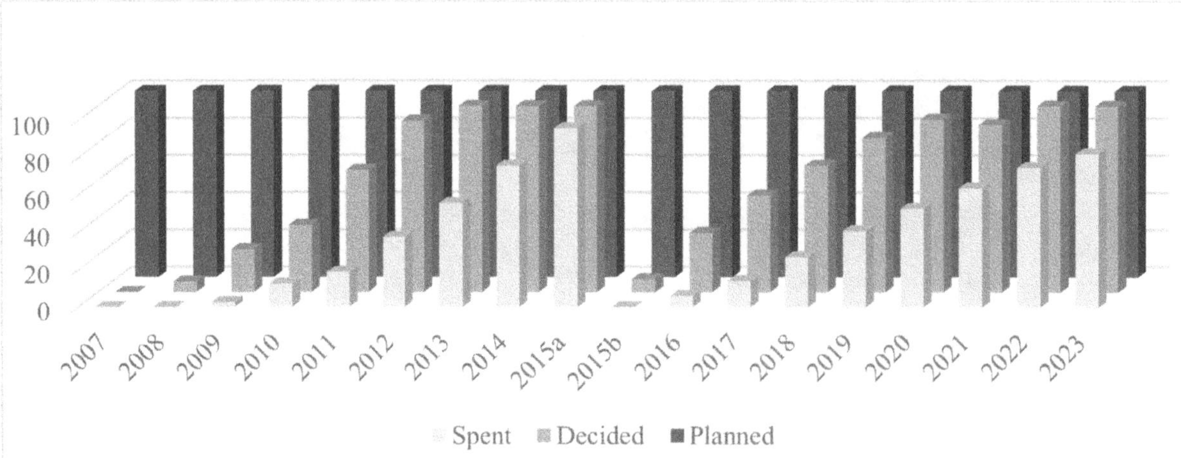


*Sources:European Commission (2024b); Ministry of Finance of the Republic of Bulgaria (2024)*

*Notes: Planned - total budget of the EU funded programs; Decided - financial resources allocated to selected projects (project pipeline); Spent - expenditure reported by the selected projects.*

Due to accelerated absorption in the second half of the period, at the end of 2013 the contracted funds reached 100% while the disbursed funds reached 55.8% of the budget. Thanks to the n+2 rule, the Bulgarian beneficiaries fully absorbed the contracted European funding within two years after the end of the programming period. The situation was almost the same in the first three years of the second programming period (2014-2020). The contracted amounts until the end of 2016 did not exceed 32% of the total budget, and the paid amounts represent only 6% of the available funds. In this regard, it is recommended to increase the absorption rate in the first years of the programming periods in order to accelerate the impact of EU funds on regional economic development.

## Empirical Evidence of the Impact of ESIF on Regional Economic Development in Bulgaria

The results from the robust least squares (RLS) estimations are reported in Table 1. As described in the previous section, six specifications of the regression equation have been constructed by using different dependent variables. The first four specifications of the model use respectively the regional GDP per inhabitant, employment rate, gross fixed capital formation and household income as dependent variables. As expected, the empirical evaluations support the insights of the conventional economic logic for a positive impact of the absorbed European funds on these key indicators of regional economic development. However, the impact is significant only on the second lag indicating that European funds have positive long-term effects on the regional GDP, employment, gross fixed capital formation and household income, but do not demonstrate significant short-term effects. It is interesting to note that the regression results do not show a significant impact of European financial resources on the real labor productivity and the share of the population living at risk of poverty, neither in the short-term, nor in the long-term. These findings call into question the effectiveness of projects supported by European funds as a tool for increasing labor productivity and reducing poverty in Bulgarian regions.

*Table 1. Results from the regression analysis*

| | Model 1 | Model 2 | Model 3 | Model 4 | Model 5 | Model 6 |
|---|---|---|---|---|---|---|
| $y_{it}$ | GDP | EMPL | GFCF | INC | POV | LAB_PROD |
| $y_{it-1}$ | 1.0354***<br>(178.02) | 0.9876***<br>(245.85) | 0.9874***<br>(77.79) | 1.0363***<br>(141.63) | 0.9841***<br>(81.3712) | 0.0474***<br>(5.4625) |
| EUF | -2.18E-08<br>(-0.1845) | 1.48E-08*<br>(1.8628) | -1.22E-06<br>(-1.3214) | -6.58E-07<br>(-0.7671) | 1.93E-10<br>(0.0185) | -1.03E-10<br>(-0.0587) |
| EUF(-1) | -1.41E-07<br>(-0.1054) | -1.31E-09<br>(-1.3647) | 2.47E-08<br>(0.2452) | 3.31E-09<br>(0.0358) | 4.35E-10<br>(0.3714) | 3.78E-10<br>(0.1887) |
| EUF(-2) | 3.34E-07***<br>(2.7568) | 2.89E-09***<br>(3.7694) | 2.12E-07***<br>(2.5886) | 1.72E-07**<br>(1.9975) | 5.64E-10<br>(0.5536) | -1.82E-09<br>(-1.0457) |
| R-squared | 0.808287 | 0.837128 | 0.634983 | 0.812962 | 0.748241 | 0.213818 |
| Adjusted R-squared | 0.801487 | 0.821673 | 0.636604 | 0.804899 | 0.733302 | 0.204232 |
| Akaike info criterion | 112.4948 | 63.6239 | 130.7037 | 96.51436 | 66.85657 | 72.93694 |
| Schwarz criterion | 124.5850 | 75.9320 | 140.4843 | 106.8407 | 79.03802 | 84.79146 |
| Rn-squared statistic | 52002.85 | 95816.78 | 9408.713 | 33569.74 | 8870.506 | 40.57700 |
| Prob(Rn-squared statistic) | 0.000000 | 0.000000 | 0.000000 | 0.000000 | 0.000000 | 0.000000 |
| Observations | 96 | 96 | 96 | 96 | 96 | 96 |

*Source:* Author's calculations
*Notes:* z- statistics shown in parentheses below coefficient;
Asterisks (*, **, ***) indicate the significance level (10%, 5%, 1%) of the coefficients.

The correlation matrix (Table 2) presents the correlations between each pair of variables, included in the regression model. The coefficients demonstrate relationships that are consistent with conventional economic wisdom. Strong positive correlations are identified among the variables regional GDP per capita, employment rate, gross fixed capital formation and household income. As expected, these key economic development variables are negatively correlated with the share of the population living at risk of poverty, indicating that increasing regional GDP, employment, investment and household income can be a powerful tool to reduce the at-risk-of-poverty rate.

*Table 2. Correlation matrix of the variables of the regression model*

| | GDP | EMPL | GFCF | INC | POV | LAB_PROD | EUF | EUF(-1) | EUF(-2) |
|---|---|---|---|---|---|---|---|---|---|
| GDP | 1.0000 | 0.8377 | 0.6544 | 0.9225 | -0.5082 | 0.1279 | 0.2324 | 0.2667 | 0.3318 |
| EMPL | 0.8377 | 1.0000 | 0.6884 | 0.8779 | -0.4877 | -0.0166 | -0.0355 | 0.0041 | 0.1552 |
| GFCF | 0.6544 | 0.6884 | 1.0000 | 0.6800 | -0.5572 | -0.0146 | 0.1763 | 0.1413 | 0.1258 |
| INC | 0.9225 | 0.8779 | 0.6800 | 1.0000 | -0.5136 | 0.0714 | 0.2068 | 0.2220 | 0.2810 |
| POV | -0.5082 | -0.4877 | -0.5572 | -0.5136 | 1.0000 | 0.0255 | -0.0324 | -0.0131 | -0.0476 |
| LAB_PROD | 0.1279 | -0.0166 | -0.0146 | 0.0714 | 0.0255 | 1.0000 | 0.0126 | 0.0336 | -0.0365 |
| EUF | 0.2324 | -0.0355 | 0.1763 | 0.2068 | -0.0324 | 0.0126 | 1.0000 | 0.6639 | 0.4500 |
| EUF(-1) | 0.2667 | 0.0041 | 0.1413 | 0.2220 | -0.0131 | 0.0336 | 0.6639 | 1.0000 | 0.7157 |
| EUF(-2) | 0.3318 | 0.1552 | 0.1258 | 0.2810 | -0.0476 | -0.0365 | 0.4500 | 0.7157 | 1.0000 |

*Source:* Author's calculations

It is noteworthy that the correlations between regional GDP and household income and European funding are positive and strengthen at the first and second lags, which is consistent with the regression results. At the same time, employment, gross fixed capital formation and labor productivity appear to be weakly related to EU funding. Logically, the correlation between European financial support and regional poverty rate is negative, but extremely weak.

The results of Pairwise Granger Causality Tests (Table 3) confirm that at the first lag there are no causal relationships between the EU funds and the key economic development indicators. At the second lag, there are bidirectional causal relationships between the regional GDP and gross fixed capital formation, and the absorbed euro funds. These findings confirm our observations and show that more developed regions with higher GDP per capita and intensive capital formation absorb larger amounts of European funding, thus exacerbating regional disparities in Bulgaria. As expected, our results indicate that European financial resources Granger cause regional employment and household income. The null hypothesis cannot be rejected for the variables labor productivity and at-risk-of-poverty rate, so it seems that there are no clear causal relationships between EU funds and these variables.

*Table 3. Pairwise Granger Causality tests*

| **Lags: 1** | | | |
|---|---|---|---|
| | | | |
| Null Hypothesis: | Obs. | F-Statistic | Prob. |
| | | | |
| EUF does not Granger Cause GDP | 102 | 0.03682 | 0.9184 |
| GDP does not Granger Cause EUF | | 2.76198 | 0.1063 |
| | | | |
| EUF does not Granger Cause EMPL | 102 | 1.03616 | 0.2801 |
| EMPL does not Granger Cause EUF | | 0.00054 | 0.9745 |
| | | | |
| EUF does not Granger Cause GFCF | 102 | 0.00235 | 0.9826 |
| GFCF does not Granger Cause EUF | | 3.42679 | 0.0624 |
| | | | |
| EUF does not Granger Cause INC | 102 | 0.02042 | 0.8974 |
| INC does not Granger Cause EUF | | 2.52447 | 0.1157 |
| | | | |
| EUF does not Granger Cause POV | 102 | 0.16484 | 0.7127 |
| POV does not Granger Cause EUF | | 3.29184 | 0.0722 |
| | | | |
| EUF does not Granger Cause LAB_PROD | 102 | 0.05187 | 0.8187 |
| LAB_PROD does not Granger Cause EUF | | 0.71664 | 0.3865 |
| | | | |
| Lags: 2 | | | |
| | | | |

continued on following page

*Table 3. Continued*

| **Lags: 1** | | | |
|---|---|---|---|
| Null Hypothesis: | Obs. | F-Statistic | Prob. |
| | | | |
| EUF does not Granger Cause GDP | 96 | 1.09271 | 0.0415 |
| GDP does not Granger Cause EUF | | 4.16154 | 0.0082 |
| | | | |
| EUF does not Granger Cause EMPL | 96 | 7.25578 | 0.0022 |
| EMPL does not Granger Cause EUF | | 0.23910 | 0.7963 |
| | | | |
| EUF does not Granger Cause GFCF | 96 | 1.60023 | 0.0054 |
| GFCF does not Granger Cause EUF | | 2.95848 | 0.0072 |
| | | | |
| EUF does not Granger Cause INC | 96 | 2.27535 | 0.0009 |
| INC does not Granger Cause EUF | | 1.41908 | 0.2427 |
| | | | |
| EUF does not Granger Cause POV | 96 | 0.44239 | 0.6341 |
| POV does not Granger Cause EUF | | 2.51473 | 0.1984 |
| | | | |
| EUF does not Granger Cause LAB_PROD | 96 | 0.32656 | 0.7296 |
| LAB_PROD does not Granger Cause EUF | | 0.43644 | 0.6417 |

*Source*: Author's calculations

The results of the analysis confirm our hypothesis that ESIF have a positive effect on regional economic development through a significant positive impact on GDP, employment, household income and gross fixed capital formation in Bulgarian regions. Our findings are consistent with conventional economic logic and are supported by the works of numerous authors. For example, confirmation of the positive impact of EU funds on regional economic growth is provided by Lolos (2009), Pellegrini et al. (2013), Maynou et al. (2016), Gagliardi and Percoco (2017), Žáček et al. (2019), Piętak (2021), Di Cataldo and Monastiriotis (2020), Stoilova and Todorov (2021), Vukašina et al. (2022), Stoilova (2023), Fidrmuc et al. (2023), Kisiała and Stępiński (2024), Bachtrögler-Unger et al. (2024), At the same time, there are several studies that challenge our findings, such as the works of Mohl and Hagen (2010), Bouayad-Agha et al. (2013), Dumciuviene et al. (2015), who claim that the impact of EU funds on regional economic growth is not so clear, and in some cases is negligible or even negative.

Noteworthy, Dumciuviene et al. (2015) report Granger causality test results consistent with our findings that more developed regions with higher GDP per capita and intensive capital formation absorb larger amounts of European funding, thereby exacerbating regional disparities. This conclusion is supported by the works of Terrasi (1999), Boldrin and Canova (2001), Cappelen et al. (2003), Ederveen et al. (2006), Dall'erba and Le Gallo (2008), Sotiriou and Tsiapa (2015), Mogila et al. (2022), Rodríguez-Pose and Novak (2013), Kersan-Škabić and Tijanić (2017), Diemer et al. (2022), Schwab (2024), Spilioti and Anastasiou (2024) who do not find clear evidence that regional policies financed by the EU funds actually reduce interregional disparities. This is recognized in the latest reports on economic, social and territorial cohesion (European Commission, 2022, 2024a), which identify a number of less developed and middle-income regions caught in a "development trap" that have suffered from economic stagnation or relative economic decline over the last 15 to 20 years. At the same time, it must be acknowledged that there are several authors whose studies contradict our findings and show evidence of a positive impact of EU funds on regional convergence, such as Fagerberg and Verspagen (1996), Beugelsdijk and Eijffinger (2005), Loddo (2006), Kyriacou and Roca-Sagalés (2012), Von Ehrlich (2024).

In line with our findings, several authors have found confirmation of the significant positive impact of EU funding on income and employment. For example, Pinho et al. (2015) report positive effects of EU support on income in a group of 137 European regions over the period 1995-2009. A recent study by Lang et al. (2022) also shows a positive impact of EU funds on household income, but argues that EU cohesion policy actually increases the incomes of wealthy households, while hardly affecting low-income households in supported regions, thus widening income inequality across European regions. These findings are consistent with the results of the standard income convergence analysis carried out by Marzinotto (2012), which confirms that while regions in the EU converge, regional income disparities within member states are increasing.

The work of Giua (2017) supports our findings and identifies a positive impact of EU regional policy on employment levels in Italian regions. This is further confirmed by a recent study by Destefanis and Rehman (2023), who find that ESIF have significant effect on employment across NUTS-2 European regions for the years 2000-2016. Ferraro et al. (2023) also argue that funding provided under the EU cohesion policy in Estonia has a positive effect on labor productivity and employment over the period 2014–2018.

Similar to our results, Dumciuviene et al. (2015) find no significant relationship between structural funds and real labor productivity in the EU for the period 2000-2014. This is confirmed by the work of Bachtrögler et al. (2020) who find evidence that EU support promoted employment but not productivity in seven European countries for the period 2007–2013. In contrast to our findings, Nemethova et al. (2019) find positive and significant impact of EU regional policy on labor productivity in less developed regions in Slovakia, but point out that the effect disappears one year after subsidy allocation.

Several studies support our findings and estimate a positive impact of EU funding on gross fixed capital formation. For example, Mohl (2016), Staehr and Urke (2022) conclude that EU-funded projects stimulate investment spending. On the opposite side are the conclusions of Del Bo and Sirtori (2016), Cantos et al. (2020), who find that financial assistance provided under the EU regional policy did not have the expected positive impact on regional public investment in Italy and Spain.

In contrast to our findings, the estimates of Ilie et al. (2024) show that there is an inverse relationship between the development funds absorbed and the percentage of people living at risk of poverty and social exclusion in rural regions of the European Union for the period 2000 – 2022. However, our conclusion about the unsignificant impact of EU funds on the population living at risk of poverty is supported by the works of EURACTIV (2010) and Farrell (2021).

## SOLUTIONS AND RECOMMENDATIONS

The findings of this study can contribute to a deeper understanding of the complexity surrounding the impact of the ESIF on regional economic development in Bulgaria as a member state and indirectly in the European Union. The empirical analysis reveals that over the period 2007-2023 all six NUTS-2 regions in Bulgaria are gradually converging with the EU-27 average in terms of key economic development indicators. The support provided by the EU funds has positive long-term effects on regional GDP, employment, gross fixed capital formation and household income, but does not demonstrate a significant impact on labor productivity and the percentage of population living at risk of poverty. In addition, regional disparities in Bulgaria persist, as more developed regions absorb larger amounts of European funding.

In this regard, the results of the study are useful for the policymakers to determine appropriate organizational and financial interventions for the next programming periods. Several solutions and recommendations can be proposed to address the challenges and maximize the benefits of EU funds for regional economic development in Bulgaria. First of all, there is a need of enhanced targeting of European funding. Financial support should be focused on lagging regions and a higher percentage of funds should be allocated to less developed NUTS-2 regions to reduce regional disparities. Policymakers can implement needs-based allocation by using data-driven approaches to identify specific development needs in each region and ensure that resources are targeted where they can have the greatest impact. In addition, there is a need to improve administrative capacity, especially in less developed regions. Capacity building initiatives in the form of training and technical assistance to regional authorities and local governments are recommended to enhance their ability to design, implement and monitor EU-funded projects. It would also be useful to reduce administrative barriers and streamline application and reporting processes to make EU funds more accessible to less developed regions.

It is recommended to promote inclusive growth by prioritizing funding for SMEs and start-ups in underdeveloped regions to encourage entrepreneurship and job creation at regional level. In addition, policymakers can design new and more effective social inclusion programs to increase investment in social infrastructure, education and healthcare to address poverty and improve living standards. Special programs can be designed, tailored to the needs of vulnerable groups. There is a need for targeted interventions for the population at risk of poverty, such as support for social enterprises and provision of housing support. Vocational training and upskilling programs should be offered to improve employability in marginalized communities.

Another useful solution is the development and implementation of programs aimed at fostering innovation and productivity. It can be expected that targeted investments in digitalization and advanced technologies will improve labor productivity, especially in traditional industries. More targeted financial support should be provided to innovation-oriented projects that promote collaboration between universities, research institutions, and businesses. Public-private partnerships should be encouraged, especially in less developed regions, to leverage private investments. It is necessary to strengthen the mechanisms for monitoring and evaluation of EU-funded projects to ensure greater accountability and effectiveness. Stronger impact assessment mechanisms would allow for adjustment of funding allocations based on performance indicators and changing regional needs over time.

Policymakers can develop and implement measures aimed at promoting cross-regional cooperation and partnerships between more developed and less developed regions to share knowledge, best practices and resources. Bulgarian regional and local authorities should be encouraged to participate in exchanges with other EU regions with successful development experiences.

These solutions and recommendations are expected to contribute to higher efficiency of financial support provided by EU funds, to reduce regional disparities and to promote more balanced and inclusive economic growth in all regions of Bulgaria.

## FUTURE RESEARCH DIRECTIONS

Like any study, our research also has territorial and temporal limitations. The scope of the study is limited to the impact of the ESIF on the key economic development indicators (GDP, employment, gross fixed capital formation, household income, labor productivity and the percentage of people living at risk of poverty) in the six regions at NUTS-2 level in Bulgaria for the period 2007-2023. Further research is needed to estimate the effects of EU funds on more indicators of the economic and social development of the Bulgarian regions. For example, a more comprehensive study could conduct sector-specific analysis on how EU funding influences agriculture, manufacturing, services, and emerging industries. Special emphasis can be placed on the role of sustainable development and green economy initiatives in regional economic growth.

In addition, it would be useful to explore why EU funds have such a negligible impact on labor productivity and poverty reduction. It may be useful to assess the reasons for the lack of significant improvement in labor productivity despite investments financed by the ESIF. In this regard, a more detailed study could examine the role of innovation, digitalization, research and development in increasing regional productivity. Another line of research could investigate why EU funding does not significantly reduce the percentage of the population living at risk of poverty and propose policies to improve its social impact. The analysis could focus on the role of education, skills development, and employment policies in improving household income and reducing poverty.

Furthermore, comparative studies between Bulgarian regions with high and low absorption rates can reveal best practices and replicable models for the effective use of EU funds. Also, comparative studies with other EU member states could compare Bulgaria's regional development trajectory with similar economies to identify good practices. It would be useful to examine how different EU regions with similar economic structures have used ESIF for long-term sustainable growth. Such comparative studies can be used as a basis for building more targeted regional development strategies, promoting balanced and inclusive economic growth in all regions of Bulgaria.

## CONCLUSION

Regional economic growth, sustainable development and cohesion are widely recognized as vital for Europe's future progress and prosperity. This is why the impact of the ESIF on regional economic development in the EU member states is attracting increasing attention in the academic community and there is significant scientific output on this topic. Our research aims to contribute to this debate by examining the effects of European funds on several key indicators of regional economic development in Bulgaria for the period 2007-2023.

The results show that that all Bulgarian regions are gradually converging with the EU-27 average in terms of the key development indicators. The support provided by the ESIF has positive long-term effects on regional GDP, employment, gross fixed capital formation and household income, but does not demonstrate a significant impact on labor factor productivity and people-at-risk-of-poverty rate. At the same time, regional disparities in Bulgaria persist and the absorption of financial resources provided by EU funds varies significantly between regions. More developed regions with higher GDP per capita and intensive capital formation absorb larger amounts of European funding, thereby exacerbating regional disparities.

Our findings have several economic and social implications. From an economic perspective, regional development in Bulgaria demonstrates uneven growth patterns. The concentration of EU funds in more developed regions perpetuates a cycle of uneven growth as these regions continue to attract more investment, capital and labor. Furthermore, the insignificant impact of European funding on labor productivity and poverty reduction points to structural challenges that hinder economic convergence. This could slow down Bulgaria's progress in closing the gap with the EU-27 average in terms of key economic development indicators. There is also a risk of creating an unhealthy dependence on external funding, especially in less developed regions, which may become overly reliant on external support without building self-sustaining economic structures.

The social implications point to the risks of increased migration, social polarization and marginalization of vulnerable groups. Persistent regional disparities can drive internal migration from poorer to wealthier regions, leading to urban overcrowding and depopulation in rural areas, thus exacerbating demographic imbalances. Inequal absorption of EU fund can create divisions between regions and social polarization, potentially undermining public trust in national and EU institutions. Without targeted interventions, people at risk of poverty may remain excluded from the benefits of economic growth, further perpetuating cycles of poverty.

The study has practical and research implications. From a practical point of view, the results of the study would be useful for policymakers in determining appropriate organizational and financial interventions for the next programming periods. Policymakers should design targeted policies to address regional disparities by directing more resources to underdeveloped regions. Needs-based allocation can be implemented to identify specific development needs in each region and ensure that resources are targeted where they can have the greatest impact. It is recommended to change the principle of distribution of EU funds. Instead of funding based on country-wide thematic programs (e.g. environment, transport, competitiveness, education and training, etc.), allocation should be made through regional programs targeting specific regions of the country to accelerate the convergence of lagging regions. Funding criteria should be adjusted to prioritize regions with lower GDP per capita, less capital formation, and higher poverty levels to ensure that EU funds effectively promote convergence and reduce disparities.

Furthermore, it is extremely important to strengthen administrative capacity in lagging regions. Capacity building initiatives in the form of training and technical assistance to regional and local authorities are highly recommended to enhance their ability to design, implement and monitor EU-funded projects. More targeted support is needed to achieve higher productivity and inclusion. Policymakers should prioritize investments in initiatives that directly improve labor productivity, such as skills development, digital transformation, and technology adoption. Developing special programs targeting vulnerable groups can help reduce poverty levels.

The main research implications point to the need for further analysis of the effectiveness of EU funding. Future research should explore why EU funds have a negligible impact on labor productivity and poverty reduction in Bulgarian NUTS-2 regions. Identifying bottlenecks or inefficiencies can guide improvements in funds allocation and management. In addition, more comprehensive comparative studies between regions with high and low absorption rates can reveal best practices and replicable models for the effective use of EU funds. Such studies can be used as a basis for building more targeted regional development strategies, promoting balanced and inclusive economic growth in all regions of Bulgaria.

## REFERENCES


Antunes, M., Viegas, M., Varum, C., & Pinho, C. (2020). The impact of structural funds on regional growth: A panel data spatial analysis. *Inter Economics*, *55*(5), 312–319. DOI: 10.1007/s10272-020-0921-1

Bachtrögler, J., Fratesi, U., & Perucca, G. (2020). The influence of the local context on the implementation and impact of EU Cohesion Policy. *Regional Studies*, *54*(1), 21–34. DOI: 10.1080/00343404.2018.1551615

Bachtrögler-Unger, J., Dolls, M., Krolage, C., Schüle, P., Taubenböck, H., & Weigand, M. (2024). New evidence on the effects of EU Regional Policy. *Economic Policy Forum*, 25(1). https://www.econpol.eu/publications/forum-2024-1-big-data-based-economic-insights/new-evidence-on-the-effects-of-eu-regional-policy

Becker, S. O., Egger, P. H., & von Ehrlich, M. (2013). Absorptive capacity and the growth and investment effects of regional transfers: A regression discontinuity design with heterogeneous treatment effects. *American Economic Journal. Economic Policy*, *5*(4), 29–77. DOI: 10.1257/pol.5.4.29

Beugelsdijk, M., & Eijffinger, S. (2005). The effectiveness of structural policy in the European union: An empirical analysis for the EU-15 in 1995-2001. *Journal of Common Market Studies*, *43*(1), 37–51. DOI: 10.1111/j.0021-9886.2005.00545.x

Boldrin, M., & Canova, F. (2001). Inequality and convergence in Europe's regions: Reconsidering European regional policies. *Economic Policy*, *32*(32), 205–253. DOI: 10.1111/1468-0327.00074

Bouayad-Agha, S., Turpin, N., & Védrine, L. (2013). Fostering the development of European regions: A spatial dynamic panel data analysis of the impact of Cohesion Policy. *Regional Studies*, *47*(9), 1573–1593. DOI: 10.1080/00343404.2011.628930

Cantos, J. M., Balsalobre-Lorente, D., & García-Nicolás, C. (2020). *Why the financial aid of the EU's regional policy does not impact on the public investment level? The case of the Spanish regions*. Public Affairs., DOI: 10.1002/pa.2295

Cappelen, A., Castellacci, F., Fagerberg, J., & Verspagen, B. (2003). The impact of EU regional support on growth and convergence in the European Union. *Journal of Common Market Studies*, *41*(4), 621–644. DOI: 10.1111/1468-5965.00438

Dall'erba, S., & Le Gallo, J. (2008). Regional convergence and the impact of European structural funds over 1989-1999: A spatial econometric analysis. *Papers in Regional Science*, *87*(2), 219–244. DOI: 10.1111/j.1435-5957.2008.00184.x

Del Bo, C. F., & Sirtori, E. (2016). Additionality and regional public finance—Evidence from Italy. *Environment and Planning C. Environment and Planning. C, Government & Policy*, *34*(5), 855–878. DOI: 10.1177/0263774X15614682

Destefanis, S., & Rehman, N. U. (2023). Investment, innovation activities and employment across European regions. *Structural Change and Economic Dynamics*, *65*, 474–490. DOI: 10.1016/j.strueco.2023.03.013

Di Cataldo, M., & Monastiriotis, V. (2020). Regional needs, regional targeting and regional growth: An assessment of EU Cohesion Policy in UK regions. *Regional Studies*, *54*(1), 35–47. DOI: 10.1080/00343404.2018.1498073

Diemer, A., Iammarino, S., Rodríguez-Pose, A., & Storper, M. (2022). The regional development trap in Europe. *Economic Geography*, *98*(5), 487–509. DOI: 10.1080/00130095.2022.2080655

Dumciuviene, D., Stundziene, A., & Startiene, G. (2015). Relationship between structural funds and economic indicators of the European union. *The Engineering Economist*, *26*(5), 507–516. DOI: 10.5755/j01.ee.26.5.8831

Durova, K. (2018). Long-Term Impact of the European Funds on Bulgaria's Economy. *Economic Alternatives*. 3, 325-333. https://www.unwe.bg/eajournal/en/journalissues/article/14172

Durova, K. (2022). The Impact of Absorbed European Funds on the Economic Growth of Bulgaria and New Member States. *Economic Archive*, 4, 17-36. https://www2.uni-svishtov.bg/NSArhiv/title.asp?title=2788

EURACTIV. (2010, October 15). EU money having little effect on poverty in Hungary (article in press). EURACTIV Hungary report. https://www.euractiv.com/section/politics/news/eu-money-having-little-effect-on-poverty-in-hungary/

European Commission. (2022, February 9). *Cohesion in Europe towards 2050: Eighth report on economic, social and territorial cohesion.* Publication Office of the European Union. https://ec.europa.eu/regional_policy/information-sources/8cohesion-report_en

European Commission. (2024a, March 27). *Ninth report on economic, social and territorial cohesion.* Publication Office of the European Union. Luxembourg. https://ec.europa.eu/regional_policy/en/information/cohesion-report/

European Commission. (2024b, November 29). *Cohesion open data platform: Country data for Bulgaria.* https://cohesiondata.ec.europa.eu/countries/BG#top

European Parliament. (2003, May 26). *Regulation (EC) No 1059/2003 of the European Parliament and of the Council of 26 May 2003 on the establishment of a common classification of territorial units for statistics (NUTS).* https://data.europa.eu/eli/reg/2003/1059/oj

Eurostat. (2024, December 4). *Data Browser.* https://ec.europa.eu/eurostat

Fagerberg, J., & Verspagen, B. (1996). Heading for divergence? Regional growth in Europe reconsidered. *Journal of Common Market Studies*, *34*(3), 431–448. DOI: 10.1111/j.1468-5965.1996.tb00580.x

Farrell, F. (2021). *ESF and the fight against poverty: The use of the European Social Fund (ESF) during 2014-2020 for combating poverty and achieving social inclusion.* The Left in the European Parliament: Brussels. https://left.eu/app/uploads/2021/12/506388-GLUE-NG-Studies-2021-EMPL.pdf

Ferraro, S., Männasoo, K., & Tasane, H. (2023). How the EU Cohesion Policy targeted at R&D and innovation impacts the productivity, employment and exports of SMEs in Estonia. *Evaluation and Program Planning*, *97*, 102221. DOI: 10.1016/j.evalprogplan.2022.102221 PMID: 36592544

Fidrmuc, J., Hulényi, M., & Zajkowska, O. (2023). The long and winding road to find the impact of EU funds on regional growth: IV and spatial analyses. *Regional Studies*, *58*(3), 583–600. DOI: 10.1080/00343404.2023.2217214

Gagliardi, L., & Percoco, M. (2017). The impact of European Cohesion Policy in urban and rural regions. *Regional Studies*, *51*(6), 857–868. DOI: 10.1080/00343404.2016.1179384

Ganev, K., & Simeonova-Ganeva, R. (2012). Effects of EU Funded Policies: Net Impact Assessment of Investments in Education and Science in Bulgaria. SSRN *Electronic Journal*. DOI: 10.2139/ssrn.2030621

Giua, M. (2017). Spatial discontinuity for the impact assessment of the EU Regional Policy: The case of Italian Objective 1 Region. *Journal of Regional Science*, *57*(1), 109–131. DOI: 10.1111/jors.12300

Ilie , R. I., Borlea, S. N., & Pricope, L. (2024). Impact of European funds upon rural development in the European Union. *Brazilian Journal of Business*, *6*(1), 273–288. DOI: 10.34140/bjbv6n1-021

Information System for Management and Monitoring of EU Funds in Bulgaria 2014-2020 (UMIS 2020). (2024, December 4). *Public information on the implementation of operational programs in Bulgaria: Database*. https://2020.eufunds.bg/en

Kersan-Škabić, I., & Tijanić, L. (2017). Regional absorption capacity of EU funds. [Ekonomska Istrazivanja]. *Ekonomska Istrazivanja*, *30*(1), 191–1208. DOI: 10.1080/1331677X.2017.1340174

Kisiała, W., & Stępiński, B. (2024). European funds and the dynamics of economic growth among EU regions: A spatial modelling approach. *Quaestiones Geographicae*, *43*(2), 67–80. DOI: 10.14746/quageo-2024-0020

Kyriacou, A., & Roca-Sagalés, O. (2012). The impact of EU structural funds on regional disparities within member states. *Environment and Planning. C, Government & Policy*, *30*(2), 267–281. DOI: 10.1068/c11140r

Lang, V., Redeker, N., & Bischof, D. (2022). *Place-based policies and inequality within regions*. OSF. https://doi.org/DOI: 10.31219/osf.io/2xmzj

Loddo, S. (2006). *Structural funds and regional convergence in Italy*. Working paper No 2006/03. CRENoS. https://crenos.unica.it/crenos/publications/structural-funds-and-regional-convergence-italy

Lolos, S. (2009). The effect of EU structural funds on regional growth: Assessing the evidence from Greece, 1990-2005. *Economic Change and Restructuring*, *42*(3), 211–228. DOI: 10.1007/s10644-009-9070-z

Marzinotto, B. (2012). *The growth effects of EU cohesion policy – a meta-analysis*. Bruegel Working paper No 14/2012. https://www.bruegel.org/working-paper/growth-effects-eu-cohesion-policy-meta-analysis

Maynou, L., Saez, M., Kyriacou, A., & Bacaria, J. (2016). The impact of structural and cohesion funds on Eurozone convergence, 1990–2010. *Regional Studies*, *50*(7), 1127–1139. DOI: 10.1080/00343404.2014.965137

Ministry of Finance of the Republic of Bulgaria. (2022, September 11). *EU Funds in Bulgaria: Assessment of the macroeconomic effects of the implementation of programs co-financed with EU funds*. https://www.minfin.bg/bg/1168

Ministry of Finance of the Republic of Bulgaria. (2024, December 14). *Budget: Statistics*. https://www.minfin.bg/en/613

Mogila, Z., Miklošovič, T., Lichner, I., Radvanský, M., & Zaleski, J. (2022). Does Cohesion Policy help to combat intra-country regional disparities? A perspective on Central European countries. *Regional Studies*, *56*(10), 1783–1795. DOI: 10.1080/00343404.2022.2037541

Mohl, P. (2016). *Empirical evidence on the macroeconomic effects of EU Cohesion Policy*. Springer., DOI: 10.1007/978-3-658-13852-3

Mohl, P., & Hagen, T. (2010). Do EU structural funds promote regional growth? New evidence from various panel data approaches. *Regional Science and Urban Economics*, *40*(5), 353–365. DOI: 10.1016/j.regsciurbeco.2010.03.005

National Statistical Institute of the Republic of Bulgaria (NSI). (2024, December 4). *Statistical data: Macroeconomic statistics*. https://www.nsi.bg/en/content/779/macroeconomic-statistics

Nemethova, V., Siranova, M., & Sipikal, M. (2019). Public support for firms in lagging regions-evaluation of innovation subsidy in Slovakia. *Science & Public Policy*, *46*(2), 173–183. DOI: 10.1093/scipol/scy046

Piętak, Ł. (2021). Structural funds and convergence in Poland. *Hacienda Publica Espanola*, *236*(1), 3–37. DOI: 10.7866/HPE-RPE.21.1.1

Pinho, C., Varum, C., & Antunes, M. (2015). Under what conditions do structural funds play a significant role in European regional economic growth? Some evidence from recent panel data. *Journal of Economic Issues*, *49*(3), 749–771. DOI: 10.1080/00213624.2015.1072382

Rodríguez-Pose, A., & Novak, K. (2013). Learning processes and economic returns in European Cohesion policy. *Investigaciones Regionales*, 25, 7–26. http://www.aecr.org/images/ImatgesArticles/2013/5/1_Rodriguez.pdf

Schwab, T. (2024). Quo Vadis, Cohesion Policy? European regional development at a crossroads. *Inter Economics*, *59*(5), 284–292. DOI: 10.2478/ie-2024-0056

Sompolska-Rzechuła, A., & Kurdyś-Kujawska, A. (2022). Assessment of the development of poverty in EU countries. *International Journal of Environmental Research and Public Health*, *19*(7), 3950. DOI: 10.3390/ijerph19073950 PMID: 35409633

Šostar, M., Ristanović, V., & de Alwis, C. (2023). Application of successful EU funds absorption models to sustainable regional development. *Economies*, 11, 220. DOI: 10.20944/preprints202306.1876.v1

Sotiriou, A., & Tsiapa, M. (2015). The asymmetric influence of structural funds on regional growth in Greece. *Environment and Planning. C, Government & Policy*, *33*(4), 863–881. DOI: 10.1177/0263774X15603905

Spilioti, N., & Anastasiou, A. (2024). European Structural and Investment Funds (ESIFs) and regional development across the European Union (EU).*Journal of Risk and Financial Management*, *17*(6), 228. DOI: 10.3390/jrfm17060228

Staehr, K., & Urke, K. (2022). The European structural and investment funds and public investment in the EU countries. *Empirica*, *49*(4), 1031–1062. DOI: 10.1007/s10663-022-09549-6 PMID: 36320380

Stoilova, D. (2023). The impact of tax structure on economic growth: New empirical evidence from Central and Eastern Europe. *Journal of Tax Reform*, *9*(2), 181–196. DOI: 10.15826/jtr.2023.9.2.136

Stoilova, D., & Todorov, I. (2021). Fiscal policy and economic growth: Evidence from Central and Eastern Europe. *Journal of Tax Reform*, *7*(2), 146–159. DOI: 10.15826/jtr.2021.7.2.095

Terrasi, M. (1999). Convergence and divergence across Italian regions. *The Annals of Regional Science*, *33*(4), 491–510. DOI: 10.1007/s001680050117

Todorov, I., Durova, K., & Aleksandrov, A. (2018). *The Economy of Bulgaria: Structural Funds, Growth and Cyclical Recurrence*. Sciendo., DOI: 10.2478/9783110619218

Unified Management Information System for the EU Structural Instruments in Bulgaria 2007-2013 (UMIS). (2024, December 4). *Public information on the implementation of operational programs in Bulgaria: Database*. https://umispublic.government.bg

Vasilev, D., Ganev, K., Simeonova-Ganeva, R., Chobanov, P., & Tsvetkov, S. (2011). Model for Impact Assessment of the Structural Funds and the Cohesion Fund of the European Union in Bulgaria: SIBILA. SSRN *Electronic Journal*. DOI: 10.2139/ssrn.2290694

Von Ehrlich, M. (2024). *The importance of EU Cohesion Policy for economic growth and convergence*. ZEW - Centre for European Economic Research, Discussion Paper No. 24-041. DOI: 10.2139/ssrn.4871714

Vukašina, M., Kersan-škabić, I., & Orlić, E. (2022). Impact of European structural and investment funds absorption on the regional development in the EU–12 (new member states). Equilibrium. *Quarterly Journal of Economics and Economic Policy*, *17*(4), 857–880. DOI: 10.24136/eq.2022.029

World Bank. (2024, May 16). Data and Statistics: Country Groups. *World Bank Database*. https://www.worldbank.org

Žáček, J., Hrůza, F., & Volčík, S. (2019). The impact of EU funds on regional economic growth of the Czech Republic. *Finance a Uver - Czech. Journal of Economics and Finance*, *69*(1), 76–94. https://journal.fsv.cuni.cz/mag/article/show/id/1429

# Section 2
# Sustainable Development and Local Attractiveness

# Chapter 7
# Social Capital in Tourism as a Key Factor of Sustainable Territorial Development: A Network Approach

**Diana López-Molina**
https://orcid.org/0000-0002-2824-2824
*University of Cuenca, Ecuador*

**Juan Ignacio Pulido-Fernández**
*University of Jaén, Spain*

## ABSTRACT

*Social capital in tourism is a key factor for sustainable territorial development. This, in turn, is related to other factors, such as environmental, economic and social factors. There are several methodologies for its measurement, such as Stakeholder Theory and the examination of interactions and relationships, known as Social Network Analysis (SNA), which are analysed in this chapter through their application in Ecuadorian cities as research context. Through these methodologies It has been possible to determine that there are different types of actors with attributes of power, legitimacy and urgency, the formation of networks or groups of actors that can also lead to greater or lesser participation and collaboration in a tourism destination.*

## INTRODUCTION

The dynamics of sustainable territorial development involves the interaction of various factors that influence the growth and well-being of a territory. It focuses on a sustainable use of resources (natural and cultural), which therefore require a balance amid economic, environmental and social aspects. In

DOI: 10.4018/979-8-3693-7081-0.ch007

recent years, innovation, technology, sustainable tourism and collaboration between actors have added to this dynamic.

The concept of sustainable development is people-centred, seeking to meet current needs with due care not to compromise or damage the capacities and needs of future generations. It refers to respect for people and the environment in which they live. Therefore, all factors that allow for true respect for this principle or conception of sustainability must be considered.

The need for a real commitment from countries to generate a change focused on sustainability resulted in the *Sustainable Development Goals*, proposed in 2015 and with a deadline for compliance, through 17 goals that seek to reduce poverty and hunger in the world and strengthen cooperation at global, regional, national and local levels (Mempel-Śnieżyk, 2014).

In this context, sustainability is recognised as a key factor of territorial development and tourism activity, although the improvement of the quality of life of the local population, which is the ultimate goal pursued, is not always achieved through these. It is possible that this may be due to a purely theoretical conception which, in many cases, has failed to land in an integral manner in a territory, as a consequence of not considering the limitations and potential of each territory, or to the fact of downplaying the importance of social capital and its participatory and collaborative processes, or even to the lack of an articulation of the dimensions of sustainability (environmental, social, economic and institutional). Therefore, the transition towards sustainable development must be based on seeking to consolidate these dimensions in the territories (Voronkova et al., 2019; Salazar et al., 2021).

All this shows the need to consider the concept of local development, focusing on territories and their specific characteristics, with the aim of improving the well-being of their residents. Through initiatives and the articulation of partnerships (Cortez, 2020), cooperation at regional or local level and cooperation networks that can lead to innovative processes (Mempel-Śnieżyk, 2014; Nguyen et al., 2022), local development becomes a key concept in current development processes.

Territorial dynamics focus on social capital and all its forms of relationships, which drive economic activities such as tourism. If tourism is considered as a local economic development strategy, the level of relationships and cooperation that exists between tourism stakeholders must be analysed (Ramukumba et al., 2012). Therefore, social capital and tourism are important factors to consider in sustainable territorial development. Thus, this chapter aims to analyse the importance of social capital in tourism as a key factor for sustainable territorial development, by applying a network approach. Therefore, the hypotheses guiding this chapter are:

> H1: It is possible to analyse the importance of social capital in tourism activity from a network approach.
>
> H2: It is possible to analyse sustainable territorial development based on the identification of stakeholders, their level of influence on other actors or groups, the relationship with other actors or groups and whether the response to their claims is timely.
>
> H3: Sustainable territorial development can be determined by the level of collaboration of actors and can influence their relational dynamics.

In order to understand the importance of social capital and its different ways of measuring it, the case study is Ecuador, a developing country that is considered an emerging tourist destination. It is located on the South American continent. It has a great potential for tourism resources, both natural and cultural, which has led to its international recognition by international organisations such as UNESCO. From a geographical point of view, Ecuador is divided into four regions: coast, highlands, east and the island region. Each region is divided into provinces and each province is made up of cantons and urban and rural parishes.

This chapter is structured in six sections. The introduction corresponds to the first section, a second section contains the literature review, a third section that shows the most important characteristics of Ecuador as a research context, a fourth section that summarises the research process used, a fifth section that shows the results obtained and a sixth section that includes the conclusions of this study.

## LITERATURE REVIEW

Sustainable development focuses on a balance with a long-term approach, an important aspect that differentiates it from the traditional model, which focuses on short-term economic growth, without considering the impacts it may have, mainly social and environmental. Some authors, such as Károly (2011), Barbosa et al. (2014), Sen (2016), Kidd (1992) and Meadows et al. (2018), consider that the term 'sustainable' arises as a reaction to social and environmental problems, the latter with greater importance (Mebratu, 1998; Banerjee, 2003), adding to this the process of globalisation that further settled the inequalities between countries. All this led to a change of conception from the traditional model to a model centred on sustainability, which was officially defined in the Brundtland Report (1987).

Therefore, sustainable territorial development emerges as an integrated approach that seeks to solve development challenges at the local and regional level. Morales et al. (2021) consider that equality is the key aspect within sustainable territorial development, supported by a framework of public policies summarised in the 2030 Sustainable Development Goals, highlighting governance, innovation and resilience. They also consider that the participation of social capital in a territory should be inclusive, seeking a common value based on collaboration that allows the solution of problems and the proposal of strategies for the improvement of the quality of life, based on the capacities of the actors.

According to Musavengane & Kloppers (2020) community resilience is built through the connections formed within social capital dynamics.Currently, the link between social capital and sustainability has led to a focus on factors that favour sustainability, such as social inclusion through social responsibility and gender equality, which are embraced by various sectors, both public and private. This approach encourages collaborative processes built on trust.

Additionally, implementing transparency in processes encourages trust between organisations and their stakeholders, thereby strengthening the social fabric and enhancing cooperation. It also emphasizes the circular economy approach for sustainable management, that requires greater cooperation and trust among the different participants in the value chain. This collaboration is a crucial element of social capital, as well as the integration of organisational structures designed for collective actions aimed at achieving sustainable development goals.

Tourism, for its part, is considered an economic activity and a development strategy, mainly in developing countries, which see in its resources an important potential, as long as sustainability and its dimensions are considered. Tourism activity takes place in a territory with resources (natural and cultural) and infrastructure (basic and complementary). This territory is characterised as an open and dynamic system in which stakeholders participate with their customs, knowledge, beliefs and power structures, collaboration processes and forms of production. This dynamic is characterised by constant transformation, which requires active management of the destination.

The COVID-19 crisis underscored the urgent need to transform the tourism sector towards more sustainable practices, including circular economy and regenerative tourism. Developing and implementing these sustainable models, which bring together a large amount of information and data to effectively manage tourist destinations. To accomplish this, we need tools that streamline information processing to support decision-making for those involved in tourism. Consequently, leveraging technological tools enables the collection, analysis, and visualization of essential data for managing tourist destinations.

The ongoing digital transformation is greatly affecting the tourism industry, altering how different stakeholders engage and work together, while also fostering innovation and the adoption of technological tools (Martínez-Peláez et al., 2023). Nevertheless, in emerging destinations, there remains a significant gap in understanding these processes and how to implement them (Zvaigzne et al., 2023).

On the other hand, the connection between social capital and sustainability emphasizes the crucial role of social interactions in various innovation processes. It's vital to implement policies that promote collaboration and encourage learning among different stakeholders, along with the necessary investments that tourist destinations require for effective implementation (Annamalah et al., 2023).

These practices of trust and action within social capital facilitate collaborative management through governance, which identifies different types of social capital and can develop strategies for its improvement, ultimately supporting the sustainability of destinations (Sabet & Khaksar, 2024). Nonetheless, it is crucial to recognize that these interactions may also lead to negative consequences (Rust et al., 2023).

Tourism also has the capacity to build trust among the stakeholders of a destination. For its development, it requires links that allow it to achieve various objectives, resulting in an interaction between people that generates trust in the actors and in the different groups (Nunkoo & Smith, 2014). Social capital has an impact on tourism and can be the basis for a participatory model of tourism management (Jumiati et al., 2024). Tourism is composed of a value chain; therefore, stakeholder participation must have a joint vision that seeks to achieve sustainable tourism through governance based on principles of collaboration and commitment (Roxas et al., 2020).

Trust towards local governments also becomes an important factor for tourism development. This trust is shown in the level of power of the stakeholders as well as the level of knowledge about the activity itself. Therefore, stakeholder involvement in planning processes and the benefits it generates should be sought, and it can lead to genuine legitimacy on the part of its stakeholders (Nunkoo, 2015).

Local development can be defined as a process of economic growth, accompanied by structural change, which is both long-term and irreversible. The results of this process include an increase in the relative productivity of a region's economy and, therefore, an increase in the per capita income of its population (Coffey & Polese, 1985, p. 86). It recognises the 'tangible and intangible' elements of a territory and achieves long-term competitiveness (Capello, 2011, p. 12).

Local development has as its setting the territory, which in turn possesses endogenous resources and its own identity. It is also centred on the participation of all its actors and collaboration between the different sectors. It is constantly innovating, always seeking a balanced development, which leads to the following dimensions: Economic, social, environmental and institutional dimension (Haddad et al., 2021).

Fayos-Solà et al. (2014) consider 'human, social-institutional capital' as key aspects for development, based on clear rules that lead to trust and cooperation between different actors. It is therefore important to note that development is undergoing a transition from an economic interest to a social interest, and is now also focused on a sustainable perspective that seeks equal living conditions for communities (Álvarez, 2014). Therefore, tourism, well planned and managed, can become a local economic development strategy focused on partnership building, local resource utilisation, governance and innovation strategies (Binns & Nel, 2002).

Social capital is a fundamental aspect of the social dimension of sustainability and comprises stakeholders and their relationships. It consists of the interaction of the subjects that make up a territory, based on norms or levels of relationship. It is classified as internal or external social capital and is an important factor in the implementation of development strategies (Fayos-Solà et al., 2014).

It can also be formal and informal, this type of social capital is mostly developed at the local level and its governance and sustainable development is determined by the formalities of its relationships (Nunkoo, 2017). Although it is not possible to analyse the totality of their interactions, it is possible to know their membership in groups or associations and this participation is focused on a common goal, characterised by 'cooperation and trust' (Stolle & Rochon, 1998).

Stakeholders have objectives and to achieve them they need to relate to other actors pursuing common goals. These relationships lead to the formation of networks. Networks can be constituted in a formal way, through agreements or norms, and in an informal way, based on trust or affinity. Stakeholder networks are dynamic, changing according to the objectives and interests of the stakeholder group. These relationships can be considered internal (cohesion) or external, either bridging or linking, the latter related to a hierarchy of power.

Nahapiet & Ghoshal (1998) consider that social capital is not all positive, it requires a high investment, mainly in 'relational and cognitive' capital, due to the size and characteristics of the relationships. On the other hand, small networks do not always favour tourism, and in the case of large networks they do not always favour sustainability (Nunkoo, 2017).

An important factor defining social capital is trust. Trust, in turn, relates to tourism activity in both positive and negative ways (Vongvisitsin et al., 2024; Nunkoo & Smith, 2014), the latter based on conflict, competition and failure to achieve results. However, the positive aspects can be worked on through all actors sharing values and objectives, achieved through stakeholder interaction and good governance (Nunkoo & Smith, 2014).

Trust, power and social capital are inherent to social relationships, minimising conflict and facilitating collaboration. All this within a framework of rule-based structures and policy guidelines, leading to an understanding of 'actions and behaviours' in tourism (Nunkoo, 2017).

For Prayitno et al. (2024), social capital is not only composed of trust, he considers that norms and networks are also important aspects. Moreover, he considers that sustainable tourism is made up of resources (cultural and natural) with a focus on planning with the aim of protecting these resources, as well as stakeholder participation. Therefore, 'general social capital can become a basic resource formed from beliefs, norms and social networks in society and encourage the development of sustainable tourism' (Prayitno et al., 2024, p. 19).

Understanding the unique traits and elements of the actors in a territory leads to understanding their social capital, as well as the unique characteristics and dynamics of each community. As Hussain et al. (2024, p. 279) point out, 'this collaborative approach helps to identify the essential components of social capital that support community well-being, resilience and self-determination, thereby reducing long-term vulnerability'.

Tourism destinations, according to Baggio et al. (2010), are considered complex systems. This system is made up of different factors. One of these factors is the set of actors and their relationships, which is considered as social capital. Therefore, its analysis allows for the design of tourist destinations taking the characteristics of the system as a reference (Baggio, 2020, p. 4), making it a key aspect within a planning process.

The social capital of a territory is understood as the set of actors (the subjects that make up a territory) and the relationships that occur between them. Social capital is presented from different typologies, such as: structural social capital, which refers to the networks and connections that exist between individuals and groups, including organisations and communities, facilitating access to resources and opportunities; Cognitive social capital, which focuses on shared norms, values and beliefs that foster cooperation and trust among members of a community, generating importance in social cohesion and conflict resolution and, finally, relational social capital, focused on interpersonal relationships and trust among actors, it is considered that high relational social capital can improve individual and social well-being (Putnam, 1995), highlighting that they have characteristics that link them together (Nahapiet & Ghoshal, 1998; García-Villaverde et al., 2021).

Moreover, it is important to understand that social networks are cultural constructs and share traditions and norms (Chan et al., 2020), and the actors' perception of these practices influences the positioning of actors in their environment (Czernek-Marszałek, 2019).

## RESEARCH CONTEXT

The analysis of social capital in tourism as a key factor in sustainable territorial development is carried out in Ecuador, a mega-diverse country crossed by the Equator and the Andes, which also allows for the formation of four regions (coast, highlands, Amazon and island region). This division is shown in Figure 1.

Ecuador has important cultural resources, mainly represented by the historic centres of the cities of Quito and Cuenca, declared by UNESCO as World Heritage Sites in 1978 and 1999 respectively, and the Qhapaq Ñan - Andean road system in 2014.

In terms of intangible heritage, the oral heritage and cultural manifestations of the Zápara people in conjunction with Peru, also recognised by UNESCO in 2008, stand out. The traditional weaving of the toquilla straw hat, recognised in 2012. The marimba music and traditional songs and dances of the Colombian region of the South Pacific and the Ecuadorian province of Esmeraldas jointly with Colombia in 2015 and the Ecuadorian pasillo in 2021 (UNESCO, 2024).

Some of its natural resources have also received international recognition, such as the Galapagos Islands, declared a World Heritage Site in 1978, and the Sangay National Park in 1983.

Ecuador also has other cultural and natural resources distributed in each of its provinces, as well as different ethnic groups that position it as a mega-diverse country. However, tourism activity has not yet managed to develop competitive advantages at a global level.

It is also important to note that each province has important tourism resources due to its geographical position and characteristics, as well as the different ethnic groups that are mostly found in the north of the country and in the east of Ecuador.

The country's tourism policy has been framed within the framework of different government plans focused on different strategic areas according to the needs of the activity. At present, these areas are based on: legal and tourism security; product development and experiences; competitiveness and national and international promotion to be developed in the short, medium and long term (MINTUR, 2024).

Ecuador has a territorial dynamic based on four regions: coast, highlands, Amazon and islands. Each region is made up of provinces and each province is made up of cantons and rural parishes (special regimes may be established). Its administration is autonomous both politically and financially, therefore, tourism activity at the level of the Autonomous Decentralised Governments is included within these characteristics.

For the administration of tourism activity, different levels are also considered: at the national level, the Ministry of Tourism is the governing body and is responsible for the planning, regulation, control and management of tourism. At a second level are the provincial governments, which have the power to plan, regulate and manage the activity. At a third level are the decentralised autonomous governments or municipalities that are in charge of planning, regulation and management, and in the case of rural parish governments, they only have the power to manage the activity. It is important to note that all these powers are developed under the guidelines of the governing body of tourism activity at the national level (CNC, 2016).

The characteristics of Ecuador's territorial dynamics, despite being decentralised, have not allowed for total autonomy of governments and have even hindered the development of policies. On the other hand, sectional governments do not have qualified human resources and resources are still less than the realities of each territory.

*Figure 1. Location and administrative division of Ecuador*

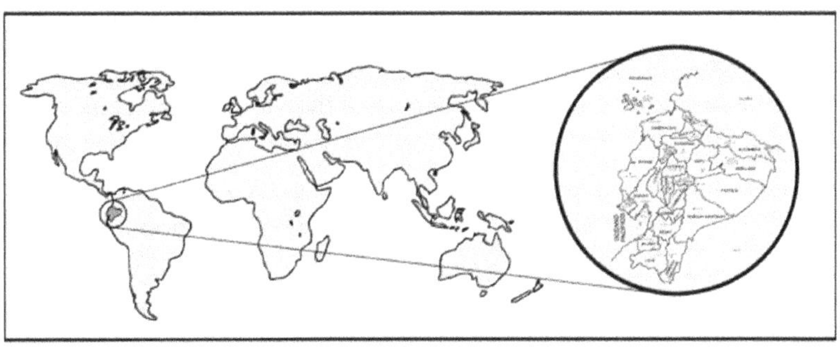

*Source: López-Molina & Pulido-Fernández (2023).*

Therefore, prior to the analysis of the social capital of Ecuador's cities, we proceeded to determine their degree of tourism development through a system of indicators applied to the twenty-four capital cities of each province. This system of indicators focused on aspects related to management, infrastructure, tourism services and tourism resources. As a result, cities with different levels of tourism development were identified, which has led to the application of different planning processes that, in some cases, have not favoured tourism activity, as well as not considering stakeholder participation as part of these processes.

## RESEARCH PROCESS

For the analysis of social capital there are methodologies that focus on actors and their characteristics, such as the Stakeholder Theory or the analysis of interactions and relationships, known as Social Network Analysis (SNA).

Stakeholder Theory identifies tourism stakeholders through attributes. Mitchell et al. (1997) establish a classification of stakeholders based on three attributes: power, legitimacy and urgency; and classify them, depending on whether they have more or fewer attributes, as latent, interested and definitive.

Social Network Analysis (SNA) is another methodology used, which focuses on examining the networks of relationships to which stakeholders in a tourism destination belong. It uses network indicators such as centrality, which determines the actors with the greatest influence and thus visibility within the destination's activity. Density is a second indicator, which depends on the number of actors in the network and the number of relationships these actors have within the network and, in turn, the level of recognition they have from other actors.

Ecuador, being a country with different geographical characteristics that define its natural and cultural attractions, has not identified a level of tourism development that can carry out effective planning processes that are in line with the reality of the territory and the reality of tourism.

As a preliminary investigation, an analysis of the level of tourism development in the capital cities of the 24 provinces of Ecuador was carried out. To this end, a system of indicators was constructed and validated through a search for and analysis of information. The system was classified into four areas: Management indicators focused on the public sector. Indicators of basic infrastructure and services. Indicators of tourism services and finally indicators of tourism resources (natural and cultural). Their validation was based on the opinion of a panel of experts on the validity and importance of each indicator.

At the end of this stage, the indicators were normalised using the methodology of the United Nations Development Programme (UNDP). The global composite index was then constructed by calculating the composite indices for each area that makes up the system of indicators. The methodology applied in previous studies by Pulido-Fernández and Sánchez-Rivero (2009) and Casado-Montilla and Pulido-Fernández (2020) was used. Finally, the groups of cities were obtained through a hierarchical cluster analysis and are shown in Table 1.

*Table 1. Level of tourism development in Ecuador's 24 provinces*

| | Cluster | | | | p-value |
|---|---|---|---|---|---|
| | 1 | 2 | 3 | 4 | |
| Municipalities | Cuenca<br>Guayaquil<br>Pto. Baq. Moreno<br>Quito | Ambato<br>Azogues<br>Esmeraldas<br>Ibarra<br>Latacunga<br>Loja<br>Macas<br>Puyo<br>Riobamba<br>Tena | Babahoyo<br>Guaranda<br>Machala<br>Nueva Loja<br>Portoviejo<br>Santa Elena<br>Tulcán | Pto. Fco. Orellana<br>Sto. Domingo<br>Zamora | |
| Management index | 92.144 (0.322) | 88.866 (3.101) | 85.740 (5.140) | 59.131 (0.0537) | 0.002a |
| Basic services index | 76.180 (4.071) | 62.810 (5.835) | 57.539 (6.591) | 68.515 (5.935) | <0.001b |
| Index of tourist services | 94.824 (3.379) | 89.605 (2.572) | 73.713 (7.820) | 81.313 (9.093) | <0.001b |
| Index of tourist resources | 85.786 (7.604) | 78.830 (3.292) | 71.827 (4.823) | 71.710 (10.030) | 0.003b |
| Global index | 88.038 (2.072) | 81.188 (1.270) | 72.664 (1.201) | 71.358 (6.055) | <0.001b |

Shown: Means (standard deviations).
Kruskal-Wallis aH.
[b]ANOVA.
Source: López-Molina & Pulido-Fernández (2023).

Group 1 includes the cities with the highest scores in all four indices and the overall index. These are the four best-positioned cities in the sample in terms of tourism. The next best positioned group of cities is found in cluster 2, with medium-high values in almost all the indices, except for basic services. The next group, cluster 3, brings together cities with lower values than the previous groups, especially in basic services, although still well positioned in management. Finally, group 4 brings together the cities with the worst scores overall, although their scores in tourism services stand out. In contrast, they have particularly low scores in management (López-Molina & Pulido-Fernández, 2023, p. 12).

After having identified the groups of cities based on their level of tourism development, the application of the different methodologies of social capital analysis was carried out. For this purpose, one city was selected for each degree of tourism development, with the aim of also finding out the possible differences between cities with different levels of development.

In the case of the group of cities with significant tourism development, the city of Cuenca was selected. From the group of cities with a medium level of development, the city of Loja was selected. From the group of cities with a low level of development, the city of Santa Elena was selected, and finally, from the group of cities with a weak level of development, the city of Zamora was selected.

Cuenca is a city located in the south of Ecuador. It is the capital of the province of Azuay. It has important natural resources found in its natural parks and forests. In relation to cultural resources, Cuenca was declared a UNESCO World Heritage Site in 1999. It also has an important intangible heritage of which the technique of weaving toquilla straw hats stands out, also declared by Unesco as Intangible Heritage of Humanity. It is also considered the third largest city in Ecuador.

Loja is also located in the south of Ecuador, in the highland region. It is the capital of the province of Loja. It has nationally important natural and cultural resources. Its tourist activity shows a seasonal tourism that focuses mainly on religious tourism, which has its peak in the month of September.

Santa Elena is a city located in the coastal region of Ecuador. It is the capital of the province of Santa Elena. Due to its geographical position, it is a city of passage to tourist attractions of sun and beach. This has led to the development of tourist activity based on communes (small groups of people) located along these attractions.

Zamora is the capital of the province of Zamora Chinchipe, which is located in the eastern region. It is a city that also has natural and cultural attractions, especially the presence of indigenous peoples of the Amazon. Therefore, it is a city of passage for the entrance to these attractions.

The identification and characteristics of the actors in each city was carried out by applying the methodology proposed by Mitchell et al. (1997). This methodology is composed of several theories such as need satisfaction (instrumental); internal value-seeking theory (moral) and resource exchange or trade-off theory (De Gooyert et al., 2017). Relationships (Yang and Bentley, 2017) and equity, with equal participation and entitlement.

Mitchell et al. (1997) propose that stakeholder types can be 'identified by the possession of one, two or all three of the following attributes: (1) the stakeholder's power to influence other actors, the group or decision making; (2) the legitimacy of the stakeholder relationship whether it consists of a formality or not; and (3) the urgency of the stakeholder's claim. This methodology produces a comprehensive typology of stakeholders based on the normative assumption that these variables define their field as entities to which their managers should pay attention' (Pulido-Fernández & López-Molina, 2023, p. 256).

These groups, in turn, form levels of relationships. These depend on the number of attributes they may have. Groups of actors with only one attribute are known as latent, which can be inactive (power), discretionary (legitimacy) and demanding (urgency) groups. The second group of relationships is made up of stakeholders with two attributes, known as: Dominant (power and legitimacy), Dependent (legitimacy and urgency) and Dangerous (power and urgency); and the last type of relationship is made up of those known as Definitive, which have the three attributes power, legitimacy and urgency.

## RESULTS

Once the level of tourism development of the twenty-four capital cities of each province in Ecuador had been determined, stakeholders and their level of participation in tourism activity were identified. The objective was to strategically analyse the stakeholder networks, carrying out a comparative study in Ecuadorian cities in order to determine whether the factors of the dynamic system also influence the level of tourism development in these cities.

The analysis was based on the importance of determining the actors and their level of participation in the cities of Ecuador, focusing on the different attributes, taking into account that they are cities that not only have different levels of tourism development, but also different planning and management processes for the activity.

Therefore, the identification, characterisation and classification of stakeholders was carried out, taking into account their level of participation in the tourism activity of the different cities. A second aspect was to analyse whether the level of tourism development of a territory can be determined through the identification of its stakeholders and their level of influence, their relationship with each other and the timely response to their claims and, finally, whether the level of stakeholder participation influences the degree of tourism development of a territory (Pulido-Fernández & López-Molina, 2023).

The application of this methodology resulted in a number of stakeholders that also has a certain relationship with the characteristics and size of each city. In the case of Cuenca, 101 stakeholders were identified, in Loja 65 stakeholders were identified, in the city of Santa Elena 44 stakeholders and in Zamora a total of 18 stakeholders.

The results show that stakeholders in a territory can be identified by their attributes (power, legitimacy and urgency). On the other hand, it could be determined that the level of stakeholder participation influences the degree of tourism development of a territory by affecting its tourism dynamics. In the case of the cities analysed, although they have a different level of tourism development (important, medium, weak and low), they show similar dynamics in stakeholder participation in tourism activity, and this is characterised by being weak. Therefore, 'knowing the power they exercise, the legitimacy with which they participate and their perception in relation to the immediate response to their claims, is a key factor for the tourism development of a territory' (Pulido-Fernández & López-Molina, 2023. p.267) and is observed in table 2.

*Table 2. Stakeholder characterisation according to Mitchell et al. (1997) by municipality and stakeholder groups*

| City | Interested parties | | | Definitive (power, legitimacy and urgency) |
|---|---|---|---|---|
| | Dominants (power and legitimacy) | Dependents (legitimacy and urgency) | Dangerous (power and urgency) | |
| Cuenca Public sector (articulator) Trade unions (demand and support) | 10, **19**, **20**, 2, 2, 29, 36, 39, 45, 46, 47, 55, 58, 74, 75, 76, 77, 97, 99 | **1**, 4, 12, 25, 44, 49, 50, 62, 70, 82, 84, 88, 91, 92 | 40, 41, 68, 101 | **2**, **5**, 7, **17**, 26, 32, 33, 34, 35, **43**, **48**, 56, 61, 63, 64, 65, 66, 67, 69, 71, 72, 78, 79, 81, 83, 85, 90, 93, 94, 95, 98 |
| Loja Public sector Trade (no major support) | 6, 13, 16, 17, 21, 22, 31, 44, 51, 54, 55, 57, 58, 60, 62 | **1**, 4, 9, 14, 30, 34, 37, 39, 41, 44, 48, 53, 57 | 62 | 3, **10**, **11**, 19, 28, 36, 38, 40, 43, 49, 51, 64 |
| Santa Elena Public sector (basic) Trade unions (not strong) Associations - Communes | 1, 4, 10, 12, 17, **18**, **20**, 21, 24, **33**, 35, 37 | 3, 5, 19, 31 | 11, 25, **36** | 1, 4, 10, 12, 17, **18**, **20**, 21, 24, 33, 35, 37 |
| Zamora Public sector (basic) Guild (chamber) Actors (own activity) | 9, 10, 15, 17 | 14 | **2**, **5** | **1**, 6, 12, 13, 18 |

Stakeholders: Public ■ Guilds and associations ■ Cultural ■ Academia ■ Private ■

Source: based on Pulido-Fernández & López-Molina (2023).

According to Table 2, the application of the methodology proposed by Mitchell et al. (1997) in the cities of Ecuador made it possible to group the actors in the different levels of relationships. The participation of actors is observed in all levels of relationships; however, the group of definitive actors is shown with a higher number in all cities, followed by the dominant groups followed by the dependent ones and at a lower level the dangerous ones. This information is necessary in the development of planning and decision-making processes, as well as in the measurement of social capital strengths.

While it is true that Stakeholder Theory focuses on identifying and analysing the actors in a tourism destination, it is also important to know the relationships of these actors, to determine the characteristics of these relationships, their level of interaction and collaboration, and to identify the central actors and, from this, also to be able to analyse whether they influence the level of tourism development.

The methodology applied for this analysis was Social Network Analysis (SNA). This methodology focuses on the analysis of networks, their types of relationships measured through network indicators that allow the direct relationships of the actors to be determined, as well as their recognition by other actors.

This methodology has also been applied in different studies by authors such as Merinero and Pulido (2009), Merinero (2011) and Ledesma et al. (2021), and is known as relational analysis.

The relational analysis in the cities of Ecuador started with the identification of the actors in each city, starting with key actors in the activity and through interviews that allowed data to be obtained from other actors with whom they are related. A second analysis was to determine the level of relationship, for which the network indicator was applied to analyse the centrality of the actors, by means of matrices and the use of Ucinet 6 software, the results were obtained for the centrality of degree of entry (indegree), which refers to the prestige that an actor has and its recognition by other actors, and the centrality of degree of exit (outdegree), which refers to the influence through the relationships that an actor has with other actors. Another network indicator that was analysed was density, which indicates the number of links a network has. 'Both aspects were analysed based on the characteristics of economic position, social prestige, political relevance, importance in the community and social contacts' (López-Molina & Pulido-Fernández, 2022, p. 27). It is shown in Figure 2.

The actors in Ecuador's cities are characterised by being actors belonging to the public sector (institutions and local governments that are responsible for managing tourism activity and the cultural sector), and, secondly, the private sector, represented mainly by tourism service companies, trade unions and academia.

According to the analysis, it was determined that there is no direct relationship between the degree of tourism development in the four Ecuadorian cities analysed and their relational dynamics. This is one of the main hypotheses maintained (and verified) by the existing scientific literature to date (Merinero & Pulido, 2009; Merinero, 2011; Pulido-Fernández & Merinero-Rodríguez, 2018).

In this study, it has been found that the opposite of what these authors suggest occurs, i.e. that the cities with the highest degree of tourism development, such as Cuenca and Loja, are also those with the lowest relational dynamics. The opposite is true for Santa Elena and Zamora (López- Molina & Pulido-Fernández, 2022, p. 27).

*Figure 2. Relational and collaborative analysis of the cities of Cuenca, Loja, Santa Elena and Zamora*

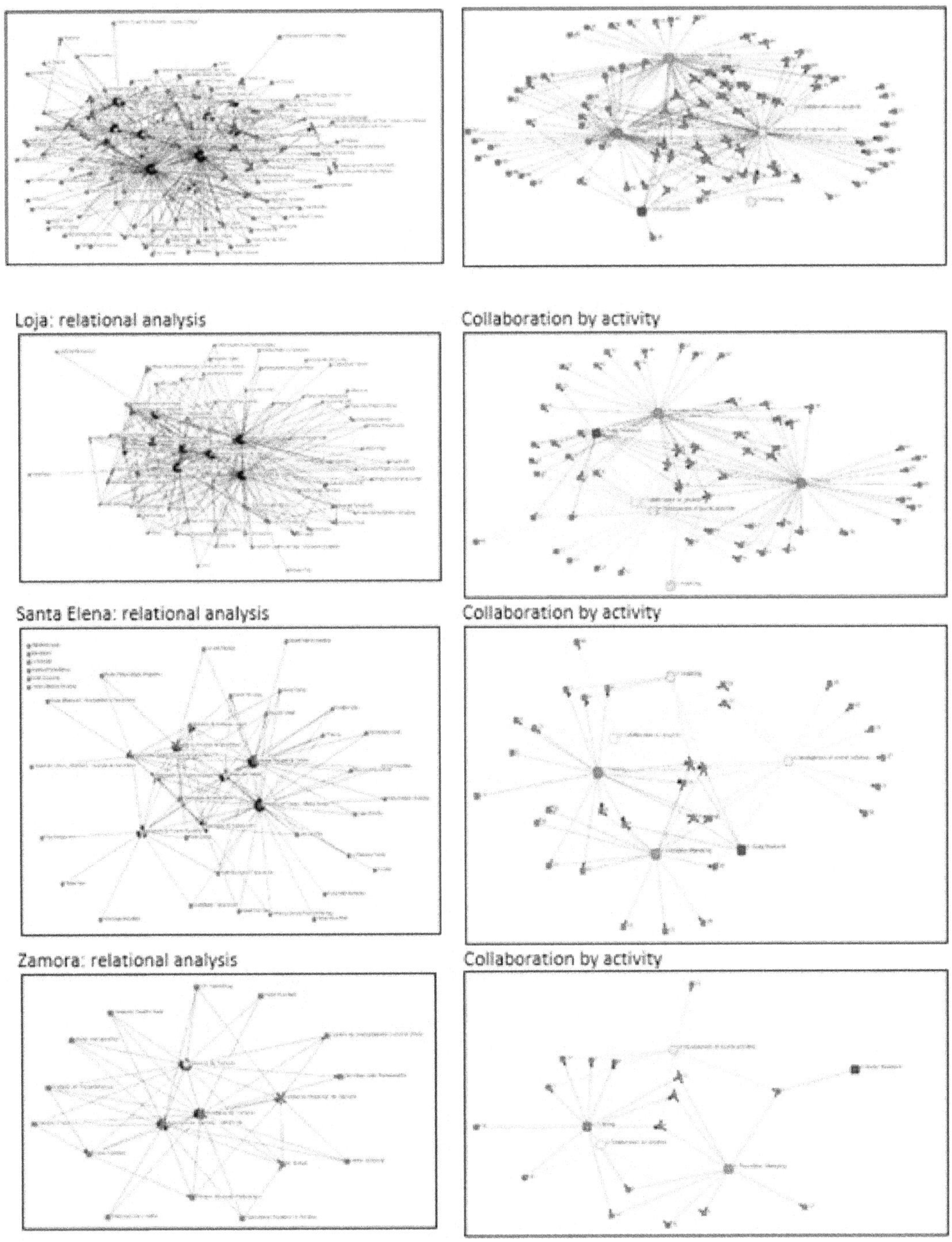

Conversely, the analysis of centrality shows that the level of tourism development is related to the central actors, therefore, this is reflected in their level of tourism development, being higher or lower according to each city. 'The centrality indicator shows a shift from the public sector to the private sector, therefore, as the tourism development of a territory increases, centrality shifts from the public sector to the private sector' (López-Molina & Pulido-Fernández, 2022, p. 28).

The Social Network Analysis (SNA) methodology was also applied in the analysis of stakeholder interaction and collaboration. For this, it was based on studies by Merinero-Rodríguez and Pulido-Fernández (2009), Pearce (2014), and Pulido-Fernández and Merinero-Rodríguez (2018) related to the analysis of collaboration and its influence on the tourism development of destinations. 'This analysis seeks to determine through network indicators (centrality and density) whether collaboration determines the structure of destinations and influences their relational dynamics, whether activities with high centrality increase the level of tourism development and whether the participation and interaction of tourism stakeholders in the different activities allows for a more meaningful relationship between them' (López-Molina & Pulido-Fernández, 2024. p. 4).

This was analysed in terms of training activities, development of tourism activities, financing, marketing and promotion, study/research, project collaboration. This allowed the analysis of the complete networks of each city, but also an analysis by layer of collaboration. Moreover, a 'statistical analysis based on the methodology applied by Cehan et al. (2021) was carried out to find out if there is a relationship between the different layers of collaboration in each city, and an ANOVA analysis of variance to determine if there are significant differences in the layers of collaboration between the cities (López-Molina & Pulido-Fernández, 2024. p. 5).

It is important that in the case of the analysed cities and their actors these present common characteristics and needs, which leads to the conclusion that interaction and collaboration is established in some cases based on a close relationship between these actors, reaffirming what authors such as Beritelli (2011) argue that relationships are characterised by being more personal than formal.

It is also important to highlight that the actors in Ecuador's cities have no interest in interacting, let alone establishing collaborative processes with other actors. However, despite this, they recognise the actors (public, private, trade, academic and cultural) and refer to them as active or passive subjects in the tourism activity of each city.

In relation to the activities in each city, it was observed that, according to their level of participation and importance of each activity according to the interests of each actor or group of actors, therefore, the association between layers of collaboration is very low. It shows that actors do not seek to participate in collaborative activities. However, 'the existence of activities in common could be a nexus for the relationship between layers of collaboration in each city' (López-Molina & Pulido-Fernández, 2024. p. 16).

## CONCLUSION

The analysis of social capital in tourism as a key factor in sustainable territorial development: from a network approach, highlights several aspects: One is that both sustainable territorial development and sustainable tourism, are characterised or based on dimensions that when applied as a whole can enable true sustainability.

These dimensions are common to each of the aspects analysed in this chapter: the environmental dimension, the economic dimension and the social dimension. Within the latter, social capital has been highlighted in recent years, focusing on the actors and their level of participation in tourism activity, which is the case here. Moreover, in order for this social capital to make a positive contribution to sustainable territorial development, it must be analysed on the basis of the reality of a territory, which is an important aspect for all the factors that can lead to sustainable development to be applied.

Social capital also shows us that the actors have a dynamic that can lead to determine a level of tourism development in these territories focused on the formation of groups of actors that have two or three attributes that define their level of participation in tourism activity, however, it is also important to bear in mind that there are many key aspects for this participation to be carried out and above all to benefit the tourist destination, This is mainly based on the level of trust that can be had, which is based on participation in governance processes, which in turn leads to a level of collaboration between stakeholders in favour of a common development of tourism activity as another factor of sustainable territorial development.

Social capital is therefore a key factor in sustainable territorial development. Just as its other dimensions are measurable, social capital can also be measurable, for which two methodologies have been proposed in this chapter: Stakeholder Theory and Social Network Analysis (SNA).

From the point of view of the Stakeholder Theory methodology, proposed by Mitchell et al., 1997, it is important to highlight that the actors of a territory can be determined and characterised through three attributes: power, legitimacy and urgency. Having two or all three attributes allows us to determine the level of participation and protagonism of the actors within the tourism activity of a territory.

The second methodology that allows us to know the actors of a territory is Social Network Analysis (SNA), which goes beyond determining and classifying the actors, this methodology allows us to analyse the level of interaction and collaboration of the actors in a tourist destination, which in many cases falls on networks of actors.

However, it is important to point out that tourism activity in Ecuador was not only affected by the pandemic, but also by a series of problems and a lack of government management, leading to a lack of participation and commitment on the part of stakeholders. This has led to the impossibility of obtaining a real articulation of stakeholders despite the ongoing crisis and the need for further strengthening in the recovery of tourism activity (López-Molina and Pulido-Fernández, 2023).

The analysis of social capital is a key factor for the development of a destination. Knowing the stakeholders of the destination and the level of relationships that exist between them allows to direct the tourism activity of a territory with strategies that favour participatory planning processes. The application of the methodologies proposed in this chapter for the analysis of the stakeholders of a destination makes it possible to understand the structure of the relationships and can determine the relational dynamics of tourism destinations.

In the case of Ecuador, it was determined that cities with a higher degree of tourism development have a lower relational dynamic, and cities with a lower degree of development have a higher relational dynamic. This is just the opposite of what, until now, has been advocated in the scientific literature on the subject (Merinero & Pulido, 2009; Merinero, 2011; Pulido-Fernández & Merinero-Rodríguez, 2018; López-Molina & Pulido-Fernández, 2022).

## REFERENCES


Alvarez, M. D. (2014). Sustainability issues. In *Tourism as an Instrument for Development: A Theoretical and Practical Study*. Emerald Group Publishing Limited. DOI: 10.1108/S2042-144320140000006001

Annamalah, S., Paraman, P., Ahmed, S., Dass, R., Sentosa, I., Pertheban, T. R., Shamsudin, F., Kadir, B., Aravindan, K. L., Raman, M., Hoo, W. C., & Singh, P. (2023). The role of open innovation and a normalizing mechanism of social capital in the tourism industry. *Journal of Open Innovation*, *9*(2), 100056. DOI: 10.1016/j.joitmc.2023.100056

Baggio, R. (2020). Tourism destinations: A universality conjecture based on network science. *Annals of Tourism Research*, *82*, 102929. DOI: 10.1016/j.annals.2020.102929

Baggio, R., Scott, N., & Cooper, C. (2010). Network science: A review focused on tourism. *Annals of Tourism Research*, *37*(3), 802–827. DOI: 10.1016/j.annals.2010.02.008

Banerjee, S. B. (2003). Who sustains whose development? Sustainable development and the reinvention of nature. *Organization Studies*, *24*(1), 143–180. DOI: 10.1177/0170840603024001341

Barbosa, G. S., Drach, P. R., & Corbella, O. D. (2014). A conceptual review of the terms sustainable development and sustainability. *Journal of Social Sciences*, *3*(2), 1.

Binns, T., & Nel, E. (2002). Tourism as a local development strategy in South Africa. *The Geographical Journal*, *168*(3), 235–247. DOI: 10.1111/1475-4959.00051

Brundtland, I. (1987). Desarrollo y cooperación económica internacional medio ambiente. Informe de la comisión mundial sobre el medio ambiente y el Desarrollo [Development and International Economic Cooperation and the Environment. Report of the World Commission on Environment and Development].

Capello, R. (2011). Location, regional growth and local development theories. *Aestimum (Firenze)*, •••, 1–25.

Cehan, A., Eva, M., & Ia u, C. (2021). A multilayer network approach to tourism collaboration. *Journal of Hospitality and Tourism Management*, *46*, 316–326. DOI: 10.1016/j.jhtm.2021.01.006

Chan, G. K., Selvadurai, S., & Aziz, R. A. (2020). The Culture Of Heritage Conservation In Malaysia: A Study Of Eco-Tourism In Langkawi. e-BANGI Journal, 17(1).

Coffey, W. J., & Polese, M. (1985). Local development: Conceptual bases and policy implications. *Regional Studies*, *19*(2), 85–93. DOI: 10.1080/09595238500185101

Cortez, J. U. (2020). Comisión Económica para América Latina y el Caribe (2019), Planificación para el desarrollo territorial sostenible en América Latina y el Caribe [Economic Commission for Latin America and the Caribbean (2019), Planning for sustainable territorial development in Latin America and the Caribbean]. *Revista de Estudios Regionales*, (117), 175–177.

Czernek-Marszałek, K. (2019). Applying mixed methods in social network research–The case of co-operation in a Polish tourist destination. *Journal of Destination Marketing & Management*, *11*, 40–52. DOI: 10.1016/j.jdmm.2018.10.004

Facultades A Gobiernos Autonomos Desarrollo Actividades Turisticas. [Powers to Autonomous Governments for the Development of Tourist Activities]. (2016, 23 de marzo). Consejo Nacional de Competencias Registro Oficial Suplemento 718 No. 0001-CNC-2016. https://www.turismo.gob.ec/wp-content/uploads/2016/04/Reg%C3%BAlense-las-facultades-y-atribuciones-de-los-GADs-Municipales-Metropolitanos-Provinciales-y-Parroquiales-Rurales-respecto-al-desarrollo-de-actividades-tur%C3%ADsticas.pdf

Fayos-Solà, E., Moraleda, L. F., & Mazón, A. I. M. (2014). Key factors for development. In *Tourism as an Instrument for Development: A Theoretical and Practical Study*. Emerald Group Publishing Limited. DOI: 10.1108/S2042-144320140000006011

García-Villaverde, P. M., Ruiz-Ortega, M. J., Hurtado-Palomino, A., De La Gala-Velásquez, B., & Zirena-Bejarano, P. P. (2021). Social capital and innovativeness in firms in cultural tourism destinations: Divergent contingent factors. *Journal of Destination Marketing & Management*, *19*, 100529. DOI: 10.1016/j.jdmm.2020.100529

Haddad, E. A., de Araújo, I. F., de Almeida Vale, V., Sandoval, H. D., Roman, P. A. G., Rodríguez, L. A. C., Jaramillo, E. A., & Lopez, L. J. G. (2021). Dimensions of local development in the Colombian Pacific Region. *Regional Science Policy & Practice*, *13*(4), 1348–1371. DOI: 10.1111/rsp3.12453

Hussain, A., Mandić, A., & Fusté-Forné, F. (2024). Transforming communities: Analyzing the effects of infrastructure and tourism development on social capital, livelihoods, and resilience in Gilgit-Baltistan, Pakistan. *Journal of Hospitality and Tourism Management*, *59*, 276–295. DOI: 10.1016/j.jhtm.2024.04.017

Jumaiti, J., Saputra, B., Frinaldi, A., & Putri, N. E. (2024). Examining the Mediating Effects of Social Capital and Community-Based Tourism on the Role of Tourism Villages in Sustainable Tourism. *Journal of Environmental Management and Tourism*, *15*(1), 176–193. DOI: 10.14505/jemt.v15.1(73).15

Károly, K. (2011). Rise and fall of the concept sustainability. *Journal of Environmental Sustainability*, *1*(1), 1–13. DOI: 10.14448/jes.01.0001

Kidd, C. V. (1992). The evolution of sustainability. *Journal of Agricultural & Environmental Ethics*, *5*(1), 1–26. DOI: 10.1007/BF01965413

López Molina, D., & Pulido-Fernández, J. I. (2022). Strategic analysis of a Tourism Stakeholder Network: A comparative study in Ecuadorian cities. *Boletín de la Asociación de Geógrafos Españoles*, (94). Advance online publication. DOI: 10.21138/bage.3283

López-Molina, D., & Pulido-Fernández, J. I. (2024). Analysis of the interaction and collaboration of the actors of a tourist destination from a network perspective. Current Issues in Tourism, 27(10), 1572-1589. p. 4

Martínez-Peláez, R., Ochoa-Brust, A., Rivera, S., Félix, V. G., Ostos, R., Brito, H., Félix, R. A., & Mena, L. J. (2023). Role of digital transformation for achieving sustainability: Mediated role of stakeholders, key capabilities, and technology. *Sustainability (Basel)*, *15*(14), 11221. DOI: 10.3390/su151411221

Meadows, D. H., Meadows, D. L., Randers, J., & Behrens, W. W. (2018). The limits to growth. In *Green planet blues* (pp. 25–29). Routledge. DOI: 10.4324/9780429493744-3

Mebratu, D. (1998). Sustainability and sustainable development: Historical and conceptual review. *Environmental Impact Assessment Review, 18*(6), 493–520. DOI: 10.1016/S0195-9255(98)00019-5

Mempel-Śnieżyk, A. (2014). Networks and cooperation for sustainable development The role of local authorities and clusters in regional development and economic growth. *European Journal of Sustainable Development, 3*(3), 111–111. DOI: 10.14207/ejsd.2014.v3n3p111

Merinero, R. (2011). Redes de actores y desarrollo turístico: estudio de caso en Portugal. Journal of Tourism Analysis [Actor networks and tourism development: a case study in Portugal. Journal of Tourism Analysis] = Revista de Análisis Turísticos, 11(1), 9–21.

Merinero-Rodríguez, R., & Pulido-Fernández, J. I. (2009). Desarrollo turístico y dinámica relacional. Metodología de análisis para la gestión activa de destinos turísticos. [Tourism development and relational dynamics. Analysis methodology for the active management of tourist destinations*] Cuadernos de Turismo, 23*, 173–194.

Ministerio de Turismo. (2024). *Sistema Nacional de Información Turística del Ecuador*. [National Tourist Information System of Ecuador]. https://servicios.turismo.gob.ec/turismo-en-cifras/

Mitchell, R. K., Agle, B. R., & Wood, D. J. (1997). Toward a theory of stakeholder identification and salience: Defining the principle of who and what really counts. *Academy of Management Review, 22*(4), 853–886. DOI: 10.2307/259247

Morales, C., Pérez, R., Riffo Pérez, L., & Williner, A. (2021). Desarrollo territorial sostenible y nuevas ciudadanías: consideraciones sobre políticas públicas para un mundo en transformación.

Musavengane, R., & Kloppers, R. (2020). Social capital: An investment towards community resilience in the collaborative natural resources management of community-based tourism schemes. *Tourism Management Perspectives, 34*, 100654. DOI: 10.1016/j.tmp.2020.100654

Nahapiet, J., & Ghoshal, S. (1998). Social Capital, Intellectual Capital, and the Organizational Advantage. *Academy of Management Review, 23*(2), 242. DOI: 10.2307/259373

Nguyen, T. Q. T., Johnson, P., & Young, T. (2022). Networking, coopetition and sustainability of tourism destinations. *Journal of Hospitality and Tourism Management, 50*, 400–411. DOI: 10.1016/j.jhtm.2022.01.003

Nunkoo, R. (2015). Tourism development and trust in local government. *Tourism Management, 46*, 623–634. DOI: 10.1016/j.tourman.2014.08.016

Nunkoo, R. (2017). Governance and sustainable tourism: What is the role of trust, power and social capital? *Journal of Destination Marketing & Management, 6*(4), 277–285. DOI: 10.1016/j.jdmm.2017.10.003

Nunkoo, R., & Smith, S. L. (2014). Trust, tourism development, and planning. In *Trust, tourism development and planning* (pp. 1–8). Routledge. DOI: 10.4324/9780203537817

Pearce, D. G. (2014). Toward an integrative conceptual framework of destinations. *Journal of Travel Research, 53*(2), 141–153. DOI: 10.1177/0047287513491334

Prayitno, G., Auliah, A., Ari, I. R. D., Effendi, A., Hayat, A., Delisa, A., Siankwilimba, E., & Hiddlestone-Mumford, J. (2024). Social capital for sustainable tourism development in Indonesia. *Cogent Social Sciences*, *10*(1), 2293310. DOI: 10.1080/23311886.2023.2293310

Pulido Fernández, J. I., & López Molina, D. (2023). Las partes interesadas en el desarrollo turístico de un territorio. Análisis de casos en Ecuador [Stakeholders in a Territory's Tourism Development: Case Studies in Ecuador]. *Investigaciones Turísticas*, (26), 251–273. DOI: 10.14198/INTURI.23156

Pulido-Fernández, J. I., & Merinero-Rodríguez, R. (2018). Destinations' relational dynamic and tourism development. *Journal of Destination Marketing & Management*, *7*, 140–152. DOI: 10.1016/j.jdmm.2016.09.008

Putnam, R. D. (1995). Bowling Alone: America's Declining Social Capital. *Journal of Democracy*, *6*(1), 65–78. DOI: 10.1353/jod.1995.0002

Ramukumba, T., Mmbengwa, V. M., Mwamayi, K. A., & Groenewald, J. A. (2012). Analysis of local economic development (LED) initiated partnership and support services for emerging tourism entrepreneurs in George municipality, Western Cape Province, RSA. *Tourism Management Perspectives*, *2*, 7–12. DOI: 10.1016/j.tmp.2011.12.006

Roxas, F. M. Y., Rivera, J. P. R., & Gutierrez, E. L. M. (2020). Mapping stakeholders' roles in governing sustainable tourism destinations. *Journal of Hospitality and Tourism Management*, *45*, 387–398. DOI: 10.1016/j.jhtm.2020.09.005

Rust, N. A., Ptak, E. N., Graversgaard, M., Iversen, S., Reed, M. S., de Vries, J. R., Ingram, J., Mills, J., Neumann, R. K., Kjeldsen, C., Muro, M., & Dalgaard, T. (2023). Social capital factors affecting uptake of sustainable soil management practices: A literature review. *Emerald Open Research*, *1*(10). Advance online publication. DOI: 10.1108/EOR-10-2023-0002

Sabet, N. S., & Khaksar, S. (2024). The performance of local government, social capital and participation of villagers in sustainable rural development. *The Social Science Journal*, *61*(1), 1–29. DOI: 10.1080/03623319.2020.1782649

Salazar, J. N., Vergara-Romero, A., Sorhegui-Ortega, R., & Garnica-Jarrin, L. (2021). Repensando el Desarrollo Sostenible en el territorio. Res non verba revista científica, [Rethinking Sustainable Development in the Territory. Res non verba, a scientific journal]. 11(1), 19-33.

Sen, A. (2016). The ends and means of sustainability. In *The Capability Approach and Sustainability* (pp. 5–19). Routledge.

Stolle, D., & Rochon, T. R. (1998). Are all associations alike? Member diversity, associational type, and the creation of social capital. *The American Behavioral Scientist*, *42*(1), 47–65. DOI: 10.1177/0002764298042001005

Vongvisitsin, T. B., Huang, W. J., & King, B. (2024). Urban community-based tourism development: A networked social capital model. *Annals of Tourism Research*, *106*, 103759. DOI: 10.1016/j.annals.2024.103759

Voronkova, O. Y., Yankovskaya, V., Kovaleva, I., Epishkin, I., Iusupova, I., & Berdova, Y. (2019). Sustainable territorial development based on the effective use of resource potential. *Entrepreneurship and Sustainability Issues*, *7*(1), 662–673. DOI: 10.9770/jesi.2019.7.1(47)

Zvaigzne, A., Mietule, I., Kotane, I., Sprudzane, S., & Bartkute-Norkuniene, V. (2023). Digital innovations in tourism: The perceptions of stakeholders. *Worldwide Hospitality and Tourism Themes*, *15*(5), 528–537. DOI: 10.1108/WHATT-06-2023-0080

# Chapter 8
# Unlock Tourism Activities Through the Identification of Cultural Heritage Tourism Opportunities for Sustainable Economic Development

**Lombuso Precious Shabalala**
https://orcid.org/0000-0001-8415-9980
*University of South Africa, South Africa*

## ABSTRACT

*Using Bushbuckridge Local Municipality as a case study, the study investigates how identifying cultural heritage tourism opportunities can unlock tourism activities that contribute to sustainable economic development. CHT is presented as a vehicle that can be utilised by the municipality and Bushbuckridge Local Economic Development Forum Management Committee (BLEDFMC) within the municipality to mitigate poverty alleviation and socio-economic development, thus addressing sustainable development. A qualitative desk study with a triangulation design was adopted for this study. Key findings revealed that a capacitated BLEDFMC is vital in leading and monitoring the process of identifying assets and opportunities, including linking these assets with key attractions in the area, supported by the municipality. It will also aim to address the primary needs of the communities and ensure fair benefits sharing in its true sense. This research advocates for a capacitated BLEDFMC that recognises the role of research, and local community participation, including the Gap analysis model.*

## 1. INTRODUCTION

"Our rich and varied cultural heritage has a profound power to help build our nation" The late honourable Nelson Rolihlahla Mandela 18 Jul 1918 - 05 Dec 2013.

The majority of cultural heritage sites are located in rural areas. This type of location often results in social and economic challenges related to job opportunities, infrastructure, and socio-economic reforms. Tourism is acknowledged as a vehicle that can help sustain both tangible and intangible elements of

DOI: 10.4018/979-8-3693-7081-0.ch008

Indigenous cultural heritage, including languages, stories, song, art, dance, hunting methods, rituals, and customs (Ruhanen et al., 2021:1). The declaration of a World Heritage Site can be viewed by some communities located near protected area sites, as an opportunity due to an increased in the number of visitors to the geographical area, which is associated with an increase in income through tourism activities (Shabalala & Ezeuduji, 2022:422). Ruhanen et al. (2021) note that socio-economic opportunities for the communities involved can be realised; however, "tourism can also present a challenge as the self-management of Indigenous cultural products and cultural identity can be problematic." On the same note, referencing Southern Africa case studies, Ndoro (2015) examined the contribution of heritage conservation efforts as a viable enterprise in providing livelihood strategies for local communities. In addition, the author discusses infrastructural development issues and the resulting job creation (Ndoro, 2015). However, in some cases, the declaration has been viewed as an answer to socioeconomic challenges faced by local communities (Ndoro, 2015:392).

Using Bushbuckridge Local Municipality (BLM) situated in Mpumalanga Province, South Africa, this paper explores how the identification of Cultural Heritage Tourism (CHT) opportunities could unlock tourism activities contributing to sustainable economic development. The focus is on how the identified CHT opportunities can be linked and presented as a vehicle that can be utilized by the Bushbuckridge Local Economic Development (BLED) Forum Management Committee in collaboration with local communities. By doing so, it is believed that mitigating poverty alleviation and socio-economic development could be realised, thus addressing sustainable development.

On that note, local government must play an important role in promoting social and economic development that aligns with constitutional requirements. Debatably, The Local Government Handbook: South Africa (2015) notes that the South African government has put in place a strategic direction pertaining to its vision of how it envisages the economy to be driven, including development courses. In addition, the same strategy outlines the government's plan for its intervention in favor of the poor and the previously marginalized people. In support of the Human Resource Development Council (HRDC) of South Africa, implementing strategies that will stimulate a culture of training and lifelong learning at individual level, organisational level and national levels of employability could assist (The Local Government Handbook: South Africa, 2015:5). In the same vein, Koma (2012:125) note that "through the local economic development policy, municipalities have assumed a central role to contribute to job creation, eradication of poverty and boost local economies. To achieve growth and development, the author advocates for a synergised and integrated approach from all the required spheres of government (Koma, 2012:125).

## 2. DESCRIPTION OF STUDY AREA

Bushbuckridge Local Municipality is in the northern part of Mpumalanga Province, South Africa. The Free Encyclopaedia (2022) notes that The Municipality falls under Ehlanzeni District, the largest local municipality in Mpumalanga province, both in terms of population and land size, established in 2000 and mainly formed by villages and rural settlements. It further indicates that the area was named Bushbuckridge owing to the large herds of bushbuck found there. "*The municipality borders the Blyde River Canyon in the west, the Kruger National Park / Sabie Sand reserves in the east; Manyeleti and Andover Game Reserves fall into its area along the northern border*" (Department of Provincial and Local Government of South Africa & Business Trust, 2007:8). This province dominates in Wildlife economy and is one the developing provinces in the country. The BLM is considered a gateway municipality to Limpopo province and other wildlife-protected areas such as Kruger National Park, Manyeleti Nature Reserve, Bushbuckridge Nature Reserve, and Mangwazi Nature Reserve, just to name a few. The municipality holds a strong history that embraces historical sites such as Mariepskop and the cultural diversity of the three indigenous tribes, namely The Tsongas, the Mapulana, and siSwati cultures. In addition, the municipality is a host to unique cultural assets, which include cultural offerings by the three prior mentioned tribes, ranging from traditional dishes, traditional regalia/attire, dances, music, language, customs/traditions, stories/poems, events, art, artifacts and so forth. Most importantly, it is understood that this municipality holds ten (10) tribal authorities. According to The Free Encyclopaedia (2022), *Commercial farming, which consists of pine /blue-gum plantations, tobacco, cotton, sub-tropical fruits, and vegetables, is practiced in the municipality.* Lastly, Beyers and Schutte (2018) note that the study area suffers from service delivery challenges, including an inadequate water supply, gravel roads, a lack of health facilities & electricity in some communities, and inadequate sanitation.

*Figure 1. Bushbuckridge municipality map*

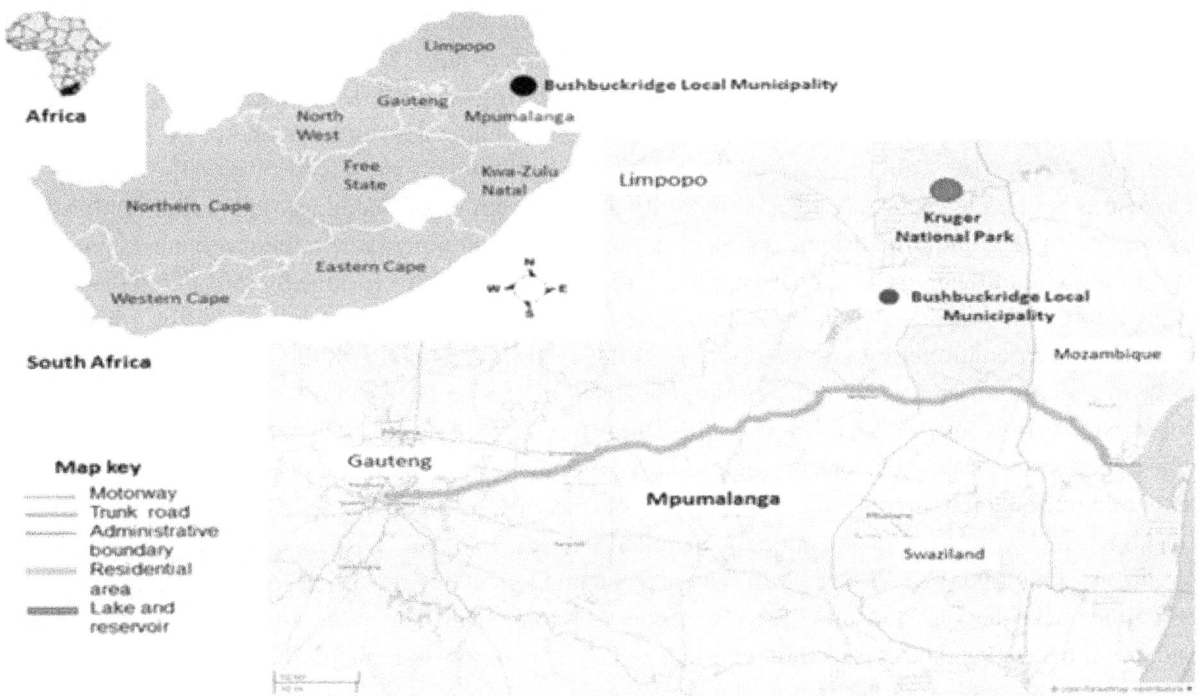


*Source: Bushbuckridge Local Municipality (2023).*

## 3. METHODOLOGY

A qualitative desk study with a triangulation design was preferred for this study. The data was gathered from different sources, which include peer-reviewed journal articles, government documents, and website media. Creswell and Creswell (2005) believe that triangulation is a popular design type in social science. This case involved Bushbuckridge Municipality (BLM) records analysis, observation during BLM engagements, and comparison with observations. It must be noted that the data from the LED Forum Launch organised by Bushbuckridge Local Municipality under the theme: "Building an inclusive economy through stakeholder participation and investor mobilisation" played a key role. The researcher then analysed and interpreted the data. Narrative analysis was adopted, whereby experiences were transcribed. Narrative analysis is a cluster of analytic methods for deciphering texts or visual data that have a storied kind. The analytic method enabled the researcher to know what to look for in the successive data sets, which led to the researcher gaining perceptive and drawing findings.

The Complexity Science Theory and the Basic Needs Theory were employed to complement the diversity. Saturation of employment of these theories is based on the nature of the study and underpins the study. Within the context of the Complexity Science Theory, a system is understood to be complex because of many challenges that are often dynamic, unpredictable, and multidimensional in nature through interconnected relationships (University of Victoria research groups, 2012). In the case of the three tribes residing in Bushbuckridge, complex issues relate to identifying the cultural heritage opportunities/assets that could be used to unlock tourism opportunities for sustainable development and economic development. Later in the paper, suggestions for resolving complex issues are presented. Within the Basic Needs Theory, as applied by de Wet (2018), community development is expanded beyond earlier applications by integrating the multidimensional nature of community development into a theory that acknowledges the complexity of the interdisciplinary approach to development. This is done by introducing a priority index into a basic needs assessment technique that enables the researcher to prioritise the "real" basic needs in a particular community (de Wet, 2018:1). Prideaux, Timothy, and Chon (2008) noted that tourism and culture in any particular geographical setting can be utilised for a variety of purposes that could extend from entertainment, preservation, information, education, profit, and propaganda, they did note that this should only be done through socio-economic development that prioritises responsible and authentic tourism and, in this way, speak directly to the various guidelines of the SDGs. In the case of Bushbuckridge communities, it cannot be disputed that several "real" basic needs require the attention of various stakeholders. This study will thus present findings in this regard, followed by suggestions on how Bushbuckridge LED Forum Management can collaborate with its Communities (Tsonga, Mapulana, and Swati people) and other stakeholders such as CPAs, and how to assist in mitigating the challenges to achieve sustainable socio-economic development.

A total of 82 delegates from 32 stakeholders attended the prior alluded LED Forum Launch organised by Bushbuckridge Local Municipality. These stakeholders suited the invitation due to their merits. Institutions of Higher Learning, such as the University of Mpumalanga and Ehlanzeni TVET College, were present as experts in academia (Teaching & Learning, research, and community engagement). People and Parks Unit and the Kruger2Canyon Biosphere Unit from South African National Parks was also represented. Youth and people living with disabilities were also represented. Local farmers were also part of the delegates including Ehlanzeni Municipality, COGTA and DEDT. Financial institutions such as Standard Bank, NYDA, SEDA and so forth were present. Businesspeople from Bushbuckridge graced the occasion through their leadership Business Chamber and SANCO. Bushbuckridge municipality procurement unit provided an overview of the services provided by their office for the businesspeople and community in general to be aware and take apply as service providers.

## 4. LITERATURE REVIEW

The South African government has put in place the National Tourism Sector Strategy (NTSS) 2016-2026 (2011), supported by the 2012 National Heritage and Cultural Tourism Strategy (NHCTS), to enable the tourism sector to accomplish its set objectives, also position itself in a competitive advantage working together with the respective communities. After all, the tourism sector contributes to job creation, transformation, and the economy. The NTSS 2016-2026 (2011) portrays tourism as one of the world's largest industries, crucial to community commercial strength. This implies that tourism has the muscle to contribute towards job creation and mutual understanding when it is well-guided and well-managed. The possible opportunities could result in socio-economic benefits for local communities (in this case, Bushbuckridge's immediate local communities). Community engagement and participation in the Sustainable Development of Cultural Heritage Tourism have become vital.

It cannot be denied that a robust connection exists between tourism and Cultural Heritage (CH), which submits to an experience related to cultural treasures. Furthermore, CH belongs to the people of a particular community, clan, or tribe. Through Cultural Heritage Tourism (CHT), many can share CH through education and unlocking CHT opportunities by identifying tourism activities/assets. Similarly, the social and economic of the action benefit the locals and the custodians of the culture. Nowadays, CH is packaged or commercialised in a way that suits and caters to a specific tourism market segment. Therefore, through research, academics in consultation with the Local Economic Development (LED) management, such as LED Forums and the communities, could play a vital role in linking the identified opportunities/assets with attractions of interest. The White Paper on Local Government (1998), cited in the Bushbuckridge Local Municipality, Local Economic Development Forum: Terms of Reference (2021:1), notes that "LED is not about creating a platform and environment where investment and entrepreneurship thrive." It further states that LED *"is responsible for taking steps to ensure that the locality's overall economic and social conditions are conducive to creating employment opportunities"*. On that note, academics should also assist in developing a more suitable management model and/or stakeholder participation model aimed at including and benefiting all stakeholders, particularly local communities/custodians of that culture. In support of the view by UNESCO (2002), the argument of a need to educate communities through the vehicle of community engagement (CE) becomes paramount. At the same time, Keitumetse (2014), Kurin (2004), and Shabalala et al (2022) advocate for community education and knowledge enhancement of their respective geographic sites, and this must include the potential commercial benefits that would proceed from the preservation of the local cultural heritage such as relics, monuments, sites, traditional dishes and traditional regalia and physical and human landscapes. Furthermore, these scholars also indicate that educated communities tend to value the heritage in such a manner that would reinforce relations between the custodians of the culture and the project managers leading the process.

The World Heritage Committee (UNESCO: 2002) is aligned with the 2030 SDG Agenda (United Nations, 2015), whereby it declared job creation and community involvement as part of key areas of performance. In acknowledgment of the declaration, the South African Government, through the National Department of Tourism (NDT, 2011), implemented the National Tourism Sector Strategy (NTSS)

2016-2026, supported by the National Heritage and Cultural Tourism Strategy (NHCTS) that was implemented in 2012. The NTSS maintains that tourism is a crucial global sector for its contribution to the gross domestic product of many countries and local trade power. This is most likely why the South African Government plays an important role in its viability and success. The strategy also recognises tourism as an industry with a massive potential role in growing the economy, as it is in accordance with the NHCTS vision. The NHCTS vision is to "*realise the global competitiveness of South African heritage and cultural resources through product development for sustainable tourism and economic development*" (NHCTS, 2012:15).

Drawing from the NHCTS vision, community participation should be encouraged as it is also about sharing knowledge and transforming the learning process in the service of people's self-development. Although the contribution of tourism to such a community is substantial, some challenges remain. Striking a balance between localisation & internalisation and CH opportunities identification could facilitate more opportunities geared towards sustainable local development and poverty alleviation and result in more meaningful benefits sharing while positively tackling a number of challenges. The challenges include issues of ownership, access, economic leakages (from the local economy and through imports), local employment, benefit distribution, social and environmental impacts, and dependency. These challenges were perceived to effectively yield positive impacts when properly addressed at the destination level with the active participation of the local communities.

The Department of Corporative Governance and Traditional Affairs (2021) defines Local Economic Development (LED) as an approach towards economic development that allows and encourages local people to work together to achieve sustainable economic growth and development, thereby bringing economic benefits and improved quality of life for all residents in a local municipal area. The "local" in economic development points to the fact that the political jurisdiction at a local level is often the most appropriate place for economic intervention as it carries alongside it the accountability and legitimacy of a democratically elected body (Department of Corporative Governance and Traditional Affairs, 2021:1). The role of a Local Economic Development Forum Management Committee (LEDFMC) becomes relevant and vital as expected to work with local municipalities and local communities. Over and above, the Department of Corporative Governance and Traditional Affairs (2021) presents the areas of support provided by the LED as follows:

- *"Development and review of national policy, strategy and guidelines on LED*
- *Providing direct and hands-on support to provincial and local government*
- *Management of the Local Economic Development Fund*
- *Management and Technical Support to Nodal Economic Development Planning*
- *Facilitating coordinating and monitoring of donor programmes*
- *Assisting with LED capacity-building processes"*

Without a doubt, the Bushbuckridge Local Economic Development Forum Management Committee (BLEDMC) should be instrumental in the process and facilitation of identifying and unlocking cultural heritage tourism activities to unleash sustainable socioeconomic development opportunities in the Bushbuckridge area. Drawing from the complexity of National Development Plan 2030, the plan sets out six interlinked priorities namely (Department of the Presidency Republic of South Africa, 2012:16):

- *"Uniting all South Africans around a common programme to achieve prosperity and equity.*

- *Promoting active citizenry to strengthen development, democracy, and accountability.*
- *Bringing about faster economic growth, higher investment, and greater labour absorption.*
- *Focusing on key capabilities of people and the state.*
- *Building a capable and developmental state.*
- *Encouraging strong leadership throughout society to work together to solve problems".*

In addition, like in many African countries, South Africa's history is dominated by colonialism, racism, apartheid, sexism, and many repulsive policies whose legacy remains severe. On that notion, a study by Gumede (2008) believes that due to the previously mentioned history, South Africans are confronted with serious economic, social, political, and even cultural challenges. Undoubtedly, societal challenges of this nature call for relevant and responsive public policies. On that notion, a study by Mkandawire (2004) advocates for the *necessity of research combining a diverse analysis strand.* In addition, the research is expected to encourage more explicit consideration in relation to policy implications for different political, economic, and social settings. It must be noted the terms political context and developmental context call for attention as narrated by Mkandawire (2001), cited in by Gumede (2008), noting that the terms 'political contexts' of social policies in 'developmental contexts', "*South Africa embarked on a concerted process of redressing the inherited imbalances, with the focus on dismantling apartheid social relations and creating a democratic society based on its constitutional principles of equity, non-racialism and non-sexism*". Over and above, the significant challenges facing the democratic government included rebuilding the institutional mechanisms and initiating and implementing legislation and policies that align with the Constitution to usher in a new era of a developmental state. Without a doubt, "*there is a need for context-sensitive research on the links between macroeconomic performance and the fundamental goal of raising human welfare. After that acknowledge the need to bridge the gap between theoretical and empirical findings and social policy making, between means and ends.*" Mkandawire (2001: iv). One cannot deny the fact that "*these massive, accumulated disadvantages (which includes representation of apartheid's legacy of inequality, poverty, and lack of national unity) have shaped the nature of South Africa's society* (Gumede, 2008: 10). Regardless, an opportunity still exists to address these accumulated disadvantages collectively sustainably.

## 5. FINDINGS AND DISCUSSION

The study's key finding indicates that a capacitated LED Forum management supported by the municipality is vital in identifying the assets and opportunities. However, it is essential to implement a stakeholder participation model as it will not only present an opportunity to identify meaningful roles and a chance for active participation of the stakeholders. Instead, it will address the communities' primary needs and ensure fair benefits sharing in its true sense.

In conjunction with the study's key finding, the paper demonstrates that community education, engagement, and involvement in sustainable socio-economic development projects from the initial stages play an important role in achieving the desired sustainable socioeconomic opportunity creation. The three tribes are in a position of Indigenous knowledge and skills through sustainable job opportunities and can improve their lives when involved. Therefore, the LED management Committee needs to consider the communities' views and advice from other stakeholders, such as academics and experts.

The findings of the chapter established that once the identification process is complete, it is important to package the identified opportunities /assets and link them with the place of interest/attraction such as Mariepskop Nature Reserve, Injaka Dam, Kruger National Park, Manyeleti Game Reserve, Bushbuckridge Nature Reserve, organised local traditional cuisine eateries, local curio shops, etc. To ensure the authenticity of products/ services as they reflect the region to the world, the involvement and participation of the custodians or owners of the cultures become vital in every stage of the process. As a result, CHT will fulfill its aim of creating sustainable development through job creation (tour guides, ambassadors, tourism monitors, CHT site managers, Indigenous cuisine eateries owners/chefs, etc.); transformation and community capacitation will also gradually take place, and benefit the previously disadvantage people in its true sense. Community development is a social process involving residents in activities designed to improve their quality of life. In the case of Bushbuckridge LED Forum, consideration of community engagement, consultation, and participation of the communities, especially in matters regarding unlocking tourism opportunities, is vital. The three tribes' participation should include identification of the products/services from all 3 BLM nodes, namely:

- South Node: geographically covers the Mkhuhlu area past Lily-dale till Kruger National Park (KNP).
- Mid-land Node: geographically covers from Dwarsloop area till Thulamahashe (Injaka Dam & Bushbuckridge Nature Reserve, etc.).
- North Node: geographically covers from Acornhoek area till Manyeleti (Mariepskop Nature Reserve, Manyeleti Nature Reserve /Game reserve).

Therefore, the study suggests recognition of the role of research and the diversity (uniqueness and the complexity of the communities during the process) that should be considered paramount. In addition, it must be understood that each node dominates a certain culture, language-wise. For instance, The Mapulana people speak the Sepulana language and have their own culture and traditions, such as celebrating Dikoma yearly. This event involves celebrating initiates coming back home after a successful initiation journey. The Tsonga people speak the Xitsonga language and have their own culture and traditions, such as hosting the Muchongolo festival yearly. This festival involves celebrating the Tsonga music, dances, cuisine, showcasing their traditional attire, etc. Therefore, the nomination of a committee for each node with traditional leaders' representation and each tribe's representation is highly suggested as it will assist with equal recognition and fair support and opportunities.

Figure 2 presents the possible sources of the CHT products /services (assets) that can be utilized in Bushbuckridge Municipality to unlock tourism activities/opportunities for socio-economic sustainable development and turn the area into an attractive and competitive municipality in the province and possibly in the country.

*Figure 2. Sources for cultural heritage tourism products/services (assets)*

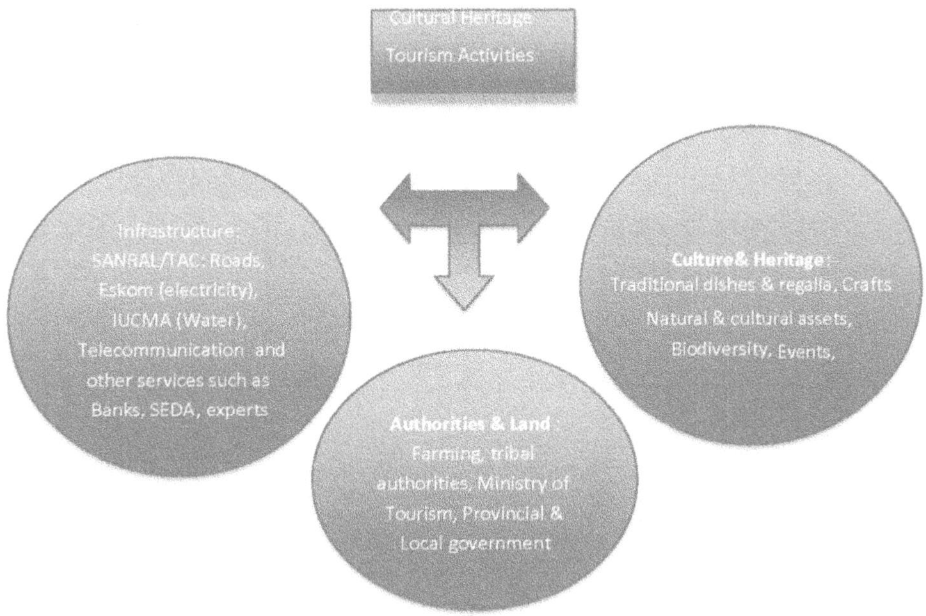


*Source: Researchers' own compilation (2023).*

In the case of BLM, the culture and heritage of the three tribes are vital. The cuisine, arts & crafts, traditional regalia/attire, language, story/customs & traditions, traditional events, etc., form part of the offerings to the tourists/travellers. These offerings will open Small and Medium Enterprises (SMEs) opportunities for locals. Natural & cultural assets such as Mariepskop, unique history, and Injaka dam. Biodiversity includes KNP, Bushbuckridge Nature Reserve, and Manyeleti. Obviously, these identified opportunities will require a piece of land, and it must be regulated and guided by policies and so forth. For instance, farmers will need a piece of land to plant indigenous ingredients and keep their livestock, which will be used by the SMMEs to prepare indigenous cuisine. Traditional authorities hold most of the land in the area, and the local people respect the traditional system. Therefore, the buy-in of the 10 traditional authorities and government support for the envisaged development is key. In addition, Infrastructure is key as proper roads granting access to the offering are required. Water, telecommunication, and electricity are crucial to tourist areas and SME operations. Obviously, other vital services required include banks and financial support, including experts such as academic instructions, SEDA, CIPC, etc., to guide and advise. Last, there is a need for a gap analysis method development to assist with quarterly performance assessment in all three nodes. Such analysis is crucial because it reveals where the business is (present state) and where it is expected to be (the target or desired state). A gap analysis is also known as a needs analysis, needs assessment, or need-gap analysis. The gap analysis will present a realistic diagnosis of each business unit from each node to determine whether business requirements or objectives are being met. In cases that are not met, steps to be taken to meet the requirements or the objectives should be determined.

*Figure 3. Gap analysis*

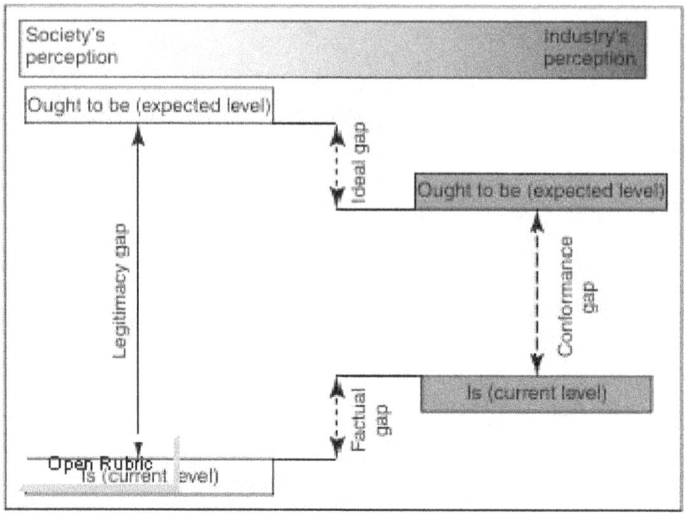


*Source: Panwar et al. (2012).*

Lastly, Mashego (2023), in her Dissertation, claims that in Bushbuckridge local Municipality, traditional leaders are only informed and consulted when the municipality is on the verge of executing a service delivery project in their areas. This claim presents an opportunity for the BLM through the LED Forum Committee to take advantage of a key resource that involves adopting a bottom-up strategy that adheres to Afrocentricity and inclusiveness.

## 6. CONCLUSION

The study's findings enlighten how an LED Forum Management Committee can utilise the identification of relevant CHT opportunities to unlock tourism activities for sustainable socio-economic development within their jurisdiction. Community participation, with traditional authorities and government support (Municipality), becomes key to the initiative's success.

Therefore, it cannot be denied that community engagement and participation come with their own challenges. However, greater sustainable benefits can be realised if managed properly. A stakeholder participation model is suggested as it will not only present an opportunity to identify meaningful roles and a chance for active participation of the stakeholders but also will ensure the preparation of a conducive environment that would attract the required resources and possibly yield results contributing to the realisation of fair benefits sharing in its true sense. The model's success depends on a stakeholder's positive attitude paired with formal & informal expertise in the field and team effort with a common goal, including resolving current burning issues if there are any. Linkage of attractions and local cultural & natural offerings from South to North (BLM - Nodes) for tourists to buy and enjoy the products and services is crucial. In addition, adopting a gap analysis model will assist with determining if each business unit of the nodes is meeting its objectives or requirements and act accordingly if not. Most importantly, the application of bottom-up strategy adhering to inclusive processes embracing Afrocentricity whereby local people & traditional leaders are involved from the initiation stage. Lastly, a capacitated LED Forum Management Committee is vital in identifying the assets and opportunities and developing the blueprint, as it can turn around the economy and positively impact the socioeconomic of the region/municipality.

## REFERENCES


Beyers, L. A., & Schutte, N. E. (2018). Guidelines for Improving Infrastructure Development in the Rural Communities of Bushbuckridge. *Studies of Tribes and Tribals*, *16*(1-2), 32–38. DOI: 10.31901/24566799.2018/16.1-2.367

Bushbuckridge Local Municipality. (2021) Local Economic Development Forum: Terms of Reference. Bushbuckridge LED Forum Launch, 10th -11th June 2021, Swadini Forever Resorts, Hoedspruit, South Africa.

Creswell, J. W., & Creswell, J. D. (2005). *Mixed methods research: Developments, debates, and dilemma*. Berrett-Koehler Publishers.

9. De Wet, S. (2018) "The basic needs theory for community development", *ResearchGate*, pp 1-14. DOI: DOI: 10.13140/RG.2.2.11882.98243

Department of Corporative Governance and Traditional Affairs. (2021). Local Economic Development (LED), [online] https://www.cogta.gov.za/index.php/local-economic-development-led/

Department of Provincial and Local Government of South Africa and Business Trsut. (2007) Nodal Economic Profiling Project Bushbuckridge Mpumalanga, [online] http://www.btrust.org.za/library/assets/uploads/documents/1_CIPPN_Bushbuckridge%20profile.PDF

Department of the Presidency Republic of South Africa. (2012) National Development Plan 2030, [online] https://www.gov.za/sites/default/files/Executive%20Summary-NDP%202030%20-%20Our%20future%20-%20make%20it%20work.pdf / https://www.gov.za/issues/national-development-plan-2030

Department of Tourism. (2011) National Tourism Sector Strategy 2016-2026. [online] www.gov.za/ites/default/files/National%20Tourism%20Sector%20Strategy%20NTSS%202016-2026.pdf

Department of Tourism. (2012) National Heritage and Cultural Tourism Strategy, [online] https://www.tourism.gov.za/AboutNDT/Branches1/domestic/Documents/National%20Heritage%20and%20Cultural%20Tourism%20Strategy.pdf

Gumede, V. (2008) "Public policy making in a post-apartheid South Africa: a preliminary perspective", *Africanus*, Vol 38, No. 2, pp 7-23, [online] https://www.vusigumede.com/content/academic%20papers/Public%20policy%20making%20(Journal%20of%20Development%20Studies%20paper,%2038,%202,%20pp%207-23).pdf

Keitumetse, S. O. (2014). Cultural Resource as Sustainability Enablers: Towards a Community-Based Cultural Heritage Resources Management (COBACHREM) Model. *Sustainability (Basel)*, *6*(1), 70–85. DOI: 10.3390/su6010070

Koma, S. B. (2012) "Local economic development in South Africa - Policy implications ", *African Journal of Public Affairs,* Vol 5, No. 3, pp 125-140, [online] https://repository.up.ac.za/bitstream/handle/2263/31727/Koma_Local%282012%29.pdf?isAllowed=y&sequence=1

*Kurin,R.(2004) "Safeguarding Intangible Cultural Heritage in the 2003 UNESCO Convention: a critical appraisal", .* Museum international, Vol 56, No. 1-2, pp 66-77, [online] .DOI: 10.1111/j.1350-0775.2004.00459.x

Lopez-Guzman, T. & Santa-Cruz, F.G. (2016) "International tourism and the UNESCO category of intangible cultural heritage", *International Journal of Culture, Tourism and Hospitality Research,* Vol 10, No. 3, pp 310-322, [online] .DOI: 10.1108/IJCTHR-03-2015-0025

Mashego, P. S. (2023) "Investigating Traditional leaders' engagement in the integrated development planning and implementation processes in Bushbuckridge local Municipality" (Master's thesis, University of Johannesburg (South Africa).

Mkandawire, T. (2001). *Social policy in a development context. Social Policy and Development Programme Paper 7.* United Nations Research Institute for Social Development.

Mkandawire, T. (2004). *Social policy in a development context.* ResearchGate., DOI: 10.1057/9780230523975

National Development Plan 2030. (2013) Executive Summary - Our future - make it work, [online] https://static.pmg.org.za/130917ndp.pdf

Ndoro, W. (2015) "World Heritage Sites in Africa: what are the benefits of nomination and inscription?". *A companion to heritage studies,* pp 392-409. DOI: 10.1002/9781118486634.ch27

Panwar, R., Hansen, E., & Kozak, R. (2012). Evaluating social and environmental issues by integrating the legitimacy gap with expectational gaps: An empirical assessment of the forest industry. *Business & Society, 53*(6), 853–875. DOI: 10.1177/0007650312438884

Prideaux, B., Timothy, D. J., & Chon, K. (2008). *Themes in Cultural and Heritage Tourism in the Asian Pacific Region.* Routledge.

Ruhanen, L., & Whitford, M. (2021). Cultural heritage and Indigenous tourism. In *Indigenous heritage* (pp. 1–13). Routledge. DOI: 10.4324/9781003142997-1

Shabalala, L. P., & Ezeuduji, I. O. (2022) "Community Involvement and participation in Sustainable Development of Cultural Heritage Tourism: A case from South Africa". Evangelos Christou & Anestis Fotiadis (Eds). Reviving tourism, in the post pandemic era. The School of Economics and Business, International Hellenic Univerity, Greece. DOI: DOI: 10.5281/zenodo.6428590

The Free Encyclopaedia. (2022) Bushbuckridge Local Municipality, [online] https://en.wikipedia.org/wiki/Bushbuckridge_Local_Municipality

The Local Government Handbook. South Africa. (2015) " A complete guide to municipalities in South Africa", 5th Ed, Yes!Media: Mowbray. ISSN: 2220-5179, [online] https://issuu.com/yesmedia/docs/lgh2015?e=5245023%2F11022032

The White Paper on Local Government – South African Government. (1998), [online] https://www.gov.za/sites/default/files/gcis_document/201409/whitepaper0.pdf

UNESCO. (2007). UNESCO-EIIHCAP regional meeting. In *Safeguarding Intangible Heritage and Sustainable Cultural Tourism: Opportunities and Challenges*. UNESCO.

United Nations. (2015) Transforming our world: the 2030 Agenda for Sustainable Development, [online] https://sustainabledevelopment.un.org/content/documents/21252030%20Agenda%20for%20Sustainable%20Development%20web.pdf

University of Victoria research groups. (2012) Complexity Science in brief, [online] https://www.uvic.ca/research/groups/cphfri/assets/doc/Complexity_science_in _brief.pdf

# Chapter 9
# The Role of Gastronomic Tourism as a Sustainable Territorial Development Strategy

**Cristina Barzallo-Neira**
https://orcid.org/0000-0002-3770-3004
*University of Cuenca, Ecuador*

**Juan Ignacio Pulido-Fernández**
*Universidad de Jaén, Spain*

## ABSTRACT

*Gastronomic tourism has grown significantly in recent years, acquiring interesting relevance due to its potential for enhancing endogenous resources in the destinations where it develops, which stimulates the local economy and promotes sustainable development. Based on the results of a survey conducted with 421 international gastronomic tourists, this chapter demonstrates that the expectations and level of satisfaction of gastronomic tourists with the experiences they enjoy during their trip influence their willingness to purchase (or recommend) a quality-certified gastronomic product, as well as their average daily expenditure during their stay at the destination. The results obtained are relevant for appraising the role of gastronomic tourism as a sustainable territorial development strategy.*

## 1 INTRODUCTION

Gastronomic tourism is positioned as one of the most demanded and valued types of travel by tourists, and it currently stands as a notable force in driving tourist movement. It has experienced significant growth in the tourism industry due to the universal enjoyment of gastronomy by visitors, who make it a significant activity in the global tourism industry.

This typology, derived from cultural tourism, focuses on the traditions and food practices of each territory. Its origin is linked to the development of wine tourism in Europe during the 20th century, while its consolidation in the 1990s was favored by globalization, the rise of culinary guides such as Michelin

DOI: 10.4018/979-8-3693-7081-0.ch009

and the growing media coverage of cuisine. In 2020, gastronomic tourism generated an estimated income of 237.7 billion dollars globally, with an annual growth projection of 14.2% until 2028 (Thongkaw et al., 2024), which shows its relevance in the tourist industry. Currently, gastronomic tourism transcends sensory enjoyment and is positioned as a strategic axis of sustainable tourism, by promoting food heritage, contributing to local development and consolidating itself as a key to the positive transformation of territories (Ferrari et al., 2022).

Its influence on travelers' decisions and its substantial contribution to the economic development of different regions has been demonstrated in various scientific studies (Fusté-Forné et al. 2021; Kokkranikal & Carabelli 2024; Rachão et al. 2023; Soonsan et al. 2023), which highlights its dynamism and the ease that gastronomic tourism has to complement other types of tourism in any territory. In the same way, its direct relationship with the principles of sustainable tourism, as well as with the Sustainable Development Goals (SDGs), establishes the need to deepen the analysis of gastronomic tourism's role as a tool for sustainable territorial development, considering that its practice encourages the intake of local products, traditional cuisine, the rational use of resources, the reduction of waste, residues, and pollutant emissions, etc.

In this context, activities that promote the local and sustainable economy of destinations through the consumption of locally sourced food, such as Km 0 experiences, those associated with products with Geographical Indications of Origin, and in general, activities that offer a taste of the local culture, are of great interest to the demand of gastronomic tourism.

From a demand perspective, gastronomic tourism encompasses an interesting array of goods and services that tourists are willing to acquire in a particular destination. Similar to other forms of tourism, it is influenced by factors such as expectations, satisfaction levels, purchasing power, time availability, and the tourist's length of stay at the destination. Paying attention to these factors allows for identifying the territory's potential and determining its influence on local development and growth opportunities for the community as a whole.

Based on the results of a survey conducted with 421 international gastronomic tourists, this chapter aims to understand to what extent tourists' expectations and satisfaction with the experiences they enjoy during their trip influence their willingness to purchase (or recommend) a quality-certified gastronomic product (e.g., olive oil, wine, ham, cheese) for later consumption at home, as well as their average daily expenditure during their stay at the destination.

The results of this research are relevant for assessing to what extent gastronomic tourism can be used as a sustainable territorial development strategy. The conclusions obtained will be very important for strengthening the strategies of gastronomic tourist destinations, aiming to enhance the value of their endogenous resources and reinforce their development, therefore contributing to the creation of opportunities in these territories without losing the essence of the destinations.

To achieve the stated objective, and after conducting a deep review of the scientific literature on the subject, which is summarized in the subsequent section, the following hypothesis is proposed: the expectations and level of satisfaction of gastronomic tourists are positively related to their willingness to purchase quality-sealed gastronomic products and their average daily spending.

## 2 LITERATURE REVIEW

Currently, the relationship between sustainability and gastronomic tourism stands out as an innovative topic in scientific research due to its academic, economic, and environmental importance. In general, tourism practices oriented towards sustainable territorial development are of high interest worldwide, since they offer viable solutions to the threats of globalization.

Gastronomic tourism, characterized by the search for authentic experiences and the appreciation of local culture (Berbel-Pineda et al. 2019; Harrington & Ottenbacher 2010), through the use of endogenous territorial resources—such as agricultural richness, culinary traditions, and native products, which play a prominent role in its configuration—(Björk & Kauppinen-Räisänen 2016; Kalpidis et al. 2024; Şengül et al. 2024a) offers an authentic experience that attracts tourists and directly influences their expectations and satisfaction levels (Liu et al. 2024; Zou et al. 2024).

Expectations, influenced by factors such as the destination's reputation, the perceived quality of local products, and the authenticity of the offer, largely determine visitors' initial perceptions (Akdag et al. 2018; Akyürek 2023). Satisfaction, in turn, is closely related with the destination's ability to meet or exceed those expectations (Liu et al. 2024; Zou et al. 2024) and impacts tourist loyalty and their willingness to recommend the destination (Correia et al. 2020; Sutiadiningsih et al. 2024). Existing studies on this relationship emphasize that a high level of satisfaction is associated with a greater tendency to purchase local products (Akdag et al. 2018; Çakir Keleş 2021) and to increase spending at the destination (Demirel & Tekeli 2022; Lima et al. 2024; Zou et al. 2024), which, in turn, highlights the importance of an offer that combines authenticity, quality, and memorable experiences.

Along the same lines, existing studies emphasize the value that gastronomic tourists place on the quality and uniqueness of local products (Akdag et al. 2018; Çakir Keleş 2021; Demirel & Tekeli 2022; Lima et al. 2024). However, scientific literature has not yet analyzed the willingness of gastronomic tourists to acquire featured products nor the increase in average spending when it comes to quality-certified products—a gap in the research. It is precisely the link between the authenticity of endogenous resources and tourist satisfaction that strengthens a destination's ability to boost its economy through tourism practices and their added value.

Regarding tourist spending, studies repeatedly highlight the trend of gastronomic tourism to generate significant economic impact on destinations (Berbel-Pineda et al. 2019; Diaconescu et al. 2016; Dorta-Afonso & Padrón-Ávila 2021; Mitchell & Hall 2003), indicating that gastronomic tourists show higher daily spending compared to other segments due to their interest in authentic local products, high-quality culinary experiences (Demirel & Tekeli 2022; Zhong et al. 2024), and experiences that promote sustainability (Şengül et al. 2024b; Sinha & Haluwalia 2024).

Concerning gastronomic products with quality certifications, various studies highlight the advantages they offer to tourist destinations, such as guaranteeing authenticity and origin (Duque et al. 2023; Getz & Robinson 2014), which translates into consumer trust and enhances the perception of value. These products also guarantee a high-quality gastronomic experience (Kivela & Crotts 2006; Millan et al. 2021) and contribute to greater satisfaction (Akdag et al. 2018; Millan et al. 2021). As they are associated with high production standards, they strengthen the identity of the destination and promote recognition of its traditions and culture. Fewer studies also refer to the added value provided by quality certifications, generally indicating that they stimulate tourist spending among travelers willing to invest in products that guarantee quality and sustainability (Armesto López & Gómez Martín 2004; Thees & Pechlaner 2019; Zhong et al. 2024).

Finally, concerning the types of research conducted on the subject, it is important to note that both qualitative and quantitative approaches are used to demonstrate that tourists who value authenticity in gastronomy tend to perceive destinations that promote endogenous development as more attractive (Akdag et al. 2018; Cunha et al. 2019; Duque et al. 2023; Sgroi 2021; Thees & Pechlaner 2019). These studies are based on the idea of a direct connection between visitors and local products, where spending contributes to cultural preservation and economic strengthening of the destination.

# 3 METHODOLOGY

## 3.1. Questionnaire and Survey

The research design incorporated both quantitative and qualitative elements to understand the sustainable behavior of gastronomic tourists. The methodology implemented was based on meticulous planning and selection of variables from the field of study, allowing for a comprehensive analysis and systematic and rigorous information processing.

A structured questionnaire was designed using Google Forms (see attached in Annex 1), including closed-ended questions to collect data on the sustainable behavior of gastronomic tourists, along with several open-ended questions to explore in detail the motivations and expectations of the demand. The questionnaire consisted of 32 questions, 25 of which were aimed at understanding behavior, spending disposition, expectations, and experiences of the respondents, while the remaining questions allowed for the creation of a sociodemographic profile of the participants.

Table 1 contains the technical details of the survey. Due to the impossibility of identifying the target population, due to a lack of adequate statistical information, a simple random sampling was conducted using 421 valid surveys.

*Table 1. Technical details of the survey*

| **Study population** | **Gastronomic tourism demand (infinite population)** |
|---|---|
| **Scope** | International |
| **Survey type** | Semi-structured questionnaire via Google Forms |
| **Sample size** | 421 valid surveys |
| **Sampling error** | 4.8% |
| **Confidence level** | 95% |
| **Survey period** | October to December 2023 |

Source: Own elaboration.

At first glance, the sample might seem limited and not representative of the entire population to be analyzed (the demand for gastronomic tourism). However, two points justify the opposite. Firstly, as detailed later, the questionnaire was applied exclusively to gastronomic tourists, that is tourists whose primary motivation for visiting a destination is to enjoy its gastronomy; so, while the sample is not large, it is indeed significant. Secondly, the spatial distribution of responses ensures representation from gastronomic tourists worldwide. In fact, for the distribution of the questionnaire, the regional division used by the World Tourism Organization was considered, resulting in the final distribution of responses shown in Table 6. In conclusion, while it is not certain that the sample is fully representative, there is a reasonable probability of representativeness.

Prior to its dissemination, the survey was validated by six experts in the field to improve, complement, and corroborate its final content. It was then distributed via email and promoted by various gastronomic tourism associations (World Food Travel Association, ITER VITIS Europe, International Wine Tourism Association, UNESCO Creative Cities Network for Gastronomy, among others) with the goal of reaching the largest possible number of international gastronomic tourists.

It is important to note that the questionnaire was not administered indiscriminately to any international tourists, only to later identify those with a gastronomic tourist profile. Instead, from the beginning, this specific profile was sought. Accordingly, the questionnaire was distributed through entities directly linked to this profile to ensure the sample was as representative as possible of the target population. This was confirmed by the response to the first question in the questionnaire: 96.9% expressed their interest in learning about the gastronomy of destinations during their vacation travels.

The online survey was distributed via email and promoted by associations of gastronomic tourism in various places (World Food Travel Association, ITER VITIS Europe, International Wine Tourism Association, UNESCO Creative Cities Network for Gastronomy, among others) to reach international gastronomic travelers.

Efforts were made to maximize participation and diversity in the sample, and no incentives were offered for completing the survey. The total number of questionnaires received exceeded the required sample size. The use of all the responses collected in the study is justified by the integrity and representativeness of the data, as well as the methodology employed in their collection. This ensured the capture of a diversity of perspectives, enhancing the validity and reliability of the results, minimizing selection bias, and maximizing the value of the resources invested in data collection.

The development of the research complies with ethical standards, ensuring the confidentiality and anonymity of the participants. Overall, it constitutes a complete and reliable framework for identifying a global profile of gastronomic tourists.

## 3.2. Methodological Tools

To address the proposed research, questions 2, 22, 23, and 25 from the questionnaire were used. These questions refer to the following aspects:

P2: To what extent does the gastronomic offer influence your choice of a destination to visit? (Likert scale: 1 - does not influence at all; 7 - influences greatly)
P22: In general, what is your level of satisfaction with the gastronomic tourism experiences you have recently enjoyed? (Likert scale: 1 - not satisfied at all; 7 - completely satisfied)
P23: If during your trips you have tasted any gastronomic product with quality seals (olive oils, wines, ham, cheese, etc.), what is the likelihood that you would buy (or recommend) it for consumption at home? (Likert scale: 1 - no likelihood; 7 - very likely)
P25: What is your average daily spending on a gastronomic tourism trip? (Ordinal scale: <50€; 50-100€; 100-200€; >200€)

The tools used to perform the statistical analysis were Spearman's rank correlation coefficient and two independent ordinal logistic regression models. The Spearman's rank correlation coefficient is a non-parametric measure of the rank rating (statistical dependence of the ranking between two variables). It is mainly used for data analysis and measures the strength and direction of the association between two ranked variables. Logistic regression is also a data analysis technique used to find the relationships between two data factors, in order to subsequently predict the value of one of those factors calculated on the other. It is used to determine a dependent variable that can only have two outcomes, that is, in situations where the outcome is binary. The model may have one or more independent variables on which it depends.

Regarding the methodological tools used, in a first step, Spearman's correlation analysis was applied—a non-parametric technique that measures the strength and direction of the association between two variables. This technique is especially useful in studies like this, where the data do not follow a normal distribution.

*Table 2. Spearman's correlation coefficients for questions 2, 22, 23, and 25*

| | P23 | P25 |
|---|---|---|
| P2 | 0.280** | 0.241** |
| P22 | 0.504** | 0.144** |

** p < 0.01; *p < 0.05

Source: Own elaboration.

In Table 2, Spearman's correlation coefficients are shown. It is important to notice that P22 shows a high and significant correlation with P23 (0.504**), although not as much with P25. In the case of P2, the correlations are lower and less significant, although still positive and statistically significant, which could indicate relevant patterns for further analysis.

*Table 3. Spearman correlation coefficients for sociodemographic questions*

| | P1 | P3 | P4 | P5 | P6 | P7 |
|---|---|---|---|---|---|---|
| P2 | 0.108* | 0.098* | 0.125* | 0.036 | 0.058 | 0.158** |
| P22 | -0.164** | 0.255** | 0.002 | 0.137** | 0.132** | 0.224** |
| P23 | -0.141** | 0.225** | 0.045 | 0.205** | 0.211** | 0.272** |
| P25 | -0.031 | 0.188** | -0.058 | 0.169** | 0.148** | 0.300** |

** p < 0.01; *p < 0.05

Source: Own elaboration.

Table 3 shows Spearman's correlation coefficients between the sociodemographic questions and questions 2, 22, 23, and 25. Regarding nationality (P1), there is a general trend toward negative correlations with several items on the scale. Variables P22, P23, and P25 show significant negative correlations with nationality, which suggests that respondents of different nationalities may score differently on these items.

Regarding age (P3), the results show significant positive correlations with P22 and P23, indicating that older respondents tend to score higher on these items. Gender (P4), on the other hand, shows a moderate influence on the evaluated items, with positive correlations.

In the case of profession-occupation (P5), significant positive correlations were identified for items P22, P23, and P25, which highlights that specific occupations tend to correlate positively with higher scores on these items. This finding suggests that occupation can considerably influence the respondents' evaluations.

The level of education (P6) also shows significant positive correlations with items P22, P23, and P25. This indicates that a higher level of education tends to be associated with higher scores on these items.

Finally, regarding monthly net income (P7), significant positive correlations are observed with items P2, P22, P23, and P25. This indicates that respondents with higher incomes tend to score higher on these items. The positive correlation with P25 is particularly strong, suggesting that income is strongly associated with higher scores on this item.

Therefore, the results presented in Table 3 show that both education level and income have a significant positive association with several dimensions of the evaluated items, while nationality and gender show more varied relationships. Correlations with age and occupation also reveal important association patterns. These findings can provide useful insights into how demographic and socioeconomic characteristics relate to the evaluations of the different items under study.

In a second step, two independent ordinal logistic regression models are proposed, which vary according to the context of the selected dependent variable:

Model 1: $\text{Logit}(Y=i) = \beta 0i + \beta 1 \times P2 + \beta 2 \times P22 + \epsilon i$

Model 2: $\text{Logit}(Y=i) = \beta 0i + \beta 1 \times P2 + \epsilon i$

From one perspective, question 23 from the questionnaire is used as the dependent variable (model 1). On the other hand, question 25 is used as the dependent variable (model 2). It is important to mention that both P23 and P25 have been identified as actions carried out by gastronomic tourists, which justify whether they are willing to purchase quality-sealed gastronomic products and whether they have higher daily average spending.

Finally, it should be noted that the development of this research complies with ethical standards, ensuring the confidentiality and anonymity of the participants. Overall, it constitutes a complete and reliable framework for identifying a global profile of gastronomic tourists.

## 4 RESULTS

### 4.1 Descriptive Analysis

This section presents a descriptive analysis of the variables under study and a sociodemographic characterization of the sample analyzed. Table 4 shows the descriptive statistics for questions 2, 22, 23, and 25.

*Table 4. Descriptive statistics for questions 2, 22, 23, and 25*

| | Mean | Media | Mode | Standard Deviation | Skewness | Kurtosis | Minimum | Maximum |
|---|---|---|---|---|---|---|---|---|
| **P2** | 4.95 | 5.00 | 5 | 1.504 | -0.472 | -0.365 | 1 | 7 |
| **P22** | 5.39 | 6.00 | 6 | 1.159 | -0.902 | 1.390 | 1 | 7 |
| **P23** | 5.39 | 6.00 | 6 | 1.479 | -1.135 | 0.962 | 1 | 7 |
| **P25** | 1.97 | 2.00 | 2 | 1.241 | 0.162 | -0.774 | 0 | 4 |

Source: Own elaboration.

From the analysis of the results, it can be concluded that respondents show a significant inclination towards purchasing or recommending gastronomic products with a quality seal (such as olive oils, wines, ham, cheese, etc.). Figure 1 shows that most respondents (79%) expressed a moderate to very high likelihood, with 35% rating their likelihood as "Very high" and 23% as "Very probable." These findings suggest a high level of confidence and appreciation for quality-sealed gastronomic products, representing significant potential for the growth of gastronomic tourism.

From an economic perspective, this behavior suggests a strong influence, as it encourages demand for high-quality products while stimulating regional production and trade. From a tourism perspective, this result highlights the role of gastronomic tourism in diversifying offerings and creating employment in sectors related to gastronomy and agriculture.

*Figure 1. Probability of buying or recommending quality-sealed gastronomic products*

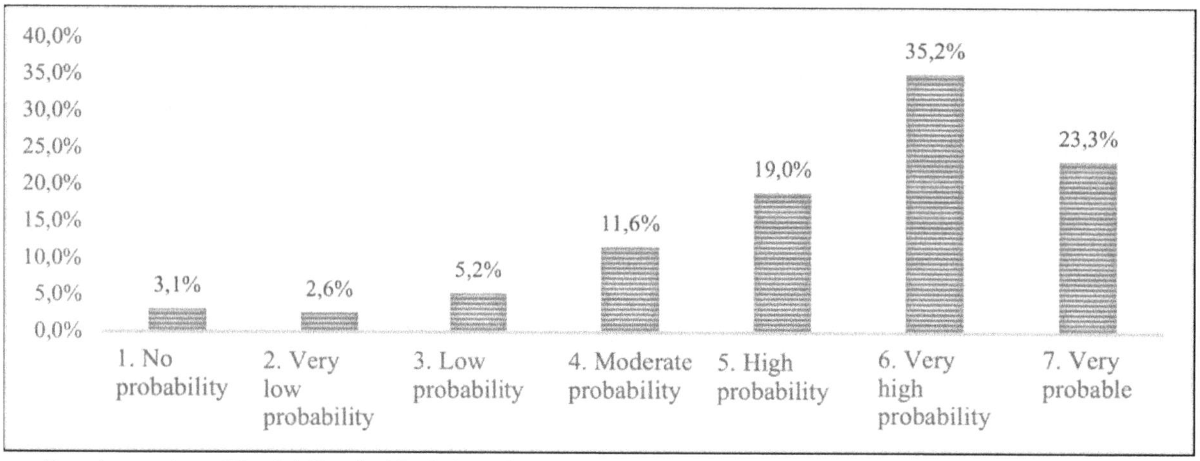


*Note: Average (out of 7) = 5.4 / Standard Deviation = 1.48*
*Source: Own elaboration.*

On the other hand, regarding the second issue analyzed (Table 5), the average daily spending for a gastronomic tourism trip varies significantly across different monetary ranges. The data shows that most respondents (almost 40%) spend between 30€ and 100€ per day on gastronomic experiences, indicating a preference for moderate spending options. However, a significant portion of respondents is also willing to spend more, with 15% assigning between 100€ and 200€ daily, and a minority spending less than 30€ or more than 200€ per day.

*Table 5. Average daily spending on a gastronomic tourism trip*

| Daily Average Spending | % |
|---|---|
| ≤€30 | 11.40 |
| €30 - €50 | 14.25 |
| €50 - €75 | 4.28 |
| €75 - €100 | 14.01 |
| €100 - €150 | 6.65 |
| €150 - €200 | 5.46 |
| €200 - €300 | 2.85 |
| €300 - €500 | 2.61 |
| Más de €500 | 0.71 |

Source: Own elaboration.

The sociodemographic characteristics of the survey (Table 6) indicate that the sample was divided between 57.72% women and 42.28% men. In terms of age, the majority group in the sample is 41-56 years old (41.09%), although two other groups also have significant representation: 25-40 years old (21.14%) and 57-75 years old (20.19%), this shows that interest in gastronomic tourism is not limited to a specific age group. Regarding nationality, the sample is well distributed across different world regions, with Europeans (24.70%) and Americans (22.10%) having the largest representation. Moreover, the majority of respondents hold high educational levels, with a master's degree being the most common qualification (42.04%). Regarding occupation, middle management employees and self-employed professionals are the most representative, each making up about 22%, followed by students at 19.71%. Lastly, in terms of monthly net income, the most represented group earns 3,000€ or more per month (22.80%), followed by those earning 2,100-3,000€ (18.05%).

*Table 6. Description of the variables related to the characteristics of the demand for gastronomic tourism*

| Gender | % | Nationality | % |
|---|---|---|---|
| Female | 57.72 | Africa | 8.08 |
| Male | 42.28 | Americas | 22.10 |
| | | South Asia | 15.91 |
| **Age** | % | East Asia & Pacific | 17.10 |
| 18-24 years | 17.34 | Europe | 24.70 |
| 25-40 years | 21.14 | Middle East | 12.11 |
| 41-56 years | 41.09 | | |
| 57-75 years | 20.19 | **Profession /Occupation** | % |
| 76-91 years | 0.24 | Businessman - High Command | 13.54 |
| | | Employee - Middle management | 22.33 |
| **Monthly Net Income** | % | Employee – Operator | 8.79 |
| < 600€ | 16.15 | Other | 10.21 |
| 600€ - 900€ | 7.60 | Professional free practice | 21.85 |

continued on following page

*Table 6. Continued*

| Gender | % | Nationality | % |
|---|---|---|---|
| 900€ - 1.200€ | 7.13 | Retired | 3.56 |
| 1.200€ - 1.500€ | 8.31 | Student | 19.71 |
| 1.500€ - 1.800€ | 8.08 | | |
| 1.800€ - 2.100€ | 11.88 | **Level of education** | % |
| 2.100€ - 3.000€ | 18.05 | Doctorate degree | 18.53 |
| 3.000€ or more | 22.80 | High school | 14.73 |
| | | Master's degree | 42.04 |
| | | Undergraduate degree | 24.70 |

Source: Own elaboration.

## 4.2 Hypothesis Testing

Based on the Spearman correlations obtained, Model 1 is proposed, with P23 as the dependent variable and P2 + P22 as independent variables. Table 7 presents the fit indices of this model.

*Table 7. Model 1 fit indices*

| Index | Value |
|---|---|
| Chi-square | 166.439 ($p < 0.05$) |
| AIC | 1231.555 |
| BIC | 1263.896 |
| McFadden's $R^2$ | 0.254 |
| Residual Deviance | 1215.555 ($p > 0.05$) |

Source: Own elaboration.

Model 1 shows a significant and appropriate fit to the data. Although the pseudo R-squared value is not extremely high, it indicates that the model is reasonably capable of explaining the variability in the dependent variable, with a 25.4%. The model improves significantly with the inclusion of the predictor variables, and the non-significant residual deviance suggests a good fit to the observed data.

The coefficients of Model 1, shown in Table 8, indicate the magnitude and direction of the influence of each independent variable on the likelihood that tourists will purchase or recommend quality-sealed gastronomic products, thus favoring sustainable territorial development.

*Table 8. Coefficients of model 1*

| Ítem | Estimate | Standard Error | t-value | p-value |
|---|---|---|---|---|
| P2 | 0.234 | 0.063 | 3.72 | 0.000** |
| P22 | 0.967 | 0.092 | 10.46 | 0.000** |
| Intercept 1 | 2.046 | 0.527 | 3.882 | 0.000** |
| Intercept 2 | 2.783 | 0.503 | 5.538 | 0.000** |
| Intercept 3 | 3.671 | 0.503 | 7.302 | 0.000** |
| Intercept 4 | 4.801 | 0.522 | 9.199 | 0.000** |
| Intercept 5 | 5.992 | 0.551 | 10.869 | 0.000** |
| Intercept 6 | 7.918 | 0.598 | 13.240 | 0.000** |

* p < 0,05; ** p < 0,01
Source: Own elaboration.

The coefficient table of Model 1 (Table 8) reveals the behavior of gastronomic tourists:

- **P2**: The estimate for P2, which measures the extent to which the gastronomic offer influences the choice of destination, is 0.234. With a p-value of 0.000, this coefficient is statistically significant. This suggests that the greater the influence of the gastronomic offer on the choice of destination, the higher the likelihood that gastronomic tourists will purchase quality-sealed gastronomic products. In other words, the more the gastronomic offer influences the choice of destination, the more likely it is that gastronomic tourists will exhibit attitudes that favor sustainable territorial development.
- **P22**: The coefficient for P22, which measures the level of satisfaction with gastronomic tourism experiences, is 0.967 with a p-value of 0.000. This coefficient is highly significant and positive, indicating that greater satisfaction with gastronomic tourism experiences is strongly associated with the willingness of gastronomic tourists to purchase quality-sealed gastronomic products. Tourists who are more satisfied with their gastronomic experiences are more likely to buy quality-sealed products.
- **Intercepts**: The intercepts are statistically significant and represent the cut-off points between the ordinal categories of willingness to buy quality-sealed gastronomic products (P23). The increasing values of the intercepts reflect the barriers that gastronomic tourists must overcome to move from one category of willingness to the next. The results indicate that the willingness categories are clearly differentiated and that the model effectively captures the differences between these categories.

Model 1 shows a reasonable fit, with a moderate ability to explain how gastronomic tourists' expectations and satisfaction levels influence their willingness to purchase quality-sealed gastronomic products. The coefficients of P2 and P22 are significant and positive, indicating that both the influence of the gastronomic offer on the choice of destination and the satisfaction with gastronomic experiences are positively related to the willingness to purchase quality-sealed gastronomic products, which ultimately shows the potential of gastronomic tourism as a strategy for sustainable territorial development. The intercepts confirm that the perception categories are clearly differentiated in the model.

From another perspective, Model 2 is proposed with P25 as the dependent variable and P2 as the independent variable. Table 9 shows the fit indices of this model.

*Table 9. Model 2 fit indices*

| Index | Value |
|---|---|
| Chi-square | 32.254 ($p < 0.05$) |
| AIC | 1247.488 |
| BIC | 1267.701 |
| McFadden's $R^2$ | 0.252 |
| Residual Deviance | 1237.488 ($p > 0.05$) |

Source: Own elaboration.

Model 2 also shows a significant and appropriate fit to the data, presenting very similar values to Model 1. Consequently, the model is reasonably capable of explaining the variability in the dependent variable, with a 25.2%. The model improves significantly with the inclusion of the predictor variable, and the non-significant residual deviance suggests a good fit to the observed data.

The coefficients of Model 2, shown in Table 10, indicate the magnitude and direction of the influence of each independent variable on the likelihood that tourists will have a higher or lower daily average spending on a gastronomic tourism trip; favoring therefore, territorial development.

*Table 10. Coefficients of Model 2*

| Item | Estimate | Standard Error | t-value | p-value |
|---|---|---|---|---|
| P2 | 0.330 | 0.062 | 5.304 | 0.000** |
| Intercept 1 | -0.313 | 0.318 | -0.985 | 0.325 |
| Intercept 2 | 0.925 | 0.315 | 2.9407 | 0.003** |
| Intercept 3 | 2.631 | 0.338 | 7.773 | 0.000** |
| Intercept 4 | 3.281 | 0.352 | 9.333 | 0.000** |

* $p < 0,05$; ** $p < 0,01$
Source: Own elaboration.

The coefficient table of Model 2 (Table 10) reveals the behavior of gastronomic tourists:

- **P2**: The estimate for P2, which measures the influence of the gastronomic offer on the choice of destination, is 0.330 with a p-value of 0.000. This coefficient is statistically significant and positive, indicating that a greater influence of the gastronomic offer is associated with higher daily average spending on gastronomic tourism (P25). In other words, when the gastronomic offer has more influence on the travel decision, the average daily spending on gastronomic tourism tends to be higher.
- **Intercepts**: The intercepts reflect the cut-off points between the ordinal categories of the dependent variable P25. The first intercept is not significant, indicating that there is no statistically significant barrier in the transition between the first category and the second category of average

daily spending. This makes sense, since the first category of this variable is the lack of response. Therefore, the results indicate that the categories are clearly differentiated, and the model effectively captures the differences between these categories.

Model 2 shows a reasonable fit, with a moderate ability to explain how the influence of the gastronomic offer (P2) relates to average daily spending on gastronomic tourism (P25). The coefficient for P2 is significantly positive, suggesting that the greater the influence of the gastronomic offer on the choice of destination, the higher the average daily spending on gastronomic tourism.

In summary, both models provide evidence that the expectations and satisfaction levels of gastronomic tourists are positively related to their willingness to purchase quality-sealed gastronomic products and their average daily spending—two key aspects of sustainable territorial development. The results of Model 1 reinforce the original hypothesis, while those of Model 2 highlight the economic importance of these attitudes. This suggests that a positive assessment of the gastronomic offer has implications both on the gastronomic tourist's willingness to purchase quality-sealed products and on their spending behavior, clearly indicating a strong relationship between the attitudes of gastronomic tourists and their contribution to sustainable territorial development.

The findings obtained demonstrate that gastronomic tourism constitutes an essential instrument for sustainable territorial development, by allowing the valorization of endogenous resources and highlighting the uniqueness of each territory. This approach also promotes the recognition of local agri-food production, strengthens territorial economies by promoting marketing circuits and sustainable practices, while at the same time giving prominence and empowerment to farmers, by recognizing their products as basic components of the local heritage. Gastronomic tourism is firmly aligned with the principles of sustainability.

## 5 DISCUSSION

Unlike previous studies, this research establishes the existence of a direct correlation between the expectations and satisfaction levels of gastronomic tourists and their willingness to purchase (or recommend) quality-sealed gastronomic products, as well as their average daily spending at the destination.

The analysis conducted in this chapter reveals that when expectations are met, or better yet, exceeded, gastronomic tourists are more willing to acquire local products with quality seals. This finding confirms results obtained by other researchers (Akdag et al. 2018; Armesto López & Gómez Martín 2004; Dancausa-Millán et al. 2022) regarding the role played by quality seals in generating trust and enhancing the perceived value of products, promoting a positive cycle of investment and consumption.

Previous studies on the subject (Berbel-Pineda et al. 2019; Correia et al. 2020; Liu et al. 2024) have focused on the economic impact generated by the tourist experience and the general spending behavior of visitors. Most of them emphasize that satisfied tourists become promoters of the destination, amplifying its impact through recommendations on social media and other channels (Getz & Robinson 2014; Sutiadiningsih et al. 2024). Moreover, they point out that the success of the economic impact depends on effective cooperation between public and private actors (Diaconescu et al. 2016; Đurkin Badurina et al. 2023; Kalpidis et al. 2024) and on investment in infrastructure, training, and promotion of local products (Şengül et al. 2024a; Zhu & Yasami 2021).

These ideas are interesting for confirming the role of gastronomic tourism as a strategy for sustainable territorial development. However, they do not allow for concrete statements about spending, as suggested by this research, which shows that the increase in average spending by these types of tourists is affected by the influence of the gastronomic offer on their choice of destination.

Similarly, the results obtained in this research show that the more the gastronomic offer influences the choice of destination, the more likely gastronomic tourists are willing to purchase (or recommend) quality-sealed gastronomic products. On this matter, the scientific literature had not previously addressed this issue, making this a noteworthy contribution of the present study.

In conclusion, these two latest contributions of the present chapter, besides being innovative, reinforce the idea already noted by other authors (Berbel-Pineda et al., 2019; Enríquez, 2024; Mora et al., 2021) regarding the importance for a destination to convey an evocative gastronomic proposal to potential clients.

Moreover, the results of this research align with previous investigations (García-Henche et al. 2024; Nie et al. 2024) by highlighting that gastronomic tourism is a mechanism for enhancing the heritage of destinations. From a territorial development perspective, it also adds evidence that quality seals play a key role by certifying the authenticity of products, creating a competitive advantage in the global tourism market by attracting more demanding tourists and ensuring that gastronomic products align with the principles of sustainability and cultural preservation.

This study reinforces the idea already proposed by other authors (Carral et al. 2020; Lima et al. 2024; Noguer-Juncà et al. 2021) that gastronomic tourism is a powerful tool for promoting sustainable territorial development, provided it is well-managed.

Additionally, in line with the results presented in other studies (Garcês 2024; Hsu et al. 2022; Nie et al. 2024), this chapter demonstrates that tourist satisfaction impacts their immediate spending and influences the reputation and promotion of the destination in the long term. This strengthens the consumption of endogenous products and encourages equitable economic development that respects local culture and natural resources.

## 6 CONCLUSION

The results obtained in this research have validated the initial hypothesis. Indeed, it has been demonstrated that the greater the influence of the gastronomic offer on the choice of destination, the more likely it is that gastronomic tourists will exhibit favorable attitudes for sustainable territorial development. Similarly, it has been shown that tourists who are more satisfied with their gastronomic experiences are more inclined to purchase quality-sealed products.

Additionally, it has been confirmed that a greater influence of the gastronomic offer is associated with higher average daily spending on gastronomic tourism. In other words, when the gastronomic offer has more influence on the decision to travel, the average daily spending on gastronomic tourism tends to be higher.

The review of the scientific literature has confirmed that quality-certified gastronomic products enhance the perceived authenticity and value of gastronomic experiences, contributing positively to tourist satisfaction.

The results of this research also confirm that gastronomic tourists who value the authenticity of the tourist offer perceive destinations that promote sustainable territorial development as more attractive. This perception aligns with the claims made in the reviewed scientific literature regarding the contribution of gastronomic tourism to cultural preservation and the economic strengthening of local communities.

Consequently, if well planned and managed, gastronomic tourism can act as a strategic tool for sustainable territorial development by integrating endogenous resources and authentic experiences. This approach improves tourist satisfaction and drives economic benefits, supporting the preservation of local culture and traditions.

As highlighted, the analysis reveals a strong inclination among respondents to purchase (or recommend) quality-sealed gastronomic products. This preference presents significant potential for the growth of gastronomic tourism, boosting demand for high-quality products and stimulating local production and trade, highlighting the role of this type of tourism in diversifying offerings and generating employment in tourist destinations.

Regarding the average daily spending of gastronomic tourists, the results indicate that almost 40% of respondents spend between 30€ and 100€ per day on gastronomic experiences, suggesting a predominant preference for moderate spending options. However, 15% of respondents are willing to spend between 100€ and 200€ daily, while a minority spend less than 30€ or more than 200€ per day. This spending pattern highlights the diversity in expectations and financial capacities among gastronomic tourists, indicating that there is a broad and segmented market within gastronomic tourism.

The sample used for this study displays notable diversity in sociodemographic characteristics. This diverse profile reflects a wide range of interest and economic capacity among gastronomic tourists. The results suggest that, to attract and satisfy gastronomic tourists, destinations have two clearly contrasting options: i) offer a diversity of experiences tailored to different ages, nationalities, education levels, and economic capacities: ii) identify a specific segment of gastronomic tourists and specialize their offer to meet the expectations and needs of that group.

Finally, it is important to mention the limitations of the study, as well as future lines of research suggested by the results. Regarding the limitations, while the sample is considered representative, a larger number of responses would have allowed for a more robust analysis of some variables. Additionally, the survey was conducted over only three months, which could introduce some bias in the responses. Regarding future lines of research, the first challenge is to expand the sample. This would allow, for example, to carry out this same study by differentiating between segments of gastronomic tourists, which would be of great interest for destinations whose strategy focuses on specialization. It is also possible to disaggregate the average daily spending according to different activities that the gastronomic tourist performs at the destination. Lastly, from the perspective of the contribution of gastronomic tourism to sustainable territorial development, it would be very interesting to know if these tourists interact directly with local producers and/or are interested in acquiring products or experiences that ensure the greatest possible multiplier effect on the local economy.

## REFERENCES


Akdag, G., Guler, O., Dalgic, A., Benli, S., & Cakici, A. C. (2018). Do tourists' gastronomic experiences differ within the same geographical region? A comparative study of two Mediterranean destinations: Turkey and Spain. *British Food Journal, 120*(1), 158–171. DOI: 10.1108/BFJ-01-2017-0017

Akyürek, S. (2023). Gastronomic festival tours in Turkey: Motivations and expectations of tourists. In *Managing Festivals for Destination Marketing and Branding*. DOI: 10.4018/978-1-6684-6356-7.ch008

Armesto López, X. A., & Gómez Martín, B. (2004). High quality agrarian food products, tourism and local development. The case of Priorat | Productos agroalimentarios de calidad, turismo y desarrollo local: El caso del Priorat. *Cuadernos Geograficos, 34*, 83–94.

Berbel-Pineda, J. M., Palacios-Florencio, B., Ramírez-Hurtado, J. M., & Santos-Roldán, L. (2019). Gastronomic experience as a factor of motivation in the tourist movements. *International Journal of Gastronomy and Food Science, 18*, 100171. Advance online publication. DOI: 10.1016/j.ijgfs.2019.100171

Björk, P., & Kauppinen-Räisänen, H. (2016). Local food: A source for destination attraction. *International Journal of Contemporary Hospitality Management, 28*(1), 177–194. DOI: 10.1108/IJCHM-05-2014-0214

Çakir Keleş, M. (2021). Gastronomy Tourism Resources and Local Food. In *Gastronomy and Hospitality Studies in Tourism.*

Carral, E. V., Del Río, M., & López, Z. (2020). Gastronomy and tourism: Socioeconomic and territorial implications in santiago de compostela-galiza (NW Spain). *International Journal of Environmental Research and Public Health, 17*(17), 1–25. DOI: 10.3390/ijerph17176173 PMID: 32854422

Correia, A., Kim, S., & Kozak, M. (2020). Gastronomy experiential traits and their effects on intentions for recommendation: A fuzzy set approach. *International Journal of Tourism Research, 22*(3), 351–363. DOI: 10.1002/jtr.2340

Cunha, S., Barroco, C., & Antunes, J. (2019). Food tourism as a differentiating factor of the destinations: The case of Portugal | O turismo gastronómico como fator diferenciador dos destinos: O caso de Portugal. *RISTI - Revista Iberica de Sistemas e Tecnologias de Informacao, 2019*(E24), 409–422.

Dancausa-Millan, G., Millán-Vázquez de la Torre, M. G., & Huete-Alcocer, N. (2022). Olive oil as a gourmet ingredient in contemporary cuisine. A gastronomic tourism proposal. *International Journal of Gastronomy and Food Science, 29*, 100548. Advance online publication. DOI: 10.1016/j.ijgfs.2022.100548

Demirel, N., & Tekeli, E. K. (2022). Foodie tourist behavior. In *Tourist Behavior*. Past, Present, and Future. DOI: 10.1201/9781003282082-10

Diaconescu, D. M., Moraru, R., & Stănciulescu, G. (2016). Considerations on gastronomic tourism as a component of sustainable local development. *Amfiteatru Economic, 18*(Specialiss), 999–1014.

Dorta-Afonso, D., & Padrón-Ávila, H. (2021). Gastronomic tourism management: identifying the potential market in the Canaries | Gestión de turismo gastronómico: identificación del mercado potencial en Canarias. *Pasos (El Sauzal), 19*(4), 725–736. DOI: 10.25145/j.pasos.2021.19.047

Duque, A. S., Barroco, C., & Martins, M. L. (2023). Certified products in the genesis of tourist routes: An opportunity to get to know the Center Region (Portugal) | Produtos certificados na génese de rotas turísticas: Uma oportunidade para conhecer a Região Centro. *Journal of Tourism and Development*, *41*, 303–315. DOI: 10.34624/rtd.v41i0.30039

Đurkin Badurina, J., Klapan, M., & Soldić Frleta, D. (2023). Stakeholders' Collaboration in the Development of an Authentic Gastronomic Offering in Rural Areas: Example of the Ravni Kotari Region in Croatia. *Sustainability (Basel)*, *15*(5), 4649. Advance online publication. DOI: 10.3390/su15054649

Enríquez, C. C. L. (2024). Gastronomic tourism scenario of an international destination bases on netnography model | cenário de turismo gastronómico de um destino internacional baseado no modelo de netnografia | el escenario del turismo gastronómico de un destino internacional basa. *New Trends in Qualitative Research*, *20*(3), 1–14. DOI: 10.36367/ntqr.20.3.2024.e1062

Ferrari, S., Nicotera, T., lo Presti, A., & Biasone, A. M. (2022). Local Development Through the Connection Between Roots Tourism, Local Food and Wine. In *Lecture Notes in Networks and Systems* (Vol. 482). LNNS., DOI: 10.1007/978-3-031-06825-6_221

Fusté-Forné, F., Ginés-Ariza, P., & Noguer-Juncà, E. (2021). Food in slow tourism: The creation of experiences based on the origin of products sold at mercat del lleó (girona). *Heritage*, *4*(3), 1995–2008. DOI: 10.3390/heritage4030113

Garcês, S. (2024). Gastronomy experiences, authenticity, and storytelling in tourism destinations: A conceptual paper. In *Cultural*. Gastronomy, and Adventure Tourism Development., DOI: 10.4018/979-8-3693-3158-3.ch009

García-Henche, B., Cuesta-Valiño, P., Durán-Álamo, P., & Penelas-Leguía, A. (2024). The role of women in maintaining the heritage value of gastronomy in Castilla-La Mancha. *International Journal of Gastronomy and Food Science*, *37*, 100987. Advance online publication. DOI: 10.1016/j.ijgfs.2024.100987

Getz, D., & Robinson, R. N. S. (2014). "Foodies" and their travel preferences. *Tourism Analysis*, *19*(6), 659–672. DOI: 10.3727/108354214X14116690097693

Harrington, R. J., & Ottenbacher, M. C. (2010). Culinary tourism-a case study of the gastronomic capital. *Journal of Culinary Science & Technology*, *8*(1), 14–32. DOI: 10.1080/15428052.2010.490765

Hsu, F. C., Agyeiwaah, E., & Scott, N. (2022). Understanding tourists' perceived food consumption values: Do different cultures share similar food values? *International Journal of Gastronomy and Food Science*, *28*, 100533. Advance online publication. DOI: 10.1016/j.ijgfs.2022.100533

Kalpidis, C., Bersimis, F., & Tsartas, P. (2024). Effect of Restaurant Attributes on Tourism Satisfaction and Loyalty: Local Gastronomy in Athens. *Springer Proceedings in Business and Economics*, 1049–1069. DOI: 10.1007/978-3-031-54338-8_63

Kivela, J., & Crotts, J. C. (2006). Tourism and Gastronomy: Gastronomy's Influence on How Tourists Experience a Destination. *Journal of Hospitality & Tourism Research (Washington, D.C.)*, *30*(3), 354–377. DOI: 10.1177/1096348006286797

Kokkranikal, J., & Carabelli, E. (2024). Gastronomy tourism experiences: The cooking classes of Cinque Terre. *Tourism Recreation Research, 49*(1), 161–172. DOI: 10.1080/02508281.2021.1975213

Lima, J., Serra, J., Borges, M. D. R., & Marujo, N. (2024). Is gastronomy important for UNESCO world heritage sites' tourists? A case study from Portugal. *Anatolia, 35*(2), 326–338. DOI: 10.1080/13032917.2023.2191268

Liu, S., Wei, C., Hu, S.-M., & Alsetoohy, O. (2024). Exploring Post-Experience Evaluation of Gastronomy Tourism Experiences Through Airbnb. *International Journal of Hospitality & Tourism Administration*, 1–28. Advance online publication. DOI: 10.1080/15256480.2024.2389532

Millan, M. G. D., De la Torre, M. G. M. V., & Rojas, R. H. (2021). Analysis of the demand for gastronomic tourism in Andalusia (Spain). *PLoS ONE, 16*(2 February). DOI: 10.1371/journal.pone.0246377

Mitchell, R., & Hall, C. M. (2003). Consuming tourists: Food tourism consumer behaviour. In *Food Tourism Around The World*. DOI: 10.4324/9780080477862

Mora, D., Solano-Sánchez, M. Á., López-Guzmán, T., & Moral-Cuadra, S. (2021). Gastronomic experiences as a key element in the development of a tourist destination. *International Journal of Gastronomy and Food Science, 25*, 100405. Advance online publication. DOI: 10.1016/j.ijgfs.2021.100405

Nie, X., Su, S., Zhao, W. M., Guan, J., & Liu, R. (2024). Examining the Effects of Food Consumption Value and Food Image on Tourists' Intention to Purchase Guilin Rice Noodles. *Journal of China Tourism Research*, 1–22. Advance online publication. DOI: 10.1080/19388160.2024.2382713

Noguer-Juncà, E., Crespi-Vallbona, M., & Fusté-Forné, F. (2021). Sociocultural and gastronomic revaluation of local products: Trumfa in the Vall de Camprodon (Catalonia, Spain). *International Journal of Gastronomy and Food Science, 26*, 100425. Advance online publication. DOI: 10.1016/j.ijgfs.2021.100425

Rachão, S., Breda, Z., de Oliveira Fernandes, C., Joukes, V., & Ferreira, C. (2023). Food-and-wine tourists' willingness to pay for co-creation experiences: A generational approach. *Journal of Hospitality and Tourism Management, 56*, 245–252. DOI: 10.1016/j.jhtm.2023.06.004

Şengül, S., Usta Dişsiz, S., & Uçkan Çakır, M. (2024a). Over-gastronomy: Conceptualisation of the problems in gastronomy. *Current Issues in Tourism*, 1–18. Advance online publication. DOI: 10.1080/13683500.2024.2390675

Şengül, S., Usta Dişsiz, S., & Uçkan Çakır, M. (2024b). Over-gastronomy: Conceptualisation of the problems in gastronomy. *Current Issues in Tourism*, 1–18. Advance online publication. DOI: 10.1080/13683500.2024.2390675

Sgroi, F. (2021). Food products, gastronomy and religious tourism: The resilience of food landscapes. *International Journal of Gastronomy and Food Science, 26*, 100435. Advance online publication. DOI: 10.1016/j.ijgfs.2021.100435

Sinha, R., & Haluwalia, S. (2024). Gastronomic delights for community growth: Unravelling the impact of sustainable tourism in Sikkim, India. *International Journal of Tourism Policy, 14*(4), 384–401. DOI: 10.1504/IJTP.2024.139729

Soonsan, N., Phakdee-auksorn, P., & Suksirisopon, P. (2023). Determining food attributes for measuring and evaluating a gastronomic destination's appeal to visitors. *Journal of Hospitality and Tourism Insights*, *6*(5), 1755–1775. DOI: 10.1108/JHTI-02-2022-0048

Sutiadiningsih, A., Mahfud, T., Dang, V. H., Purwidiani, N., Rachma Wati, G., & Dewi, I. H. P. (2024). THE ROLE OF GASTRONOMY TOURISM ON REVISIT AND RECOMMENDATION INTENTIONS: THE MEDIATION ANALYSIS OF TOURIST SATISFACTION. *Geo Journal of Tourism and Geosites*, *52*(1), 195–202. DOI: 10.30892/gtg.52118-1195

Thees, H., & Pechlaner, H. (2019). Tourism along the new silk road. Prospects for integrated development of regions and destinations | Tourismus entlang der Neuen Seidenstraße: Chancen für eine integrierte Regional-und Destinationsentwicklung. *Geographische Rundschau*, *71*(6), 12–17.

Thongkaw, B., Kongbuamai, N., Chinnakum, W., & Chaiboonsri, C. (2024). The Impact of Gastronomic Tourism on the Regional Economy of Thailand: Examined by the Dynamic I-O Model after the Decline of COVID-19. *Economies*, *12*(7), 180. Advance online publication. DOI: 10.3390/economies12070180

Zhong, L., Liu, J., Morrison, A. M., & Yang, L. (2024). Peking duck, anyone? An analysis of international tourist food perceptions and influence factors. *International Journal of Gastronomy and Food Science*, *37*, 100980. Advance online publication. DOI: 10.1016/j.ijgfs.2024.100980

Zhu, H., & Yasami, M. (2021). DEVELOPING GASTRONOMIC RESOURCES: PRACTICES of UNESCO CREATIVE CITIES of GASTRONOMY. *Geo Journal of Tourism and Geosites*, *39*(4 supplement), 1406–1414. DOI: 10.30892/gtg.394spl11-784

Zou, H., Zheng, Y., Zhang, Y., & Liu, Y. (2024). A Geospatial Perspective on the Factors Influencing Tourist Dining Satisfaction. *Journal of Geovisualization and Spatial Analysis*, *8*(2), 25. Advance online publication. DOI: 10.1007/s41651-024-00186-0

## APPENDIX: SURVEY TO DETERMINE THE BEHAVIOR OF GASTRONOMIC TOURISTS

Behavior, willingness to spend, expectations, and experiences

1. When you travel for holidays, do you show interest in getting to know the gastronomy from the places you visit?
   a. Yes
   b. No
2. To what extent does the gastronomic offer influence when choosing a destination for your visit? (Likert scale: 1it does not influence at all; 7 it influences a lot)

*Table 11.*

| Does not influence at all | 1 | 2 | 3 | 4 | 5 | 6 | 7 | It influences a lot |
|---|---|---|---|---|---|---|---|---|

3. Have you ever made a trip with the only purpose of enjoying the gastronomic offer of this destination?
   a. Yes
   b. No
4. If you are influenced by the gastronomic offer when choosing a destination, what factors do you value most about this offer? (Likert scale: 1 the least rated; 7 the most rated)

*Table 12.*

| Assessment (1 to 7) | Factors |
|---|---|
| | Prestige of the local gastronomy |
| | Existing environment in certain areas |
| | Price – Quality relationship |
| | Variety in the gastronomic offer |
| | Interest in local gastronomy (identity) |
| | Existence of vegetarian or vegan gastronomic establishments |
| | Existence of establishments with quality labels (Michelin, Sol Repsol and others) |

5. What is your motivation for gastronomic tourism activities? (multi-response)
   a. The very act of traveling
   b. Cultural enrichment
   c. Enjoying the gastronomy
   d. Having new experiences
   e. Getting out from the routine

f. Work
g. Shopping & Leisure
h. Other..............................................................

6. Which of the following factors motivate you the most when trying the gastronomy of a destination? (Likert scale: 1 motivates the least; 7 motivates the most)

*Table 13.*

| Assessment (1 to 7) | Factors |
|---|---|
| | Fame of a certain gastronomic product |
| | Trying different flavors from the ones you already know |
| | Enjoying a unique experience |
| | Consuming products in their production and processing environment |
| | Appearance, taste and smell of the food |
| | Eating healthy dishes |
| | Existence of a quality restaurant offer |
| | Existence of products with Appellation of Origin or Protected Designation of Origin |

7. Do you usually search the internet for recommendations/reviews before going to a gastronomic establishment?
   a. Yes
   b. No
8. If the answer to the previous question is "Yes", do the comments / reviews you read on internet really influence you when choosing the establishment you finally attend?
   a. Yes
   b. No
9. What are the information sources consulted prior to your arrival at your destination? (multi-response)
   a. Destination's official website
   b. Family and friends' recommendations
   c. Review websites (Tripadvisor, Booking, and others)
   d. Google reviews
   e. Social media
   f. Travel blogs & magazines
   g. Travel agencies
   h. Doesn't look for information before arriving at the destination
10. What are the periods of time you allocate for gastronomic tourism? (multi-response)
    a. Weekdays
    b. Weekends
    c. Holidays or vacations
11. How often do you go on gastronomic trips?
    a. Once a year

b. Two or three times a year
c. More than three times a year

12. What are the gastronomic tourism activities that you prefer to do in a destination? (multi-response)
    a. Learn about specific products or techniques
    b. Eating or drinking in restaurants
    c. Eating or drinking at production sites (wineries, vineyards, plants, etc.)
    d. Eating or drinking in others (street entrepreneurships, etc.)
    e. Visiting food markets
    f. Buying local products
    g. Carrying out tastings
    h. Visiting wineries, industries or themed museums
    i. Attending gastronomic events
    j. Workshops or cooking courses
    k. Other:.........................................................................
13. When you do gastronomic tourism, what complementary activities do you do? (multi-response)
    a. Visiting the destination (population centers, cities, communities)
    b. Visits to cultural sites
    c. Visits to family or friends
    d. Nature activities
    e. Health & Wellness Activities
    f. Shopping & Leisure
    g. Rest
    h. Other. .......................................................................
14. When you do food tourism, do you share your opinion or experience on social media?
    a. Yes
    b. No
15. When you do food tourism, how much are you willing to spend on the following activities:

*Table 14.*

| | **I would not spend anything** | **I would spend less than 10 €** | **I would spend 11 to 20 €** | **I would spend 21 to 35 €** | **I would spend 36 to 50 €** | **I would spend 51 to 100 €** | **I would spend 101 to 150 €** | **I would spend more than 150 €** |
|---|---|---|---|---|---|---|---|---|
| À la carte food menu | | | | | | | | |
| Tasting menu | | | | | | | | |
| Visiting a food industry and tasting the product | | | | | | | | |
| Cooking Workshop | | | | | | | | |
| Gastronomic Tour | | | | | | | | |

continued on following page

*Table 14. Continued*

| | I would not spend anything | I would spend less than 10 € | I would spend 11 to 20 € | I would spend 21 to 35 € | I would spend 36 to 50 € | I would spend 51 to 100 € | I would spend 101 to 150 € | I would spend more than 150 € |
|---|---|---|---|---|---|---|---|---|
| Buying local products | | | | | | | | |
| Gastronomic event | | | | | | | | |

16. When you do gastronomic tourism, do you interact directly with local producers?
    a. Yes
    b. No
    c. Other. ..........................................................................
17. When you do gastronomic tourism, do you actively participate in the activities offered?
    a. Yes
    b. No
    c. Other. ..........................................................................
18. When visiting a tourist destination, are you worried that you won't find vegan or vegetarian food options? (Likert scale: 1 it does not worry you at all; 7 it worries you extremely)

*Table 15.*

| It does not worry you at all | 1 | 2 | 3 | 4 | 5 | 6 | 7 | It worries you extremely |
|---|---|---|---|---|---|---|---|---|

19. How decisive is it that you have a vegan or vegetarian food offer to choose or discard the destination? (Likert scale: 1 not at all determinant; 7 totally determining)

*Table 16.*

| Not at all determinant | 1 | 2 | 3 | 4 | 5 | 6 | 7 | Totally determining |
|---|---|---|---|---|---|---|---|---|

20. When you do gastronomic tourism, to what extent would you be willing to pay more, compared to what is usually your budget, to enjoy a gastronomic experience?

*Table 17.*

| | 1 Nothing | 2 A Little | 3 Moderate | 4 Plenty | 5 A lot |
|---|---|---|---|---|---|
| Cooking classes and gastronomic workshops | | | | | |
| Meals at home of local families | | | | | |
| Lunch at featured restaurants (with special distinctions) | | | | | |
| Tastings and specialized tastings | | | | | |
| Gastronomic events | | | | | |
| Exclusive dining experiences (Unusual sites, themed events) | | | | | |
| Experience the destination's traditional localgastronomy | | | | | |
| Food tours | | | | | |
| Visits to local markets and food producers | | | | | |

21. When you do gastronomic tourism, to what extent would you be willing to pay more, compared to what is usually your budget for enjoying a gastronomic experience based on:

*Table 18.*

| | 1 Nothing | 2 A Little | 3 Moderate | 4 Plenty | 5 A lot |
|---|---|---|---|---|---|
| Zero-kilometer-products | | | | | |
| Destination´s traditional cuisine | | | | | |
| Spaces that demonstrate sociocultural authenticity and local heritage. | | | | | |
| Direct interaction with the community. | | | | | |
| Consumption of natural, healthy and seasonal origin products. | | | | | |
| Sustainable production (rational use of resources, reduction of waste, residues and polluting emissions). | | | | | |
| Products with special distinctions, and/or services with certified good practices. | | | | | |
| Vegetarian or vegan food | | | | | |
| Local services and fair trade. | | | | | |

22. Overall, what is your level of satisfaction with the gastronomic tourism experiences you have enjoyed lately? (Likert scale: 1 not at all satisfied; 7 totally satisfied)

*Table 19.*

| Not at all satisfied | 1 | 2 | 3 | 4 | 5 | 6 | 7 | Totally satisfied |
|---|---|---|---|---|---|---|---|---|

23. If, during your trips, you have tasted any gastronomic product with quality seals (olive oils, wines, ham, cheese, etc.), indicate how likely (Likert scale: 1 no probability; 7 strongly probable) you are to buy (or recommend) it later for home consumption.

*Table 20.*

| No probability | 1 | 2 | 3 | 4 | 5 | 6 | 7 | (Strongly probable) you are to buy (or recommend) it later for home consumption. |
|---|---|---|---|---|---|---|---|---|

24. What is the usual average budget of a food tourism trip for you?
25. What is the usual average DAILY expenditure of a gastronomic tourism trip for you?

Sociodemographic information

1. Nationality
2. Place of habitual residence
3. Age
   a. 18-24 years old
   b. 25-40 years
   c. 41-56 years
   d. 57-75 years
   e. 76-91 years
4. Sex
   a. Male
   b. Female
   c. Other (specify):
5. Profession - Occupation
   a. Student
   b. Professional free practice
   c. Employee - Operator
   d. Employee - Middle management
   e. Businessman - High Command
   f. Household chores
   g. Unemployed
   h. Retired
   i. Other (specify)
6. Level of Education
   a. No education
   b. Primary school
   c. High school
   d. Undergraduate degree
   e. Master's degree
   f. Doctorate degree

7. Monthly Net Income
    a. < 600€
    b. 600€ - 900€
    c. 900€ – 1.200€
    d. 1.200€ - 1.500€
    e. 1.500€ - 1.800€
    f. 1.800€ - 2.100€
    g. €2,100 - €3,000
    h. €3,000 or more

# Chapter 10
# Urban Vitality and Sustainability of Heritage Manifestations:
## Interdisciplinary Analysis of the Andador 20 de Noviembre and the Pilgrimage of Zapopan, Jalisco

**Rogelio Martínez Cárdenas**
https://orcid.org/0000-0001-5572-9825
*University of Guadalajara, Mexico*

**Francisco Partida Hoy**
https://orcid.org/0000-0003-2319-3282
*University of Guadalajara, Mexico*

## ABSTRACT

*Urban vitality is key to preserving and revitalizing heritage spaces, ensuring the history, culture, and identity of a place remain vibrant while promoting social integration and economic growth. The Andador 20 de Noviembre in Zapopan, Jalisco, Mexico, exemplifies this as a central axis of the city's historical and cultural life, offering a hub for social interaction through its commercial, gastronomic, and cultural activities. The Pilgrimage of Zapopan, a UNESCO-recognized event, further enhances this vitality by attracting millions and boosting the local economy. The interplay between the urban vitality of Andador 20 de Noviembre and the pilgrimage underscores the necessity of keeping such heritage spaces active. These places serve not only as historical witnesses but also as catalysts for social, cultural, and economic development. The study highlights the importance of preserving and promoting these spaces as dynamic centers of urban life, enriching the experiences of both inhabitants and visitors.*

## 1. INTRODUCTION

Already in 1961, Jane Jacobs, in her book The Life and Death of Cities, asked: "What is the first thing that comes to mind when thinking about a city? Its streets. When the streets of a city offer interest, the entire city offers interest; "When they look sad, the whole city looks sad." (Jacobs 2011, 34).

DOI: 10.4018/979-8-3693-7081-0.ch010

Jacobs knew that the complexity of cities, as well as their understanding, cannot be reduced to simple buildings and roads to travel through them, since their materiality is not everything (Delclòs-Alió, X., & Miralles-Guasch, C. 2018). He knew that behind the vitality of some neighborhoods and cities, as well as the apathy and monotony of others, there is a series of elements, policies and intrinsic relationships that can be studied and explained. Urban vitality is the quality of those spaces in cities that are capable of attracting heterogeneous people for different types of activities during varied hours. (Mouratidis, 2020; Beltrán Rodríguez, 2016).

Why do some open public spaces such as plazas, walkways, boardwalks and promenades, manage to attract heterogeneous people and activities and remain with great urban vitality throughout the year and others do not? What type of spatial elements, architectural, environmental, historical and sociocultural, can we find in them that promote citizen use and appropriation? What are the benefits that these public spaces bring to the communities and cities where they are located? These and other questions guide and outline the present work, relating them specifically to the *Andador 20 de Noviembre* and its historical relationship with the Pilgrimage of the *Romería*, in the city of Zapopan, Jalisco, Mexico (Kang, Fan, & Jiao, 2021) .

First of all, it must be considered that the *Andador 20 de noviembre* belongs to the type of open public and pedestrian spaces located in the historic center of its municipality. It is very notable that the *Andador 20 de noviembre*, since its pedestrianization, has gained urban vitality, manifested in a greater flow of people, influx of tourists, cultural activities, gastronomic offer and provision of better urban services; It can be argued that the rich cultural life it boasts results from the following fact: The spaces for cultural presentations are located in strategic areas with extensive symbolic, historical and economic capital. The historic centers, which have the aforementioned capitals in addition to a high architectural heritage, bring together a good part of the urban cultural offer. (Ramírez Kuri, 2016).

In addition to the importance linked to the aforementioned capitals, there is still an important reason to highlight; namely, that open pedestrian public spaces (closed to motorized traffic) in urban centrality are the primary setting for citizen interaction; They are spaces of coexistence and protest, of work and leisure, of demonstration and meeting; of socialization where ties are woven and interwoven between people who may or may not know each other previously, and which make it possible to carry out multiple commercial, recreational, political, artistic and cultural activities (Ayala García & Tami Cortés, 2020; Berroeta Torres, 2012).

And not only buildings are habitable, but also spaces, since habitability is a condition limited to the specific attributes of habitable spaces so that they are useful, functional, intelligible and significant (Organista 2021). However, not everything is perfect, since the "tourism" of urban space implies changes that are not necessarily well received by local inhabitants, who see their neighborhood continually saturated with people and activities that can be stressful. In addition, businessmen and government agents take advantage of these spaces to make questionable real estate investments, which are also not consulted with citizens and represent extra pressure for their inhabitants (Reyes, 2024; Sampaio de Almeida et al., 2024; Ecologistas en Acción, 2020).

*Figure 1. Different views of the Andador 20 de noviembre (a)*

*Photos of the authors.*

*Figure 2. Different views of the Andador 20 de noviembre (b)*

*Photos of the authors.*

*Figure 3. Different views of the Andador 20 de noviembre (c)*

*Photos of the authors.*

## 2. Urban Architectural Dimension

The *Andador 20 de noviembre* is the pedestrian route in the center of Zapopan, which ends in the Plaza de las Américas and this, in turn, in the Basilica Menor of Zapopan, the most emblematic and visited building of this municipality, since it is the destination of one of the largest religious pilgrimages in the state of Jalisco, the Zapopan Pilgrimage, which brings together, every October 12, almost two million people (Figure 5). In this way, the vector line or architectural spatial axis is integrated as follows: Andador 20 de noviembre > Plaza de las Américas > Basilica Menor, whose direction of movement remains from east to west, changing in amplitude and concentration, from a relatively narrow road (20 m), until its widening and width in the Plaza de las Américas (100 m).

*Figure 4. Map of the historic center of Zapopan, Jalisco, where you can see 20 de Noviembre Street (Andador) that goes from Av. De los Laureles, in the East of the map, to Emiliano Zapata Street, where the Plaza de the Americas, to the West. Source: Guadalajara City Council, 2023. Taken from: https://mapa.guadalajara.gob.mx/geomap*

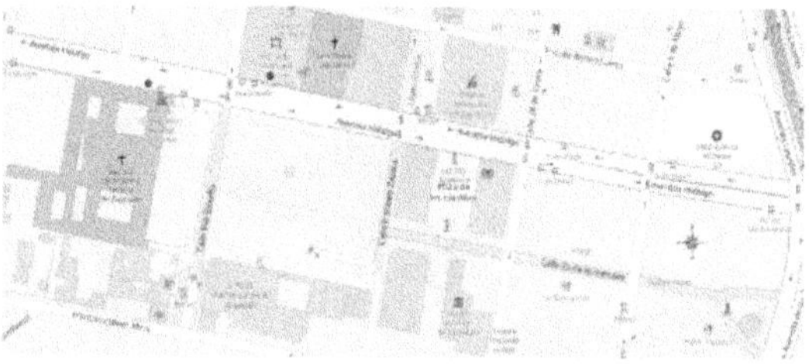

Based on the previous map, the main buildings and spaces linked to the *Andador 20 de noviembre* are shown schematically below, which is its compositional axis, spatially speaking. As already mentioned, it has a mainly east-west direction because the most important visual culmination is the Basilica.

In the northern part, the most significant space is the Plaza de los Caudillos and in the southern part the Zapopan Art Museum, in the western part there are two: the Plaza de las Américas and the Basilica building and, in the east, the Arcos de Ingreso and its surrounding fountain, as well as the new Zapopan Art Museum, under construction, called MAZ+.

*Figure 5. Plaza de las Américas and Basílica Menor de Zapopan during the Pilgrimage in 2023.*

*Taken from: https://siker.com.mx/sin-categoria/romeria-de-zapopan-2023-convoca-a-2-2-millones-de-devotos/*

*Figure 6. Schematic representation of the Andador November 20 with its main spaces and buildings. Outline by authors.*

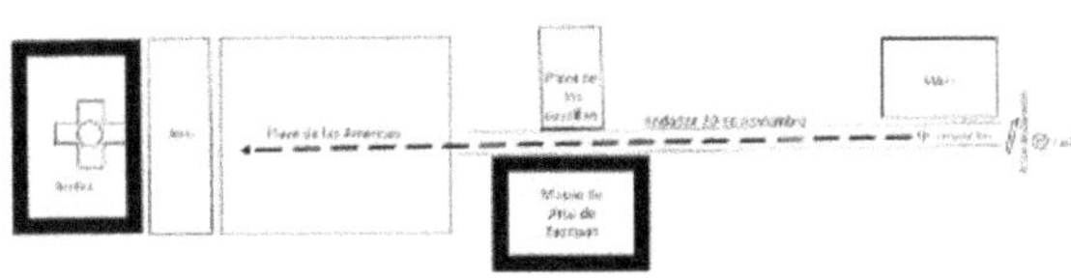

The *Andador 20 de noviembre* measures 260 meters in length, from the Monument of the Arches of Zapopan, to the beginning of the Plaza de las Américas; and has a width of 20 meters; Plaza de los Caudillos measures 54 m long by 30 m wide and Plaza de las Américas measures 140 m long by 100 m wide.

The most significant monuments are the Entrance Arch and its surrounding fountain. The entrance arch was built in 1981 and completed the following year. It was, both the project and its execution, the work of Guillermo González Ibarra, although the sculptures and reliefs are the work of his wife María del Carmen Rábago. At the foot of the monument there is a bronze plaque that, among other information, says that:

> "Its decoration stages the history of Zapopan. The pre-Hispanic era appears on its left vertical face; the right side represents contemporary Zapopan; The rear faces recreate the arrival of the Spanish and the work carried out by the Franciscan missionaries. On the left side, on a plinth, is the sculpture that represents Topiltzintli, child god of corn, and on the right side, the goddess of corn.; At the top, a hunting target symbolizes triumph. At its top there stands an eagle like that of the national coat of arms."

Likewise, octagonal in shape, entirely in quarry, and with four bodies, the fountain in front of the Entrance Arch is a sculptural element in perfect condition that provides freshness and luminosity at the beginning of the route of this walkway. Its first body is the superficial pool whose function is to receive the waters of the three upper bodies. The second body is a plate that is both a container and a source of jets in the form of arches that point to the center of the sculptural group.

*Figure 7. Face of the Entrance Arch: Corresponding to the east face. Likewise, you can see the octagonal fountain in the foreground*

*Photos of the authors, 2023.*

*Figure 8. Face of the Entrance Arch: Next to the west face. You can see the octagonal fountain in the background*

*Photos of the authors, 2023.*

It should be noted that on the vertical face of this body some bas-reliefs of aquatic leaves stand out. The third body is a carved quarry glass with figures of children in a lump that hold, kneeling, like small Atlases, the entire weight of the crown of the cup. Thin jets of water rise from this glass until they reach approximately two meters in height from its base. Finally, at the top there is a smaller cup, in the highest part of which we find a stone pine cone from which water gushes out without reaching great heights, being the zenithal finish of the sculpture.

Towards the west and following the schematic representation (Figure 5) we will find the Zapopan Art Museum, the work of architects María Emilia Orendain and Enrique Toussaint, inaugurated in 2002. It has three temporary exhibition rooms: the Juan Soriano room, the Juan Barragán room and the Manuel Álvarez Bravo room, and a multidisciplinary auditorium named after Juan José Arreola, as well as a bookstore and store.

It also has a main courtyard in the center of the museum that is used for various activities. The building is modern and functional; Its discreet main façade does not exceed the heights of the surrounding buildings excessively, so it is integrated into the street as a whole.

The structure of this façade is made of concrete in which four enormous red folding doors stand out, which also have the function of lattices. At the top there is a stylized circular glass pediment that rises from a metal beam, and whose roof is a thin reinforced concrete barrel vault.

The rooms are spacious, equipped and well lit. The experience that the viewer or user has is of finding themselves in a space of exquisite architectural workmanship. The curatorship also stands out for its search for new expressions, media and formats, with local, national and foreign artists; information that is available on its official page https://maz.zapopan.gob.mx/#where you can consult the history of its exhibitions.

*Figure 9. Facade of the Zapopan Museum of Art (MAZ).*

*Source: https://guadalajaramidestino.com/el-maz-trae-de-vuelta-al-salon-independiente/, 2022.*

*Figure 10. Interior of a room of the Zapopan Museum of Art.*

*Source: https://guadalajaramidestino.com/el-maz-trae-de-vuelta-al-salon-independiente/, 2022.*

In front of this museum is the Plaza de los Caudillos; an esplanade that contains at its southern end a monument to Mexicanness: the eagle of the national coat of arms. This square is surrounded by two neo colonial-style porticoed buildings, where cafes and small food and beverage businesses, mainly, meet. The Plaza de los Caudillos is also a passage between the Andador 20 de Noviembre and Av. Hidalgo, the main motorized road in the center of Zapopan, where the Municipal Palace and other prominent buildings of the municipality are located. The esplanade has a stone plinth that rises one meter above the Andador.

*Figure 11. Plaza de los Caudillos.*

*Partida, 2023.*

*Figure 12. Graph of Satisfaction with the quality of six public services in the Guadalajara Metropolitan Area. Scale from 1 to 5.*

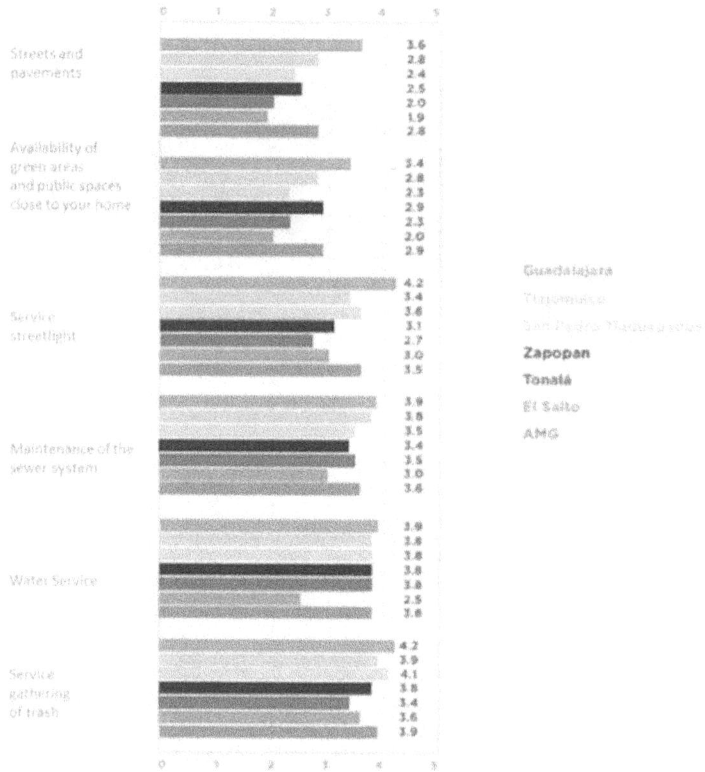


*Source: Seventh citizen perception survey on quality of life 2020. Jalisco cómo Vamos. Citizen Observatory*

According to official information from the Zapopan City Council, in 2017, with an investment of 19.8 million pesos, the Andador 20 de Noviembre was renovated. The actions carried out in this work include the equipment and LED lighting of the entrance fountain to the Andador 20 de Noviembre and the lighting of the Zapopan Arches, as well as the change of paving stone for semi-polished concrete tiling, and the construction of planter-bench, also made of polished concrete.

Likewise, public lighting was replaced with the use of LED lights, and the necessary adjustments were made for universal accessibility in this passage, so that all people can enjoy the local cultural and gastronomic offering. A 4-inch drinking water line was also constructed; Storm drains were built and the Irving-type grates were replaced, and the stormwater network was rehabilitated. The access steps to Plaza de los Caudillos were repaired and stages were built, in addition to placing platforms to promote cultural activities. The trees were transplanted and the existing trees were treated.

It is not unusual to observe, then, in this set of articulated and equipped spaces and buildings, citizens and visitors engaged in different and varied activities typical of the historical, commercial and sociocultural complexity of the site. There are pedestrians who are passing through and take advantage of the pedestrian path to "cut" the path or, on the contrary, to make it more interesting. There are diners, tourists, merchants, street artists and people who come for some good or service. The most important and significant thing about the Andador is, precisely, what its name indicates, that 20 de Noviembre Street has been pedestrianized. From that decision, people appropriated it, and today what was yesterday just another street for cars overflowing with urban vitality.

Finally, it is worth mentioning in this section that, during the time of our fieldwork at the site, the new MAZ+ headquarters was being built, so this brief description and analysis of the urban-architectural dimension does not take into account this building. However, we can advance some data, taking into account the journalistic information alluding to this development. In this sense, according to a note by Sarah Ochoa, in Diario Mural, on June 13, 2021:

> [...] the project, endorsed since 2020 by the Plenary of the Zapopan City Council, considers the construction of a museum, a gastronomic corridor and a housing development where the Zapopan Shopping Center square -Plaza Arcos- was previously located. File 199/2020 of the opinion, the land located at the intersection of Calle Hidalgo and Avenida Laureles, next to the Arcos de Zapopan, has the project approved since October 30, 2020 by the Cabildo. According to the document, of the 25,080 square meters of land, 14,630 square meters can be built. The developers plan to allocate 2,800 square meters to house a museum, 4,770 for mixed use and 5,376 for residential use. The Municipality approved the proposal by "Tierra y Armonía" to create a private trust that will be in charge of carrying out the civil works and management, where the municipal Government will participate with 86.33 percent of the land.

The journalist also warns of social discontent over this work, since neighborhood groups spoke out because the space previously occupied by Plaza Arcos was used as a public space, specifically for a park. In the end, the municipal government of Zapopan decided on the construction of the MAZ+, as part of a larger project called the Zapopan Center Museum District.

*Figure 13. Isometric projection of the Zapopan Museum District project*

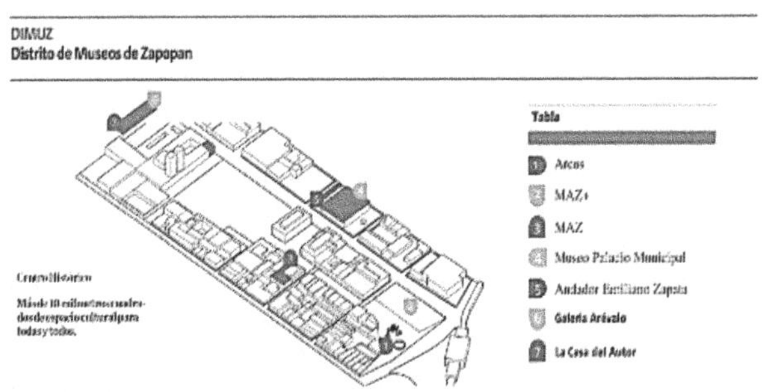


*Source: Zapopan City Council, 2021, https://www.milenio.com/cultura/centro-zapopan-museos-palacio-municipal-plaza-arcos*

It is no secret that urban policies and projects respond to different public and private interests. A power such as private economic capital can, together with the government sector, make a vision for the development of cities prevail, timely presenting a series of benefits, accompanied by strong media socialization.

Museum or park? It is a question whose answer cannot be univocal, but in the current socio-urban reality, it is far from being just a healthy democratic exercise, such as citizen consultation. Each block, each neighborhood of the cities, is commonly a trench dispute, where the powers represented in individuals or groups, maintain a permanent struggle for their interests.

## 3. SOCIOECONOMIC DIMENSION

From the observation and registration of the buildings in the Andador 20 de Noviembre, the following uses and economic activities can be found:

*Figure 14. Type and number of businesses on Andador November 20.*

| Tipo de espacio o servicios | Cantidad |
|---|---|
| Restaurants | 15 |
| Coffee shops | 5 |
| Ice Cream Vendors | 3 |
| Banks | 2 |
| Foreign Exchange Businesses | 2 |
| Parcel | 1 |
| Goods and Appliances Store | 2 |
| Preschool and Primary School | 1 |
| Nucleus of Dental Surgeons | 1 |
| "Miraculous Potions" Store | 1 |
| Bags and Backpacks Store | 1 |
| Contemporary Museum | 2 |
| Wixárrica Art Museum | 1 |
| Parishes | 2 |
| Stationery | 2 |
| Grocery stores | 4 |
| Law Firm | 1 |
| Pharmacy | 2 |
| Juice and Preparation Sales | 3 |
| Institute of Higher Studies | 1 |
| Aesthetics | 2 |
| Tlapaleria | 1 |
| Municipal Comptroller | 1 |
| Political Party House | 1 |
| Bookshop | 1 |
| Music Store | 1 |
| Handicraft shop | 1 |
| Municipal administrative unit | 1 |
| Optics | 1 |
| pubs | 3 |
| "Botaneros" Centers | 3 |
| Hotel | 2 |
| Parking lots | 3 |

*Source: Partida, 2023.*

Due to the quality and quantity of its services, there is considerable recreational and commercial activity throughout the week in Andador 20 de Noviembre. The prices of dishes in restaurants, for example, vary between 80 and 300 pesos, so people from different sectors and socioeconomic possibilities gather at the place to taste a dish. There are restaurants serving Mexican snacks, seafood, roast meats, Italian, Greek, Japanese food... and a long list of fast food. As can be seen in the previous image, the predominant establishments on the Andador are commerce and services; This is consistent with the information published by the National Statistical Directory of Economic Units (DENUE) of INEGI, about the municipality, in Zapopan, Municipal Diagnosis, August 2022:

The municipality of Zapopan has 52,239 economic units as of May 2022 and its distribution by sectors reveals a predominance of establishments dedicated to services, these being 47.59% of the total in the municipality. It occupies position 2 of the total number of companies established in the state and number 2 in the regional ranking. (*Diagnóstico Municipal*, agosto 2022: p.38).

The 2019 economic censuses recorded that, in the municipality of Zapopan, the three most important subsectors in the generation of gross census added value were the Food Industry; Manufacture of computing, communication, measurement and other electronic equipment, components and accessories; and Retail trade of motor vehicles, spare parts, fuels and lubricants, which together generated 27.5% of the total gross census value added registered in 2019 in the municipality (Municipal Diagnosis, August 2022: p. 39) (*Diagnóstico Municipal,* agosto 2022: p. 39)

As in the rest of the world, derived from the COVID 19 pandemic, many of the economic activities linked to commerce and services, as well as leisure in public places decreased significantly in Zapopan. However, by June 2022 the Mexican Social Security Institute (IMSS) announced that there are a total of 442,958 insured workers in the municipality, that is, an annual increase of 37,657 workers compared to 2021. According to the records of the IMSS, the economic group with the most jobs registered within the municipality of Zapopan was that of professional and technical services, which in June 2022 registered a total of 63,836 workers, concentrating 14.41% of the total in the municipality. In this way, the economic recovery has been very firm since the official end of the COVID 19 Pandemic and the historic center of the municipality is proof of this. It is worth mentioning that Zapopan, currently, is the municipality with the highest GDP per capita and HDI in Jalisco, as well as one of the 50 municipalities with the highest HDI and GDP per capita in Mexico.[1].

Now that people can go out into the streets more calmly and safely, the bustle has returned to the Andador 20 de Noviembre, which, in the afternoons, is filled with people and sociocultural activities, thus corroborating what Fenochio and Dillingham assured about public spaces and the squares, in the sense that they are the place of commerce, the meeting place par excellence where people chat and live together, the place for a casual meeting or for flirting during the serenade; the agora for the concentration of protesters and complainants. The meeting point where community events are discussed, the place of memories, the space for solace and recreation, the mirror of the city. And I would add that it is the preferred place for tourists who are interested in knowing part of the historical and cultural aspects of the cities and an important point for the development of commercial and service socio economic activity. A very important part of the urban vitality of this studied space is the Zapopan Pilgrimage, which has been a World Cultural Heritage since 2018.

*Figure 15. Dancers in the Pilgrimage of Zapopan*

*Source: Martínez, 2022.*

## 4. INTANGIBLE HERITAGE

The term heritage has experienced a significant change in its conceptualization over time, evolving from a paradigm that referred to the realm of the particular, in which parents inherit assets to their descendants, to a collective we, where assets They acquire a social dimension as a representation of events and cultural processes from previous times (Demanget, 2002).

The conception of heritage as social property is a product of the historical, social and political changes that humanity experienced in the 18th century, consisting of the disappearance of the King-State as a result of the triumph of the French Revolution. With the modification of the political-social regime, an enormous amount of property ceased to be the personal heritage of noble families and royalty, and became property of the republic; no link to a particular person. As a result of this inheritance received by the nascent State, and aware of the intrinsic value of the architectural and artistic heritage that the nobility had held, it was forced to assume responsibility for the safeguarding of all properties and collections seized as part of the new social contract.

Heritage, or concern for the past, is a modern Eurocentric concept, centered around the meta-narrative of nationalism as an ideology of belonging, legitimation and national identity. (Alvarado-Sizzo & López López, 2018, p. 31)

In the last quarter of the 20th century, concern for heritage conservation increased "the destruction caused to cities, civil buildings and population centers by the countries that participated in the Second World War, causing an important awareness about "the need to preserve not only peace, which for five long years was forgotten, but also the cultural manifestations of the afflicted nations." (Torres Aguilar, 2015, p. 20)

The United Nations Educational, Scientific and Cultural Organization (UNESCO) carried out the Convention on International Cooperation in the Protection of the Cultural and Natural Heritage of Mankind in 1972, with the aim of protecting world heritage (UNESCO, 1972). Subsequently, in 2003, it created the Convention for the Safeguarding of Intangible Cultural Heritage, conceiving it as follows:

> [...]the uses, representations, expressions, knowledge and techniques - along with the instruments, objects, artifacts and cultural spaces that are inherent to them - that communities, groups and in some cases individuals recognize as an integral part of their cultural heritage. This intangible cultural heritage, which is transmitted from generation to generation, is constantly recreated by communities and groups based on their environment, their interaction with nature and their history, instilling in them a sense of identity and continuity and thus contributing to promoting respect of cultural diversity and human creativity. (UNESCO, 2003)

The United Nations Organization has established clear criteria to value heritage and grant it the world heritage mark (UNESCO, 2006); However, this has not limited a debate regarding the determination of what should be called heritage and the use made of it. The current in favor of the declaration of heritage considers that it is a positive strategy, in which heritage has a neutral status and its only purpose is to transmit customs and cultural landscapes to future generations.

The negative view perceives heritage as a conscious manipulation of history, about what is good to remember and what should be forgotten, designed with the intention of generating visitors willing to spend money (Hubbard & Lilley, 2000). It does not try to separate heritage from its historical or cultural legacy (a link that will always keep the present and past together), it is precisely that quality that is considered to be used to generate a marketable product, turning heritage into a desirable object to be visited. (supply segment) interest that is commodified by the tourism sector (demand segment) (Bhardwaj, 1997; Cohen, 1988; Collins-Kreiner, 2016).

Religion is a relevant component of heritage. "Immovable sacred or religious heritage is a thematic sub-group that can be defined based on the destination or use that a community makes of said construction. The buildings destined for the abode of the gods are the sacred architecture par excellence" (Gudefin, 2006, pp. 96–97). An undoubted fact is that individuals come to sacred places for various motivations, from the faithful who congregate as part of the beliefs or obligations imposed on them by their religion, to those who arrive in search of experiencing a transcendental experience, and others. They arrive attracted by the cultural or natural value that is preserved in the sacred space.

Religious places are spaces of great cultural interest, since they allow us to encounter the symbolic and ontological value with which they were built, since they represent the mystical thought of a particular era. Which is shown in the different architectural elements, construction materials and dimensions with which the buildings were erected, as well as in the designs of the ornamental items, paintings and sculptures that they contain inside. However, "cultural heritage in religious matters is not kept only to protect it and, in any case, to show it on certain occasions. Rather, it must be recognized that it has a rich meaning and that therefore it is possible to use it" (José & Arancibia, 2015, p. 261). Sacred places, in addition to their identity function, are places where cult activities are carried out that include rituals and festivals, and combine elements of material and intangible heritage that represent the local culture.

> "the importance of intangible cultural heritage, a crucible of cultural diversity and guarantor of sustainable development, as highlighted in the UNESCO Recommendation on the Safeguarding of Traditional and Popular Culture of 1989, as well as in the Universal Declaration of UNESCO on Cultural Diversity of 2001 and in the Istanbul Declaration of 2002, approved by the Third Round Table of Ministers of Culture, Considering the profound interdependence that exists between intangible cultural heritage and material cultural and natural heritage" (UNESCO, n.d.)

This new vision of cultural heritage allowed the Latin American, African and Asian regions to have greater representation in the world heritage panorama, because they have a wide variety of traditions that remain alive after several centuries and are signs of their imaginary collective.

## 5. POPULAR RELIGIOSITY

Both anthropology and sociology of religion have debated the conceptual differentiation of the terms religion, spirituality and popular religiosity (Bobineau et al., 2000; Bourdieu, 1971; Bréchon, 2021; Grignon, 1977; Hervieu-Léger, 2002), however, in this work the idea proposed by Renée de la Torre (2013) will be used, so we will refer to popular religiosity as the space

"where even today a mixture is generated between various religious systems: indigenous worldviews familiar with magic, curanderismo, animism and "paganism", Catholicism articulating devotion to saints and virgins, miracles and ritualism, but also new age spirituality and neo-esoteria"(Tower, 2013, p.

*Table 1. Differences between religion, spirituality and religiosity*

| | Religion | Spirituality | Religiosity |
|---|---|---|---|
| System | Structured | Personal | Semi-structured |
| Composition | Group | Individual | Communal |
| Spatiality | Purpose-built public spaces (most of the time) | No specific place | Open public spaces (streets, squares, etc.) |
| Organization | Institutional | Individual | Group |

**Source**: Martínez, 2024.

To speak of religiosity in the specifically Mexican case is to refer to a religious environment very different from the European or even Anglo-Saxon space. Even when the Mexican population was evangelized under the European Catholic tradition and particularly in the Spanish one, the inhabitants of the original communities managed to keep many of their festive customs alive, although with a different meaning, by managing to incorporate them as practices in the Catholicism that they evangelizing friars proclaimed.

In this way, a Catholic-pre-Columbian syncretism emerges and later also incorporates part of the imagination of the black population (Juárez Huet, 2009; Ricard, 1986; Saldivar Arellano, 2013) who was brought as slaves to work in the Spanish haciendas and mines that They were the most relevant economic activities during the 16th and 17th centuries. Therefore, many current religious expressions, especially in the Catholic religious festivities that take place in Mexico, are a mixture of manifestations that make them unique, even when they are solemnities that the Catholic religion celebrates urbi et orbi.

"We are a ritual people. And this trend benefits our imagination as much as our sensitivity, always tuned and awake. The art of the Festival, debased almost everywhere, is preserved intact among us. In few places in the world you can experience a spectacle similar to that of the great religious festivals of Mexico, with their violent, sour and pure colors, their dances, ceremonies, fireworks, unusual costumes and the inexhaustible cascade of surprises from the fruits, sweets and objects that are sold those days in squares and markets.

Our calendar is full of parties. On certain days, whether in the most remote places or in the big cities, the entire country prays, shouts, eats, gets drunk [...] time suspends its race, stops and instead of pushing us towards a tomorrow that is always unattainable and liar, offers us a round and perfect present, of dance and revelry, of communion and feasting with the most ancient and secret of Mexico." (Paz, 1992, p. 18)

Thus, popular religiosity transforms public space, particularly streets and sidewalks, into non-institutionalized sacred spaces, through a mixture that includes the practice of ancestral rituals, the use of Catholic images and statuettes, candles, banners, and, above all, the music, both in melodies accompanied by lyrics that praise the Catholic imagination, and sometimes include words or prayers in Nahuatl. But above all with a rhythmic sound without vocal accompaniment that serves for the participants to dance as a way of venerating the image or images that occupy the main place on the altar that is set up for the occasion.

> "Within their beliefs, the temple is not necessary to venerate God or the Virgin, since devotion and a lump figure, divine image or crucifix is enough before which to carry out your prayer materialized with the body" (Córdova Ortega, 2023, p.13)

The public space understood as the place inhabited by everyone and at the same time by no one ceases to be *terra nullius*, to temporarily be a communal space, where the neighborhood is revived based on the religious celebration; "[the] public space…could be defined as a space of and for public relations, that is, for those that occur between individuals who physically coincide and pass through places of transit and who have to carry out a series of accommodations and mutual adjustments to adapt to the ephemeral association they establish" (Delgado, 2011, p. 17)

It is not about individual people, popular religiosity is an act of group-type territorial appropriation, which can go even beyond the neighborhood, as well as cultural resistance that allows the tradition that has been modified day to day to be kept in force., where even new generations make ancestral practices their own and are integrated as a single whole that clearly marks the difference between the profane and the sacred.

## 6. LA ROMERÍA DE ZAPOPAN (THE ZAPOPAN PILGRIMAGE)

On October 12th of each year, the city of Guadalajara experiences a religious celebration that transforms its daily life. This is the pilgrimage of the Virgin of Zapopan, a centenary event, since its beginnings date back to the year 1734. Given the importance that this event has for the population of this city, it was recognized in 2018 by the United Nations Educational, Scientific and Cultural Organization (UNESCO) as intangible cultural heritage.

However, and UNESCO recognizes it in this way, in reality it is not an event that takes place only on one day, but rather it includes an entire ritual cycle that begins in the month of May and culminates every October 12. On this date, the journey made by the image of the Virgin takes place from the Guadalajara cathedral to the Sanctuary located in the municipality of Zapopan. During the months covered by the ritual cycle, different temples in the city become places to welcome this Virgin, so that her community of faithful can be close to her.

Throughout this period of time, different streets that make up part of the public space of the Guadalajara city become spaces of pilgrimage where faithful Catholics, dancers, religious people, musical groups, etc. converge in an orderly manner to accompany the Marian image. to the temple that receives the pilgrim image that day.

Due to the number of Catholic temples that the city of Guadalajara has, some temples may appear in one year and not the next. However, there are several temples that are always included as part of the tour. The number of temples visited during this period ranges between 175 and 180, with the list changing each year, which modifies the route that the pilgrim image follows throughout the city.

The data for the last two years are:

*Table 2. Temples and Deaneries visited by the Virgin of Zapopan in Guadalajara in 2022 and 2023*

| | 2022 | | 2023 | |
|---|---|---|---|---|
| **Month** | **Temples visited** | **Deaneries** | **Temples visited** | **Deaneries** |
| May | 18 | 3 | 17 | 4 |
| June | 39 | 7 | 37 | 8 |
| July | 42 | 6 | 41 | 6 |
| August | 25 | 4 | 34 | 5 |
| September | 44 | 5 | 37 | 7 |
| October | 11 | 2 | 10 | 2 |
| **Total** | **179** | **27** | **176** | **32** |

Source: Authors' elaboration based on the 2022 and 2023 programs of visits of the Virgin of Zapopan.

*Figure 16. Spaces visited by the effigy of the virgin in the Guadalajara Metropolitan Area*

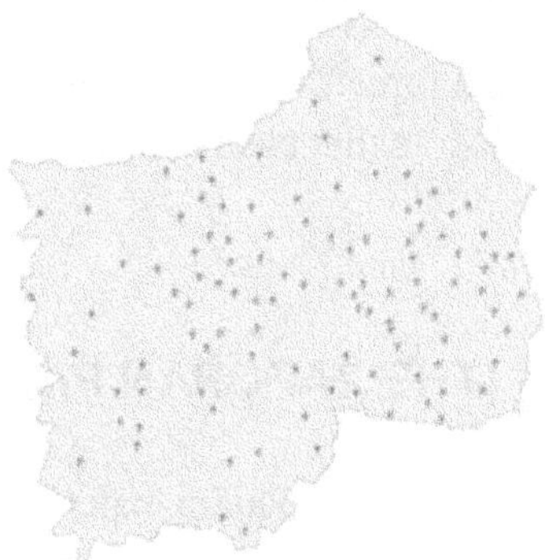

*Source: Martínez, 2024.*

*Figure 17. Spaces not visited by the effigy of the virgin in the Guadalajara Metropolitan Area*

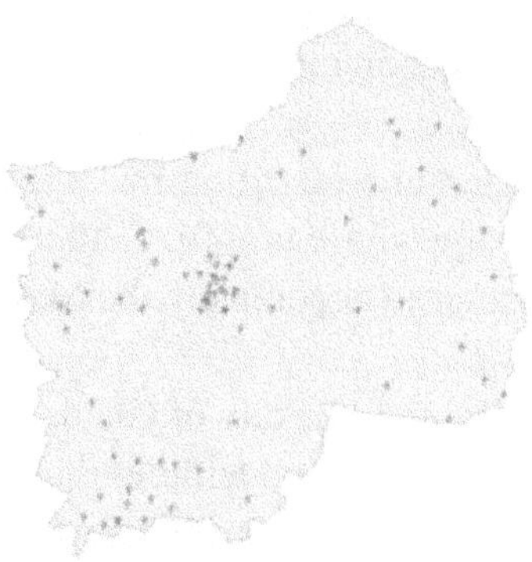

*Source: Martínez, 2024.*

## 7. THE PILGRIMAGE

The last stop on the annual tour that the virgin makes through the city of Guadalajara is always the Cathedral. Prior to the pilgrimage, a series of activities are carried out that begin on the afternoon of October 11. The first ritual event is what is known as the "Mass of Sponsorship", with this religious act a renewal of the patronage that John Paul II granted in 1989 to the Virgin over the Archdiocese of Guadalajara is carried out. This liturgy is celebrated in Plaza Tapatía, an open-air esplanade that is located in an area near the cathedral at the back. Once this ceremony is over, the image returns in procession to be placed inside the cathedral building where it spends the night.

From the afternoon and throughout the night of the eleventh, groups of pilgrims begin to arrive to accompany the image along the nearly nine kilometers that separate the cathedral of Guadalajara from the Basilica of Zapopan. The commercial portals around the cathedral, normally empty during the nights, from the eleventh to the twelfth of October, are transformed into a verbena for the enjoyment of pilgrims and dancers waiting outside the cathedral building.

You can see food stalls where entire families eat and live together, along with pilgrims who calm their appetite while talking or enjoying the dances of the groups that arrive and make an "offering in movement" (as they call their dances) before starting the pilgrimage. You can also see stalls and sellers of souvenirs of various kinds. It seems curious that among food and souvenir stalls there are others selling footwear, specifically sandals, because it is a tradition that many pilgrims make the route barefoot. This phenomenon occurs more frequently in women, who often come accompanied by their babies to present them to the virgin and thank her for having had a successful birth. Under the portals of the buildings surrounding the cathedral, you can see people sleeping waiting for the Virgin to start the tour.

*Figure 18. Images of the night of the Pilgrimage*

*Source: Martínez, 2022.*

At the same time that the verbena is held in the surroundings of the cathedral, in different parts of the city, the different native dance groups that participated in the pilgrimage carried out their last rehearsal, which they called "real rehearsal". Unlike the other rehearsals they carry out during the year, and mainly from July or August, this one is very formal. All the participants wear their complete attire, although most during the pilgrimage will use a new one ordered to be made especially for the occasion.

In the rehearsal, an altar is placed with flowers and candles that are offered by the participants of the group. On this altar is placed a replica of the image of the Virgin of Zapopan that at the end of the rehearsal will be transferred along with the flowers and candles, to the place where the dancers will rest upon their arrival in Zapopan, once the tour is over; because they will continue to dance throughout the twelfth day.

This rehearsal, depending on each group, begins between eleven at night and two in the morning, lasting two hours. The last rite prior to the pilgrimage takes place on the twelfth of October at five in the morning, when a mass is officiated in the Cathedral to bid farewell to the Virgin of the city of Guadalajara. At the end of this, at approximately 6 in the morning, the pilgrimage formally begins, a journey that will take the Virgin back to the Basilica of Zapopan, where she resides most of the year. However, the pilgrimage begins even before the image leaves the cathedral temple. Between three and four in the morning the contingent of people begins to walk along the route that will be traveled later by the image of the virgin. This beginning occurs naturally by the pilgrims who wish to receive it at the time of their arrival at the Basilica of Zapopan.

Although there is no regulation of the distance that pilgrims must travel to consider that they have made the pilgrimage, it can be observed that different contingents of both people who make the tour on foot, or on horseback, (the latter arrive around three in the morning), arrive in the surroundings of the cathedral to formally begin what for them is the route. The organized contingent, religious groups and dancers, begin to place themselves in the places arranged for each of them around four in the morning, to begin the tour the first contingent at approximately five in the morning. The places are previously assigned by the organizing committee of the pilgrimage, so each group is clear about the place from which it must depart. (Government of Zapopan, 2023) (Gobierno de Zapopan, 2023)

The barracks that always lead the pilgrimage is the *Cuartel de Danzas Autóctonas de Zapopan*, and the group of dancers that begins the tour is that of Apaches María de la O, since the invocation of the Virgin of Zapopan is that of La Expectación or de la O. 71 groups participated in this barracks, five of them guest dances that are not affiliated with the barracks. The second contingent was composed of the Royal Union of Native Dances of Jalisco Barracks.

The third contingent is made up of various religious groups that make up the official escort of the Virgin. Behind them, the Virgin is transported in a decorated vehicle that allows the image to be seen by the people who form the streets along the route. The fourth and last contingent is also made up of dancers, belonging to the Chimalhuacan Dance Barracks of the State of Jalisco, which contributed 62 groups.

Even when the first group of Apache María de la O begins the tour at five in the morning, the Zapopan Virgin arrives at the basilica shortly before 11 in the morning, because during the tour she makes different stops so that people can see the image up close, and even when the groups of dancers perform the entire tour performing their dances, at the moments when the carriage of the Virgin stops, they take the opportunity to revive their "prayer in movement" with more elaborate and complex steps. The tour concludes with the entrance of the Virgin to the walkway of November 20 that leads to the Plaza de la Américas, which ends in the atrium of the basilica. (Government of Zapopan, 2023) (Gobierno de Zapopan, 2023a).

## 8. CONCLUSION

As has been revealed in this multidimensional approach in socio-urban research, a comprehensive vision of public space better explains how some variables and elements of micro-spatial systems are related. A denser and more detailed understanding of public space and its phenomenology necessarily results in a life and urban reality that is better socialized, shared and appropriated by citizens.

In this sense, in Mexico religious expressions in public spaces are common and diverse. There is a deep-rooted Marian devotion, the Virgin of Guadalupe is considered the patron saint of Mexicans, however, devotion to the Virgin of Zapopan is the main one among the faithful of the Metropolitan Area of Guadalajara, which is why so many manifestations of devotion are carried out. to this image.

The Andador 20 de Noviembre is a fundamental space in these activities, as it is one of the main access and transit routes for the various groups that arrive to celebrate the Virgin during the Zapopan Pilgrimage. This, combined with the great urban vitality of the historic center of this municipality, gives this space a unique multidimensional and syncretic character, where recreational, commercial, cultural, religious activities, among others, take place.

The public space that by definition belongs to everyone, at the time of the celebration, during the period of two hours, is a sacred space, of worship, which is respected by passers-by, both those who do so in vehicles and those who go walking Even those who do not profess the same belief maintain respect for the celebration, understanding that it is an important tradition in the city.

People are also increasingly aware that quality of life and respect for the environment and social and cultural diversity are the true wealth of human settlements. Therefore, the urban elements that citizens and visitors value are those related to urban and environmental services, cultural offerings, popular traditions, gastronomy, historic buildings and/or quality architecture, and timely and adequate mobility. All of this attracts people to public spaces, and this also constitutes their vitality.

All this is present in this small corner of the planet that is the centrality of Zapopan, where the Andador is a key urban piece; So people have taken advantage of it and today it is in good health.

For this reason, it can be stated that it is environmental health, social coexistence and the quality of citizen life, what this type of space contributes to cities and where we can observe a possible path forward for the sustainable development of our communities.

## REFERENCES


Ayala García, C., & Tami Cortés, M. D. (2020). La arquitectura, el espacio público y el derecho a la ciudad. Entre lo físico y lo vivencial [Architecture, public space, and the right to the city. Between the physical and the experiential]. *Revista de Arquitectura*, *22*(1), 11–25.

Beltrán Rodríguez, M. (2016). La importancia de la vitalidad urbana [The importance of urban vitality]. *Ciudades*, (19), 169–182.

Berroeta Torres, H., & Vidal Moranta, T. (2012). La historia de la ciudad es la de sus espacios públicos [The history of the city is that of its public spaces]. *Revista de Urbanismo*, (26), 1–15.

Camacho, O. Mariel (2021). "Las relaciones socio–espaciales en la habitabilidad de conjuntos de vivienda social", en *Revista Internacional de Ciencias Sociales Interdisciplinares*, Vol. 10, núm. 1, Common Ground Research Networks, Estados Unidos de América.

Delclòs-Alió, X., & Miralles-Guasch, C. (2018). Looking at Barcelona through Jane Jacobs's eyes: Mapping the basic conditions for urban vitality in a Mediterranean conurbation. *Land Use Policy*, *75*, 505–517. DOI: 10.1016/j.landusepol.2018.04.026

Ecologistas en Acción. (2020). Turismo en ciudades. *Informe sobre el impacto del turismo en entornos urbanos*. [Ecologists in Action. (2020). Tourism in cities. Report on the impact of tourism in urban environments].

Gobierno de Zapopan. (2023, octubre 13). *Asisten a la Romería 2023 más de dos millones de feligreses*. [More than two million parishioners will attend the 2023 Pilgrimage]. Noticias. https://www.zapopan.gob.mx/v3/noticias/asisten-la-romeria-2023-mas-de-dos-millones-de-feligreses#:~:text=La%20edici%C3%B3n%20289%20de%20Romer%C3%ADa,corte%20del%20Operativo%20Romer%C3%ADa%202023

Gobierno de Zapopan. (2023a, octubre). https://www.zapopan.gob.mx/v3/noticias/zapopan-reconoce-danzantes-en-su-dia#:~:text=El%2027%20de%20septiembre%20de,portadoras%20de%20la%20tradici%C3%B3n%20hacen

Instituto de Información Estadística y Geográfica de Jalisco. (2022). Zapopan, Diagnóstico Municipal, agosto. Gobierno del Estado de Jalisco. [Jalisco Institute of Statistical and Geographic Information. (2022). Zapopan, Municipal Diagnosis, August. Government of the State of Jalisco].

Jacobs, J. (2011). *Vida y muerte de las grandes ciudades [Life and death of great cities]*. Capitán Swing.

Kang, C., Fan, D., & Jiao, H. (2021). Validating activity, time, and space diversity as essential components of urban vitality. *Environment and Planning. B, Urban Analytics and City Science*, *48*(8), 2255–2270. DOI: 10.1177/2399808320919771

Ramírez Kuri, Patricia (2016). *La reinvención del espacio público en la ciudad fragmentada*, Instituto de Investigaciones Sociales, [The Reinvention of Public Space in the Fragmented City, Institute for Social Research]. UNAM.

López, B. Esteban (2022). La orientación oficial del "desarrollo" atenta contra la transmisión del patrimonio biocultural comunitario, en *Revista Internacional de Ciencias Sociales Interdisciplinares*, [The official orientation of "development" threatens the transmission of community biocultural heritage, in International Journal of Interdisciplinary Social Sciences in the Fragmented City, Institute for Social Research]. Vol. 10, núm. 2, Common Ground Research Networks, Estados Unidos de América.

Mouratidis, K. (2020). "Built environment, urban vitality and social cohesion: Do vibrant neighborhoods foster strong communities?", en *Landscape and Urban Planning*. Diciembre. https://www.sciencedirect.com/science/article/pii/S0169204620301225

Programa de las Naciones Unidas para el Desarrollo. (2022). Informe de desarrollo humano municipal 2010 – 2020. Una década de transformaciones locales en México.[United Nations Development Programme. (2022). Municipal Human Development Report 2010–2020. A Decade of Local Transformations in Mexico] PNUD México.

Rendón, A. Mario (2006). Zapopan: ¿una identidad guadalajarizada? en *Estudios Jaliscienses*, núm. [A Guadalajaran identity? In Estudios Jaliscienses, no.65]. El Colegio de Jalisco, 5-19.

Reyes, E. (2024). Turistificación: el impacto en las comunidades urbanas. [Touristification: The Impact on Urban Communities]. *BNZero.*

Safa, P. (2000). "El estudio de las identidades vecinales: una propuesta metodológica". ["The study of neighborhood identities: a methodological proposal."]. *Revista Universidad de Guadalajara*, http://www.cge.udg.mx/revistaudg/rug19/articulo3.html

Sampaio de Almeida, D., Simões, R., Brito e Abreu, F., Lopes, A., & Boavida-Portugal, I. (2024). A Carrying Capacity Calculator for Pedestrians Using OpenStreetMap Data: Application to Urban Tourism and Public Spaces. *arXiv preprint arXiv:2406.16781.*

## ENDNOTE

1 https://www.undp.org/es/mexico/publicaciones/informe-de-desarrollo-humano-municipal-2010-2020-una-decada-de-transformaciones-locales-en-mexico-0

# Chapter 11
# Sustainable Development and the Attractiveness of Development Regions

**Mihai Alexandru Botezatu**
https://orcid.org/0000-0002-0218-5243
*Romanian-American University, Romania*

**Alexandru Tăbu că**
https://orcid.org/0000-0003-0630-7751
*Romanian-American University, Romania*

**Iuliu Marin Ivănescu**
https://orcid.org/0009-0002-1663-2873
*Romanian-American University, Romaniaw*

## ABSTRACT

*The study demonstrates, through empirical research on the development regions in Romania, that the average monthly income per household can be an element for evaluating the attractiveness of the regions for an adult, especially a young person, who is looking for a suitable job or an area in which to settle down and build a future. We considered factors that might be correlated with economic development in the region (GDP/place at the regional level, population occupancy rate, investments, turnover of active companies, tourist accommodation capacity, the employed population with higher education in the region). We built simple and multiple linear regression models, with data series from 2007-2019, obtained by processing data from the Statistical Yearbook of Romania (2008-2020). We concluded that all these factors are correlated with the size of the average monthly income indicator on a regional household. The results were interpreted and explained.*

DOI: 10.4018/979-8-3693-7081-0.ch011

## 1. INTRODUCTION

Sustainable development, defined by the Brundtland Report (WCED, 1987) as "development that meets the needs of the present, without compromising the ability of future generations to meet their own needs", showed all nations and organizations that intensive development, without limits in the consumption of resources can no longer continue, as it is necessary to ensure the competitiveness of all organizations under the conditions of ensuring the protection of the environment, limited natural resources and local communities.

At the global level, UN specialists and researchers have identified three dimensions of the sustainable development of an organization: economic, social and environmental (UN, 1992; UN, 2010), and have established concrete measures for their implementation in the field of climate change, of transport (UN, 2019; UN, 2016), of waste recycling and clean energy production (Madlener et al., 2011), of re-technology and digitization of production and services (Gherghina et al., 2021; Răileanu, 2018), of social protection (Commission of the European Communities, 2002).

All this was taken over and transposed into strategies, action plans, directives, decisions regarding sustainable development within the European Union countries (European Commission, 2005, 2015).

The strong technological development and the economic growth of production and services have required the finding of solutions to ensure sustainable development, both at the level of organizations, which ensure their economic competitiveness, as well as at the level of society, of communities from different geographical areas. This means achieving, on a territorial level, "a fair distribution of resources and opportunities for the current and future generations", as well as the collective responsibility for the limited use of natural resources (Jovovic et al., 2017) and for the social protection of different local communities (National Strategy for Sustainable Development of Romania 2013-2020-2030). Every organization, of any type and size, is involved in the process of ensuring sustainable development at the local and national level, through economic development measures, simultaneously with measures to improve the quality of people's lives and social cohesion, for the protection of the environment and natural resources, which are practically limited.

Romania, as an EU member country, has taken over and applied all EU requirements in the field of sustainable regional development (Government of Romania, 2008). In Romania, 8 development regions are recognized, unevenly developed, as demonstrated in studies and reports requested by the European Commission, with very different natural resources (agricultural land, forests, waters, mineral resources, urban agglomerations, etc.), with local communities which have a very different standard of living and development opportunities.

In these conditions, we found that both existing authorities at the world, European, national, or regional level, as well as specialists, economists, researchers studied and analyzed factors that directly influence sustainable economic growth (Satyro et al., 2017), the development and competitiveness of companies, the standard of living of communities, re-technology and digitization (Botezatu et al, 2021), innovation and research (Gonzalez-Loureiro et al,2012; Niebel,2018), education (Pirnau et al,2020) and health. All these are regulations or studies aimed mainly at stimulating the business environment, measures to protect the environment and communities, equal opportunities, reducing unemployment and gaps between development regions. That is why they are mainly addressed to businessmen, investors, local and central administration, political decision-makers, who can influence, in the desired sense, the identified influencing factors.

A region's attractiveness is a rather new concept and the associated scientific literature includes studies that would mainly connect a region's attractiveness by its economic and social development. This is appropriate if we are referring to the attractiveness of a region as seen by an investor. However, if we are taking into consideration the point of view of a family with several members, including children and seniors, the attractiveness of a region that would provide them with various possibilities for a better life or provide them with the social well-being they deserve cannot be linked only to economic development.

Economic development and attractiveness of a region are not identical concepts, but they are closely linked, because the attractiveness of a region is to a large extent conditioned by its degree of development (Nakamura, 2023). And yet, a region can be highly developed economically, it can be attractive to investors and business people, but not be sufficiently attractive for a citizen looking for a job or for a place to settle down. Why? Because he and/or members of his family may have a specialization in a field of activity that does not exist in the region, may have children who want a certain direction in their education, may be engaged in freelancing activities that have no market share in the area, or may be engaged in various household activities that are beneficial to their livelihood by increasing their income or reducing household expenses. In situations like these cases a region that is highly developed economically that would be attractive to investors in various types of production or service companies may not be as attractive to a simple citizen, especially a young person who would be looking for a region in which to build a future, a family, a job. Add to this the special interest given by both the EU (European Commission, 2017,2020,2023) and the OECD (OECD, 2021,2022) to the concept of regional attractiveness which should be as accurately defined and measured as possible in order to provide the best possible information to those interested or concerned about this. This requires to establish performance criteria, measurable indicators that can assess these criteria in order to better guide any citizen looking for a place of residence, work and development, who wishes to settle in a region with sustainable and competitive economic development, capable of ensuring their well-being (Balkytė et al., 2010).

We did not find any studies that examine local development from the perspective of a citizen, seeking a suitable area to establish a residence. We consider that within a family, members may have different specializations, career fields, income level expectations, and requirements for new job opportunities or starting their own businesses.

The problem is therefore that one should identify, through a measurable and easy-to-understand indicator, which is the most attractive region for him and what are the factors that influence this attractiveness of the regions.

The different, uneven development of the existing development regions in any country, the opportunity for the emergence of better jobs, in more "attractive" areas, put in front of those interested a multitude of tempting offers, apparently suitable, a whole network of options. For them, first of all, our study can be a guide for choosing the most suitable region, which will ensure them both for the present and for the future, a good life.

Therefore, we assess the attractiveness of the regions, perceived by those who want to establish their residence or place of work in a developing region of the country through the *average monthly household income indicator*, an indicator that is easy to understand and compare, with very different values in the 8 development regions in Romania.

Thus, we construct simple and multiple linear regression models using data series from 2007 to 2019, derived from processing and synthesizing information from the Statistical Yearbook of Romania. The results will be interpreted and explained.

The research will show why the indicator - *average monthly income per household at the regional level* can serve as an information support for a young person/adult in choosing the area, the region in which to settle for the future. This means that it can also serve as an indicator of regional attractiveness for interested citizens. Considering the objective of the research our objective, the work is addressed to the decision-makers, governmental or of the local or central administration, who, in order to increase the attractiveness of some regions, to reduce the gaps in development and living standards in the analyzed regions, can take measures and can influence these factors, if known.

## 2. LITERATURE REVIEW AND WORKING HYPOTHESES

### 2.1. Literature Review Regarding the Attractiveness of Development Regions

The international bodies and those of the EU paid special attention to the concept of regional development, they developed directives, laws, decisions, measures to influence the development of the regions and reduce the development gaps between them. Specialists start from the idea that the development region does not represent a summation of active companies and all types of activities and services carried out in the area, but is a complex, dynamic system, with complex interdependencies and relationships, in all environments: economic, social, environmental, cultural, ethnic, religious, political, etc. Thus, the development of the regions, in the 3 major dimensions, economic, social, and environmental, has been evaluated and analyzed by many researchers, economists and specialists, interested in measuring and possibly directly stimulating businesspeople, investors, the level livelihood of the population, protection of the environment and communities, education and employment in the development regions (Boumahdi et al., 2023).

The researchers went further with the analysis and calculations, they defined complex, composite indicators to measure the level of development of the regions (Li et al., 2009; Manea et al., 2016; Salvati et al., 2014; Shi et al., 2019; Kocmanova et al., 2012; Botha et al., 2020), in order to explain the differences in their development and thus present them to the decision-makers, who can improve the inequalities of development and standard of living in the regions.

EU statistics confirm that there are large disparities between regions in both developed and less developed countries, with direct economic and social effects. Regional policy measures, combined with those of cohesion, should stimulate investments and especially those in infrastructure and high technology, green technology (Botha et al., 2022) and digitization, employment rate and structure of employment, level and structure of education, innovation, research, and development (Constantin et al., 2007). The paper analyzes the increased influence of the competitiveness of human resources, given the level of education and specialization in the development of the regions.

Recently, more and more emphasis has been placed on a broad and integrated vision of society and the economy, which simultaneously concerns sustainable development, competitiveness, and the well-being of society (Balkytė et al., 2010).

As a result, new development models appear, which increasingly consider, in a developed region, the social well-being, the degree of satisfaction of the members of the local communities.

We believe that a more economically developed region will ensure a greater attractiveness for investors, a lower risk for investments and, as a result, will determine a multiplication of economic development - which will then be reflected in higher household incomes of the population. In these conditions, the

European Commission, as well as the Division for Regional Development Policies of the OECD, have addressed, in their studies and research, a variety of topics, including the one regarding the attractiveness of development regions, very different recently, with large gaps between these. In order to stimulate specific structural changes, required by new specializations/jobs on the labor market, in the adult education and training system, the low performances in research and innovation, the European Commission has launched and will develop a new EU mechanism: "the mechanism of stimulation and capitalization of talents" (European Commission, 2023). Practically, this mechanism means attracting human resources with the appropriate skills and abilities for the fields developed within each region. Only in this way is it possible to diversify production adapted to regional specifics, to make services accessible, to increase the efficiency of all activities, including local administration, for the attraction and efficient use of cohesion funds at the local level (Hallin et al, 2016; Gavrila-Paven et al, 2022).

Analyzing the development, wealth and very different performance of development regions in economically developed countries, OECD researchers (OECD, 2022) realized that it is difficult to indicate the most performing, most attractive region, without specifying the performance criteria that are of interest to a given moment a certain authority. This is because every entity interested in a performing region has in mind a certain field of activity (industry, construction, tourism, IT&C, research-innovation, education, etc.), environmental protection or local communities. Under these conditions, the OECD researchers propose a composite index and a methodology for its calculation, built on the basis of 14 indicators that characterize the attractiveness of 6 domains: Economic, Tourism and culture, Land and housing, Education, Connectivity, Natural environment.

The purpose of the calculated indicator is not to achieve a ranking of the regions, but a process of diagnosing them, considering indicators that characterize both the natural resources, the environment, and their development as a result of all the activities carried out. Moreover, in order to evaluate the performance profile and international attractiveness of the regions, the OECD developed in (OECD, 2021) a dashboard of regional attractiveness with approximately 60 indicators, from the fields of: business environment, knowledge, human resources and infrastructure, under the conditions of ensuring a sustainable development in all these fields.

The work (Achten et al., 2020) analyzes the effect that the unequal spatial location and extent of regions has on economic activities, and (Hirte et al., 2020) studies the effect of international trade on regional income inequality, demonstrating that these are elements determinants of economic activities and, implicitly, of the attractiveness of the regions. The article (Moyo et al., 2022) studied for regions in South Africa the effect of human capital formation represented by the level of education, on poverty and inequality, of unequal economic opportunities.

D. Nakamura in his book (Nakamura, 2023) used the social welfare function to evaluate the attractiveness of regions. He shows that all the elements of sustainable development, the economic, social and environmental infrastructure of the regions directly influence the accessibility of households to goods and services and, implicitly, the attractiveness of the regions for the population. The study (Garofoli, 2016) presents the interaction between economy, society and territory, demonstrating the active role of territory, of local resources in regional development, based on the production of knowledge and specific resources, on quality and innovation.

Many researchers have defined and analyzed the attractiveness of regions by the size and degree of safety of investments made in various regions of the world (South Africa, China, Russian Federation, Ukraine, Poland) (Roswinna, 2020; Rodionov et al., 2021; Kurikov et al., 2022; Myakshin et al., 2021; Bagautdinova et al., 2014; Godlewska-Majkowska, 2018; Sikorska-Wolak et al., 2020).

There are studies that have analyzed the influence of tourism on the attractiveness of regions, of cross-border tourism, which requires increasing accessibility to the transport network, recognizing and promoting areas as tourist destinations, measures for infrastructure development (Stach et al., 2014).

The article (Nyborg Storm, 2022) analyzes how theaters contribute to the attractiveness of a region in Denmark, and preferences for culture and art are very varied, depending on the type of region.

In Canada, the administration of the province of Quebec (Horakova, 2021) and in China (Hu B et al., 2020) the attraction of regional talents considers four aspects: regional development, industry development, income growth and attractive regional environment. The level of economic development, the quality of people's lives and the level of tertiary industrial development have a great impact on the attractiveness of talents. Talents (high level specialists in different fields of economic, social and cultural sectors) also pay a lot of attention to regional medical, educational and transportation indicators.

The European Commission, concerned with eliminating or at least reducing these inequalities in development, standard of living and opportunities for local communities, has constantly supported, through cohesion policies, the sustainable development of regions (European Commission, 2017), by supporting infrastructure, protection environment and re-technology, social protection in the poorer regions.

Recently, more and more international and European bodies, researchers and specialists use the concept of regional attractiveness, and less of their economic development, to emphasize the need to increase social well-being, the well-being of all community members, regardless of their status. For Europe, the attractiveness of regions is a theme of the European Union Strategy for employment and economic growth, Europe 2020 (European Commission, 2010) and the Territorial Agenda 2030 (European Commission, 2020). The ESPON 2013 program (ESPON, 2013) supports, first of all, the development of cohesion policy and the ability of regions to attract those resources that include specialized human capital. This means that the EU puts human capital at the center of its concerns of eliminating disparities between regions and considers that the average annual rate of net migration and the average annual rate of tourist arrivals (from the country or from outside it) can be indicators of regional attractiveness.

Romania adopted, together with the EU countries, all these measures, created its own regional development policy, considering all the indicators defined for regional attractiveness (European Commission, 1997; Antonescu, 2013).

## 2.2. Literature Review Regarding the Influence of the Level of Education to Development Level at Regional Level

Starting from the idea that without education it is not possible to ensure a human capital according to the requirements of new technologies, of digitalization and the expansion of communication systems, of new specializations and trades, a series of researchers and specialists in the field have analyzed the impact of education on economic development in general, but also on the regional one. Research show (Marquez-Ramos et al., 2018; Valero, 2021) that universities train highly qualified specialists through bachelor's, master's, and doctoral studies. They also possess a rich academic research resource (teaching staff and researchers) who, together with the business environment, carry out research-development and innovation in EU countries.

Educational performance is positively correlated with the economic growth of regions (Rodríguez-Pose et al., 2010), but the impact of income levels is unclear. The study (Titu, et al., 2013) supports the promotion, within all education and professional training units, of an education for sustainable development, which identifies, develops, and implements actions to support the creative and innovative regional entrepreneurial effort, through cooperation between the public and private sectors.

The study for Guangdong province in China (Yun Sun et al., 2021) appreciates that the results demonstrated the importance of education, especially for the impact on economic growth, and the article (Bertoletti et al., 2022) argues that the profile of higher education, the internationalization of students and the development of academic research has a direct impact on regional development. Education and regional economic development support each other in the Russian Federation (Yingkai Ma, 2022) and decision-makers are recommended to align education systems with regional development priorities (Stepus et al., 2022). The study (Pirnau et al., 2019) demonstrates the indissoluble link between education and employment, through the continuous adaptation of the educational system to the requirements of the labor market, to the specific requirements of current employers, in the conditions of the increasingly extensive digitization of activities.

The studies carried out show that also in Romania there is an interdependence between regional development and the development of the education system (Popescu et al., 2009), and the development and diversification of higher education, of the specializations offered, (Botezatu, 2020) the increase of its quality and management they have a direct impact on the regions (Pantilie, 2015), as their strategic development resource (Leontieva et al., 2021).

The article (Grant, 2017) studies the influence on regional development of a very low level of education in countries such as India, Indonesia, and the Syrian Arab Republic. The implications are in both directions: there are young people who will do hard, risky, and poorly paid work, but also regions that do not possess highly specialized human resources, with skills to stimulate economic growth. Ensuring that all young people obtain at least a good primary and lower secondary education is vital to providing countries with the skilled human resources they need for development (Kusuma, 2020).

## 2.3. Working Hypotheses

We chose the *average monthly income of a household at the regional level* as the dependent variable, an indicator that can be more easily perceived by a person as attractive or not when one wants to choose the region where he will establish his residence or is looking for a place of suitable work. We chose this different approach, which looks at the attractiveness of the regions not only for the business environment and investors, for tourists and politicians or local decision-makers, but also for the citizen (young or adult) who chooses where to work or settle for the future.

We have taken into consideration some of the factors of economic development to show that a development region may be attractive to many citizens, but not to all of them. This is due to the fact that a family may have members with different skills and specializations, thus it would search for more diverse criteria to judge the attractiveness of regions as it may have different income sources from being involved in more activities/services, it may be interested in diverse paths for the future of their children and so on.

In accordance with the previously studied literature, the following research hypotheses are formulated:

- Hypothesis 1 (H1). The GDP/capita value at the regional level is correlated with *average monthly household income at the regional level.*
- Hypothesis 2 (H2). The value of the Gross Investments of local units active in industry, construction, trade, and other services in a territorial profile with 0-9 employed persons (micro-enterprises) is in correlation with the *average monthly income of a household at the regional level.*

- Hypothesis 3 (H3). The employment rate of the regional population is correlated with the *average monthly income of a household at the regional level.*
- Hypothesis 4 (H4). The turnover of local units active in industry, construction, trade and other services in a territorial profile, Total, is correlated with the *average monthly income of a household at a regional level.*
- Hypothesis 5 (H5). The employed population, in a territorial profile, with a higher education level, is correlated with the *average monthly income of a household at the regional level.*
- Hypothesis 6 (H6). The capacity of tourist accommodation at the regional level is correlated with the *average monthly income of a household at the regional level.*

## 3. RESEARCH DESIGN

### 3.1. Description of Data and Variables

With the exception of the Bucharest-Ilfov region, the development regions in Romania group together 4-6 counties (administrative units), being very different, both in terms of the level of economic development, given by the number, structure and specificity of active companies, the specificity of the environment (relief, infrastructure, plant crops, waters, forests, etc.), as well as the level of living and training of the population, its age structure and level of education, customs, culture, ethnic and religious affiliation of these communities. All this makes the development regions extremely complex, dynamic, and difficult to analyze systems, in which the competitive advantage of organizations of any kind, included in the globalization process, is created and supported locally, only under the conditions of a sustainable development (Porter, 1992; 1996).

The data were collected from the Statistical Yearbooks of Romania for the period 2007-2019 (National Institute of Statistics, 2023), through complex processing and synthesis, for the 8 regions of regional development in Romania. Starting from the development inequalities of the regions in Romania and from the different level of education of the population, we considered that the *average monthly household income* indicator at the regional level could be more easily understood and compared by any citizen, when evaluating the attractiveness of the regions, when he has to decide where he will settle or where he will migrate for a job and/or a better life. The paper investigates the relationship between the dependent variable the *average monthly income of a household at the regional level* and the independent variables presented in table 1, in order to estimate to what extent these factors influence the attractiveness of development regions.

*Table 1. List of used variables*

| No. | Variable name | Variable type | The meaning of the variable |
|---|---|---|---|
| 1. | $Y_a$ | Dependent variable $Y_j$, j=a,..h | Average monthly income per household in the region North-Wes (Lei) |
| 2. | $Y_b$ | | Average monthly income per household in the region Center (Lei) |
| 3. | $Y_c$ | | Average monthly income per household in the region North-East (Lei) |
| 4. | $Y_d$ | | Average monthly income per household in the region South-East (Lei) |
| 5. | $Y_e$ | | Average monthly income per household in the region South-Muntenia (Lei) |
| 6. | $Y_f$ | | Average monthly income per household in the region Bucharest-Ilfov (Lei) |
| 7. | $Y_g$ | | Average monthly income per household in the region South-West Oltenia (Lei) |
| 8 | $Y_h$ | | Average monthly income per household in the region West (Lei) |
| | | For each region j with j=a,..h defined above, we define the independent variables: | |
| 9. | $X1_j$ | Independent variables $Xi_j$, with i=1,..6 j=a,..h | Regional GDP per person (PIB/pers), in Lei |
| 10. | $X2_j$ | | Gross investments of local units active in industry, construction, trade and other services in a territorial profile with 0-9 employed persons, in million Lei |
| 11. | $X3_j$ | | Turnover of local units active in industry, construction, trade and other services in territorial profile, Total, in million Lei |
| 12. | $X4_j$ | | Employment rate of the population of working age 15-64 years |
| 13. | $X5_j$ | | Employed population, in territorial profile, with higher education level (number of people) |
| 14. | $X6_j$ | | Tourist accommodation capacity (number of places) |

Source: Processing by the authors

## 3.2. The Econometric Framework

For the study of these dependencies, corresponding to the 6 formulated hypotheses, we first used the simple linear regression econometric model. Then, in order to verify the simultaneous influence of several factors among those mentioned, as suggested by the empirical data analysis at the level of the 8 regions, we built multiple linear regression models.

The proposed generic model $M_{i,j}$ with j=a,..h for the 8 regions; i=1,..6 for the 6 independent variables considered has the below form:

$$Y_j = C_{i,j} + A_{i,j} * Xi_j + E_{i,j} \qquad (1)$$

with j=a,..h; i=1,..,6 for the 6 independent variables; where:

- $Y_j$ represents the dependent variable - Average monthly income per household in the region j
- $Xi_j$ represents the independent variable i for the development region j, as described in Table 1.
- $C_{i,j}$, $A_{i,j}$ are the parameters of the regression model.
- $E_{i,j}$ is the random error variable (residue);

Thus, model $\mathbf{M}_{i,j}$ of linear regression verifies, for Romania, the hypothesis i, with i=1,..,6, if it exists, a dependency between the average monthly income per household in region j, with j= a,..,h (dependent variable) and the independent variable $Xi_j$, with i=1,..6 from the same region (X1, X2, X3, X4, X5 and X6).

We checked estimated linear regression models for each development region (Ma,..,Mh) and each of the 6 factors (X1, ..X6) considered, corresponding to the 6 formulated hypotheses (H1-H6). Thus, for the region a (Ya), North – West, the general simple regression model has the format:

$$Ya = C_i + A_i * Xi + E_i \quad i=1,..,6 \text{ for the 6 independent variables} \tag{2}$$

Thus, the model **Ma1** verifies the dependency of variable Ya, which represents the average monthly household income from region **a**, on the independent variable X1 – GDP/pers from the region, having the format:

$$Ya = C_1 + A_1 * X1 + E_1 \tag{3}$$

Model **Ma2** verifies the dependency of variable Ya, which represents the average monthly household income in region **a**, on the independent variable X2 – Gross investments of local units active in industry, construction, trade, and other services in a territorial profile with 0-9 employed persons, from the region, having the format:

$$Ya = C_2 + A_2 * X2 + E_2 \tag{4}$$

Model **Ma3** verifies the dependency of variable Ya on the independent variable X3 – The turnover of active local units in industry, construction, trade, and other services in the region, having the format:

$$Ya = C_3 + A_3 * X3 + E_3 \tag{5}$$

Model **Ma4** verifies the dependency of variable Ya on the independent variable X4 – The employment rate of the population of working age 15-64 years in the region, having the format:

$$Ya = C_4 + A_4 * X4 + E_4 \tag{6}$$

Model **Ma5** verifies the dependency of variable Ya on the independent variable X5 – The employed population, with a higher level of education in the region, having the format:

$$Ya = C_5 + A_5 * X5 + E_5 \tag{7}$$

Model **Ma6** verifies the dependency of variable Ya on the independent variable X6 – Tourist accommodation capacity in the region, having the format:

$$Ya = C_6 + A_6 * X6 + E_6 \tag{8}$$

We have continued the study for region ***a*** with the simultaneous verification of the influence of several factors on the considered dependent variable, using the general format in the expression (2).

The general model **Mjk** represents the model Mk of multiple regression in region **j** (j=a,..,h), for the study of the simultaneous influence of several factors **Xi**, cu **i**=1,..,6, and has the generic format:

$$Yj = C_{j,k}+A_{j,k,1}*X1_j+A_{j,k,2}*X2_j+A_{j,k,3}*X3_j+A_{j,k,4}*X4_j+A_{j,k,5}*X5_j+A_{j,k,6}*X6_j+E_{j,k} \quad (9)$$

Thus, model **Ma7** (Table 3) verifies for region **a** the simultaneous dependency of variable Ya on the independent variables X1 and X4, having the format:

$$Ya = C_{a,7}+A_{a,7,1}*X1_a+A_{a,7,4}*X4_a+E_{a,7} \quad (10)$$

We continued the study by proceeding in a similar way for all other regions (b,..,h). Table 3 presents the parameter estimates from valid simple and/or multiple linear regression models, which attests to the influence of the independent variables considered on the dependent variable Y in each region. The data is presented for just 3 NUTS2 Romanian development regions out of 8, as the results are similar for the rest of the 5 development regions.

## 3.3 A Preliminary Data Analysis

A descriptive statistic of the variables used is summarized in Table 2.

*Table 2. Statistical description of the variables*

| Var | Regions | Mean | Maximum | Minimum | Std. Dev | Skewness | Kurtosis | Jarque -Bera |
|---|---|---|---|---|---|---|---|---|
| | North - West | 2930.315 | 5191.92 | 1718.89 | 976.2782 | 1.203898 | 3.529072 | 3.291924 |
| | Center | 2898.202 | 5041.06 | 1700.67 | 942.1523 | 1.132505 | 3.377939 | 2.856267 |
| | North - East | 2397.914 | 3859.68 | 1544.43 | 627.9517 | 1.197254 | 3.652342 | 3.336243 |
| Y | South - East | 2484.682 | 4257.41 | 1546.26 | 759.7299 | 1.241702 | 3.570133 | 3.516686 |
| | South - Muntenia | 2665.713 | 4305.63 | 1637.5 | 753.0177 | 1.131145 | 3.370369 | 2.84653 |
| | Bucharest - Ilfov | 3858.035 | 6960.57 | 2208.07 | 1395.122 | 1.241561 | 3.393564 | 3.423761 |
| | South - West Oltenia | 2513.374 | 4209.88 | 1529.64 | 723.2279 | 1.163756 | 3.64611 | 3.160498 |
| | West | 2881.618 | 4839.98 | 1706.97 | 834.6632 | 1.113332 | 3.683979 | 2.93901 |
| | North - West | 33305.93 | 60981.6 | 21284.3 | 12692.64 | 0.905343 | 2.734426 | 1.814103 |
| | Center | 34868.53 | 62046.1 | 22618.8 | 12438.45 | 0.86728 | 2.742161 | 1.66572 |
| | North - East | 24092.68 | 56572.1 | 14649.3 | 11631.3 | 1.773261 | 5.706475 | 10.7807 |
| X1 | South - East | 31308.04 | 61661 | 18738.2 | 12219.49 | 1.129462 | 3.892873 | 3.19581 |
| | South - Muntenia | 30914.65 | 73147.6 | 19648.08 | 14586.03 | 1.9797 | 6.503687 | 15.14103 |
| | Bucharest - Ilfov | 85720.82 | 146775.2 | 55079.3 | 28706.17 | 0.801537 | 2.610784 | 1.474058 |
| | South - West Oltenia | 27060.29 | 42589.6 | 17752.8 | 8980.591 | 0.660452 | 2.046973 | 1.437068 |
| | West | 37650.25 | 56507.8 | 25602.4 | 11094.36 | 0.528041 | 1.899256 | 1.260431 |
| | North - West | 3067.231 | 5080 | 1711 | 1091.572 | 0.412912 | 2.025363 | 0.883947 |
| | Center | 2682 | 4410 | 1528 | 922.7153 | 0.540689 | 2.108706 | 1.063715 |

continued on following page

*Table 2. Continued*

| Var | Regions | Mean | Maximum | Minimum | Std. Dev | Skewness | Kurtosis | Jarque -Bera |
|---|---|---|---|---|---|---|---|---|
| | North - East | 1907.231 | 3652 | 1154 | 730.4498 | 1.058575 | 3.393921 | 2.511978 |
| X2 | South - East | 2464.692 | 4740 | 1377 | 997.2219 | 0.902503 | 1.769989 | 0.820153 |
| | South - Muntenia | 1925.615 | 2633 | 1320 | 513.2817 | 0.386288 | 1.366696 | 1.7683 |
| | Bucharest - Ilfov | 15611.46 | 23223 | 7502 | 5089.533 | -0.339063 | 1.850759 | 0.964497 |
| | South - West Oltenia | 854.9231 | 1392 | 549 | 294.7096 | 0.619331 | 1.821217 | 1.583734 |
| | West | 2520.769 | 4219 | 1416 | 995.1504 | 0.486765 | 1.870533 | 1.204373 |
| | North - West | 118754.3 | 185544 | 78103 | 32285.65 | 0.756916 | 2.556054 | 1.348087 |
| | Center | 126874.2 | 197026 | 81065 | 35697.72 | 0.640693 | 2.370745 | 1.10387 |
| | North - East | 80585.92 | 121565 | 56108 | 19588.18 | 0.750901 | 2.634483 | 1.294047 |
| X3 | South - East | 107644.9 | 142626 | 79453 | 16734.55 | 0.380067 | 3.003143 | 0.312983 |
| | South - Muntenia | 135621.5 | 192480 | 90116 | 30871.31 | 0.437323 | 2.435869 | 0.58676 |
| | Bucharest - Ilfov | 397027.1 | 588009 | 278275 | 86319.7 | 0.89804 | 3.07478 | 1.750392 |
| | South - West Oltenia | 64193.62 | 95490 | 48426 | 14141.59 | 1.031102 | 3.126764 | 2.312244 |
| | West | 97333 | 144512 | 60716 | 27671.71 | 0.374462 | 1.88552 | 0.976599 |
| | North - West | 63.08462 | 67 | 59.8 | 2.525815 | 0.291585 | 1.964195 | 0.765364 |
| | Center | 56.81538 | 60.8 | 52.8 | 2.680748 | -0.057648 | 1.626781 | 1.028638 |
| | North - East | 67.96923 | 73.1 | 64.6 | 2.635458 | 0.541475 | 2.257327 | 0.934021 |
| X4 | South - East | 57.15385 | 60.4 | 54.4 | 1.744331 | 0.064108 | 2.258355 | 0.306841 |
| | South - Muntenia | 61.14615 | 64.9 | 56.4 | 2.466311 | -0.261969 | 2.265747 | 0.440721 |
| | Bucharest - Ilfov | 65.88462 | 72.3 | 62.2 | 3.382762 | 0.829792 | 2.238025 | 1.806365 |
| | South - West Oltenia | 61.05385 | 64 | 55.7 | 2.490855 | -1.242557 | 3.497064 | 3.47905 |
| | West | 59.01538 | 60.6 | 57.2 | 1.080776 | -0.005976 | 1.919069 | 0.632967 |
| | North - West | 200.2308 | 249 | 150 | 33.56127 | 0.103113 | 1.57269 | 1.126528 |
| | Center | 180.6923 | 216 | 140 | 29.15586 | 0.060552 | 1.413987 | 1.370473 |
| | North - East | 193.3077 | 234 | 179 | 16.18325 | 1.536452 | 4.334214 | 6.079056 |
| X5 | South - East | 149 | 166 | 119 | 13.75984 | -0.769079 | 2.755646 | 1.313889 |
| | South - Muntenia | 177.2308 | 203 | 142 | 20.0173 | -0.597534 | 2.181886 | 1.136145 |
| | Bucharest - Ilfov | 419.3846 | 537 | 325 | 65.40074 | 0.15783 | 2.05521 | 0.537479 |
| | South - West Oltenia | 146 | 155 | 120 | 9.327379 | -1.692433 | 5.691042 | 10.12864 |
| | West | 138.8462 | 151 | 113 | 12.00587 | -0.842112 | 2.654288 | 1.601236 |
| | North - West | 31565 | 40897 | 26103 | 5135.711 | 0.766363 | 2.200046 | 1.619137 |
| | Center | 55362.62 | 71038 | 35380 | 13709.55 | -0.196813 | 1.422622 | 1.431659 |
| | North - East | 25260.62 | 31469 | 18414 | 4683.748 | -0.002366 | 1.632285 | 1.013278 |
| X6 | South - East | 110793.8 | 136875 | 95587 | 16587.05 | 0.748533 | 1.692792 | 2.139582 |
| | South - Muntenia | 26039.23 | 31529 | 13747 | 5132.401 | -1.033552 | 3.381449 | 2.393314 |
| | Bucharest - Ilfov | 21718.69 | 24294 | 18937 | 1520.173 | 0.124371 | 2.326976 | 0.278868 |
| | South - West Oltenia | 18662.69 | 22927 | 14973 | 2492.447 | 0.131988 | 2.124553 | 0.452883 |
| | West | 26060.46 | 30664 | 20447 | 3442.18 | -0.156629 | 1.788302 | 0.848436 |

Source: Processing by the authors

At first glance, the average household income (Y) has average values that do not differ much (between 2397.91 in the Yc region and 3858.03 in the Yf region). A closer analysis reveals that the value of the income per household varies in a very wide range, from the maximum value of 6960.57 in the Yf region and 5191.92 in the Ya region, to the minimum value of 1544.43 in Yc and 1529.64 in the Yg region respectively. We appreciate that this represents a very large difference in income per household, which directly affects the standard of living of the respective households. The graph of the values of the indicator Y, which measures the average income per household, is presented in Fig. 1.

*Figure 1. The graph of the average income per household in the period 2007-2019 in the regions of Romania*

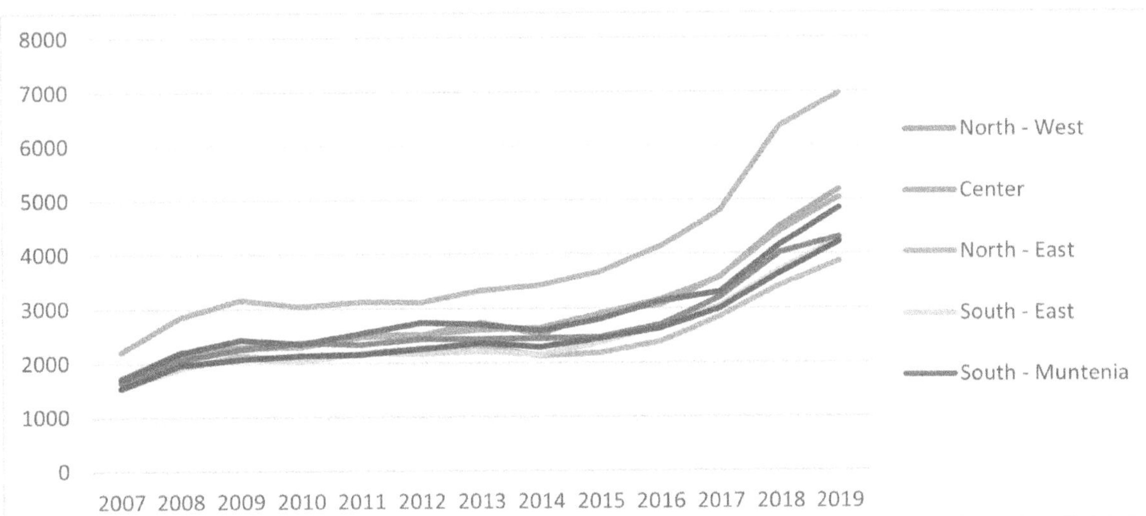


Analyzing the average value of the GDP/place indicator expressed in lei/inhabitant (X1) by region, it exceeds in the Yf region (85721 lei) by 2.45 times the next value, in terms of size, belonging to the Yb region (34869 lei) and by 3.56 times the smallest, 24093 lei of the Yc region. It is observed that X1 registers the highest value in the Yf region, of 146,775 lei and the minimum of 55,079 lei, followed at a great distance by the Ya region with 60,982 lei - maximum and minimum value of 21,284 lei. The lowest values are recorded in the Yc region, where the maximum is 24,092 lei, and the minimum is 14,649 lei. The GDP/place indicator shows an uneven development of the 8 regions, which is not exactly reflected (in terms of size) on the average income per household. This means that, for a correct assessment of the regional attractiveness, measured by the average income per household, other indicators must also be considered.

Analyzing the gross investments made by local units active in industry, construction, trade and other services with 0-9 employed persons, in a territorial profile, it is found that the X2 indicator has the highest average value in the Yf Bucharest-Ilfov region (15611 million lei) being 18.3 times higher than the average value for the Yg region (South - West Oltenia) of 854.9 million lei.

The graph of the values of the indicator X1 (GDP/place) which assesses the economic development of the regions is presented in Fig. 2.

*Figure 2. Graph of GDP/place values in the period 2007-2019 in the regions of Romania*

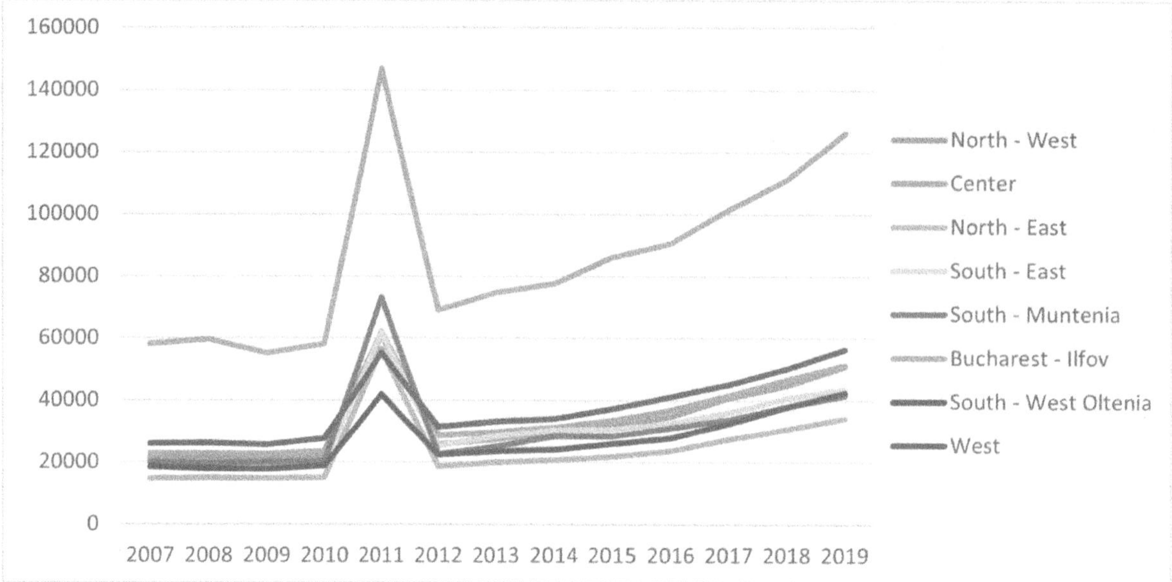


The range of values for the maximum value, with the highest value in the Yf region (23223 million lei) and the lowest in the Yg region of 549 million lei, shows that the Yg region is characterized by the lack of attractiveness for investors in the creation and development of businesses micro. The graph of the values of the X2 indicator that assesses the attractiveness of the regions for investors is presented in Fig. 3. It is found that the Bucharest-Ilfov region (Yf) presents a much higher attractiveness than all other regions for the creation and development through investments of micro enterprises (with 0-9 employees). Comparing this graph to graph 1, it can be seen that this big difference in value is not exactly transmitted to the average household income indicator, which means that there are other indicators that reduce this influence, and they should be taken into analysis.

*Figure 3. Graph of the values Gross investments made by active local units with 0-9 people employed, in the period 2007-2019, in the regions of Romania*

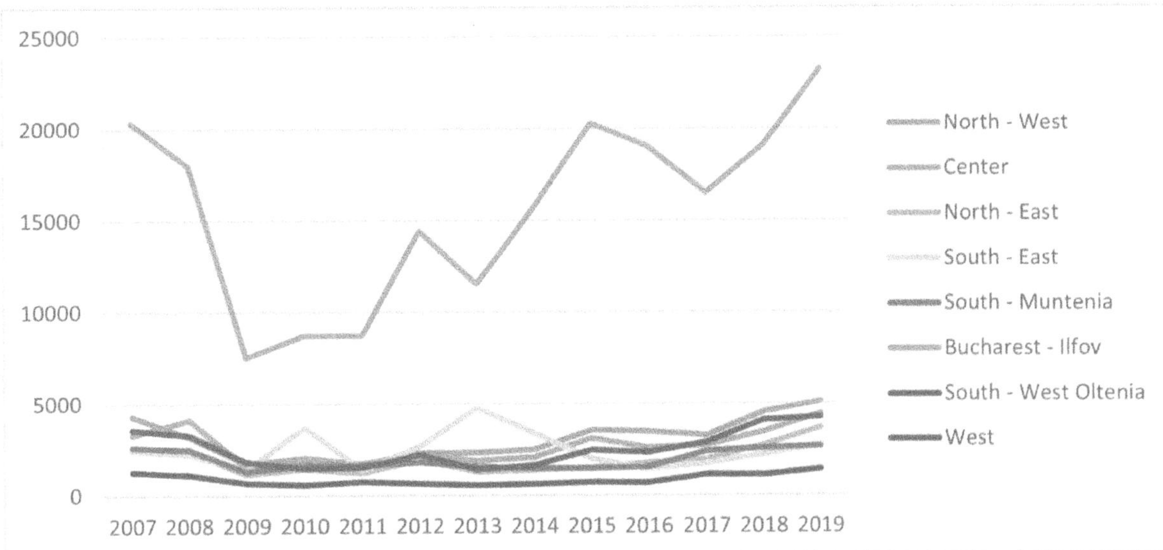


The indicator Total turnover of active companies in the regions (X3) shows that the Yf region has companies with a turnover 3.34 times higher than the next region in terms of value (397,027 million lei compared to the Ya region with 118,754 million lei) and 6.18 times compared to the region with the lowest average Yg value (64194 million lei). Their value varied between the maximum value of 588009 (Yf region) and the minimum value of 48426 in the Yg region. The graph of the values of the X3 indicator that assesses the attractiveness of the regions for entrepreneurs is presented in Fig. 4.

*Figure 4. Chart of values Total Turnover of active companies in the period 2007-2019 in the regions of Romania*

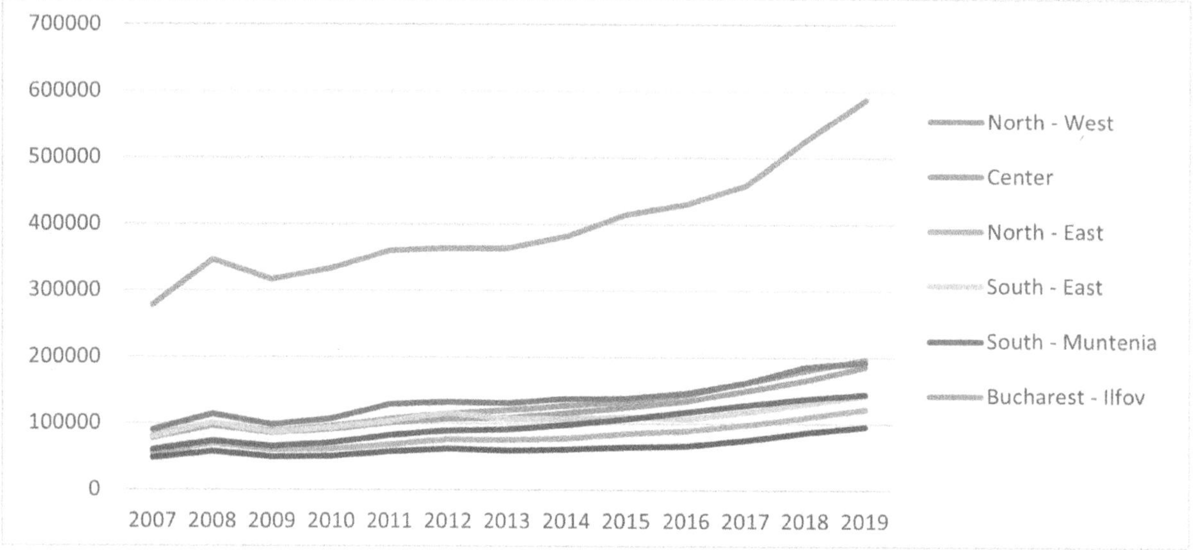


The indicator Employment rate of the working age population 15-64 years old, regionally (X4) has a different evolution in the 8 regions. X4 has a higher average value in the Yc region (67.97) compared to the developed regions Yf and Ya, with average values of the same indicator of 65.9 and 63.08, respectively. The same order also exists regarding the maximum and minimum values of the X4 indicator. This means that, although the employment rate of the population is higher in reg Yc, the incomes per household remain lower, because the wages are lower, being performed less well-paid activities, which require a poorly specialized or unskilled labor force. It may not be possible to obtain additional sources of household income, so that household income remains at a lower level than in the Yf region. The graph of the values of the X4 indicator regarding the employment rate of the population is presented in Fig. 5.

*Figure 5. Graph of the values of the Population Employment Rate in the period 2007-2019 in the regions of Romania*

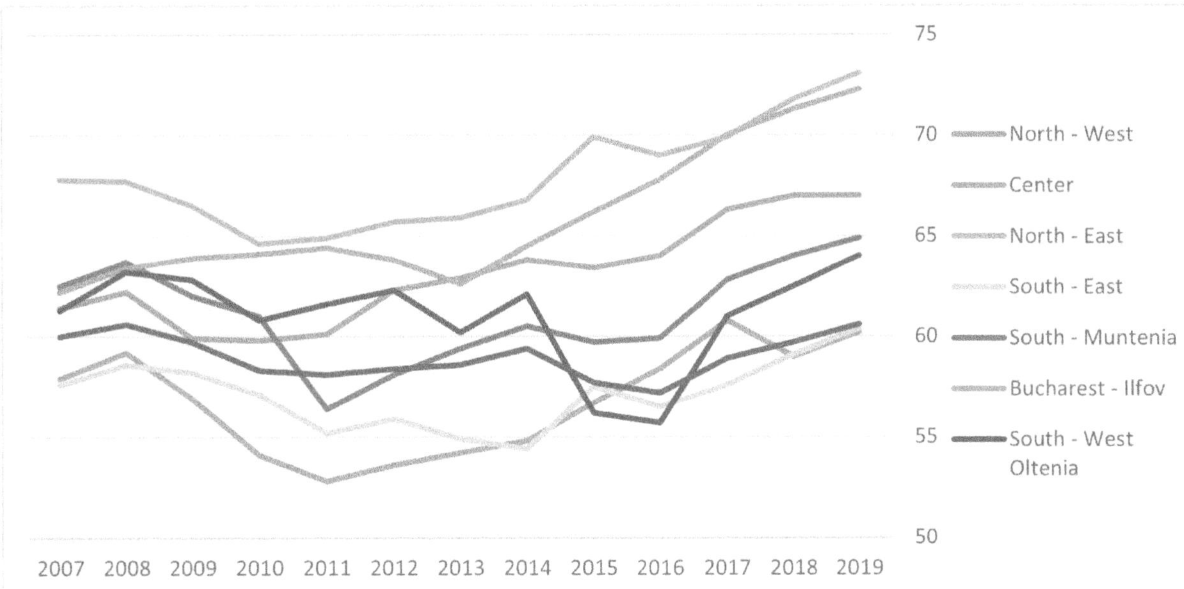


The employed population, in territorial profile, with a higher education level (number of people), X5, shows a structure of highly specialized activities, which benefits from an average number of about 420 thousand people with higher education in the Yf region, 3 times more compared to about 139 thousand in the Yh region. The graph of the values of the X5 indicator regarding the number of the population with higher education in the region is presented in Fig. 6.

*Figure 6. Graph of the values of the employed population, in territorial profile, with higher education level (number of people) in the period 2007-2019 in the regions of Romania*

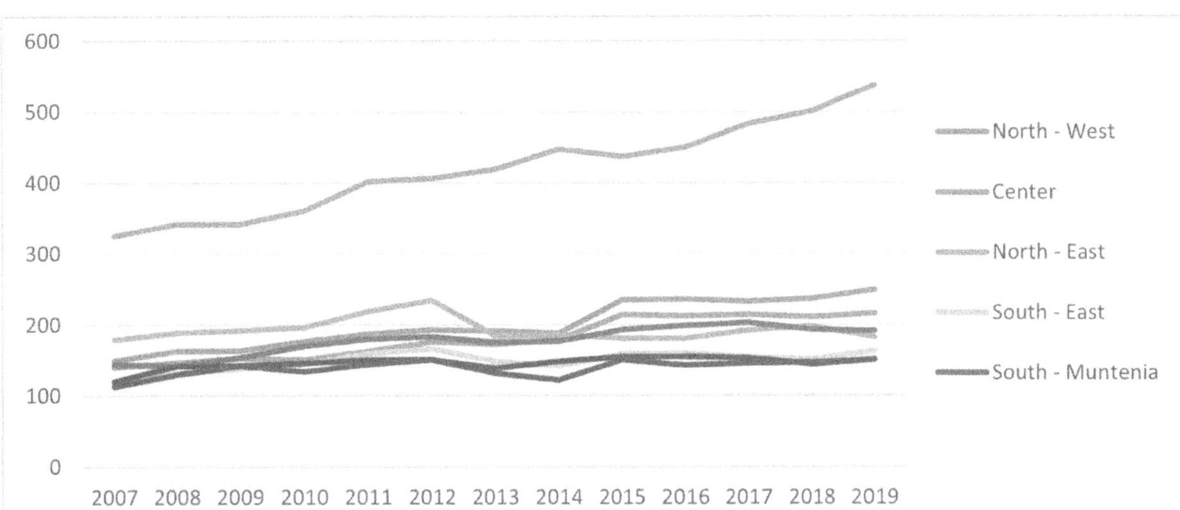

The analysis of the values of the indicator X6 - The accommodation capacity offered at the territorial level (fig 7), shows a big difference between the South-East region, with an average value of 110793.8 places, compared to the next region, Center, with 55362.62 and then the following regions with values between 18662 (South -West Oltenia) and 31565 (North–West). This means that the X6 indicator can influence the average household income, especially in regions where it has high values.

*Figure 7. Graph of values of accommodation capacity in territorial profile, (number of places) in the period 2007-2019 in the regions of Romania*

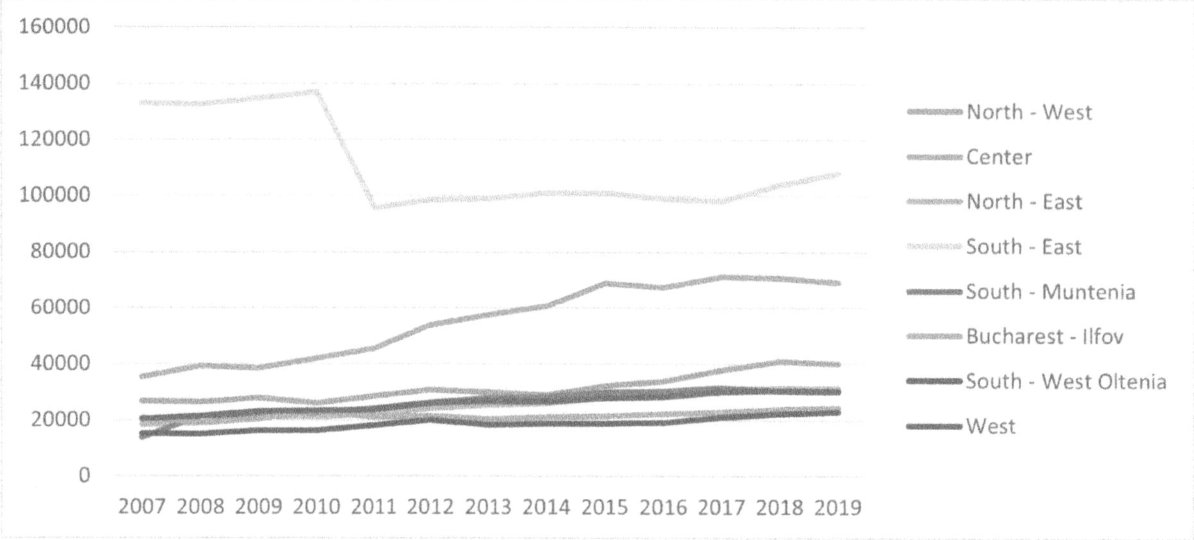


## 4. THE RESULTS OF THE REGRESSION MODELS

From the primary analysis of the data, we noticed that a single indicator does not cover all the aspects that contribute to the assessment of the standard of living, of the well-being of a region, to the attractiveness of the region for human resources, for citizens who wish to seek a better job or to settle in the region. Therefore, we considered it necessary to consider several indicators, to check to what extent the models built on their basis are valid and explain the large differences in development and living standards between the 8 regions in Romania.

We built and verified the models for each development region in Romania (8) and each considered factor (6). We thus checked the correctness of the formulated hypotheses (H1- H6). The centralizer of the parameter estimates obtained for part of the valid linear regression models, which shows the influence of the 6 independent variables on the *average gross monthly income per household* in 3 development regions in Romania is presented in Table 3.

*Table 3. Centralizer of parameter estimates obtained for selected valid linear regression models*

| Var<br>Model | C | X1 | X2 | X3 | X4 | X5 | X6 | R-squared | Adjusted Rsquared | F-statistic |
|---|---|---|---|---|---|---|---|---|---|---|
| **Region Ya - North - West** | | | | | | | | | | |
| Ma1 | 1277.263 †<br>(2.0325) | 0.0496 *<br>(2.8013) | | | | | | 0.4164 | 0.3633 | 7.84 |
| Ma2 | 1142.479 †<br>(1.7231) | | 0.5829 *<br>(2.8498) | | | | | 0.4247 | 0.3724 | 8.12 |
| Ma3 | -581.5542 *<br>(-2.4895) | | | 0.0296***<br>(15.5379) | | | | 0.9564 | 0.9525 | 241.42 |
| Ma4 | -18118***<br>(-4.8780) | | | | 333.65***<br>(5.6711) | | | 0.7451 | 0.7219 | 32.16 |
| Ma5 | -2070.52 *<br>(-2.2703) | | | | | 24.97***<br>(5.5541) | | 0.7371 | 0.7132 | 30.84 |
| Ma6 | -<br>2740.613***<br>(-4.5797) | | | | | | 0.1796***<br>(9.5916) | 0.8932 | 0.8835 | 92.00 |
| Ma7 | -<br>15439.41***<br>(-4.6180) | 0.0255 *<br>(2.3249) | | | 277.70 *<br>(5.0278) | | | 0.8345 | 0.8014 | 25.22 |
| Ma8 | -11616.31 *<br>(-2.4761) | | | | 188.02 †<br>(2.0650) | 13.41 †<br>(1.9570) | | 0.8157 | 0.7788 | 22.13 |
| **Region Yb - Center** | | | | | | | | | | |
| Mb1 | 1214.887 †<br>(1.8728) | 0.0483 *<br>(2.7432) | | | | | | 0.4062 | 0.3522 | 7.52 |
| Mb2 | 1543.059 †<br>(2.0419) | | 0.5053 †<br>(1.8886) | | | | | 0.2449 | 0.1762 | 3.56 |
| Mb3 | -7709.042 †<br>(-1.5097) | | | | 186.69 †<br>(2.0795) | | | 0.2822 | 0.2169 | 4.32 |
| Mb4 | -1886.26 †<br>(-1.8470) | | | | | 26.47***<br>(4.7410) | | 0.6714 | 0.6415 | 22.47 |
| Mb5 | -8335.81 †<br>(-2.1900) | 0.0454<br>**<br>(3.1386) | | | 169.89 *<br>(2.5340) | | | 0.6384 | 0.5661 | 8.82 |
| **Region Yf - Bucharest - Ilfov** | | | | | | | | | | |
| Mf1 | -<br>2408.305***<br>(-5.6588) | | | 0.0158***<br>(15.0419) | | | | 0.9536 | 0.9494 | 226.26 |
| Mf2 | -<br>22163.52***<br>(-9.3843) | | | | 394.95***<br>(11.0313) | | | 0.9171 | 0.9096 | 121.69 |
| Mf3 | -4159.337 **<br>(-3.4368) | | | | | 19.11***<br>(6.6986) | | 0.8031 | 0.7852 | 44.87 |
| Mf4 | -11620.13 **<br>(-3.4197) | | 0.0763 †<br>(1.5656) | | | | 0.6578 **<br>(4.0304) | 0.7133 | 0.6559 | 12.43 |
| Mf5 | -8172.311 *<br>(-2.9951) | | | | | 14.31 **<br>(3.5870) | 0.2775 †<br>(1.6159) | 0.8439 | 0.8127 | 27.02 |

Source: Processed by the authors.

Note: ***, **, *, † highlights statistical significance for the levels of 0.1%, 1%, 5% and 10%. Values of the t statistic are given in parentheses. The description of the variables is made in Table no. 1.

We have synthesized the results for all 8 Romanian regions in order to verify the existence of a correlation between the analyzed factors and the selected indicator "average household income at regional level" for measuring the attractiveness of a development region.

We see that, if valid simple linear regression models were found for an influence factor, it was not included in multiple models except to highlight the influence of other factors. For some influencing factors, no valid simple linear regression models were found, and their influence was highlighted through multiple models in which they participate as independent variables, along with other factors.

## 5. DISCUSSIONS

The study identifies and analyzes the correlation of some factors of economic development and the structure of the employed population with the attractiveness of development regions in Romania, viewed and analyzed based on the perception of the citizen - young or adult, who wants to choose the area for residence or a place of work.

From the empirical results of the valid models for the **Ya (North-West)** region, listed in Table 3, the following can be found:

- From the model **Ma1**, the estimated value of the coefficient of determination (R-square) shows that the variation in the value of the independent variable X1 explains the variation in the dependent variable (Ya) in proportion of 41,64%. For each increment by 100 Lei of the regional GDP/place value (X1), average gross monthly household income (Ya) increases by approximately 5 Lei.
- From the model **Ma2**, the estimated value of the coefficient of determination (R-square) shows that the variation in the value of the independent variable X2 explains the variation in the dependent variable (Ya) in proportion of 42,47%. For each increment by 100 million Lei of the gross investment value of local units active in industry, construction, trade and other services in a territorial profile with 0-9 employed persons (X2), average gross monthly household income (Ya) increases by 58 Lei.
- From the model **Ma3**, the estimated value of the coefficient of determination (R-square) shows that the variation in the value of the independent variable X3 explains the variation in the dependent variable (Ya) in proportion of 95,64%. For each increment of 100 million Lei of the of the turnover value of local units active in industry, construction, trade and other services in a territorial profile (X3), average gross monthly income per household (Ya) increases by 3 Lei.
- From the model **Ma4**, the estimated value of the coefficient of determination (R-square) shows that the variation in the value of the independent variable X4 explains the variation in the dependent variable (Ya) in proportion of 74,51%. For each increment of 1% of the value of the Employment Rate of the population of working age 15-64 years in territorial profile (X4), average gross monthly income per household (Ya) increases by 333,65 Lei.
- From the model **Ma5**, the estimated value of the coefficient of determination (R-square) shows that the variation in the value of the independent variable X5 explains the variation in the dependent variable (Ya) in proportion of 73,71%. For each increment of 10 persons of the value of the Employed population, in territorial profile, with a higher level of education (X5), average gross monthly income per household (Ya) increases by 249 Lei.

- From the model **Ma6**, the estimated value of the coefficient of determination (R-square) shows that the variation in the value of the independent variable X6 explains the variation in the dependent variable (Ya) in proportion of 89,32%. For each increment of 100 places for the value of tourist accommodation capacity in territorial profile (X6), average gross monthly income per household (Ya) increases by 17 Lei.

From the empirical results of the valid models for the **Yb (Center)** region, listed in Table 3, the following can be found:

- From model **Mb1**, the estimated value of the coefficient of determination (R-square) shows that the variation in the value of the independent variable X1 explains the variation in the dependent variable (Yb) in proportion of 40,62%. For each increment by 100 Lei of the value of X1, average gross monthly income per household (Yb) increases by 5 Lei.
- From model **Mb2**, the estimated value of the coefficient of determination (R-square) shows that the variation in the value of the independent variable X2 explains the variation in the dependent variable (Yb) in proportion of 24,49%. For each increment of 100 million Lei of the value of X2, average gross monthly income per household (Yb) increases by 50 Lei.
- From model **Mb3**, the estimated value of the coefficient of determination (R-square) shows that the variation in the value of the independent variable X4 explains the variation in the dependent variable (Yb) in proportion of 28,22%. For each increment by 1% of the value of X4, average gross monthly income per household (Yb) increases by 186,69 Lei.
- From model **Mb4**, the estimated value of the coefficient of determination (R-square) shows that the variation in the value of the independent variable X5 explains the variation in the dependent variable (Yb) in proportion of 67,14%. For each increment by 10 persons of the value of X5, average gross monthly income per household (Yb) increases by 264,7 Lei.

No valid regression models were found to attest to the influence of the factors The turnover value of local units active in industry, construction, trade, and other services in a territorial profile (X3) and Tourist accommodation capacity in a territorial profile (X6) on Income gross monthly average per household (Yb).

From the empirical results of the valid models for the **Yf region (Bucharest - Ilfov)**, listed in Table 3, the following can be found:

- From model **Mf4**, the estimated value of the coefficient of determination (R-square) shows that the variation in the value of the independent variables X2 with X6 explains the variation in the dependent variable (Yf) in proportion of 71,33%. For each increment of 100 million Lei of the value of X2, average gross monthly income per household (Yf) increases by 7 Lei.
- From model **Mf1**, the estimated value of the coefficient of determination (R-square) shows that the variation in the value of the independent variable explains the variation in the dependent variable (Yf) in proportion of 95,36%. For each increment of 100 million Lei of the value of X3, average gross monthly income per household (Yf) increases by 2 Lei.
- From model **Mf2**, the estimated value of the coefficient of determination (R-square) shows that the variation in the value of the independent variable X4 explains the variation in the dependent

variable (Yf) in proportion of 91,71%. For each increment of 1% of the value of X4, average gross monthly income per household (Yf) increases by 395 Lei.

- From model **Mf3**, the estimated value of the coefficient of determination (R-square) shows that the variation in the value of the independent variable X5 explains the variation in the dependent variable (Yf) in proportion of 80,31%. For each increment of 10 people of the value of X5, average gross monthly income per household (Yf) increases by 191 Lei.
- From model **Mf4**, the estimated value of the coefficient of determination (R-square) shows that the variation in the value of the independent variables X6 with X2 explains the variation in the dependent variable (Yf) in proportion of 71,33%. For each increment of 100 places of the value of X6, average gross monthly income per household (Yf) increases by 65,78 Lei.

No valid regression models were found to attest to the influence of the regional GDP/person value factor (X1) on the average gross monthly income per household (Yf).

The obtained results show that the studied indicators (X1...X6) are significant from a statistical point of view, which leads us to validate the formulated hypotheses H1-H6. Validated models are those with p-values lower than 0.10, identified in table 3 by: *** for $p<0.001$, ** $p<0.01$, * $p<0.05$, † $p<0.10$. The presented results show that all six independent variables taken into account (X1, .., X6) have a direct and significant impact on the dependent variable - the average gross monthly income per household Y, with different values for the analyzed development regions in Romania. In conclusion, we can accept that the hypotheses H1, H2, H3, H4, H5 and H6 are verified.

## 6. CONCLUSIONS

The study identifies and analyzes to what extent the considered indicators influence the standard of living, the social well-being of the communities living in the regions of Romania, the attractiveness of the regions, reflected by the average gross income per household in the respective regions. The research considered Romania with its 8 development regions, with unequal access to natural resources and different degrees of development, less addressed in research by specialists in sustainable territorial development.

This different level of development of the regions is perceived and analyzed not only by the business environment, investors of all kinds, local or central administrations or politicians, but also by citizens from the country or outside it, when they want to look for a job or residence, a place of residence or in which to build one's future. That's why we chose this different approach, we analyzed the attractiveness of the regions through an indicator that is easier to understand, analyze and compare for any interested citizen, young person, or adult, namely the *average gross monthly income per household*, at the level of the regions. I have not found works that do this research, but there are a series of studies that show the influence of the factors analyzed on the economic development of the regions and the employment rate of the population, leading to their attractiveness for investors, to the development of specific forms of education or tourist activities.

Therefore, the results confirm the working hypotheses H1-H6 and are in accordance with those presented by a number of specialists in other studies that have targeted region attractiveness for investors. The study mainly aims the general population interested in finding an attractive region to settle in, as well as a family with diverse and divergent studies, activities, abilities and competencies interested as well in finding such a region.

Thus, the level of economic development of a region, reflected by the regional GDP/person (X1), is correlated with the attractiveness of regions for citizens, in accordance with other studies (Hu B et al., 2020) that analyzed medical, educational and transport indicators at the territorial level. In accordance with the results of other research, study shows that the investments made by micro-enterprises (X2) have an important multiplier effect on economic development at the regional level, in accordance with those specified by (Gherghina et al., 2020) and it is correlated with the growth of the average gross monthly income per household in all the analyzed regions. Investments increase the attractiveness of regions and by diversifying production and services offered to communities (Rodionov et al., 2021; Kurikov et al., 2022), by implementing high technologies or by computerizing some activities, by ensuring environmental protection and quality in all areas of activity (Botezatu, 2020), of the turnover of all companies in the region (X3) which correlates with the average household income in the region.

The employment rate at the regional level (X4) is correlated with the average income per household in the region, being influenced by the use of modern technologies, the computerization of production and services (Gherghina et al, 2021), the variation in the number of the population and the appearance of some new jobs, etc.

Human resource with a higher level of training at the regional level (X5) is correlated with the average income per household in the region, in accordance with another research (Constantin et al., 2007; Marquez-Ramos et al., 2018; Valero, 2021; Moyo et al., 2022). The human resource with higher education has better distributed key competencies and specialization sectors and approaches various, highly technological and/or computerized fields, which leads to a strong influence on the average income per household in the region. This influence could be at the attention of local or central decision-makers in order to achieve the development and diversification of higher education, of the specializations offered in close interdependence with the type of activities carried out by companies in the region, as well as of investments, according to (Popescu et al., 2009; Pirnau et al., 2019).

The accommodation capacity (X6) in the region, the development of different types of tourism are correlated with the average household income. They can thus constitute important sources of increasing regional attractiveness, especially if they have tourist potential and promote this potential (Stach et al., 2014).

Moreover, the marriage rates and instability are correlated with economic development factors such as employment rate, level of development, growth rate of ICT employment, and risk of poverty (Botha et al., 2023).

We consider that the research results are useful both theoretically and especially for practitioners, who can be decision-makers or citizens looking for a region to work in or to settle down in the future. Theoretically, the results obtained are consistent with those obtained by research that modeled, at the regional level, the behavior of sustainable economic, social and environmental development, identifying and explaining the factors that influence it.

Changing the approach and putting in the center of attention the citizen interested in finding an attractive region for him, we considered as the dependent variable *the average household income at regional level.*

One could ask why did we take this indicator into consideration. We have done this because it can be larger, more composite, as it includes in its standard definition more income sources than just employee wages or entrepreneurial revenues, both as individuals and as members of a household or family.

Average income for a household can be higher and more stable than the sum of the incomes of its members, either employees or entrepreneurs, as it can include a lot more income sources or facilities to reduce household expenditures. For reference, other sources of income could include craftsmen activities, household activities that would reduce household maintenance expenditures (raising cattle/poultry, growing vegetables, orchards cultivation, bee hives, and so on). As such, this paper has the goal to emphasize the importance of the specific measurable indicator called *"average household income at regional level"* and actually proves that the factors considered in this research through the above – defined and described models are supporting this.

It was found that the 6 influencing factors on the *average household income at regional level* considered by us do not have the same influence in all regions, their intensity differs, and the simultaneous influence of several factors is specific to each region. Under these conditions, research results can be used at least by:

- citizens, who can see in the results presented in Tables 2 and 3 data regarding the statistical values of the 6 indicators in the regions of Romania, but also their direct influence on the indicator that may directly interest them, the *average income per household at the regional level.* Depending on their own interests and wishes regarding their future, interested citizens, especially young people, can choose the most attractive region in which to settle and to start a family.
- local or central administration decision-makers, governors, or parliamentarians, who can increase the attractiveness of regions for citizens, especially young people, through concrete public policies and actions to stimulate the analyzed factors, thus reducing the gaps between regions according to the EU cohesion policy (European Commission, 2020; 2023).
- bodies and institutions of all forms of schooling, at local and central level, which have the opportunity to promote the results of this study, to make them known to young people in any form of schooling, to inform them, to teach them to opt for the region they he considered her attractive.

As future research directions, the current work should be developed by exploring the relationships between the types of activities and services developed at the territorial level, the specializations offered by the secondary and higher education system and the attractiveness of the regions, measured by the *average household income at the regional level.*

Also, based on the data obtained, through the selection and interpretation of the results, an "Indicative Guide for evaluating the attractiveness of regions" could be created, addressed primarily to those who follow an intermediate or final form of schooling in a field, but also young graduates or citizens interested in choosing a better job or a region where they can settle down and possibly build their future.

We believe that through the results obtained in the conducted research, it can even contribute to the motivation of young people in choosing the directions of training in the educational process, when they want to settle in a certain region. On the other hand, they can have access to objective, measurable indicators when they want to choose a region of residence, in which to work and/or found a family.

Through all this we consider that this study leads (at the national or local level) to increasing the importance given to young people or citizens of any age, providing them with an objective tool for evaluating the attractiveness of regions, but also to the responsibility of the decision-making factors towards citizens.

This research can thus contribute to the mutual influence of citizens, the business environment, and administrative and political decision-makers as a solution for effective measures to reduce inequities and gaps in the sustainable development of the regions of the country and, implicitly, the living standards of the communities, which will also increase the social welfare and the attractiveness of the respective regions.

## REFERENCES


Achten, S., & Lessmann, C. (2020). Spatial inequality, geography and economic activity. *World Development, 136*, 105114. https://www.sciencedirect.com/science/article/abs/pii/S0305750X20302412. DOI: 10.1016/j.worlddev.2020.105114

Antonescu, D. (2013), Politica de dezvoltare regională a României în etapa postaderare, Bucureşti, Academia Română, Institutul Naţional de Cercetări Economice, [Romania's regional development policy in the post-accession stage, Bucharest, Romanian Academy, National Institute of Economic Research]. ISSN: 2285 – 7036

Bagautdinova, N. G., Galeeva, G. M., Fazlieva, E. P., & Arzhantseva, N. V. (2014), Investment Attractiveness of the Region as the Factor in the Formation of Competitive Advantages Mediterranean Journal of Social Sciences, Vol 5, No 28 (2014), ISSN 2039-2117(Online), DOI: DOI: 10.5901/mjss.2014.v5n28p9

Balkytė, A., & Tvaronavičienė, M. (2010). Perception of competitiveness in the context of sustainable development: Facets of "sustainable competitiveness". *Journal of Business Economics and Management, 11*(2), 341–365. www.jbem.vgtu.lt. DOI: 10.3846/jbem.2010.17

Bertoletti, A., Berbegal-Mirabent, J., & Agasisti, T. (2022). Higher education systems and regional economic development in Europe: A combined approach using econometric and machine learning methods, Socio-Economic Planning Sciences, Vol 82. *Socio-Economic Planning Sciences, 101231*, 101231. Advance online publication. DOI: 10.1016/j.seps.2022.101231

Botezatu, M. A. (2020). Organizational Sustainability, Modern Management and IT&C Impact on Local Development. In *Monograph:Enterprise in the Global Economy: Challenges of the Current Global Environment, 4th Int. e-conference "Enterprises in the Global Economy" EGE, (14th october 2019)* (pp. 62–69). Filodiritto Publisher.

Botezatu, M. A., Ivanescu, I. M., Ivanescu, M. M., & Diaconescu, F. (2021), Challenges of Digital Economies: An Analysis of the Factors that Influence Economic Development of the EU Member States, in Under the Pressure of Digitalization: Challenges and Solutions at Organizational and Industrial Levels, First Edition, Pag: 32-39, ISBN: 979-12-80225-27-6, 5th Edition International e-conference "Enterprises in the Global Economy *under Pandemic*" EGE, (December 14th, 2020), https://www.webofscience.com/wos/woscc/full-record/WOS:000683887600005

Botha, I., Botezatu, M.A., Coancă, M. (2020), Innovative Calculation Model for Evaluating Regional Sustainable Development, Economic Computation and Economic Cybernetics Studies and Research, Vol. 54, Issue 3/2020, pg.5-24, DOI: DOI: 10.24818/18423264/54.3.20.01

Botha, I., Botezatu, M. A., Tabusca, A., & Hosszu, A. (2023), *Economic factors correlated with marriage and divorce rates in European Union countries*, Economic Computation and Economic Cybernetics Studies and Research, Issue 3/2023; Vol. 57, pg. 133-150, ISSN: 0424-267X, ASE Publishing, DOI: , https://ecocyb.ase.ro/Articles2023_3.htmDOI: 10.24818/18423264/57.3.23.08

Botha, I., Gherghina, . C., Simionescu, L. N., Botezatu, M. A., & Coculescu, C. (2022), Investigating the drivers of renewable energy production: Panel data evidence for Central and Eastern European Countries, Economic Computation and Economic Cybernetics Studies and Research, Vol. 56, Issue 1/2022, pg. 5-22, eISSN 1842–3264, ASE Publishing, DOI: , https://ecocyb.ase.ro/nr2022_1/CONTENTS_2022_1.pdfDOI: 10.24818/18423264/56.1.22.01

Boumahdi, I., & Zaoujal, N. (2023). Regional Well-Being Disparities in Morocco and its OECD Partners [SpringerLink]. *Social Indicators Research, 167*(1-3), 183–211. DOI: 10.1007/s11205-023-03097-7 PMID: 37304458

Commission of the European Communities. (2002). *Corporate Social Responsibility: A business contribution to Sustainable Development.*

Constantin, D. L., & Dimian, G. C. (2007), Competitivitatea regiunilor din România în contextul integrării în Uniunea Europeană, Jurnalul Economic, nr. 24, https://core.ac.uk/download/pdf/6231368.pdf

Ευροπεαν Χομμισσιον. (2021), Τηε Διγιταλ Εχονομψ ανδ Σοχιετψ Ινδεξ (ΔΕΣΙ), [European Commission. (2021), The Digital Economy and Society Index (DESI)]. https://digital-strategy.ec.europa.eu/en/policies/desi

ESPON. (2013), Attractiveness of Regions to Migrants and Visitors, https://www.espon.eu/topics-policy/publications/maps-month/attractiveness-regions-migrants-and-visitors

European Comission. (2005), “Report of the European Comission for the Council and the European parliament regarding the Sustainable Development Strategy”, Bruxelles, December European Commission, (2015), A Digital Single Market Strategy for Europe, *COM(2015) 192 fina*

European Commission. (1997), Carta Verde. Politica de Dezvoltare Regionala in Romania. Guvernul Romaniei, Program Phare. Bucuresti, https://www.adrbi.ro/media/1665/carta_verde_politica_de_dezvoltare_regionala.pdf

European Commission. (2010), Europa 2020, http://publications.europa.eu/resource/cellar/6a915e39-0aab-491c-8881-147ec91fe88a.0022.02/DOC_1

European Commission. (2017), Competitiveness in low-income and low-growth regions. The lagging regions report, Brussels, 10.4.2017 SWD(2017) 132 final, COMMISSION STAFF WORKING DOCUMENT, https://edz.bib.uni-mannheim.de/edz/pdf/swd/2017/swd-2017-0132-en.pdf

European Commission. (2020), Territorial Agenda 2030, A future for all places, https://territorialagenda.eu

European Commission. (2023), Strasbourg, 17.1.2023 final Communication From The Commission To The European Parliament, The Council, The European Economic And Social Committee And The Committee Of The Regions Harnessing talent in Europe’s regions, https://ec.europa.eu/regional_policy/sources/communication/harnessing-talents/harnessing-talents-regions_en.pdf

Garofoli, G. (2016). Local Development in Europe: Theoretical Models and International Comparisons. *European Urban and Regional Studies, 9*(3), 2016. DOI: 10.1177/096977640200900303

Gavrila-Paven, I., & Wainberg, D. (2022), Influence of Projects Financed by the Regional Operational Program on the Economic Performance of Companies, Economic Computation and Economic Cybernetics Studies and Research, Vol. 56, Issue 2/2022, pg 273-289, https://ecocyb.ase.ro/nr2022_2/CONTENTS_2022_2.pdf

Gherghina, . C., Botezatu, M. A., Hosszu, A., & Simionescu, L. N. (2020). Small and Medium-Sized Enterprises (SMEs): The Engine of Economic Growth through Investments and Innovation. *Sustainability (Basel)*, *12*(1), 347. Advance online publication. DOI: 10.3390/su12010347

Gherghina, S. C., Botezatu, M. A., & Simionescu, L. N. (2021). Exploring the Impact of Electronic Commerce on Employment Rate: Panel Data Evidence from European Union Countries. *Journal of Theoretical and Applied Electronic Commerce Research*, *2021*(16), 3157–3183. DOI: 10.3390/jtaer16070172

Godlewska-Majkowska, H. (2018). Polarity of the Regional Space – the Dilemma of Shaping the Investment Attractiveness of Poland. *Studies of the Industrial Geography Commission of the Polish Geographical Society*, *32*(4), 110–122. DOI: 10.24917/20801653.324.6

Gonzalez-Loureiro, M., & Pita-Castelo, J. (2012). A model for assessing the contribution of innovative SMEs to economic growth: The intangible approach. *Economics Letters*, *116*(3), 312–315. DOI: 10.1016/j.econlet.2012.03.028

Government of Romania. (2008), "National Sustainable Development Strategy for Romania", pp. 29- 32 available at: http://www.insse.ro/cms/files/IDDT%202012/StategiaDD.pdf

Grant, C. (2017), The Contribution of Education to Economic Growth, K4D Helpdesk Report, https://assets.publishing.service.gov.uk/media/5b9b87f340f0b67896977bae/K4D_HDR_The_Contribution_of_Education_to_Economic_Growth_Final.pdf

Hallin, G., & Malmberg, A. (2016). Attraction, Competition and Regional Development in Europe. *European Urban and Regional Studies*, *3*(4), 2016. DOI: 10.1177/096977649600300404

Hirte, G., Lessmann, C., & Seide, A. (2020). International trade, geographic heterogeneity and interregional inequality. *European Economic Review*, *127*(August), 103427. DOI: 10.1016/j.euroecorev.2020.103427

Horakova, S. (2021), Map of regional attractiveness, The Quebec City Metropolitan Community, https://hub.polirural.eu/news/-/blogs/map-of-regional-attractiveness

Hu, B., Liu, Y., Zhang, X., & Dong, X. (2020). Understanding regional talent attraction and its influencing factors in China: From the perspective of spatiotemporal pattern evolution. *PLoS One*, *15*(6), e0234856. DOI: 10.1371/journal.pone.0234856 PMID: 32555616

Jovovic, R., Draskovic, M., Delibasic, M., & Jovovic, M. (2017). The concept of sustainable regional development – institutional aspects, policies and prospects. *Journal of International Students*, *10*(1), 255–266. DOI: 10.14254/2071-8330.2017/10-1/18

Kocmanova, A., & Docekalova, M. (2012). Construction of the Economic Indicators of Performance in Relation to Environmental, Social and Corporate Governance (ESG) Factors. *Acta Universitatis Agriculturae et Silviculturae Mendelianae Brunensis*, *60*(4), 195–206. DOI: 10.11118/actaun201260040195Kurikov, V., & Tashlanova, Y. (2022), The practice of state regional support for the development of investment attractiveness (on the example of the Khanty-Mansiysk Autonomous Okrug–Yugra), SHS Web Conf, Vol 141, 2022, IV International Scientific and Practical Conference "Modern Management Trends and Digital Economy: from Regional Development to Global Economic Growth" (MTDE 2022), 01013, iunie 2022, DOI: 10.1051/shsconf/202214101013

Leontieva L.S., Avilkina S.V. (2021), The Higher Education System as a Strategic Resource for Regional Development, Gosudarstvennoe upravlenie. Elektronnyy vestnik, (86):200–219, DOI: 10.24412/2070-1381-2021-86-200-219

Li, F., Liu, X. S., Hu, D., Wang, R. S., Yang, W. R., Li, D., & Zhao, D. (2009). Measurement Indexes and an Evaluation Approach for Assessing Urban Sustainable Development: A Case Study for China's Jining City. *Landscape and Urban Planning*, *90*(3-4), 134–142. DOI: 10.1016/j.landurbplan.2008.10.022

Madlener, R., & Sunak, Y. (2011). Impacts of urbanization on urban structures and energy demand: What can we learn for urban energy planning and urbanization management? *Sustainable Cities and Society*, *2011*(1), 45–53. DOI: 10.1016/j.scs.2010.08.006

Manea, D., Titan, E., Boboc, C., & Anoaica, A. (2016), *Logistic Regression in Modelling Some Sustainable Development Phenomena*; Economic Computation and Economic Cybernetics Studies and Research, Vol. 50, Issue 3, 83-100, ISSN 1842–3264; ASE Publishing

Marquez-Ramos, L., & Mourelle, E. (2018), Education and economic growth: an empirical analysis of nonlinearities, Applied Economic Analysis, Vol 27 Iss 79, pp 21-45, ISSN: 2632-7627, DOI: DOI: 10.1108/AEA-06-2019-0005

Moyo, C., Mishi S. & Ncwadi, R. (2022), Human capital development, poverty and income inequality in the Eastern Cape province, Development Studies Research, Volume 9, 2022 - Issue 1, Pages 36-47, DOI: 10.1080/21665095.2022.2032236

Myakshin, V., & Grishina, I. (2021), Assessment of the Region Investment Attractiveness in Complex Relationship with Sustainable Development on the Basis of the Balanced Scorecard, In Proceedings of the International Scientific and Practical Conference on Sustainable Development of Regional Infrastructure (ISSDRI 2021), pag 388-395, ISBN: 978-989-758-519-7, DOI: DOI: 10.5220/0010591103880395

Nakamura, D. (2023), Attractiveness of Regions and Sustainable Regional Economic System, As a Measure of Social Welfare Function, vol 75, Book Apr 2024, https://link.springer.com/book/9789812878540

National Institute of Statistics. 2023, Statistical Yearbooks of Romania, Available online: https://insse.ro/cms/en/content/statistical-yearbooks-romania

Niebel, T. ICT and economic growth – Comparing developing, emerging and developed countries, World Development, Volume 104, 2018, Pages 197-211, ISSN 0305-750X, DOI: 10.1016/j.worlddev.2017.11.024

OECD. (2021), What makes a region attractive in the new global environment? How to measure and monitor, Issues Note, 29th November 2021, Rethinking Regional Attractiveness Webinar Series, https://www.oecd.org/regional/Issues-note%20-region-attractive-new-global-environment.pdf

OECD. (2022), Measuring the attractiveness of regions, OECD Regional Development Papers no 36, ISSN: 27094065 (online), DOI: 10.1787/267a6231-en

Pantilie, A. (2015). Education, Mandatory Condition in the Regional Economic Development of Romania, 2015. *International Journal of Academic Research in Economics and Management Sciences, 4*(1). Advance online publication. DOI: 10.6007/IJAREMS/v4-i1/1468

Pirnau, M., Ciocardia, R. M. C., Pirnau, C., Ghiculescu, L. D., & Marinescu, N. (2019), *2019* The Identification of Intelligent Interactions between Education and Labour Force Market, *11th International Conference on Electronics, Computers and Artificial Intelligence (ECAI)*, Pitesti, Romania, pp. 1-6, Publisher: IEEE april 2020, DOI: 10.1109/ECAI46879.2019.9042048

Popescu, C. C., Diaconu, L. (2009), The Relationship Between the Level of Education and the Development State of a Country, Analele Ştiinłifice ale Universitălii „ALEXANDRU IOAN CUZA" din IaşI Tomul LVI Ştiinte Economice 2009

Porter, M. E. (1992). *Competitive advantage: Creating and sustaining superior performance.* PA Consulting Group.

Porter, M. E. (1996). *Competitive Advantage.* Agglomeration Economies, and Regional Policy.

Pratita Vajar Kusuma. (2020), The Impact of Education on Regional Economic Performance in Indonesia, International Journal of Economics, Business and Accounting Research (IJEBAR), Vol 4, No 03, E-ISSN: 2614-1280, http://jurnal.stie-aas.ac.id/index.php/IJEBAR

Răileanu, S. M. (2018). New insights from a multilevel approach to the regional digital divide in the European Union. *Telecommunications Policy, 42*(6), 452–463. DOI: 10.1016/j.telpol.2018.03.007

Rodionov, D. G., Konnikov, E. A., & Nasrutdinov, M. N. (2021). A transformation of the approach to evaluating a region's investment attractiveness as a consequence of the COVID-19 pandemic. *Economies, 9*(59), 1–20. DOI: 10.3390/economies9020059

Rodríguez-Pose, A., & Tselios, V. (2010), Inequalities in income and education and regional economic growth in western Europe, *The Annals of Regional Science*, vol 44, pag 349–375, https://link.springer.com/article/10.1007/s00168-008-0267-2

Roswinna, W. (2020). Increasing The Potential Region Attractiveness In The Development Order Investation. *Sosiohumaniora, 22*(3), 341–347. DOI: 10.24198/sosiohumaniora.v22i3.28499

Salvati, L., & Carlucci, M. (2014). A Composite Index of Sustainable Development at the Local Scale: Italy as a Case Study. *Ecological Indicators, 2014*(43), 162–171. DOI: 10.1016/j.ecolind.2014.02.021

Satyro, W. C., Sacomano, J. B., Contador, J. C., Almeida, C. M., & Giannetti, B. F. (2017). Process of strategy formulation for sustainable environmental development: Basic model. *Journal of Cleaner Production, 2017*(166), 1295–1304. DOI: 10.1016/j.jclepro.2017.08.128

Shi, Y., Ge, X., Yuan, X., Wang, Q., Kellett, J., Li, F., & Ba, K. (2019). An Integrated Indicator System and Evaluation Model for Regional Sustainable Development. *Sustainability (Basel), 11*(7), 2183. DOI: 10.3390/su11072183

Strategia Naţională pentru Dezvoltare Durabilă a României Orizonturi 2013–2020–2030, https://www.mmediu.ro/beta/domenii/dezvoltare-durabila/strategia-nationala-a-romaniei-2013-2020-2030/

Sikorska-Wolak, I., Zawadka, J., & Krzyżanowska, K. (2020), The Investment Attractiveness Of Regions As One Of Entrepreneurship Development Factors, Economic and Regional Studies (Studia Ekonomiczne i Regionalne), vol. 13(2), p.170-183, ISSN 2083-3725, DOI: 10.2478/ers-2020-0012

Stach, E., Matoga, L., & Pawłowska, A. (2014), Evaluation of Tourist Attractiveness of the Communes in Chełm County in the Context of the Development of Cross-Border Tourism, Barometr Regionalny Tom 12 nr 3 Nyborg Storm, H. (2022), Cultural Institutions and Attractiveness: How Cultural Institutions Contribute to the Development of Regions and Local Communities, https://research.cbs.dk/en/publications/cultural-institutions-and-attractiveness-how-cultural-institution

Stepus, I. S., Averyanov, A. O., & Gurtov, V. A. (2022). Indicators of the Interrelation between the Education System and the Labor Market: Development and Testing. *Integra Educativa, 26*(4), 594–612. DOI: 10.15507/1991-9468.109.026.202204.594-612

Sun, Y., Qin, Y., Hu, Y., Wang, S., & Bi, X. (2021), The Correlation Analysis of Education Level and Regional Economic Growth Quality in Guangdong Province, Advances in Social Science, Education and Humanities Research, vol 598, *Proceedings of the 7th International Conference on Social Science and Higher Education (ICSSHE 2021)*, DOI: DOI: 10.2991/assehr.k.211122.116

Titu, M. A., Pirnau, C., & Pirnau, M. (2013), Creativity, Education and Quality for Sustainable Development, the real Support for the Innovative Cluster's European Network, 8th Research/Expert Conference with International Participations "QUALITY 2013", Neum, B&H, June 06 – 08, 2013, pp 19-24, https://quality.unze.ba/zbornici/QUALITY%202013/004-Q13-111.pdf

United Nations. (1992), AGENDA 21, Conference on Environment & Development, Rio de Janerio, Brazil, 3 to 14 June 1992, https://sustainabledevelopment.un.org/content/documents/Agenda21.pdf

United Nations. (2010), The Sustainable Development Goals 2030 Agenda, https://sustainabledevelopment.un.org/

United Nations. (2016), High-level Advisory Group on Sustainable Transport, Mobilizing Sustainable Transport for Development, https://sustainabledevelopment.un.org/index.php?page=view&type=400&nr=2375&menu=35

United Nations. (2019), The Climate Technology Centre and Network (CTCN), Climate Strategies 2020, December 10, 2019, https://www.ctc-n.org/news/new-publication-climate-strategies-2020

Valero, A. (2021), Education and economic growth, Centre for Economic Performance, London School of Economics and Political Science, Discussion Paper No.1764, ISSN 2042-2695

WCED (World Commission on Environment and Development). (1987), Our common future: The Brundtland report, Oxford University Press 1987, p. 43

Yingkai, M. (2022). Research on the Influence of Educational Resources on Regional Economic Development, SHS Web of Conferences 151, 01005 (2022). *EMSD*, *2022*(dec). Advance online publication. DOI: 10.1051/shsconf/202215101005

# Chapter 12
# Low Carbon Tourism:
## A Content Analysis With Mapping Technique

**Jesús Claudio Pérez Gálvez**
https://orcid.org/0000-0002-6204-2412
*University of Cordoba, Spain*

**Jaime José Orts Cardador**
https://orcid.org/0000-0002-1229-8161
*University of Cordoba, Spain*

**Elena Carvajal Trujillo**
https://orcid.org/0000-0001-7444-4059
*Univeristy of Huelva, Spain*

## ABSTRACT

*Low Carbon Tourism has elicited significant academic interest in recent years due its important role in the promotion of environmentally responsible destinations. The appearance of different climate problems, such as the generalised increase in temperatures, droughts or rising sea levels, has challenged the current economic model, with tourism being of the main economic actors responsible for this situation. The main objective of this article is to identify the lines of research related to Low Carbon Tourism through the application of mapping techniques. The content analysis performed, by applying the VOSviewer tool for the 2010-2024 period, allows the identification of four relevant lines of research: Sustainable Development in Tourism; Relationship between Carbon Footprint and Tourism; Effects of Climate Change in Tourism and Low Carbon Tourism in China; with Sustainable Development in Tourism; and Effects of Climate Change on Tourism being the lines with the greatest academic impact and relevance in the final years of the period that is the subject of this study.*

DOI: 10.4018/979-8-3693-7081-0.ch012

## 1. INTRODUCTION

Traditionally, the success of tourism has been assessed on the basis of economic results obtained by the industry and the growth indicators for the region, such as employment creation, the arrival of tourists and the creation of companies (Koh et al., 2022; Fakfare & Wattanacharoensil, 2023). Even though these indicators have commonly been accepted by tourist professionals as a benefit (Fakfare & Wattanacharoensil, 2023), in recent years, different negative external factors surrounding this industry, such as over-crowding in traditional destinations (McKinsey & Company and World Travel & Tourism Council, 2017), excessive energy consumption (Shakouri et al., 2017) and the emission of carbon dioxide and other greenhouse gases into the atmosphere (Mishra et al., 2022). In this last case, the significant increase of carbon dioxide emissions in the last 50 years has been accepted by the scientific community as the main reason for climate change and environmental degradation (Friedlingstein et al, 2006; Kocak et al., 2020). Specifically, in 2013, the tourism sector contributed to 8% of the total production of carbon in the last decade, which represents 4.3 billion tonnes of CO2 emissions (Lenzen et al., 2018). Recently, the World Travel and Tourism Council (WTTC), United Nations Environment Programme (UNEP) & United Nations Framework Convention on Climate Change (UNFCCC) (2021), in its "net zero" report, estimated that, for 2019, tourism would be responsible for between 8% and 11% of the volume of emissions, which means 3.9 to 5.4 billion tonnes of CO2 emissions. Additionally, the World Tourism Organization (UNWTO) and International Transport Forum (ITF), in their latest report which analyses the transport-related CO2 emissions of the tourism sector, predict an increase in emissions by 25% in 2030 and, specifically, 45% in international travel (UNWTO, 2019).

In this context, climate change is becoming a challenge for the tourism sector and should undergo drastic changes in the future with the aim of adapting to the increasing risk of decarbonisation policies (Scott et al., 2012; Lenzen et al., 2018). The UNWTO recommends establishing these new strategies not only in the realm of transport, but also through the development of new tourism activities in which all the parties involved act according to the planet's objectives, as it is an economic sector which contributes enormously to global pollution (Lenzen et al., 2018; Mishra et al., 2022). As a result, these questions shall control the debate regarding tourist development and travel options in the near future (Scott et al., 2012; Mishra et al., 2022).

Low Carbon Tourism (LCT) was initially proposed at the World Economic Forum, "Go to Low-carbon Travel and Tourism Industry," in May 2009 as a new form of sustainable tourism that co-ordinates tourism experience with the reduction of carbon produced in tourists' activities, with the aim of acquiring greater social, economic and environmental benefits for our society (Wang et al., 2019; Bhaktikul et al., 2021). Since then, numerous researchers have explored the negative consequences that tourist activities have on the environment (Mahadew & Appadoo, 2019; Tian et al., 2020; Wang et al., 2021).

The main objective of this paper is to analyse the structure and trends of Low-Carbon Tourism between 2010 and 2024 using visualisation tools (VOSviewer). From the collection of documents in WoS, VOSviewer has made it possible to visualise keyword co-occurrence networks. Feng et al. (2017) highlight the ability of VOSviewer to facilitate pragmatic data analysis through its robust graphical interface. This interface enables the generation of maps that visually represent the relationships between individual units of analysis (Donthu et al., 2021). These analyses will enable the following intermediate research objectives to be achieved

O1: Describe the state of research in low-carbon tourism, identifying the most productive journals, institutions and authors.

O2: Identify current lines and future research opportunities in low-carbon tourism through keyword co-occurrence analysis.

## 2. LITERATURE REVIEW

### 2.1. The Challenges in Tourism for Low Carbon

On the basis of agreements adopted at the United Nation Climate Change Conference (2022), called "COP27", and the Paris Climate Agreement (2015) the different parties have been urged to achieve climate neutrality, limiting global warming to 1.5° and reducing greenhouse effect emissions by 43% before 2030 (Paris Climate Agreement, 2015; United Nation Climate Change, 2022). Accordingly, the different economic sectors have been requested to participate in carbon neutrality, with tourism being among them (UNWTO, 2019; UNWTO, 2021). As such, climate change represents a big challenge for tourism development, as its economic activity shall be conditioned by it in the coming years (Cho et al., 2016; Zha et al., 2019), especially when tourism is one of the main industries that produces CO2 emissions and contributes to climate change (Hall et al., 2013; Gössling et al., 2016).

Gössling (2000) is one of the pioneering researchers in analysing the impact of CO2 emissions caused by tourism. Since then, numerous researchers have considered this topic to be one of the main challenges that the tourism industry currently faces (Zha et al., 2019). Among other research, the CO2 emissions of tourist transport (Becken et al., 2003; Gössling et al., 2005; Luo et al., 2018), tourist accommodation (Filimonaou et al., 2011; Lai et al., 2015) or tourist activities (Dawson et al., 2010; Sung et al., 2021) should be highlighted. In the recent study by Gössling et al. (2023), the authors show how a decarbonisation policy in tourism has to be a priority. We may see an example of this in Figure 1, in which the red curve shows the growth of predicted emissions in the tourist industry, in comparison with the scenario presented in the WTCC-UNEP-UNFCCC "net zero" report (2021; green line) and the scenario presented by the Intergovernmental Panel on Climate Change (IPCC) (2022, blue line), which will be necessary in order to achieve the target of 1.5 °C. As a result, we are talking about an average decarbonisation of 8%-10% per year (Friedlingstein et al., 2022). However, this falls short in a context in which a continuous yearly growth of 3% is estimated for the aviation sector and 5% for the remaining tourism-related sectors, which according to estimations, shall double CO2 emissions between 2023 and 2050 (Gössling et al., 2023).

*Figure 1. Expectation of growth in CO2 in tourism-related sector*

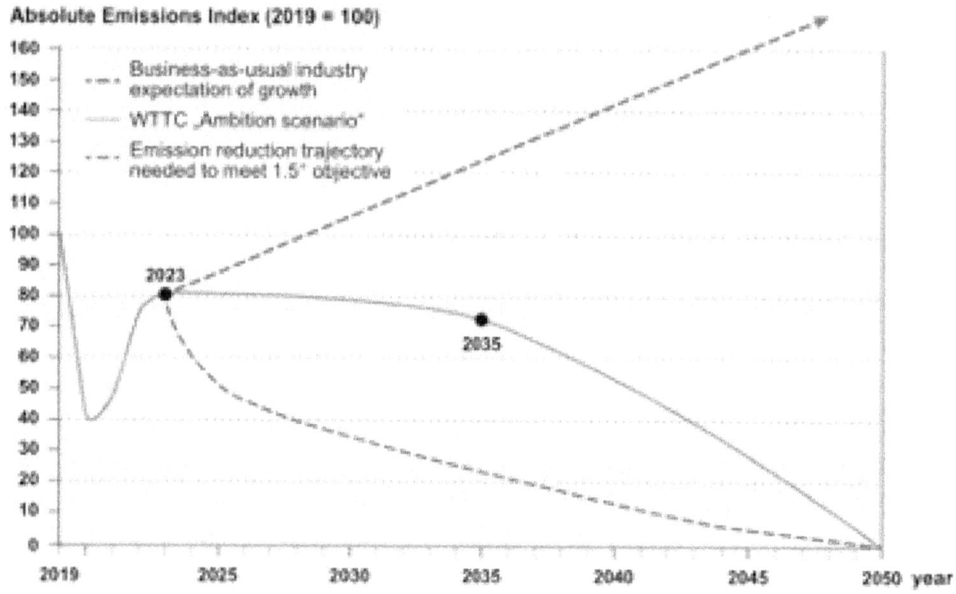


*Source: Gössling et al. (2023) based in WTTC-UNEP-UNFCCC (2021) and IPCC (2022).*

Gössling & Higham (2021) maintain a series of challenges for sustainable tourism. First of all, the new sharing economy platforms for booking accommodation (e.g. Booking, AirBnB), transport (e.g. Uber, Cabify) or leisure (e.g. TripAdvisor, Atrapalo), have contributed to the decrease in the average length of a stay in tourist destinations (Gössling & Hall, 2019). This implies that tourists have a greater responsibility of undertaking a greater number of trips during different tourism seasons, which impacts negatively on sustainability. From the UNWTO data (2011, 2017), Gössling *et al.* (2019) analysed the average stay in 32 tourist destinations in the 1995-2015 period, concluding that it has decreased from 5.4 to 4.6 days. Similarly, the cost of flights decreased by 60% between 1998 and 2008 (International Air Transport Association, 2019), allowing international tourism to increase from 531 million in 1995 to 1.326 billion in 2017 (UNWTO, 2018). As such, it is imperative to change the current tourism model to a sustainable one, which, at the same time, is economically attractive in the long term (Gössling & Higham, 2021).

## 2.2. The Importance of Low Carbon in Tourism

Given the challenge facing different actors to reduce carbon emissions by half by 2030 and to reach net zero emissions before 2050 (UNWTO, 2021), the managers of tourist destinations are considering how to address this challenge (Gössling & Higham, 2021). Tourism is an industry with a high demand for electricity, water and fuel (Fakfare & Wattanacharoensil, 2023) and, as a result, it has a negative reputation for going against the demands of the planet (Becken, 2017). Geels et al., (2017) analysed the process for the transition to sustainable tourism, reaching the conclusion that two components were required: first, the weakness of the existing system and, second, the alternative shown by means of a niche innovation. As we may observe, the weakness of the current system has been shown, by means of the phenomenon of overtourism and pollution (Milano et al., 2019; Gössling & Higham, 2021). Therefore, it is necessary to establish an economic alternative for the development of destinations' economies, by means of promoting new policies, the development of new technology and changes in individual behaviour (Becken, 2017; Geels et al., 2017).

The individual behaviour of tourists affects the emissions generated by the tourism industry (Lee &Jan, 2019). Therefore, it would be necessary to reduce the distance travelled (Gössling et al., 2023), use alternative means of transport (Peeters et al., 2016), stay longer in the destination (Rico et al., 2019) or use environmentally friendly products (Dickinson et al., 2011). Filimonau et al. (2013) analysed the environmental impact in the Algarve region and highlighted the change in the tourism model, as the aviation sector was the most responsible for emissions (80.8%) and hotel stays (13.4%). Along the same lines, the study by Wang et al. (2021) concludes that an imminent change in the transport model is necessary, as it contributes to about 52% of the current pollution from Chinese tourism. Seetanah & Fauzel (2018) analysed the environmental impact of tourism on 18 islands with high tourism demand from 1989 to 2016. They found a high correlation between island pollution and tourism demand.

On the one hand, we found studies analysing the adoption of alternative transport and, more generally, other new forms of sustainable entertainment in the tourism industry. For example, the adoption of alternative energy in aviation (Gössling & Humpe, 2023), the implementation of policies by policy makers (Geels et al., 2017; Thongdejsri & Nitivattananon, 2019), the intended use of green hotels (Teng et al, 2018), the reduction of air travel by tourists (Filimonau et al., 2013; Mahadew & Appadoo, 2019) or, more generally, the use of alternative means of transport by tourists (Singh et al., 2023), such as electric vehicles (Higueras-Castillo et al., 2022), hydrogen vehicles (Kar et al., 2022) or bicycles (Chopdar et al., 2022). On the other hand, there are studies that focus on the individual behaviour of tourists and its impact on the environment. For example, the promotion of low-carbon tours by travel agencies (Sung et al., 2021), the introduction of slow travel, a movement that advocates the use of environmentally friendly transport, short distance travel or connection with the local community (Manthiou et al., 2022), the alteration of the natural habitat of native animals (Dawson et al., 2010; Belicia & Islam, 2010; Belicia & Islam, 2018), the use of the sharing economy (Gössling & Hall, 2019) or the acceptance of this new form of tourism by potential tourists (Fakfare & Wattanacharoensil, 2023). In conclusion, in order to reverse the negative process of the current tourism model, it is necessary to change the behaviour of tourists and adopt alternatives. Therefore, it is necessary to raise climate awareness and encourage consumers to develop new attitudes, values, sensitivity and knowledge about this current issue (Eames et al., 2008; Horng et al., 2013).

The current literature has acknowledged that the CO2 emissions caused by the tourism sector is a standard way of measuring environmental impact (Wu & Shi, 2011; Tang et al., 2014; Paramati et al., 2018; Satrovic & Muslija, 2019; Kocak et al., 2020; Wangzhou et al., 2022). The studies urge the different stakeholders to establish measures with the aim of changing the tourism model towards a sustainable model (Gössling & Higham, 2021). In this context, Low Carbon Tourism is a new form of sustainable tourism which has the aim of maximising the tourist experience by reducing energy use, CO2 and, in general, less pollution in the process of transport, accommodation, tourist visits and other tourist entertainment, at the same time as introducing new technology that pollutes less, with the aim of creating social, economic and environmental benefits (Su, 2019; Bhaktikul et al., 2021). Table 1 summarises the most relevant research that has analysed the impact of CO2 from different tourist services.

The different studies indicate that it is urgent to change the behaviour of tourists and to adopt alternatives in transport with the aim of reversing the negative process of the current tourism model. As such, it is necessary to increase climate awareness and encourage consumers to develop new attitudes, values, sensitivity and knowledge regarding this current problem (Eames et al., 2008; Horng et al., 2013).

Given the growth in research in this current topic, the recent interest by scientific academia and the importance of the introduction of Low Carbon Tourism, an analysis that enables the identification of the main research lines until now becomes necessary.

*Table 1. Literature of Low Carbon Tourism*

| Source | Purpose of the study | Methodology | Tourist Service |
|---|---|---|---|
| Xu et al. (2011) | Development of a low-carbon tourism system | Quantitative: Fuzzy differential equations | World natural and cultural heritage areas |
| Cheng et al. (2013) | Evaluation index system for low-carbon tourism attractions through expert survey | Quantitative: Delphi method and the analytic hierarchy process | National park |
| Tsai et al. (2014) | Analysis of CO2 emissions in different types of tourist accommodation | Quantitative: CO2 analysis | International tourist hotels, standard tourist hotels, general hotels, and homestay facilities |
| Scott et al. (2015) | Analysis of CO2 emissions in different tourism industry | Quantitative: CO2 analysis | Tourism industries: accommodation, activities, car, air |
| Huang et al. (2017) | Analysis of CO2 emissions in tour traffic flow | Quantitative: CO2 analysis | Car |
| Teng et al. (2018) | Tourists questionary | Quantitative: CB-SEM | Hotels environmentally friendly |
| Zhang & Zhang (2018) | Analysis of the impact of carbon taxes on the tourism industry | Quantitative: General Equilibrium Model (CGE) | Tourism industries: air transport, transport via road, and accommodation. |
| Sung et al. (2021) | Determine the intention of travel agencies to promote low-carbon travel. | Quantitative: PLS-SEM | Low-Carbon tours |
| Mishra et al. (2022) | Assessment and selection of most suitable low-carbon tourism strategy | Quantitative: Additive ratio assessment (ARAS) framework | Tourism industries in general |

Source: own elaboration.

## 3. METHODOLOGY

Bibliometrics is a field of study in library and information science that uses a quantitative approach with the aim of examining the bibliographic contents of a given field of study and presenting the most important results in a systematic way (Mártinez-López et al., 2018; Pritchard, 1969). In the tourism field, bibliometric analysis has been widely used – for example, in cultural tourism (Kohler & Digiampietri, 2021), ecotourism (Mishra et al., 2021), ethnocentrism (Orts-Cardador et al., 2023), sustainable tourism (Hernández-Garrido et al., 2023) and for analyzing new trends in tourism (Qian et al., 2019). Despite the academic relevance of Low Carbon Tourism, due to the rise and growing relevance of the sustainable tourism, there are only three works that analyze this type of tourism from the point of view of bibliometrics (Mishra et al., 2022). However, this article only analyses the publications of this scientific discipline until 2021 and our article identifies three new lines of research: *Sustainable Development in Tourism; Low Carbon Tourism in China;* and *Effects of Climate Change in Tourism.*

With the aim of visualising the most relevant research topics of Low Carbon Tourism, the Visualization of Similarities Viewer (VOSviewer) tool has been used. It is a software tool widely used by scientific literature (Liu et al., 2022) whose aim is to create, visualise and explore maps of a specific topic (Van Eck & Waltman, 2022). The Web of Science (WoS) was used to perform the analysis, due to providing access to the articles published by the main publishers: Elsevier, Emerald, Springer, MDPI, Wiley, Taylor and Francis, among others (De Oliveira et al., 2019). At the same time, it includes studies published in the most prestigious and rigorous scientific journals (Zupic & Carter, 2015). Accordingly, the main researchers who perform bibliometric studies in the category of "hospitality, leisure, sport and tourism," use this database due to its reliability (Molina-Collado et al., 2022).

The search was performed on the 31st of May 2024, with the first research being for 2010. The key words chosen and the search consultation used were ("Low Carbon Tourism"). A total of 217 documents were obtained. Following the recommendations of Liu et al. (2022) and Bhukya & Paul (2023), the exploration was limited to publications in scientific journals, including early-access articles. The search for the terms under study was applied to the topic (title, abstract, authors' keywords and keywords plus) of the documents. In order to eliminate incorrect data and merge abbreviated terms with complete terms or synonyms, the thesaurus files were applied (Van Eck & Waltman, 2022). Likewise, in order to reduce the influence of those publications that have a high number of authors, keywords, institutions or countries, fractional counting of bibliometric links was applied (Khanra et al., 2021). As a result, applying these filters, we obtained a sample of 111 documents.

Developing a protocol is a critical step in conducting a correct bibliometric analysis (Busalim, 2016; Acikgoz et al., 2024). This protocol is generally used in the field of "hospitality, leisure, sport and tourism" (Nandasena et al., 2022; Herold et al., 2024) in order to minimize any potential research bias (Moher et al., 2010; Acikgoz et al., 2024). In this context, the PRISMA (Preferred Reporting Items for Systematic Reviews and Meta-Analyses) statement, which was developed by Moher et al. (2010), is a tool that serves to present the findings in a more reliable way and involves four stages, namely identification, screening, eligibility and inclusion (Moher et al., 2010). The research questions and review protocol performed for this study are depicted in Figure 2.

*Figure 2. PRISMA model. Preferred Reporting Items for Systematic Review and Meta-Analysis (PRISMA) flowchart for the keywords used in the literature review.*

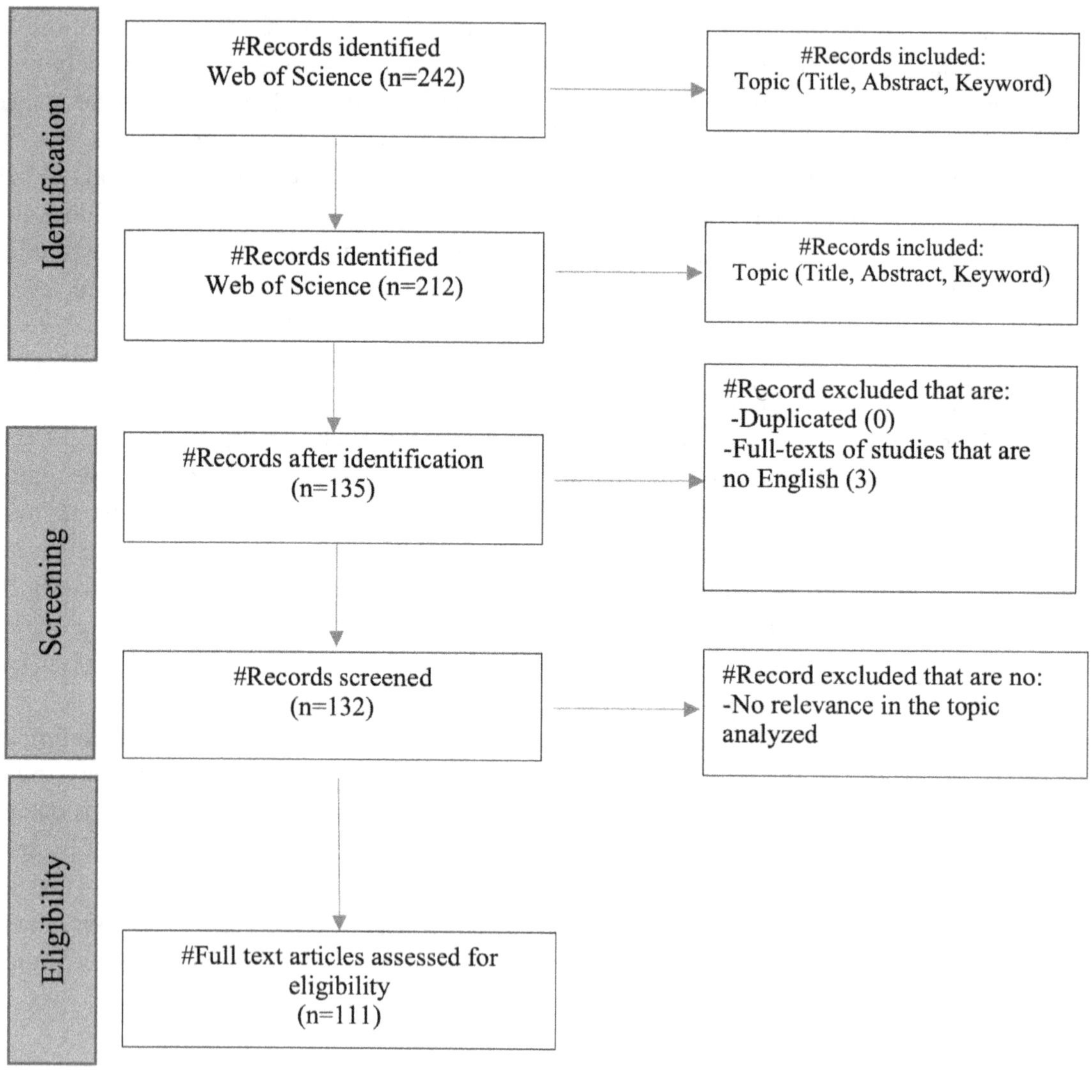


*Source: Own elaboration*

## 4. FINDINGS

### 4.1. Descriptive Analysis

In our analysis, a total of 111 articles were obtained from 56 journals as shown in Table 2. The first article to analyse Low-Carbon Tourism was that of Mundet & Coenders (2010), which analysed the development of greenways and/or trails as an alternative system to the car that allows respect for the environment. To achieve this goal, they surveyed 1,261 users along a 106 km greenway in Spain that connects the Pyrenees with the Mediterranean. The results show how open tourists are to changes in tourism and illustrate the potential importance of greenways in a future low-carbon tourism strategy that adapts to climate change.

*Table 2. Summary of data.*

| Web of Science | Record Count |
|---|---|
| Articles | 111 |
| Keywords | 394 |
| Citations | 2172 |
| Journals | 56 |
| Authors | 311 |
| Institutions | 181 |
| Countries | 25 |
| Study time | 2010-2024 |

Source: own elaboration.

The Figure 3 shows that is an upward trend in the number of publications over time, with a maximum production in 2022 with 19 publications and with a higher number of citations in 2021 with 571 citations.

*Figure 3. Number of publications and citations from 2010 to 2024*

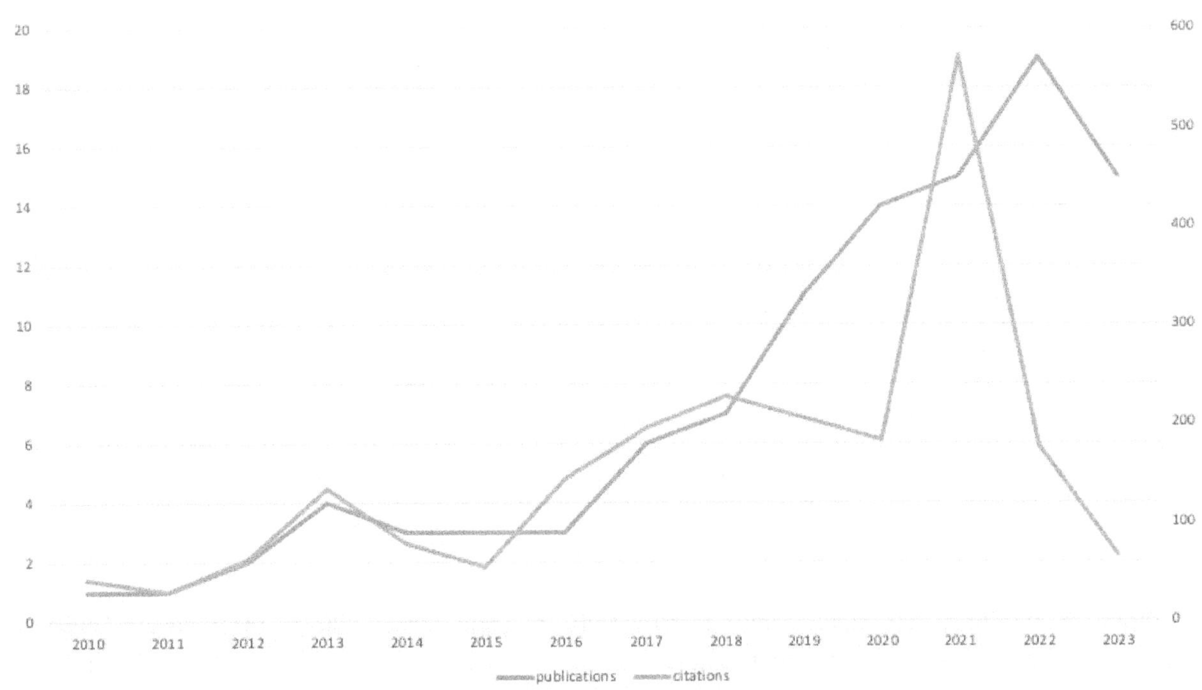


*Source: own elaboration.*

Table 3 shows the top 10 journals that have analyzed sustainable behavior by tourists with a total of 55 articles (49,6% of the total sample). The journals are indexed in several categories, being *Hospitality, Leisure, Sport & Tourism*; *Environmental Sciences* and *Green & Sustainable Science & Technology* the main categories. This indicates that the subject matter analyzed is multidisciplinary and focused on both tourism and the environment. Within the top 10, *Sustainability* and *Asia Pacific Journal of Tourism Research* stand out as the journals with the highest number of articles published. However, in relation to citations per article, being the indicator that really indicates the scientific impact (Agramunt et al., 2020), *Tourism Management* and *Journal of Sustainable Tourism* stand out, coinciding with its high scientific impact. Finally, it should be noted that all the journals have a high Journal Citation Report (JCR) and Scimago Journal Rank (SJR), which indicates the thematic relevance of the field analyzed.

*Table 3. Top ten journals by number of papers in the Web of Science data.*

| Journals | Category JCR 2023 (Quartil) | Papers | Cites | C/P | First Paper | Last Paper | JCR (2023) | SJR (2023) |
|---|---|---|---|---|---|---|---|---|
| Sustainability | GSST (Q3)<br>ES (Q2) | 21 | 145 | 6,90 | 2014 | 2024 | 3,3 | 0,67 |
| Asia Pacific Journal of Tourism Research | HLST (Q1) | 6 | 126 | 21,00 | 2014 | 2024 | 4,3 | 1,05 |
| Journal of Sustainable Tourism | GSST (Q2)<br>HLST (Q1) | 5 | 237 | 47,40 | 2010 | 2017 | 6,9 | 2,82 |
| Journal of Cleaner Production | EE (Q1)<br>ES (Q1)<br>GSST (Q1) | 5 | 187 | 37,40 | 2017 | 2024 | 9,7 | 2,06 |
| Current Issues in Tourism | HLST (Q1) | 5 | 82 | 16,40 | 2012 | 2023 | 5,7 | 1,92 |
| Environment Development and Sustainability | ES (Q2)<br>GSST (Q2) | 3 | 60 | 20,00 | 2021 | 2022 | 4,7 | 0,89 |
| International Journal of Environmental Research and Public Health | PEOH-SCIE (Q2)<br>PEOH-SSCI (Q1)<br>ES (Q2) | 3 | 32 | 10,67 | 2017 | 2022 | 4,61 | 0,81 |
| International Journal of Low-Carbon Technologies | EF (Q3)<br>THER (Q2) | 3 | 27 | 9,00 | 2019 | 2022 | 2,4 | 0,5 |
| Tourism Management | ES (Q1)<br>HLST (Q1)<br>MG (Q1) | 2 | 111 | 55,50 | 2013 | 2013 | 10,9 | 3,35 |
| Tourism Review | HLST (Q1) | 2 | 34 | 17 | 2019 | 2023 | 7,3 | 1,76 |
| **Total** | | **55** | **1058** | | | | | |

*Note*: C/P (average citation per paper); First Paper (year first published); Last Paper (year last published). Categories (JCR database): GSST (Green & Sustainable Science & Technology); HLST (Hospitality, Leisure, Sport & Tourism); ES (Environmental Studies); Management (MG); Engineering, Environmental (EE); Environmental Sciences (ES); Public, Environmental & Occupational Health-Science Citation Index Expanded (PEOH-SCIE); Public, Environmental & Occupational Health- Social Sciences Citation Index (PEOH-SSCI); EF (Energy & Fuels); THER (Thermodynamics); EC (Economic); Psychology, Multidisciplinary (PM).

Source: own elaboration.

Table 4 shows the most productive authors in the field analyzed. Researchers from China and Thailand stand out in terms of scientific production and number of citations. Specifically, Jiekuan Zhang from the Guilin Tourism University (China) and Yan Zhang from the Xinyang Normal University (China) are the authors with the highest number of citations and the highest number of publications. However, in relation to citations per article, Jeou-Shyan Horng of the Chih Chien University (Taiwan) and Yan Zhang of Xinyang Normal University (China) stand out.

*Table 4. Top ten authors by number of papers in the Web of Science data.*

| Author/s | Papers | Cites | C/P | First Paper | Last Paper | University | h-index (WoS) |
|---|---|---|---|---|---|---|---|
| Zhang, Jiekuan | 8 | 313 | 39,13 | 2017 | 2022 | Guilin Tourism University (China) | 16 |
| Zhang, Yan | 6 | 215 | 35,83 | 2018 | 2020 | Xinyang Normal University (China) | 8 |
| Tang, Zi | 4 | 20 | 5,00 | 2021 | 2024 | Harbin University Commerce (China) | 7 |
| Horng, Jeou-Shyan | 3 | 121 | 40,33 | 2013 | 2018 | Chih Chien University (Taiwan) | 29 |
| Luo, Yuyan | 3 | 34 | 11,33 | 2014 | 2022 | Chengdu University of Technology (China) | 11 |
| Zhang, Cheng | 3 | 29 | 9,67 | 2020 | 2024 | University of Science & Technology of China (China) | 9 |
| Fakfare, Pipatpong | 3 | 21 | 7,00 | 2023 | 2024 | Bangkok University (Thailand) | 13 |
| Wattanacharoensil, Walanchalee | 3 | 21 | 7,00 | 2023 | 2024 | Bangkok University (Thailand) | 8 |
| Huang, Tianyue | 3 | 19 | 6,33 | 2021 | 2022 | Harbin University of Commerce (China) | 2 |
| Liao, Zhixue | 3 | 14 | 4,67 | 2013 | 2014 | Southwestern University of Finance & Economics (China) | 9 |

*Note*: C/P (average citation per paper); First Paper (year first published); Last Paper (year last published).
Source: own elaboration.

The analysis of co-authorship networks for the joint period (2010–2024) has identified four networks for scientific collaboration. All of these networks are national in nature, with two being intra-institutional and two being inter-institutional (Figure 4). According to Donthu et al. (2021), they have only considered authors that have published five or more papers as having a link strength $\geq 2$.

The first network (yellow color) emerges in the year 2018 and finally in 2022. The researchers are Jiekuan Zhang from the Guilin Tourism University (China) and Yan Zhang from the Xinyang Normal University (China). Therefore, this network has a national and inter-institutional nature. This network is characterized by the fact that it is formed by the most productive and cited author (Table 4). Similarly, it is the network with the highest academic impact (528 citations and 38 in citation rate).

The second network (green color) emerges in the year 2013 and finally in 2020. The researchers are Yuyan Luo from the Chengdu University of Technology (China) and Liao, Zhixue Liao from the Southwestern University of Finance & Economics (China). Therefore, this network has a national and inter-institutional nature. This network has a medium academic impact (48 citations and 8 in citation rate).

The fourth network (blue color) emerges in the year 2023 and it is currently active (2024). The researchers are Pipatpong Fakfare and Walanchalee Wattanacharoensil from the Bangkok University (Thailand). Therefore, this network has a national and intra-institutional nature. This network has a low academic impact because it is currently formed (42 citations and 7 in citation rate).

Finally, the third network (red color) emerges in the year 2021 and it is currently active (2024). The researchers are Zi Tang and Tianyue Huang from the Harbin University Commerce (China). Therefore, this network has a national and intra-institutional nature. As well as the blue network, this network has a low academic impact because it is currently formed (39 citations and 6 in citation rate).

*Figure 4. Co-authorship networks 2010-2024*

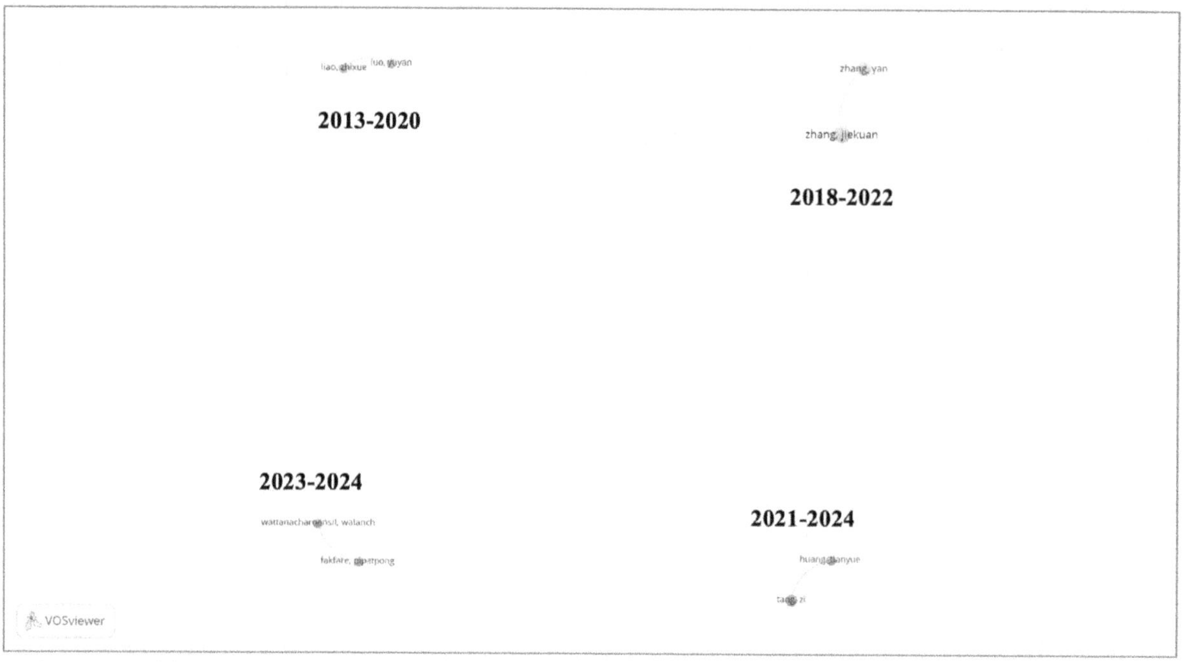


*Source: own elaboration with Web of Science (2024) processed with VOSviewer software*

Table 5 shows the most influential and productive institutions in the field analyzed. As with the authors, China universities stand out for their scientific production. In terms of productivity by number of articles published, Sichuan University (China) and the Xinyang Normal University (China) stand out. However, the institutions with the greatest influence in terms of citations per article are Jinwen University of Science and Technology (China) and Xinyang Normal University (China). It is noteworthy that the majority of the institutions have published in the last two years, which indicates that the subject matter is current. Finally, it is remarkable that in terms of scientific productivity among universities and authors, Chinese universities have a dominant presence in this scientific field.

*Table 5. Top ten Institutions by papers in the Web of Science data*

| University | Country | Papers | Cites | C/P | First Paper | Last Paper | SIR (2023) |
|---|---|---|---|---|---|---|---|
| Sichuan University | China | 8 | 140 | 17,50 | 2011 | 2024 | 24 |
| Xinyang Normal University | China | 5 | 150 | 30,00 | 2018 | 2022 | 2124 |
| Guilin Tourism University | China | 4 | 66 | 16,50 | 2020 | 2022 | 849 |
| Chengdu University of Technology | China | 4 | 34 | 8,50 | 2014 | 2020 | 1632 |
| Harbin University of Commerce | China | 4 | 20 | 5,00 | 2021 | 2024 | 3623 |
| Jinwen University of Science and Technology | China | 3 | 121 | 40,33 | 2013 | 2018 | 2200 |
| National Taiwan Normal University | Taiwan | 3 | 89 | 29,67 | 2012 | 2018 | 832 |
| Southwestern University of Finance and Economics | China | 3 | 34 | 11,33 | 2020 | 2023 | 2184 |
| Bangkok University | Thailand | 3 | 21 | 7,00 | 2023 | 2024 | 1582 |
| China University of Mining and Technology | China | 3 | 4 | 1,33 | 2020 | 2022 | 240 |

*Note*: C/P (average citation per paper); First Paper (year first published); Last Paper (year last published). SIR (Scimago Institution Ranking).

Source: own elaboration.

## 4.2. Content Analysis

The key words of the documents provide useful information regarding its man content and allow the identification of the main research topics and future lines of study (Callon et al., 1991; Liu et al., 2015). According to Liu et al. (2015), the content analysis is applied by means of the <<author keywords>> provided by WoS. From a minimum co-occurrence number of 3, the content analysis shows the relevance for four research lines: *Sustainable Development in Tourism* (red cluster); *Relationship between Carbon Footprint and Tourism* (green cluster); *Effects of Climate Change in Tourism* (blue cluster) and *Low Carbon Tourism in China* (yellow cluster) (Figure 5).

The content analysis shows the relevance of the research related to *Sustainable Development in Tourism* (red cluster) and, to a lesser extent, to *Relationship between Carbon Footprint and Tourism* (green cluster) for the entirety of the period between 2010 and 2024. The analysis by sub-periods through the overlay map (Figure 6) shows that *Sustainable Development in Tourism* (red cluster) and *Effects of Climate Change on Tourism* (blue cluster) are the lines with greater relevance and academic impact in the years between 2020 and 2024. These new research lines emerge after 2020 due to a large part of the articles being published in this period (67 articles).

*Relationship between Carbon Footprint and Tourism* analyses the negative effects of tourism activities for the carbon footprint. Carbon footprint refers to the amount of hidden greenhouse gases emissions in the daily consumption of a person (Whittlesea & Owen, 2012). In the tourism industry, the carbon footprint is especially relevant due to all the tourism activities, in one way or another, affecting the emission of greenhouse gases (food, accommodation, purchases or transport) (Rico et al., 2019). The article with most academic relevance is that by Luo et al. (2021), which analyses the carbon footprint in the Xingwen Geopark (China), a destination which introduced a policy of low-carbon construction consistent in high-yield buildings to avoid excessive energy consumption. The results show that the current scenario of the park is not ideal because, even though it is promoting low carbon tourism, the number of tourists is growing exponentially. The authors recommend reducing the carbon footprint by means such as restricting the number of tourists, the introduction of responsible tourism products or investment in environmental protection.

*Figure 5. Keywords network 2010-2024*

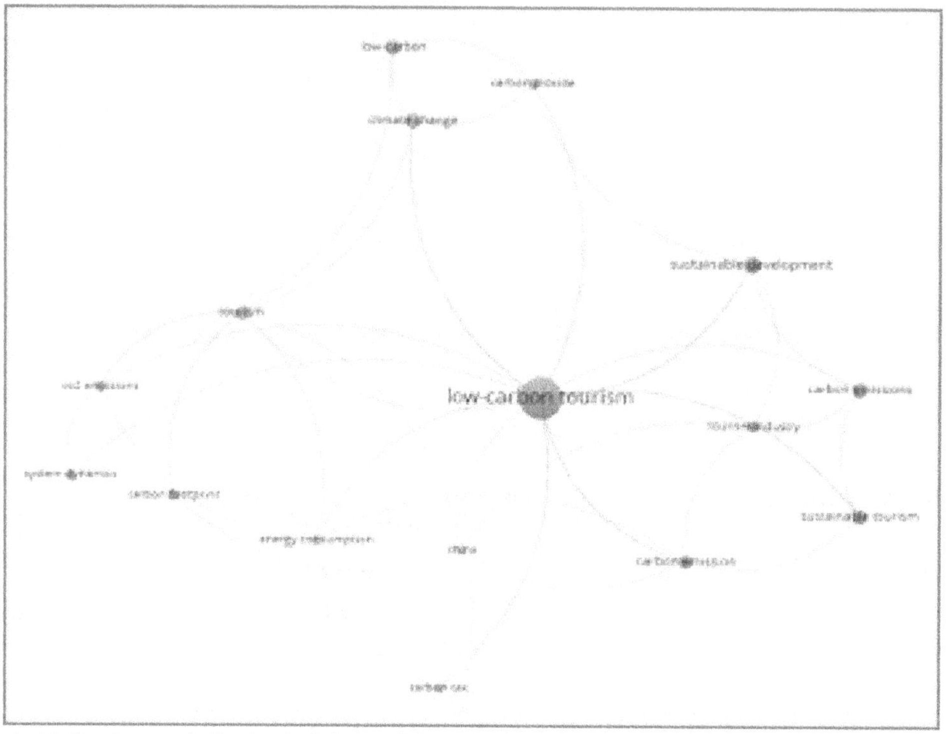


*Note: Sustainable Development in Tourism (red cluster); Relationship between Carbon Footprint and Tourism (green cluster); Effects of Climate Change on Tourism (blue cluster) and Low Carbon Tourism in China (yellow cluster).*

*Source: own elaboration with Web of Science (2024) processed with VOSviewer software*

*Low Carbon Tourism in China* analyses the effect of low-emission tourism policies in China through carbon taxes, the reduction of energy consumption by tourists and tourist destinations, or the participation of the local community in tourism planning. China has an exceptional biodiversity and a unique historic heritage, being in 2023 the country with the second highest number of World Heritage Sites (UNESCO, 2023). However, China is the country with the most CO2 emissions in 2022, having a total of 12,667.428 megatonnes (Datos Macro, 2022), putting its biodiversity at risk. As a result, decarbonisation policies in the Asian country are undergoing change in the tourism model, due to the negative repercussion of tourism on environmental sustainability, with the aim of preserving this heritage and environmental legacy. One of the articles with the most impact is that by Zhang & Zhang (2019) who analyse the introduction of the carbon tax on energy consumption in the tourism sector. The results show that this tax has no long-term effect. This is due to the fact that, even though the tax had a limited short-term effect, in the end, the tourism industries returned to previous pollution levels as a result of there being no energy alternative. As such, the authors recommend that the solution goes through the optimisation of the existing energy structure and reduces the current excessive dependence on fossil fuels, through the use of renewable sources.

*Effects of Climate Change in Tourism* analyses the negative effects of climate change on tourism. The risks associated with climate change have a negative effect on tourism activities; for example, the degradation of natural assets and damage to tourism infrastructure, as well as erosion on the beaches; increase of the cost of food and energy or drought; or the restriction of destinations to adapt to climate change (Scott et al., 2019). The results of the article by Gössling & Higham (2021) show how tourist destinations have a key role to play in the reduction of emissions, as they consist of groups of tourism actors that may work towards decarbonisation and, at the same time, meet secondary goals of increasing profitability and resilience. The authors recommend that the managers of tourist destinations understand the effects of climate change and the emissions of greenhouse effect on their businesses, changing the current approach of mass tourism to an environmentally sustainable approach.

Sustainable Development in Tourism analyses the role of the development of sustainable tourism through activities that allow for the existence of a balance between the economic benefits of tourism and environmental protection (Sung et al., 2021). The relationship between the environment and tourism should be a symbiotic relationship; however, tourist activities may lead to environmental degradation (Skanavis & Sakellari 2011). These activities are composed of eco-friendly vehicles and flights, green and ecological hotels or sustainable tourist attractions (Filimonau et al., 2013). One of the articles with the most academic relevance is that by Tang & Huang (2021), which analyses the existing relationship between tourism, economic growth and CO2 emissions in China. The results show that tourist development, both national and international, has contributed to greater CO2 emissions. As a result, the authors recommend establishing policies restricting tourism, especially in peak season, in order to reduce the destination's burden.

*Figure 6. Overlay map keywords network 2010-2024*

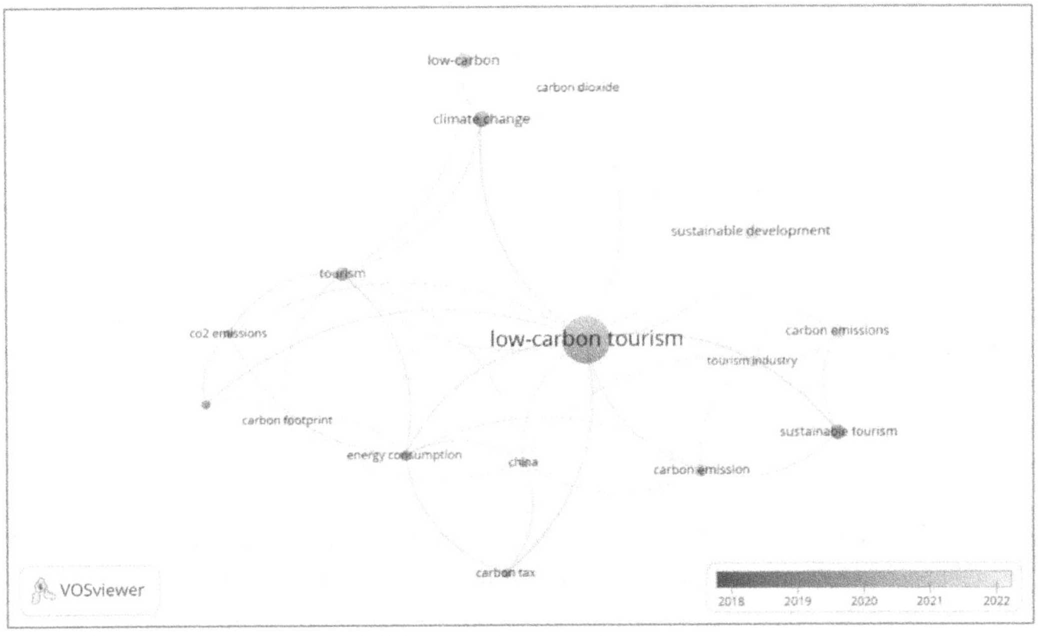


*Source: own elaboration with Web of Science (2024) processed with VOSviewer software*

## 5. CONCLUSION

The Intergovernmental Panel on Climate Change recommends that the global economy should decarbonise in the next 30 years (IPCC, 2018). Tourism is an economic sector closely involved in this imperative due to being one of the main contributors to the emission of carbon dioxide (Gössling & Higham, 2021). Additionally, the rapid expansion of tourism has not been linked to sustainability policies, which has had a multiplying effect on pollution (Dolnicar et al., 2019). Proof of this is that, between 2009 and 2013, tourism has been responsible for 8% of all greenhouse effect emissions (Lenzen et al., 2018). As a result, tourist destinations perform a fundamental role in the reduction of emissions and this occurs because the different destination managers understand the risks of climate change and pollution for their economic sector (Scott et al., 2019). The new imperative of low carbon emissions obligates the prioritisation of value over volume and rethinking the mechanisms of value generation (Oklevik et al. 2019). Therefore, Low Carbon Tourism, which prioritises sustainability and low emission of greenhouse gases, is an alternative to the pollution of mass tourism.

The main aim of this research is to visualise the relevant research topics in the realm of Low Carbon Tourism between the years 2010 and 2024, which shall help researchers, politicians and destination marketing organisations (DMO) to better understand the existing studies and future research topics in the realm of LCT. The use of VOSviewer is a new analysis tool for scientific literature, versus traditional analysis models, which enables graphically visualizing key topics and establishing future challenges in this scientific field. Table 1 shows that the methodology applied to analyse the impact of CO2 in the realm of tourism is diverse. The description of the state of Low-Carbon Tourism (O1) shows a growing academic interest in this scientific field, with an increase in scientific production since 2018 (Figure 3). During the period analysed, China was the country that contributed most to research on low-carbon tourism, with Sichuan University, Xinyang Normal University (China) and Jinwen University of Science and Technology standing out (Tables 4 and 5). In this line, there are co-authorship networks in which the main collaborative networks are formed by authors from China, all of these networks having been created recently (Figure 4). The identification of current lines and future research opportunities in Low-Carbon Tourism (O2) has enabled the identification of four relevant research lines: *Sustainable Development in Tourism* (red cluster); *Relationship between Carbon Footprint and Tourism* (green cluster); *Effects of Climate Change in Tourism* (blue cluster) and *Low Carbon Tourism in China* (yellow cluster) (Figure 5), with *Sustainable Development in Tourism* and *Effects of Climate Change on Tourism* being the lines with most academic impact and relevance in the recent years of this period that is the subject of this study (Figure 6).

This study has diverse practical applications. First of all, tourist services should encourage services that are eco-friendly and have a smaller carbon footprint (electric vehicles, saving water, self-sufficient energy, solar panels, green or ecological hotels…). As a result, governments may introduce a series of policies, such as grants for renewable energies and electric vehicles, carbon taxes, hydrocarbon taxes or issuing ecological certifications for hotels. Secondly, it is observed that short distances, recurring trips and international trips negatively influence tourism sustainability. As such, it is recommended that tourist government policies are focused on the growth of national tourism and increasing the duration of tourist stays. In Spain, this is being undertaken through the 2030 Sustainable Tourism Strategy for Spain which encourages the three pillars of sustainability: socio-economic, environmental and regional. Thirdly, touristification is causing the displacement of residents from an area and other negative consequences (destruction of historic heritage, both tangible and intangible, loss of air quality, or the increase in housing prices) as a result of mass tourism (Jover & Díaz-Parra, 2020). Accordingly, Low Carbon Tourism may be an alternative to avoid seasonality and to promote sustainable destinations, far from large urban areas. Fourth, China is the country with the greatest impact on CO2 in the world, putting its cultural and environmental diversity at risk. As such, politicians and managers of tourist destinations should establish public policies with the aim of reducing CO2 emissions. The results of the study by Zhang & Zhang (2019) show how policies introduced in this country, such as carbon tax, have no long-term effects on the reduction of emissions. Accordingly, we recommend the introduction of other policies in this country, such as optimising the current energy structure and reducing the excessive dependence on fossil fuels, by means of introducing alternative energies, such as solar or wind energy. Fifthly, destination managers can introduce new technologies that contribute to LCT (solar energy, electric cars or recycled water). Medina-Jimenez et al. (2024) analyse the potential of the Canary Islands to replace internal combustion engine rental car fleets with electric vehicles. The results highlight the confidence of destination managers in the introduction of these electric cars, provided that bureaucratic barriers are reduced and the number of charging points is increased. Similar conclusions are drawn in the article by Funsho-Idowu (2022), who recommends the introduction of electric vehicles in destinations as they are more efficient than internal combustion vehicles. In this respect, the authors recommend that policies in tourist destinations should focus on improving infrastructure to facilitate the use of these electric cars by tourists in the future. Gössling & Lund-Durlacher (2021) analyse the energy production of 30 hotels in Austria. Among the measures to be taken, the authors recommend the introduction of measures such as thermal insulation of buildings, introduction of solar energy, introduction of alternative transport or electrification of vehicles. Rodríguez-Pérez et al. (2021) analyse the introduction of a series of measures in tourism in the Canary Islands with the aim of reducing the carbon footprint, such as renewable water, biogas and the introduction of solar and wind energy.

With regard to emerging trends in LCT, it is important to highlight the challenges of implementing LCT strategies, as outlined by Gossling & Higham (2021). The authors discuss the three main pillars of decarbonisation policies: introducing new fiscal policies, reducing emissions (e.g. by increasing the number of trips or eco-efficient travel) and adding value to travel (e.g. by buying local and organic products). However, the main challenges for the implementation of decarbonisation policies are the lack of adequate public infrastructure (e.g. charging points for electric vehicles), lack of institutional support, diminishing returns, the emergence of new technologies facilitating the purchase of tourism services, and poor consumer adaptation. In this respect, future studies should analyse the innovations that different destinations and tourism services can introduce to be in line with low-carbon policies. In addition, new studies should analyse the policies that different policy actors would introduce to promote decarbonisation in destinations. For example, several authors have highlighted the need to remove bureaucratic barriers, provide subsidies to destinations to promote sustainability, or introduce new taxes to incentivise emission reductions (Zhang & Zhang, 2020; Leh et al., 2023; Wang et al., 2024).

With regard to the social and cultural dimensions, there are many individual actions that tourists can take to reduce their carbon footprint, such as paying a surcharge on flights to make the trip CO2 neutral (called a footprint), as introduced by some airlines such as Iberia or railway companies such as Iryo, reducing the number of stays during the year, recycling and reducing expenses during the trip, and using alternative or electric transport. The results of the study by Carvajal-Trujillo et al. (2024) show that the intention to adopt sustainable behaviour is not always translated into actual behaviour during the holiday. Therefore, the authors recommend that future studies analyse how destinations should promote sustainable behaviour among tourists.

Finally, as with every study, there are limitations. First of all, Web of Science (WoS) was the database used to analyse the sample, and it may be the case that relevant field studies are not included. Therefore, there is a bias towards Anglo-Saxon literature. In this sense, new studies may include work from other databases so as to include Spanish-language journals (for example, Scielo). This may be useful for comparing the results obtained and exploring new concepts and new trends in research related to Low Carbon Tourism. Secondly, in the future, new bibliometric computer programmes such as SciMAT or Bibliometrix may be used to improve bibliometric analysis, for example, by performing longitudinal analysis. Thirdly, meta-analysis is a powerful tool that does not allow the supplementation of bibliometric analysis due to it allowing the summary of results from different empirical studies on the effect of an independent variable (Sos et al., 2021). Therefore, future studies should use this tool to analyse the existing relationships of tourist behaviour in the context of Low Carbon Tourism.

Regarding the future lines of research; first of all, Gössling & Higham (2021) recommend that future public policies introduce measures to avoid the environmental impact of tourism and to follow the path of decarbonisation, such as measuring the impact of the intensity of carbon by companies and the need to introduce new performance indicators, such as the relationship between profits and emissions. Secondly, Zhang & Zhang (2019) recommend expanding the analysis of different public decarbonisation policies (technology, legislation, carbon commerce systems and carbon taxes) into a wider geographical range than that undertaken by these authors. Accordingly, it would be interesting for future studies to address the analysis of different public policies on energy consumption in different countries and compare the results. Thirdly, there is a lack of research regarding the socio-demographic nature of tourists and their relationship with LCT use. As such, regarding the results of the study by Tomasi et al. (2021), we deem it necessary that future research addresses the study of LCT from a generational, gender or geographic perspective. Finally, we generally find the problem that LCT is an alternative with a greater cost than traditional tourism. As such, future studies should address how to motivate potential tourists to use this type of tourism (Dai et al., 2022; Shie et al., 2022). For example, the managers of these destinations should not promote this type of tourism by emphasising the environmental aspect, but also through the promotion of personal health or the sustainable tourist realm (Zhang et al., 2020). Finally, in this study we only considered "*Low Carbon Tourism**" as a search query. Future studies can broaden the scope of the research by adding other keywords, such as *eco-efficiency of tourism* or *responsible behaviour*.

To summarise the main contribution of this paper, we have presented Figure 7:

*Figure 7. Main contributions of the current manuscript*

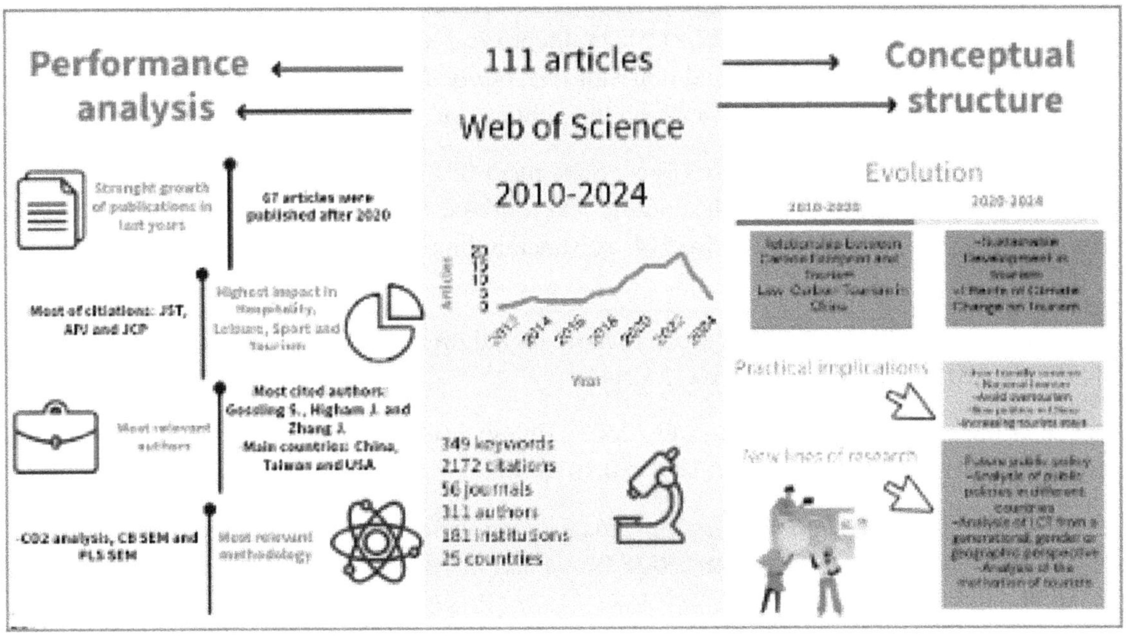


*Source: own elaboration*

## REFERENCES


Acikgoz, F., Stylos, N., & Lythreatis, S. (2024). Identifying capabilities and constraints in utilizing blockchain technology in hospitality and tourism. *International Journal of Contemporary Hospitality Management*, *36*(10), 3493–3514. Advance online publication. DOI: 10.1108/IJCHM-07-2023-1083

Acikgoz, F., Stylos, N., & Lythreatis, S. (2024, September 02). Identifying capabilities and constraints in utilizing blockchain technology in hospitality and tourism. *International Journal of Contemporary Hospitality Management*, *36*(10), 3493–3514. Advance online publication. DOI: 10.1108/IJCHM-07-2023-1083

Becken, S. (2017). Evidence of a low-carbon tourism paradigm? *Journal of Sustainable Tourism*, *25*(6), 832–850. DOI: 10.1080/09669582.2016.1251446

Becken, S., Simmons, D. G., & Frampton, C. (2003). Energy use associated with different travel choices. *Tourism Management*, *24*(3), 267–277. DOI: 10.1016/S0261-5177(02)00066-3

Belicia, T. X. Y., & Islam, M. S. (2018). Towards a decommodified wildlife tourism: Why market environmentalism is not enough for conservation. *Societies (Basel, Switzerland)*, *8*(3), 59. DOI: 10.3390/soc8030059

Bhaktikul, K., Aroonsrimorakot, S., Laiphrakpam, M., & Paisantanakij, W. (2021). Toward a low-carbon tourism for sustainable development: A study based on a royal project for highland community development in Chiang Rai, Thailand. *Environment, Development and Sustainability*, *23*(7), 10743–10762. DOI: 10.1007/s10668-020-01083-4

Bhukya, R., & Paul, J. (2023). Social influence research in consumer behavior: What we learned and what we need to learn?–A hybrid systematic literature review. *Journal of Business Research*, *162*, 113870. DOI: 10.1016/j.jbusres.2023.113870

Busalim, A. H., & Hussin, A. R. C. (2016). Understanding social commerce: A systematic literature review and directions for further research. *International Journal of Information Management*, *36*(6), 1075–1088. DOI: 10.1016/j.ijinfomgt.2016.06.005

Callon, M., Courtial, J. P., & Laville, F. (1991). Co-word analysis as a tool for describing the network of interactions between basic and technological research: The case of polymer chemistry. *Scientometrics*, *22*(1), 155–205. DOI: 10.1007/BF02019280

Carvajal-Trujillo, E., Pérez-Gálvez, J. C., & Orts-Cardador, J. J. (2024). Exploring tourists' pro-environmental behavior: a bibliometric analysis over two decades (1999–2023). *Journal of Tourism Futures*. DOI: 10.1108/JTF-02-2024-0033

Cheng, Q., Su, B., & Tan, J. (2013). Developing an evaluation index system for low-carbon tourist attractions in China–A case study examining the Xixi wetland. *Tourism Management*, *36*, 314-320http:// DOI: 10.1016/j.tourman.2012.10.019

Cho, Y. J., Wang, Y., & Hsu, L. L. I. (2016). Constructing Taiwan's low-carbon tourism development suitability evaluation indicators. *Asia Pacific Journal of Tourism Research*, *21*(6), 658–677. DOI: 10.1080/10941665.2015.1068193

Chopdar, P. K., Lytras, M. D., & Visvizi, A. (2022). Exploring factors influencing bicycle-sharing adoption in India: A UTAUT 2 based mixed-method approach. *International Journal of Emerging Markets, 18*(11), 5109–5134. DOI: 10.1108/IJOEM-06-2021-0862

Dai, Y. Y., Shie, A. J., Chu, J. H., & Wu, Y. C. J. (2022). Low-carbon travel motivation and constraint: Scales development and validation. *International Journal of Environmental Research and Public Health, 19*(9), 5123. DOI: 10.3390/ijerph19095123 PMID: 35564516

Datos Macro. (2022). *CO2 emissions in China*. Datos Macro 2022. https://datosmacro.expansion.com/energia-y-medio-ambiente/emisiones-co2/china

Dawson, J., Stewart, E. J., Lemelin, H., & Scott, D. (2010). The carbon cost of polar bear viewing tourism in Churchill, Canada. *Journal of Sustainable Tourism, 18*(3), 319–336. DOI: 10.1080/09669580903215147

Dawson, J., Stewart, E. J., Lemelin, H., & Scott, D. (2010). The carbon cost of polar bear viewing tourism in Churchill, Canada. *Journal of Sustainable Tourism, 18*(3), 319–336. DOI: 10.1080/09669580903215147

De Oliveira, O. J., da Silva, F. F., Juliani, F., Barbosa, L. C. F. M., & Nunhes, T. V. (2019). Bibliometric method for mapping the state-of-the-art and identifying research gaps and trends in literature: An essential instrument to support the development of scientific projects. In Kunosic, S., & Zerem, E. (Eds.), *Scientometrics recent advances* (pp. 47–64). IntechOpen., DOI: 10.5772/intechopen.85856

Dickinson, J. E., Lumsdon, L. M., & Robbins, D. (2011). Slow travel: Issues for tourism and climate change. *Journal of Sustainable Tourism, 19*(3), 281–300. DOI: 10.1080/09669582.2010.524704

Dolnicar, S., Knezevic Cvelbar, L., & Grün, B. (2019). A sharing-based approach to enticing tourists to behave more environmentally friendly. *Journal of Travel Research, 58*(2), 241–252. DOI: 10.1177/0047287517746013 PMID: 30662098

Donthu, N., Kumar, S., Mukherjee, D., Pandey, N., & Lim, W. M. (2021). How to conduct a bibliometric analysis: An overview and guidelines. *Journal of Business Research, 133*, 285–296. DOI: 10.1016/j.jbusres.2021.04.070

Eames, C., Cowie, B., & Bolstad, R. (2008). An evaluation of characteristics of envi- ronmental education practice in New Zealand schools. *Environmental Education Research, 14*(1), 35–51. DOI: 10.1080/13504620701843343

Fakfare, P., & Wattanacharoensil, W. (2023). Low-carbon tourism: determining domestic tourist perception from Thailand: TOURISM AGENDA 2030. *Tourism Review, 78*(2), 496–516. DOI: 10.1108/TR-12-2021-0537

Feng, Y., Zhu, Q., & Lai, K. H. (2017). Corporate social responsibility for supply chain management: A literature review and bibliometric analysis. *Journal of Cleaner Production, 158*, 296–307. DOI: 10.1016/j.jclepro.2017.05.018

Filimonau, V., Dickinson, J., Robbins, D., & Reddy, M. V. (2013). The role of 'indirect' greenhouse gas emissions in tourism: Assessing the hidden carbon impacts from a holiday package tour. *Transportation Research Part A, Policy and Practice, 54*, 78–91. DOI: 10.1016/j.tra.2013.07.002

Fontan Kohler, A., & Antonio Digiampietri, L. (2021). Cultural tourism: Bibliometric and social network analysis of Brazilian tourism field, 1990-2018. *Pasos (El Sauzal), 19*(4). Advance online publication. DOI: 10.25145/j.pasos.2021.19.054

Friedlingstein, P., Cox, P., Betts, R., Bopp, L., von Bloh, W., Brovkin, V., Cadule, P., Doney, S., Eby, M., Fung, I., Bala, G., John, J., Jones, C., Joos, F., Kato, T., Kawamiya, M., Knorr, W., Lindsay, K., Matthews, H. D., & Zeng, N. (2006). Climate–carbon cycle feedback analysis: Results from the C4MIP model intercomparison. *Journal of Climate, 19*(14), 3337–3353. DOI: 10.1175/JCLI3800.1

Friedlingstein, P., O'sullivan, M., Jones, M. W., Andrew, R. M., Gregor, L., Hauck, J., Le Quéré, C., Luijkx, I. T., Olsen, A., Peters, G. P., Peters, W., Pongratz, J., Schwingshackl, C., Sitch, S., Canadell, J. G., Ciais, P., Jackson, R. B., Alin, S. R., Alkama, R., & Zheng, B. (2022). Global carbon budget 2022. *Earth System Science Data, 14*(11), 4811–4900. DOI: 10.5194/essd-14-4811-2022

Funsho Idowu, O., Adedoyin, F. F., Bekun, F. V., & Balsalobre-Lorente, D. (2022). Modeling the environmental implications of car ownership and energy consumption in the UK: Evidence from NARDL model. *International Journal of Sustainable Transportation, 16*(12), 1097–1109. DOI: 10.1080/15568318.2021.1969708

Geels, F. W., Sovacool, B. K., Schwanen, T., & Sorrell, S. (2017). Sociotechnical transitions for deep decarbonization. *Science, 357*(6357), 1242–1244. DOI: 10.1126/science.aao3760 PMID: 28935795

Gössling, S. (2000). Tourism–sustainable development option? [Opens in a new window]. *Environmental Conservation, 27*(3), 223–224. DOI: 10.1017/S0376892900000242

Gössling, S., Balas, M., Mayer, M., & Sun, Y. Y. (2023). A review of tourism and climate change mitigation: The scales, scopes, stakeholders and strategies of carbon management. *Tourism Management, 95*, 104681. DOI: 10.1016/j.tourman.2022.104681

Gössling, S., Balas, M., Mayer, M., & Sun, Y. Y. (2023). A review of tourism and climate change mitigation: The scales, scopes, stakeholders and strategies of carbon management. *Tourism Management, 95*, 104681. DOI: 10.1016/j.tourman.2022.104681

Gössling, S., & Higham, J. (2021). The low-carbon imperative: Destination management under urgent climate change. *Journal of Travel Research, 60*(6), 1167–1179. DOI: 10.1177/0047287520933679

Gössling, S., & Humpe, A. (2023). Net-zero aviation: Time for a new business model? *Journal of Air Transport Management, 107*, 102353. DOI: 10.1016/j.jairtraman.2022.102353

Gössling, S., & Humpe, A. (2023). Net-zero aviation: Time for a new business model? *Journal of Air Transport Management, 107*, 102353. DOI: 10.1016/j.jairtraman.2022.102353

Gössling, S., & Lund-Durlacher, D. (2021). Tourist accommodation, climate change and mitigation: An assessment for Austria. *Journal of Outdoor Recreation and Tourism, 34*, 100367. DOI: 10.1016/j.jort.2021.100367

Gössling, S., & Michael Hall, C. (2019). Sharing versus collaborative economy: How to align ICT developments and the SDGs in tourism? *Journal of Sustainable Tourism, 27*(1), 74–96. DOI: 10.1080/09669582.2018.1560455

Gössling, S., & Michael Hall, C. (2019). Sharing versus collaborative economy: How to align ICT developments and the SDGs in tourism? *Journal of Sustainable Tourism, 27*(1), 74–96. DOI: 10.1080/09669582.2018.1560455

Gössling, S., Peeters, P., Ceron, J. P., Dubois, G., Patterson, T., & Richardson, R. B. (2005). The eco-efficiency of tourism. *Ecological Economics, 54*(4), 417–434. DOI: 10.1016/j.ecolecon.2004.10.006

Gössling, S., Ring, A., Dwyer, L., Andersson, A.-C., & Hall, C. M. (2016). Optimizing or maximizing growth? A challenge for sustainable tourism. *Journal of Sustainable Tourism, 24*(4), 527–548. DOI: 10.1080/09669582.2015.1085869

Gössling, S., Scott, D., & Hall, C. M. (2018). Global trends in length of stay: Implications for destination management and climate change. *Journal of Sustainable Tourism, 26*(12), 2087–2101. DOI: 10.1080/09669582.2018.1529771

Hall, C. M., Scott, D., & Gössling, S. (2013). The primacy of climate change for sustainable international tourism. *Sustainable Development (Bradford), 21*(2), 112–121. DOI: 10.1002/sd.1562

Hernández-Garrido, R., Orts-Cardador, J., & Perez-Calañas, C. (2023). The Role of Management in Sustainable Tourism: A Bibliometric Analysis Approach. *Sustainability (Basel), 15*(12), 9712. DOI: 10.3390/su15129712

Herold, F., Theobald, P., Gronwald, T., Kaushal, N., Zou, L., de Bruin, E. D., Bherer, L., & Müller, N. G. (2024). Alexa, let's train now!—A systematic review and classification approach to digital and home-based physical training interventions aiming to support healthy cognitive aging. *Journal of Sport and Health Science, 13*(1), 30–46. DOI: 10.1016/j.jshs.2023.01.004 PMID: 36736727

Higueras-Castillo, E., García-Maroto, I., Muñoz-Leiva, F., & Liébana-Cabanillas, F. (2022). Modelling sustainable mobility adoption from the urban population view (SMAUP model): The moderating effect of household size. *Research in Transportation Business & Management, 45*, 100878. DOI: 10.1016/j.rtbm.2022.100878

Horng, J. S., Hu, M. L. M., Teng, C. C. C., Hsiao, H. L., & Liu, C. H. S. (2013). Development and validation of the low-carbon literacy scale among practitioners in the Taiwanese tourism industry. *Tourism Management, 35*, 255–262. DOI: 10.1016/j.tourman.2012.08.001

Horng, J. S., Hu, M. L. M., Teng, C. C. C., Hsiao, H. L., & Liu, C. H. S. (2013). Development and validation of the low-carbon literacy scale among practitioners in the Taiwanese tourism industry. *Tourism Management, 35*, 255–262. DOI: 10.1016/j.tourman.2012.08.001

Huang, Z., Cao, F., Jin, C., Yu, Z., & Huang, R. (2017). Carbon emission flow from self-driving tours and its spatial relationship with scenic spots–A traffic-related big data method. *Journal of Cleaner Production, 142*, 946–955. DOI: 10.1016/j.jclepro.2016.09.129

Intergovernmental Panel on Climate Change (IPCC). (2022). Intergovernmental Panel on Climate Change. https://www.ipcc.ch/

International Air Transport Association. (2019). Annual Review 2019. https://www.iata.org/contentassets/c81222d96c9a4e0bb4ff6ced0126f0bb/iata-annual-review-2019.pdf

Jover, J., & Díaz-Parra, I. (2020). Gentrification, transnational gentrification and touristification in Seville, Spain. *Urban Studies (Edinburgh, Scotland)*, *57*(15), 3044–3059. DOI: 10.1177/0042098019857585

Kar, S. K., Bansal, R., & Harichandan, S. (2022). An empirical study on intention to use hydrogen fuel cell vehicles in India. *International Journal of Hydrogen Energy*, *47*(46), 19999–20015. DOI: 10.1016/j.ijhydene.2022.04.137

Koçak, E., Ulucak, R., & Ulucak, Z. Ş. (2020). The impact of tourism developments on CO2 emissions: An advanced panel data estimation. *Tourism Management Perspectives*, *33*, 100611. DOI: 10.1016/j.tmp.2019.100611

Koh, E., Fakfare, P., & Pongwat, A. (2022). The limits of Thai hospitality–Perceived impact of tourism development on residents' well-being in Chiang Mai. *International Journal of Tourism Cities*, *8*(1), 187–209. DOI: 10.1108/IJTC-03-2020-0055

Kohler, A., & Digiampietri, L. (2021). Cultural tourism: Bibliometric and social network analysis of Brazilian tourism field, 1990-2018. *Pasos (El Sauzal)*, *19*(4). Advance online publication. DOI: 10.25145/j.pasos.2021.19.054

Lai, J. H. (2015). Carbon footprints of hotels: Analysis of three archetypes in Hong Kong. *Sustainable Cities and Society*, *14*, 334–341. DOI: 10.1016/j.scs.2013.09.005

Lee, T. H., & Jan, F. H. (2019). The low-carbon tourism experience: A multidimensional scale development. *Journal of Hospitality & Tourism Research (Washington, D.C.)*, *43*(6), 890–918. DOI: 10.1177/1096348019849675

Leh, F. C., Mohd Isa, N. K., Ibrahim, M. H., Ibrahim, M., Mohd Yunos, M. Y., & Ibrahim, J. A. (2023). A Literature Review of Low-Carbon Urban Tourism Indicators and Policy. *Pertanika Journal of Social Science & Humanities*, *31*(2), 655–681. Advance online publication. DOI: 10.47836/pjssh.31.2.10

Lenzen, M., Sun, Y. Y., Faturay, F., Ting, Y. P., Geschke, A., & Malik, A. (2018). The carbon footprint of global tourism. *Nature Climate Change*, *8*(6), 522–528. DOI: 10.1038/s41558-018-0141-x

Liu, X., Zeng, Y., He, J., & Li, Z. (2022). Value cocreation research in tourism and hospitality: A comparative bibliometric analysis. *International Journal of Contemporary Hospitality Management*, *34*(2), 663–686. DOI: 10.1108/IJCHM-05-2021-0666

Liu, Z., Yin, Y., Liu, W., & Dunford, M. (2015). Visualizing the intellectual structure and evolution of innovation systems research: A bibliometric analysis. *Scientometrics*, *103*(1), 135–158. DOI: 10.1007/s11192-014-1517-y

Luo, F., Becken, S., & Zhong, Y. (2018). Changing travel patterns in China and 'carbon footprint' implications for a domestic tourist destination. *Tourism Management*, *65*, 1–13. DOI: 10.1016/j.tourman.2017.09.012

Luo, Y., Mou, Y., Wang, Z., Su, Z., & Qin, Y. (2021). Scenario-based planning for a dynamic tourism system with carbon footprint analysis: A case study of Xingwen Global Geopark, China. *Journal of Cleaner Production*, *254*, 119999. DOI: 10.1016/j.jclepro.2020.119999

Mahadew, R., & Appadoo, K. A. (2019). Tourism and climate change in Mauritius: Assessing the adaptation and mitigation plans and prospects. *Tourism Review*, *74*(2), 204–215. DOI: 10.1108/TR-12-2017-0203

Manthiou, A., Klaus, P., & Luong, V. H. (2022). Slow tourism: Conceptualization and interpretation–A travel vloggers' perspective. *Tourism Management*, *93*, 104570. DOI: 10.1016/j.tourman.2022.104570

Martínez-López, F. J., Merigó, J. M., Valenzuela-Fernández, L., & Nicolás, C. (2018). Fifty years of the European Journal of Marketing: A bibliometric analysis. *European Journal of Marketing*, *52*(1/2), 439–468. DOI: 10.1108/EJM-11-2017-0853

McKinsey & Company and World Travel & Tourism Council. (2017). *Managing overcrowding in tourist destinations.* World travel & tourism council. www.mckinsey.com/industries/travel-transport-and-logistics/our-insights/coping-with-success-managing-overcrowding-in- tourism-destinations

Medina-Jiménez, I., Ramos-Real, F. J., Vielma, J. E. L., & Calero-García, F. (2024). Designing an integrative strategy to introduce electric vehicles in the tourism sector in an outermost region of the European Union. *Sustainable Energy Technologies and Assessments*, *72*, 104071. DOI: 10.1016/j.seta.2024.104071

Milano, C., Cheer, J. M., & Novelli, M. (Eds.). (2019). *Overtourism: Excesses, discontents and measures in travel and tourism.* CABI. DOI: 10.1079/9781786399823.0000

Mishra, A. R., Chandel, A., & Saeidi, P. (2022). Low-carbon tourism strategy evaluation and selection using interval-valued intuitionistic fuzzy additive ratio assessment approach based on similarity measures. *Environment, Development and Sustainability*, *24*(5), 7236–7282. DOI: 10.1007/s10668-021-01746-w PMID: 34493927

Mishra, H. G., Pandita, S., Bhat, A. A., Mishra, R. K., & Sharma, S. (2022). Tourism and carbon emissions: A bibliometric review of the last three decades: 1990–2021. *Tourism Review*, *77*(2), 636–658. DOI: 10.1108/TR-07-2021-0310

Mishra, H. G., Pandita, S., Bhat, A. A., Mishra, R. K., & Sharma, S. (2022). Tourism and carbon emissions: A bibliometric review of the last three decades: 1990–2021. *Tourism Review*, *77*(2), 636–658. DOI: 10.1108/TR-07-2021-0310

Moher, D., Liberati, A., Tetzlaff, J., & Altman, D. G.Prisma Group. (2010). Preferred reporting items for systematic reviews and meta-analyses: The PRISMA statement. *International Journal of Surgery*, *8*(5), 336–341. DOI: 10.1016/j.ijsu.2010.02.007 PMID: 20171303

Molina-Collado, A., Santos-Vijande, M. L., Gómez-Rico, M., & Madera, J. M. (2022). Sustainability in hospitality and tourism: A review of key research topics from 1994 to 2020. *International Journal of Contemporary Hospitality Management*, *34*(8), 3029–3064. DOI: 10.1108/IJCHM-10-2021-1305

Mundet, L., & Coenders, G. (2010). Greenways: A sustainable leisure experience concept for both communities and tourists. *Journal of Sustainable Tourism*, *18*(5), 657–674. DOI: 10.1080/09669581003668524

Nandasena, R., Morrison, A. M., & Coca-Stefaniak, J. A. (2022). Transformational tourism–a systematic literature review and research agenda. *Journal of Tourism Futures*, *8*(3), 282–297. DOI: 10.1108/JTF-02-2022-0038

Oklevik, O., Gössling, S., Hall, C. M., Jacobsen, J. K. S., Grøtte, I. P., & McCabe, S. (2020). Overtourism, optimisation, and destination performance indicators: A case study of activities in Fjord Norway. In *Tourism and Degrowth* (pp. 60–80). Routledge. DOI: 10.4324/9781003017257-4

Orts-Cardador, J. J. O., Pérez-Gálvez, J. C., Gomez-Casero, G., & Alba, C. A. J. (2023). Tourist ethnocentrism: A bibliometric analysis based on Web of Science (WoS). *Family and Consumer Sciences Research Journal*, *52*(1), 38–52. DOI: 10.1111/fcsr.12488

Paramati, S. R., Alam, M. S., & Lau, C. K. M. (2018). The effect of tourism investment on tourism development and CO2 emissions: Empirical evidence from the EU nations. *Journal of Sustainable Tourism*, *26*(9), 1587–1607. DOI: 10.1080/09669582.2018.1489398

Paris Climate Agreement. (2015). https://unfccc.int/es/acerca-de-las-ndc/el-acuerdo-de-paris

Pritchard, A. (1969). Statistical bibliography or bibliometrics. *The Journal of Documentation*, *25*, 348–349.

Qian, J., Law, R., Wei, J., & Wu, Y. (2019). Trends in global tourism studies: A content analysis of the publications in tourism management. *Journal of Quality Assurance in Hospitality & Tourism*, *20*(6), 753–768. DOI: 10.1080/1528008X.2019.1658149

Rico, A., Martínez-Blanco, J., Montlleó, M., Rodríguez, G., Tavares, N., Arias, A., & Oliver-Solà, J. (2019). Carbon footprint of tourism in Barcelona. *Tourism Management*, *70*, 491–504. DOI: 10.1016/j.tourman.2018.09.012

Rodríguez-Pérez, M. L., Mendieta-Pino, C. A., Ramos-Martín, A., León-Zerpa, F. A., & Déniz-Quintana, F. A. (2022). Inventory of water–energy–waste resources in rural houses in Gran Canaria Island: Application and potential of renewable resources and mitigation of carbon footprint and GHG. *Water (Basel)*, *14*(8), 1197. DOI: 10.3390/w14081197

Satrovic, E., & Muslija, A. (2019). The empirical evidence on tourism-urbanization-CO2 emissions nexus. [AHTR]. *Advances in Hospitality and Tourism Research*, *7*(1), 85–105. DOI: 10.30519/ahtr.484287

Scott, D., Gössling, S., & Hall, C. M. (2012). International tourism and climate change. *Wiley Interdisciplinary Reviews: Climate Change*, *3*(3), 213–232. DOI: 10.1002/wcc.165

Scott, D., Gössling, S., Hall, C. M., & Peeters, P. (2016). Can tourism be part of the decarbonized global economy? The costs and risks of alternate carbon reduction policy pathways. *Journal of Sustainable Tourism*, *24*(1), 52–72. DOI: 10.1080/09669582.2015.1107080

Scott, D., Hall, C. M., & Gössling, S. (2019). Global tourism vulnerability to climate change. *Annals of Tourism Research*, *77*, 49–61. DOI: 10.1016/j.annals.2019.05.007

Scott, D., Peeters, P., & Gössling, S. (2010). Can tourism deliver its "aspirational" greenhouse gas emission reduction targets? *Journal of Sustainable Tourism*, *18*(3), 393–408. DOI: 10.1080/09669581003653542

Seetanah, B., & Fauzel, S. (2018). Investigating the impact of climate change on the tourism sector: Evidence from a sample of island economies. *Tourism Review*, *74*(2), 194–203. DOI: 10.1108/TR-12-2017-0204

Shakouri, B., Khoshnevis Yazdi, S., & Ghorchebigi, E. (2017). Does tourism development promote CO2 emissions? *Anatolia*, *28*(3), 444–452. DOI: 10.1080/13032917.2017.1335648

Shie, A. J., Dai, Y. Y., Shen, M. X., Tian, L., Yang, M., Luo, W. W., Wu, Y. J., & Su, Z. H. (2022). Diamond model of green commitment and low-carbon travel motivation, constraint, and intention. *International Journal of Environmental Research and Public Health, 19*(14), 8454. DOI: 10.3390/ijerph19148454 PMID: 35886303

Singh, V., Singh, T., Higueras-Castillo, E., & Liebana-Cabanillas, F. J. (2023). Sustainable road transportation adoption research: A meta and weight analysis, and moderation analysis. *Journal of Cleaner Production, 392*, 136276. DOI: 10.1016/j.jclepro.2023.136276

Skanavis, C., & Sakellari, M. (2011). International tourism, domestic tourism and environmental change: Environmental education can find the balance. *Tourismos, 6*(1), 233–249.

Su, J. (2019). Impact of tourism resource development based on low-carbon mode: A case study of Guizhou ethnic areas. *Ecological Processes, 8*(1), 1–7. DOI: 10.1186/s13717-019-0176-6

Sung, P. L., Hsiao, T. Y., Huang, L., & Morrison, A. M. (2021). The influence of green trust on travel agency intentions to promote low-carbon tours for the purpose of sustainable development. *Corporate Social Responsibility and Environmental Management, 28*(4), 1185–1199. DOI: 10.1002/csr.2131

Tang, Z., & Huang, T. (2021). Carbon dioxide emission measurement and its spatiotemporal evolution of tourism industry in Heilongjiang province, China. *Advances in Meteorology, 2021*(1), 1458373. DOI: 10.1155/2021/1458373

Tang, Z., Shang, J., Shi, C., Liu, Z., & Bi, K. (2014). Decoupling indicators of CO2 emissions from the tourism industry in China: 1990–2012. *Ecological Indicators, 46*, 390–397. DOI: 10.1016/j.ecolind.2014.06.041

Teng, C. C., Lu, A. C. C., & Huang, T. T. (2018). Drivers of consumers' behavioral intention toward green hotels. *International Journal of Contemporary Hospitality Management, 30*(2), 1134–1151. Advance online publication. DOI: 10.1108/IJCHM-04-2017-0203

Thongdejsri, M., & Nitivattananon, V. (2019). Assessing impacts of implementing low-carbon tourism program for sustainable tourism in a world heritage city. *Tourism Review, 74*(2), 216–234. DOI: 10.1108/TR-04-2017-0082

Tian, C., Peng, J., Zhang, W., Zhang, S., & Wang, J. (2020). Tourism environmental impact assessment based on improved AHP and picture fuzzy PROMETHEE II methods. *Technological and Economic Development of Economy, 26*(2), 355–378. DOI: 10.3846/tede.2019.11413

Tomasi, S., Zubaryeva, A., Pizzirani, C., Dal Col, M., & Balest, J. (2021). Propensity to choose electric vehicles in cross-border alpine regions. *Sustainability (Basel), 13*(8), 4583. DOI: 10.3390/su13084583

Tsai, K. T., Lin, T. P., Hwang, R. L., & Huang, Y. J. (2014). Carbon dioxide emissions generated by energy consumption of hotels and homestay facilities in Taiwan. *Tourism Management, 42*, 13-21http:// DOI: 10.1016/j.tourman.2013.08.017

UNESCO. (2023). UNESCO World Heritage List. https://whc.unesco.org/es/list/

United Nation Climate Change. (2022). *UN Climate Change Conference.* UN (enviromental programme). https://www.unep.org/events/conference/un-climate-change-conference-unfccc-cop-27#:~:text=In%20November%202022%2C%20Egypt%20will,the%20way%20for%20future%20ambition

UNWTO. (2018). World Tourism Organization. *International tourism results in 2017: highest in seven years.*https://www.unwto.org/es/press-release/2018-01-15/resultados-del-turismo-internacional-en-2017-los-mas-altos-en-siete-anos

UNWTO. (2019). World Tourism Organization and International Transport Forum (2019). *Transport-related $CO_2$ Emissions of the Tourism Sector – Modelling Results,* UNWTO, Madrid. DOI: 10.18111/9789284416660

UNWTO. (2021). Transforming Tourism for Climate Action. https://www.unwto.org/sustainable-development/climate-action

Van Eck, N. J., & Waltman, L. (2022). *VOSviewer Manual. Manual for VOSviewer Version 1.6.v8.* https://www.vosviewer.com/documentation/Manual_VOSviewer_1.6.18.pdf

Wang, Q., Mao, Z., Xian, L., & Liang, Z. (2019). A study on the coupling coordination between tourism and the low-carbon city. *Asia Pacific Journal of Tourism Research, 24*(6), 550–562. DOI: 10.1080/10941665.2019.1610002

Wang, S., Cao, W., Du, J., Tang, P., Fu, H., Tang, Z., & Li, J. (2021). Assessing the environmental impact of China's tourism activities: A tourism heat footprint method. *Environmental Science and Pollution Research International, 28*(43), 61176–61188. DOI: 10.1007/s11356-021-15082-z PMID: 34169419

Wang, Y., Chen, J., Ren, X., & Tao, D. (2024). Low-carbon strategy and tourism development. *Current Issues in Tourism, 27*(21), 3458–3477. DOI: 10.1080/13683500.2023.2266100

Wangzhou, K., Wen, J. J., Wang, Z., Wang, H., Hao, C., & Andlib, Z. (2022). Revealing the nexus between tourism development and CO2 emissions in Asia: Does asymmetry matter? *Environmental Science and Pollution Research International, 29*(52), 79016–79024. DOI: 10.1007/s11356-022-21339-y PMID: 35705760

Whittlesea, E. R., & Owen, A. (2012). Towards a low carbon future–the development and application of REAP Tourism, a destination footprint and scenario tool. *Journal of Sustainable Tourism, 20*(6), 845–865. DOI: 10.1080/09669582.2012.680699

WTCC-UNEP-UNFCCC. (2021). *Transforming Tourism for Climate Action.* UNWTO: Sustainable development climate action. https://action.wttc.org/climate-environment

Wu, P., & Shi, P. (2011). An estimation of energy consumption and CO2 emissions in tourism sector of China. *Journal of Geographical Sciences, 21*(4), 733–745. DOI: 10.1007/s11442-011-0876-z

Xu, J., Yao, L., & Mo, L. (2011). Simulation of low-carbon tourism in world natural and cultural heritage areas: An application to Shizhong District of Leshan City in China. *Energy Policy, 39*(7), 4298–4307. DOI: 10.1016/j.enpol.2011.04.047

Zha, J., He, L., Liu, Y., & Shao, Y. (2019). Evaluation on development efficiency of low-carbon tourism economy: A case study of Hubei Province, China. *Socio-Economic Planning Sciences*, *66*, 47–57. DOI: 10.1016/j.seps.2018.07.003

Zhang, B., Chen, H., Du, Z., & Wang, Z. (2020). Does license plate rule induce low-carbon choices in residents' daily travels: Motivation and impacts. *Renewable & Sustainable Energy Reviews*, *124*, 109780. DOI: 10.1016/j.rser.2020.109780

Zhang, J., & Zhang, Y. (2018). Carbon tax, tourism CO2 emissions and economic welfare. *Annals of Tourism Research*, *69*, 18–30. DOI: 10.1016/j.annals.2017.12.009

Zhang, J., & Zhang, Y. (2019). Exploring the impacts of carbon tax on tourism-related energy consumption in China. *Sustainable Development (Bradford)*, *27*(3), 296–303. DOI: 10.1002/sd.1900

Zhang, J., & Zhang, Y. (2020). Assessing the low-carbon tourism in the tourism-based urban destinations. *Journal of Cleaner Production*, *276*, 124303. DOI: 10.1016/j.jclepro.2020.124303

Zupic, I., & Čater, T. (2015). Bibliometric methods in management and organization. *Organizational Research Methods*, *18*(3), 429–472. DOI: 10.1177/1094428114562629

## KEY TERMS AND DEFINITIONS

**Bibliometrics:** A variant of systematic literature reviews that involves the application of quantitative and statistical techniques based on various bibliographic data.

**Climate Change:** Long-term changes in temperature and weather patterns. These changes can be caused by nature (solar activity or volcanic eruptions) or by human activity itself, mainly through the burning of fossil fuels such as coal, oil and gas.

**Low Carbon Tourism:** A new form of sustainable tourism that balances the tourist experience with the reduction of the carbon produced by tourists' activities, with the aim of achieving greater social, economic and environmental benefits for our society.

**Sustainability:** A societal goal so that people and other living things can coexist on Earth for a long period of time. It is based on three pillars: environmental, economic and social.

**Tourism:** The set of actions carried out by people when they move and stay for a limited period of time in places other than their usual environment for different reasons (leisure, business or culture, among others).

**VOSviewer:** Computer software for the construction and visualisation of bibliometric networks. The networks created can be citation, bibliographic coupling, co-citation or co-authorship networks based on journals, researchers, references or publications.

**Web of Science:** Online scientific information platform provided by Clarivate Analytics, consisting of various databases such as Science Citation Index (SCI) or Social Sciences Citation Index (SSCI).

# Section 3
# Sustainable Development and Innovative Solutions

# Chapter 13
# Re-Thinking the Cultural Heritage Sustainability in the AI Era:
## From Virtualization to Authenticity

**Marco Tregua**
https://orcid.org/0000-0003-1579-7676
*University of Naples Federico II, Italy*

**Davide Bizjak**
https://orcid.org/0000-0003-2219-6983
*University of Naples Federico II, Italy*

## ABSTRACT

*This chapter aims to explore the impact of AI and its generative version on the sustainable development of Cultural Heritage. Narrowly, generative AI is the first technological innovation capable of producing creative work through textual or vocal input. Therefore, this is both an innovative opportunity for museums and other cultural sites as well as a relevant challenge, since sometimes the use of new digital technologies make visitors behaviour too quickly changing for firms to react. The chapter addresses the origins and a brief historical overview of AI, then explore the concepts of authenticity and sustainability concerning the use of AI. Therefore, four cases are examined to understand the possible fields of application and its effects. Finally, the guiding principles that could contribute to the sustainability of Cultural Heritage will be discussed, considering AI both as a support tool and as a preservation factor in itself.*

## INTRODUCTION

This chapter aims to explore the impact of AI and its generative version on the sustainable development of Cultural Heritage. The fundamental distinction between these two concepts lies in the fact that, while CH embodies the advancement of millennia-old techniques, ranging from artifacts to museums

DOI: 10.4018/979-8-3693-7081-0.ch013

and their related symbolic and social significance (UNESCO, 2003), AI appears poised to fulfill a desire for creativity that does not necessarily involve traditional technical knowledge (McCarthy et al., 1956).

If we were to project into the future, we might envision AI itself becoming part of the cultural heritage for future generations (Marcus and Davis, 2019). Although the development techniques for AI languages have a long history, dating back to the mid-20th century (Turing, 1950), their potential applications are still largely unknown and only recently have they seen widespread adoption (Brynjolfsson and McAfee, 2017). Narrowly, generative AI is the first technological innovation capable of producing creative work through textual or vocal input (commonly known as a prompt), delivering a result anticipated by its creator. Previous technological innovations have typically served as tools to support creative work, allowing humans to explore new creative pathways (Negroponte, 1995), or they have enabled the same work to be performed with greater precision or increased productivity (Autor et al., 2003). Additionally, digital technologies have been frequently meant as supportive to service provision in cultural heritage; indeed, digitally-driven provision is common nowadays – both onsite and online – leading to new visitors engagement mechanisms (Milic, 2022); therefore, this is both an innovative opportunity for museums and other cultural sites as well as a relevant challenge, since sometimes the use of new digital technologies make visitors behaviour too quickly changing for firms to react. In order to join the debate on new digital technologies in cultural heritage, this chapter addresses the impact of AI on Cultural Heritage, attempting to answer the following questions:

- In what ways can generative AI support the promotion, preservation, and value creation of cultural heritage?
- And, consequently: Is there a potential for generative AI to be disruptive in the development of a sustainable cultural heritage?

To address the above mentioned questions, the chapter will be structured as follows:

The first paragraph addresses the origins and a brief historical overview of AI, which, although of great interest today, has a very long history rooted in the earliest computing machines. The second paragraph is aimed to explore the concepts of authenticity and sustainability concerning the use of AI in the field of Cultural Heritage in museums, in order to outline the potential threats of AI in managing the dialectical trade-off between authenticity and sustainability. Therefore, four cases of European museums using AI technologies will be examined to understand the possible fields of application. Finally, the guiding principles that could contribute to the sustainability of Cultural Heritage will be discussed, considering AI both as a support tool and as a preservation factor in itself.

## 1. AI: NOT A NEW BRAND CONTENT

The challenge of imagining and designing a shared framework where artificial intelligence (AI) and cultural heritage can contribute to mutual, sustainable development is multifaceted. AI operates with a forward-looking orientation, using present-day data to create future outputs, while cultural heritage management focuses on preserving the past, emphasizing social learning over technological advances. Despite these differences, both fields fundamentally rely on historical knowledge. It is precisely this reliance on the past that makes it important to revisit the key milestones in AI's evolution and explore how this technological domain can intersect with heritage practices.

The origins of AI are often traced back to Alan Turing's concept of a "universal machine" in 1936, followed by his famous Turing Test in 1950, which aimed to evaluate whether a machine could exhibit human-like intelligence (Turing, 1950). Since then, AI has evolved considerably, beginning with rule-based systems in the mid-20th century, such as John McCarthy's introduction of the term "artificial intelligence" at the 1956 Dartmouth Conference (McCarthy et al., 1956). Early achievements laid the foundation for more sophisticated AI applications in the late 20th and early 21st centuries, particularly with the rise of deep learning and neural networks, powered by the growing availability of big data (LeCun et al., 2015). These developments have increasingly influenced various social spheres, raising complex debates about AI's impact on human life and culture. One of the most transformative subsets of AI in recent years has been generative AI, which creates new content—such as text, images, or even 3D models—by learning patterns from existing datasets (Goodfellow et al., 2014). These models, including Generative Adversarial Networks (GANs) and transformer-based models like GPT, have opened unprecedented possibilities in fields like cultural heritage preservation. By analyzing historical photographs, documents, or architectural plans, AI can generate highly accurate reconstructions of historical sites or artifacts that have been damaged or lost (Li et al., 2020). Additionally, new digital technologies do represent a way to set innovative service provision, thus offering more insightful services as well as opportunities better aligned to what more pressing consumers have been asking for; indeed, digital strategies for museums and cultural heritages sites are yet to be fully set, due to the quickness of the change that the new technologies brought (Pinto et al., 2022); the need to react quickly is also expressed with reference to what visitors do before proper changes might be set: this is due to the digital literacy of some visitors, as it acts before proper service design strategies are full in force (Milic, 2022). All in all, service provision is being infused with digital technologies changing the full range of services as well as the whole service context, making museums and cultural sites constantly changing (Romanelli, 2020). The models embedding Generative AI are yet to be fully explored, but it is already evident that service design considerations are flourishing (Kun et al., 2024) and that they serve not only as research and educational tools but also help mitigate the risks associated with the physical deterioration of cultural assets.

## 2. CULTURAL HERITAGE AND DIGITAL TECHNOLOGIES: A TRADEOFF BETWEEN AUTHENTICITY AND SUSTAINABILITY

Museums and cultural heritage institutions are still struggling with the implementation of new digital technologies, as chatbots, virtual, augmented and mixed reality, and 3D printing systems, due to constraints depending on multiple elements. Among these elements, affordability is limiting the use of new solutions, while curators are still wondering how to counteract the risk on authenticity (Komarac et al., 2020), how to deal with the interplay between *on-site* and *online* visit experience (Morse et al., 2022), as well as the need for specialized competences to renew the offering of cultural heritage institutions (Taormina and Baraldi, 2023). The feasibility of activities based on artificial intelligence in cultural heritage is even trickier than the other digital technologies, due to the newness it embeds; indeed, Griffin et al., (2023) highlighted the need of new and specific competence to implement artificial intelligence, that in most cases are still to be developed. Anyway, accessibility, enjoyment, and sustainability are some of the key advantages expected from the implementation of artificial intelligence (Chung et al., 2018).

Apart from highlighting the variety of benefits that can be achieved through the implementation of digital technologies (Navarrete, 2013), scholars also stressed the risk of losing authenticity. Authenticity is a key feature of cultural heritage and it leads to visitors satisfaction (Gao et al., 2020), because its perception have an effect on time meanings, since it creates nostalgia; thus, nostalgia bridges authenticity and satisfaction. In line with this, authenticity has been addressed as a key goal for governments too, since it can act as a lever to favour a proper perception of intangible cultural heritage. The call for actions addressed to public agencies (Su et al., 2020) considers authenticity as the characteristic balancing the need to ensure protection of cultural heritage and the risk of commodification, as this latter depends on the risk of offering artefacts that would only mock the real content of cultural heritage. The risk recalled derives from the extant debate on the authenticity of heritage tourism, since several scholars (e.g., Thomson and Vester, 2016) referred to the so-called staged authenticity: it mirrors the condition in which cultural elements from an area are expressed in a forced – and sometimes fake – way to show the content that tourists should see according to tourism service providers, instead of showing reality as it is. Staged authenticity – as well as authenticity on its own – is also recalled with reference to the introduction of digital technologies, to assess their effects. Indeed, scholars (Chhabra, 2019) suggest that the introduction of digital technologies may lead to digital toxicity, thus with potentially harmful effects on authenticity and its dimensions. This is true, since, besides giving the chance to facilitate enriched and augmented experiences, the use of technologies can transform in an unnatural way the context in which cultural heritage is experienced (Were, 2015). The main suggestion to maintain the proper cultural context is to keep the cultural framework (García-Almeida, 2019), therefore the role of curators and managers in cultural heritage is crucial (Farrelly et al., 2019). Digital technologies are also meant to protect the authenticity of cultural heritage when dealing with the opportunities depending on blockchain (Trček, 2022), while other technologies still need to be properly implemented, as competences might lack (Kastenholz and Gronau, 2022) and preserving heritage doesn't mean to necessarily keep authenticity in the offering (Li et al., 2024). With reference to artificial intelligence, the reshaping of offerings in cultural heritage domain stimulated the scholarly debate with some authors asserting that authenticity is jeopardized – as recalled above in Chhabra, 2019 –, while some other authors seeing the potential of such new tools in keeping the authenticity (Kaur and Rai, 2024). Authenticity is also a challenge encompassing time for several reasons, namely (a) time is part of what shapes a visitor experience (Chronis, 2005); (b) time contributes to shape artworks meaning together with other contextual elements (Farrelly et al., 2019); and (c) time affects the integrity of artworks, thus their authenticity (Jokilehto, 1994). Moreover, time has been considered in multiple ways in relation to cultural heritage besides authenticity; first and foremost, time is strictly related to cultural heritage due to the artworks being completed in the past, shaping exhibitions in the present, and being protected in order to favour the use in future as referred to by a multitude of scholars (e.g., Orbasli and Woodward, 2009). Anyway, this is as much a complete as a way too general interpretation of cultural heritage, since what makes the relationship between cultural heritage and time more intricated is meaning. Indeed, Smith (2009) referred to cultural heritage as something beyond remainders of the past, namely it shapes a social practice centered on the past to create meanings today. Therefore, it is not a simple time positioning, but the meaningfulness of cultural heritage is strictly dependent on time. What makes this concept even more hot in scholarly debate was the theoretical framing introduced by Hodges (2009), since he focused on the anthropology of time, as the conceptualization of the manner in which the past is infused in cultural practices framed in today's time context. According to Hodges, the interplay between human practices and historical processes creates – and nuances – the heritage experience over time. Human practices are related to the past and in society, indeed, tourists use to visit historic places since they recognized their historical value, but such visits occur in a context made by society; this latter refers to social practices that affect how cultural heritage is experienced, adding even more relevance to time. As a matter of fact, social practices in visiting museum and other heritage sites are not to be meant as alike over time: digital heritage and digital tools are such examples, since looking at the practitioners angle, key actors in this domain – as UNESCO – stress the relevance of digital technologies in various activities in cultural heritage (e.g., The UNESCO Programme on Cultural and Digital Technologies, launched in 2022 with the support and funding of the Kingdom of Saudi Arabia). Similarly, scholars addressed the same, and the debate is quite well established (Parry, 2007), leading to a recode effect digital technologies can have on museums. Anyway, the debate continued over time, due to the novel technologies that were then launched. The recalling of technologies – especially digital ones – and their changing over time mirror the conceptualizations of practices; this is due to practices being emerging and in cultural heritage domain, scholars describe them as "unruly, mutable, and open to multiplicity" (Jones and Yarrow, 2022: 24). More in detail, Jones and Yarrow (2022) built on previous studies, referring to the practices in cultural heritage as the processes leading to meaning elaboration from visitors. The achievement of meanings depends on the value cultural heritage holds today, but this depends on what value it has from the past, namely the memorial value. This latter is given by the author(-s) of the artwork (Riegl, 1996). Anyway, recent studies referred to the material value even in different ways; more in detail memorial value might represent (Meneghin et al., 2023) either the attachment of a community due to emotions and empathy, or he combination of roles of individual and collectivity in shaping cultural heritage meaning.

The debate on time is intertwined with the one on authenticity, since the main aim of curators should be to retaining cultural heritage authenticity over time (Farrelly et al., 2019). Anyway, this task is more complicated when it comes to intangible cultural heritage, since offerings and experiences are shaped around a multitude of elements that can be subject to change over time. While this risk is mitigated in tangible cultural heritage, since the cultural and artistic characteristics of an item of cultural heritage last over time, in case proper processes of either conservation or restoration are put in place (Ehteshami and Soltaninehad, 2020)

Finally, the suitability of digital technologies also depends on the features of local context, as well as of users; while the first might be easily framed (Li et al., 2024) – besides it is not static –, users can't be categorized, since their context of origin might be very much varied. To sum up, the debate is still open, different postures are valuable and should be further assessed, and calls for further research have been called for (e.g., Kastenholz and Gronau, 2022).

## 2.1 AI's Threats and Opportunities for Cultural Heritage

AI's application in cultural heritage extends beyond preservation. For instance, AI can assist in restoring damaged artifacts by generating plausible reconstructions of missing sections, offering a scientifically-informed hypothesis of the original appearance (Sourla et al., 2022). Furthermore, AI-generated replicas reduce the need for handling fragile artifacts, thereby promoting their long-term sustainability. Virtual reality (VR) environments generated by AI can also simulate historical settings, providing immersive experiences that educate the public while reducing the environmental impact of tourism (Palmas et al., 2021). Additionally, AI has the potential to break down language barriers by generating multilingual content, enhancing global accessibility and inclusivity. However, while the integration of AI into cultural heritage offers many benefits, it also poses significant challenges, particularly in terms of maintaining authenticity. AI-generated reconstructions, no matter how accurate, remain approximations. This raises concerns about the possible distortion of cultural context and meaning (Were, 2015). Social scientists and heritage professionals must engage in careful curation and ethical considerations to ensure that AI's contributions complement rather than detract from the cultural significance of heritage.

The environmental impact of AI, particularly large models used for generative art or language processing, poses a significant challenge to sustainability. These models require vast computational resources, which in turn consume considerable energy. For instance, training a single large AI model can emit as much carbon dioxide as five cars over their lifetimes (Strubell et al., 2019). This energy-intensive process raises concerns when AI is applied in cultural heritage projects, where the environmental footprint may undermine the benefits of digital preservation. Generative AI used for virtual reconstructions or digital art production can require high-performance computing, often involving energy sources that are not renewable (Bender et al., 2021). In cases where the environmental costs exceed the conservation benefits, such as reducing physical handling of artifacts or democratizing access through virtual exhibits, the sustainability of AI-driven cultural projects is questionable. Therefore, it is crucial to evaluate the ecological trade-offs of these technologies and explore energy-efficient alternatives, such as low-carbon data centers or optimizing model design, to ensure that AI contributes positively to both cultural preservation and environmental sustainability.

## 3. CURRENT AND FUTURE APPLICATION OF GEN-AI TO CH

The progress and the interest in artificial intelligence led to additional opportunities and challenges, thus shifting the attention of some scholars in what's on and what's next in cultural heritage domain. Indeed, recent studies addressed the contributions of artificial intelligence – albeit still potential in some cases – on cultural heritage, stressing the importance it might have in studying (Mesanza-Moraza et al., 2020), restoring (Li et al., 2021), conserving (Hajebi and Hajebi, 2021), categorizing (Souibgui et al., 2023), and protecting (Quan et al., 2024) cultural heritage. Parallel to those contributions, new issues arose, as it is with authorship and the related rights of artworks (Stork, 2022). A recent literature review on the implementation of artificial intelligence into cultural heritage shows the contribution of computer science techniques to cultural heritage domain (Mishra and Lourenço, 2024). The authors highlighted the potential of new techniques in protecting the artworks and the cultural heritage sites, as well as in preventing the potential damages due to weather conditions and the passing of time. Additionally, they focused on the training of professionals to identify such damages and planning the due maintenance. In a different vein Bogdanovych et al. (2010) had been pioneers in assessing the contribution of artificial intelligence to service design, reenactment, and preservation of cultural heritage allowed by new techniques. Moreover, they considered the support to learning goals for visitors, and the setting of a new model combining the preservation of culture and the stimulation of visitors, thus aiming to solve the hugely debated dilemma for curators in preferring use – through visits – over preservation or the other way around.

The analysis of some evidence from different context is useful to shed light on this debate; the analysis of recent implementations of artificial intelligence on cultural heritage refers to multiple countries, thus it is suitable to address the questions arising on the role of the local context (Were, 2015; Li et al.,

2024). Anyhow, scholars stressed the need to further research on this topic, because the use of artificial intelligence in cultural heritage is still in its infancy, thus there are several issues to be still addressed, beyond the potential uses; such issues refer to the adaptability of new digital technologies to different cultural sites (Allal-Chérif, 2022), the performance achieved through artificial intelligence in cultural sites preservation (Bi and Nasir, 2024), and the impacts on visitor experience, due to the multiple effects on the visit, as well as because of the variety of visitors with reference to their knowledge, their background, and previous experience (Harisanty et al., 2024). Consequently, we investigated a multitude of case studies from different geographical contexts and addressing different spheres of heritage in the offering to shed some more light on the use of new digital technologies – mostly artificial intelligence – and address the aforementioned gaps. The cases have been investigated by triangulating multiple sources to decrease the subjectivity based on single sources, and increasing the reliability of the analysis.

## 3.1 I-Muse Project

The role of artificial intelligence in museums is multifaceted, enhancing personalization, operational efficiency, visitor interaction, and even educational outcomes. Through advanced algorithms, real-time data processing, and dynamic content management, AI is transforming museums from static repositories of knowledge into interactive, living spaces where culture is experienced in a deeply personal and engaging way.

Artificial intelligence (AI) is transforming the museum experience, enhancing both visitor engagement and operational efficiency. The I-Muse project, a collaboration between the Università degli Studi di Torino, Politecnico di Torino, and Synesthesia, showcases the pivotal role of AI in revolutionizing how museums interact with the public. Through sophisticated algorithms like CoreAI and V-Predict, AI plays a fundamental role in personalizing and optimizing the museum journey for visitors. At the heart of this innovation is CoreAI, an artificial intelligence system that personalizes itineraries based on the visitor's preferences. Visitors can select specific TAGs—such as topics, artists, or art styles—that align with their interests, and CoreAI uses these inputs to curate a customized museum tour. This allows for a highly individualized experience, where visitors are guided to the artworks and exhibits that are most relevant to them, creating an enriching and meaningful connection with the cultural content. Moreover, AI facilitates a more dynamic interaction between visitors and museums. Traditional museum experiences are often static, where visitors passively absorb information. AI, however, enables a more interactive and engaging encounter. With technologies like iBeacons, sensors that communicate with visitors' mobile devices, museums can provide real-time, context-aware information. When a visitor approaches a specific artwork, the AI-driven system delivers relevant data, enhancing understanding and appreciation. This ability to offer tailored information creates an adaptive museum experience that evolves based on the visitor's movements and interests.

The V-Predict algorithm further underscores the operational advantages of AI in museums by analyzing historical visitor data to forecast attendance trends. Predicting visitor numbers enables museums to better manage foot traffic, allocate resources, and enhance crowd control, particularly during peak visiting times. By anticipating how many visitors are expected at any given time, museums can ensure a smoother, more enjoyable experience for all attendees. Additionally, it allows for more efficient staff management and helps in maintaining optimal exhibit conditions, such as lighting and climate control, which can be crucial for preserving delicate artworks.

In addition to personalizing visitor experiences and improving operational logistics, AI offers curators unprecedented flexibility in managing and updating exhibit information. The integration of DatoCMS, a content management system, allows museum staff to autonomously update digital content, such as exhibit descriptions and multimedia elements, in real-time. This means that exhibits can be constantly refreshed with the latest information, keeping the museum content current and engaging. Curators no longer need to rely on static, printed descriptions but can offer dynamic, multimedia content that is accessible instantly through the mobile app. This enhances the educational value of museum visits, as the information provided is always up-to-date and can be tailored to various visitor demographics.

Furthermore, AI in museums opens the door to a new dimension of interaction: gamification. The I-Muse app integrates interactive games designed by Garycom, which encourage visitors to engage with exhibits in a playful and educational manner. By turning museum visits into interactive experiences, AI fosters deeper visitor engagement and learning. The integration of AI with gaming elements makes the museum more accessible, especially for younger audiences, providing an immersive and entertaining way to connect with cultural heritage.

## 3.2 Musée de Quai

The Musée du Quai Branly – in Paris (France) – is at the forefront of using artificial intelligence to create a more personalized, interactive, and efficient museum experience. By integrating AI across various aspects of museum operations—from personalized tours and educational tools to curatorial practices and visitor management—the museum is setting a new standard for how cultural institutions can harness technology to enrich the visitor experience and preserve the integrity of their collections. Museum of Tomorrow. The museum, known for its extensive collection of non-European art and artifacts, has adopted AI as part of a broader digital transformation strategy aimed at making its exhibits more accessible, personalized, and interactive for a diverse global audience. By incorporating AI, the museum is revolutionizing how visitors interact with exhibits, offering new ways to explore and understand the museum's vast collections from Africa, Asia, Oceania, and the Americas. One of the key ways AI is transforming the visitor experience at the Musée du Quai Branly is through the use of personalized tours. Utilizing algorithms similar to recommendation systems in digital platforms, the museum's AI-driven tools analyze visitor preferences, behaviors, and past interactions to curate customized tours. This allows visitors to engage more deeply with exhibits that align with their specific interests, whether it be certain regions, periods, or art forms. By analyzing data collected from mobile apps and website interactions, the AI system can suggest a unique path through the museum, helping visitors discover hidden gems and lesser-known artifacts that might otherwise be overlooked. This personalized approach not only enriches the visitor experience but also fosters a deeper emotional connection to the art and artifacts, as the museum can highlight content most relevant to each individual's tastes and curiosities.

In addition to personalization, AI at the Musée du Quai Branly also enhances the educational component of museum visits. The museum's AI tools are integrated into interactive displays and mobile applications that provide visitors with detailed, real-time information about the exhibits. For example, when a visitor approaches a particular artifact, sensors can trigger an AI-driven response, offering a wealth of contextual information about the object, such as its historical significance, cultural background, and the techniques used in its creation. This system turns a passive viewing experience into an active learning journey, where visitors can delve deeper into the stories behind the artifacts, aided by the museum's extensive digital archives and multimedia content. The AI's ability to adapt and respond to the visitor's real-time queries also enhances the sense of immersion, making the experience more engaging and informative.

On the operational side, AI has been instrumental in managing the museum's vast collections and improving curatorial practices. The Musée du Quai Branly has integrated AI-powered systems to assist in the cataloging and preservation of its artifacts. By leveraging machine learning algorithms, the museum can better track the condition of delicate artifacts, predict maintenance needs, and ensure proper preservation techniques are employed. AI systems are also used to automate routine tasks, such as updating digital records and ensuring the accuracy of exhibit descriptions, allowing curators to focus on more creative and strategic aspects of exhibit planning. This integration of AI into the museum's operations ensures that its vast and diverse collection is meticulously managed, reducing the risk of human error and streamlining curatorial workflows. Moreover, the museum has explored AI's potential in visitor flow management and crowd control. By using predictive analytics, AI can forecast visitor numbers based on historical data and current trends, helping the museum to optimize staff allocation, improve visitor safety, and ensure a smooth and enjoyable experience for everyone. During peak times or special exhibitions, AI systems can dynamically adjust the flow of visitors through the museum, preventing overcrowding and enhancing the overall quality of the visit.

## 3.3 Collección Solo: The SOLO Collection

The SOLO collection is hosted in Madrid (Spain) and consists of artworks – mostly paintings, but also multimedia artifacts – from contemporary art mixing different cultures, styles, and trends. The collection stimulates the knowledge of different cultures from multiple countries and artistic styles and is prone to show the contribution of new media and artificial intelligence to visitors. Innovation is the essence of this exhibition, since the founders scout for talents from around the world and stimulate them in setting artworks with innovative approaches, including artificial intelligence. The exhibition takes place in Madrid and the building hosting the artworks is shaped as a labyrinth to make it more versatile to a constantly update collection.

SOLO Collection hosts artworks created with artificial intelligence and the curators claimed that image generation tools is a form of conceptual art and one can't generalize on AI-based contents being far from creative, where creativity is a humankind feature. In order to further stimulate the embedding of artificial intelligence into artworks they hired artists already experienced in AI-based artworks to support newcomers in this field. This is achieved through both single artists cooperation and agreement with other museums and collective in other countries. The project summarizing the efforts to drive artificial intelligence into artworks is named Onkaos and led to the creation of a platform offering several services to artists. The support offered by SOLO Collection expands beyond the art itself, as it embeds marketing strategies, blockchain certificates, and legal help.

Additionally, most of the attention SOLO Collection founders paid to artificial intelligence is mirrored in an award they assign every year. This award is attributed to the artist expressing the best effort in combining creativity with artificial intelligence and having a media art as an outcome. This initiative is partnered by Goldsmiths University, Artnet, Google Arts & Culture, and the University Pompeu Fabra. These partnerships were necessary to bring together multiple competences to be integrated into the SOLO Collection organization; indeed, the Goldsmiths University contributed through its Department of Computing to set new practices for arts creation through machine learning and artificial intelligence. Artnet transferred knowledge on the art market, thus helping both buyers and sellers in navigating the market, especially in a moment of change as the introduction of artificial intelligence into this business. Google Arts & Culture is a pioneer in the domain of new digital technologies into art and collaborated by sharing knowledge on how to preserve and share culture through new tools. Finally, the University Pompeu Fabra joined the SOLO Collection in assigning the award through the Department of Communication, due to the experience in arranging a film festival with movies produced with artificial intelligence. The award has been attributed in both 2023 and 2024 and the artworks were added to the collection and are temporarily exhibited even in other collaborating institutions.

The SOLO Collection has recently launched a new attraction, namely a dog-like robot embedding ChatGPT; this robot has been trained with all the description of the artworks and every time a visitor asks for information the robot provides observations. Therefore, the hybridization of art forms is constantly deployed at SOLO Collection, since its philosophy is to combine sculpture and painting in their traditional forms with artificial intelligence. Finally, in order to further stress the vision behind the collection, an operational fiction is exhibited to describe the history of the museum, depict the key features on the ongoing collection, and help visitors in imagining the future of the collection.

### 3.4 American Alliance of Museums' Center for the Future of Museums

American Alliance of Museums' Center plays a relevant role in the activities carried out at museums in the United States, not only for its being a coordinating body, but also due to its effort in relation to artificial intelligence in cultural heritage. The Alliance represents the entire domain of museums in the United States, therefore it incorporates over 35,000 institutions and professionals. The key strategic goals of the Alliance are to enforce the impact of museums and culture on society and community, to fight racism, to expand and celebrate the museum community, and to generally ensure equity in culture domain, thus favouring change, building leadership, and making business models viable.

The posture of the Alliance on artificial intelligence embeddedness in cultural heritage is addressed by Elizabeth Merritt, the founding direction of the Center for the Future of Museums, that is part of the Alliance. She is also in charge for the strategic foresight, therefore dealing with artificial intelligence is something she could not have skipped. Due to the role of the Alliance in cultural industry in the United States, an event was arranged to debate about the expected impacts of new digital technologies in this domain, with specific reference to artificial intelligence. The overview that emerged from the event led to consider a bright and a dark side for artificial intelligence in cultural heritage: it is seen as a tool that can smooth the operations into cultural heritage sites – including museums – making the efforts of professionals more directly addressed to added value activities than to repetitive tasks; anyway, concerns on ethics and authors' rights are mentioned in the statements of the American Alliance of Museums' Center for the Future of Museums, since the use of AI should be somewhat limited.

Elizabeth Merritt published the outcome of the simulation of an *interview* to ChatGPT, stressing the potential implementations in a museum activities, as well as the effects on visitors' experience, and a comparison with other recent innovative technologies. Additionally, what emerged as particularly relevant from the generative power of ChatGPT during the interview is the capability to depict a forward-looking strategy, besides lots of questions arise from this approach, due to the high standardization that usually affects contents generated in such way.

However, the Alliance started the implementation of artificial intelligence in its Center for the Future of Museums; indeed, an artificial intelligence application was launched to allow visitors to interact with historical figures at the museum, like if visitors were allowed to interview a painter from the past; additionally, the application allows visitors to interact with artworks and oral histories about the artworks themselves and the artists that made them. Still, the members of the strategic team of the Alliance questioned the responsibilities of running the cultural service via artificial intelligence and how to assess the value brought to visitors in experience shaped by the application.

The use of such applications is mirrored also at different levels, since the Alliance recognizes the potential of artificial intelligence in using algorithms to sort elements of a collection, thus supporting the tagging of artworks as well as the outfitting of a museum. The advantage AI-applications embeds is the capability to identify visual elements, colours, and other descriptive elements that would make easier for curators to combine artworks for a thematic visit. Therefore, consistency in both the collection and the catalogue of a museum is the key results of such implementation.

Finally, the Alliance also experienced the use of artificial intelligence in strategizing for cultural heritage. Indeed, the opportunity to analyse data in a more interactive way can favour the analyses on visitors' behaviour to assess and predict their experiences, as well as can simplify facilities management, thus improving the quality of services offered and the business efficiency.

## 4. CREATIVITY AND TECHNIQUE FROM BEING OXYMORON TO THE INTERPLAY FOR SUSTAINABILITY

The integration of Artificial Intelligence (AI) into the preservation, accessibility, and enhancement of cultural heritage is reshaping how we engage with and sustain this invaluable global asset. Techniques and creativity are intertwined in this process, allowing AI to offer both innovative and practical solutions in various cultural heritage sectors and addressing different issues, including contrasting ones. From enhancing visitor experiences to preserving artifacts, AI is playing an increasingly crucial role in ensuring that cultural heritage is not only preserved but also made more accessible to broader audiences. The application of AI in cultural heritage can be categorized into four primary areas: enhancing the visitor experience, facilitating broader access, supporting the conservation process, and improving museum management.

### 4.1 Enhancing the Visitor Experience

One of the primary ways AI is applied to cultural heritage is by virtualizing or augmenting the visitor experience. This approach primarily focuses on place-based technologies that enrich how individuals interact with cultural sites. For instance, AI is used to create immersive experiences that enhance the visit itself, providing digital apps or infrastructural support to make the journey through cultural heritage sites more engaging and informative. A good example of this is the Core AI technology used in the I-Muse project. I-Muse integrates AI-powered digital guides, augmented reality, and interactive maps that offer visitors a personalized and enriched tour of the museum or cultural site. The Musée du Quai Branly in Paris also utilizes similar AI-driven solutions to provide visitors with a more tailored and educational experience through interactive exhibits and AI-driven recommendations based on visitor preferences. Similarly, the visitors at American museums are being increasingly encouraged in using artificial intelligence to add contents and information to their visits, since a simulated dialogue with the artist is being launched.

The main impact of AI in this domain occurs during the visit itself, where digital applications and virtual reality can create a more engaging and interactive environment. By offering visitors enhanced interactivity, AI helps bridge the gap between the physical and digital, making cultural sites more immersive. These technologies also offer accessibility benefits, allowing individuals who cannot physically visit the sites to engage in virtual tours and interactive experiences, which expand the museum's reach globally. Thus, AI's role in enhancing the visitor experience not only enriches cultural understanding but also democratizes access to heritage.

## 4.2 Facilitating Broader Access to Cultural Heritage

Beyond enhancing the physical visit, AI technologies also facilitate broader and more generalized access to cultural heritage. AI-powered platforms can disseminate cultural content globally, offering virtual access to historical sites, museum collections, and even specific artifacts that may not be physically available to the public. An easier access to culture and its detailed content is brought by the dog-like robot at SOLO Collection, since it offers additional information to visitors asking for more advanced information on either an artist or an artwork. Similarly, the V-Predict at I-Muse project allows museums' users to customize their visits according to their own interests, as well as getting insights on the meaningful ties among artworks. A similar recommendation system is offered at Musée du Quai to stimulate the observation of less known artworks and getting an updated journey on the basis of the personal preferences. In addition to expanding access, AI can help bridge linguistic and cultural barriers by offering real-time translation of content. Machine translation systems powered by AI enable international visitors to access information about cultural heritage in their native languages, thus fostering a more inclusive cultural experience. As such, AI contributes to the democratization of cultural heritage, making it more accessible to diverse global audiences and enabling individuals from all walks of life to engage with and appreciate the world's cultural assets.

## 4.3 Supporting Conservation Efforts

AI also plays a vital role in the sustainability of cultural heritage through its applications in the conservation and restoration of artifacts. AI-driven technologies, such as drones and advanced image recognition software, allow curators and conservators to design more accurate and efficient restoration processes. Drones, for instance, can capture detailed images of heritage sites from difficult angles, providing comprehensive data that aids in the structural analysis of buildings or statues. Additionally, AI-based algorithms can analyze these images to detect signs of wear, damage, or environmental degradation, helping conservators prioritize areas that need immediate attention. This is one of the main reasons why Google Arts & Culture partnered SOLO Collection to set practices to both preserving culture and share it via new technologies; similarly, the V-Predict algorithm measure key metrics of museums – including peak hours, the level of lighting and temperature, and the expected effects on artifacts – to manage the access to the museum in a way that would decrease the risk of affecting the most delicate artworks. Similarly, the technologies in use at Musée du Quai are helpful in preserving the collection through a maintenance program, the updating of digital record, and the optimization of the decision-making process to limit the risk of making mistakes due to the limited view on some issues that the human mind might have. Another area where AI contributes is in the restoration of paintings and other artworks. Machine learning algorithms are increasingly used to analyze the composition of paintings and predict the most accurate methods for restoration. AI can analyze the chemical composition of pigments, identify historical trends in artistic techniques, and even simulate the effects of different restoration materials over time. This not only speeds up the restoration process but also ensures the preservation of cultural artifacts with higher precision.

### 4.4 Optimizing Museum Management and Operations

Lastly, AI has a significant impact on the sustainability of cultural heritage through its role in museum management and operations. Administrative tasks, such as inventory management, archiving, and communication, are being streamlined by AI technologies, improving efficiency and reducing operational costs. Museums are increasingly adopting AI-powered systems to manage their vast collections, automate ticketing processes, and even curate exhibitions. More in detail, the flow management at Musée du Quai to contrast overcrowding and favour a better experience to visitors, and the ease of use of content management systems at I-Muse project allowing staff to manage digital content and update the system with live information are some tangible examples of how daily operations might be run through new AI-based technologies. These technologies allow museum staff to focus more on curatorial and educational activities rather than on time-consuming administrative tasks; indeed, business efficiency is one of the expected goals at the American Alliance of Museums in the United States, since relevant but routinary tasks as facility management can be performed in a more efficient way through the new digital technologies. AI can also assist in audience engagement by analyzing visitor data to tailor marketing strategies and enhance communication with visitors. Machine learning algorithms can predict visitor preferences based on past behavior, enabling museums to offer personalized recommendations and improve visitor satisfaction. This contributes to a more sustainable business model for museums, as they can attract a wider audience and generate additional revenue through targeted offerings.

## 5. IMPLICATIONS AND CONCLUSIONS

This chapter assessed how artificial intelligence can support the multiple goals in cultural heritage domain, ranging from promotion to preservation, thus attaining an all-around sustainable set of operation in cultural heritage sites. When answering the questions related to this topic, another issue emerges, namely how to keep the authenticity of the cultural content, since authenticity is not only a fundamental value for the preservation but also for the sustainability of cultural heritage. Exploring the concept of authenticity allowed us to understand that the value of a single artifact is not solely based on its intrinsic worth. Its value is represented indeed by the interest that the heritage element has generated over time. Although AI would allow the use of tools that prevent the natural decay of cultural heritage, the reliance on the virtualization of both visits and the heritage itself risks threatening its authenticity (Komarac et al., 2020), potentially compromising its value over time. The contribution of artificial intelligence to visits mirrors the opportunity of being aligned with the goals of authenticity and – at the same time – allowing the spreading of additional content. Indeed, the enhancement of the visitor experience is achieved through the addition of extra-content instructed by the new digital technologies, while still keeping the context as it is- Therefore, this interplay between content and context shows the new trend in enriching the visits in museums, but it also shapes a strategy keeping authenticity as a key goal. Such a consideration corroborates the value of contents driven by artificial intelligence as scholars already stressed (Goodfellow et al., 2014), but also takes good consideration of authenticity in visit, thus contrasting the problem of digital toxicity (Chhabra, 2019).

The achievement of a broader access to cultural heritage is the second area this research highlights, therefore the contribution of this chapter to the extant literature stands in making the access democratized. Therefore, the evidence and the deriving analysis are in line with the potential of enriching the experience – as per Bender et al. (2021) – but advances the knowledge in this debate, since artificial intelligence emerges as the way to expand the access in ways other than virtual reconstructions of damaged buildings; indeed, the provision of additional content and the personalization of visits according to what visitors expressed as their interest while visiting are two relevant ways to expand the access to cultural heritage, as well as the value of the visitor experience itself. Therefore, the variety of effects referred to from scholars (e.g., Bi and Nasir, 2024) has been concretely observed in this research, paving the way for further analyses on the assessment of visitors perceptions. This would also further link extant studies, by recalling the memorial value (Meneghin et al., 2023) because emotions and empathy – at both a personal and a community level – can be stimulated by the customization of the visit according to one's interest, background and previous experience. This would also make the museum management sustainable in terms of long-term goals, since the visits would be better appreciated in terms of both viability of the digital technology advancements and with reference to the value of sharing knowledge about cultural heritage.

The support to conservation process is favoured by the AI-based tools since they can monitor risk factors in a more efficient way then human beings would do; measuring the temperature, checking the effect of lighting, and predicting the peak hours would be unbearable for human beings, no matter how they would try, especially in combining the predictions of such variables. Thus, the new tools are supportive for management, as well as for conservation. This consideration addresses the need for assessment as recommended by Ehteshami and Soltaninehad (2020) and expand such view since it does not consider conservation as a goal on its own, but combined with the daily management of cultural heritage sites.

The process of understanding whether AI-related technologies are truly disruptive still appears to be a long one. It is a technology that originates in a specific sector and shows the potential to contribute significantly to many areas of application, including the one analyzed in this chapter. However, it has yet to be proven whether AI has the ability to make incumbents obsolete.

Finally, the improvements in museum management are addressed because of the potentiality in data analysis that artificial intelligence tools hold; indeed, they support both daily processes as well as the decision-making process, getting to a point where human efforts would not be enough to properly assess the effects on museums. Therefore, the support to data processing is very valuable, thus is it supportive of the tasks and efforts required to curators and managers (Farrelly et al., 2019) and makes the doubts addressed by other scholars (e.g., Kastenholz and Gronau, 2022) fading away. This is due to the ease of use that new tools and technologies have already achieved, mostly because of the fine tuning of tasks to be performed. As a consequence, this also opens up to additional research efforts to describe what will come next, including potential advances in the ease of use for curators, managers, and the whole staff of museums. Such a combination of goals would result in being supportive to the time challenges, since time affects the integrity of artworks (Jokilehto, 1994) and AI-based technologies can contrast such a risk and predict what to do even before the risks will be evident. This advantage would be also helpful in shaping the time of the visit context in a new way, thus making artworks lasting longer and having artworks travelling over time along with the information they bring; in such a way, visitors would assign a meaning to the artworks and the visit, in a context protecting both the physical essence of artworks (Kun et al., 2024)and their authenticity (Kaur and Rai, 2024).

It is hoped, therefore, that the debate on the use of AI for the management and sustainability of cultural heritage will not only consider how AI can support a more comprehensive dissemination and preservation but also take into account the temporal factor. This is, therefore, a specific issue to be addressed within the field of cultural value; the perception of authenticity has been stressed by scholars (e.g., Navarrete, 2013; Gao et al., 2020) as a driver of satisfaction. Furthermore, it should be noted that every element we are accustomed to understanding as virtual, actually involves a physical artifact, which we are not used to seeing and which resides in the data processing centers that are rapidly growing and spreading worldwide. It is thus legitimate to wonder whether the material assets of technological advancements in recent years may themselves become, in the long run, elements of cultural heritage.

## 6. LIMITATIONS AND FURTHER RESEARCH

The evidence of this study as well as the research gaps addressed in recent studies (e.g., Bi and Nasir, 2024; Harisanty et al., 2024) suggest that we should start questioning right away the fact that the evidence of past centuries intertwine and interact with the material assets that, in the coming centuries, will in turn become part of cultural heritage. This research offers a view leaning on different cultural and geographical context, as well as takes into account different levels of implementation of artificial intelligence tools; this is an advantage since it offers a view that is limitedly biased by the features of the research context, still would benefit from further investigations on other cultural heritage sites and additional tools. These latter would emerge in the upcoming time, thus the novelty of the opportunities should be addressed in future studies. Moreover, contrasting the business view adopted by the authors of this research with the visitors perception might shed additional light on what to expect from the use of artificial intelligence tools. As a consequence, museums curators and managers can increase their awareness of the expected effects of new tools, thus leading to the assessment of both authenticity and sustainability of museums management.

This sets very ambitious goals for research in the field of cultural heritage sustainability. The greatest challenge will probably be working on the comparison between concrete – and onsite – testimonies that narrate a past-present and evidence of the present that use the past as a source for their elaborations, and which in the future will become witnesses of our current time, for which, hopefully, we are going to be accountable from today onwards.

## REFERENCES


Allal-Chérif, O. (2022). Intelligent cathedrals: Using augmented reality, virtual reality, and artificial intelligence to provide an intense cultural, historical, and religious visitor experience. *Technological Forecasting and Social Change*, *178*, 121604. DOI: 10.1016/j.techfore.2022.121604

Autor, D. H., Levy, F., & Murnane, R. J. (2003). The skill content of recent technological change: An empirical exploration. *The Quarterly Journal of Economics*, *118*(4), 1279–1333. DOI: 10.1162/003355303322552801

Bender, E. M., Gebru, T., McMillan-Major, A., & Shmitchell, S. (2021). On the dangers of stochastic parrots: Can language models be too big? *FAccT '21: Proceedings of the 2021 ACM Conference on Fairness, Accountability, and Transparency*. DOI: 10.1145/3442188.3445922

Bi, H., & Nasir, N. B. M. (2024). Innovative Approaches to Preserving Intangible Cultural Heritage through AI-Driven Interactive Experiences. *Academic Journal of Science and Technology*, *12*(2), 81–84. DOI: 10.54097/98nre954

Brynjolfsson, E., & McAfee, A. (2017). *The second machine age: Work, progress, and prosperity in a time of brilliant technologies*. W.W. Norton & Company.

Chhabra, D. (2019). Authenticity and the authentication of heritage: Dialogical perceptiveness. *Journal of Heritage Tourism*, *14*(5-6), 389–395. DOI: 10.1080/1743873X.2019.1644340

Chronis, A. (2017). Coconstructing heritage at the Gettysburg storyscape. In *The Political Nature of Cultural Heritage and Tourism* (pp. 87–107). Routledge.

Chung, N., Lee, H., Kim, J. Y., & Koo, C. (2018). The role of augmented reality for experience-influenced environments: The case of cultural heritage tourism in Korea. *Journal of Travel Research*, *57*(5), 627–643. DOI: 10.1177/0047287517708255

Ehteshami, A., & Soltaninejad, M. (2020). The concept of authenticity in restoration analysis of monitoring and restoration in the authenticity preservation of cultural heritage. *Advances in Anthropology*, *10*(2), 81–96. DOI: 10.4236/aa.2020.102006

Farrelly, F., Kock, F., & Josiassen, A. (2019). Cultural heritage authenticity: A producer view. *Annals of Tourism Research*, *79*, 102770. DOI: 10.1016/j.annals.2019.102770

Gao, J., Lin, S. S., & Zhang, C. (2020). Authenticity, involvement, and nostalgia: Understanding visitor satisfaction with an adaptive reuse heritage site in urban China. *Journal of Destination Marketing & Management*, *15*, 100404. DOI: 10.1016/j.jdmm.2019.100404

Goodfellow, I., Pouget-Abadie, J., Mirza, M., Xu, B., Warde-Farley, D., Ozair, S., & Bengio, Y. (2014). Generative adversarial nets. *Advances in Neural Information Processing Systems*, •••, 27.

Griffin, G., Wennerström, E., & Foka, A. (2023). AI and Swedish Heritage Organisations: Challenges and opportunities. *AI & Society*, •••, 1–14.

Harisanty, D., Obille, K. L. B., Anna, N. E. V., Purwanti, E., & Retrialisca, F. (2024). Cultural heritage preservation in the digital age, harnessing artificial intelligence for the future: A bibliometric analysis. *Digital Library Perspectives*, *40*(4), 609–630. DOI: 10.1108/DLP-01-2024-0018

Jokilehto, J. (1994). Questions about 'authenticity'. *ICOMOS Scientific Journal*, *3*, 69–75.

Jones, S., & Yarrow, T. (2022). *The object of conservation: An ethnography of heritage practice*. Routledge. DOI: 10.4324/9781315622385

Kastenholz, E., & Gronau, W. (2022). Enhancing competences for co-creating appealing and meaningful cultural heritage experiences in tourism. *Journal of Hospitality & Tourism Research (Washington, D.C.)*, *46*(8), 1519–1544. DOI: 10.1177/1096348020951637

Kaur, N., & Rai, M. (2024). Role of Digital Technology and Education for Transformation of Cultural Heritage. In *Digital Cultural Heritage* (pp. 206–221). CRC Press. DOI: 10.1201/9781032630564-11

Kitchin, R. (2014). *The Data Revolution: Big Data, Open Data, Data Infrastructures and Their Consequences*. SAGE Publications.

Komarac, T., Ozretic-Dosen, D., & Skare, V. (2020). Managing edutainment and perceived authenticity of museum visitor experience: Insights from qualitative study. *Museum Management and Curatorship*, *35*(2), 160–181. DOI: 10.1080/09647775.2019.1630850

Kun, P., Freiberger, M. A., Løvlie, A. S., & Risi, S. (2024, July). GenFrame–Embedding Generative AI Into Interactive Artifacts. In *Proceedings of the 2024 ACM Designing Interactive Systems Conference* (pp. 714-727). DOI: 10.1145/3643834.3660750

LeCun, Y., Bengio, Y., & Hinton, G. (2015). Deep learning. *Nature*, *521*(7553), 436–444. DOI: 10.1038/nature14539 PMID: 26017442

Li, M., Sun, X., Zhu, Y., & Qiu, H. (2024). Real in virtual: The influence mechanism of virtual reality on tourists' perceptions of presence and authenticity in museum tourism. *International Journal of Contemporary Hospitality Management*, *36*(11), 3651–3673. DOI: 10.1108/IJCHM-07-2023-0957

Li, X., Fu, Y., & Liu, B. (2020). AI-driven digital reconstruction of historical architectures for cultural heritage. *Heritage Science*, *8*(1), 1–12.

Li, Y., Jiao, L., & Zhou, M. (2024). How does cultural heritage destination digitalization influence tourists' attitudes? The role of constructive authenticity and technology-destination fit. *Journal of Travel & Tourism Marketing*, *41*(2), 221–234. DOI: 10.1080/10548408.2024.2311328

Marcus, G., & Davis, E. (2019). *Rebooting AI: Building artificial intelligence we can trust*. Pantheon Books.

Mayer-Schönberger, V., & Cukier, K. (2013). *Big Data: A Revolution That Will Transform How We Live, Work, and Think*. Eamon Dolan/Houghton Mifflin Harcourt.

McCarthy, J., Minsky, M. L., Rochester, N., & Shannon, C. E. (1956). A proposal for the Dartmouth Summer Research Project on Artificial Intelligence. *AI Magazine*, *27*(4), 12. http://jmc.stanford.edu/articles/dartmouth/dartmouth.pdf

Meneghin, E., Longhi, A., & Segre, G. (2023). Cultural heritage in non-urban areas: Identifying and understanding values. *Il Capitale Culturale*, *28*, 59–72.

Milic, N. (2022). Digitalising the museum. In *Handbook of research on museum management in the digital era* (pp. 138–154). IGI Global. DOI: 10.4018/978-1-7998-9656-2.ch008

Mishra, M., & Lourenço, P. B. (2024). Artificial intelligence-assisted visual inspection for cultural heritage: State-of-the-art review. *Journal of Cultural Heritage*, *66*, 536–550. DOI: 10.1016/j.culher.2024.01.005

Morse, C., Landau, B., Lallemand, C., Wieneke, L., & Koenig, V. (2022). From #museumathome to #athomeatthemuseum: Digital museums and dialogical engagement beyond the COVID-19 pandemic. [JOCCH]. *ACM Journal on Computing and Cultural Heritage*, *15*(2), 1–29. DOI: 10.1145/3480955

Navarrete, T. (2013). Digital cultural heritage. In *Handbook on the economics of cultural heritage* (pp. 251–271). Edward Elgar Publishing. DOI: 10.4337/9780857931009.00023

Negroponte, N. (1995). *Being digital*. Knopf.

Orbaslı, A., & Woodward, S. (2009). Tourism and heritage conservation. *The SAGE handbook of tourism studies*, 314-332.

Palmas, G., Rafanelli, M., & Lanza, C. (2021). AI and the future of cultural heritage: Virtual museums and cultural tourism. *Journal of Cultural Heritage*, *48*, 124–134.

Parry, R. (2007). *Recoding the museum: Digital heritage and the technologies of change*. Routledge. DOI: 10.4324/9780203347485

Pinto, M., Tregua, M., Gaeta, G. L., & Bifulco, F. (2022). The Long Way Towards Digitization: A Multivariate Analysis on Italian Museums. In *Handbook of Research on Museum Management in the Digital Era* (pp. 331-351). IGI Global. DOI: 10.4018/978-1-7998-9656-2.ch018

Radford, A., Wu, J., Child, R., Luan, D., Amodei, D., & Sutskever, I. (2019). Language models are unsupervised multitask learners. *OpenAI Blog, 1*(8).

Riegl, A. (1996). The modern cult of monuments: its essence and its development. *Historical and philosophical issues in the conservation of cultural heritage*, 69, 83.

Romanelli, M. (2020). Museums and technology for value creation. *Technology and Creativity: Production, Mediation and Evaluation in the Digital Age*, 181-210.

Smith, M. K. (2009). *Issues in cultural tourism studies*. Routledge. DOI: 10.4324/9780203869857

Sourla, S., Bampoulis, P., & Ioannidis, S. (2022). AI in cultural heritage preservation: Challenges and solutions. *Journal of Digital Heritage*, *10*(2), 78–88.

Strubell, E., Ganesh, A., & McCallum, A. (2019). Energy and policy considerations for deep learning in NLP. *Proceedings of the 57th Annual Meeting of the Association for Computational Linguistics*. DOI: 10.18653/v1/P19-1355

Su, J. (2020). Managing intangible cultural heritage in the context of tourism: Chinese officials' perspectives. *Journal of Tourism and Cultural Change*, *18*(2), 164–186. DOI: 10.1080/14766825.2019.1604720

Taormina, F., & Baraldi, S. B. (2023). Museums and digital technology: a literature review on organizational issues. *Rethinking Culture and Creativity in the Digital Transformation*, 69-87.

Thomsen, R. C., & Vester, S. P. (2016). Towards a semiotics-based typology of authenticities in heritage tourism: Authenticities at Nottingham Castle, UK, and Nuuk Colonial Harbour, Greenland. *Scandinavian Journal of Hospitality and Tourism, 16*(3), 254–273. DOI: 10.1080/15022250.2015.1084148

Tim, Y., Ouyang, T., & Zeng, D. (2020). Back to the future: Actualizing technology affordances to transform Emperor Qin's terracotta warriors Museum. *Information & Management, 57*(8), 103271. DOI: 10.1016/j.im.2020.103271

Trček, D. (2022). Cultural heritage preservation by using blockchain technologies. *Heritage Science, 10*(1), 6. DOI: 10.1186/s40494-021-00643-9

Turing, A. M. (1950). Computing machinery and intelligence. *Mind, 59*(236), 433–460. DOI: 10.1093/mind/LIX.236.433

UNESCO. (2003). *Convention for the safeguarding of the intangible cultural heritage*. Retrieved from https://ich.unesco.org/en/convention

UNESCO. (2022). *Protecting cultural heritage through technology*. Retrieved from: https://www.unesco.org/en/digital-culture-and-technology

Were, G. (2015). Digital heritage and the problem of authenticity. *Museum Anthropology, 38*(2), 133–142. DOI: 10.1111/muan.12058

Were, G. (2015). Digital heritage in a Melanesian context: Authenticity, integrity and ancestrality from the other side of the digital divide. *International Journal of Heritage Studies, 21*(2), 153–165. DOI: 10.1080/13527258.2013.842607

# Chapter 14
# Industrial Parks in Europe: Challenges for Sustainable Territorial Development

**Maria Bogren**
https://orcid.org/0000-0002-8969-4752
*Nord University, Norway*

**Anna Sörensson**
https://orcid.org/0000-0001-5261-8169
*Mid Sweden University, Sweden & Inland Norway University, Norway*

**Charlotta Faith-Ell**
*Mid Sweden University, Sweden*

**Marta Lindvert**
https://orcid.org/0000-0003-3417-6963
*Nord University, Norway*

**Anna-Maria Jansson**
https://orcid.org/0009-0004-5542-4844
*Mid Sweden University, Sweden*

## ABSTRACT

*This is a study of industrial parks in Europe and their impact on the places where they are established. The European Union's strategy, the Green Deal, is pushing the green transition in Europe, and large-scale industrial parks are being established in territorial regions in the name of this transition. The aim of this chapter is to explore the challenges and opportunities with industrial parks from the perspective of sustainable territorial development. The study was conducted as a case study where five territorial areas in Europe (located in Finland, Norway, Sweden, Estonia and Italy) were studied. Data collection was conducted with semi-structured interviews, internet sources, and on-site observations. The results show the importance of communication and interaction between the stakeholders. Another result is that culture and language play a significant role in this process. Moreover, when building sustainable communities, well-functioning infrastructure and good services are essential. This study contributes to knowledge about challenges and opportunities when establishing industrial parks. Both managers and*

DOI: 10.4018/979-8-3693-7081-0.ch014

*officials from municipalities can benefit from this study.*

## INTRODUCTION

Europe is undergoing a green transition, while large industrial parks are simultaneously being established. Large-scale industrial parks are important contributions to regional development, providing jobs and economic growth, which are especially important in rural territorial regions (Falahatdoost & Wang, 2022). A major establishment, often more commonly referred to as an industrial park, is defined based on the United Nations Industrial Development Organization (UNIDO) definition (UNIDO, 2024). UNIDO defines industrial parks as geographically demarcated areas intended for industrial development, characterized by the provision of infrastructure, facilities, and services specifically tailored to the needs of industrial tenants. These parks are designed to promote industrial growth and competitiveness, foster economic development, and create employment opportunities (UNIDO, 2024).

In Asia, large industrial parks have emerged quickly over the past 20 years, but it is only now that a similar development is occurring in rural Europe (Lyu et al., 2022). Many of the industrial parks are located in rural areas, where there is access to cheap land and green energy. Some of them are strongly connected with the ongoing green transition, while others are not. The EU Green Deal is the European Union's strategy to achieve climate neutrality by 2050. It aims to transform the EU into a sustainable economy by reducing greenhouse gas emissions, promoting renewable energy, and fostering innovation in clean technologies. The plan includes initiatives for energy efficiency, circular economy, biodiversity protection, sustainable agriculture, and pollution reduction. It also seeks to balance environmental goals with economic growth, ensuring a just transition that supports workers and regions most affected by the shift to a green economy. The Brundtland Commission Report (1987) is often described as an important milestone for sustainable development and shed light on sustainable development in terms of economic growth, environmental protection, and social equality. The United Nations took this further and formulated the 17 Sustainable Development Goals (SDGs) (United Nations, 2015), with Goal 8 addressing the need for decent working conditions and economic growth, and Goal 11 addressing the need for sustainable cities and communities, specifically relevant for this book chapter. When an industrial park is established in a municipality, on the one hand, it is positive since it creates work opportunities. On the other hand, it also requires services and infrastructure that the municipality is expected to provide. The territorial places for such an establishment thereby face both opportunities and challenges.

Industrial parks play a vital role in bolstering rural areas of different countries and have created a significant challenge concerning regional disparities (Falahatdoost & Wang, 2022). Research on different types of industrial parks reveals a variety of approaches and models implemented across different regions (Petrushenko et al., 2021). Traditional industrial parks focus primarily on providing infrastructure and facilities for manufacturing and industrial activities (Lambert & Boons, 2002). They typically offer standardized lots or buildings for lease or sale to companies engaged in production, assembly, or warehousing. Research on traditional industrial parks often assesses factors such as land availability, utility infrastructure, workforce availability, and economic incentives offered by local governments to attract businesses (Ablonczy-Mihályka & Kecskés, 2015). In our study, both traditional industrial parks and other large establishments are included, but we name them all as industrial parks. The common denominator is that they have an impact on the surrounding society.

When a new industrial park is initiated, it brings several significant challenges to the region in terms of managing social resources as well as physical preconditions and demands (Dong et al., 2021; Sörensson et al., 2024). One of the most pressing challenges is the need for infrastructure. The local municipality faces numerous demands to meet the needs of the industrial park, including access to and use of land, transportation for goods and employees, and housing for those moving to the area for work. If employees bring their families, additional demands arise, such as the need for more schools and recreational activities for all family members. The local government must be prepared to address these complex and diverse requirements to ensure successful integration of the new industrial activity into the community. Therefore, the aim of this chapter is to explore the challenges and opportunities with industrial parks from the perspective of sustainable territorial development.

## THEORETICAL FRAMEWORK

This section is structured based on three areas. Firstly, sustainable development for industrial parks is presented, followed by stakeholders' involvement in sustainable territorial development. Thirdly and lastly, functional regions and land use transport interaction are included.

### Sustainable Development for Industrial Parks

Sustainable development is now a prerequisite for creating long-term prosperity, social justice, and preserving the environment for future generations (Sörensson et al., 2024). By integrating economic, social, and environmental aspects into different areas in rural communities, societies can develop in a way that benefits both people in that place and the planet (Elkington, 1994). This means that growth and development can no longer come at the expense of natural resources or social rights but must balance these factors to achieve sustainability at all levels. The United Nation has, through Agenda 2030, placed a strong focus on sustainable development for future progress. Agenda 2030 is designed to guide toward sustainable development by balancing economic growth, social inclusion, and environmental protection. It highlights the need for a shift in how we approach development, ensuring that future generations can meet their needs without compromising the health of the planet (The Brundtland Commission Report, 1987). By addressing critical issues such as poverty, inequality, climate change, and resource depletion, Agenda 2030 sets clear goals for sustainable progress, making it essential for countries and their stakeholders to align their policies and actions with this vision to achieve a better and more sustainable future for all (United Nations, 2015).

This chapter focuses primarily on Agenda 2030's SDG8 (decent working conditions and economic growth) and SDG11 (sustainable cities and communities). Regarding SDG8, related to decent working conditions and economic growth, the United Nations (2024a) states that: "Decent work means opportunities for everyone to get work that is productive and delivers a fair income, security in the workplace, and social protection for families, better prospects for personal development and social integration". Entrepreneurship and encouragement for enterprises of different sizes are important goals for this, as well as to provide decent and secure working conditions for all employees: men and women of different ages, migrant workers, and persons with disabilities. In the context of sustainable territorial development, the working conditions for employees from different countries become an important issue to handle. Regarding SDG 11, related to sustainable cities and communities, the United Nations (2024b) has set up goals for "adequate, safe, and affordable housing and basic services" and "access to safe, affordable, accessible, and sustainable transport systems for all". Besides that, they also stress the importance of "inclusive and sustainable urbanization" and emphasize the efforts "to protect and safeguard the world's cultural and natural heritage". All these aspects are important when large industrial parks are being established in new areas. New inhabitants need housing, functioning transportation systems, and other services.

## Stakeholders' Involvement in Sustainable Territorial Development

When studying the establishment of large industrial parks in terms of sustainability, one needs to look at this from a broad and inclusive perspective since there are many stakeholders as well as aspects that affect each other. One way of approaching this is with a systems perspective to include the involved companies, the employees, the inhabitants, and the officials at the municipality. For an industrial park, there are several key stakeholders with diverse interests in its operations (Awan et al., 2021; Sörensson et al., 2024). Stakeholder theory suggests that each group requires tailored information to meet their specific needs, such as reports on sustainability and its impact (Sörensson & Jansson, 2016).

The primary stakeholders for an industrial park include not just investors and tenants but also local communities, government agencies, employees, suppliers, and NGOs. This can create challenges since different stakeholders may demand different types of information (Waligo et al., 2013). Consequently, the industrial park must prioritize its communications based on the significance of each stakeholder, often influenced by factors such as regulatory requirements, community relations, or financial contributions. Stakeholders obtain their information from a variety of sources, including environmental assessments, regulatory filings, public disclosures, and community outreach initiatives (Dumay et al., 2010). To an increasing extent, industrial parks are adopting diverse goals such as SDGs, sharing different information with different stakeholders. These goals might range from profit maximization and fostering innovation to promoting environmental responsibility, supporting local economies, and ensuring compliance with regulations. Communication is often aimed at government bodies, environmental organizations, and the local community (Sörensson & Jansson, 2016). Earlier studies in Asia highlight the importance of intersectoral collaboration and different stakeholders' understanding of sustainability (Ma & Chang, 2019) as well as the local governments' coordinating function among all involved stakeholders (Zhang et al., 2021).

Ben-Eli (2018) proposed five core sustainability principles. Together, these principles offer a holistic approach to sustainability, urging society to balance environmental stewardship, economic stability, social equity, and ethical consciousness in pursuit of a sustainable future. The last two bullet points are relevant for the analysis in this chapter:

- The Material Domain (the flow of materials and energy)
- The Economic Domain (a framework for defining, creating, and managing wealth),
- The Domain of Life (appropriate behaviour in relation to all other species),
- The Social Domain (the basis for social interactions),
- The Spiritual Domain (attitudes, value orientation and code of ethics).

Concerning the fourth principle, Ben-Eli (2018) argues that societies, much like ecological and living systems, rely on diversity and internal variety for their resilience, long-term viability, and overall health. This underscores the importance of fostering open processes, adaptive structures, diverse expressions, and the principle of equality for all individuals as the foundational pillars of a healthy social order. These elements are crucial for sustaining a robust and dynamic society. The fifth principle reflects a fundamental aspect of human nature—the inherent desire to push beyond boundaries and limitations. Throughout history, humans have sought to expand their understanding of the world, both physically and intellectually, in pursuit of a deeper sense of purpose, meaning, and completeness. This drive for transcendence is not just about personal or material advancement, but about reaching a higher state of consciousness and harmony with the world around us. Ben-Eli's (2018) five core sustainability principles can be useful for industrial parks as they provide a structured framework to guide their operations toward long-term sustainability. Sustainability can be understood as a state of a system, shaped by specific structures that maintain its balance. This perspective differs fundamentally from the common view of sustainability as simply a normative goal to aspire to (Ben-Eli, 2018).

The European Commission puts forward the importance of local development for a successful territorial development (European Union, 2024). This is about mobilizing resources within the territory and empowering local political institutions and connecting relevant stakeholders in the community. From their study of rural areas in Spain, Ruiz Pulpón and Canizares Ruiz (2020) highlight how important it is that different stakeholders collaborate – through collaborative governance – when it comes to value, development, and income of existing natural and cultural resources. The results from their study showed weaknesses in transport infrastructure which prevented visitors from coming, an aging population which caused problems in the labour market, and an absence of business culture on site that could hinder development. Medeiros (2020) proposed five dimensions of territorial sustainable development: circular economy, social environmental awareness, environmental conservation, a global governance sustainability focus, and a global spatial planning sustainability focus. Medeiros' (2020) five dimensions of territorial sustainable development provide a holistic framework for achieving sustainable outcomes by considering the economic, environmental, social, institutional, and spatial dynamics of a specific territory. The framework ensures that development is balanced, equitable, and beneficial to both current and future generations, with special attention to reducing inequalities and protecting the environment.

## Functional Regions and Land Use Transport Interaction

Good accessibility for people and goods is a prerequisite for successful industrial parks. This means that the transport system plays a crucial role in maintaining regional cohesion with regards to e.g. culture, work opportunities, education, and leisure. This means that factors to consider when planning industrial parks are functional regions and the land use and transport interaction (LUTI).

A functional region is an economically integrated geographical area characterized by frequent intra-regional interactions (OECD, 2020). The European Union also uses the concept of a functional area (European Commission, 2024). These regions play a crucial role in urban planning and transport systems (Andersson, 2008). However, since their boundaries are based on commuting between municipalities, their distribution does not always coincide with territorial boundaries at a higher administrative level (OECD, 2002). When many municipalities share a common labour, service, and housing market, the regional economy is considered integrated. Similarly, businesses in the region can share a pool of labour and business services. This creates a local market for labour and services for both households and businesses. Therefore, a well-connected regional transport system is essential for businesses and households in a region to share a common economic environment, resulting in low travel costs and short travel times

(Andersson, 2008). This means that the integration of land-use and transport planning is essential for achieving resilient and sustainable outcomes (Faith-Ell et al., 2020).

Also, for the development of industrial parks, OECD (2020) argues that functional regions can be found in both urban and rural areas. Furthermore, Faith-Ell et al. (2024) show in their study the importance of functional interrelatedness, i.e., the land-use transport interaction, as well as institutional interdependencies, i.e., multi-level governance for a well-functioning region. Local and regional authorities often initiate many land-use developments, such as housing, offices, and industrial parks. These developments interact with policies for large-scale infrastructure projects (Bertolini et al., 2005; Faith-Ell et al., 2024). This means that the integration of transport and land use planning is crucial for achieving sustainable development (Bertolini et al., 2005). One way to explain and predict the relationship between land use and transportation is the application of Land use and transport interaction (LUTI). By applying the concept of LUTI to regional planning, factors such as industry, employment, population, and flows or trips between different activities in an area can be considered (Faith-Ell et al., 2020; Faith-Ell et al., 2024; Le et al., 2023). Another approach for furthering functional regions or areas could be to use the Toolkit for functional areas, developed by the European Commission (2024).

## METHOD

The study was designed with a qualitative and explorative approach using cases in five countries: Finland, Norway, Sweden, Estonia, and Italy. The cases were selected based on the following criteria: a large industrial park has been established in a (most often small) location and has become a large workplace for the inhabitants as well as for the incoming workforce. We wanted to investigate how this development affected the territory, and applied a multiple case embedded design (Yin, 2009).

In the northern countries: Finland, Norway, and Sweden, one case in each country was included. In Estonia and Italy, there were multiple cases included in the sample.

*Figure 1. Cases in five countries*

## Finland

The first industrial case is located in a small municipality in the south-west of Finland, with around 6,000 inhabitants. The municipality has around 400 businesses, including everything from small local companies to large companies. However, the industry is dominated by one major actor, operating in the energy sector. The company was established in 2005 and is currently employing a significant portion of the local population. In addition, many inhabitants work in closely related service- and industry sectors.

## Norway

The second case is located in Northern Norway, in a municipality with approximately 26,000 inhabitants. The industrial park was established in 1999, although there has been significant industrial activity for much longer. The industrial park hosts around 100 companies, ranging from small startups to large companies. It is known for its diversity of industries, such as metal production, engineering, and technology firms. Many of them strongly focus on sustainable and green practices. Approximately 2,500 people are employed at the industrial park.

### Sweden

The Swedish case is located in the middle of the country, in a municipality with around 6,800 inhabitants. Historically, the area was dominated by agriculture, forestry, and wood businesses. From the 1950s onward, the focus on industrial production has become increasingly important, and the municipality is today relatively industry-heavy. There are around 780 companies operating in different industries, such as manufacturing, food, plastics, services and trade, and e-commerce. The most important private employers are three companies, employing approximately 350, 180, and 125 people respectively.

### Estonia

In Estonia, the case did not consist of one single municipality, but a region with several industrial establishments, spread over several municipalities. The first sub-case, A) is a science- and industrial park that was established in 2007, with a focus on renewable energy, cleantech, and environmental technologies. The park hosts around 30 companies and employs several hundred people. The second, B) is an industrial park that was established in the 2000s, where diverse industries are represented, including manufacturing, logistics, and services. Around 20 companies employ a few hundred people. The third, C) is an industrial park that was developed in the early 2000s, focusing on logistics, manufacturing, and various industrial services. Several hundred people are employed at approximately 50 companies. The final and fourth sub-case, D) is an industrial park that was established in the 1990s, focusing on oil shale processing, chemical industry, and energy production. Around 40 companies employ several hundred people.

### Italy

As for Estonia, the Italian case consists of a region, representing several industrial establishments. The first sub-case, A) is a technology park, established in 2017, focusing on innovation and technology, with a strong emphasis on sustainability, renewable energy, and digitalization. It hosts over 70 companies and research institutions, providing jobs for several hundred people. The second, B) is part of a larger group with multiple subsidiaries. It is a manufacturing company producing high-tech components for the automotive and energy sectors. It employs over 1,000 people across different locations. The third, C) operates as a single company, with a global presence. It was established in 1860 and produces machinery and equipment for powder metallurgy and ceramic industries. Several hundred people are employed.

## Data Collection

Three different techniques were used to collect data. First, and most importantly, we conducted semi-structured interviews with key informants from municipalities and companies. An interview guide was used, covering central themes that were relevant for all cases. At the same time, the interview guide gave room for follow-up questions, which were sometimes case-specific. Interviews lasted around one hour and were conducted on-site or through Teams. The interviews were, with consent from the interviewees, recorded, transcribed verbatim, and translated to English if needed. Second, in parallel with conducting interviews, we made site visits to some of the industrial parks. This gave us a firsthand impression of the specific environments of the cases, which was valuable during the process of analysing interview data. Third, we used written and electronic sources of data, mainly from relevant web pages. Although the interviews are our primary source of data, we regard the other sources of data as important to understand the overall contexts, which were important to understand and analyse the cases. Neither the industrial parks nor informants are presented with real names in the findings.

## Data Analysis

Inspired by Braun and Clarke (2006), a thematic analysis was carried through. The following steps were taken: 1) data were sorted into codes, 2) these codes were sorted into themes, both predefined based on theory, and emerging from the data, 3) themes were categorized into aggregated dimensions, 4) the aggregated dimensions were analysed in relation to the overall purpose of the study.

The aggregated dimensions and underlying themes are summarized below, and further discussed in the findings section:

*Table 1. Overview of data*

| Expressions creating provisional categories/first order codes | Main themes | Aggregate dimensions |
|---|---|---|
| *Statements about;* The importance of communication between different levels and different actors, open dialogue with local community<br>*Statements about;* How to avoid cultural clashes, cultural understanding needs to go both ways, to provide information in English/other relevant languages<br>*Statements about*; Branding the industrial park in a positive way, use branding for cultural events, festivals, targeting tourism | -Stakeholder communication<br>-Culture and language<br>-Territorial area branding | *Communication and interaction* |
| *Statements about*; The importance of building adequate physical infrastructure, including roads, flight routes, bus routes, supporting car-pooling, and bicycle lanes<br>*Statements about*; Balancing land use between industrial premises and residences, energy supply, importance of quick decisions/less bureaucracy from the municipality side, social planning<br>*Statements about*; Offering an attractive environment for both 'fly-in-fly-out' and permanent residents, to create cultural/social arenas for ex-pats, including their families, the role of churches for religious inclusion | -Mobility and transportation<br>-Land use and housing provision<br>-Leisure activities | *Infrastructure and services* |

# FINDINGS

The findings section is structured in the following way: Firstly, the aggregate dimension *Communication and interaction* is addressed with its three main themes (Stakeholder communication, Culture and language, Territorial area branding) that have a connection to SDG 8 related to decent working conditions. Secondly, the aggregate dimension *Infrastructure and services* is addressed with its three main themes (Mobility and transportation, Land use and housing provision, Leisure activities) connected to SDG 11 about sustainable cities and communities.

## Communication and Interaction

When a large industrial park is established in a municipality, there are many stakeholders to consider and engage in dialogue with. To provide good working conditions (SDG 8) for both inhabitants and incoming (and hopefully future inhabitants) workforce there are several aspects to consider.

### Stakeholder Communication

Results from the study showed that strong cooperation is required between the different stakeholders at the site where an industrial establishment is to be established. Communication and interaction are therefore identified as important factors. It is about communication between different levels, such as micro, meso, and macro, but also between different stakeholders on site. For example, it is important to keep the inhabitants updated, inform the incoming workforce about the working and living conditions in a new place/country, and have a good dialogue between officials at the municipality and business owners.

All informants emphasize the importance of maintaining open communication with the local population. It is not sufficient merely to communicate adequately; rather, it is advisable to exceed what is perceived to be the actual need. This is even more crucial in cases involving establishments that provoke any form of concern due to the production that will be carried out. The more information provided, the less fear and a greater understanding and acceptance of the establishment. One informant talks about the need to inform local inhabitants about the establishment and the safety surrounding the project, but also about the importance of "silent" information that comes from people working on the site.

> "I can truly say that for example, we haven't got any family who doesn't know some who had worked or working at the moment in XXX and that silent information is very important. It creates a strong trust, when you got official information and the silent information supports that official information."

The informants also highlighted the importance of communication with foreign labourers at an early stage. An example provided by the Swedish informant was when foreign labourers were found fishing from private docks at cottages, which caused dissatisfaction among the local population. The information about accessibility to land was then necessary. In Sweden people have the right to public access in nature (Allemansrätten), but this does not include access to private land. By communicating about the rules and regulations of the specific location (in the new country), future problems with the local population can be minimized. The Finnish informant expressed it like this:

> "But of course, of course, when people come from other countries to Finland, we have our culture here and they have their own culture. Of course it needed a lot of information."

The informants also put forward that it is important for the stakeholders from the business community and the officials from the municipality (including the municipality's business development unit and others) to engage in close dialogue, so that the municipality understands the ongoing developments in the business community and the current and future needs therein. Consistent efforts from the municipality, disseminating information through various media about the developments in the community, have been identified as a key success factor. This has had significance, not only for the establishment itself but also for the broader business environment in the municipality.

In one of the municipalities, it is mentioned that they have employed the use of "narrative" for many years as a tool to foster inclusivity among all stakeholders (municipal officials, entrepreneurs, and employees) regarding the community's affairs. By "narrative," it is meant that they continuously communicate, through various media, what is happening within the municipality with the aim of engendering a sense of participation among all. Through this narrative, they have succeeded in cultivating a feeling among business owners that they operate within a context, in a society progressing positively, resulting in forward-thinking, and today there is talk of a particular "spirit":

"The basic idea is that if, for example, you see yourself working in a context in a society that is heading in a positive direction, you tend to make more forward-looking and positive decisions during the day."

This has also led to businesses seeking to establish themselves in the municipality.

## Culture and Language

National cultures and languages also play a central role when it comes to communication and interaction. Many of the places that have received a large establishment experience clashes between cultures and language barriers. For example, the "Swedish way" is not always obvious to outsiders, and the cultural habits and behaviours from other countries are not always so easy to understand for Swedes. Therefore, the information goes both ways – newcomers in a country need to learn more about the existing culture, and the national employees in an industrial park need to learn more about the cultures of employees from other countries. This can avoid misunderstandings and cultural clashes in the workplace.

Since the industrial parks often have employees from many countries, the informants put forward that information needs to be provided in English or in languages that are understood among most employees. Moreover, the municipalities are emphasized to inform a larger number of individuals at the industrial parks at the same time. Not speaking the language in the country where you work can be a barrier in many ways. One example that was mentioned is when having to take your child to a doctor and explain the symptoms.

When it comes to language, one way for the municipalities to facilitate for new inhabitants is to provide a website with relevant languages spoken by the incoming workforce. This can reduce the workload for the municipality. One informant from the municipality explained about their website:

"We have at a lot of information in different kind of languages: English, German, French, Polish, etcetera. You need information on the Internet site in different languages."

Another solution mentioned by municipality informants is to make sure that the initial contact at the municipality (switchboard or equivalent) has language skills and thus can facilitate for others within the municipal operations. Some of the cases have designated contact persons in the workplace who function as facilitators in their contacts and dialogues with the municipality.

## Territorial Area Branding

How the place brand is communicated is interesting, since the industrial park or factory often becomes the "name" and not the municipality. The majority of those we interviewed emphasize that an establishment always becomes larger than initially anticipated. One informant highlights that an establishment can become synonymous with a place rather than the municipality. This naturally affects the municipality, which may thereby lose "control" over what the place represents. The establishment becomes larger than the individual municipality and may, in some cases, involve an entire region. One of the informants expressed how the establishment became dominant:

"Because XXX sails up and becomes almost like a classic mill [The town is an old mill town] with us, that is, they become so dominant."

When there is a significant influx of labour to a location, especially if it occurs over an extended period, an identity is created among the residents where industry and society are closely interconnected. In one of the cases studied, this is highlighted as central regarding how the hometown is perceived, both among municipal residents and outsiders. For some of the cases the identity has been reinforced in a positive way. In Norway, the studied case has become closely linked to the development of local culture, including cultural events. The Norwegian informant explains:

> "It does something to a place when the whole town is built around this industry. It reflects in the culture and the understanding of how industry and society are interconnected. And you can see it, for example, in the various cultural offerings we have [giving examples of music bands with industry-related names]. We have festivals like XXX, which plays on the [industry sector], obviously, but also the fact that people from different places meet and create a new life. [...] ... there are so many references [to the industry] everywhere. Industrial identity is very strong among people, and you can see it very clearly in the cultural life."

These examples can contribute to an understanding of the mutual dependence of industry and society at large.

## Infrastructure and Services

A large establishment sets demands on infrastructure and services in the territorial area where they establish. In order to develop sustainable places (SDG11) there are many issues a municipality needs to address.

### Mobility and Transportation

Many aspects of mobility need to be taken care of, for example, flight lines, bus routes, cycle paths, and ports that are deep enough for large and heavy transports. In some cases, there have been close dialogues with the municipality about suitable new bus routes. Some companies have even offered direct bus services for their employees.

However, several cases indicate that the most common mode of transportation is by car. In some instances, carpooling to the workplace also occurs. Three cases (Estonia, Italy, and Sweden) highlight extensive commuting distances of up to 100 kilometres one way. The explanation in these cases is that a larger community is approximately 100 kilometres from the establishment (i.e., a larger pool of potential employees). This highlights the importance of functional regions in the development of industrial parks. The Estonian interviews also highlight the need for detailed mobility studies as commuting patterns often do not match projections. The Estonian informant stated that:

> *"All presumptions were just not true, in XXX County, the idea is a radial public transport model. However, in fact, we proved that the employment pendulum is circulating around XXX. But no public transportation is taking this into consideration."*

In several cases, the workforce commuted from other municipalities than expected. Furthermore, there were instances of a domino effect where an industrial establishment in one municipality (B) attracted labour from a nearby municipality. This, in turn, attracted labour from the next municipality, and so forth. The mobility study conducted in the two Estonian cases B and C revealed that the public transportation system did not correspond to the travel patterns resulting from the establishments. Consequently, commuting was done by car. This example highlights that a LUTI approach could have contributed to a more sustainable transport system if it had been applied.

In Italy, new bus routes have been created, with the establishment engaging in close dialogue with the municipality regarding the timing and locations of bus routes (based on working hours). In Finland, direct buses to the industrial park are offered by the establishment. These direct buses provided by the company for employees have been a simple way for employees to return home after work. However, there has been one major problem with this, as it creates chaotic situations when a bus with many people simultaneously stops to buy dinner at the local grocery store:

> "There was about 40 people in one bus, and it transported those people to work and when the day was ended, they bring them back to the houses and for shopping. Imagine the food market when 40 men came to shop for something for the evening. Quite long, long queue, you know, when they go to pay."

For the industrial park in Finland, where a large proportion of the workforce comes from abroad, this has led to the introduction of new flight routes. However, representatives from the municipalities also emphasize the benefits of such flight routes for the local population. The new flight routes have resulted in increased travel for the local population to a greater extent than expected.

The case in Sweden has encountered challenges in constructing requested bicycle paths and new exits, which are requested by the establishment to facilitate, but primarily to create safer, transportation. However, there have been challenges with the Swedish Transport Administration to gain approval for these requests. The informant from the establishment explained:

> "We had no knowledge of such issues, and I had no established contacts. But now we were so troublesome so we could get out of it, but there were a lot of harsh words and there were people who had to work on vacation to have meetings and so on to arrange this because otherwise XXX won't get started with the construction and it must be ready by Black Week in the autumn. But the Swedish Transport Administration only said that: now we are going on vacation, so we will continue the process in the autumn."

National and regional transport planning is conducted in four-year cycles. This means that the municipality needs to have a long-term planning readiness for industrial establishments, in which the needs for exits and bicycle paths have been secured through collaboration with the Swedish Transport Administration.

In some cases, it is crucial for the industry to utilize maritime transport, which necessitates the availability of ports deep enough for large/heavy vessels. In the Norwegian case, the municipality and the industry have collaborated and decided to build a deep-water quay together. This is part of the municipality's development plan, consisting of seven strategic areas. The Norwegian informant says:

> "The thematic plan for business development is a regulatory plan and strategy, really, which the municipal council adopted [...]. But they had seven strategic focus areas: XXX factory was one of them, deep-water quay, that is, a quay with sufficient depth, airport, XXX industrial park, that is simply a new industrial park in the neighboring municipality, hospital..."

The informant concludes by reflecting on the collaboration between the industrial park and the municipality:

> "In many of the central issues, we are very coordinated and in agreement, and work well together."

## Land Use and Housing Provision

Requests for land are of interest for both industrial premises and residences. For what purpose land can be used varies between the studied cases, but mostly a certain amount of bureaucracy is involved regarding industrial land. Companies emphasize the importance of clear and well-established dialogue with representatives from the municipalities to jointly create favourable conditions regarding land needs or changes in land use. Rapid action by municipalities can influence establishments to choose a location. One example involved acquiring land and making a decision in either eight months or three weeks, as recounted by one of the informants. Close dialogue between the establishment and the municipality becomes crucial. All cases in the study stress the importance of a well-integrated approach of land use planning as well as the consideration of functional regions.

Besides land for the establishment, land is also needed for houses for the employees, both for those who wish to bring their family to the place and live there together and for those who choose to commute; fly in – fly out. This is a challenge for the municipalities in several ways. First, housing is needed. Second, they need to consider how to avoid segregation. In some of the cases, the companies (with help of the municipalities) have reached out directly to homeowners asking for renting possibilities. This can be both summer cottages and rooms in houses. Others have actively identified abandoned houses, and the case in Finland has provided barrack housing close to the workplace, specifically for the group of "fly-in, fly-out" personnel. The advantage of barracks near the workplace is that commuting to and from work is reduced. The Finnish informant described the situation:

> "Ok, in one era, those workers were mainly single men and there were some parks, you know that kind of. There was block buildings for those people, and some people bought their own house here."

Several of the municipalities are aware of the need for social planning to avoid and reduce segregation. The results show that foreign workers prefer to live in the same place (a place becomes known for its international population). In such locations, businesses targeting the international population have often emerged. Even traditional grocery stores have adapted to the international population in terms of food offerings. However, an example from Estonia shows that it is not certain that an industrial establishment reduces social disparities. One industrial park (D) was partly aimed at reducing segregation in eastern Estonia, but instead the workers chose not to move their families to the vicinity of the industrial park and instead they commuted longer distances or commuted on a weekly basis. This shows that there is a risk that socially strong groups choose to commute instead of settling in areas with socially weaker groups.

Another crucial thing when deciding where to establish a large industrial park is to have a secured energy supply, preferably near transmission stations. Otherwise, there is a risk of bottlenecks because an establishment area may be limited by the amount of electricity that can be allocated. Currently, there is an upgrade to the transmission network in Sweden, and therefore, there is an incentive for municipalities to advocate for the placement of transmission stations in close proximity to establishment areas.

Among the examined cases, it is evident that comprehensive and detailed planning plays a significant role. It may transpire that in cases where there is a high demand for housing, companies wishing to build, and land designated for residential purposes, the plan poses an obstacle. The land is zoned for industrial use, making residential construction impossible without a change in zoning. This proves to be a lengthy process with long timeframes, serving as a hindrance to the establishment's expansion.

In Estonia, an informant raises the issue of competition between different industrial establishments. That is to say, one industrial establishment may outcompete another. The case highlighted was the C industrial area, which thrives while the industrial area on the other side of the highway performs poorly.

The main reason for the challenges of the second area was considered to be a lack of access to the highway. The other industrial area had slightly less favourable access to direct exits compared to C, causing it to lose attractiveness.

### Leisure Activities

Services in the form of Leisure activities do not always come up when first discussing a large establishment but are essential for the employees, both "fly in - fly out" staff and those who have moved to a place. Especially the "fly in - fly out" staff are often overlooked but need to occupy themselves during evenings or other times when they are not working. Informants emphasize the importance of creating meaningful activities for this group as well.

Many of the examined cases have also focused on offering activities within the company premises. Some companies provide a gym at the factory, while others create an attractive expat environment with international cultural events. To make it attractive for the incoming workforce from other countries and their accompanying family members, the informants stress that it is important to contribute to a positive "expat environment". This could, for example, involve offering social activities involving people from different nationalities and activities that facilitate people settling in and feeling comfortable.

In Norway, the informant talks about how the municipality has a specific project, consisting of several packages to attract qualified competence, from other areas in Norway and from abroad:

> "It [the project] consists of different approaches. One is about attractiveness, reputation, communication, and it ranges from overall attractiveness to more direct contact with, for example, students. Simply to increase attractiveness. And then there is a part about onboarding, which is precisely about welcoming people in a good way. And the municipality has done some work there. They offer relocation services; you can contact them if you are a newcomer and have questions, and you will, because it is very difficult to move to Norway from many countries, especially from outside the EEA. Onboarding also involves, for example, creating a community, trying to create a bit of an expat environment, preferably with many different nationalities, those kinds of concrete activities."

Collaborations with churches in the surroundings are also common. In the case of people moving in with different cultural backgrounds, it may also mean that they celebrate religious holidays differently from those typically celebrated in the country of the established industrial park. One informant highlighted the importance of collaborating with entities outside the municipality. An example from Sweden was that the church lends out its premises to other religious groups to celebrate their holidays.

## DISCUSSION

This chapter has explored challenges and opportunities with industrial parks from the perspective of sustainable territorial development. SDG8 sheds light on decent working conditions and economic growth, and SDG11 focuses on sustainable cities and communities. These two SDGs will guide the discussion in the first and main part of this section. At the end, a broader system perspective will frame the discussion.

*Figure 2. Industrial parks' sustainable territorial development (own creation)*

To create sustainable workplaces and communities containing economic, environmental, and social aspects, the region's various stakeholders need to be included in the process. The foundation for this is having effective communication, not just one-way but through interaction (Ben-Eli, 2018). Security in the workplace is one aspect highlighted in SDG8. For employees, this can be connected to reliable information about laws and rules in society and in the country in question. For inhabitants living close to an industrial park, it can be of great value to get information about, for example, security issues. By involving stakeholders early in the process of establishing an industrial park, resistance to the changes that an industrial park brings will be reduced. The importance of communication and interaction has been highlighted as a key contribution from this study, which previous research also emphasized (Ruiz Pulpon & Canizares Ruiz, 2020).

In SDG8, several aspects regarding decent working conditions are listed, such as productive work with a fair income, security in the workplace, and possibilities for personal development and social integration. In our study, cultural habits and language issues have been central in the answers from the informants. Some of the industrial parks and the municipalities have made great efforts to provide information in different languages so that the new workers and inhabitants will feel included and safe in society. However, not so much has come forward about how the establishment provides opportunities for personal development in the workplace or how to take advantage of cultural differences among the employees.

The results show that some of the cases have "provided" a new identity to the territory, where the name of the industrial park is now also used for the place or the region. SDG8 focuses on decent working conditions and economic growth, which here can be seen as a possible and positive growth for the territory in a broader sense.

In SDG11, sustainable cities and communities are in focus, where access to safe, affordable, accessible and sustainable transport systems for all is highlighted. From the results, we can see that issues regarding mobility and transportation are high on the agenda for the industrial parks and municipalities.

The municipalities are working hard to meet the demands from the establishments to create infrastructure that facilitates commuting for staff at the industrial site. Andersson (2008) emphasized the importance of infrastructure to create a well-connected regional transport system. However, results from this study show that commuting distances are significantly longer than expected, with some reaching nearly 100 kilometres one way. To create a sustainable society in line with SDG 11, it is essential to consider the integration between land use and transport planning (Faith-Ell et al., 2020). The cases in the study show the importance of considering functional areas as well as applying a LUTI approach to the planning of new industrial areas.

Besides accessible and sustainable transport systems for all, SDG11 sheds light on adequate, safe and affordable housing, basic services, as well as the importance of inclusive and sustainable urbanization. To provide housing for employees close to the industrial parks has been an important issue to solve for the establishments and municipalities. One challenge is that different employees seek different types of housing. When the available housing does not match their preferences, it often leads to long commuting distances. The findings also show that cultural background plays a role, with people choosing to settle in areas where the population shares the same cultural, often linguistic, backgrounds. This is despite a longer distance to commute for work. The way people choose to settle down presents a major challenge for the municipalities. Their aim is often to increase the number of residents, but this study indicates that this is not always the outcome. Thus, it indirectly leads to social segregation, and sustainable communities are not achieved.

For industrial parks, it is crucial to adopt a holistic approach, recognizing that entire families, not just individual employees, often move to the region. This affects not only housing but also the types of leisure activities that need to be provided. From a stakeholder perspective, family members are often overlooked, as they are usually not considered primary stakeholders (Ben-Eli, 2018; Sörensson et al., 2024). SDG11 emphasizes the significance of inclusive and sustainable urbanization, along with the protection of cultural and natural heritage. Achieving this goal requires balancing the development of inclusive and sustainable communities for all inhabitants while integrating new cultures and at the same time preserving the cultural and natural heritage of the area.

Medeiros' (2020) work is relevant for the establishment and management of industrial parks, particularly in rural areas. Industrial parks, while offering significant economic opportunities, also raise challenges that need to be addressed from a sustainability perspective by municipalities. There are notable differences between the studied cases in terms of the extent and quality of communication with the surrounding community concerning sustainable territorial development. In some instances, companies in Italy have taken independent action to address various challenges related to their establishment, often due to difficulties in resolving issues collaboratively with local authorities. For example, permitting processes have been slow and cumbersome in dialogues with municipal governments. Another challenge that differs across cases is the level and structure of communication with foreign workers. Cases with a higher proportion of international employees have encountered greater difficulties. Additionally, approaches to integrating foreign labour vary. In one case, the company explicitly avoided hiring individuals who did not speak the national language, citing significant cultural and linguistic challenges that hinder workplace integration. Transportation practices also reveal both similarities and differences. In most cases, employees commute approximately 100 kilometres one way daily, often carpooling with colleagues. However, Finland stands out as an exception, offering a direct bus service to and from the workplace. This solution, however, led to congestion in the residential area when the bus arrived, as many employees simultaneously visited local grocery stores to purchase dinner supplies.

## CONCLUSIONS AND IMPLICATIONS

We have explored challenges and opportunities with industrial parks from the perspective of sustainable territorial development. The conclusion of this study is that stakeholder involvement is essential when aiming to build a sustainable community. Different stakeholders have varying demands, making communication and interaction crucial. The diverse cultural backgrounds of these stakeholders add complexity to the process. Therefore, municipalities must understand not only these challenges but also take advantage of the opportunities that arise when establishing industrial parks. For example, the development of infrastructure, new sustainable residential areas, and cultural influences from new inhabitants, which can contribute to the development of regions.

To better understand the developments in (especially) rural communities related to industrial parks, more research is needed to explore the challenges and opportunities they bring. This could include examining contextual differences, as previous studies mainly focused on Chinese industrial parks in Asia, have only partially addressed. As new industrialization emerges in territorial areas in Europe, it is essential to investigate whether this leads to sustainable territorial development. Since this is an ongoing process in Europe, and the outcomes and effects of large industrial parks are not finalized at the moment, it would be of interest to perform follow-up studies investigating several SDGs.

This study has practical implications for managers and CEOs of establishing companies as well as for officials at municipalities who are involved in plans for land use, housing, transportation, schools, and so forth. Another category that is involved in the process of hiring workers for industrial parks is employees working in Human Resources, especially those who handle new employees from many different countries.

## REFERENCES


Ablonczy-Mihályka, L., & Kecskés, P. (2015). Changing principles how to define and regulate the term 'industrial park': The case of Hungary, Romania and Bulgaria. *The Central European Journal of Regional Development and Tourism*, *7*(3), 101–112. DOI: 10.32725/det.2015.036

Andersson, Å. E. (2008). Regionförstoring för tillväxt och jobb. [Regional expansion for growth and jobs] In *Handelskammarens rapport 3 2008*. Handelskammaren.

Awan, U., Sroufe, R., & Shahbaz, M. (2021). Industry 4.0 and the circular economy: A literature review and recommendations for future research. *Business Strategy and the Environment*, *30*(4), 2038–2060. DOI: 10.1002/bse.2731

Ben-Eli, M. U. (2018). Sustainability: Definition and five core principles, a systems perspective. *Sustainability Science*, *13*(5), 1337–1343. DOI: 10.1007/s11625-018-0564-3

Bertolini, L., Le Clercq, F., & Kapoen, L. (2005). Sustainable accessibility: A conceptual framework to integrate transport and land use plan-making. Two test-applications in the Netherlands and a reflection on the way forward. *Transport Policy*, *12*(3), 207–220. DOI: 10.1016/j.tranpol.2005.01.006

Braun, V., & Clarke, V. (2006). Using thematic analysis in psychology. *Qualitative Research in Psychology*, *3*(2), 77–101. DOI: 10.1191/1478088706qp063oa

Dong, H., Zhang, L., Geng, Y., Li, P., & Yu, C. (2021). New insights from grey water footprint assessment: An industrial park level. *Journal of Cleaner Production*, *285*, 124915. DOI: 10.1016/j.jclepro.2020.124915

Dumay, J., Guthrie, J., & Farneti, F. (2010). GRI sustainability reporting guidelines for public and third sector organizations: A critical review. *Public Management Review*, *12*(4), 531–548. DOI: 10.1080/14719037.2010.496266

Elkington, J. (1994). Towards the sustainable corporation: Win-win-win business strategies for sustainable development. *California Management Review*, *36*(2), 90–100. DOI: 10.2307/41165746

European Commission (2024). *Functional Areas in the EU, Methodological Toolkit to improve governance, coordination, planning, and implementation processes across jurisdictional boundaries.*

European Union (2024). Capacity4dev, Public Sector Reform & Decentralisation https://capacity4dev.europa.eu/groups/public-pubsector-reform-decentralisation/info/33-working-definition-territorial-development_en (Accessed 18 July, 2024)

Faith-Ell, C., Arts, J., & Kalle, H. (2024). Towards sustainable and inclusive corridors: Rethinking planning of infrastructure and spatial development. *10th Conference of Transportation Research Arena - Transport Transitions: Advancing Sustainable and Inclusive Mobility*, 15-18 April 2024, RDS, Dublin. Springer.

Faith-Ell, C., Kalle, H., & Arts, J. (2020). Connecting the dots: Rethinking large-scale corridor infrastructure planning. *The 8th Transport Research Arena TRA 2020*, April 27-30, Helsinki, Finland.

Falahatdoost, S., & Wang, X. (2022). Industrial Park Role as a Catalyst for Regional Development: Zooming on Middle East Countries. *Land (Basel)*, *11*(8), 1357. DOI: 10.3390/land11081357

Lambert, A. J. D., & Boons, F. A. (2002). Eco-industrial parks: Stimulating sustainable development in mixed industrial parks. *Technovation*, *22*(8), 471–484. DOI: 10.1016/S0166-4972(01)00040-2

Le, H., Gurry, F., & Lennox, J. (2023). An application of land use, transport, and economy interaction model. *Research in Transportation Economics*, *99*, 101294. Advance online publication. DOI: 10.1016/j.retrec.2023.101294

Lyu, Y., Liu, Y., Guo, Y., Sang, J., Tian, J., & Chen, L. (2022). Review of green development of Chinese industrial parks. *Energy Strategy Reviews*, *42*, 100867. DOI: 10.1016/j.esr.2022.100867

Ma, C. C., & Chang, H. P. (2019). Environmental consciousness in local sustainable development: A case study of the anti-idling policy in Taiwan. *Sustainability (Basel)*, *11*(16), 4442. DOI: 10.3390/su11164442

Medeiros, E. (2020). Portugal 2020: An effective policy platform to promote sustainable territorial development? *Sustainability (Basel)*, *12*(3), 1126. DOI: 10.3390/su12031126

OECD (2002), *Redefining Territories: The Functional Regions*, OECD Regional Development Studies, OECD Publishing. .DOI: 10.1787/9789264196179-en

OECD. (2020). *Delineating Functional Areas in All Territories. OECD Territorial Reviews.* OECD Publishing., DOI: 10.1787/07970966-

Petrushenko, M., Burkynskyi, B., Shevchenko, H., & Baranchenko, Y. (2021). Towards sustainable development in a transition economy: The case of eco-industrial parks in Ukraine. *Environment and Ecology*, *12*(1), 149–164. DOI: 10.21511/ee.12(1).2021.13

Ruiz Pulpon, A. R., & Canizares Ruiz, M. D. C. (2020). Enhancing the territorial heritage of declining rural areas in Spain: Towards integrating top-down and bottom-up approaches. *Land (Basel)*, *9*(7), 216. DOI: 10.3390/land9070216

Sörensson, A., Faith-Ell, C., Jansson, A., Lindvert, M., Bogren, M., & Lundström, A. (2024). Samhällsutveckling i norra Sverige – från småföretag till stora etableringar. [Community development in northern Sweden – from small businesses to large establishments] In Bäckström, I., Fredman, P., Giritli-Nygren, K., Niskanen, K., Olofsson, A., Nilsson, H.-E., & Lindbäck, K. (Eds.), *Globala utmaningar – lokala lösningar: Forskning för en hållbar samhällsutveckling i norra Sverige* [Global challenges – local solutions: Research for a sustainable community development in northern Sweden]. (pp. 109–111). Mid Sweden University.

Sörensson, A., & Jansson, A. M. (2016). Sustainability reporting among Swedish tourism service providers: Information differences between them. *WIT Transactions on Ecology and the Environment*, *201*, 103–113. DOI: 10.2495/ST160091

The Brundtland Commission Report. (1987). *Our common future.* Oxford University Press.

UNIDO. (2024). The United Nations Industrial Development Organization's Industrial Park Platform. https://ipp.unido.org/industrial-parks-overview

United Nations. (2015). *Sustainable Development Goals.*

United Nations. (2024a). *Sustainable Development Goals 8*. https://www.un.org/sustainabledevelopment/economic-growth/

United Nations. (2024b). *Sustainable Development Goals 11*. https://www.un.org/sustainabledevelopment/cities/

Waligo, V., Clarke, J., & Hawkins, R. (2013). Implementing sustainable tourism: A multi-stakeholder involvement management framework. *Tourism Management*, *36*, 342–353. DOI: 10.1016/j.tourman.2012.10.008

Yin, R. K. (2009). *Case study research: Design and methods*. SAGE Publications.

Zhang, F., Chung, C. K. L., Lu, T., & Wu, F. (2021). The role of the local government in China's urban sustainability transition: A case study of Wuxi's solar development. *Cities (London, England)*, *117*, 103294. DOI: 10.1016/j.cities.2021.103294

# Chapter 15
# Vernacular Architecture: A Climate Change Mitigation and Adaptation Strategy

**Jayati Talapatra**
https://orcid.org/0000-0002-2673-0218
*Independent Researcher, India*

## ABSTRACT

*Vernacular Architecture, which focusses on creating structures suitable to a specific region, keeping its climate, soil and other local conditions in mind, is a solution to meet growing infrastructure needs while keeping Green House Gas and pollutant emissions in check. Moreover, the use of local materials and labour in construction, encourages decentralised growth of industries and increase in employment opportunities across a larger spread of land. Vernacular architecture is increasingly being adopted by countries across the world. This paper presents an overview of key examples of such structures and their contribution to local economy and environment. Recent ecological disaster in Joshimath has forced a relook at traditional architectural practices of the hill state of Uttarakhand- Koti Banal. The earthquake in Bhuj in 2001 and the recent earthquake in Turkey, showed the importance of resilient structures that vernacular architecture may provide. This paper will focus on important vernacular architecture styles of India and Central Asia.*

## INTRODUCTION

The biggest humanitarian crisis that we face today, is the triple-pronged planetary crisis of Climate Change, Biodiversity Loss and Pollution. The Intergovernmental Panel on Climate Change (IPCC) has provided evidence that exceeding the 1.5 degree Celsius target would mean irreversible, catastrophic planetary damage putting all life at risk. For the first time since the Industrial revolution, the earth saw temperatures exceeding 1.5 degree Celsius over pre-industrial levels in 2024. An urgent need to reduce Green House Gas (GHG) emissions by 45% by 2030, on base year of 2010, was agreed upon by world leaders and climate experts in the Conference of Parties (COP), United Nation's Climate Change Conventions held in the past few years. However, emissions have instead increased by 15% since 2010. Recent ecological disaster in Joshimath in North India has forced a relook at traditional architectural practices of the hill state of Uttarakhand- Koti Banal. The earthquake in Bhuj in 2001 and the recent earthquake

DOI: 10.4018/979-8-3693-7081-0.ch015

in Turkey, showed the importance of resilient structures that vernacular architecture may provide. This paper will focus on important vernacular architecture styles of India and Central Asia.

For a developing country like India, with ambitions to be categorised as 'Developed nation' by 2047, infrastructure development is non-negotiable – being a key enabler for economic growth. However, with mounting global pressure to reduce emissions, focusing on 'Sustainable Infrastructure' is the only path ahead. Agrarian economies, like India and many parts of Central Asia, further benefit from vernacular architecture in addressing challenges of seasonal unemployment and agriculture waste utilisation among others. The region, especially Northern Indian subcontinent, suffers from severe air pollution through large parts of the year. Stubble burning is a significant contributor to the crisis. Vernacular structures can utilise stubble as building material and reduce the two-pronged problem of pollution due to stubble burning and green house gas emissions from use of cement – one of the most carbon intensive material globally.

Buildings are both responsible for and most susceptible to Climate Change, especially in highly vulnerable and low income countries such as the Indian Subcontinent, which is the focus area for the chapter. According to a report by the World Green Building Council (WGBC), the world's largest network actioning work on sustainable buildings, states that while built spaces only occupy 2% of the Planet, our cities produce 70% of all Greenhouse Gas emissions and consume almost half of the earth's resources extracted globally (Jackson 2023). Additional 1.2 km square of built area is expected to be added by 2030 from 2023 as urban expansion outpaces human population growth, as per the same report. Low-income countries are disproportionately impacted by Climate Change as they are typically located in regions most vulnerable to heat stress while having limited financial resources to deal with it. These countries are presently on the path to economic development, post liberation from colonial rulers. Infrastructure development is a critical enabler of economic progress, leading to large scale building and construction activities in these regions. While the need to build sustainably is a crucial and an important element of Nationally Determined Contributions (NDC) of all signatory countries of the Paris Agreement (2015), it is more pronounced for the countries of the Global South. Fortunately, these countries also have a rich tradition of structures which were climate resilient as well as low on energy and resource use. Therefore, revisiting Vernacular Architecture methods may be a solution to the present need to build sustainably.

## VERNACULAR ARCHITECTURE

As part of a research project called 'Encyclopedia of Vernacular Architecture of the World' Architect Paul Oliver defines vernacular architecture as an architecture that encompasses peoples' dwellings and other structures, built in relation to their specific environment and resources using traditional techniques. It is built to reflect the economy, lifestyle, values and needs of a specific culture (Oliver 2006).

Rudofsky defines vernacular architecture as one where local people, without any conventional training in architecture or construction, create structures which carry the local signature of a place (Rudofsky 1964).

The first structures built on earth date back to 9500 – 8000 BCE, in South East of Turkey. Gobekli Tepe, most likely to have been a temple for hunters to hone their skills, still has its pillars and carvings visible, after more than 10,000 years. It is important to note that Gobekli Tepe is in a one of the most seismically active zones in the world and would have experienced varying range of earthquakes, over the 10,000 years of its existence. While this structure has suffered some damages over time, Cairn of Barnenez, in South of France, the second oldest structure in the world built in 4800 BCE, stands almost intact. Built as a Tumulus, a human-made mound to provide passage to after life, the Cairn of Barnanez has an intricate system of underground passage tombs, all of which have retained their original structure over more than 6000 years. Much younger but more popular structures such as the temples and pyramids of Egypt have also maintained their originally structures remarkably well, over thousands of years.

While a recent earthquake in Turkey flattened buildings and damaged structures in an area of 350,000 square kilometres, the ancient structure of Gobekli Tepe in the same region managed to weather 10,000 years with much higher resilience. Ancient structures are able to stand up to natural calamities much more effectively than newer cement-concrete structures (Oliver 2006).

What makes these structures more robust and resilient than modern buildings?

Some common elements found in all pre-industrialisation era structures, are extensive use of natural materials including stones, rocks and even grass, as in the case of Cairn of Barnanez (Forestell 2021). Newer structures built over the last 1000 to 1500 years, also have colours, embedded stones and motifs in their walls, some of which can still be seen in the Mughal era monuments in the Indian Subcontinent, mosques of Central Asia and other structures of the time. While layered stones formed most of the Before Common Era structures, in the Common Era, stones have also been increasingly covered with natural paints and locally acquired precious stones/gems to increase their aesthetic value. Whether in the BCE or in the last 2000 years, the structures that have survived attacks, both human and natural, are those that have used natural materials and can be categorised under Vernacular Architecture, as per the definition above. In sharp contrast, newer constructions, like the buildings in Himachal Pradesh in India which crumbled to the ground during recent floods in 2023, have been constantly in need of repair and often, reconstruction.

As per the Emergency Events Database, EM-DAT, the number of extreme weather events have increased exactly three-fold over the four decades. There were 1300 such events in 1975-84 and 3900 in 2005-2014 (ADB Economics Working Paper Series 2015). The rate of increase has spiked in the past decade along with record-breaking high temperatures each year. From 2000 to 2015, 1 million people are estimated to have died and $1.7 trillion have been lost due to natural calamities (Guha-Sapir, Below and Hoyois 2015). A large percentage of the cost of damage is due to destruction of built structures. Constant reconstruction, especially around coastal areas, have become the norm. It is important to note that 70% of all Green House Gas (GHG) emissions come from construction and operation of Infrastructure and buildings themselves are responsible for 30% of the world's resource and energy consumption (United Nations Regional Information Centre 2022). Therefore, the sector which contributes the most to climate change, infrastructure, is also the one that suffers most from the impact of it.

Can built-spaces be made to be more resilient to the impact of climate change while reducing its energy and resource footprint?

## RESEARCH QUESTIONS

Hypothesis of this paper is that Vernacular Architecture is both a climate adaptation and mitigation strategy.

In this paper the following five vernacular architecture styles of Asia will be studied. Two styles from India and three from neighbouring countries have been chosen for the paper as all these regions experience natural disasters in the form of earthquakes or floods or droughts. Their location makes them more prone to extreme weather conditions arising out of Climate Change.

1. Traditional Farm houses of Bhutan. Bhutanese structures are traditionally made with local materials like stones, timber and rammed earth as well as bamboo in regions which grow it. These houses have lime-plastered walls and typically do not have nails and bolts but use timber-joining techniques to hold beams together. The author felt these structures were able to retain warmth created during the day through the night, when she stayed in one of these houses in Phobjikha valley in Bhutan.
2. Kath-kuni style of Himachal Pradesh, India. Like the above, these structures use locally available materials and use similar timber-joining techniques. While there are differences in appearance due to cultural elements, there are large similarities between the two styles of architecture as both exist in the mountainous regions, on either side of the Himalayan range. The author has experienced the isothermal nature of a Kath-kuni home during her stay in Dharamshala, Himachal Pradesh.
3. Wind-towers and Cisterns of Iran. Wind-towers and Cisterns are key elements in traditional architecture of Iran. Both are passive cooling structures. Wind-towers are vertical shafts, rising above structures like chimneys, using circulation principles to keep the interiors cool. Cisterns use evaporation techniques to achieve cooling. These zero-carbon emitting, natural cooling systems have gained prominence in recent years, as extreme heat is becoming an increasing occurrence across the world.
4. Bamboo Stilt houses of Assam, India. Assam region of India is prone to flooding every year. Building bamboo homes raised on stilts is a Nature-based Solution to the increasingly frequent and virulent flooding that the region is experiencing. These structures have bamboo slats as floors. The author has experienced the ventilating effect of these floors which is critical in a place with high humidity conditions through most of the year.
5. Indigenous and Tropical Modernist structures of Sri Lanka. Indigenous structures of Sri Lanka use local material and is influenced by Buddhist principles of connecting with nature. Application of Modernist architecture principles of minimalism and functionality to tropical regions, led to the creation of Tropical Modernist structures of Sri Lanka. Key element of these structures is the interplay between nature and the structure. The author has experienced the seamless blending of building and nature as well as the impact of the style on maximising natural lighting and ventilation, in Colombo, Sri Lanka.

Each of the above style will be studied to answer the following two questions:

Question 1: Is the style suitable to meet with extreme weather events, as compared to standard structures

Question 2: Is the style able to reduce GHG emissions and resource use, as compared to standard structures

The author has defined 'Standard Structures' to be the cement-concrete structures that do not demonstrate any of the parameters of vernacular architecture, namely, unique to the local culture and values and use of local materials and labour.

## METHODOLOGY

The above mentioned five styles were chosen as areas of study based on the following criteria:

Author's personal experience in living in four of the five habitats. Author has not personally experienced the Wind-towers and Cisterns of Iran.

Climate Vulnerability Index which rates all the five countries of this study, as 'Highly Vulnerable' making climate change and mitigation as critical need for survival in these countries. Climate Vulnerability Index (CVI) is a globally acknowledged rapid assessment tool that assesses Climate Vulnerability of places.

The Wind-towers and Cisterns of Iran were chosen for their relevance to the region in focus, which is South East Asia. Both these architectural elements moderate temperatures with minimal use of energy and use earth as basic building material, which is a commonly used material this region. Also, evaporation techniques are being looked at with renewed focus as an efficient means of cooling in the dry region of the Indian Subcontinent.

Post decision on the five styles chosen for further study, the following actions were taken.

Secondary Research: An understanding of Vernacular Architecture and its relationship with Climate Change, was gathered through a review of relevant publications in both Climate Change and Architecture. Secondary data on all five styles has been gathered through a review of relevant publications.

Primary Research: Author has collated her personal experience with four of the five styles mentioned, during her visits to Bhutan, Himachal Pradesh and Assam in India and Sri Lanka. Author has gathered primary data on Tropical Modernist Structures of Sri Lanka from two architects who have worked with Sri Lankan architect, Geoffrey Bawa, a leading architect who incorporated traditional Sri Lankan building styles into Modern Structures. Author has gathered primary data on Kath-Kuni style of architecture through an architect working at reviving this building form in Himachal Pradesh, India.

Secondary and Primary data has been analysed to arrive at some conclusion on whether Vernacular Architecture can act as a Mitigation as well as/or an Adaptation strategy for Climate Change.

Research has been qualitative in nature and data gathered directly from source has been through interviews.

Globally, energy demand and consequent GHG emissions from buildings has been increasing as per all reports on Energy Consumption. United Nation's Status Report on Buildings and Construction, state that 34% of global energy demand and 37% of Energy and Process-driven CO2 demand came from this sector in 2022 (UNEP 2024). The report also elaborates on the relevance of Nature-based solutions (NbS) in lowering heat-island effects, where built-up areas are hotter than those left to nature, as well as managing water and air quality. Some examples of Nature-based solutions in architecture, are green roofs, permeable pavements and rain gardens. Biophilic designs as another low energy solutions is also mentioned in the report. While using the same principles as NbS, Biophilic designs mimic nature in a way that increases engagement and connection of inhabitants to the natural world. Both the above mentioned approaches are central to vernacular architecture, where natural and local building materials are used and buildings are nature inspired, allowing interaction between dwellers and the space around them. World Green Building Council's paper called The Circular Built Environment lays emphasis on Nature-inspired buildings as both a mitigation and adaptation solution (Jackson 2023). It additionally points out the relevance of such building in reducing biodiversity loss, an important contributor to Climate Change.

There is a scarcity of peer-reviewed publications on the use of Vernacular Architecture in Climate Change mitigation and adaptation, though sufficient research exists on the role of nature-inspired buildings and its role in adaptation and mitigation. There is some research that brings out the importance of Vernacular architecture in reducing environmental damage but specifics are missing (Zong et al 2024). Proceeds from the 'Heritage2020 International Conference on Vernacular Architecture in World Heritage Sites' organised in Spain presented a number of case studies that showed the resilience of Vernacular Structures in the face of natural calamities like floods and landslides, the frequency of which are increasing due to Climate Change (Vegas et al 2022).

Case Studies of Vernacular Architecture in different countries, show the innate ability of such traditional structures to respond to climate. Indonesian traditional structures are considered to be 'breathing buildings', made with natural materials such as timber, bamboo and palm sheets, which cool the spaces inside (Rajendra 2021). Indonesian vernacular structures also have high roofs to allow circulation. Additionally, most of them are raised on stilts to allow cooling of the floor as well as deal with increasing floods and rise of water levels in low-lying areas of Bali, Indonesia.

Case study of Vernacular architecture in Chile brings out variations within the same country, based on different climatic conditions (Pareti et al 2022). Use of stilts in temperature control and flood resilience is also found in Chiloe Island in the Chile, surrounded by the Pacific Ocean. The stilts also ensure that fungus and algae growth due to constant humidity is prevented. In sharp contrast, the Atacama Desert region in Chile has Ayllus, which are adobes with compact mud walls of 25 cm thickness. These walls trap day heat and release it during the night when the desert gets cold.

One conclusive study found during Literature Review was a comparative study between a modern and a vernacular structure in Minna Niger State, Nigeria (Dada and Alibaba 2023). The study used a simulation software, EnergyPlus for assessment and forecasting of thermal comfort in both kinds of structures. The study concluded that the vernacular structure showed higher thermal comfort up to 50% more than the modern structure, during peak heat times. Vegetation, courtyard and use of natural materials were mentioned as key features of the vernacular structure, which minimised its environmental footprint while substantially reducing heat within the premise.

As the focus of this chapter is South East Asia, a review of vernacular agriculture in South East Asian region was carried out which presented similar facts as above. Most house in the whole of this region use Mud as primary material, especially in the rural areas. A research on mud houses in Sri Lanka and Bangladesh shows important learnings from such traditional structures, for designing energy efficient buildings (Mehjabeen 2020).

Deeper study of vernacular architecture of the five regions in the subcontinent, are presented below.

## KATH-KUNI ARCHITECTURE, HIMACHAL PRADESH, INDIA

Landslides caused by rain, led to the complete destruction of 27 buildings and partial damage of 87, in August 2023, in one district of Himachal Pradesh, India, according to the state's Disaster Management Authority (https://hpsdma.nic.in/). At least 367 people lost their lives in this incidence of landslide along. Similar landslides followed by vast-scale destruction of property and lives was observed in other parts of the state earlier this year. Landslides following rains, have become a norm in the hill-states of Himachal Pradesh and Uttarakhand, located in the North of India.

In January 2023, buildings in Joshimath in the state of Uttarakhand, India, developed cracks and became uninhabitable, according the daily The Indian Express, January 8, 2023 edition. Land subsidence, the sinking of ground, has led to the displacement of people from Joshimath and surrounding areas, according to experts from National Disaster Management Authority (https://ndma.gov.in/) and IIT Roorkee (https://www.iitr.ac.in/).

6000 lives were lost in another district of Uttarakhand, when Glacial Lake Outburst Flood (GLOF) hit Kedarnath in June 2013. Experts attribute rampant heavy construction in this fragile ecosystem which also has high seismic activity, to the destruction (Agrawal and Chauhan 2023). Kedarnath is home to an ancient temple built between 9th and 11th century. The temple attracts lakhs of tourists each year and uncontrolled construction has been taking place to accommodate tourists, despite the area being a fragile ecosystem. According to a report and recommendation of future construction in the area, Wadia Institute of Himalayan Geology states that the area can only support light construction, like the traditional hill structures that were used earlier (Bhambri et al 2015). It is important to note that the more than 1000 year temple has survived the 2013 floods as well as annual flooding and devastation that occurs in the region every year. Additionally, being in a highly active seismic zone, the temple is likely to have faced earthquakes in its long years of existence. But the structure stands more or less intact till date. The temple is an example of the ancient Koti Banal style of architecture, native to the region and similar to Kath-kuni style described below. Buildings made in the Koti Banal style have survived landslides and earthquakes much more than other buildings, even during the devastating Uttarkashi earthquake of 1991, where close to 90,000 buildings were either partially or completely destroyed (Rautela and Joshi 2007).

Kath-kuni Architecture derives its name from Kath, meaning wood and Kuni, meaning corner. It is the traditional architecture form of Himachal Pradesh and surrounding areas. It is primarily a timber-laced dry masonry construction which uses local stones and wood, layered on top of each other, to create structures that are suitable for hilly conditions. The absence of cement makes these structures flexible and more earth-quake resistant than rigid concrete structures. Additionally, non-linear wall behaviour, ductility, allow the stone and stone-timber to deform vertically when the base is shaken, preventing the structure from collapse (Marloes 2018).

According to United Nations Environment Program's report on 'Greening Cement', the cement industry contributes up to 8% of global GHG emissions (UNEP 2010). Kath-kuni structures use locally grown deodar trees, slate and other local stones, which do not require energy intensive cement or steel. Additionally, the practice is centuries-old and passed down over generations. Therefore local people are employed for the construction, making Kath-kuni buildings are good source of livelihood for the locals.

Construction Debris is a leading cause of land, soil, air and water contamination. Use of natural materials such as sustainably harvested wood and local stones ensure that end-of-life of the building does not damage the environment. Another key environmental benefit of kath-kuni is the absence of paints and binders. Volatile Organic Compounds in paints and binders are toxic for living beings and a significant contributor to pollution.

New construction in the region is not using Kath-kuni or Koti-Banal form of buildings today. Post-disaster reconstruction, commissioned by the National Disaster Management Authority, have involved steel frames and concrete rather than traditional materials (Arya 1994). The reason for this is the need for quick turn-around which is not possible with the traditional styles, which are labour intensive. Another reason is the reduction in forest cover required to provide wood for the buildings. Sustainably managed forests are few and steadily on the decline in the mountains.

The solution presented by expert groups has been to infuse new materials, such as bamboo and in certain cases concrete slabs, to reinforce the traditional forms (Chandalavada and Srikonda 2018). There is sufficient evidence to demonstrate the resilience of Kath-kuni structures in the face of natural disasters. Also, resource and energy footprint of such structures is a fraction of concrete buildings. In terms of social benefits, these structures provide local employment in terms of labour and in promoting tourism.

## BAMBOO STILT STRUCTURES OF MAJULI, ASSAM

Majuli is the world's largest inhabited river island, is located in the Brahmaputra river in Assam, India. It originally comprised 15 large islands, which have over the years been reduced to 1 main island and 25 thinly populated small islands, due to the constant erosion by the river Brahmaputra. The island is severely prone to floods and is water-logged through a large part of the year, making travel by boat a common practice. Majuli also experiences frequent earthquakes and large ones in 1897 and 1950 were further responsible for reducing the size of Majuli to its present state (UNESCO World Heritage Centre).

The architecture of Majuli is an interesting mix of traditional styles of neighbouring states and countries. Multiple tribes, of mongoloid origin, came to this island from as far as Mongolia and China in the 16$^{th}$ century, the largest of which is the Mising tribe of Majuli. A traditional Mising hut is made predominantly of bamboo along with wood, reed, cane and thatch (Salam and Dasgupta 2021). To cope with constant flooding, soft alluvial soil and wild animals, these huts are raised on bamboo stilts. The floor of the hut is perforated and allows for natural ventilation and reduces chances of mold that can form in high humidity conditions. The second largest tribe in Majuli is the Deuri. Their houses also use same architectural principles as the Mising house, with an additional raised granary, for protecting grains from the moisture laden ground, flooding and animals. SonowalKacharis make up a majority of the remaining population of the district. Their houses follow a similar pattern using bamboo and other local vegetation except that the houses are not built on stilts but on a raised plinth. While the other tribes make their walls with enmeshed bamboo and other natural vegetation, the Sonowal Kacharis use cow dung and mud to plaster the walls over the bamboo as reinforcement.

Critical elements of vernacular architecture of Majuli that make it suitable to adapt to climate change related excessive rainfall and rising waters of the Brahmaputra, are its raised structure on bamboo stilts, the extensive use of bamboo, reeds and other vegetation which are more resilient to constant rain and the sloping roof structures. High ductility of bamboo also makes these structures more resilient during earth quakes than rigid concrete structures (Barman, Roy and Dasgupta 2020).

As in all vernacular architecture styles, the use of local materials in Majuli Bamboo-Stilt architecture, reduce GHG emission. Additionally, the avoidance of cement and paints in such structures further prevent air, water, soil contamination. Clay created by locally sourced mud and cow-dung also exhibit anti-termite properties, reducing the dependence of chemical insecticides (Salam and Dasgupta 2021). Along with skylights, these huts have perforated floors for better ventilation reducing dependence on electricity. A unique feature of these huts, especially the ones made by Deuri, is the placement of pigsty under the hut. Organic waste is reused in the slurry fed to pigs, making it a completely circular process.

Both the above examples of vernacular architecture show an ability to deal with natural disasters, whether caused by climate change or otherwise, better than other structures. The material used and the techniques employed make these structures low on GHG emission while polluting the environment much less than modern structures. As in the case of Kath-kuni style, the vernacular architecture of Majuli provides employment to the locals and these houses, along with the instruments used to create them, are now a tourist attraction in Assam.

To further understand the environmental impact of vernacular structures, vernacular architectural styles of three other countries are presented.

## VERNACULAR ARCHITECTURE OF IRAN

Iranian vernacular architecture takes into account the hot and dry climate of most of Iran, and focusses on creating spaces that are cool and protected from the sun and wind. One way that the structures here differ from the ones mentioned above, is the focus on building close to each other, so that a large part of the outer boundary walls are protected by other houses on either side (Mohammadabadi and Ghoreshi 2011). The houses tend to have a central courtyard which ideally has a water body. The water body helps keep the surrounding structure cool and also works as a connection between the rooms on either side. A common open area for socialisation in the centre of the house, is found in most vernacular architecture styles, including those in South of India. Like most traditional structures of the region, material used is mud or clay. Adobe structures, made of clay and natural vegetation, are common in dry and hot regions. The ability of such structures to protect inhabitants from harsh desert conditions, has been proven over centuries (Bahadori and Haghighat 1986). Most of these structures have a domed roof, which helps reflect back sunlight.

A defining feature of traditional Iranian architecture is wind-tunnels. Wind-tunnels are placed on roofs to bring in cool air from above inside buildings (Mohammadabadi and Ghoreshi 2011). At times, the tunnels are sunk into the ground to cool the air contained in it, and then emerge as air vents inside the buildings. This ancient form of ventilation has been found to be an effective way of cooling inside buildings and at the same time keeping the air in constant circulation, removing any indoor pollution.

Cisterns, called 'Ab-Anbar' in Iran, are water reservoirs, built deep in the ground and covered by mud-brick domes (Kazemi and Shirvani 2011). The oldest Ab-Anbars have been found from second century BCE and have helped keep water cool through centuries (Yousefi and Nocera 2021). The water is collected from a higher level, sometimes at the base of a mountain, and moved down by gravity to these cisterns. The Mud-brick dome protects it from sun and the porous walls allow the water to cool. Such structures have helped provide relief in the form of naturally cooled water, over other parts of the Arabian desert. Another structure attributed to Iran but also found all the way up to East Europe, is the Ice-House (Kazemi and Shirvani 2011). The process of storing ice in rammed earth mud-brick structures is centuries old and can be traced back to China in eighth century BCE.

At the United Nations Convention to Combat Desertification (UNCCD) COP15 in Abidjan, the body declared 40% of ice-free land on earth, to be degraded and turning into desert (UNFCCC 2022). Wind-tunnels, cisterns and ice-houses have been keeping water and air cool for centuries without the use of energy, in harsh desert areas.

Vernacular architecture is defined as architecture that uses natural materials and as per the examples above, focuses on natural means of cooling/heating, light, and ventilation. The structures are created keeping in mind local climate and from the above, we see their ability to adapt to climate.

To understand vernacular architecture from a societal mindset or culture point of view, the traditional villages of Sri Lanka were studied.

## INDIGENOUS SETTLEMENTS OF SRI LANKA

Traditional Sri Lanka settlement deeply reflected the principles of Buddhism – namely sharing, compassion and balance (Dayaratne 2018). The Buddhist tenets of 'middle-path' and minimalism are reflected in the creation of settlements around common agricultural land, common forests and common sources of water. A strong belief in living in harmony with nature is demonstrated through the practice of conserving fertile land for growing food and never building on them. Even boulders that lay in the path of settlement, are not moved or broken but built around.

Weva, lake, and Dagoba, temple, are central to traditional Sri Lankan settlements. While temples were built with stones and built to last long, houses were built of perishable material like straw and mud. While lime plastering was observed, it was not common practice. The Sinhalese believed that their homes were not required to last long as that reflected an 'ego'- a vice. Circularity was embedded in their lives and the walls of the houses too disintegrated into natural debris, that could go back into the earth. It is observed that most structures did have a more permanent wooden skeleton which lasted longer than the outside walls.

An important element of traditional Sri Lankan settlements were the commons. In all cases a water reservoir and in some cases a forest. The Sinhalese believed that each individual needs to give their best to the preservation of the commons but take from it, only according to their need.

Geoffrey Bawa, a Sri Lankan architect credited with reviving vernacular architecture through his Modern Regionalist form of building in the 1960s, embraced the ethos of Sri Lankan settlements in his work (Robson 2019). Rejecting modern buildings that do not work well in tropical climate, he went back to structures which keep the rain and heat out through overhangs and porous building materials. Kandalama Hotel built over an ancient reservoir on a ridge, is an excellent example of how traditional wisdom can be incorporated in a modern structure. Bawa's hope for this structure was to give it back to the ridge that is sits on, at the end of its life, imbibing circularity - a cornerstone of traditional Sinhalese construction.

The rapid adoption of Glass-Chrome-Steel architecture in tropical regions is leading to high GHG emissions as these structures trap heat and require intense air-conditioning. Understanding Tropical Modernist structures is important to apply the minimalism of modernism while adapting to the high heat and humidity conditions of the tropics.

## TRADITIONAL FARMHOUSES OF BHUTAN

Bhutan has a rich architectural heritage which has been carefully preserved by monarchies which have ruled this kingdom for centuries. Heritage structures like the Dzongs (fortresses) and Choetens (Stupas) have stood the test of time. The oldest fortress in Bhutan, Simtokha Dzong, was built in the $16^{th}$ century and is still structurally intact. Owing to a strong focus on cultural identity by the present King, one can observe widespread use of traditional wear and ancient forms of entertainment such as archery, along with the existence of traditional farmhouses, still being built in the same manner for the past many centuries. The present King has also laid down measures to maintain the vernacular architecture of the region. In 2014, the Ministry of Works and Human Settlement, Royal Government of Bhutan, released the 'Bhutanese Architecture Guidelines' which presents methods that can be adopted for building sustainably, learning from the vernacular structures of the kingdom (https://www.moit.gov.bt/wp-content/uploads/2010/11/Bhutan-Arch-Guidelines-final-2014.pdf). While building facades still follow vernacular styles, there has been use of modern building materials such as cement and a shift towards use of technology for heating and ventilation (Yip 2000). On the other hand, emphasis on eco-tourism has encouraged the Bhutanese people to continue the practice of living in and building Traditional Farmhouses.

A typical Bhutanese farmhouse is a rectangular structure with a stone foundation, which may be as high as 80 cm to prevent dampness from entering the house. The ground floor is traditionally a barn meant for animals and storing hay. Pitched timber roofs allow quick disbursement of heavy rain water that Bhutan receives during summer monsoons.

Most of the structures are made of rammed earth, trapping heat during the day and keeping the house warm at night. Additional heat is provided by the kitchen which is in the centre of the house with stove fuelled with firewood. It is found that the living space situated about the barn also receive heat from the animals in the ground floor. While rammed earth is more commonly used for building walls, Central and East Bhutan farmhouses also use stone masonry, as a response to local material availability and climatic conditions. The practice of creating the rammed mud walls with a wooden rammer on moist earth continues till present day. The 80-100 cm thick mud walls provide both stability and resilience to earth quakes and tremors (Dorji 2019). Bhutan lies in the 'most active seismic zone' of 4 and 5 and its traditional practice of thick rammed mud walls has helped keep structures standing through earthquakes. Traditional farmhouses do not apply plaster or paint to their mud walls. Therefore there is no discharge of chemical contaminants of wall paints.

A traditional Bhutanese Farmhouse is a good example of biophilic construction, where nature, including animals, food crops, foodgrains, fodder, along with humans, exist in the same space. The harmonious co-existence of all species is deeply embedded in the official religion of Bhutan, Buddhism. Such structures not only provide sustainable dwellings for the Bhutanese but also exemplify their belief system (Lim 2006).

## FINDINGS

The five styles of vernacular architecture show that they help in climate change mitigation through the following ways:

Use of natural materials. All the structures studies use combinations of stones, wood, mud and other local vegetation. Cement production is one of the most GHG emitting processes, and releases upto 8% of the world's CO2 as per International Energy Agency (https://www.iea.org/energy-system/industry/cement). While unsustainable use of wood can lead to deforestation, these structures seem to last long and therefore it is possible to use wood sustainably in buildings. Recycling wood for construction is being looked at favourably now by architecture firms promoting use of locally acquired wood over cement and concrete. Additionally, toxic leaching of material from construction debris, is not a part of vernacular structures. The structures biodegrade at end of life as do construction waste material, if any.

Isothermal building materials. Most of the structures studied above, use mud as a reinforcing layer over bamboo or wood or directly as mud-brick walls. The porous nature of mud makes it easier to keep structures cool. Ice-houses and cisterns also use this property to keep water cool.

Natural light and ventilation. While all the structures above are created to utilise natural light, the perforated bamboo floors of Majuli and Wind-towers of Iran are exemplars of natural ventilation. Of the total energy footprint of buildings, 18% is used in heating, cooling and lighting as per International Energy Agency.

Absence of paints. Other than some structures in traditional Sri Lankan settlements, all other structures have no paint. The Sri Lankan structures have used lime plaster in some instances which has negligible toxicity. Modern wall paints contain Volatile Organic Compounds which are a significant contributor to air, water and soil pollution. According to the World Health Organisation (WHO), widespread use of Lead has led to extensive environmental damage and public health problems. Some of the problems stated by the organisation are kidney damage, stillbirth, premature birth and low birthrate, among those exposed to high VOC paints. Other solvents like Toluene and Xylene affect the nervous system adversely (WHO 2023).

The structures are also found to be Climate adaptable in the following ways:

Resilience of natural materials and structure. While earthquakes are not a consequence of Climate Change, the structures above, especially the ones in active seismic zones, were found to be much more resilient to jolts than rigid cement structures. Ductility of bamboo and the layering of the construction material made them flexible and easier to resist damage. The material is also more suitable to handle extreme heat conditions expected as a result of climate change. However, Sri Lankan traditional huts were found to be destructible, disintegrating into the ground in consistent heavy downpour. Water storage in Iranian cisterns appear to be a suitable way to deal with water scarcity situations. Overhangs and stilts provide protection against heavy rainfall and frequent flooding in Majuli.

The five examples above prove what is commonly said of vernacular architecture i.e. it is less resource and carbon intensive than one based on modern designs (Jadhav 2007). Social aspects of vernacular architecture become clear on studying the above styles. Renowned Egyptian architect, Hassan Fathy, talked about the demise of vernacular architecture, saying "Until the collapse of cultural frontiers in last century, there were distinctive local shapes and details in architecture, and the buildings of every locality were the beautiful children of a happy marriage between the imagination of people and the demands of their countryside" (Fathy 2000). All literature on the above styles lamented the loss of a sense of uniqueness and identity, as a result of rapidly disappearing vernacular structures. A strong appeal to retain them and revive them by incorporating modern tools, is recommended by all the authors studied for this paper. They cite increased tourism and reduced damage due to climate change as leading reasons but underlying their appeals, is a need to provide dignity and pride to the local artisans who have created these structures for centuries over multiple generations.

An intangible benefit that the author personally experienced in Bhutan, Assam, Himachal and Sri Lankan structures mentioned above, was the constant connect with nature. The homes in these spaces allowed sun, air and in the cases of Assam and Bhutan, even animals, become part of the main dwelling. Trees, shrubs and water bodies are an important part of the home design, encouraging human and non-human species to coexist together. While the focus of this paper is Climate Change, the role of biodiversity in mitigating climate change cannot be ignored. According to experts at the Stockholm

Resilience Centre, the body that researches and provides inputs on maintaining a liveable planet, loss of biodiversity will make the planet inhabitable even if we achieve Net-Zero in GHG emissions (Stockholm Resilience Centre 2023). Human habitation has created a barrier between nature and people and this barrier has increased manifold with the introduction of modern steel-glass-cement structures (Mancuso 2020). Vernacular architecture reduces this barrier, making it easier for inhabitants to feel connected and consequently, more responsible towards Nature. This sense of responsibility is an important step towards Climate Change mitigation.

## DISCUSSION

The chapter was aimed at establishing a relationship between Climate Change and Vernacular Architecture. During the research, multiple other aspects of vernacular architecture emerged, which are presented below as questions:

Does Vernacular Architecture lead to the creation of an unique identity for its people? The definition of Vernacular Architecture emerges from identity of a place and its people. Through the case studies, the converse appeared to be true as well. People identified themselves with their local and traditional structures. A loss of such structures may then imply a loss of unique identity. A possible area of research could be the reason behind disassociation from one's unique identity and the growing need to conform to a global template.

Does Vernacular Architecture lead to a sustainable mindset among its users? It may be accepted that vernacular architecture is more sustainable on multiple aspects and more suitable to dealing with and slowing Climate Change. However, the biophilic nature of vernacular structures has nature-connect as core design principle. Research exists to show that exposure and consequent connection to nature are critical enablers for a sustainable mindset (Zelenski 2015). Therefore, vernacular structures may also promote sustainable behaviour among those living in or using them.

## RESEARCH SHORTCOMINGS

To truly understand the impact of vernacular architecture, styles from all over the world should be researched. This paper only looks at five styles clustered in and around India. Other climatic, social and economic conditions have not been studied. Financial viability of reviving such techniques can be an area of further research.

## CONCLUSION

The adage 'Old is Gold' appears to be true for architecture, not just in terms of suitability for local climatic conditions and resilience to unforeseen natural events, but also in terms of pride for the local community. There is revived interest in using local materials and traditional designs in building, led by architects like Hassan Fathy, Geoffrey Bawa and in India, BV Doshi, Charles Correa and Benny Kuriokose to name a few. Rutland based Stonemasonry Company and architect Amin Taha are bringing stones, abundantly available and used for centuries, back into construction in England.

Vernacular architecture takes time and is labour intensive. Moreover, the techniques used for centuries are slowly getting lost due to low demand, intensifying the challenge of building vernacular. Application of efficient designs and modern building tools on local materials while incorporating traditional wisdom, could yet be a possibility.

As people increasingly realise that the built spaces they occupy, impact their well-being, productivity, happiness and in many cases, a sense of identity, the chances of shifting to buildings which are unique and natural will get higher.

"Whatever good things we build, end up building us", Jim Rohn. Architect.

## REFERENCES


Aamirah, S., & Arpan, D. (2021) Tales of traditions, aspects of adaptations and stories of sustenance of the largest river island in the world. Elementary Education Online. Vol 20. Issue 1.

Adrian, J. (2023). *The Circular Built Environment Playbook*. World Green Building Council.

Barman Amal, Roy Madhumita, Dasgupta Arpan (2020) Vernacular architecture of Majuli, Assam-meaning, model and metaphor in integrating the environmental, socio-economic and cultural realms. International Journal of Creative Research Thoughts. Vol 8. Issue 7.

Anom, R. (2021) Contemporary Challenges of the Indonesian Vernacular Architecture in addressing Climate Change. IOP Conference Series: Earth and Environment Rautela Piyoosh, Joshi Girish Chandra (2007) Earthquake safe Koti Banal Architecture of Uttarakhand, India. Disaster Mitigation and Management Centre. Department of Disaster Management. Uttarakhand India.

Arya, A. S. (1994) Earthquake Engineering. Tenth World Congress. Rotterdam. ISBN 90 5410 060 5

Bahadori, M. N., & Fariborz, H. (1986). Thermal performance of adobe structures with domed roofs and moist internal surfaces. *Solar Energy*, *36*(4), 365–375. DOI: 10.1016/0038-092X(86)90154-4

Bhambri, R., Mehta, M., Dobhal, D. P., & Gupta, A. K. (2015). *Glacier Lake Iniventory of Uttarakhand.* Wadia Institute of Himalayan Geology.

Dada, A. D., & Alibaba, H. Z. (2023). Comparison analysis between the components of vernacular and modern architectures for sustainable housing in Niger State. *IOP Conference Series. Earth and Environmental Science*, *1210*(1), 012011. DOI: 10.1088/1755-1315/1210/1/012011

Robinson David (2019) Geoffrey Bawa: The master architect of Sri Lanka. STIRworld.

Fazeleh, Y., & Francesco, N. (2021). *The role of Ab-Anbars in the vernacular architecture of Iran with emphasis on the performance of Wind-catchers in hot and dry climate*. Energy Efficiency in Historic Buildings. Special Issue

Ghayour, K. A., & Hossein, S. A. (2011). An overview of some vernacular techniques in Iranian sustainable architecture in reference to Cisterns and Ice Houses. *Journal of Sustainable Development*, *4*(1), •••.

Guha-Sapir, D., Below, R., & Hoyois, P. (2015). *EM-DAT: International Disaster Database*. Universitécatholique de Louvain—CRED.

Jadhav, R. (2007). Green architecture in India: Combining modern technology with traditional methods. *UN Chronicle*, *154*(2), 66–71.

Karthik, C., & Ramesh, S. (2021). Vernacular Practices: An appraisal for sustainability for housing in Uttarakhand and Himachal Pradesh, India. *International Journal of Humanities and Social Science*, *10*(1), •••.

Lim Regina Mapua. (2006). *Cultural Sustainability and Development: Drukpa and Burman Vernacular Architecture*. Ashgate Publishing Limited.

Mancuso, S. (2020). *Tree Stories*. Editori Laterza.

Nihal, P. (1995). *Critical Vernacularism: The subversion of universalising trends in architecture. Binghamton University*. State University of New York.

Pareti, S., Valdebenito, V., Rudolph, L., & Bustamante, C. (2022). Green energy and environmental sustainability on Vernacular Architecture. The case of Ayllus of Atacama Desert and stilt houses of Chiloé. *IOP Conference Series. Earth and Environmental Science, 1094*(1), 012003. DOI: 10.1088/1755-1315/1094/1/012003

Paul, O. (2006). *Built to meet needs: Cultural issues in vernacular architecture*. Routledge.

Ranjith, D. (2018). *Toward sustainable development: Lessons from vernacular settlements of Sri Lanka. Frontiers of Architectural Research*. South East University.

Rudofsky, B. (1964). *Architecture without Architects: A short introduction to non-pedigreed architecture*. University of New Mexico Press.

Sabrina, M., Nuzhat, F., & Shariful, S. (2020) Vernacular Architecture of South Asia: Exploring Passive Design Strategies of Traditional Houses in Warm Humid Climate of Bangladesh and Sri Lanka. *Proceedings of the International Conference of Contemporary Affairs in Architecture and Urbanism-ICCAUA*. 3. 216-226. DOI: 10.38027/N212020ICCAUA316262

Samuel, D. (2022). *Kath Kuni Architecture: Origin and Development*. Amazing Architecture.

Sandhya, A., & Singh, C. A. (2023). *A decade after the floods, is Kedarnath safer?* The Third Pole.

Stockholm Resilience Centre Annual Report (2023) Investing in Resilience. Stockholm University.

United Nations Climate Change (2022) Growing desertification demonstrates need for adaptation plans

United Nations Environment Program (2010) Greening cement production has a big role to play in reducing Green House Gas emissions

United Nations Environment Program (2024) Global Status Report for Buildings and Construction United Nations Regional Information Centre for Western Europe (2022) Sustainable Infrastructure: a synergy between climate mitigation and economic growth

Van der Zanden Marloes. (2018). *Assessment of the seismic performance and sustainability of the Kath Kuni building style in the Indian Himalaya*. Delft University of Technology.

Vegas, F., Mileto, C., Escobar, A. H., & de Miguel, M. L. (2022). Sustainability, Risks and Resilience of Vernacular Architecture. *International Journal of Architectural Heritage, 16*(6), 817–819. DOI: 10.1080/15583058.2022.2067435

Vinod, T., & Ramon, L. (2015) Global Increase in Climate related disasters. ADB Economics Working Paper Series. No. 466

World Health Organisation Fact Sheet (August 2023) Lead Poisoning

UNESCO World Heritage Convention (2004) River Island Majuli mid-stream in Brahmaputra river in Assam

Yip Christopher, L. (2000) Bhutan: Its Architectural Heritage and Change. ACSA 2000 International Conference. Hong Kong. China.

Zelenski John, M., Dopko Raelyne, L., & Capaldi Colin, A. (2015). Cooperation is in our Nature: Nature Exposure may promote Cooperative and Environmentally Sustainable Behavior. *Journal of Environmental Psychology*, *42*, 24–31. DOI: 10.1016/j.jenvp.2015.01.005

Zong, J., Wan Mohamed, W. S., Zaky Jaafar, M. F., & Ujang, N. (2024). Sustainable development of vernacular architecture: A systematic literature review. *Journal of Asian Architecture and Building Engineering*, •••, 1–17. DOI: 10.1080/13467581.2024.2399685

## KEY TERMS AND DEFINITIONS

**Climate Change:** Climate Change is a shift in Earth's climate which is a result of atmospheric conditions like presence of Greenhouse Gases and other factors.

**Climate Change Adaptation:** Climate Change Adaptation is the process of adapting to consequences of Climate Change such as sea level rise, extreme weather events and forest fires.

**Climate Change Mitigation:** Climate Change Mitigation is the process of reducing Climate Change through reduction on Greenhouse Gases and increasing carbon sinks.

**Greenhouse Gases:** Greenhouse Gases are those gases that trap heat in the Earth's atmosphere and increase the temperature of the earth. Major Greenhouse gases are Carbon Dioxide, Methane and fluorinated gases.

**Indigenous:** Indigenous means belonging to a certain place.

**Isothermal:** Isothermal is the process which ensures temperature remains constant.

**Natural Materials:** Natural materials are those that are derived directly from Nature.

**Nature-Based Solutions:** Solutions that utilise ecosystems to provide provisioning services such as air, water, soil quality management.

**Vernacular Architecture:** Vernacular Architecture is the architecture of a certain place, using local materials and styles.

# Compilation of References

Aamirah, S., & Arpan, D. (2021) Tales of traditions, aspects of adaptations and stories of sustenance of the largest river island in the world. Elementary Education Online. Vol 20. Issue 1.

Abdullah, N., Hussin, A., & Hadi, M. (2015). The determinants of trade and trade direction of Arab Maghreb Union. *Journal of Economic Cooperation and Development*, *36*(3), 123–148.

Ablonczy-Mihályka, L., & Kecskés, P. (2015). Changing principles how to define and regulate the term 'industrial park': The case of Hungary, Romania and Bulgaria. *The Central European Journal of Regional Development and Tourism*, *7*(3), 101–112. DOI: 10.32725/det.2015.036

Abreu, R., David, F., & Crowther, D. (2005). Corporate social responsibility is urgently needed in health care. *Social Responsibility Journal*, *1*(3/4), 225–240. DOI: 10.1108/eb045813

Abu-Fadil, M., Torrent, J., & Grizzle, A. (2016). Opportunities for media and information literacy in the Middle East and North Africa. *The International Clearinghouse on Children, Youth & Media at Nordicom*, University of Gothemburg. (pp. 55-115).

Academy of Marketing Science (AMS) World Marketing Congress (WMC), Vol. 617, Springer, .DOI: 10.1007/978-3-030-02568-7_165

Acar, S., & Dogruel, F. (2012). Sources of inequality in selected MENA countries. *Structural Change and Economic Dynamics*, *23*(3), 276–285. DOI: 10.1016/j.strueco.2012.03.004

Achten, S., & Lessmann, C. (2020). Spatial inequality, geography and economic activity. *World Development*, *136*, 105114. https://www.sciencedirect.com/science/article/abs/pii/S0305750X20302412. DOI: 10.1016/j.worlddev.2020.105114

Acikgoz, F., Stylos, N., & Lythreatis, S. (2024). Identifying capabilities and constraints in utilizing blockchain technology in hospitality and tourism. *International Journal of Contemporary Hospitality Management*, *36*(10), 3493–3514. Advance online publication. DOI: 10.1108/IJCHM-07-2023-1083

Adrian, J. (2023). *The Circular Built Environment Playbook*. World Green Building Council.

Afshardoost, M., & Eshaghi, M. S. (2020). Destination image and tourist behavioral intentions: A meta-analysis. *Tourism Management*, *81*, 104154. DOI: 10.1016/j.tourman.2020.104154

Agencia Andaluza de la Energía. *Ayudas a la financiación*. 2024b. Available online: https://www.agenciaandaluzadelaenergia.es/es/todos-los-programas. Accessed on 17 September 2024.

Agencia Andaluza de la Energía. *INFO-ENERGÍA*. 2024a. Available online: https://www.agenciaandaluzadelaenergia.es/info-web/loginController. Accessed on 4 July 2024.

Agencia Andaluza de la Energía. *La Bioenergía en Andalucía*. 2020. Available online: https://www.agenciaandaluzadelaenergia.es/sites/default/files/Documentos/3_2_0068_20_LA_BIOENERGIA_EN_ANDALUCIA.PDF. Accessed on 4 July 2024.

Aghazadeh, H., Beheshti Jazan Abadi, E., & Zandi, F. (2022). Branding advantage of agri-food companies in competitive export markets: A resource-based theory. *British Food Journal*, *124*(7), 2039–2060. DOI: 10.1108/BFJ-08-2021-0952

Akdag, G., Guler, O., Dalgic, A., Benli, S., & Cakici, A. C. (2018). Do tourists' gastronomic experiences differ within the same geographical region? A comparative study of two Mediterranean destinations: Turkey and Spain. *British Food Journal*, *120*(1), 158–171. DOI: 10.1108/BFJ-01-2017-0017

Akyürek, S. (2023). Gastronomic festival tours in Turkey: Motivations and expectations of tourists. In *Managing Festivals for Destination Marketing and Branding*. DOI: 10.4018/978-1-6684-6356-7.ch008

Al Doghan, M. A., & Zakariya, A. (2022). Developing positive health behavior among employees: Exploring role of green work environment in healthcare sector. *AgBioForum*, *24*(3), 84–96.

Alizadeh, M. (2020). Analysis of economic convergence of Islamic Justice in selected Islamic Countries. *Journal of Economic Structures*, *9*(1), 24. Advance online publication. DOI: 10.1186/s40008-020-00191-8

Allal-Chérif, O. (2022). Intelligent cathedrals: Using augmented reality, virtual reality, and artificial intelligence to provide an intense cultural, historical, and religious visitor experience. *Technological Forecasting and Social Change*, *178*, 121604. DOI: 10.1016/j.techfore.2022.121604

Almeida, C. C. (2004). Cities Marketing. Management And Development, (12), 9-45. Retrieved from https://doi.org/DOI: 10.7559/gestaoedesenvolvimento.2004.104

Alsip, P. J., Hartig, J. H., Krantzberg, G., Williams, K. C., & Wondolleck, J. (2021). Evolving institutional arrangements for use of an ecosystem approach in restoring Great Lakes Areas of Concern. *Sustainability*, *13*(3), 1532. DOI: 10.3390/su13031532 PMID: 34676112

Alvarez, I., & Ossorio, A. (2019). Spain, Israel and Palestine. History of encounters and disagreements. *Hispania*, *79*(261), 221–248. DOI: 10.3989/hispania.2019.008

Alvarez, M. D. (2014). Sustainability issues. In *Tourism as an Instrument for Development: A Theoretical and Practical Study*. Emerald Group Publishing Limited. DOI: 10.1108/S2042-144320140000006001

Andersson, Å. E. (2008). Regionförstoring för tillväxt och jobb. [Regional expansion for growth and jobs] In *Handelskammarens rapport 3 2008*. Handelskammaren.

Annamalah, S., Paraman, P., Ahmed, S., Dass, R., Sentosa, I., Pertheban, T. R., Shamsudin, F., Kadir, B., Aravindan, K. L., Raman, M., Hoo, W. C., & Singh, P. (2023). The role of open innovation and a normalizing mechanism of social capital in the tourism industry. *Journal of Open Innovation*, *9*(2), 100056. DOI: 10.1016/j.joitmc.2023.100056

Anom, R. (2021) Contemporary Challenges of the Indonesian Vernacular Architecture in addressing Climate Change. IOP Conference Series: Earth and Environment Rautela Piyoosh, Joshi Girish Chandra (2007) Earthquake safe Koti Banal Architecture of Uttarakhand, India. Disaster Mitigation and Management Centre. Department of Disaster Management. Uttarakhand India.

Antonescu, D. (2013), Politica de dezvoltare regională a României în etapa postaderare, Bucureşti, Academia Română, Institutul Naţional de Cercetări Economice, [Romania's regional development policy in the post-accession stage, Bucharest, Romanian Academy, National Institute of Economic Research]. ISSN: 2285 – 7036

Antunes, M., Viegas, M., Varum, C., & Pinho, C. (2020). The impact of structural funds on regional growth: A panel data spatial analysis. *Inter Economics*, *55*(5), 312–319. DOI: 10.1007/s10272-020-0921-1

Apocada del Hoyo, M. (2016). Middle East and the great powers. International Relations and the Cold War, 1945-1948. Retrieved from https://dialnet.unirioja.es/servlet/dctes?codigo=155576

Apuuli, K. (2021). The competing mediations in the post-Qaddafi Libyan political crisis. *International Negotiation*, *8*(1), 1–31. DOI: 10.1163/15718069-bja10019

Armesto López, X. A., & Gómez Martín, B. (2004). High quality agrarian food products, tourism and local development. The case of Priorat | Productos agroalimentarios de calidad, turismo y desarrollo local: El caso del Priorat. *Cuadernos Geograficos*, *34*, 83–94.

Arora, S. (2015). Micromax Informatics Ltd: Marketing strategy for emerging markets. *Emerald Emerging Markets Case Studies*, *5*(5), 1–22. DOI: 10.1108/EEMCS-06-2014-0158

Arranz, M., & Martín, J. (2009). The factors of socio-economic development and territorial of Morocco: The contribution of the remittances from migrants. *Annales de Géographie*, *29*(2), 9–35.

Artetxe, A. (2016). The European Union and Spain in their relationship with the Maghreb: The cases of Morocco and Algeria. Retrieved from http://hdl.handle.net/10810/18490

Arya, A. S. (1994) Earthquake Engineering. Tenth World Congress. Rotterdam. ISBN 90 5410 060 5

Attard, J., McMahon, H., Doody, P., Belfrage, J., Clark, C., Ugarte, J. A., Pérez-Camacho, M. N., Cuenca Martín, M. S., Giráldez Morales, A. J., & Gaffey, J. (2020). Mapping and Analysis of Biomass Supply Chains in Andalusia and the Republic of Ireland. *Sustainability (Basel)*, *12*(11), 4595. DOI: 10.3390/su12114595

Autor, D. H., Levy, F., & Murnane, R. J. (2003). The skill content of recent technological change: An empirical exploration. *The Quarterly Journal of Economics*, *118*(4), 1279–1333. DOI: 10.1162/003355303322552801

Awan, U., Sroufe, R., & Shahbaz, M. (2021). Industry 4.0 and the circular economy: A literature review and recommendations for future research. *Business Strategy and the Environment*, *30*(4), 2038–2060. DOI: 10.1002/bse.2731

Ayala García, C., & Tami Cortés, M. D. (2020). La arquitectura, el espacio público y el derecho a la ciudad. Entre lo físico y lo vivencial [Architecture, public space, and the right to the city. Between the physical and the experiential]. *Revista de Arquitectura*, *22*(1), 11–25.

Ayuntamiento de Sevilla. *Plan de Acción por el Clima y la Energía Sostenible (PACES)*. 2016. Available online: https://www.sevilla.org/servicios/economia/agencia-energia-sostenibilidad/documentos/paces-2016-aprobado.pdf. Accessed on 14 September 2024.

Azevedo, A. (2009). Are you proud to live here? – A residents oriented place marketing audit (attachment, self-esteem and identity). In *38th European Marketing Academy Conference* (pp. 26-29).

Babshetti, V., Singh, J., & Yaragol, P. (2022). The impact of COVID-19 on the socio-economic indicators of the selected Asian countries. *India Quarterly*, *78*(1), 28–46. DOI: 10.1177/09749284211068162

Bachtrögler, J., Fratesi, U., & Perucca, G. (2020). The influence of the local context on the implementation and impact of EU Cohesion Policy. *Regional Studies*, *54*(1), 21–34. DOI: 10.1080/00343404.2018.1551615

Bachtrögler-Unger, J., Dolls, M., Krolage, C., Schüle, P., Taubenböck, H., & Weigand, M. (2024). New evidence on the effects of EU Regional Policy. *Economic Policy Forum*, 25(1). https://www.econpol.eu/publications/forum-2024-1-big-data-based-economic-insights/new-evidence-on-the-effects-of-eu-regional-policy

Badri, M., Davis, D. & Davis, D. (2000). Operations strategy, environmental uncertainty, and performance: a path analytic model of industries in developing countries. *Omega, 28(2):155-173.* doi: 00041-9.DOI: 10.1016/S03050483(99)

Badri, M., & Alshare, K. (2008). A path analytic model and measurement of the business value of e-government: An international perspective. *International Journal of Information Management*, *28*(6), 524–535. DOI: 10.1016/j.ijinfomgt.2006.10.004

Bagautdinova, N. G., Galeeva, G. M., Fazlieva, E. P., & Arzhantseva, N. V. (2014), Investment Attractiveness of the Region as the Factor in the Formation of Competitive Advantages Mediterranean Journal of Social Sciences, Vol 5, No 28 (2014), ISSN 2039-2117(Online), DOI: DOI: 10.5901/mjss.2014.v5n28p9

Baggio, R. (2020). Tourism destinations: A universality conjecture based on network science. *Annals of Tourism Research*, *82*, 102929. DOI: 10.1016/j.annals.2020.102929

Baggio, R., Scott, N., & Cooper, C. (2010). Network science: A review focused on tourism. *Annals of Tourism Research*, *37*(3), 802–827. DOI: 10.1016/j.annals.2010.02.008

Bagozzi, R., & Heatherton, T. (1994). A general approach to representing multifaceted personality construct: Application to state self-esteem? *Structural Equation Modeling*, *1*(1), 35–67. DOI: 10.1080/10705519409539961

Bahadori, M. N., & Fariborz, H. (1986). Thermal performance of adobe structures with domed roofs and moist internal surfaces. *Solar Energy*, *36*(4), 365–375. DOI: 10.1016/0038-092X(86)90154-4

Bajaj, H. (2018). Corporate Governance: At the Crossroads? *Governance and Governed: Multi-Country Perspectives on State. Social Development*, •••, 189–205.

Balkytė, A., & Tvaronavičienė, M. (2010). Perception of competitiveness in the context of sustainable development: Facets of "sustainable competitiveness". *Journal of Business Economics and Management*, *11*(2), 341–365. www.jbem.vgtu.lt. DOI: 10.3846/jbem.2010.17

Ballings, M., McCullough, H., & Bharadwaj, N. (2018). Cause marketing and customer profitability. *Journal of the Academy of Marketing Science*, *46*(2), 234–251. DOI: 10.1007/s11747-017-0571-4

Baloglu, S., & McCleary, K. W. (1999). A model of destination image formation. *Annals of Tourism Research, 26*(4), 868–897. DOI: 10.1016/S0160-7383(99)00030-4

Banerjee, S. B. (2003). Who sustains whose development? Sustainable development and the reinvention of nature. *Organization Studies, 24*(1), 143–180. DOI: 10.1177/0170840603024001341

Barauskaite, G., & Streimikiene, D. (2021). Corporate social responsibility and financial performance of companies: The puzzle of concepts, definitions and assessment methods. *Corporate Social Responsibility and Environmental Management, 28*(1), 278–287. DOI: 10.1002/csr.2048

Barbosa, G. S., Drach, P. R., & Corbella, O. D. (2014). A conceptual review of the terms sustainable development and sustainability. *Journal of Social Sciences, 3*(2), 1.

Barman Amal, Roy Madhumita, Dasgupta Arpan (2020) Vernacular architecture of Majuli, Assam- meaning, model and metaphor in integrating the environmental, socio-economic and cultural realms. International Journal of Creative Research Thoughts. Vol 8. Issue 7.

Barman, A. (2021). "New playbook: Is Plaeto out to disrupt kids' sneaker market dominated by Bata, Nike and Campus?", Economic Times (12th November 2021), Accessed on 23rd December 2021 from, https://economictimes.indiatimes.com

Barros, C., & Gama, R. (2009). Territorial marketing as an instrument for valuing rural spaces: An application in the Schist Villages network. *Caderno de Geografia, 28*(29), 93–106.

Bassil, C., Saleh, A., & Anwar, S. (2019). Terrorism and tourism demand: A case study of Lebanon, Türkiye and Israel. *Current Issues in Tourism, 22*(1), 50–70. DOI: 10.1080/13683500.2017.1397609

Beck, D. F., & Ferasso, M. (2022). Image of cities as a tool for urban governance in Mercosur: contributions of city and urban branding. ReMark - Brazilian Marketing Magazine, 21(1), 9–28. DOI: 10.5585/remark.v21i1.19354

Becken, S. (2017). Evidence of a low-carbon tourism paradigm? *Journal of Sustainable Tourism, 25*(6), 832–850. DOI: 10.1080/09669582.2016.1251446

Becken, S., Simmons, D. G., & Frampton, C. (2003). Energy use associated with different travel choices. *Tourism Management, 24*(3), 267–277. DOI: 10.1016/S0261-5177(02)00066-3

Becker, S. O., Egger, P. H., & von Ehrlich, M. (2013). Absorptive capacity and the growth and investment effects of regional transfers: A regression discontinuity design with heterogeneous treatment effects. *American Economic Journal. Economic Policy, 5*(4), 29–77. DOI: 10.1257/pol.5.4.29

Belicia, T. X. Y., & Islam, M. S. (2018). Towards a decommodified wildlife tourism: Why market environmentalism is not enough for conservation. *Societies (Basel, Switzerland), 8*(3), 59. DOI: 10.3390/soc8030059

Beltrán Rodríguez, M. (2016). La importancia de la vitalidad urbana [The importance of urban vitality]. *Ciudades*, (19), 169–182.

Bender, E. M., Gebru, T., McMillan-Major, A., & Shmitchell, S. (2021). On the dangers of stochastic parrots: Can language models be too big? *FAccT '21: Proceedings of the 2021 ACM Conference on Fairness, Accountability, and Transparency*. DOI: 10.1145/3442188.3445922

Ben-Eli, M. U. (2018). Sustainability: Definition and five core principles, a systems perspective. *Sustainability Science, 13*(5), 1337–1343. DOI: 10.1007/s11625-018-0564-3

Bentler, P., & Yuan, K. (1999). Structural Equation Modeling with Small Samples: Test Statistics. *Multivariate Behavioral Research, 34*(2), 181–197. DOI: 10.1207/S15327906Mb340203 PMID: 26753935

Berbel, J., & Posadillo, A. (2018). Review and analysis of alternatives for the valorisation of agro-industrial olive oil by-products. *Sustainability (Basel), 10*(1), 237. DOI: 10.3390/su10010237

Berbel-Pineda, J. M., Palacios-Florencio, B., Ramírez-Hurtado, J. M., & Santos-Roldán, L. (2019). Gastronomic experience as a factor of motivation in the tourist movements. *International Journal of Gastronomy and Food Science, 18*, 100171. Advance online publication. DOI: 10.1016/j.ijgfs.2019.100171

Berger-Walliser, G., & Scott, I. (2018). Redefining corporate social responsibility in an era of globalization and regulatory hardening. *American Business Law Journal, 55*(1), 167–218. DOI: 10.1111/ablj.12119

Berroeta Torres, H., & Vidal Moranta, T. (2012). La historia de la ciudad es la de sus espacios públicos [The history of the city is that of its public spaces]. *Revista de Urbanismo*, (26), 1–15.

Bertoletti, A., Berbegal-Mirabent, J., & Agasisti, T. (2022). Higher education systems and regional economic development in Europe: A combined approach using econometric and machine learning methods, Socio-Economic Planning Sciences, Vol 82. *Socio-Economic Planning Sciences, 101231*, 101231. Advance online publication. DOI: 10.1016/j.seps.2022.101231

Bertolini, L., Le Clercq, F., & Kapoen, L. (2005). Sustainable accessibility: A conceptual framework to integrate transport and land use plan-making. Two test-applications in the Netherlands and a reflection on the way forward. *Transport Policy, 12*(3), 207–220. DOI: 10.1016/j.tranpol.2005.01.006

Beugelsdijk, M., & Eijffinger, S. (2005). The effectiveness of structural policy in the European union: An empirical analysis for the EU-15 in 1995-2001. *Journal of Common Market Studies, 43*(1), 37–51. DOI: 10.1111/j.0021-9886.2005.00545.x

Beyers, L. A., & Schutte, N. E. (2018). Guidelines for Improving Infrastructure Development in the Rural Communities of Bushbuckridge. *Studies of Tribes and Tribals, 16*(1-2), 32–38. DOI: 10.31901/24566799.2018/16.1-2.367

Bhaktikul, K., Aroonsrimorakot, S., Laiphrakpam, M., & Paisantanakij, W. (2021). Toward a low-carbon tourism for sustainable development: A study based on a royal project for highland community development in Chiang Rai, Thailand. *Environment, Development and Sustainability, 23*(7), 10743–10762. DOI: 10.1007/s10668-020-01083-4

Bhambri, R., Mehta, M., Dobhal, D. P., & Gupta, A. K. (2015). *Glacier Lake Iniventory of Uttarakhand*. Wadia Institute of Himalayan Geology.

Bhukya, R., & Paul, J. (2023). Social influence research in consumer behavior: What we learned and what we need to learn?–A hybrid systematic literature review. *Journal of Business Research, 162*, 113870. DOI: 10.1016/j.jbusres.2023.113870

Bi, H., & Nasir, N. B. M. (2024). Innovative Approaches to Preserving Intangible Cultural Heritage through AI-Driven Interactive Experiences. *Academic Journal of Science and Technology*, *12*(2), 81–84. DOI: 10.54097/98nre954

Binns, T., & Nel, E. (2002). Tourism as a local development strategy in South Africa. *The Geographical Journal*, *168*(3), 235–247. DOI: 10.1111/1475-4959.00051

Björk, P., & Kauppinen-Räisänen, H. (2016). Local food: A source for destination attraction. *International Journal of Contemporary Hospitality Management*, *28*(1), 177–194. DOI: 10.1108/IJCHM-05-2014-0214

Björner, E., & Aronsson, L. (2022). Decentralized place branding through multiple authors and narratives: The collective branding of a small town in Sweden. *Journal of Marketing Management*, *38*(13-14), 1587–1612. DOI: 10.1080/0267257X.2022.2043415

Blain, C., Levy, S. E., & Ritchie, J. R. B. (2005). Destination Branding: Insights and Practices from Destination Management Organizations. *Journal of Travel Research*, *43*(4), 328–338. DOI: 10.1177/0047287505274646

Boldrin, M., & Canova, F. (2001). Inequality and convergence in Europe's regions: Reconsidering European regional policies. *Economic Policy*, *32*(32), 205–253. DOI: 10.1111/1468-0327.00074

Bollen, K., & Hoyle, R. (2012). Latent Variables in Structural Equation Modeling. In Hoyle, R. H. (Ed.), *Handbook of Structural Equation Modeling* (Vol. 1, pp. 56–67). The Guilford Press., DOI: 10.1177/0049124189017003004

Botezatu, M. A., Ivanescu, I. M., Ivanescu, M. M., & Diaconescu, F. (2021), Challenges of Digital Economies: An Analysis of the Factors that Influence Economic Development of the EU Member States, in Under the Pressure of Digitalization: Challenges and Solutions at Organizational and Industrial Levels, First Edition, Pag: 32-39, ISBN: 979-12-80225-27-6, 5th Edition International e-conference "Enterprises in the Global Economy *under Pandemic*" EGE, (December 14th, 2020), https://www.webofscience.com/wos/woscc/full-record/WOS:000683887600005

Botezatu, M. A. (2020). Organizational Sustainability, Modern Management and IT&C Impact on Local Development. In *Monograph:Enterprise in the Global Economy: Challenges of the Current Global Environment, 4th Int. e-conference "Enterprises in the Global Economy" EGE, (14th october 2019)* (pp. 62–69). Filodiritto Publisher.

Botha, I., Botezatu, M. A., Tabusca, A., & Hosszu, A. (2023), *Economic factors correlated with marriage and divorce rates in European Union countries*, Economic Computation and Economic Cybernetics Studies and Research, Issue 3/2023; Vol. 57, pg. 133-150, ISSN: 0424-267X, ASE Publishing, DOI: , https://ecocyb.ase.ro/Articles2023_3.htmDOI: 10.24818/18423264/57.3.23.08

Botha, I., Botezatu, M.A., Coancă, M. (2020), Innovative Calculation Model for Evaluating Regional Sustainable Development, Economic Computation and Economic Cybernetics Studies and Research, Vol. 54, Issue 3/2020, pg.5-24, DOI: DOI: 10.24818/18423264/54.3.20.01

Botha, I., Gherghina, . C., Simionescu, L. N., Botezatu, M. A., & Coculescu, C. (2022), Investigating the drivers of renewable energy production: Panel data evidence for Central and Eastern European Countries, Economic Computation and Economic Cybernetics Studies and Research, Vol. 56, Issue 1/2022, pg. 5-22, eISSN 1842–3264, ASE Publishing, DOI: , https://ecocyb.ase.ro/nr2022_1/CONTENTS_2022_1.pdfDOI: 10.24818/18423264/56.1.22.01

Bouayad-Agha, S., Turpin, N., & Védrine, L. (2013). Fostering the development of European regions: A spatial dynamic panel data analysis of the impact of Cohesion Policy. *Regional Studies*, *47*(9), 1573–1593. DOI: 10.1080/00343404.2011.628930

Bouizgar, M., Aarabe, M., Khizzou, N. B., Alla, L., & Benjelloun, A. (2025). Smart Territorial Marketing and Promotion of Customer Engagement Towards the Territorial Brand: A Systematic Review of Literature. *Sustainable and Intelligent Territorial Marketing and Entrepreneurship*, 129-158.

Boumahdi, I., & Zaoujal, N. (2023). Regional Well-Being Disparities in Morocco and its OECD Partners [SpringerLink]. *Social Indicators Research*, *167*(1-3), 183–211. DOI: 10.1007/s11205-023-03097-7 PMID: 37304458

Bouyghrissi, S., Murshed, M., Jindal, A., Berjaoui, A., Mahmood, H., & Khanniba, M. (2022). The importance of facilitating renewable energy transition for Abating CO2 emissions in Morocco. *Environmental Science and Pollution Research International*, *29*(14), 20752–20767. DOI: 10.1007/s11356-021-17179-x PMID: 34741744

Bradbrook, C. (2018). Theoretical foundations for CI applications. In *Using collective impact to bring community change* (pp. 17–38). Routledge. DOI: 10.4324/9781315545073-2

Bradley, O. J., & Botchway, G. O. (2018). Communicating corporate social responsibility (CSR) in the coffee industry: An examination of indicators disclosed. *Sustainability Accounting. Management and Policy Journal*, *9*(2), 139–164.

Braun, E. (2008, October 30). City Marketing: Towards an Integrated Approach (No. EPS-2008-142-ORG). ERIM Ph.D. Series Research in Management. Erasmus Research Institute of Management. Retrieved from http://hdl.handle.net/1765/13694

Braun, V., & Clarke, V. (2006). Using thematic analysis in psychology. *Qualitative Research in Psychology*, *3*(2), 77–101. DOI: 10.1191/1478088706qp063oa

Breeze, B., & Wiepking, P. (2020). Different drivers: Exploring employee involvement in corporate philanthropy. *Journal of Business Ethics*, *165*(3), 453–467. DOI: 10.1007/s10551-018-4093-x

Brito, C., & Correia, R. (2012). Regions as Networks: Towards a Conceptual Framework of Territorial Dynamics. In *International Trade from Economic and Policy Perspective* (p. 17). IntechOpen.

Browne, M., & Cudeck, R. (1993). *Alternative ways of assessing model fit.* In S. Publication (Ed.), Testing structural equation model (pp. 136-162). Bollen, K.A. & Long, J.S. DOI: 10.1177/0049124192021002005

Brown, M. E., Rizzuto, T., & Singh, P. (2019). Strategic compatibility, collaboration and collective impact for community change. *Leadership and Organization Development Journal*, *40*(4), 421–434. DOI: 10.1108/LODJ-05-2018-0180

Brown, M., & Moore, T. L. (2019). Addressing complex public problems through coalition-based approaches: Collective impact and the CEP competencies. *The International Journal of Research on Service-Learning and Community Engagement*, *7*(1). Advance online publication. DOI: 10.37333/001c.11491

Brown, S., Brison, N., & Bennett, G. (2020). Corporate Social Marketing: An analysis of consumer response to Nike's campaign featuring Colin Kaepernick. *Global Sport Business Journal*, *8*(1), 33–50.

Brundtland, I. (1987). Desarrollo y cooperación económica internacional medio ambiente. Informe de la comisión mundial sobre el medio ambiente y el Desarrollo [Development and International Economic Cooperation and the Environment. Report of the World Commission on Environment and Development].

Bryden, J. M., Efstratoglou, S., Ferenczi, T., Johnson, T., Knickel, K., Refsgaard, K., & Thomson, K. J. (2012). Multifunctionality, sustainable territorial development and rural policies in Europe: Some concluding reflections. In *Towards Sustainable Rural Regions in Europe* (pp. 302–320). Routledge. DOI: 10.4324/9780203831403

Brynjolfsson, E., & McAfee, A. (2017). *The second machine age: Work, progress, and prosperity in a time of brilliant technologies*. W.W. Norton & Company.

Busalim, A. H., & Hussin, A. R. C. (2016). Understanding social commerce: A systematic literature review and directions for further research. *International Journal of Information Management*, *36*(6), 1075–1088. DOI: 10.1016/j.ijinfomgt.2016.06.005

Bushbuckridge Local Municipality. (2021) Local Economic Development Forum: Terms of Reference. Bushbuckridge LED Forum Launch, 10th -11th June 2021, Swadini Forever Resorts, Hoedspruit, South Africa.

BW Online Bureau. (2021). 'Plaeto To Power Untapped Indian Market for Kids' Footwear', Business World, December 3, http://www.businessworld.in Accessed on December 22, 2021.

Çakir Keleş, M. (2021). Gastronomy Tourism Resources and Local Food. In *Gastronomy and Hospitality Studies in Tourism*.

Calgary Homeless Foundation. (2021). Guiding the Fight Against Homelessness. *Focus (San Francisco, Calif.)*, *2025*, •••. https://www.calgaryhomeless.com/discover-learn/our-approach/plans/

Calgary Youth Sector Refresh Steering Committee. (2017). Calgary Plan to Prevent and End Youth Homelessness–2017 Refresh. *Available at:*http://homelesshub. ca/sites/default/files/Youth_Plan_Refresh_2017. pdf

Callon, M., Courtial, J. P., & Laville, F. (1991). Co-word analysis as a tool for describing the network of interactions between basic and technological research: The case of polymer chemistry. *Scientometrics*, *22*(1), 155–205. DOI: 10.1007/BF02019280

Camacho, O. Mariel (2021). "Las relaciones socio–espaciales en la habitabilidad de conjuntos de vivienda social", en *Revista Internacional de Ciencias Sociales Interdisciplinares*, Vol. 10, núm. 1, Common Ground Research Networks, Estados Unidos de América.

Cantos, J. M., Balsalobre-Lorente, D., & García-Nicolás, C. (2020). *Why the financial aid of the EU's regional policy does not impact on the public investment level? The case of the Spanish regions*. Public Affairs., DOI: 10.1002/pa.2295

Capello, R. (2011). Location, regional growth and local development theories. *Aestimum (Firenze)*, •••, 1–25.

Cappelen, A., Castellacci, F., Fagerberg, J., & Verspagen, B. (2003). The impact of EU regional support on growth and convergence in the European Union. *Journal of Common Market Studies*, *41*(4), 621–644. DOI: 10.1111/1468-5965.00438

Cappelli, P., Singh, H., Singh, J., & Useem, M. (2010). The India way: Lessons for the US. *The Academy of Management Perspectives*, *24*(2), 6–24. DOI: 10.5465/amp.24.2.6

Cardoza, D., Romero, I., Martínez, T., Ruíz, E., Gallego, F. J., López-Linares, J. C., Manzanares, P., & Castro, E. (2021). Location of Biorefineries Based on Olive-Derived Biomass in Andalusia, Spain. *Energies*, *14*(11), 3052. DOI: 10.3390/en14113052

Caridad, J. (2016). *Path Analysis. Structural models with AMOS*. (pp. 47-72). EDF, S.L.

Carral, E. V., Del Río, M., & López, Z. (2020). Gastronomy and tourism: Socioeconomic and territorial implications in santiago de compostela-galiza (NW Spain). *International Journal of Environmental Research and Public Health*, *17*(17), 1–25. DOI: 10.3390/ijerph17176173 PMID: 32854422

Carvajal-Trujillo, E., Pérez-Gálvez, J. C., & Orts-Cardador, J. J. (2024). Exploring tourists' pro-environmental behavior: a bibliometric analysis over two decades (1999–2023). *Journal of Tourism Futures*. DOI: 10.1108/JTF-02-2024-0033

Cehan, A., Eva, M., & Ia u, C. (2021). A multilayer network approach to tourism collaboration. *Journal of Hospitality and Tourism Management*, *46*, 316–326. DOI: 10.1016/j.jhtm.2021.01.006

Cerezo, J., & Fruet, V. (2022). *Spanish and International Economy* (pp. 60-86). EDF, S.L.

Cham, T., Lim, Y., & Sigala, M. (2021). Marketing and social influences, hospital branding, and medical tourists' behavioral intention: Before- and after-service consumption perspective. *International Journal of Tourism Research*. Advance online publication. DOI: 10.1002/jtr.2489

Chan, G. K., Selvadurai, S., & Aziz, R. A. (2020). The Culture Of Heritage Conservation In Malaysia: A Study Of Eco-Tourism In Langkawi. e-BANGI Journal, 17(1).

Chan, C., Berger, J., & Van Boven, L. (2012). Identifiable but Not Identical: Combining Social Identity and Uniqueness Motives in Choice. *The Journal of Consumer Research*, *39*(3), 561–573. DOI: 10.1086/664804

Chatterjee, S. R. (2016). Corporate social responsibility in India: From traditional ethos to contemporary transitions. *Key Initiatives in Corporate Social Responsibility: Global Dimension of CSR in Corporate Entities*, 303-323.

Chavan, M., Gowan, S., & Vogeley, J. (2023). Collaborative corporate social responsibility praxis: Case studies from India. *Social Responsibility Journal*, *19*(2), 229–248. DOI: 10.1108/SRJ-06-2021-0216

Cheng, Q., Su, B., & Tan, J. (2013). Developing an evaluation index system for low-carbon tourist attractions in China–A case study examining the Xixi wetland. *Tourism Management, 36*, 314-320http:// DOI: 10.1016/j.tourman.2012.10.019

Chen, X., & Huang, R. (2018). The impact of diverse corporate social responsibility practices on consumer product evaluations. *Journal of Product and Brand Management, 27*(6), 701–715. DOI: 10.1108/JPBM-01-2017-1390

Chernev, A., & Blair, S. (2015). Doing well by doing good: The benevolent halo of corporate social responsibility. *The Journal of Consumer Research, 41*(6), 1412–1425. DOI: 10.1086/680089

Cheung, M. L., Pires, G., Rosenberger, P. J.III, Leung, W. K. S., & Chang, M. K. (2021). The role of social media elements in driving co-creation and engagement. *Asia Pacific Journal of Marketing and Logistics, 33*(10), 1994–2018. DOI: 10.1108/APJML-03-2020-0176

Chhabra, D. (2019). Authenticity and the authentication of heritage: Dialogical perceptiveness. *Journal of Heritage Tourism, 14*(5-6), 389–395. DOI: 10.1080/1743873X.2019.1644340

Chipp, K., & Maphalala, J. (2019). When elephants fight: South African washing powder wars. *Emerald Emerging Markets Case Studies, 9*(1), 1–24. DOI: 10.1108/EEMCS-02-2018-0031

Chopdar, P. K., Lytras, M. D., & Visvizi, A. (2022). Exploring factors influencing bicycle-sharing adoption in India: A UTAUT 2 based mixed-method approach. *International Journal of Emerging Markets, 18*(11), 5109–5134. DOI: 10.1108/IJOEM-06-2021-0862

Cho, Y. J., Wang, Y., & Hsu, L. L. I. (2016). Constructing Taiwan's low-carbon tourism development suitability evaluation indicators. *Asia Pacific Journal of Tourism Research, 21*(6), 658–677. DOI: 10.1080/10941665.2015.1068193

Chronis, A. (2017). Coconstructing heritage at the Gettysburg storyscape. In *The Political Nature of Cultural Heritage and Tourism* (pp. 87–107). Routledge.

Chung, N., Lee, H., Kim, J. Y., & Koo, C. (2018). The role of augmented reality for experience-influenced environments: The case of cultural heritage tourism in Korea. *Journal of Travel Research, 57*(5), 627–643. DOI: 10.1177/0047287517708255

Clifford, J., & Barnes, K. (2022). Why and what to measure? The justification for social impact measurement. *Social impact measurement for a sustainable future: The power of aesthetics and practical implications*, 49-73.

Cocchini, A. (2021). A decade of war in Syria: Current situation and possible outcomes. *UNISCI, 2021*(57), 149–183. DOI: 10.31439/UNISCI-124

Coffey, W. J., & Polese, M. (1985). Local development: Conceptual bases and policy implications. *Regional Studies, 19*(2), 85–93. DOI: 10.1080/09595238500185101

Cohen, S. & Jaïdi, L. (2013). *Morocco: Globalization and its consequences.* Routledge. DOI: 10.4324/9781315810904

Colombo, S., & Soler, E. (2021). Europe and the 'New' Middle East: Geopolitical shifts and strategic choices. *Journal of Balkan & Near Eastern Studies, 23*(3), 403–422. DOI: 10.1080/19448953.2021.1888246

Commission of the European Communities. (2002). *Corporate Social Responsibility: A business contribution to Sustainable Development.*

Consejería de Empleo y Desarrollo Tecnológico de la Junta de Andalucía. *Plan Energético de Andalucía 2003-2006.* 2003. Available online: https://www.agenciaandaluzadelaenergia.es/sites/default/files/1129906106388_plean2003-20061.pdf. Accessed on 4 July 2024.

Consejería de Industria. Energía y Minas. *Estrategia Energética de Andalucía 2030.* 2022. Available online: https://www.agenciaandaluzadelaenergia.es/sites/default/files/Documentos/Planificaci%C3%B3n/estrategia_energetica_andalucia_2030-8_junio_2022_def.pdf. Accessed on 4 July 2024.

Consejería de Medio Ambiente y Ordenación del Territorio de la Junta de Andalucía. *Actuaciones de la Junta de Andalucía en cambio climático/COP21.* 2018. Available online: https://www.juntadeandalucia.es/medioambiente/site/portalweb/menuitem.30d4b35a97db5c61716f2b105510e1ca/?vgnextoid=355466afc1141510VgnVCM2000000624e50aRCRD&vgnextchannel=4c770f000a421510VgnVCM2000000624e50aRCRD&vgnextfmt=portalwebSinMenu. Accessed on 14 September 2024.

Consejería de Medio Ambiente y Ordenación del Territorio de la Junta de Andalucía. *Medio Ambiente en Andalucía. Informe 1994.* 1994. Available online: http://www.juntadeandalucia.es/medioambiente/portal_web/ima/1994/ima94_ret.pdf. Accessed on 4 July 2024.

Consejería de Medio Ambiente. *Estrategia Andaluza de Desarrollo Sostenible: Agenda 21 Andalucía.* 2004. Available online: https://www.famp.es/export/sites/famp/.galleries/documentos-consejo-andaluz-gobiernos-locales/DOC-AGENDA-21.pdf. Accessed on 14 September 2024.

Consejería de Medio Ambiente. *Plan Andaluz de Acción por el Clima.* 2007. Available online: https://www.juntadeandalucia.es/medioambiente/portal/documents/20151/1009070/plan_accion_clima_mitigacion.pdf/bfcd49a4-1220-f59e-b5a6-6d221b3ee8f9. Accessed on 14 September 2024.

Consejería de Medio Ambiente. *Programa Andaluz de Adaptación al Cambio Climático.* 2010. Available online: https://www.juntadeandalucia.es/export/drupaljda/programa_adaptacion_clima.pdf. Accessed on 14 September 2024.

Constantin, D. L., & Dimian, G. C. (2007), Competitivitatea regiunilor din România în contextul integrării în Uniunea Europeană, Jurnalul Economic, nr. 24, https://core.ac.uk/download/pdf/6231368.pdf

Contreras, M. M., Romero, I., Moya, M., & Castro, E. (2020). Olive-derived biomass as a renewable source of value-added products. *Process Biochemistry (Barking, London, England), 97*, 43–56. DOI: 10.1016/j.procbio.2020.06.013

Cooper, M. (2006). *Demographic trends and implications for the city of Calgary.* Calgary, Alberta: Canadian Policy Research Networks. Corporation for Ohio Appalachian Development (COAD), available at: https://coadinc.org/

Correia, R., & Brito, C. (2011). The importance of marketing for tourism development: The case of Montalegre. Tourism and Development Magazine. ISSN 1645-9261. 16, p. 127-143

Correia, A., Kim, S., & Kozak, M. (2020). Gastronomy experiential traits and their effects on intentions for recommendation: A fuzzy set approach. *International Journal of Tourism Research, 22*(3), 351–363. DOI: 10.1002/jtr.2340

Cortez, J. U. (2020). Comisión Económica para América Latina y el Caribe (2019), Planificación para el desarrollo territorial sostenible en América Latina y el Caribe [Economic Commission for Latin America and the Caribbean (2019), Planning for sustainable territorial development in Latin America and the Caribbean]. *Revista de Estudios Regionales*, (117), 175–177.

Cosquer, M., & Jousselme, C. (2023). The experience of parents in Ronald McDonald houses in France. *Archives de Pédiatrie, 30*(4), 219–225. DOI: 10.1016/j.arcped.2023.02.004 PMID: 36990937

Creswell, J. W., & Creswell, J. D. (2005). *Mixed methods research: Developments, debates, and dilemma*. Berrett-Koehler Publishers.

Cunha, S., Barroco, C., & Antunes, J. (2019). Food tourism as a differentiating factor of the destinations: The case of Portugal | O turismo gastronómico como fator diferenciador dos destinos: O caso de Portugal. *RISTI - Revista Iberica de Sistemas e Tecnologias de Informacao, 2019*(E24), 409–422.

Czernek-Marszałek, K. (2019). Applying mixed methods in social network research–The case of co-operation in a Polish tourist destination. *Journal of Destination Marketing & Management, 11*, 40–52. DOI: 10.1016/j.jdmm.2018.10.004

D'Auria, A., Russo Spena, T., & Bifulco, F. (2021). Proximity marketing and context-information awareness. In *Digital Transformation in the Cultural Heritage Sector: Challenges to Marketing in the New Digital Era* (pp. 161–180). Springer International Publishing. DOI: 10.1007/978-3-030-63376-9_8

D'Auria, A., Tregua, M., & Vallejo-Martos, M. C. (2018). Modern conceptions of cities as smart and sustainable and their commonalities. *Sustainability (Basel), 10*(8), 2642. DOI: 10.3390/su10082642

Dada, A. D., & Alibaba, H. Z. (2023). Comparison analysis between the components of vernacular and modern architectures for sustainable housing in Niger State. *IOP Conference Series. Earth and Environmental Science, 1210*(1), 012011. DOI: 10.1088/1755-1315/1210/1/012011

Dai, Y. Y., Shie, A. J., Chu, J. H., & Wu, Y. C. J. (2022). Low-carbon travel motivation and constraint: Scales development and validation. *International Journal of Environmental Research and Public Health, 19*(9), 5123. DOI: 10.3390/ijerph19095123 PMID: 35564516

Dall'erba, S., & Le Gallo, J. (2008). Regional convergence and the impact of European structural funds over 1989-1999: A spatial econometric analysis. *Papers in Regional Science, 87*(2), 219–244. DOI: 10.1111/j.1435-5957.2008.00184.x

Dallabrida, V., Tomporoski, A., & Sakr, M. (2016). From territorial marketing to territory branding: Theoretical concepts, analyzes and prospects for the Planalto Norte Catarinense. *Interactions (Campo Grande), 17*. Advance online publication. DOI: 10.20435/1984-042X-2016-v.17-n.4(10)

Dancausa-Millan, G., Millán-Vázquez de la Torre, M. G., & Huete-Alcocer, N. (2022). Olive oil as a gourmet ingredient in contemporary cuisine. A gastronomic tourism proposal. *International Journal of Gastronomy and Food Science, 29*, 100548. Advance online publication. DOI: 10.1016/j.ijgfs.2022.100548

Das, A., Gujre, N., Devi, R. J., & Mitra, S. (2021). A review on traditional ecological knowledge and its role in natural resources management: North East India, a cultural paradise. *Environmental Management*, •••, 1–22. PMID: 34791537

Dash, A. (2024). Smart mobility in smart cities: transforming the experiences of citizens into the future of smart cities. *Transforming Government: People. Process and Policy*, *18*(2), 287–302.

Dash, M., & Shetty, R. (2012). The Impact of Global Recession on the Foreign Exchange Exposure of Indian Readymade Apparel Manufacturing Companies. *Asian Journal of Research in Business Economics and Management*, *2*(5), 169–177.

Das, J. K., Taneja, S., & Arora, H. (Eds.). (2021). *Corporate social responsibility and sustainable development: Strategies, practices and business models*. Taylor & Francis. DOI: 10.4324/9780429295997

Datos Macro. (2022). *CO2 emissions in China*. Datos Macro 2022. https://datosmacro.expansion.com/energia-y-medio-ambiente/emisiones-co2/china

Dawson, J., Stewart, E. J., Lemelin, H., & Scott, D. (2010). The carbon cost of polar bear viewing tourism in Churchill, Canada. *Journal of Sustainable Tourism*, *18*(3), 319–336. DOI: 10.1080/09669580903215147

de Agricultura, C. Pesca y Desarrollo Rural de la Junta de Andalucía. *Estrategia Andaluza de Bioeconomía Circular*. 2018. Available online: https://www.juntadeandalucia.es/export/drupaljda/Estrategia_Andaluza_Bioeconomia_Circular_EABC_18.09.2018.pdf. Accessed on 14 September 2024.

de Agricultura, C. Pesca y Desarrollo Rural de la Junta de Andalucía. *Plan Estratégico para la Agroindustria de Andalucía Horizonte 2020*. 2017. Available online: https://www.juntadeandalucia.es/export/drupaljda/Propuesta_Plan_Agroindustria_Andaluza_Horizonte_2020_2017_11_30.pdf. Accessed on 14 September 2021.

de Agricultura, C., Pesca, A., & de la Junta de Andalucía, D. R. *Aforo de la producción de olivar en Andalucía – Campaña 2023/2024*. 2023. Available online: https://www.juntadeandalucia.es/sites/default/files/inline-files/2023/10/Estimacion_ACEITE_MESA_2023_24.pdf. Accessed on 4 July 2024.

De Chiara, A. (2015). From stakeholder engagement to the collective-impact approach for sustainability paths in complex problems. *Sinergie Italian Journal of Management*, *33*(Jan-Apr), 57–91.

De Chiara, A. (2017). Collective Impact Approach: A "Tool" for Managing Complex Problems and Business Clusters Sustainability. *Metropolitan Universities*, *28*(4), 101–114. DOI: 10.18060/21739

de Empleo, C. Empresa y Comercio de la Junta de Andalucía. *Estrategia Energética de Andalucía 2020*. 2013. Available online: https://www.agenciaandaluzadelaenergia.es/EEA/files/assets/basic-html/index.html#1. Accessed on 4 July 2024.

de Innovación, C. Ciencia y Empresa de la Junta de Andalucía. *Plan Andaluz de Sostenibilidad Energética 2007-2013*. 2007. Available online: https://www.agenciaandaluzadelaenergia.es/sites/default/files/2_pasener_2007-2013_documento_completo.pdf. Accessed on 4 July 2024.

De Moor, A. (2018). A community network ontology for participatory collaboration mapping: Towards collective impact. *Information (Basel)*, *9*(7), 151. DOI: 10.3390/info9070151

De Noni, I., Orsi, L., & Zanderighi, L. (2014). Attributes of Milan influencing city brand attractiveness. *Journal of Destination Marketing & Management, 3*(4), 218–226. DOI: 10.1016/j.jdmm.2014.06.001

De Oliveira, O. J., da Silva, F. F., Juliani, F., Barbosa, L. C. F. M., & Nunhes, T. V. (2019). Bibliometric method for mapping the state-of-the-art and identifying research gaps and trends in literature: An essential instrument to support the development of scientific projects. In Kunosic, S., & Zerem, E. (Eds.), *Scientometrics recent advances* (pp. 47–64). IntechOpen., DOI: 10.5772/intechopen.85856

De Toni, A., Vizzarri, M., Di Febbraro, M., Lasserre, B., Noguera, J., & Di Martino, P. (2021). Aligning Inner Peripheries with rural development in Italy: Territorial evidence to support policy contextualization. *Land Use Policy, 100*, 104899. DOI: 10.1016/j.landusepol.2020.104899

De Vries, E. L., & Duque, L. C. (2018). Small but sincere: How firm size and gratitude determine the effectiveness of cause marketing campaigns. *Journal of Retailing, 94*(4), 352–363. DOI: 10.1016/j.jretai.2018.08.002

Del Bo, C. F., & Sirtori, E. (2016). Additionality and regional public finance—Evidence from Italy. *Environment and Planning C. Environment and Planning. C, Government & Policy, 34*(5), 855–878. DOI: 10.1177/0263774X15614682

Delclòs-Alió, X., & Miralles-Guasch, C. (2018). Looking at Barcelona through Jane Jacobs's eyes: Mapping the basic conditions for urban vitality in a Mediterranean conurbation. *Land Use Policy, 75*, 505–517. DOI: 10.1016/j.landusepol.2018.04.026

Demeterova, B. (2023). Urban and Regional Planning for Territorial Cohesion. In *Public Policies for Territorial Cohesion* (pp. 129–143). Springer International Publishing. DOI: 10.1007/978-3-031-26228-9_7

Demirel, N., & Tekeli, E. K. (2022). Foodie tourist behavior. In *Tourist Behavior*. Past, Present, and Future. DOI: 10.1201/9781003282082-10

Department of Corporative Governance and Traditional Affairs. (2021). Local Economic Development (LED), [online] https://www.cogta.gov.za/index.php/local-economic-development-led/

Department of Provincial and Local Government of South Africa and Business Trsut. (2007) Nodal Economic Profiling Project Bushbuckridge Mpumalanga, [online] http://www.btrust.org.za/library/assets/uploads/documents/1_CIPPN_Bushbuckridge%20profile.PDF

Department of the Presidency Republic of South Africa. (2012) National Development Plan 2030, [online] https://www.gov.za/sites/default/files/Executive%20Summary-NDP%202030%20-%20Our%20future%20-%20make%20it%20work.pdf / https://www.gov.za/issues/national-development-plan-2030

Department of Tourism. (2011) National Tourism Sector Strategy 2016-2026. [online] www.gov.za/ites/default/files/National%20Tourism%20Sector%20Strategy%20NTSS%202016-2026.pdf

Department of Tourism. (2012) National Heritage and Cultural Tourism Strategy, [online] https://www.tourism.gov.za/AboutNDT/Branches1/domestic/Documents/National%20Heritage%20and%20Cultural%20Tourism%20Strategy.pdf

Destefanis, S., & Rehman, N. U. (2023). Investment, innovation activities and employment across European regions. *Structural Change and Economic Dynamics, 65*, 474–490. DOI: 10.1016/j.strueco.2023.03.013

Di Cataldo, M., & Monastiriotis, V. (2020). Regional needs, regional targeting and regional growth: An assessment of EU Cohesion Policy in UK regions. *Regional Studies, 54*(1), 35–47. DOI: 10.1080/00343404.2018.1498073

Diaconescu, D. M., Moraru, R., & Stănciulescu, G. (2016). Considerations on gastronomic tourism as a component of sustainable local development. *Amfiteatru Economic, 18*(Specialiss), 999–1014.

Diamantis, D., & Puhr, R. (2022). Corporate social responsibility and work–life balance provisions for employee quality of life in hospitality and tourism settings. *Worldwide Hospitality and Tourism Themes, 14*(3), 207–209. DOI: 10.1108/WHATT-02-2022-0026

Dick, W. (2015). Naandi Foundation: Delivering High Quality Elementary Education in India. In *Experiencing Innovation in Asia: Cases in Business Model Development* (pp. 27-44).

Dickinson, J. E., Lumsdon, L. M., & Robbins, D. (2011). Slow travel: Issues for tourism and climate change. *Journal of Sustainable Tourism, 19*(3), 281–300. DOI: 10.1080/09669582.2010.524704

Diemer, A., Iammarino, S., Rodríguez-Pose, A., & Storper, M. (2022). The regional development trap in Europe. *Economic Geography, 98*(5), 487–509. DOI: 10.1080/00130095.2022.2080655

Dolnicar, S., Knezevic Cvelbar, L., & Grün, B. (2019). A sharing-based approach to enticing tourists to behave more environmentally friendly. *Journal of Travel Research, 58*(2), 241–252. DOI: 10.1177/0047287517746013 PMID: 30662098

Dong, H., Zhang, L., Geng, Y., Li, P., & Yu, C. (2021). New insights from grey water footprint assessment: An industrial park level. *Journal of Cleaner Production, 285*, 124915. DOI: 10.1016/j.jclepro.2020.124915

Donthu, N., Kumar, S., Mukherjee, D., Pandey, N., & Lim, W. M. (2021). How to conduct a bibliometric analysis: An overview and guidelines. *Journal of Business Research, 133*, 285–296. DOI: 10.1016/j.jbusres.2021.04.070

Dörr, S., & Lautermann, C. (2024). Beyond direct stakeholders: The extensive scope of Societal Corporate Digital Responsibility (CDR). *Organizational Dynamics, 53*(2), 101057. DOI: 10.1016/j.orgdyn.2024.101057

Dorta-Afonso, D., & Padrón-Ávila, H. (2021). Gastronomic tourism management: identifying the potential market in the Canaries | Gestión de turismo gastronómico: identificación del mercado potencial en Canarias. *Pasos (El Sauzal), 19*(4), 725–736. DOI: 10.25145/j.pasos.2021.19.047

Drennan, J., Bianchi, C., Cacho-Elizondo, S., Louriero, S., Guibert, N., & Proud, W. (2015). Examining the role of wine brand love on brand loyalty: A multi-country comparison. *International Journal of Hospitality Management, 49*, 47–55. DOI: 10.1016/j.ijhm.2015.04.012

Duarte, A., Braga, V., Marques, C., & Sá, A. A. (2020). Geotourism and territorial development: A systematic literature review and research agenda. *Geoheritage, 12*(3), 65. DOI: 10.1007/s12371-020-00478-z

Dudaklı, N., Felekoğlu, B., & Baykasoğlu, A. (2022). Building blocks of the reverse innovation process. *Innovation (Abingdon), 35*(2), 196–223. DOI: 10.1080/13511610.2021.1925527

Dumay, J., Guthrie, J., & Farneti, F. (2010). GRI sustainability reporting guidelines for public and third sector organizations: A critical review. *Public Management Review, 12*(4), 531–548. DOI: 10.1080/14719037.2010.496266

Dumciuviene, D., Stundziene, A., & Startiene, G. (2015). Relationship between structural funds and economic indicators of the European union. *The Engineering Economist, 26*(5), 507–516. DOI: 10.5755/j01.ee.26.5.8831

Duque, A. S., Barroco, C., & Martins, M. L. (2023). Certified products in the genesis of tourist routes: An opportunity to get to know the Center Region (Portugal) | Produtos certificados na génese de rotas turísticas: Uma oportunidade para conhecer a Região Centro. *Journal of Tourism and Development, 41*, 303–315. DOI: 10.34624/rtd.v41i0.30039

Đurkin Badurina, J., Klapan, M., & Soldić Frleta, D. (2023). Stakeholders' Collaboration in the Development of an Authentic Gastronomic Offering in Rural Areas: Example of the Ravni Kotari Region in Croatia. *Sustainability (Basel), 15*(5), 4649. Advance online publication. DOI: 10.3390/su15054649

Durova, K. (2018). Long-Term Impact of the European Funds on Bulgaria's Economy. *Economic Alternatives*. 3, 325-333. https://www.unwe.bg/eajournal/en/journalissues/article/14172

Durova, K. (2022). The Impact of Absorbed European Funds on the Economic Growth of Bulgaria and New Member States. *Economic Archive*, 4, 17-36. https://www2.uni-svishtov.bg/NSArhiv/title.asp?title=2788

Dutta, D. (2015). Adam Smith theory of development in Economics (Main Features). Retrieved from http://www.economicsdiscussion.net/econo mics-2/adam-smith-theory-of-development-in-economics-main-features/4514

Eames, C., Cowie, B., & Bolstad, R. (2008). An evaluation of characteristics of envi- ronmental education practice in New Zealand schools. *Environmental Education Research, 14*(1), 35–51. DOI: 10.1080/13504620701843343

Easterling, D. (2013). Getting to collective impact: How funders can contribute over the life course of the work. *The Foundation Review, 5*(2), 7. DOI: 10.9707/1944-5660.1157

Ecologistas en Acción. (2020). Turismo en ciudades. *Informe sobre el impacto del turismo en entornos urbanos*. [Ecologists in Action. (2020). Tourism in cities. Report on the impact of tourism in urban environments].

Ehteshami, A., & Soltaninejad, M. (2020). The concept of authenticity in restoration analysis of monitoring and restoration in the authenticity preservation of cultural heritage. *Advances in Anthropology, 10*(2), 81–96. DOI: 10.4236/aa.2020.102006

Elkington, J. (1994). Towards the sustainable corporation: Win-win-win business strategies for sustainable development. *California Management Review, 36*(2), 90–100. DOI: 10.2307/41165746

Elosua, P. (2011). Subjective values of quality-of-life dimensions in elderly people. A SEM preference model approach. *Social Indicators Research, 104*(3), 427–437. DOI: 10.1007/s11205-010-9752-y

English, W. (2024). Can Welfare Economics Justify Corporate Philanthropy? Proposing the Philanthropy Multiplier as a Metric for Evaluating Corporate Philanthropic Expenditures. *Business Ethics Quarterly*, *34*(3), 440–470. DOI: 10.1017/beq.2023.2

Enríquez, C. C. L. (2024). Gastronomic tourism scenario of an international destination bases on netnography model | cenário de turismo gastronómico de um destino internacional baseado no modelo de netnografia | el escenario del turismo gastronómico de un destino internacional basa. *New Trends in Qualitative Research*, *20*(3), 1–14. DOI: 10.36367/ntqr.20.3.2024.e1062

Eshuis, J., & Ripoll González, L. (2025). Conceptualising place branding in three approaches: Towards a new definition of place brands as embodied experiences. *Journal of Place Management and Development*, *18*(1), 61–79. DOI: 10.1108/JPMD-11-2023-0109

ESPON. (2013), Attractiveness of Regions to Migrants and Visitors, https://www.espon.eu/topics-policy/publications/maps-month/attractiveness-regions-migrants-and-visitors

EURACTIV. (2010, October 15). EU money having little effect on poverty in Hungary (article in press). EURACTIV Hungary report. https://www.euractiv.com/section/politics/news/eu-money-having-little-effect-on-poverty-in-hungary/

Europa Press. *Junta y Gobierno constituyen la Sociedad Andaluza para la Valorización de la biomasa "pionera en Europa"*. 2006. Available online: https://www.europapress.es/andalucia/innova-00232/noticia-innova-junta-gobierno-constituyen-sociedad-andaluza-valorizacion-biomasa-pionera-europa-20061101160415.html. Accessed on 14 September 2024.

European Comission. (2005), "Report of the European Comission for the Council and the European parliament regarding the Sustainable Development Strategy", Bruxelles, December European Commission, (2015), A Digital Single Market Strategy for Europe, *COM(2015) 192 fina*

European Commission (2024). *Functional Areas in the EU, Methodological Toolkit to improve governance, coordination, planning, and implementation processes across jurisdictional boundaries.*

European Commission. (1997), Carta Verde. Politica de Dezvoltare Regionala in Romania. Guvernul Romaniei, Program Phare. Bucuresti, https://www.adrbi.ro/media/1665/carta_verde_politica_de_dezvoltare_regionala.pdf

European Commission. (2010), Europa 2020, http://publications.europa.eu/resource/cellar/6a915e39-0aab-491c-8881-147ec91fe88a.0022.02/DOC_1

European Commission. (2017), Competitiveness in low-income and low-growth regions. The lagging regions report, Brussels, 10.4.2017 SWD(2017) 132 final, COMMISSION STAFF WORKING DOCUMENT, https://edz.bib.uni-mannheim.de/edz/pdf/swd/2017/swd-2017-0132-en.pdf

European Commission. (2020), Territorial Agenda 2030, A future for all places, https://territorialagenda.eu

European Commission. (2022, February 9). *Cohesion in Europe towards 2050: Eighth report on economic, social and territorial cohesion.* Publication Office of the European Union. https://ec.europa.eu/regional_policy/information-sources/8cohesion-report_en

European Commission. (2023), Strasbourg, 17.1.2023 final Communication From The Commission To The European Parliament, The Council, The European Economic And Social Committee And The Committee Of The Regions Harnessing talent in Europe's regions, https://ec.europa.eu/regional_policy/sources/communication/harnessing-talents/harnessing-talents-regions_en.pdf

European Commission. (2024a, March 27). *Ninth report on economic, social and territorial cohesion.* Publication Office of the European Union. Luxembourg. https://ec.europa.eu/regional_policy/en/information/cohesion-report/

European Commission. (2024b, November 29). *Cohesion open data platform: Country data for Bulgaria.* https://cohesiondata.ec.europa.eu/countries/BG#top

European Parliament. (2003, May 26). *Regulation (EC) No 1059/2003 of the European Parliament and of the Council of 26 May 2003 on the establishment of a common classification of territorial units for statistics (NUTS).* https://data.europa.eu/eli/reg/2003/1059/oj

European Union (2024). Capacity4dev, Public Sector Reform & Decentralisation https://capacity4dev.europa.eu/groups/public-pubsector-reform-decentralisation/info/33-working-definition-territorial-development_en (Accessed 18 July, 2024)

Eurostat. (2024, December 4). *Data Browser.* https://ec.europa.eu/eurostat

Evans, D., Bratton, S., & McKee, J. (2021). *Social Media Marketing.* AG Printing & Publishing.

Ευροπεαν Χομμισσιον. (2021), Τηε Διγιταλ Εχονομψ ανδ Σοχιετψ Ινδεξ (ΔΕΣΙ), [European Commission. (2021), The Digital Economy and Society Index (DESI)]. https://digital-strategy.ec.europa.eu/en/policies/desi

Facultades A Gobiernos Autonomos Desarrollo Actividades Turisticas. [Powers to Autonomous Governments for the Development of Tourist Activities]. (2016, 23 de marzo). Consejo Nacional de Competencias Registro Oficial Suplemento 718 No. 0001-CNC-2016. https://www.turismo.gob.ec/wp-content/uploads/2016/04/Reg%C3%BAlense-las-facultades-y-atribuciones-de-los-GADs-Municipales-Metropolitanos-Provinciales-y-Parroquiales-Rurales-respecto-al-desarrollo-de-actividades-tur%C3%ADsticas.pdf

Fagerberg, J., & Verspagen, B. (1996). Heading for divergence? Regional growth in Europe reconsidered. *Journal of Common Market Studies, 34*(3), 431–448. DOI: 10.1111/j.1468-5965.1996.tb00580.x

Faith-Ell, C., Kalle, H., & Arts, J. (2020). Connecting the dots: Rethinking large-scale corridor infrastructure planning. *The 8th Transport Research Arena TRA 2020*, April 27-30, Helsinki, Finland.

Faith-Ell, C., Arts, J., & Kalle, H. (2024). Towards sustainable and inclusive corridors: Rethinking planning of infrastructure and spatial development. *10th Conference of Transportation Research Arena - Transport Transitions: Advancing Sustainable and Inclusive Mobility*, 15-18 April 2024, RDS, Dublin. Springer.

Fakfare, P., & Wattanacharoensil, W. (2023). Low-carbon tourism: determining domestic tourist perception from Thailand: TOURISM AGENDA 2030. *Tourism Review, 78*(2), 496–516. DOI: 10.1108/TR-12-2021-0537

Falahatdoost, S., & Wang, X. (2022). Industrial Park Role as a Catalyst for Regional Development: Zooming on Middle East Countries. *Land (Basel), 11*(8), 1357. DOI: 10.3390/land11081357

Farooq, Q., Fu, P., Liu, X., & Hao, Y. (2021). Basics of macro to microlevel corporate social responsibility and advancement in triple bottom line theory. *Corporate Social Responsibility and Environmental Management*, *28*(3), 969–979. DOI: 10.1002/csr.2069

Farrell, F. (2021). *ESF and the fight against poverty: The use of the European Social Fund (ESF) during 2014-2020 for combating poverty and achieving social inclusion*. The Left in the European Parliament: Brussels. https://left.eu/app/uploads/2021/12/506388-GLUE-NG-Studies-2021-EMPL.pdf

Farrelly, F., Kock, F., & Josiassen, A. (2019). Cultural heritage authenticity: A producer view. *Annals of Tourism Research*, *79*, 102770. DOI: 10.1016/j.annals.2019.102770

Fazeleh, Y., & Francesco, N. (2021). *The role of Ab-Anbars in the vernacular architecture of Iran with emphasis on the performance of Wind-catchers in hot and dry climate*. Energy Efficiency in Historic Buildings. Special Issue

Feng, Y., Zhu, Q., & Lai, K. H. (2017). Corporate social responsibility for supply chain management: A literature review and bibliometric analysis. *Journal of Cleaner Production*, *158*, 296–307. DOI: 10.1016/j.jclepro.2017.05.018

Ferrari, S., Nicotera, T., lo Presti, A., & Biasone, A. M. (2022). Local Development Through the Connection Between Roots Tourism, Local Food and Wine. In *Lecture Notes in Networks and Systems* (Vol. 482). LNNS., DOI: 10.1007/978-3-031-06825-6_221

Ferraro, S., Männasoo, K., & Tasane, H. (2023). How the EU Cohesion Policy targeted at R&D and innovation impacts the productivity, employment and exports of SMEs in Estonia. *Evaluation and Program Planning*, *97*, 102221. DOI: 10.1016/j.evalprogplan.2022.102221 PMID: 36592544

Ferreira, J., & Coelho, A. (2020). Dynamic capabilities, innovation and branding capabilities and their impact on competitive advantage and SME's performance in Portugal: The moderating effects of entrepreneurial orientation. *International Journal of Innovation Science*, *12*(3), 255–286. DOI: 10.1108/IJIS-10-2018-0108

Fidrmuc, J., Hulényi, M., & Zajkowska, O. (2023). The long and winding road to find the impact of EU funds on regional growth: IV and spatial analyses. *Regional Studies*, *58*(3), 583–600. DOI: 10.1080/00343404.2023.2217214

Filimonau, V., Dickinson, J., Robbins, D., & Reddy, M. V. (2013). The role of 'indirect' greenhouse gas emissions in tourism: Assessing the hidden carbon impacts from a holiday package tour. *Transportation Research Part A, Policy and Practice*, *54*, 78–91. DOI: 10.1016/j.tra.2013.07.002

Fletcher, R. A., Long, R. E., & Schumann, W. (Eds.). (2023). *Engaging Appalachia: A Guidebook for Building Capacity and Sustainability*. University Press of Kentucky. DOI: 10.2307/j.ctv3596zs0

Floress, K., Connolly, S., Halvorsen, K. E., Egan, A., Schuler, T., Hill, A., DeSenze, P., Fenimore, S., & Karriker, K. (2018). Implementing landscape scale conservation across organizational boundaries: Lessons from the central Appalachian region, United States. *Environmental Management*, *62*(5), 845–857. DOI: 10.1007/s00267-018-1081-y PMID: 30046845

Folta, S. C., Kuder, J. F., Goldberg, J. P., Hyatt, R. R., Must, A., Naumova, E. N., Nelson, M. E., & Economos, C. D. (2013). Changes in diet and physical activity resulting from the Shape Up Somerville community intervention. *BMC Pediatrics*, *13*(1), 1–9. DOI: 10.1186/1471-2431-13-157 PMID: 24093936

Fontan Kohler, A., & Antonio Digiampietri, L. (2021). Cultural tourism: Bibliometric and social network analysis of Brazilian tourism field, 1990-2018. *Pasos (El Sauzal)*, *19*(4). Advance online publication. DOI: 10.25145/j.pasos.2021.19.054

Fordham, A. E., Robinson, G. M., & Blackwell, B. D. (2017). Corporate social responsibility in resource companies–Opportunities for developing positive benefits and lasting legacies. *Resources Policy*, *52*, 366–376. DOI: 10.1016/j.resourpol.2017.04.009

Fourie, J., Rossello, J., & Santana, M. (2020). Fatal attraction: How security threats hurt tourism. *Journal of Travel Research*, *59*(2), 209–219. DOI: 10.1177/0047287519826208

Fox, A., Mwangi, C. G., Pachucki, M., Wells, R., Dasgupta, B., Thoma, H., Dunton, S., & Kimball, E. (2023). Rethinking Backbones in Collective Impact: Examining a Broadening STEM Participation Program as a Feminist Matrix Organization. *Innovative Higher Education*, *48*(5), 925–947. DOI: 10.1007/s10755-023-09660-x

Franco, F. (2001). The Muslim conquest of the Maghreb and Al-Andalus according to the Mozarabic chronicles. Retrieved from http://hdl.handle.net/10045/25131

Friedlingstein, P., Cox, P., Betts, R., Bopp, L., von Bloh, W., Brovkin, V., Cadule, P., Doney, S., Eby, M., Fung, I., Bala, G., John, J., Jones, C., Joos, F., Kato, T., Kawamiya, M., Knorr, W., Lindsay, K., Matthews, H. D., & Zeng, N. (2006). Climate–carbon cycle feedback analysis: Results from the C4MIP model intercomparison. *Journal of Climate*, *19*(14), 3337–3353. DOI: 10.1175/JCLI3800.1

Friedlingstein, P., O'sullivan, M., Jones, M. W., Andrew, R. M., Gregor, L., Hauck, J., Le Quéré, C., Luijkx, I. T., Olsen, A., Peters, G. P., Peters, W., Pongratz, J., Schwingshackl, C., Sitch, S., Canadell, J. G., Ciais, P., Jackson, R. B., Alin, S. R., Alkama, R., & Zheng, B. (2022). Global carbon budget 2022. *Earth System Science Data*, *14*(11), 4811–4900. DOI: 10.5194/essd-14-4811-2022

Fuhrman, E. (2009). Green mountain coffee roasters gives a one-two punch; Single-cup brewers fuel specialty coffee success. *Beverage Industry*, *100*(3), 29–35.

Fundación para la Eficiencia Energética (FEE). *Crece en Andalucía el consumo de biomasa en el sector residencial.* 2016. Available online: https://www.eseficiencia.es/2016/09/07/crece-en-andalucia-el-consumo-de-biomasa-en-el-sector-residencial. Accessed on 14 September 2024.

Funsho Idowu, O., Adedoyin, F. F., Bekun, F. V., & Balsalobre-Lorente, D. (2022). Modeling the environmental implications of car ownership and energy consumption in the UK: Evidence from NARDL model. *International Journal of Sustainable Transportation*, *16*(12), 1097–1109. DOI: 10.1080/15568318.2021.1969708

Fusté-Forné, F., Ginés-Ariza, P., & Noguer-Juncà, E. (2021). Food in slow tourism: The creation of experiences based on the origin of products sold at mercat del lleó (girona). *Heritage*, *4*(3), 1995–2008. DOI: 10.3390/heritage4030113

Gagliardi, L., & Percoco, M. (2017). The impact of European Cohesion Policy in urban and rural regions. *Regional Studies, 51*(6), 857–868. DOI: 10.1080/00343404.2016.1179384

Gallant, L. (2013). Product (RED): The case against consumerism as a form of aid. *Te Canadian Undergraduate Journal of Development Studies*, *X*(I), 22.

Ganev, K., & Simeonova-Ganeva, R. (2012). Effects of EU Funded Policies: Net Impact Assessment of Investments in Education and Science in Bulgaria. SSRN *Electronic Journal*. DOI: 10.2139/ssrn.2030621

Gao, F. (2020). Cause marketing: Product pricing, design, and distribution. *Manufacturing & Service Operations Management*, *22*(4), 775–791. DOI: 10.1287/msom.2019.0772

Gao, J., Lin, S. S., & Zhang, C. (2020). Authenticity, involvement, and nostalgia: Understanding visitor satisfaction with an adaptive reuse heritage site in urban China. *Journal of Destination Marketing & Management*, *15*, 100404. DOI: 10.1016/j.jdmm.2019.100404

Garcês, S. (2024). Gastronomy experiences, authenticity, and storytelling in tourism destinations: A conceptual paper. In *Cultural*. Gastronomy, and Adventure Tourism Development., DOI: 10.4018/979-8-3693-3158-3.ch009

García Martín, J. F., Cuevas, M., Feng, C. H., Álvarez Mateos, P., Torres García, M., & Sánchez, S. (2020). Energetic Valorisation of Olive Biomass: Olive-Tree Pruning, Olive Stones and Pomaces. *Processes (Basel, Switzerland)*, *8*(5), 511. DOI: 10.3390/pr8050511

García-Henche, B., Cuesta-Valiño, P., Durán-Álamo, P., & Penelas-Leguía, A. (2024). The role of women in maintaining the heritage value of gastronomy in Castilla-La Mancha. *International Journal of Gastronomy and Food Science*, *37*, 100987. Advance online publication. DOI: 10.1016/j.ijgfs.2024.100987

García-Maraver, A., Zamorano, M., Ramos-Ridao, A., & Díaz, L. F. Analysis of olive grove residual biomass potential for electric and thermal energy generation in Andalusia (Spain). Renewable and Sustainable Energy Reviews, 2012, 16(1), 745-751.

García-Villaverde, P. M., Ruiz-Ortega, M. J., Hurtado-Palomino, A., De La Gala-Velásquez, B., & Zirena-Bejarano, P. P. (2021). Social capital and innovativeness in firms in cultural tourism destinations: Divergent contingent factors. *Journal of Destination Marketing & Management*, *19*, 100529. DOI: 10.1016/j.jdmm.2020.100529

Gardberg, N. A., Zyglidopoulos, S. C., Symeou, P. C., & Schepers, D. H. (2019). The impact of corporate philanthropy on reputation for corporate social performance. *Business & Society*, *58*(6), 1177–1208. DOI: 10.1177/0007650317694856

Garofoli, G. (2016). Local Development in Europe: Theoretical Models and International Comparisons. *European Urban and Regional Studies*, *9*(3), 2016. DOI: 10.1177/096977640200900303

Garson, D. (2008). Path Analysis with structural equation model. *In Path Analysis* (pp.1- 21). Academia. Accelerating the world's research.

Gavrila-Paven, I., & Wainberg, D. (2022), Influence of Projects Financed by the Regional Operational Program on the Economic Performance of Companies, Economic Computation and Economic Cybernetics Studies and Research, Vol. 56, Issue 2/2022, pg 273-289, https://ecocyb.ase.ro/nr2022_2/CONTENTS_2022_2.pdf

Geels, F. W., Sovacool, B. K., Schwanen, T., & Sorrell, S. (2017). Sociotechnical transitions for deep decarbonization. *Science, 357*(6357), 1242–1244. DOI: 10.1126/science.aao3760 PMID: 28935795

Getz, D., & Robinson, R. N. S. (2014). "Foodies" and their travel preferences. *Tourism Analysis, 19*(6), 659–672. DOI: 10.3727/108354214X14116690097693

Ghayour, K. A., & Hossein, S. A. (2011). An overview of some vernacular techniques in Iranian sustainable architecture in reference to Cisterns and Ice Houses. *Journal of Sustainable Development, 4*(1), •••.

Gherghina, . C., Botezatu, M. A., Hosszu, A., & Simionescu, L. N. (2020). Small and Medium-Sized Enterprises (SMEs): The Engine of Economic Growth through Investments and Innovation. *Sustainability (Basel), 12*(1), 347. Advance online publication. DOI: 10.3390/su12010347

Gherghina, S. C., Botezatu, M. A., & Simionescu, L. N. (2021). Exploring the Impact of Electronic Commerce on Employment Rate: Panel Data Evidence from European Union Countries. *Journal of Theoretical and Applied Electronic Commerce Research, 2021*(16), 3157–3183. DOI: 10.3390/jtaer16070172

Ginesta, X., & San Eugenio, J. (2020). Rethinking Place Branding From a Political Perspective: Urban Governance, Public Diplomacy, and Sustainable Policy Making. *The American Behavioral Scientist,* •••, 1–18. DOI: 10.1177/0002764220975066

Giua, M. (2017). Spatial discontinuity for the impact assessment of the EU Regional Policy: The case of Italian Objective 1 Region. *Journal of Regional Science, 57*(1), 109–131. DOI: 10.1111/jors.12300

Gobierno de Zapopan. (2023, octubre 13). *Asisten a la Romería 2023 más de dos millones de feligreses.* [More than two million parishioners will attend the 2023 Pilgrimage]. Noticias. https://www.zapopan.gob.mx/v3/noticias/asisten-la-romeria-2023-mas-de-dos-millones-de-feligreses#:~:text=La%20edici%C3%B3n%20289%20de%20Romer%C3%ADa,corte%20del%20Operativo%20Romer%C3%ADa%202023

Gobierno de Zapopan. (2023a, octubre). https://www.zapopan.gob.mx/v3/noticias/zapopan-reconoce-danzantes-en-su-dia#:~:text=El%2027%20de%20septiembre%20de,portadoras%20de%20la%20tradici%C3%B3n%20hacen

Godlewska-Majkowska, H. (2018). Polarity of the Regional Space – the Dilemma of Shaping the Investment Attractiveness of Poland. *Studies of the Industrial Geography Commission of the Polish Geographical Society, 32*(4), 110–122. DOI: 10.24917/20801653.324.6

Gonzalez-Loureiro, M., & Pita-Castelo, J. (2012). A model for assessing the contribution of innovative SMEs to economic growth: The intangible approach. *Economics Letters, 116*(3), 312–315. DOI: 10.1016/j.econlet.2012.03.028

Goodfellow, I., Pouget-Abadie, J., Mirza, M., Xu, B., Warde-Farley, D., Ozair, S., & Bengio, Y. (2014). Generative adversarial nets. *Advances in Neural Information Processing Systems,* •••, 27.

Gordon, R., Russell-Bennett, R., & Lefebvre, R. C. (2016). Social marketing: The state of play and brokering the way forward. *Journal of Marketing Management, 32*(11-12), 1059–1082. DOI: 10.1080/0267257X.2016.1199156

Gössling, S. (2000). Tourism–sustainable development option? [Opens in a new window]. *Environmental Conservation, 27*(3), 223–224. DOI: 10.1017/S0376892900000242

Gössling, S., Balas, M., Mayer, M., & Sun, Y. Y. (2023). A review of tourism and climate change mitigation: The scales, scopes, stakeholders and strategies of carbon management. *Tourism Management, 95*, 104681. DOI: 10.1016/j.tourman.2022.104681

Gössling, S., & Higham, J. (2021). The low-carbon imperative: Destination management under urgent climate change. *Journal of Travel Research, 60*(6), 1167–1179. DOI: 10.1177/0047287520933679

Gössling, S., & Humpe, A. (2023). Net-zero aviation: Time for a new business model? *Journal of Air Transport Management, 107*, 102353. DOI: 10.1016/j.jairtraman.2022.102353

Gössling, S., & Lund-Durlacher, D. (2021). Tourist accommodation, climate change and mitigation: An assessment for Austria. *Journal of Outdoor Recreation and Tourism, 34*, 100367. DOI: 10.1016/j.jort.2021.100367

Gössling, S., & Michael Hall, C. (2019). Sharing versus collaborative economy: How to align ICT developments and the SDGs in tourism? *Journal of Sustainable Tourism, 27*(1), 74–96. DOI: 10.1080/09669582.2018.1560455

Gössling, S., Peeters, P., Ceron, J. P., Dubois, G., Patterson, T., & Richardson, R. B. (2005). The eco-efficiency of tourism. *Ecological Economics, 54*(4), 417–434. DOI: 10.1016/j.ecolecon.2004.10.006

Gössling, S., Ring, A., Dwyer, L., Andersson, A.-C., & Hall, C. M. (2016). Optimizing or maximizing growth? A challenge for sustainable tourism. *Journal of Sustainable Tourism, 24*(4), 527–548. DOI: 10.1080/09669582.2015.1085869

Gössling, S., Scott, D., & Hall, C. M. (2018). Global trends in length of stay: Implications for destination management and climate change. *Journal of Sustainable Tourism, 26*(12), 2087–2101. DOI: 10.1080/09669582.2018.1529771

Gouveia, M., Aragonez, T., & Saur-Amaral, I. (2015). The Image of the Central Region: The Perspective of its Residents. *Tourism & Management Studies, 11*(2), 93–102. DOI: 10.18089/tms.2015.11212

Government of Romania. (2008), "National Sustainable Development Strategy for Romania", pp. 29- 32 available at: http://www.insse.ro/cms/files/IDDT%202012/StategiaDD.pdf

Government of Spain. Ministry of Foreign Affairs, European Union and Cooperation (2021). Maghreb and Middle East. Retrieved from https://www.exteriores.gob.es/es/PoliticaExterior/Paginas/MagrebOrienteProximo.asp

Govindarajan, V., & Euchner, J. (2012). Reverse innovation. *Research Technology Management, 55*(6), 13–17. DOI: 10.5437/08956308X5506003

Govindarajan, V., & Ramamurti, R. (2018). *Reverse innovation in health care: How to make value-based delivery work*. Harvard Business Press.

Grant, C. (2017), The Contribution of Education to Economic Growth, K4D Helpdesk Report, https://assets.publishing.service.gov.uk/media/5b9b87f340f0b67896977bae/K4D_HDR_The_Contribution_of_Education_to_Economic_Growth_Final.pdf

Grbac, B., & Lončarić, D. (2009). Ethics, social responsibility and business performance in a transition economy. *EuroMed Journal of Business*, *4*(2), 143–158. DOI: 10.1108/14502190910976501

Griffin, G., Wennerström, E., & Foka, A. (2023). AI and Swedish Heritage Organisations: Challenges and opportunities. *AI & Society*, •••, 1–14.

Groizard, J., Mohanad, I., & Santana, M. (2022). Political upheavals, tourism flight, and spillovers: The case of the Arab Spring. *Journal of Travel Research*, *61*(4), 921–939. DOI: 10.1177/00472875211002652

Guha-Sapir, D., Below, R., & Hoyois, P. (2015). *EM-DAT: International Disaster Database*. Universitécatholique de Louvain—CRED.

Gumede, V. (2008) "Public policy making in a post-apartheid South Africa: a preliminary perspective", *Africanus*, Vol 38, No. 2, pp 7-23, [online] https://www.vusigumede.com/content/academic%20papers/Public%20policy%20making%20(Journal%20of%20Development%20Studies%20paper,%2038,%202,%20pp%207-23).pdf

Haddad, E. A., de Araújo, I. F., de Almeida Vale, V., Sandoval, H. D., Roman, P. A. G., Rodríguez, L. A. C., Jaramillo, E. A., & Lopez, L. J. G. (2021). Dimensions of local development in the Colombian Pacific Region. *Regional Science Policy & Practice*, *13*(4), 1348–1371. DOI: 10.1111/rsp3.12453

Hall, C. M., Scott, D., & Gössling, S. (2013). The primacy of climate change for sustainable international tourism. *Sustainable Development (Bradford)*, *21*(2), 112–121. DOI: 10.1002/sd.1562

Hallin, G., & Malmberg, A. (2016). Attraction, Competition and Regional Development in Europe. *European Urban and Regional Studies*, *3*(4), 2016. DOI: 10.1177/096977649600300404

Han, C. M., Kim, K. A., & Nam, H. (2020). Can corporate philanthropy change consumers' perceptions of Japanese multinationals and reduce animosity toward them? *Asia Pacific Journal of Marketing and Logistics*, *32*(1), 65–85. DOI: 10.1108/APJML-09-2018-0383

Handel, K. (2012). *Planned Bullyhood: The Truth Behind the Headlines about the Planned Parenthood Funding Battle with Susan G. Komen for the Cure*. Simon and Schuster.

Han, H., & Hyun, S. S. (2015). Customer retention in the medical tourism industry: Impact of quality, satisfaction, trust, and price reasonableness. *Tourism Management*, *46*, 20–29. DOI: 10.1016/j.tourman.2014.06.003

Hanlan, J., Fuller, D., & Wilde, S. (2006). Destination Decision Making: The Need for a Strategic Planning and Management Approach. *Tourism and Hospitality Planning & Development*, *3*(3), 209–221. DOI: 10.1080/14790530601132385

Hanleybrown, F., Kania, J., & Kramer, M. (2012). *Channeling change: Making collective impact work*. FSG.

Hardin, R. (2016). Collective contradictions of corporate environmental conservation. *The Anthropology of Corporate Social Responsibility*, 179-198.

Harisanty, D., Obille, K. L. B., Anna, N. E. V., Purwanti, E., & Retrialisca, F. (2024). Cultural heritage preservation in the digital age, harnessing artificial intelligence for the future: A bibliometric analysis. *Digital Library Perspectives*, *40*(4), 609–630. DOI: 10.1108/DLP-01-2024-0018

Harrington, R. J., & Ottenbacher, M. C. (2010). Culinary tourism-a case study of the gastronomic capital. *Journal of Culinary Science & Technology*, *8*(1), 14–32. DOI: 10.1080/15428052.2010.490765

Hart, R. A. (2013). *Children's participation: The theory and practice of involving young citizens in community development and environmental care*. Routledge. DOI: 10.4324/9781315070728

Helm, R. C., Carter, H. R., Ford, R. G., Fry, D. M., Moreno, R. L., Sanpera, C., & Tseng, F. S. (2014). Overview of efforts to document and reduce impacts of oil spills on seabirds. *Handbook of Oil Spill Science and Technology*, 429-453.

Hernández-Garrido, R., Orts-Cardador, J., & Perez-Calañas, C. (2023). The Role of Management in Sustainable Tourism: A Bibliometric Analysis Approach. *Sustainability (Basel)*, *15*(12), 9712. DOI: 10.3390/su15129712

Hernando de Larramendi, M. (2019). Doomed regionalism in a eedrawn Maghreb? The changing shape of the rivalry between Algeria and Morocco in the post-2011 era. *Journal of North African Studies*, *24*(3), 506–531. DOI: 10.1080/13629387.2018.1454657

Herold, F., Theobald, P., Gronwald, T., Kaushal, N., Zou, L., de Bruin, E. D., Bherer, L., & Müller, N. G. (2024). Alexa, let's train now!—A systematic review and classification approach to digital and home-based physical training interventions aiming to support healthy cognitive aging. *Journal of Sport and Health Science*, *13*(1), 30–46. DOI: 10.1016/j.jshs.2023.01.004 PMID: 36736727

Hervani, A. A., Sarkis, J., & Helms, M. M. (2017). Environmental goods valuations for social sustainability: A conceptual framework. *Technological Forecasting and Social Change*, *125*, 137–153. DOI: 10.1016/j.techfore.2017.07.015

Hickel, J., Dorninger, C., Wieland, H., & Suwandi, I. (2022). Imperialist Appropriation in the World Economy: Drain from the Global South through Unequal Exchange, 1990–2015. *Global Environmental Change*, *73*, 102467. DOI: 10.1016/j.gloenvcha.2022.102467

Higueras-Castillo, E., García-Maroto, I., Muñoz-Leiva, F., & Liébana-Cabanillas, F. (2022). Modelling sustainable mobility adoption from the urban population view (SMAUP model): The moderating effect of household size. *Research in Transportation Business & Management*, *45*, 100878. DOI: 10.1016/j.rtbm.2022.100878

Hiller, J. S. (2013). The benefit corporation and corporate social responsibility. *Journal of Business Ethics*, *118*(2), 287–301. DOI: 10.1007/s10551-012-1580-3

Hirte, G., Lessmann, C., & Seide, A. (2020). International trade, geographic heterogeneity and interregional inequality. *European Economic Review, 127*(August), 103427. DOI: 10.1016/j.euroecorev.2020.103427

Hoeffler, S., Bloom, P. N., & Keller, K. L. (2010). Understanding stakeholder responses to corporate citizenship initiatives: Managerial guidelines and research directions. *Journal of Public Policy & Marketing, 29*(1), 78–88. DOI: 10.1509/jppm.29.1.78

Horakova, S. (2021), Map of regional attractiveness, The Quebec City Metropolitan Community, https://hub.polirural.eu/news/-/blogs/map-of-regional-attractiveness

Horng, J. S., Hu, M. L. M., Teng, C. C. C., Hsiao, H. L., & Liu, C. H. S. (2013). Development and validation of the low-carbon literacy scale among practitioners in the Taiwanese tourism industry. *Tourism Management, 35*, 255–262. DOI: 10.1016/j.tourman.2012.08.001

Hospers, G.-J. (2009). Lynch, Urry and city marketing: Taking advantage of the city as a built and graphic image. *Place Branding and Public Diplomacy, 5*(3), 226–233. DOI: 10.1057/pb.2009.10

Hsu, F. C., Agyeiwaah, E., & Scott, N. (2022). Understanding tourists' perceived food consumption values: Do different cultures share similar food values? *International Journal of Gastronomy and Food Science, 28*, 100533. Advance online publication. DOI: 10.1016/j.ijgfs.2022.100533

Huang, Z., Cao, F., Jin, C., Yu, Z., & Huang, R. (2017). Carbon emission flow from self-driving tours and its spatial relationship with scenic spots–A traffic-related big data method. *Journal of Cleaner Production, 142*, 946–955. DOI: 10.1016/j.jclepro.2016.09.129

Hu, B., Liu, Y., Zhang, X., & Dong, X. (2020). Understanding regional talent attraction and its influencing factors in China: From the perspective of spatiotemporal pattern evolution. *PLoS One, 15*(6), e0234856. DOI: 10.1371/journal.pone.0234856 PMID: 32555616

Hughes, A. (2015). Retailers, corporate ethics and fair trade. In *Handbook of research on fair trade* (pp. 298–315). Edward Elgar Publishing. DOI: 10.4337/9781783474622.00027

Huntington, H. P. (2000). Using traditional ecological knowledge in science: Methods and applications. *Ecological Applications, 10*(5), 1270–1274. DOI: 10.1890/1051-0761(2000)010[1270:UTEKIS]2.0.CO;2

Hussain, A., Mandić, A., & Fusté-Forné, F. (2024). Transforming communities: Analyzing the effects of infrastructure and tourism development on social capital, livelihoods, and resilience in Gilgit-Baltistan, Pakistan. *Journal of Hospitality and Tourism Management, 59*, 276–295. DOI: 10.1016/j.jhtm.2024.04.017

Huynh, H. T. N., Trieu, H. D. X., Van Nguyen, P., Tran, T. G., & Lam, L. N. H. (2021). Explaining Brand Equity in the Information Technology Sector in Vietnam. *Administrative Sciences, 11*(128), 1–25. DOI: 10.3390/admsci11040128

Ibrahiem, D., & Hanafy, S. (2021). Do energy security and environmental quality contribute to Renewable Energy? The Role of Trade Openness and Energy Use in North African Countries. *Renewable Energy, 179*, 667–678. DOI: 10.1016/j.renene.2021.07.019

Idowu, S. O., & Kasum, A. S. (2016). *People, Planet and Profit: Socio-Economic Perspectives of CSR.* Routledge. DOI: 10.4324/9781315599915

Ilie , R. I., Borlea, S. N., & Pricope, L. (2024). Impact of European funds upon rural development in the European Union. *Brazilian Journal of Business*, *6*(1), 273–288. DOI: 10.34140/bjbv6n1-021

Information System for Management and Monitoring of EU Funds in Bulgaria 2014-2020 (UMIS 2020). (2024, December 4). *Public information on the implementation of operational programs in Bulgaria: Database*. https://2020.eufunds.bg/en

Insch, A., & Florek, M. (2010). Marketing cities: Controversies, contradictions and consequences - A special issue of the Journal of Town and City Management. *Journal Of Town & City Management*, *1*(3), 233–238.

Instituto de Información Estadística y Geográfica de Jalisco. (2022). Zapopan, Diagnóstico Municipal, agosto. Gobierno del Estado de Jalisco. [Jalisco Institute of Statistical and Geographic Information. (2022). Zapopan, Municipal Diagnosis, August. Government of the State of Jalisco].

Intergovernmental Panel on Climate Change (IPCC). (2022). Intergovernmental Panel on Climate Change. https://www.ipcc.ch/

International Air Transport Association. (2019). Annual Review 2019. https://www.iata.org/contentassets/c81222d96c9a4e0bb4ff6ced0126f0bb/iata-annual-review-2019.pdf

Io, M.-U., & Wan, P. Y. K. (2017). Relationships between Tourism Experiences and Place Attachment in the Context of Casino Resorts. *Journal of Quality Assurance in Hospitality & Tourism*, *19*(1), 45–65. DOI: 10.1080/1528008X.2017.1314801

Jacobs, J. (2011). *Vida y muerte de las grandes ciudades [Life and death of great cities]*. Capitán Swing.

Jadhav, R. (2007). Green architecture in India: Combining modern technology with traditional methods. *UN Chronicle*, *154*(2), 66–71.

James, M. L. (2013). Sustainability and integrated reporting: Opportunities and strategies for small and midsize companies. *The Entrepreneurial Executive*, *18*, 17.

Jano Reiss, M., Rotem, A., Gridinger, O., Tzur, Y., Reichman, G., Berenbaum, R., & Tziraki, C. (2022). Health and wellbeing (SDG3) in urban design and spatial planning–a retrospective roadmap towards the collective impact model. *Cities & Health*, *6*(5), 993–1003. DOI: 10.1080/23748834.2022.2147469

Ji, X., Dong, F., Zheng, C., & Bu, N. (2022). The influences of international trade on sustainable economic growth: An economic policy perspective. *Sustainability (Basel)*, *14*(5), 1–15. DOI: 10.3390/su14052781

Johansen, P. H., Ejrnæs, R., Kronvang, B., Olsen, J. V., Præstholm, S., & Schou, J. S. (2018). Pursuing collective impact: A novel indicator-based approach to assessment of shared measurements when planning for multifunctional land consolidation. *Land Use Policy*, *73*, 102–114. DOI: 10.1016/j.landusepol.2018.01.040

Jokilehto, J. (1994). Questions about 'authenticity'. *ICOMOS Scientific Journal*, *3*, 69–75.

Jones, P., Comfort, D., & Hillier, D. (2006). Healthy eating and the UK's major food retailers: A case study in corporate social responsibility. *British Food Journal*, *108*(10), 838–848. DOI: 10.1108/00070700610702091

Jones, S., & Yarrow, T. (2022). *The object of conservation: An ethnography of heritage practice*. Routledge. DOI: 10.4324/9781315622385

Jover, J., & Díaz-Parra, I. (2020). Gentrification, transnational gentrification and touristification in Seville, Spain. *Urban Studies (Edinburgh, Scotland)*, *57*(15), 3044–3059. DOI: 10.1177/0042098019857585

Jovovic, R., Draskovic, M., Delibasic, M., & Jovovic, M. (2017). The concept of sustainable regional development – institutional aspects, policies and prospects. *Journal of International Students*, *10*(1), 255–266. DOI: 10.14254/2071-8330.2017/10-1/18

Judelsohn, A., Hoey, L., Shapiro, L. F., & Colasanti, K. (2022). Incorporating shared measurement in social change initiatives: Benefits, challenges, and lessons learned. *Community Development Journal: An International Forum*, *57*(3), 533–551. DOI: 10.1093/cdj/bsab009

Jue, M. (2019). Fluid Cuts: The Anti-visual Logic of Surfactants after Deepwater Horizon. *Configurations*, *27*(4), 525–544. DOI: 10.1353/con.2019.0034

Jumaiti, J., Saputra, B., Frinaldi, A., & Putri, N. E. (2024). Examining the Mediating Effects of Social Capital and Community-Based Tourism on the Role of Tourism Villages in Sustainable Tourism. *Journal of Environmental Management and Tourism*, *15*(1), 176–193. DOI: 10.14505/jemt.v15.1(73).15

Kalpidis, C., Bersimis, F., & Tsartas, P. (2024). Effect of Restaurant Attributes on Tourism Satisfaction and Loyalty: Local Gastronomy in Athens. *Springer Proceedings in Business and Economics*, 1049–1069. DOI: 10.1007/978-3-031-54338-8_63

Kang, C., Fan, D., & Jiao, H. (2021). Validating activity, time, and space diversity as essential components of urban vitality. *Environment and Planning. B, Urban Analytics and City Science*, *48*(8), 2255–2270. DOI: 10.1177/2399808320919771

Kania, J., Hanleybrown, F., Juster, J. S., Edmondson, J., Hecht, B., Bartczak, L., & White, E. (2014). Collective insights on collective impact. *Stanford Social Innovation Review*, *12*(4), 1–24.

Kania, J., & Kramer, M. (2011). *Collective impact*. FSG.

Karmann, M., Martinez, Z., Meier-Dörnberg, J., & Santos, V. (2022). An assessment of FSC certification solutions for smallholders and community-managed forests. In *Routledge Handbook of Community Forestry* (pp. 237–255). Routledge. DOI: 10.4324/9780367488710-19

Károly, K. (2011). Rise and fall of the concept sustainability. *Journal of Environmental Sustainability*, *1*(1), 1–13. DOI: 10.14448/jes.01.0001

Kar, S. K., Bansal, R., & Harichandan, S. (2022). An empirical study on intention to use hydrogen fuel cell vehicles in India. *International Journal of Hydrogen Energy*, *47*(46), 19999–20015. DOI: 10.1016/j.ijhydene.2022.04.137

Karthik, C., & Ramesh, S. (2021). Vernacular Practices: An appraisal for sustainability for housing in Uttarakhand and Himachal Pradesh, India. *International Journal of Humanities and Social Science*, *10*(1), •••.

Kastenholz, E., & Gronau, W. (2022). Enhancing competences for co-creating appealing and meaningful cultural heritage experiences in tourism. *Journal of Hospitality & Tourism Research (Washington, D.C.)*, *46*(8), 1519–1544. DOI: 10.1177/1096348020951637

Kaur, N., & Rai, M. (2024). Role of Digital Technology and Education for Transformation of Cultural Heritage. In *Digital Cultural Heritage* (pp. 206–221). CRC Press. DOI: 10.1201/9781032630564-11

Kavaratzis, M. (2004). From city marketing to city branding: Towards a theoretical framework for developing city brands. *Place Branding*, *1*(1), 58–73. DOI: 10.1057/palgrave.pb.5990005

Kavaratzis, M., & Ashworth, G. (2006). City branding: An effective assertion of identity or a transient marketing trick? *Place Branding and Public Diplomacy*, *2*(3), 183–194. DOI: 10.1057/palgrave.pb.5990056

Kavaratzis, M., & Ashworth, G. (2008). Place marketing: How did we get here and where are we going? *Journal of Place Management and Development*, *1*(2), 150–165. DOI: 10.1108/17538330810889989

Keitumetse, S. O. (2014). Cultural Resource as Sustainability Enablers: Towards a Community-Based Cultural Heritage Resources Management (COBACHREM) Model. *Sustainability (Basel)*, *6*(1), 70–85. DOI: 10.3390/su6010070

Keller, K. L., & Kotler, P. (2015). Holistic marketing: a broad, integrated perspective to marketing management. In *Does marketing need reform?: Fresh Perspectives on the Future* (pp. 308-313). Routledge.

Kersan-Škabić, I., & Tijanić, L. (2017). Regional absorption capacity of EU funds. [Ekonomska Istrazivanja]. *Ekonomska Istrazivanja*, *30*(1), 191–1208. DOI: 10.1080/1331677X.2017.1340174

Kidd, C. V. (1992). The evolution of sustainability. *Journal of Agricultural & Environmental Ethics*, *5*(1), 1–26. DOI: 10.1007/BF01965413

Kieffer, E. L., & Socolof, J. (2024). *Rural Arts Management*. Taylor & Francis. DOI: 10.4324/9781003365853

Kim, J.-H. (2014). The antecedents of memorable tourism experiences: The development of a scale to measure the destination attributes associated with memorable experiences. *Tourism Management*, *44*, 34–45. DOI: 10.1016/j.tourman.2014.02.007

Kim, K., Cheong, Y., & Lim, J. S. (2015). Choosing the right message for the right cause in social cause advertising: Type of social cause message, perceived company–cause fit and the persuasiveness of communication. *International Journal of Advertising*, *34*(3), 473–494. DOI: 10.1080/02650487.2015.1006081

Kisiała, W., & Stępiński, B. (2024). European funds and the dynamics of economic growth among EU regions: A spatial modelling approach. *Quaestiones Geographicae*, *43*(2), 67–80. DOI: 10.14746/quageo-2024-0020

Kitchin, R. (2014). *The Data Revolution: Big Data, Open Data, Data Infrastructures and Their Consequences*. SAGE Publications.

Kivela, J., & Crotts, J. C. (2006). Tourism and Gastronomy: Gastronomy's Influence on How Tourists Experience a Destination. *Journal of Hospitality & Tourism Research (Washington, D.C.)*, *30*(3), 354–377. DOI: 10.1177/1096348006286797

Koçak, E., Ulucak, R., & Ulucak, Z. Ş. (2020). The impact of tourism developments on CO2 emissions: An advanced panel data estimation. *Tourism Management Perspectives, 33*, 100611. DOI: 10.1016/j.tmp.2019.100611

Koch, P. (2023). Where limits to growth are tangible: The olive sector in Jaén and its bioeconomic future. *Sustainability Science, 18*(2), 661–674. DOI: 10.1007/s11625-022-01236-6

Kocmanova, A., & Docekalova, M. (2012). Construction of the Economic Indicators of Performance in Relation to Environmental, Social and Corporate Governance (ESG) Factors. *Acta Universitatis Agriculturae et Silviculturae Mendelianae Brunensis, 60*(4), 195–206. DOI: 10.11118/actaun201260040195Kurikov, V., & Tashlanova, Y. (2022), The practice of state regional support for the development of investment attractiveness (on the example of the Khanty-Mansiysk Autonomous Okrug–Yugra), SHS Web Conf, Vol 141, 2022, IV International Scientific and Practical Conference "Modern Management Trends and Digital Economy: from Regional Development to Global Economic Growth" (MTDE 2022), 01013, iunie 2022, DOI: 10.1051/shsconf/202214101013

Koh, E., Fakfare, P., & Pongwat, A. (2022). The limits of Thai hospitality–Perceived impact of tourism development on residents' well-being in Chiang Mai. *International Journal of Tourism Cities, 8*(1), 187–209. DOI: 10.1108/IJTC-03-2020-0055

Kokkranikal, J., & Carabelli, E. (2024). Gastronomy tourism experiences: The cooking classes of Cinque Terre. *Tourism Recreation Research, 49*(1), 161–172. DOI: 10.1080/02508281.2021.1975213

Kolleck, N. (2019). The power of third sector organizations in public education. *Journal of Educational Administration, 57*(4), 411–425. DOI: 10.1108/JEA-08-2018-0142

Kolotouchkina, O., Ripoll González, L., & Belabas, W. (2024). Smart cities, digital inequalities, and the challenge of Inclusion. *Smart Cities, 7*(6), 3355–3370. DOI: 10.3390/smartcities7060130

Koma, S. B. (2012) "Local economic development in South Africa - Policy implications ", *African Journal of Public Affairs,* Vol 5, No. 3, pp 125-140, [online] https://repository.up.ac.za/bitstream/handle/2263/31727/Koma_Local%282012%29.pdf?isAllowed=y&sequence=1

Komarac, T., Ozretic-Dosen, D., & Skare, V. (2020). Managing edutainment and perceived authenticity of museum visitor experience: Insights from qualitative study. *Museum Management and Curatorship, 35*(2), 160–181. DOI: 10.1080/09647775.2019.1630850

Kotek, K., Schoenberg, A. M., & Schwand, C. (2018). CSR behavior: Between altruism and profit maximization. *Innovation Management and Corporate Social Responsibility: Social Responsibility as Competitive Advantage*, 159-169.

Kotler, P., & Gertner, D. (2011). A place marketing and place branding perspective revisited. Destination Brands, 33–53. DOI: 10.1016/B978-0-08-096930-5.10003-5

Kotler, P., & Gertner, D. (2002). Country as brand, product, and beyond: A place marketing and brand management perspective. *Journal of Brand Management, 9*(4), 249–261. DOI: 10.1057/palgrave.bm.2540076

Kotler, P., Haider, D. H., & Rein, I. (1993). *Marketing Places: Attracting Investment, Industry, and Tourism to Cities, States and Nations*. Free Press.

Kotler, P., & Zaltman, G. (1971). Social marketing: An approach to planned social change. *Journal of Marketing*, *35*(3), 3–12. DOI: 10.1177/002224297103500302 PMID: 12276120

Kujawa, K. (2021). Turkish-Russian Cooperation: Implications for NATO. *Journal of International Students*, *14*(2), 194–207. DOI: 10.14254/2071-8330.2021/14-2/13

Kumar, A., & Verma, A. (2021). Optimal techno-economic sizing of a solar-biomass-battery hybrid system for off-setting dependency on diesel generators for microgrid facilities. *Journal of Energy Storage*, *36*, 102251. DOI: 10.1016/j.est.2021.102251

Kun, P., Freiberger, M. A., Løvlie, A. S., & Risi, S. (2024, July). GenFrame–Embedding Generative AI Into Interactive Artifacts. In *Proceedings of the 2024 ACM Designing Interactive Systems Conference* (pp. 714-727). DOI: 10.1145/3643834.3660750

Kuo, A., & Rice, D. H. (2015). The impact of perceptual congruence on the effectiveness of cause-related marketing campaigns. *Journal of Consumer Psychology*, *25*(1), 78–88. DOI: 10.1016/j.jcps.2014.06.002

Kuo, Y. F., Lin, C. S., & Liu, L. T. (2022). The effects of framing messages and cause-related marketing on backing intentions in reward-based crowdfunding. *Journal of Retailing and Consumer Services*, *64*, 102799. DOI: 10.1016/j.jretconser.2021.102799

*Kurin,R.(2004) "Safeguarding Intangible Cultural Heritage in the 2003 UNESCO Convention: a critical appraisal"*, . Museum international, Vol 56, No. 1-2, pp 66-77, [online] .DOI: 10.1111/j.1350-0775.2004.00459.x

Kyriacou, A., & Roca-Sagalés, O. (2012). The impact of EU structural funds on regional disparities within member states. *Environment and Planning. C, Government & Policy*, *30*(2), 267–281. DOI: 10.1068/c11140r

Lages, R., Sousa, B., & Azevedo, A. (2018). Positioning and image in tourist destination marketing contexts: Case study applied to the city of Braga. *European Journal of Applied Business Management*, (Special Issue), 15–32.

Lai, J. H. (2015). Carbon footprints of hotels: Analysis of three archetypes in Hong Kong. *Sustainable Cities and Society*, *14*, 334–341. DOI: 10.1016/j.scs.2013.09.005

Laimer, P. (2010). Basic Concepts and Definitions: Travel and Tourism (Domestic and International). In Paper on Regional Workshop for the CIS Countries on Tourism Statistics: Challenges and Good Practices. UNWTO/UNSD WS Moldova (Vol. 29).

Lambert, A. J. D., & Boons, F. A. (2002). Eco-industrial parks: Stimulating sustainable development in mixed industrial parks. *Technovation*, *22*(8), 471–484. DOI: 10.1016/S0166-4972(01)00040-2

Lancendorfer, K. M., & Reece, B. B. (2010). Can you market God? A case study of the 'God Speaks' social marketing campaign. *International Journal of Nonprofit and Voluntary Sector Marketing*, *15*(4), 324–338. DOI: 10.1002/nvsm.401

Lang, V., Redeker, N., & Bischof, D. (2022). *Place-based policies and inequality within regions.* OSF. https://doi.org/DOI: 10.31219/osf.io/2xmzj

Lartey, F. M. (2020). Ethical Challenges of Complex Products: Case of Goldman Sachs and the Synthetic Collateralized Debt Obligations. *International Business Research, 13*(6), 115–115. DOI: 10.5539/ibr.v13n6p115

LeChasseur, K. (2018). Re-examining power and privilege in collective impact. In *Collective Impact and Community Development Issues* (pp. 70–85). Routledge. DOI: 10.4324/9781315112916-6

LeCun, Y., Bengio, Y., & Hinton, G. (2015). Deep learning. *Nature, 521*(7553), 436–444. DOI: 10.1038/nature14539 PMID: 26017442

Lee, N. R. (2020). The future of social marketing: Let's get it in orbit by 2025! *Social Marketing Quarterly, 26*(1), 3–13. DOI: 10.1177/1524500419889141

Lee, T. H., & Jan, F. H. (2019). The low-carbon tourism experience: A multidimensional scale development. *Journal of Hospitality & Tourism Research (Washington, D.C.), 43*(6), 890–918. DOI: 10.1177/1096348019849675

Le, H., Gurry, F., & Lennox, J. (2023). An application of land use, transport, and economy interaction model. *Research in Transportation Economics, 99*, 101294. Advance online publication. DOI: 10.1016/j.retrec.2023.101294

Leh, F. C., Mohd Isa, N. K., Ibrahim, M. H., Ibrahim, M., Mohd Yunos, M. Y., & Ibrahim, J. A. (2023). A Literature Review of Low-Carbon Urban Tourism Indicators and Policy. *Pertanika Journal of Social Science & Humanities, 31*(2), 655–681. Advance online publication. DOI: 10.47836/pjssh.31.2.10

Lenzen, M., Sun, Y. Y., Faturay, F., Ting, Y. P., Geschke, A., & Malik, A. (2018). The carbon footprint of global tourism. *Nature Climate Change, 8*(6), 522–528. DOI: 10.1038/s41558-018-0141-x

Leontieva L.S., Avilkina S.V. (2021), The Higher Education System as a Strategic Resource for Regional Development, Gosudarstvennoe upravlenie. Elektronnyy vestnik, (86):200–219, DOI: 10.24412/2070-1381-2021-86-200-219

LeSage, T., Timur, A., & Pawlicki, D. (2021). A case study on the use of the SDGs with a collective impact initiative in Southwest Florida. The foundation review, 13(4), 6.

Li, F., Liu, X. S., Hu, D., Wang, R. S., Yang, W. R., Li, D., & Zhao, D. (2009). Measurement Indexes and an Evaluation Approach for Assessing Urban Sustainable Development: A Case Study for China's Jining City. *Landscape and Urban Planning, 90*(3-4), 134–142. DOI: 10.1016/j.landurbplan.2008.10.022

Lim Regina Mapua. (2006). *Cultural Sustainability and Development: Drukpa and Burman Vernacular Architecture.* Ashgate Publishing Limited.

Li, M., Sun, X., Zhu, Y., & Qiu, H. (2024). Real in virtual: The influence mechanism of virtual reality on tourists' perceptions of presence and authenticity in museum tourism. *International Journal of Contemporary Hospitality Management, 36*(11), 3651–3673. DOI: 10.1108/IJCHM-07-2023-0957

Lima, J., Serra, J., Borges, M. D. R., & Marujo, N. (2024). Is gastronomy important for UNESCO world heritage sites' tourists? A case study from Portugal. *Anatolia*, *35*(2), 326–338. DOI: 10.1080/13032917.2023.2191268

Linderman, A. (2019). Systemic Collective Impact and Rapid City's Ongoing Success Story. *Interdisciplinary Journal of Partnership Studies*, *6*(2), 5–5. DOI: 10.24926/ijps.v6i2.2206

Lindström, S., & Vanhala, S. (2013). Performance in local government HRM: The role of external customers. *Baltic Journal of Management*, *8*(3), 252–268. DOI: 10.1108/BJOM-10-2012-0094

Liu, S., Wei, C., Hu, S.-M., & Alsetoohy, O. (2024). Exploring Post-Experience Evaluation of Gastronomy Tourism Experiences Through Airbnb. *International Journal of Hospitality & Tourism Administration*, 1–28. Advance online publication. DOI: 10.1080/15256480.2024.2389532

Liute, A., & De Giacomo, M. R. (2022). The environmental performance of UK-based B Corp companies: An analysis based on the triple bottom line approach. *Business Strategy and the Environment*, *31*(3), 810–827. DOI: 10.1002/bse.2919

Liu, X., Zeng, Y., He, J., & Li, Z. (2022). Value cocreation research in tourism and hospitality: A comparative bibliometric analysis. *International Journal of Contemporary Hospitality Management*, *34*(2), 663–686. DOI: 10.1108/IJCHM-05-2021-0666

Liu, Z., Yin, Y., Liu, W., & Dunford, M. (2015). Visualizing the intellectual structure and evolution of innovation systems research: A bibliometric analysis. *Scientometrics*, *103*(1), 135–158. DOI: 10.1007/s11192-014-1517-y

Li, X., Fu, Y., & Liu, B. (2020). AI-driven digital reconstruction of historical architectures for cultural heritage. *Heritage Science*, *8*(1), 1–12.

Li, Y., Jiao, L., & Zhou, M. (2024). How does cultural heritage destination digitalization influence tourists' attitudes? The role of constructive authenticity and technology-destination fit. *Journal of Travel & Tourism Marketing*, *41*(2), 221–234. DOI: 10.1080/10548408.2024.2311328

Loddo, S. (2006). *Structural funds and regional convergence in Italy*. Working paper No 2006/03. CRENoS. https://crenos.unica.it/crenos/publications/structural-funds-and-regional-convergence-italy

Lolos, S. (2009). The effect of EU structural funds on regional growth: Assessing the evidence from Greece, 1990-2005. *Economic Change and Restructuring*, *42*(3), 211–228. DOI: 10.1007/s10644-009-9070-z

López Molina, D., & Pulido-Fernández, J. I. (2022). Strategic analysis of a Tourism Stakeholder Network: A comparative study in Ecuadorian cities. *Boletín de la Asociación de Geógrafos Españoles*, (94). Advance online publication. DOI: 10.21138/bage.3283

López, B. Esteban (2022). La orientación oficial del "desarrollo" atenta contra la transmisión del patrimonio biocultural comunitario, en *Revista Internacional de Ciencias Sociales Interdisciplinares*, [The official orientation of "development" threatens the transmission of community biocultural heritage, in International Journal of Interdisciplinary Social Sciences in the Fragmented City, Institute for Social Research]. Vol. 10, núm. 2, Common Ground Research Networks, Estados Unidos de América.

Lopez-Guzman, T. & Santa-Cruz, F.G. (2016) "International tourism and the UNESCO category of intangible cultural heritage", *International Journal of Culture, Tourism and Hospitality Research*, Vol 10, No. 3, pp 310-322, [online] .DOI: 10.1108/IJCTHR-03-2015-0025

López-Molina, D., & Pulido-Fernández, J. I. (2024). Analysis of the interaction and collaboration of the actors of a tourist destination from a network perspective. Current Issues in Tourism, 27(10), 1572-1589. p. 4

Lopez, R. (2015). *Fight against antisemitism and promotion of religious tolerance in Argentina. The creation of the State of Israel*. Democratic Bridge Program of CADAL.

Loureiro, S. M. C., & Kaufmann, H. R. (2012). Explaining Love of Wine Brands. *Journal of Promotion Management, 18*(3), 329–343. DOI: 10.1080/10496491.2012.696460

Loutskina, E., Yemen, G., Mead, J., Loutskina, E., & Yemen, G. (2024). Impact Makers (A): The Newman's Own of Management Consulting. *Darden Business Publishing Cases*, 1-25.

Luo, F., Becken, S., & Zhong, Y. (2018). Changing travel patterns in China and 'carbon footprint' implications for a domestic tourist destination. *Tourism Management, 65*, 1–13. DOI: 10.1016/j.tourman.2017.09.012

Luo, Y., Mou, Y., Wang, Z., Su, Z., & Qin, Y. (2021). Scenario-based planning for a dynamic tourism system with carbon footprint analysis: A case study of Xingwen Global Geopark, China. *Journal of Cleaner Production, 254*, 119999. DOI: 10.1016/j.jclepro.2020.119999

Lyu, Y., Liu, Y., Guo, Y., Sang, J., Tian, J., & Chen, L. (2022). Review of green development of Chinese industrial parks. *Energy Strategy Reviews, 42*, 100867. DOI: 10.1016/j.esr.2022.100867

Ma, C. C., & Chang, H. P. (2019). Environmental consciousness in local sustainable development: A case study of the anti-idling policy in Taiwan. *Sustainability (Basel), 11*(16), 4442. DOI: 10.3390/su11164442

Madlener, R., & Sunak, Y. (2011). Impacts of urbanization on urban structures and energy demand: What can we learn for urban energy planning and urbanization management? *Sustainable Cities and Society, 2011*(1), 45–53. DOI: 10.1016/j.scs.2010.08.006

Magrizos, S., & Harris, L. C. (2023). Crisis induced CSR innovation: CSR implementation in B2B firms before and after COVID-19. *Industrial Marketing Management, 115*, 44–56. DOI: 10.1016/j.indmarman.2023.09.009

Mahadew, R., & Appadoo, K. A. (2019). Tourism and climate change in Mauritius: Assessing the adaptation and mitigation plans and prospects. *Tourism Review, 74*(2), 204–215. DOI: 10.1108/TR-12-2017-0203

Maier, K. (2012). The pursuit of balanced territorial development: The realities and complexities of the cohesion agenda. In Territorial Development, Cohesion and Spatial Planning (pp. 266-290). Routledge.

Malik, O. R. (2017). When Davids start becoming Goliaths: Unique capabilities of emerging-market multinational enterprises and how they foster growth in developed markets? *International Journal of Technology Management, 74*(1-4), 45–69. DOI: 10.1504/IJTM.2017.083594

Mancuso, S. (2020). *Tree Stories*. Editori Laterza.

Mandayam, G., Nandan, M., & Bowen, E. (2023). Convergence of community social work practice, collective impact, and design thinking: What, why, and how? *Journal of Social Work : JSW*, *23*(5), 916–938. DOI: 10.1177/14680173231166112

Manea, D., Titan, E., Boboc, C., & Anoaica, A. (2016), *Logistic Regression in Modelling Some Sustainable Development Phenomena*; Economic Computation and Economic Cybernetics Studies and Research, Vol. 50, Issue 3, 83-100, ISSN 1842–3264; ASE Publishing

Manser, K., Hillebrand, B., Woolthuis, R. K., Ziggers, G. W., Driessen, P. H., & Bloemer, J. (2016). An activities-based approach to network management: An explorative study. *Industrial Marketing Management*, *55*, 187–199. DOI: 10.1016/j.indmarman.2015.10.004

Manthiou, A., Klaus, P., & Luong, V. H. (2022). Slow tourism: Conceptualization and interpretation–A travel vloggers' perspective. *Tourism Management*, *93*, 104570. DOI: 10.1016/j.tourman.2022.104570

Marcus, G., & Davis, E. (2019). *Rebooting AI: Building artificial intelligence we can trust*. Pantheon Books.

Marôco, A. L., Nogueira, F., Gonçalves, S. P., & Marques, I. C. (2022). Work-family interface in the context of social responsibility: A systematic literature review. *Sustainability (Basel)*, *14*(5), 3091. DOI: 10.3390/su14053091

Marquez-Ramos, L., & Mourelle, E. (2018), Education and economic growth: an empirical analysis of nonlinearities, Applied Economic Analysis, Vol 27 Iss 79, pp 21-45, ISSN: 2632-7627, DOI: DOI: 10.1108/AEA-06-2019-0005

Marquina, J., Colinet, M. J., & Pablo-Romero, M. D. P. (2021a). The economic value of olive sector biomass for thermal and electrical uses in Andalusia (Spain). *Renewable & Sustainable Energy Reviews*, *148*, 111278. DOI: 10.1016/j.rser.2021.111278

Marquina, J., Colinet, M. J., & Pablo-Romero, M. D. P. (2021b). Measures to Promote Olive Grove Biomass in Spain and Andalusia: An Opportunity for Economic Recovery against COVID-19. *Sustainability (Basel)*, *13*(20), 11318. DOI: 10.3390/su132011318

Martínez-López, F. J., Merigó, J. M., Valenzuela-Fernández, L., & Nicolás, C. (2018). Fifty years of the European Journal of Marketing: A bibliometric analysis. *European Journal of Marketing*, *52*(1/2), 439–468. DOI: 10.1108/EJM-11-2017-0853

Martínez-Peláez, R., Ochoa-Brust, A., Rivera, S., Félix, V. G., Ostos, R., Brito, H., Félix, R. A., & Mena, L. J. (2023). Role of digital transformation for achieving sustainability: Mediated role of stakeholders, key capabilities, and technology. *Sustainability (Basel)*, *15*(14), 11221. DOI: 10.3390/su151411221

Marzinotto, B. (2012). *The growth effects of EU cohesion policy – a meta-analysis*. Bruegel Working paper No 14/2012. https://www.bruegel.org/working-paper/growth-effects-eu-cohesion-policy-meta-analysis

Mashego, P. S. (2023) "Investigating Traditional leaders' engagement in the integrated development planning and implementation processes in Bushbuckridge local Municipality" (Master's thesis, University of Johannesburg (South Africa).

Ma, W., de Jong, M., Hoppe, T., & de Bruijne, M. (2021). From city promotion via city marketing to city branding: Examining urban strategies in 23 Chinese cities. *Cities (London, England)*, *116*, 103269. DOI: 10.1016/j.cities.2021.103269

Mawejje, J., & Odhiambo, N. (2022). The determinants and cyclicality of fiscal policy: Empirical evidence from East Africa. *Inter Economics*, *169*, 55–70. DOI: 10.1016/j.inteco.2021.12.001

Mayer-Schönberger, V., & Cukier, K. (2013). *Big Data: A Revolution That Will Transform How We Live, Work, and Think*. Eamon Dolan/Houghton Mifflin Harcourt.

Maynou, L., Saez, M., Kyriacou, A., & Bacaria, J. (2016). The impact of structural and cohesion funds on Eurozone convergence, 1990–2010. *Regional Studies*, *50*(7), 1127–1139. DOI: 10.1080/00343404.2014.965137

McCarthy, J., Minsky, M. L., Rochester, N., & Shannon, C. E. (1956). A proposal for the Dartmouth Summer Research Project on Artificial Intelligence. *AI Magazine*, *27*(4), 12. http://jmc.stanford.edu/articles/dartmouth/dartmouth.pdf

McGregor, D. (2004). Traditional ecological knowledge and sustainable development: Towards coexistence. *In the way of development: Indigenous peoples, life projects and globalization*, 72-91.

McKinsey & Company and World Travel & Tourism Council. (2017). *Managing overcrowding in tourist destinations*. World travel & tourism council. www.mckinsey.com/industries/travel-transport-and-logistics/our-insights/coping-with-success-managing-overcrowding-in- tourism-destinations

Meadows, D. H., Meadows, D. L., Randers, J., & Behrens, W. W. (2018). The limits to growth. In *Green planet blues* (pp. 25–29). Routledge. DOI: 10.4324/9780429493744-3

Mebratu, D. (1998). Sustainability and sustainable development: Historical and conceptual review. *Environmental Impact Assessment Review*, *18*(6), 493–520. DOI: 10.1016/S0195-9255(98)00019-5

Medeiros, E. (2020). Portugal 2020: An effective policy platform to promote sustainable territorial development? *Sustainability (Basel)*, *12*(3), 1126. DOI: 10.3390/su12031126

Medeiros, E. (2021). The territorial dimension of the united nations sustainable development goals. *Area*, *53*(2), 292–302. DOI: 10.1111/area.12681

Medina-Jiménez, I., Ramos-Real, F. J., Vielma, J. E. L., & Calero-García, F. (2024). Designing an integrative strategy to introduce electric vehicles in the tourism sector in an outermost region of the European Union. *Sustainable Energy Technologies and Assessments*, *72*, 104071. DOI: 10.1016/j.seta.2024.104071

Mempel-Śnieżyk, A. (2014). Networks and cooperation for sustainable development The role of local authorities and clusters in regional development and economic growth. *European Journal of Sustainable Development*, *3*(3), 111–111. DOI: 10.14207/ejsd.2014.v3n3p111

Meneghin, E., Longhi, A., & Segre, G. (2023). Cultural heritage in non-urban areas: Identifying and understanding values. *Il Capitale Culturale*, *28*, 59–72.

Menéndez, J. A., Fernández-Tresguerres, L. G., Villanueva, S. F., Durán, M., Montes-Morán, M. A., & Arenillas, A. (2018). *Report on the availability of Biomass Sources in Spain: vineyards and olive groves*. Digital CSIC.

Meneses, R. (2022). The tension between Morocco and Algeria: A stoked historic rivalry for Western Sahara and the 'gas war'. *CEIPAZ, 2021-2022*, 157–170.

Menon, M., & Guha, S. (2021). Role of Corporate in Promoting Social Enterprises. In *In Search of Business Models in Social Entrepreneurship: Concepts and Cases* (pp. 119–148). Springer Singapore. DOI: 10.1007/978-981-16-0390-7_6

Merinero, R. (2011). Redes de actores y desarrollo turístico: estudio de caso en Portugal. Journal of Tourism Analysis [Actor networks and tourism development: a case study in Portugal. Journal of Tourism Analysis] = Revista de Análisis Turísticos, 11(1), 9–21.

Merinero-Rodríguez, R., & Pulido-Fernández, J. I. (2009). Desarrollo turístico y dinámica relacional. Metodología de análisis para la gestión activa de destinos turísticos. [Tourism development and relational dynamics. Analysis methodology for the active management of tourist destinations*] Cuadernos de Turismo*, *23*, 173–194.

Merk, J. (2014). The rise of tier 1 firms in the global garment industry: Challenges for labour rights advocates. *Oxford Development Studies*, *42*(2), 259–277. DOI: 10.1080/13600818.2014.908177

Michail, N. (2021). The impact of conflict on the exchange rate of developing economies. *Review of Development Economics*, *25*(2), 916–930. DOI: 10.1111/rode.12749

Milano, C., Cheer, J. M., & Novelli, M. (Eds.). (2019). *Overtourism: Excesses, discontents and measures in travel and tourism*. CABI. DOI: 10.1079/9781786399823.0000

Milic, N. (2022). Digitalising the museum. In *Handbook of research on museum management in the digital era* (pp. 138–154). IGI Global. DOI: 10.4018/978-1-7998-9656-2.ch008

Millan, M. G. D., De la Torre, M. G. M. V., & Rojas, R. H. (2021). Analysis of the demand for gastronomic tourism in Andalusia (Spain). *PLoS ONE, 16*(2 February). DOI: 10.1371/journal.pone.0246377

Millesen, J. (2015). Understanding collective impact in a rural funding collaborative: Collective grantmaking in Appalachian Ohio. *The Foundation Review*, *7*(4), 12. DOI: 10.9707/1944-5660.1271

Ministerio de Agricultura. Pesca y Alimentación. *Encuesta sobre Superficies y Rendimientos de Cultivos (ESYRCE)*. 2023. Available online: https://www.mapa.gob.es/es/estadistica/temas/estadisticas-agrarias/agricultura/esyrce/default.aspx. Accessed on 4 July 2024.

Ministerio de Agricultura. Pesca y Alimentación. *Material vegetal*. 2024. Available online: https://www.mapa.gob.es/app/MaterialVegetal/fichaMaterialVegetal.aspx?idFicha=6. Accessed on 10 September 2024.

Ministerio de Turismo. (2024). *Sistema Nacional de Información Turística del Ecuador*. [National Tourist Information System of Ecuador]. https://servicios.turismo.gob.ec/turismo-en-cifras/

Ministry of Finance of the Republic of Bulgaria. (2022, September 11). *EU Funds in Bulgaria: Assessment of the macroeconomic effects of the implementation of programs co-financed with EU funds.* https://www.minfin.bg/bg/1168

Ministry of Finance of the Republic of Bulgaria. (2024, December 14). *Budget: Statistics.* https://www.minfin.bg/en/613

Ministry of National Education. Morocco (2014). Statistics of education indicators. Retrieved from https://www.men.gov.ma/Fr/Pages/Indices-sysp%C3%A9dag.aspx

Minton, E. A. (2020). Reducing crimes against wildlife through promoting animal–human continuity beliefs: The role of consumers' religiosity. *Psychology and Marketing*, *37*(12), 1731–1742. DOI: 10.1002/mar.21415

Mishra, A. R., Chandel, A., & Saeidi, P. (2022). Low-carbon tourism strategy evaluation and selection using interval-valued intuitionistic fuzzy additive ratio assessment approach based on similarity measures. *Environment, Development and Sustainability*, *24*(5), 7236–7282. DOI: 10.1007/s10668-021-01746-w PMID: 34493927

Mishra, H. G., Pandita, S., Bhat, A. A., Mishra, R. K., & Sharma, S. (2022). Tourism and carbon emissions: A bibliometric review of the last three decades: 1990–2021. *Tourism Review*, *77*(2), 636–658. DOI: 10.1108/TR-07-2021-0310

Mishra, M., & Lourenço, P. B. (2024). Artificial intelligence-assisted visual inspection for cultural heritage: State-of-the-art review. *Journal of Cultural Heritage*, *66*, 536–550. DOI: 10.1016/j.culher.2024.01.005

Mitchell, R., & Hall, C. M. (2003). Consuming tourists: Food tourism consumer behaviour. In *Food Tourism Around The World*. DOI: 10.4324/9780080477862

Mitchell, R. K., Agle, B. R., & Wood, D. J. (1997). Toward a theory of stakeholder identification and salience: Defining the principle of who and what really counts. *Academy of Management Review*, *22*(4), 853–886. DOI: 10.2307/259247

Mkandawire, T. (2001). *Social policy in a development context. Social Policy and Development Programme Paper 7.* United Nations Research Institute for Social Development.

Mkandawire, T. (2004). *Social policy in a development context.* ResearchGate., DOI: 10.1057/9780230523975

Mogila, Z., Miklošovič, T., Lichner, I., Radvanský, M., & Zaleski, J. (2022). Does Cohesion Policy help to combat intra-country regional disparities? A perspective on Central European countries. *Regional Studies*, *56*(10), 1783–1795. DOI: 10.1080/00343404.2022.2037541

Moher, D., Liberati, A., Tetzlaff, J., & Altman, D. G.Prisma Group. (2010). Preferred reporting items for systematic reviews and meta-analyses: The PRISMA statement. *International Journal of Surgery*, *8*(5), 336–341. DOI: 10.1016/j.ijsu.2010.02.007 PMID: 20171303

Mohl, P. (2016). *Empirical evidence on the macroeconomic effects of EU Cohesion Policy*. Springer., DOI: 10.1007/978-3-658-13852-3

Mohl, P., & Hagen, T. (2010). Do EU structural funds promote regional growth? New evidence from various panel data approaches. *Regional Science and Urban Economics, 40*(5), 353–365. DOI: 10.1016/j.regsciurbeco.2010.03.005

Molina-Collado, A., Santos-Vijande, M. L., Gómez-Rico, M., & Madera, J. M. (2022). Sustainability in hospitality and tourism: A review of key research topics from 1994 to 2020. *International Journal of Contemporary Hospitality Management, 34*(8), 3029–3064. DOI: 10.1108/IJCHM-10-2021-1305

Monaco, S. (2024). Introduction: Integrating Territorial Identity into SDGs. In *Identity, Territories, and Sustainability: Challenges and Opportunities for Achieving the UN Sustainable Development Goals* (pp. 1-14). Emerald Publishing Limited.

Moorman, C. (2020). Commentary: Brand activism in a political world. *Journal of Public Policy & Marketing, 39*(4), 388–392. DOI: 10.1177/0743915620945260

Mora, D., Solano-Sánchez, M. Á., López-Guzmán, T., & Moral-Cuadra, S. (2021). Gastronomic experiences as a key element in the development of a tourist destination. *International Journal of Gastronomy and Food Science, 25*, 100405. Advance online publication. DOI: 10.1016/j.ijgfs.2021.100405

Morales, C., Pérez, R., Riffo Pérez, L., & Williner, A. (2021). Desarrollo territorial sostenible y nuevas ciudadanías: consideraciones sobre políticas públicas para un mundo en transformación.

Morse, C., Landau, B., Lallemand, C., Wieneke, L., & Koenig, V. (2022). From #museumathome to #athomeatthemuseum: Digital museums and dialogical engagement beyond the COVID-19 pandemic. [JOCCH]. *ACM Journal on Computing and Cultural Heritage, 15*(2), 1–29. DOI: 10.1145/3480955

Mouratidis, K. (2020). "Built environment, urban vitality and social cohesion: Do vibrant neighborhoods foster strong communities?", en *Landscape and Urban Planning*. Diciembre. https://www.sciencedirect.com/science/article/pii/S0169204620301225

Moyo, C., Mishi S. & Ncwadi, R. (2022), Human capital development, poverty and income inequality in the Eastern Cape province, Development Studies Research, Volume 9, 2022 - Issue 1, Pages 36-47, DOI: 10.1080/21665095.2022.2032236

Mundet, L., & Coenders, G. (2010). Greenways: A sustainable leisure experience concept for both communities and tourists. *Journal of Sustainable Tourism, 18*(5), 657–674. DOI: 10.1080/09669581003668524

Musavengane, R., & Kloppers, R. (2020). Social capital: An investment towards community resilience in the collaborative natural resources management of community-based tourism schemes. *Tourism Management Perspectives, 34*, 100654. DOI: 10.1016/j.tmp.2020.100654

Myakshin, V., & Grishina, I. (2021), Assessment of the Region Investment Attractiveness in Complex Relationship with Sustainable Development on the Basis of the Balanced Scorecard, In Proceedings of the International Scientific and Practical Conference on Sustainable Development of Regional Infrastructure (ISSDRI 2021), pag 388-395, ISBN: 978-989-758-519-7, DOI: DOI: 10.5220/0010591103880395

Nahapiet, J., & Ghoshal, S. (1998). Social Capital, Intellectual Capital, and the Organizational Advantage. *Academy of Management Review, 23*(2), 242. DOI: 10.2307/259373

Nakamura, D. (2023), Attractiveness of Regions and Sustainable Regional Economic System, As a Measure of Social Welfare Function, vol 75, Book Apr 2024, https://link.springer.com/book/9789812878540

Nandasena, R., Morrison, A. M., & Coca-Stefaniak, J. A. (2022). Transformational tourism–a systematic literature review and research agenda. *Journal of Tourism Futures*, *8*(3), 282–297. DOI: 10.1108/JTF-02-2022-0038

National Development Plan 2030. (2013) Executive Summary - Our future - make it work, [online] https://static.pmg.org.za/130917ndp.pdf

National Institute of Statistics. 2023, Statistical Yearbooks of Romania, Available online: https://insse.ro/cms/en/content/statistical-yearbooks-romania

National Statistical Institute of the Republic of Bulgaria (NSI). (2024, December 4). *Statistical data: Macroeconomic statistics*. https://www.nsi.bg/en/content/779/macroeconomic-statistics

Navarrete, T. (2013). Digital cultural heritage. In *Handbook on the economics of cultural heritage* (pp. 251–271). Edward Elgar Publishing. DOI: 10.4337/9780857931009.00023

Ndoro, W. (2015) "World Heritage Sites in Africa: what are the benefits of nomination and inscription?". *A companion to heritage studies*, pp 392-409. DOI: 10.1002/9781118486634.ch27

Negroponte, N. (1995). *Being digital*. Knopf.

Něměcková, T., Melnikovová, L., & Piskunova, N. (2021). Russia's return to Africa: A comparative study of Egypt, Algeria, and Morocco. *The Journal of Modern African Studies*, *59*(3), 367–390. DOI: 10.1017/S0022278X21000070

Nemethova, V., Siranova, M., & Sipikal, M. (2019). Public support for firms in lagging regions-evaluation of innovation subsidy in Slovakia. *Science & Public Policy*, *46*(2), 173–183. DOI: 10.1093/scipol/scy046

Newmeyer, C. E., Obeng, E., & Hulland, J. (2020). Joining forces for doing good: Getting the international cause-alliance right. *International Marketing Review*, *37*(5), 829–839. DOI: 10.1108/IMR-04-2019-0122

Nguyen, T. Q. T., Johnson, P., & Young, T. (2022). Networking, coopetition and sustainability of tourism destinations. *Journal of Hospitality and Tourism Management*, *50*, 400–411. DOI: 10.1016/j.jhtm.2022.01.003

Niebel, T. ICT and economic growth – Comparing developing, emerging and developed countries, World Development, Volume 104, 2018, Pages 197-211, ISSN 0305-750X, DOI: 10.1016/j.worlddev.2017.11.024

Nie, X., Su, S., Zhao, W. M., Guan, J., & Liu, R. (2024). Examining the Effects of Food Consumption Value and Food Image on Tourists' Intention to Purchase Guilin Rice Noodles. *Journal of China Tourism Research*, 1–22. Advance online publication. DOI: 10.1080/19388160.2024.2382713

Nihal, P. (1995). *Critical Vernacularism: The subversion of universalising trends in architecture. Binghamton University*. State University of New York.

Njoya, E., & Ragab, A. (2022). Economic impacts of public air transport investment: A case study of Egypt. *Sustainability (Basel)*, *14*(5), 2651. DOI: 10.3390/su14052651

Noguer-Juncà, E., Crespi-Vallbona, M., & Fusté-Forné, F. (2021). Sociocultural and gastronomic revaluation of local products: Trumfa in the Vall de Camprodon (Catalonia, Spain). *International Journal of Gastronomy and Food Science, 26*, 100425. Advance online publication. DOI: 10.1016/j.ijgfs.2021.100425

Novta, N., & Pugacheva, E. (2021). The macroeconomic costs of conflict. *Journal of Macroeconomics, 68*, 103286. Advance online publication. DOI: 10.1016/j.jmacro.2021.103286

Nunkoo, R. (2015). Tourism development and trust in local government. *Tourism Management, 46*, 623–634. DOI: 10.1016/j.tourman.2014.08.016

Nunkoo, R. (2017). Governance and sustainable tourism: What is the role of trust, power and social capital? *Journal of Destination Marketing & Management, 6*(4), 277–285. DOI: 10.1016/j.jdmm.2017.10.003

Nunkoo, R., & Smith, S. L. (2014). Trust, tourism development, and planning. In *Trust, tourism development and planning* (pp. 1–8). Routledge. DOI: 10.4324/9780203537817

O'Neill, M. (2020). Increasing community engagement in collective impact approaches to advance social change. *Community Development (Columbus, Ohio), 51*(1), 17–35. DOI: 10.1080/15575330.2020.1714684

O'Day, J. A., & Smith, M. S. (2016). Equality and Quality in US Education: Systemic Problems, Systemic Solutions. Policy Brief. *Education Policy Center at American Institutes for Research.*

OECD (2002), *Redefining Territories: The Functional Regions*, OECD Regional Development Studies, OECD Publishing. .DOI: 10.1787/9789264196179-en

OECD. (2020). *Delineating Functional Areas in All Territories. OECD Territorial Reviews.* OECD Publishing., DOI: 10.1787/07970966-

OECD. (2021), What makes a region attractive in the new global environment? How to measure and monitor, Issues Note, 29th November 2021, Rethinking Regional Attractiveness Webinar Series, https://www.oecd.org/regional/Issues-note%20-region-attractive-new-global-environment.pdf

OECD. (2022), Measuring the attractiveness of regions, OECD Regional Development Papers no 36, ISSN: 27094065 (online), DOI: 10.1787/267a6231-en

Oklevik, O., Gössling, S., Hall, C. M., Jacobsen, J. K. S., Grøtte, I. P., & McCabe, S. (2020). Overtourism, optimisation, and destination performance indicators: A case study of activities in Fjord Norway. In *Tourism and Degrowth* (pp. 60–80). Routledge. DOI: 10.4324/9781003017257-4

Onifade, S. T., & Haouas, I. (2023). Assessing environmental sustainability in top Middle East travel destinations: Insights on the multifaceted roles of air transport amidst other energy indicators. *Environmental Science and Pollution Research International, 30*(45), 101911–101926. DOI: 10.1007/s11356-023-29183-4 PMID: 37653199

Orbaslı, A., & Woodward, S. (2009). Tourism and heritage conservation. *The SAGE handbook of tourism studies*, 314-332.

Orts-Cardador, J. J. O., Pérez-Gálvez, J. C., Gomez-Casero, G., & Alba, C. A. J. (2023). Tourist ethnocentrism: A bibliometric analysis based on Web of Science (WoS). *Family and Consumer Sciences Research Journal, 52*(1), 38–52. DOI: 10.1111/fcsr.12488

Ossorio-Aravena, J. C., Rodríguez-Segura, F. J., Frolova, M., Terrados-Cepeda, J., & Muñoz-Cerón, J. (2022). How much solar PV, wind and biomass energy could be implemented in short-term? A multi-criteria GIS-based approach applied to the province of Jaén, Spain. *Journal of Cleaner Production, 366*, 132920. DOI: 10.1016/j.jclepro.2022.132920

Özturan, P., & Grinstein, A. (2022). Can the marketing department benefit from socially responsible marketing activities? The role of legitimacy and customers' interest in social responsibility. *European Journal of Marketing, 56*(2), 400–441. DOI: 10.1108/EJM-09-2020-0670

Palmas, G., Rafanelli, M., & Lanza, C. (2021). AI and the future of cultural heritage: Virtual museums and cultural tourism. *Journal of Cultural Heritage, 48*, 124–134.

Pandey, P. K., & Bajpai, N. (2024). Mapping the research pattern of cause-related marketing: A bibliometric analysis of publications during 2000-2020. *Journal of Nonprofit & Public Sector Marketing, 36*(3), 271–298. DOI: 10.1080/10495142.2022.2133066

Pandey, P., & Yadav, R. (2020). Danone India: The challenges of expanding into an emerging market. *South Asian Journal of Business and Management Cases, 9*(2), 189–197. DOI: 10.1177/2277977920911904

Panjwani, S., Graves-Boswell, T., Garney, W. R., Muraleetharan, D., Spadine, M., & Flores, S. (2023). Evaluating collective impact initiatives: A systematic scoping review. *The American Journal of Evaluation, 44*(3), 406–423. DOI: 10.1177/10982140221130266

Pantilie, A. (2015). Education, Mandatory Condition in the Regional Economic Development of Romania, 2015. *International Journal of Academic Research in Economics and Management Sciences, 4*(1). Advance online publication. DOI: 10.6007/IJAREMS/v4-i1/1468

Panwar, R., Hansen, E., & Kozak, R. (2012). Evaluating social and environmental issues by integrating the legitimacy gap with expectational gaps: An empirical assessment of the forest industry. *Business & Society, 53*(6), 853–875. DOI: 10.1177/0007650312438884

Paramati, S. R., Alam, M. S., & Lau, C. K. M. (2018). The effect of tourism investment on tourism development and CO2 emissions: Empirical evidence from the EU nations. *Journal of Sustainable Tourism, 26*(9), 1587–1607. DOI: 10.1080/09669582.2018.1489398

Pareti, S., Valdebenito, V., Rudolph, L., & Bustamante, C. (2022). Green energy and environmental sustainability on Vernacular Architecture. The case of Ayllus of Atacama Desert and stilt houses of Chiloé. *IOP Conference Series. Earth and Environmental Science, 1094*(1), 012003. DOI: 10.1088/1755-1315/1094/1/012003

Paris Climate Agreement. (2015). https://unfccc.int/es/acerca-de-las-ndc/el-acuerdo-de-paris

Parry, R. (2007). *Recoding the museum: Digital heritage and the technologies of change*. Routledge. DOI: 10.4324/9780203347485

Partnerships, S., & Andreasen, A. R. (2009). Cross-Sector Marketing Alliances. *Nonprofits & Business*, 155.

Paul, O. (2006). *Built to meet needs: Cultural issues in vernacular architecture*. Routledge.

Pearce, D. G. (2014). Toward an integrative conceptual framework of destinations. *Journal of Travel Research, 53*(2), 141–153. DOI: 10.1177/0047287513491334

Pedroza, L. (2020). *Lean Brands: Catch Customers, Drive Growth, and Stand Out in All Markets*. Red Wheel/Weiser.

Pérez, A., & Rodríguez del Bosque, I. (2015). Corporate social responsibility and customer loyalty: Exploring the role of identification, satisfaction and type of company. *Journal of Services Marketing, 29*(1), 15–25. DOI: 10.1108/JSM-10-2013-0272

Petrushenko, M., Burkynskyi, B., Shevchenko, H., & Baranchenko, Y. (2021). Towards sustainable development in a transition economy: The case of eco-industrial parks in Ukraine. *Environment and Ecology, 12*(1), 149–164. DOI: 10.21511/ee.12(1).2021.13

Pfajfar, G., Shoham, A., Małecka, A., & Zalaznik, M. (2022). Value of corporate social responsibility for multiple stakeholders and social impact–Relationship marketing perspective. *Journal of Business Research, 143*, 46–61. DOI: 10.1016/j.jbusres.2022.01.051

Piętak, Ł. (2021). Structural funds and convergence in Poland. *Hacienda Publica Espanola, 236*(1), 3–37. DOI: 10.7866/HPE-RPE.21.1.1

Pike, S. (2005). Tourism destination branding complexity. *Journal of Product and Brand Management, 14*(4), 258–259. DOI: 10.1108/10610420510609267

Pike, S. (2017). Destination positioning and temporality: Tracking relative strengths and weaknesses over time. *Journal of Hospitality and Tourism Management, 31*, 126–133. DOI: 10.1016/j.jhtm.2016.11.005

Pinho, C., Varum, C., & Antunes, M. (2015). Under what conditions do structural funds play a significant role in European regional economic growth? Some evidence from recent panel data. *Journal of Economic Issues, 49*(3), 749–771. DOI: 10.1080/00213624.2015.1072382

Pinto, M., Tregua, M., Gaeta, G. L., & Bifulco, F. (2022). The Long Way Towards Digitization: A Multivariate Analysis on Italian Museums. In *Handbook of Research on Museum Management in the Digital Era* (pp. 331-351). IGI Global. DOI: 10.4018/978-1-7998-9656-2.ch018

Pirnau, M., Ciocardia, R. M. C., Pirnau, C., Ghiculescu, L. D., & Marinescu, N. (2019), *2019* The Identification of Intelligent Interactions between Education and Labour Force Market, *11th International Conference on Electronics, Computers and Artificial Intelligence (ECAI)*, Pitesti, Romania, pp. 1-6, Publisher: IEEE april 2020, DOI: 10.1109/ECAI46879.2019.9042048

Poço, TB (2017). City brand management and the effect on place connection: a case study on the Viana do Castelo brand. [Master's Dissertation in Service Management, Faculty of Economics, University of Porto].

Popescu, C. C., Diaconu, L. (2009), The Relationship Between the Level of Education and the Development State of a Country, Analele Ştiinłifice ale Universitălii „ALEXANDRU IOAN CUZA" din IaşI Tomul LVI Ştiinte Economice 2009

Popovic, S. G., Dobricic, M., & Savic, S. V. (2021). Challenges of sustainable spatial development in the light of new international perspectives-The case of Montenegro. *Land Use Policy, 105*, 105438.

Porter, M. E. (1992). *Competitive advantage: Creating and sustaining superior performance*. PA Consulting Group.

Porter, M. E. (1996). *Competitive Advantage*. Agglomeration Economies, and Regional Policy.

Postema, J. (2021). *The Middle East: U.S. policy, foreign assistance and key issues*. Nova Science Publishers, Inc., Retrieved from https://pesquisa.bvsalud.org/global-literature-on-novel-coronavirus-2019-ncov/resource/pt/covidwho-1469274

Powell, D., & Piggin, J. (2021). Teaching young people about health?. *Critical Pedagogies in Physical Education, Physical Activity and Health*.

Pownall, C. (2015). Social and Environmental Threats. In *Managing Online Reputation: How to Protect Your Company on Social Media* (pp. 37–51). Palgrave Macmillan UK.

Prahalad, C. K. (2005). *The Fortune at the Bottom of the Pyramid*. Financial Times/Prentice Hall.

Prahalad, C. K. (2012). Bottom of the pyramid as a source of breakthrough innovations. *Journal of Product Innovation Management*, *29*(1), 6–12. DOI: 10.1111/j.1540-5885.2011.00874.x

Pratita Vajar Kusuma. (2020), The Impact of Education on Regional Economic Performance in Indonesia, International Journal of Economics, Business and Accounting Research (IJEBAR), Vol 4, No 03, E-ISSN: 2614-1280, http://jurnal.stie-aas.ac.id/index.php/IJEBAR

Prayag, G. (2010). Images as Pull Factors of a Tourist Destination: A Factor-Cluster Segmentation Analysis. *Tourism Analysis*, *15*(2), 213–226. DOI: 10.3727/108354210X12724863327768

Prayitno, G., Auliah, A., Ari, I. R. D., Effendi, A., Hayat, A., Delisa, A., Siankwilimba, E., & Hiddlestone-Mumford, J. (2024). Social capital for sustainable tourism development in Indonesia. *Cogent Social Sciences*, *10*(1), 2293310. DOI: 10.1080/23311886.2023.2293310

Prideaux, B., Timothy, D. J., & Chon, K. (2008). *Themes in Cultural and Heritage Tourism in the Asian Pacific Region*. Routledge.

Priporas, C. V., Stylos, N., & Kamenidou, I. E. (2020). City image, city brand personality and generation Z residents' life satisfaction under economic crisis: Predictors of city-related social media engagement. *Journal of Business Research*, *119*, 453–463. DOI: 10.1016/j.jbusres.2019.05.019

Pritchard, A. (1969). Statistical bibliography or bibliometrics. *The Journal of Documentation*, *25*, 348–349.

Programa de las Naciones Unidas para el Desarrollo. (2022). Informe de desarrollo humano municipal 2010 – 2020. Una década de transformaciones locales en México.[United Nations Development Programme. (2022). Municipal Human Development Report 2010–2020. A Decade of Local Transformations in Mexico] PNUD México.

Provincia Autonoma di Trento Assessorato alle infrastruture e all'ambiente (2018), Trentino sostenibile verso l'Agenda [Autonomous Province of Trento Department of Infrastructure and Environment (2018), Sustainable Trentino towards the Agenda] 2030, available at: https://www.mase.gov.it/sites/default/files/archivio/allegati/CReIAMO_PA/L2WP1/peer_learning_visit/8_Cattani_Progetto_CPA_L2WP1_Workshop_13giugno.pdf

Pulido Fernández, J. I., & López Molina, D. (2023). Las partes interesadas en el desarrollo turístico de un territorio. Análisis de casos en Ecuador [Stakeholders in a Territory's Tourism Development: Case Studies in Ecuador]. *Investigaciones Turísticas*, (26), 251–273. DOI: 10.14198/INTURI.23156

Pulido-Fernández, J. I., & Merinero-Rodríguez, R. (2018). Destinations' relational dynamic and tourism development. *Journal of Destination Marketing & Management*, *7*, 140–152. DOI: 10.1016/j.jdmm.2016.09.008

Putnam, R. D. (1995). Bowling Alone: America's Declining Social Capital. *Journal of Democracy*, *6*(1), 65–78. DOI: 10.1353/jod.1995.0002

Qian, J., Law, R., Wei, J., & Wu, Y. (2019). Trends in global tourism studies: A content analysis of the publications in tourism management. *Journal of Quality Assurance in Hospitality & Tourism*, *20*(6), 753–768. DOI: 10.1080/1528008X.2019.1658149

Quarter, J., Mook, L., & Armstrong, A. (2017). *Understanding the social economy: A Canadian perspective*. University of Toronto Press.

Qu, H., Kim, L. H., & Im, H. H. (2011). A model of destination branding: Integrating the concepts of the branding and destination image. *Tourism Management*, *32*(3), 465–476. DOI: 10.1016/j.tourman.2010.03.014

Rachão, S., Breda, Z., de Oliveira Fernandes, C., Joukes, V., & Ferreira, C. (2023). Food-and-wine tourists' willingness to pay for co-creation experiences: A generational approach. *Journal of Hospitality and Tourism Management*, *56*, 245–252. DOI: 10.1016/j.jhtm.2023.06.004

Radford, A., Wu, J., Child, R., Luan, D., Amodei, D., & Sutskever, I. (2019). Language models are unsupervised multitask learners. *OpenAI Blog*, *1*(8).

Răileanu, S. M. (2018). New insights from a multilevel approach to the regional digital divide in the European Union. *Telecommunications Policy*, *42*(6), 452–463. DOI: 10.1016/j.telpol.2018.03.007

Rainisto, S. (2003) Success factors of place marketing: a study of place marketing practices in Northern Europe and the United States. Retrieved from https://urn.fi/urn:nbn:fi:tkk-000746

Ramamurthy, V. S., & Srivastava, D. K. (2021). A Multidimensional Approach to Sustainable Rural Development. *Science and Culture*, *87*(9-10), 351–360. DOI: 10.36094/sc.v87.2021.A_Multidimensional_Approach_to_Sustainable.Ramamurthy.351

Ramírez Kuri, Patricia (2016). *La reinvención del espacio público en la ciudad fragmentada*, Instituto de Investigaciones Sociales, [The Reinvention of Public Space in the Fragmented City, Institute for Social Research]. UNAM.

Ramukumba, T., Mmbengwa, V. M., Mwamayi, K. A., & Groenewald, J. A. (2012). Analysis of local economic development (LED) initiated partnership and support services for emerging tourism entrepreneurs in George municipality, Western Cape Province, RSA. *Tourism Management Perspectives*, *2*, 7–12. DOI: 10.1016/j.tmp.2011.12.006

Ranjith, D. (2018). *Toward sustainable development: Lessons from vernacular settlements of Sri Lanka. Frontiers of Architectural Research*. South East University.

Rendón, A. Mario (2006). Zapopan: ¿una identidad guadalajarizada? en *Estudios Jaliscienses*, núm. [A Guadalajaran identity? In Estudios Jaliscienses, no.65]. El Colegio de Jalisco, 5-19.

Reyes, E. (2024). Turistificación: el impacto en las comunidades urbanas. [Touristification: The Impact on Urban Communities]. *BNZero.*

Rico, A., Martínez-Blanco, J., Montlleó, M., Rodríguez, G., Tavares, N., Arias, A., & Oliver-Solà, J. (2019). Carbon footprint of tourism in Barcelona. *Tourism Management*, *70*, 491–504. DOI: 10.1016/j.tourman.2018.09.012

Ricoy, C. (2005). Adam Smith's theory of economic growth. *Economy and Development*, *138*(1), 11–47.

Riegl, A. (1996). The modern cult of monuments: its essence and its development. *Historical and philosophical issues in the conservation of cultural heritage*, 69, 83.

Rizzi, P., & Dioli, I. (2010). Strategic planning, place marketing and city branding: The Italian case. *Journal Of Town & City Management*, *1*(3), 300–317.

Robinson David (2019) Geoffrey Bawa: The master architect of Sri Lanka. STIRworld.

Robins, S., Gready, P., Aloui, A., Andrieu, K., Hamza, H., & Ferchichi, W. (2022). Transitional justice from the margins: Collective reparations and Tunisia's Truth and Dignity Commission. *Political Geography*, *94*, 102565. Advance online publication. DOI: 10.1016/j.polgeo.2021.102565

Rodionov, D. G., Konnikov, E. A., & Nasrutdinov, M. N. (2021). A transformation of the approach to evaluating a region's investment attractiveness as a consequence of the COVID-19 pandemic. *Economies*, *9*(59), 1–20. DOI: 10.3390/economies9020059

Rodrigues, A., Reis, J., Pinto, F., & Lucas, D. (2021). Mass movement risk in a Portuguese municipality: Tabuaço case study. *Proceedings of the Institution of Civil Engineers-Forensic Engineering*, *173*(3), 65–73. DOI: 10.1680/jfoen.20.00018

Rodrigues, D., Sousa, B., Gomes, S., Oliveira, J., & Lopes, E. (2023). Exploring consumer behavior and brand management in the automotive sector: Insights from a digital and territorial perspective. *Administrative Sciences*, *13*(2), 36. DOI: 10.3390/admsci13020036

Rodríguez, G., Lama, A., Rodríguez, R., Jiménez, A., Guillén, R., & Férnandez-Bolaños, J. (2008). Olive stones an attractive source of bioactive and valuable compunds. *Bioresource Technology*, *99*(13), 5261–5269. DOI: 10.1016/j.biortech.2007.11.027 PMID: 18160280

Rodríguez-Lizana, A., Ramos, A., Pereira, M. J., Soares, A., & Castro Ribeiro, M. (2023). Assessment of the Spatial Variability and Uncertainty of Shreddable Pruning Biomass in an Olive Grove Based on Canopy Volume and Tree Projected Area. *Agronomy (Basel)*, *13*(17), 1697. DOI: 10.3390/agronomy13071697

Rodríguez-Pérez, M. L., Mendieta-Pino, C. A., Ramos-Martín, A., León-Zerpa, F. A., & Déniz-Quintana, F. A. (2022). Inventory of water–energy–waste resources in rural houses in Gran Canaria Island: Application and potential of renewable resources and mitigation of carbon footprint and GHG. *Water (Basel)*, *14*(8), 1197. DOI: 10.3390/w14081197

Rodríguez-Pose, A., & Novak, K. (2013). Learning processes and economic returns in European Cohesion policy. *Investigaciones Regionales*, 25, 7–26. http://www.aecr.org/images/ImatgesArticles/2013/5/1_Rodriguez.pdf

Rodríguez-Pose, A., & Tselios, V. (2010), Inequalities in income and education and regional economic growth in western Europe, *The Annals of Regional Science*, vol 44, pag 349–375, https://link.springer.com/article/10.1007/s00168-008-0267-2

Rodríguez-Pose, A. (2013). Do institutions matter for regional development? *Regional Studies*, *47*(7), 1034–1047. DOI: 10.1080/00343404.2012.748978

Román-Collado, R., & Colinet, M. J. (2021). Energy efficiency's key role in explaining the performance of energy consumption in Andalusia (Spain). *Environmental Science and Pollution Research International*, *28*(16), 20188–20208. DOI: 10.1007/s11356-020-11829-2 PMID: 33410050

Romanelli, M. (2020). Museums and technology for value creation. *Technology and Creativity: Production, Mediation and Evaluation in the Digital Age*, 181-210.

Romero-García, J. M., Sánchez, A., Rendón-Acosta, G., Martínez-Patiño, J. C., Ruiz, E., Magaña, G., & Castro, E. (2016). An olive tree pruning biorefinery for co-producing high value-added bioproducts and biofuels: Economic and energy efficiency analysis. *BioEnergy Research*, *9*(4), 1086–1070. DOI: 10.1007/s12155-016-9786-3

Roseland, M. (2000). Sustainable community development: Integrating environmental, economic, and social objectives. *Progress in Planning*, *54*(2), 73–132. DOI: 10.1016/S0305-9006(00)00003-9

Roseta, P., Sousa, B. B., & Roseta, L. (2020). Determiners in the consumer's purchase decision process in ecotourism contexts: A Portuguese case study. *Geosciences*, *10*(6), 224. DOI: 10.3390/geosciences10060224

Rosúa, J. M., & Pasadas, M. Biomass potential in Andalusia, from grapevines, olives, fruit trees and poplar, for providing heating in homes. Renewable and Sustainable Energy Reviews, 2012, 16(6), 4190-4195.

Roswinna, W. (2020). Increasing The Potential Region Attractiveness In The Development Order Investation. *Sosiohumaniora*, *22*(3), 341–347. DOI: 10.24198/sosiohumaniora.v22i3.28499

Roxas, F. M. Y., Rivera, J. P. R., & Gutierrez, E. L. M. (2020). Mapping stakeholders' roles in governing sustainable tourism destinations. *Journal of Hospitality and Tourism Management*, *45*, 387–398. DOI: 10.1016/j.jhtm.2020.09.005

Rubin, N., & Franck, L. (2017). The role of Ronald McDonald House Charities® in keeping families close. *Pediatric Nursing*, *43*(4), 202.

Rudofsky, B. (1964). *Architecture without Architects: A short introduction to non-pedigreed architecture*. University of New Mexico Press.

Ruhanen, L., & Whitford, M. (2021). Cultural heritage and Indigenous tourism. In *Indigenous heritage* (pp. 1–13). Routledge. DOI: 10.4324/9781003142997-1

Ruiz Pulpon, A. R., & Canizares Ruiz, M. D. C. (2020). Enhancing the territorial heritage of declining rural areas in Spain: Towards integrating top-down and bottom-up approaches. *Land (Basel)*, *9*(7), 216. DOI: 10.3390/land9070216

Rust, N. A., Ptak, E. N., Graversgaard, M., Iversen, S., Reed, M. S., de Vries, J. R., Ingram, J., Mills, J., Neumann, R. K., Kjeldsen, C., Muro, M., & Dalgaard, T. (2023). Social capital factors affecting uptake of sustainable soil management practices: A literature review. *Emerald Open Research*, *1*(10). Advance online publication. DOI: 10.1108/EOR-10-2023-0002

Sabet, N. S., & Khaksar, S. (2024). The performance of local government, social capital and participation of villagers in sustainable rural development. *The Social Science Journal*, *61*(1), 1–29. DOI: 10.1080/03623319.2020.1782649

Saboori, B., Mahdavian, S. M., & Radmehr, R. (2024). Assessing the environmental impact of institutional quality at aggregate and disaggregate levels: The role of renewable and non-renewable energy consumption and trade in MENA countries. *Sustainable Environment*, *10*(1), 2426833. Advance online publication. DOI: 10.1080/27658511.2024.2426833

Sabrina, M., Nuzhat, F., & Shariful, S. (2020) Vernacular Architecture of South Asia: Exploring Passive Design Strategies of Traditional Houses in Warm Humid Climate of Bangladesh and Sri Lanka. *Proceedings of the International Conference of Contemporary Affairs in Architecture and Urbanism-ICCAUA*. 3. 216-226. DOI: 10.38027/N212020ICCAUA316262

Sabri, O. (2018). The detrimental effect of cause-related marketing parodies. *Journal of Business Ethics*, *151*(2), 517–537. DOI: 10.1007/s10551-016-3232-5

Safa, P. (2000). "El estudio de las identidades vecinales: una propuesta metodológica". ["The study of neighborhood identities: a methodological proposal."]. *Revista Universidad de Guadalajara*, http://www.cge.udg.mx/revistaudg/rug19/articulo3.html

Saha, S., Ranjan, K. R., Pappu, R., & Akhlaghpour, S. (2023). Corporate giving and its impact on consumer evaluations: A meta-analysis. *Journal of Business Research*, *158*, 113656. DOI: 10.1016/j.jbusres.2023.113656

Salazar, J. N., Vergara-Romero, A., Sorhegui-Ortega, R., & Garnica-Jarrin, L. (2021). Repensando el Desarrollo Sostenible en el territorio. Res non verba revista científica, [Rethinking Sustainable Development in the Territory. Res non verba, a scientific journal]. 11(1), 19-33.

Salvati, L., & Carlucci, M. (2014). A Composite Index of Sustainable Development at the Local Scale: Italy as a Case Study. *Ecological Indicators*, *2014*(43), 162–171. DOI: 10.1016/j.ecolind.2014.02.021

Sampaio de Almeida, D., Simões, R., Brito e Abreu, F., Lopes, A., & Boavida-Portugal, I. (2024). A Carrying Capacity Calculator for Pedestrians Using OpenStreetMap Data: Application to Urban Tourism and Public Spaces. *arXiv preprint arXiv:2406.16781*.

Samuel, D. (2022). *Kath Kuni Architecture: Origin and Development*. Amazing Architecture.

Sánchez, J. (2016). Human Development Index (HDI). Retrieved from https://economipedia.com/definiciones/indice-desarrollo-humano.html

Sánchez-Martínez, J. D., & Paniza Cabrera, A. (2015). The olive monoculture in the south of Spain. *Eruopean Journal of Geography*, *6*(3), 16–29.

Sánchez-Torné, I., Morán-Álvarez, J. C., & Pérez-López, J. A. (2020). The importance of corporate social responsibility in achieving high corporate reputation. *Corporate Social Responsibility and Environmental Management*, *27*(6), 2692–2700. DOI: 10.1002/csr.1993

Sandhya, A., & Singh, C. A. (2023). *A decade after the floods, is Kedarnath safer?* The Third Pole.

Santos, V., Ramos, P., Sousa, B., Almeida, N. and Valeri, M. (2022), "Factors influencing touristic consumer behavior", Journal of Organizational Change Management, Vol. 35 No. 3, pp . 409-429. DOI: 10.1108/JOCM-02-2021-0032

Satrovic, E., & Muslija, A. (2019). The empirical evidence on tourism-urbanization-CO2 emissions nexus. [AHTR]. *Advances in Hospitality and Tourism Research*, *7*(1), 85–105. DOI: 10.30519/ahtr.484287

Satyro, W. C., Sacomano, J. B., Contador, J. C., Almeida, C. M., & Giannetti, B. F. (2017). Process of strategy formulation for sustainable environmental development: Basic model. *Journal of Cleaner Production*, *2017*(166), 1295–1304. DOI: 10.1016/j.jclepro.2017.08.128

Schartel Dunn, S., & Nisbett, G. S. (2023). When celebrity endorsements collide with social activism: Exploring athlete celebrity endorsements, social issues and brand perception. *International Journal of Sports Marketing & Sponsorship*, *24*(3), 558–569. DOI: 10.1108/IJSMS-01-2023-0010

Schwab, T. (2024). Quo Vadis, Cohesion Policy? European regional development at a crossroads. *Inter Economics*, *59*(5), 284–292. DOI: 10.2478/ie-2024-0056

Scott, D., Gössling, S., & Hall, C. M. (2012). International tourism and climate change. *Wiley Interdisciplinary Reviews: Climate Change*, *3*(3), 213–232. DOI: 10.1002/wcc.165

Scott, D., Gössling, S., Hall, C. M., & Peeters, P. (2016). Can tourism be part of the decarbonized global economy? The costs and risks of alternate carbon reduction policy pathways. *Journal of Sustainable Tourism*, *24*(1), 52–72. DOI: 10.1080/09669582.2015.1107080

Scott, D., Hall, C. M., & Gössling, S. (2019). Global tourism vulnerability to climate change. *Annals of Tourism Research*, *77*, 49–61. DOI: 10.1016/j.annals.2019.05.007

Scott, D., Peeters, P., & Gössling, S. (2010). Can tourism deliver its "aspirational" greenhouse gas emission reduction targets? *Journal of Sustainable Tourism*, *18*(3), 393–408. DOI: 10.1080/09669581003653542

Seetanah, B., & Fauzel, S. (2018). Investigating the impact of climate change on the tourism sector: Evidence from a sample of island economies. *Tourism Review*, *74*(2), 194–203. DOI: 10.1108/TR-12-2017-0204

Semenescu, G. (2014). From Local Urban Development to Cooperation and Territorial Cohesion. Annals Constantin Brancusi U. Targu Jiu, Letters & Soc. Sci. Series, 100.

Semosa, P., & Kanayo, O. (2021). Is there a nexus between inflation, exchange rate and unemployment in South Africa: An econometric analysis? *Montenegrin Journal of Economics*, *17*(1), 45–58. DOI: 10.14254/1800-5845/2021.17-1.3

Sen, A. (2016). The ends and means of sustainability. In *The Capability Approach and Sustainability* (pp. 5–19). Routledge.

Şengül, S., Usta Dişsiz, S., & Uçkan Çakır, M. (2024a). Over-gastronomy: Conceptualisation of the problems in gastronomy. *Current Issues in Tourism*, 1–18. Advance online publication. DOI: 10.1080/13683500.2024.2390675

Sertakova, E., Koptseva, N., Kolesnik, M., Libakova, N., Luzan, V., & Sergeeva, N. (2016). Brand-management of Siberian cities: Krasnoyarsk as a case study. *International Review of Management and Marketing*, *6*(S5), 185–191.

Sghaier, I. (2021). Remittances and economic growth in MENA Countries: The role of financial development. *Economic Alternatives*, *2021*(1), 43–59. DOI: 10.37075/EA.2021.1.03

Sgroi, F. (2021). Food products, gastronomy and religious tourism: The resilience of food landscapes. *International Journal of Gastronomy and Food Science*, *26*, 100435. Advance online publication. DOI: 10.1016/j.ijgfs.2021.100435

Shabalala, L. P., & Ezeuduji, I. O. (2022) "Community Involvement and participation in Sustainable Development of Cultural Heritage Tourism: A case from South Africa". Evangelos Christou & Anestis Fotiadis (Eds). Reviving tourism, in the post pandemic era. The School of Economics and Business, International Hellenic Univerity, Greece. DOI: DOI: 10.5281/zenodo.6428590

Shakouri, B., Khoshnevis Yazdi, S., & Ghorchebigi, E. (2017). Does tourism development promote CO2 emissions? *Anatolia*, *28*(3), 444–452. DOI: 10.1080/13032917.2017.1335648

Sharifi, A., Allam, Z., Bibri, S. E., & Khavarian-Garmsir, A. R. (2024). Smart cities and sustainable development goals (SDGs): A systematic literature review of co-benefits and trade-offs. *Cities (London, England)*, *146*, 104659. DOI: 10.1016/j.cities.2023.104659

Shen, N., Au, K., & Li, W. (2020). Strategic alignment of intangible assets: The role of corporate social responsibility. *Asia Pacific Journal of Management*, *37*(4), 1119–1139. DOI: 10.1007/s10490-019-09681-1

Shie, A. J., Dai, Y. Y., Shen, M. X., Tian, L., Yang, M., Luo, W. W., Wu, Y. J., & Su, Z. H. (2022). Diamond model of green commitment and low-carbon travel motivation, constraint, and intention. *International Journal of Environmental Research and Public Health*, *19*(14), 8454. DOI: 10.3390/ijerph19148454 PMID: 35886303

Shi, Y., Ge, X., Yuan, X., Wang, Q., Kellett, J., Li, F., & Ba, K. (2019). An Integrated Indicator System and Evaluation Model for Regional Sustainable Development. *Sustainability (Basel)*, *11*(7), 2183. DOI: 10.3390/su11072183

Shoori, M., Bijan, A., & Ejazi, E. (2021). Security implications of Russian arms exports to West Asian countries (Iran, Egypt, Syria, and Iraq). *Central Eurasia Studies*, *14*(2), 25–46. DOI: 10.22059/jcep.2022.320197.449990

Sikorska-Wolak, I., Zawadka, J., & Krzyżanowska, K. (2020), The Investment Attractiveness Of Regions As One Of Entrepreneurship Development Factors, Economic and Regional Studies (Studia Ekonomiczne i Regionalne), vol. 13(2), p.170-183, ISSN 2083-3725, DOI: 10.2478/ers-2020-0012

Singh, R., Bakshi, M., & Mishra, P. (2015). Corporate social responsibility: Linking bottom of the pyramid to market development? *Journal of Business Ethics*, *131*(2), 361–373. DOI: 10.1007/s10551-014-2283-8

Singh, V., Singh, T., Higueras-Castillo, E., & Liebana-Cabanillas, F. J. (2023). Sustainable road transportation adoption research: A meta and weight analysis, and moderation analysis. *Journal of Cleaner Production*, *392*, 136276. DOI: 10.1016/j.jclepro.2023.136276

Sinha, R., & Haluwalia, S. (2024). Gastronomic delights for community growth: Unravelling the impact of sustainable tourism in Sikkim, India. *International Journal of Tourism Policy*, *14*(4), 384–401. DOI: 10.1504/IJTP.2024.139729

Skanavis, C., & Sakellari, M. (2011). International tourism, domestic tourism and environmental change: Environmental education can find the balance. *Tourismos*, *6*(1), 233–249.

Smith, M. K. (2009). *Issues in cultural tourism studies*. Routledge. DOI: 10.4324/9780203869857

Smith, S. M., & Alcorn, D. S. (1991). Cause marketing: A new direction in the marketing of corporate responsibility. *Journal of Consumer Marketing*, *8*(3), 19–35. DOI: 10.1108/07363769110035054

Soltero, V. M., Román, L., Peralta, M. E., & Chacartegui, R. (2020). Sustainable biomass pellets using trunk wood from olive groves at the end of their life cycle. *Energy Reports*, *6*, 2627–2640. DOI: 10.1016/j.egyr.2020.09.017

Sompolska-Rzechuła, A., & Kurdyś-Kujawska, A. (2022). Assessment of the development of poverty in EU countries. *International Journal of Environmental Research and Public Health*, *19*(7), 3950. DOI: 10.3390/ijerph19073950 PMID: 35409633

Soonsan, N., Phakdee-auksorn, P., & Suksirisopon, P. (2023). Determining food attributes for measuring and evaluating a gastronomic destination's appeal to visitors. *Journal of Hospitality and Tourism Insights*, *6*(5), 1755–1775. DOI: 10.1108/JHTI-02-2022-0048

Sörensson, A., Faith-Ell, C., Jansson, A., Lindvert, M., Bogren, M., & Lundström, A. (2024). Samhällsutveckling i norra Sverige – från småföretag till stora etableringar. [Community development in northern Sweden – from small businesses to large establishments] In Bäckström, I., Fredman, P., Giritli-Nygren, K., Niskanen, K., Olofsson, A., Nilsson, H.-E., & Lindbäck, K. (Eds.), *Globala utmaningar – lokala lösningar: Forskning för en hållbar samhällsutveckling i norra Sverige* [Global challenges – local solutions: Research for a sustainable community development in northern Sweden]. (pp. 109–111). Mid Sweden University.

Sörensson, A., & Jansson, A. M. (2016). Sustainability reporting among Swedish tourism service providers: Information differences between them. *WIT Transactions on Ecology and the Environment*, *201*, 103–113. DOI: 10.2495/ST160091

Šostar, M., Ristanović, V., & de Alwis, C. (2023). Application of successful EU funds absorption models to sustainable regional development. *Economies*, 11, 220. DOI: 10.20944/preprints202306.1876.v1

Sotiriou, A., & Tsiapa, M. (2015). The asymmetric influence of structural funds on regional growth in Greece. *Environment and Planning. C, Government & Policy*, *33*(4), 863–881. DOI: 10.1177/0263774X15603905

Sourla, S., Bampoulis, P., & Ioannidis, S. (2022). AI in cultural heritage preservation: Challenges and solutions. *Journal of Digital Heritage*, *10*(2), 78–88.

Sousa, B., & Simões, C. (2018). "An approach on place attachment, involvement and behavioral intentions in Iberian marketing contexts: the case of Galicia-North Portugal Euroregion: an abstract", in Rossi, P. and Krey, N. (Eds), Finding New Ways to Engage and Satisfy Global Customers, Proceedings of the 2018

Sousa, B., & Rocha, A. T. (2019). The role of attachment in public management and place marketing contexts: A case study applied to Vila de Montalegre (Portugal). *International Journal of Public Sector Performance Management*, *5*(2), 189–205. DOI: 10.1504/IJPSPM.2019.099094

Spilioti, N., & Anastasiou, A. (2024). European Structural and Investment Funds (ESIFs) and regional development across the European Union (EU*).Journal of Risk and Financial Management*, *17*(6), 228. DOI: 10.3390/jrfm17060228

Stach, E., Matoga, L., & Pawłowska, A. (2014), Evaluation of Tourist Attractiveness of the Communes in Chełm County in the Context of the Development of Cross-Border Tourism, Barometr Regionalny Tom 12 nr 3 Nyborg Storm, H. (2022), Cultural Institutions and Attractiveness: How Cultural Institutions Contribute to the Development of Regions and Local Communities, https://research.cbs.dk/en/publications/cultural-institutions-and-attractiveness-how-cultural-institution

Staehr, K., & Urke, K. (2022). The European structural and investment funds and public investment in the EU countries. *Empirica*, *49*(4), 1031–1062. DOI: 10.1007/s10663-022-09549-6 PMID: 36320380

Starostka-Patyk, M., Tomski, P., & Zawada, M. (2015). Diversity management as a part of corporate social responsibility policy. *Procedia Computer Science*, *65*, 1038–1045. DOI: 10.1016/j.procs.2015.09.055

Stepus, I. S., Averyanov, A. O., & Gurtov, V. A. (2022). Indicators of the Interrelation between the Education System and the Labor Market: Development and Testing. *Integra Educativa*, *26*(4), 594–612. DOI: 10.15507/1991-9468.109.026.202204.594-612

Stockholm Resilience Centre Annual Report (2023) Investing in Resilience. Stockholm University.

Stoilova, D. (2023). The impact of tax structure on economic growth: New empirical evidence from Central and Eastern Europe. *Journal of Tax Reform*, *9*(2), 181–196. DOI: 10.15826/jtr.2023.9.2.136

Stoilova, D., & Todorov, I. (2021). Fiscal policy and economic growth: Evidence from Central and Eastern Europe. *Journal of Tax Reform*, *7*(2), 146–159. DOI: 10.15826/jtr.2021.7.2.095

Stojanovic, A., Milosevic, I., Arsic, S., Urosevic, S., & Mihajlovic, I. (2020). Corporate social responsibility as a determinant of employee loyalty and business performance. *Journal of Competitiveness*, *12*(2), 149–166. DOI: 10.7441/joc.2020.02.09

Stolle, D., & Rochon, T. R. (1998). Are all associations alike? Member diversity, associational type, and the creation of social capital. *The American Behavioral Scientist*, *42*(1), 47–65. DOI: 10.1177/0002764298042001005

Strategia Naţională pentru Dezvoltare Durabilă a României Orizonturi 2013–2020–2030, https://www.mmediu.ro/beta/domenii/dezvoltare-durabila/strategia-nationala-a-romaniei-2013-2020-2030/

Strubell, E., Ganesh, A., & McCallum, A. (2019). Energy and policy considerations for deep learning in NLP. *Proceedings of the 57th Annual Meeting of the Association for Computational Linguistics*. DOI: 10.18653/v1/P19-1355

Suarez, A., & Gwozdz, W. (2023). On the relation between monocultures and ecosystem services in the Global South: A review. *Biological Conservation*, *278*, 109870. DOI: 10.1016/j.biocon.2022.109870

Su, J. (2019). Impact of tourism resource development based on low-carbon mode: A case study of Guizhou ethnic areas. *Ecological Processes*, *8*(1), 1–7. DOI: 10.1186/s13717-019-0176-6

Su, J. (2020). Managing intangible cultural heritage in the context of tourism: Chinese officials' perspectives. *Journal of Tourism and Cultural Change*, *18*(2), 164–186. DOI: 10.1080/14766825.2019.1604720

Sung, P. L., Hsiao, T. Y., Huang, L., & Morrison, A. M. (2021). The influence of green trust on travel agency intentions to promote low-carbon tours for the purpose of sustainable development. *Corporate Social Responsibility and Environmental Management*, *28*(4), 1185–1199. DOI: 10.1002/csr.2131

Sun, Y., Qin, Y., Hu, Y., Wang, S., & Bi, X. (2021), The Correlation Analysis of Education Level and Regional Economic Growth Quality in Guangdong Province, Advances in Social Science, Education and Humanities Research, vol 598, *Proceedings of the 7th International Conference on Social Science and Higher Education (ICSSHE 2021)*, DOI: DOI: 10.2991/assehr.k.211122.116

Sutiadiningsih, A., Mahfud, T., Dang, V. H., Purwidiani, N., Rachma Wati, G., & Dewi, I. H. P. (2024). THE ROLE OF GASTRONOMY TOURISM ON REVISIT AND RECOMMENDATION INTENTIONS: THE MEDIATION ANALYSIS OF TOURIST SATISFACTION. *Geo Journal of Tourism and Geosites*, *52*(1), 195–202. DOI: 10.30892/gtg.52118-1195

Szarleta, E. (2017). Capacity building for social innovation: A collective impact approach. *Metropolitan Universities*, *28*(4), 81–100. DOI: 10.18060/21744

Tamburini, F. (2021). The COVID-19 outbreak in North Africa: A legal analysis. *Journal of Asian and African Studies*, *56*(7), 1738–1754. DOI: 10.1177/0021909620983586 PMID: 38603075

Tang, Z., & Huang, T. (2021). Carbon dioxide emission measurement and its spatiotemporal evolution of tourism industry in Heilongjiang province, China. *Advances in Meteorology*, *2021*(1), 1458373. DOI: 10.1155/2021/1458373

Tang, Z., Shang, J., Shi, C., Liu, Z., & Bi, K. (2014). Decoupling indicators of CO2 emissions from the tourism industry in China: 1990–2012. *Ecological Indicators*, *46*, 390–397. DOI: 10.1016/j.ecolind.2014.06.041

Taormina, F., & Baraldi, S. B. (2023). Museums and digital technology: a literature review on organizational issues. *Rethinking Culture and Creativity in the Digital Transformation*, 69-87.

Teng, C. C., Lu, A. C. C., & Huang, T. T. (2018). Drivers of consumers' behavioral intention toward green hotels. *International Journal of Contemporary Hospitality Management*, *30*(2), 1134–1151. Advance online publication. DOI: 10.1108/IJCHM-04-2017-0203

Terrasi, M. (1999). Convergence and divergence across Italian regions. *The Annals of Regional Science*, *33*(4), 491–510. DOI: 10.1007/s001680050117

Thabit, Q., Nassour, A., & Nelles, M. (2020). Potentiality of Waste-to-Energy Sector Coupling in the MENA Region: Jordan as a Case Study. *Energies 2020, Vol. 13, Page 2786, 13(11),* 2786. DOI: 10.3390/en13112786

The Appalachian Regional Commission (ARC). available at: https://www.arc.gov/

The Brundtland Commission Report. (1987). *Our common future.* Oxford University Press.

The Free Encyclopaedia. (2022) Bushbuckridge Local Municipality, [online] https://en.wikipedia.org/wiki/Bushbuckridge_Local_Municipality

The Local Government Handbook. South Africa. (2015) " A complete guide to municipalities in South Africa", 5th Ed, Yes!Media: Mowbray. ISSN: 2220-5179, [online] https://issuu.com/yesmedia/docs/lgh2015?e=5245023%2F11022032

The White Paper on Local Government – South African Government. (1998), [online] https://www.gov.za/sites/default/files/gcis_document/201409/whitepaper0.pdf

Thees, H., & Pechlaner, H. (2019). Tourism along the new silk road. Prospects for integrated development of regions and destinations | Tourismus entlang der Neuen Seidenstraße: Chancen für eine integrierte Regional-und Destinationsentwicklung. *Geographische Rundschau, 71*(6), 12–17.

Thomsen, R. C., & Vester, S. P. (2016). Towards a semiotics-based typology of authenticities in heritage tourism: Authenticities at Nottingham Castle, UK, and Nuuk Colonial Harbour, Greenland. *Scandinavian Journal of Hospitality and Tourism, 16*(3), 254–273. DOI: 10.1080/15022250.2015.1084148

Thongdejsri, M., & Nitivattananon, V. (2019). Assessing impacts of implementing low-carbon tourism program for sustainable tourism in a world heritage city. *Tourism Review, 74*(2), 216–234. DOI: 10.1108/TR-04-2017-0082

Thongkaw, B., Kongbuamai, N., Chinnakum, W., & Chaiboonsri, C. (2024). The Impact of Gastronomic Tourism on the Regional Economy of Thailand: Examined by the Dynamic I-O Model after the Decline of COVID-19. *Economies, 12*(7), 180. Advance online publication. DOI: 10.3390/economies12070180

Tian, C., Peng, J., Zhang, W., Zhang, S., & Wang, J. (2020). Tourism environmental impact assessment based on improved AHP and picture fuzzy PROMETHEE II methods. *Technological and Economic Development of Economy, 26*(2), 355–378. DOI: 10.3846/tede.2019.11413

Tim, Y., Ouyang, T., & Zeng, D. (2020). Back to the future: Actualizing technology affordances to transform Emperor Qin's terracotta warriors Museum. *Information & Management, 57*(8), 103271. DOI: 10.1016/j.im.2020.103271

Titu, M. A., Pirnau, C., & Pirnau, M. (2013), Creativity, Education and Quality for Sustainable Development, the real Support for the Innovative Cluster's European Network, 8th Research/Expert Conference with International Participations "QUALITY 2013", Neum, B&H, June 06 – 08, 2013, pp 19-24, https://quality.unze.ba/zbornici/QUALITY%202013/004-Q13-111.pdf

Todorov, I., Durova, K., & Aleksandrov, A. (2018). *The Economy of Bulgaria: Structural Funds, Growth and Cyclical Recurrence.* Sciendo., DOI: 10.2478/9783110619218

Tomasi, S., Zubaryeva, A., Pizzirani, C., Dal Col, M., & Balest, J. (2021). Propensity to choose electric vehicles in cross-border alpine regions. *Sustainability (Basel), 13*(8), 4583. DOI: 10.3390/su13084583

Torre, A., & Wallet, F. (2015). Towards new paths for regional and territorial development in rural areas. *European Planning Studies, 23*(4), 650–677. DOI: 10.1080/09654313.2014.945812

Torres, A. (2013). US diplomacy and the North African 'War of the Sands' (1963). *Journal of North African Studies, 18*(2), 324–348. DOI: 10.1080/13629387.2013.767041

Torrús-Castillo. Calero, J.; García-Ruíz, R. Does olive cultivation sequester carbon?: Carbon balance along a C input gradient. Agriculture, Ecosystems & Environment, 2023, 358, 108707.

Trček, D. (2022). Cultural heritage preservation by using blockchain technologies. *Heritage Science, 10*(1), 6. DOI: 10.1186/s40494-021-00643-9

Truong, V. D. (2014). Social marketing: A systematic review of research 1998–2012. *Social Marketing Quarterly, 20*(1), 15–34. DOI: 10.1177/1524500413517666

Truong, V. D. (2017). Government-led macro-social marketing programs in Vietnam: Outcomes, challenges, and implications. *Journal of Macromarketing, 37*(4), 409–425. DOI: 10.1177/0276146716660833

Tsai, K. T., Lin, T. P., Hwang, R. L., & Huang, Y. J. (2014). Carbon dioxide emissions generated by energy consumption of hotels and homestay facilities in Taiwan. *Tourism Management, 42*, 13-21http:// DOI: 10.1016/j.tourman.2013.08.017

Turing, A. M. (1950). Computing machinery and intelligence. *Mind, 59*(236), 433–460. DOI: 10.1093/mind/LIX.236.433

Turner, S., Merchant, K., Kania, J., & Martin, E. (2012). Understanding the value of backbone organizations in collective impact. *Stanford Social Innovation Review*, •••, 1.

Tyner, E. H., & Boyer, T. A. (2020). Applying best-worst scaling to rank ecosystem and economic benefits of restoration and conservation in the Great Lakes. *Journal of Environmental Management, 255*, 109888. DOI: 10.1016/j.jenvman.2019.109888 PMID: 31790870

Uche, C., & Khalid, S. (2023). The effect of organised hypocrisy: Compensation committees and fair compensation in the Ghanaian mining industry. *Critical Perspectives on Accounting, 95*, 102509. DOI: 10.1016/j.cpa.2022.102509

Udir Mišič, K., & Podnar, K. (2018). Perception of city management, fellow residents, and Perceived External Prestige (PEP) as antecedents of city affective commitment - The city marketing perspective. *Cities (London, England)*. Advance online publication. DOI: 10.1016/j.cities.2018.04.016

UNESCO World Heritage Convention (2004) River Island Majuli mid-stream in Brahmaputra river in Assam

UNESCO. (2003). *Convention for the safeguarding of the intangible cultural heritage*. Retrieved from https://ich.unesco.org/en/convention

UNESCO. (2007). UNESCO-EIIHCAP regional meeting. In *Safeguarding Intangible Heritage and Sustainable Cultural Tourism: Opportunities and Challenges*. UNESCO.

UNESCO. (2022). *Protecting cultural heritage through technology*. Retrieved from: https://www.unesco.org/en/digital-culture-and-technology

UNESCO. (2023). UNESCO World Heritage List. https://whc.unesco.org/es/list/

UNIDO. (2024). The United Nations Industrial Development Organization's Industrial Park Platform. https://ipp.unido.org/industrial-parks-overview

Unified Management Information System for the EU Structural Instruments in Bulgaria 2007-2013 (UMIS). (2024, December 4). *Public information on the implementation of operational programs in Bulgaria: Database*. https://umispublic.government.bg

United Nation Climate Change. (2022). *UN Climate Change Conference*. UN (enviromental programme). https://www.unep.org/events/conference/un-climate-change-conference-unfccc-cop-27#:~:text=In%20November%202022%2C%20Egypt%20will,the%20way%20for%20future%20ambition

United Nations Climate Change (2022) Growing desertification demonstrates need for adaptation plans

United Nations Environment Program (2010) Greening cement production has a big role to play in reducing Green House Gas emissions

United Nations Environment Program (2024) Global Status Report for Buildings and Construction United Nations Regional Information Centre for Western Europe (2022) Sustainable Infrastructure: a synergy between climate mitigation and economic growth

United Nations. (1992), AGENDA 21, Conference on Environment & Development, Rio de Janerio, Brazil, 3 to 14 June 1992, https://sustainabledevelopment.un.org/content/documents/Agenda21.pdf

United Nations. (2010), The Sustainable Development Goals 2030 Agenda, https://sustainabledevelopment.un.org/

United Nations. (2015) Transforming our world: the 2030 Agenda for Sustainable Development, [online] https://sustainabledevelopment.un.org/content/documents/21252030%20Agenda%20for%20Sustainable%20Development%20web.pdf

United Nations. (2015). *Sustainable Development Goals.*

United Nations. (2016), High-level Advisory Group on Sustainable Transport, Mobilizing Sustainable Transport for Development, https://sustainabledevelopment.un.org/index.php?page=view&type=400&nr=2375&menu=35

United Nations. (2019), The Climate Technology Centre and Network (CTCN), Climate Strategies 2020, December 10, 2019, https://www.ctc-n.org/news/new-publication-climate-strategies-2020

United Nations. (2024a). *Sustainable Development Goals 8*. https://www.un.org/sustainabledevelopment/economic-growth/

United Nations. (2024b). *Sustainable Development Goals 11*. https://www.un.org/sustainabledevelopment/cities/

University of Victoria research groups. (2012) Complexity Science in brief, [online] https://www.uvic.ca/research/groups/cphfri/assets/doc/Complexity_science_in _brief.pdf

UNWTO. (2018). World Tourism Organization. *International tourism results in 2017: highest in seven years.*https://www.unwto.org/es/press-release/2018-01-15/resultados-del-turismo-internacional-en-2017-los-mas-altos-en-siete-anos

UNWTO. (2019). World Tourism Organization and International Transport Forum (2019). *Transport-related $CO_2$ Emissions of the Tourism Sector – Modelling Results,* UNWTO, Madrid. DOI: 10.18111/9789284416660

UNWTO. (2021). Transforming Tourism for Climate Action. https://www.unwto.org/sustainable-development/climate-action

Valdani, E., & Ancari, F. (2001). Marketing Places. A Resource-Based Approach and Empirical Evidence from the European Experience. SDA Bocconi, Research Division Working Paper, 01/55.

Valero, A. (2021), Education and economic growth, Centre for Economic Performance, London School of Economics and Political Science, Discussion Paper No.1764, ISSN 2042-2695

Van der Zanden Marloes. (2018). *Assessment of the seismic performance and sustainability of the Kath Kuni building style in the Indian Himalaya.* Delft University of Technology.

Van Eck, N. J., & Waltman, L. (2022). *VOSviewer Manual. Manual for VOSviewer Version 1.6.v8.* https://www.vosviewer.com/documentation/Manual_VOSviewer_1.6.18.pdf

Vasilev, D., Ganev, K., Simeonova-Ganeva, R., Chobanov, P., & Tsvetkov, S. (2011). Model for Impact Assessment of the Structural Funds and the Cohesion Fund of the European Union in Bulgaria: SIBILA. SSRN *Electronic Journal.* DOI: 10.2139/ssrn.2290694

Vegas, F., Mileto, C., Escobar, A. H., & de Miguel, M. L. (2022). Sustainability, Risks and Resilience of Vernacular Architecture. *International Journal of Architectural Heritage, 16*(6), 817–819. DOI: 10.1080/15583058.2022.2067435

Velázquez-Martí, B., Fernández-González, E., López-Cortés, I., & Salazar-Hernández, D. M. (2011). Quantification of the residual biomass obtained from pruning of trees in Mediterranean olive groves. *Biomass and Bioenergy, 35*(7), 3208–3217. DOI: 10.1016/j.biombioe.2011.04.042

Venugopal, P., & Agrawal, D. (2023). Can corporate social responsibility make business sense? framework based on itc e-choupal. In *Strategic Corporate Responsibility and Green Management: Perspectives and Issues in Emerging Economies* (pp. 69-81). Emerald Publishing Limited.

Vinerean, A. (2013). Consumer behavior in tourism and the influencing factors of the decision making process. *Revista Economica, 65*(2), 186–198.

Vinod, T., & Ramon, L. (2015) Global Increase in Climate related disasters. ADB Economics Working Paper Series. No. 466

Virtanen, P., Ristikari, T., & Niemelä, M. (2021). Collective Impact Partnership and Backbone Organizations as Enablers of Children's Well-Being. *Partnerships for the Goals*, 183-196.

Völlers, P., Yavan, N., & Franz, M. (2021). The reaction of foreign firms to institutional changes: The case of German Direct Investment in Türkiye. *Applied Geography (Sevenoaks, England)*, *134*, 102503. Advance online publication. DOI: 10.1016/j.apgeog.2021.102503

Von Ehrlich, M. (2024). *The importance of EU Cohesion Policy for economic growth and convergence*. ZEW - Centre for European Economic Research, Discussion Paper No. 24-041. DOI: 10.2139/ssrn.4871714

Vongvisitsin, T. B., Huang, W. J., & King, B. (2024). Urban community-based tourism development: A networked social capital model. *Annals of Tourism Research*, *106*, 103759. DOI: 10.1016/j.annals.2024.103759

Voronkova, O. Y., Yankovskaya, V., Kovaleva, I., Epishkin, I., Iusupova, I., & Berdova, Y. (2019). Sustainable territorial development based on the effective use of resource potential. *Entrepreneurship and Sustainability Issues*, *7*(1), 662–673. DOI: 10.9770/jesi.2019.7.1(47)

Vuignier, R. (2017). Place branding & place marketing 1976–2016: A multidisciplinary literature review. *International Review on Public and Nonprofit Marketing*, *14*(4), 447–473. DOI: 10.1007/s12208-017-0181-3

Vukašina, M., Kersan-škabić, I., & Orlić, E. (2022). Impact of European structural and investment funds absorption on the regional development in the EU–12 (new member states). Equilibrium. *Quarterly Journal of Economics and Economic Policy*, *17*(4), 857–880. DOI: 10.24136/eq.2022.029

Waligo, V., Clarke, J., & Hawkins, R. (2013). Implementing sustainable tourism: A multi-stakeholder involvement management framework. *Tourism Management*, *36*, 342–353. DOI: 10.1016/j.tourman.2012.10.008

Wang, C. (2021). Monopoly with corporate social responsibility, product differentiation, and environmental R&D: Implications for economic, environmental, and social sustainability. *Journal of Cleaner Production*, *287*, 125433. DOI: 10.1016/j.jclepro.2020.125433

Wang, H., Sua, L. S., & Dolar, B. (2024). CAMELS-DEA in assessing the role of major factors in achieving higher efficiency levels: Evidence from Turkish banks. *Applied Economics*, •••, 1–18. DOI: 10.1080/00036846.2024.2339186

Wang, Q., Mao, Z., Xian, L., & Liang, Z. (2019). A study on the coupling coordination between tourism and the low-carbon city. *Asia Pacific Journal of Tourism Research*, *24*(6), 550–562. DOI: 10.1080/10941665.2019.1610002

Wang, S., Cao, W., Du, J., Tang, P., Fu, H., Tang, Z., & Li, J. (2021). Assessing the environmental impact of China's tourism activities: A tourism heat footprint method. *Environmental Science and Pollution Research International*, *28*(43), 61176–61188. DOI: 10.1007/s11356-021-15082-z PMID: 34169419

Wang, Y., Chen, J., Ren, X., & Tao, D. (2024). Low-carbon strategy and tourism development. *Current Issues in Tourism*, *27*(21), 3458–3477. DOI: 10.1080/13683500.2023.2266100

Wangzhou, K., Wen, J. J., Wang, Z., Wang, H., Hao, C., & Andlib, Z. (2022). Revealing the nexus between tourism development and CO2 emissions in Asia: Does asymmetry matter? *Environmental Science and Pollution Research International*, *29*(52), 79016–79024. DOI: 10.1007/s11356-022-21339-y PMID: 35705760

Wani, M. J. G., Alamir, I. A., Ghazwani, M., Ahmed, I., Alkaraan, F., & Khan, M. A. (2024). Asymmetric Effect of Green Energy and Economic Growth on the Environmental Deterioration and the Environmental Kuznets Curve Validation in MENA Countries. *International Journal of Finance & Economics*, ijfe.3079. Advance online publication. DOI: 10.1002/ijfe.3079

WCED (World Commission on Environment and Development). (1987), Our common future: The Brundtland report, Oxford University Press 1987, p. 43

Weaver, L., & Cabaj, M. (2018). Collective impact 3.0: Extending the collective impact vision for community change 1. Using collective impact to bring community change, 97-112.

Weaver, L. (2019). *The Journey of Collective Impact: Contributions to the Field from Tamarack Institute*. FriesenPress.

Were, G. (2015). Digital heritage and the problem of authenticity. *Museum Anthropology*, *38*(2), 133–142. DOI: 10.1111/muan.12058

Were, G. (2015). Digital heritage in a Melanesian context: Authenticity, integrity and ancestrality from the other side of the digital divide. *International Journal of Heritage Studies*, *21*(2), 153–165. DOI: 10.1080/13527258.2013.842607

White, L. A. (2018). Social marketing in the Caribbean: Philosophy, programs, projects, and pedagogy. *Social Marketing Quarterly*, *24*(1), 35–44. DOI: 10.1177/1524500417752311

White, P. (2009). Building a sustainability strategy into the business. *Corporate Governance (Bradford)*, *9*(4), 386–394. DOI: 10.1108/14720700910984936

Whittlesea, E. R., & Owen, A. (2012). Towards a low carbon future–the development and application of REAP Tourism, a destination footprint and scenario tool. *Journal of Sustainable Tourism*, *20*(6), 845–865. DOI: 10.1080/09669582.2012.680699

Wolniak, R., & Stecuła, K. (2024). Artificial Intelligence in Smart Cities—Applications, Barriers, and Future Directions: A Review. *Smart Cities*, *7*(3), 1346–1389. DOI: 10.3390/smartcities7030057

World Bank. (2021a). Economic data of Middle East and North Africa (MENA) countries. Retrieved from https://data.worldbank.org/region/middle-east-and-north-africa

World Bank. (2021b). Country data of Middle East and North Africa (MENA). Retrieved from https://data.worldbank.org/country/

World Bank. (2024, May 16). Data and Statistics: Country Groups. *World Bank Database*. https://www.worldbank.org

World Health Organisation Fact Sheet (August 2023) Lead Poisoning

WTCC-UNEP-UNFCCC. (2021). *Transforming Tourism for Climate Action.* UNWTO: Sustainable development climate action. https://action.wttc.org/climate-environment

Wu, P., & Shi, P. (2011). An estimation of energy consumption and CO2 emissions in tourism sector of China. *Journal of Geographical Sciences*, *21*(4), 733–745. DOI: 10.1007/s11442-011-0876-z

Xu, J., Yao, L., & Mo, L. (2011). Simulation of low-carbon tourism in world natural and cultural heritage areas: An application to Shizhong District of Leshan City in China. *Energy Policy*, *39*(7), 4298–4307. DOI: 10.1016/j.enpol.2011.04.047

Yang, F. F., Li, X., & Choe, Y. (2022). What constitutes a favorable destination brand portfolio? Through the lens of coherence. *Tourism Management*, *90*, 104480. DOI: 10.1016/j.tourman.2021.104480

Yingkai, M. (2022). Research on the Influence of Educational Resources on Regional Economic Development, SHS Web of Conferences 151, 01005 (2022). *EMSD*, *2022*(dec). Advance online publication. DOI: 10.1051/shsconf/202215101005

Yin, R. K. (2009). *Case study research: Design and methods.* SAGE Publications.

Yip Christopher, L. (2000) Bhutan: Its Architectural Heritage and Change. ACSA 2000 International Conference. Hong Kong. China.

You, L., & Hon, L. C. (2021). Testing the effects of reputation, value congruence and brand identity on word-of-mouth intentions. *Journal of Communication Management (London)*, *25*(2), 160–181. DOI: 10.1108/JCOM-10-2020-0119

Žáček, J., Hrůza, F., & Volčík, S. (2019). The impact of EU funds on regional economic growth of the Czech Republic. *Finance a Uver - Czech. Journal of Economics and Finance*, *69*(1), 76–94. https://journal.fsv.cuni.cz/mag/article/show/id/1429

Zelenski John, M., Dopko Raelyne, L., & Capaldi Colin, A. (2015). Cooperation is in our Nature: Nature Exposure may promote Cooperative and Environmentally Sustainable Behavior. *Journal of Environmental Psychology*, *42*, 24–31. DOI: 10.1016/j.jenvp.2015.01.005

Zenker, S., Braun, E., & Petersen, S. (2017). Branding the destination versus the place: The effects of brand complexity and identification for residents and visitors. *Tourism Management*, *58*, 15–27. DOI: 10.1016/j.tourman.2016.10.008

Zenker, S., & Jacobsen, B. P. (2015). *Inter-Regional Place Branding. Best Practices, Challenges and Solutions.* Springer International Publishing. DOI: 10.1007/978-3-319-15329-2

Zha, J., He, L., Liu, Y., & Shao, Y. (2019). Evaluation on development efficiency of low-carbon tourism economy: A case study of Hubei Province, China. *Socio-Economic Planning Sciences*, *66*, 47–57. DOI: 10.1016/j.seps.2018.07.003

Zhang, B., Chen, H., Du, Z., & Wang, Z. (2020). Does license plate rule induce low-carbon choices in residents' daily travels: Motivation and impacts. *Renewable & Sustainable Energy Reviews*, *124*, 109780. DOI: 10.1016/j.rser.2020.109780

Zhang, F., Chung, C. K. L., Lu, T., & Wu, F. (2021). The role of the local government in China's urban sustainability transition: A case study of Wuxi's solar development. *Cities (London, England)*, *117*, 103294. DOI: 10.1016/j.cities.2021.103294

Zhang, H., Fu, X., Cai, L. A., & Lu, L. (2014). Destination image and tourist loyalty: A meta-analysis. *Tourism Management*, *40*, 213–223. DOI: 10.1016/j.tourman.2013.06.006

Zhang, J., & Zhang, Y. (2018). Carbon tax, tourism CO2 emissions and economic welfare. *Annals of Tourism Research*, *69*, 18–30. DOI: 10.1016/j.annals.2017.12.009

Zhang, J., & Zhang, Y. (2019). Exploring the impacts of carbon tax on tourism-related energy consumption in China. *Sustainable Development (Bradford)*, *27*(3), 296–303. DOI: 10.1002/sd.1900

Zhang, J., & Zhang, Y. (2020). Assessing the low-carbon tourism in the tourism-based urban destinations. *Journal of Cleaner Production*, *276*, 124303. DOI: 10.1016/j.jclepro.2020.124303

Zhang, M., Cui, Y., ter Avest, E., & van Dijk, M. P. (2018). Adoption of voluntary approach: Can voluntary approach generate collective impacts for China achieving ambitious energy efficiency targets? *Energy & Environment*, *29*(2), 281–299. DOI: 10.1177/0958305X17744491

Zhong, L., Liu, J., Morrison, A. M., & Yang, L. (2024). Peking duck, anyone? An analysis of international tourist food perceptions and influence factors. *International Journal of Gastronomy and Food Science*, *37*, 100980. Advance online publication. DOI: 10.1016/j.ijgfs.2024.100980

Zhu, H., & Yasami, M. (2021). DEVELOPING GASTRONOMIC RESOURCES: PRACTICES of UNESCO CREATIVE CITIES of GASTRONOMY. *Geo Journal of Tourism and Geosites*, *39*(4 supplement), 1406–1414. DOI: 10.30892/gtg.394spl11-784

Zientara, P., Kujawski, L., & Bohdanowicz-Godfrey, P. (2015). Corporate social responsibility and employee attitudes: Evidence from a study of Polish hotel employees. *Journal of Sustainable Tourism*, *23*(6), 859–880. DOI: 10.1080/09669582.2015.1019511

Zong, J., Wan Mohamed, W. S., Zaky Jaafar, M. F., & Ujang, N. (2024). Sustainable development of vernacular architecture: A systematic literature review. *Journal of Asian Architecture and Building Engineering*, •••, 1–17. DOI: 10.1080/13467581.2024.2399685

Zou, H., Zheng, Y., Zhang, Y., & Liu, Y. (2024). A Geospatial Perspective on the Factors Influencing Tourist Dining Satisfaction. *Journal of Geovisualization and Spatial Analysis*, *8*(2), 25. Advance online publication. DOI: 10.1007/s41651-024-00186-0

Zupic, I., & Čater, T. (2015). Bibliometric methods in management and organization. *Organizational Research Methods*, *18*(3), 429–472. DOI: 10.1177/1094428114562629

Zvaigzne, A., Mietule, I., Kotane, I., Sprudzane, S., & Bartkute-Norkuniene, V. (2023). Digital innovations in tourism: The perceptions of stakeholders. *Worldwide Hospitality and Tourism Themes*, *15*(5), 528–537. DOI: 10.1108/WHATT-06-2023-0080

# About the Contributors

**Anna D'Auria** is an Assistant Professor of Management at the University of Naples L'Orientale and holds a PhD in Tourism management from the University of Naples Federico II. She was visiting scholar and professor at the University of Jaén in Spain, at the University of Sczczin in Poland and at the University of Skövde in Sweden. She participated in national and international conferences, published books on Tourism management and Innovation and sustainability, and book chapters on Tourism and Innovation management. Sha also published scientific papers on international academic journal as Journal of Service Theory and Practice, Knowledge Management Research & Practice, International Journal of Entrepreneurial Behavior & Research, and Sustainability Science. Her main areas of research are Tourism and Destination management, Innovation and Smart city, International business, Sustainable development and Sustainable city.

**Javier Sánchez-Rivas García** is a Doctor in Economics from the University of Seville since 2009, and currently Vice Dean of Institutional Relations of the Faculty of Law. Member of the Seville Tourism Sustainability Committee. Permanent professor of the International Master's Degree in Management and Conservation of Historical Sites of the Faculty of Architecture of the Universidad Michoacana de San Nicolás de Hidalgo since 2019. Author of 10 international book chapters on the legal protection, management and enhancement of historical-cultural heritage and author of twenty international research articles. Permanent Professor-Researcher at the Mexican Universities of Guadalajara and Michoacana de San Nicolás de Hidalgo. Principal investigator of 8 research contracts for knowledge transfer on the sustainability of cultural heritage in the tourism sector and team member of 8 International Research Projects.

***

**Cristina Barzallo-Neira** is PhD in Economics, Business and Legal Sciences from the University of Jaén (Spain). Professor-researcher in gastronomic tourism at the University of Cuenca (Ecuador). She studied a Master's Degree in Tourism Planning and a Specialist Course in Pedagogy. And completed her postgraduate training studying Gastronomic Tourism at the Basque Culinary Center. Her main research interests focus on gastronomic tourism and cultural tourism. She is author and co-author of several scientific articles in high-impact international journals and book chapters in publishers of international prestige.

**Davide Bizjak**, PhD, is Associate Professor in Organization Studies at the University of Naples Federico II, Italy, and he is a former Research Trainee at the University of Essex, UK. His primary research interests lie in the areas of Arts Organisations, Organisational Identity, and Arts

Entrepreneurship. He has been awarded several prizes and research grants, EURAM Grant Scheme 2019, and Best Reviewer at the EURAM Conference – SIG 01 (Paris 2016). He is SIG chair of EURAM's "Business for society". He actively serves as a reviewer for several international journals and conferences, and has published extensively on the abovementioned areas.

**Maria Bogren** is Associate Professor of Organization and Leadership at Nord University Business School in Steinkjer, Norway. She previously held a position at Mid Sweden University in Östersund, Sweden, where she received her PhD and was later appointed as Associate Professor of Business Administration. Bogren's research interests are broad, encompassing areas such as Working Life Research, Entrepreneurship, Sustainability, and Marketing. She contributed to the research project "Large Sustainable Establishments" and is currently the project leader of the research project "Limitless Competence" with researchers from Norway and Sweden. Additionally, she collaborates with researchers in Spain, focusing on both Entrepreneurship and Sustainability, and is a member of The Institute for Sustainable Social Development (INDESS) at the University of Cadiz, Spain.

**Elena Carvajal-Trujillo** is an Associate professor of Marketing in the Faculty of Business Science Management and Tourism, University of Huelva (Spain). She received her Ph.D. in Business Administration from University of Seville in Spain. Her research interests include Internet marketing, consumer behavior and tourism marketing. Her research has appeared in journal as Journal of Retailing and Consumer Services, Tourism Management, Tourism Management Perspectives, International Journal of Hospitality Management, among others.

**Alessandra De Chiara** is a Full Professor of Business Economics and Management and teaches International Business Economics and Management and Corporate Strategies for Sustainable Development. Her research focuses on sustainability and corporate social responsibility, with particular attention to supply chains, clusters, and local systems. Specifically, her studies explore stakeholder engagement in sustainability strategies, CSR communication and standards, and new consumption models in the circular economy. She is the Coordinator of the Master's Program in International Relations and the Rector's Delegate for Sustainability at the University of Naples L'Orientale.

**Charlotta Faith-Ell** is Assistant Professor in Environmental Science at Mid Sweden University in Östersund, Sweden. She received her PhD in Natural Resources Science at KTH Royal Institute of Technology, Stockholm, Sweden. She has more than 20 years of experience in both practical work and research within the realm of sustainable urban development. She contributed to the research project "Large Sustainable Establishments" and is currently involved in several projects, focusing on industrial establishments and transport planning.

**Iuliu Marin Ivănescu** is a Lecturer at the School of International Business. He has been invited as Erasmus Professor by universities in Finland, Germany, Austria, Spain, etc. The areas of interest are: International Trade and Trade Policies, Economic Diplomacy.

**Anna-Maria Jansson** is lecturer in Business Administration at Mid Sweden University in Östersund, Sweden. She received her licentiate thesis at Luleå University of Technology in 2008. Jansson's research interests encompass areas such as Accounting, Auditing and Sustainability. She contributed to the research project "Large Sustainable Establishments" and is currently in the project "Pre-study about attractive residential areas in connection with large sustainable establishments" with researchers from Mid Sweden University.

**Marta Lindvert** is Associate Professor in Entrepreneurship at Nord University Business School, Bodø, Norway. She previously held a position at Mid Sweden University in Östersund, Sweden, where she received her PhD in Business Administration. Her main research interests include entrepreneurial financing and resource mobilization, particularly from a gender perspective. She is also interested in the role of different contexts for entrepreneurship and has conducted field studies in a variety of countries, often working with qualitative methods and inspired by ethnographic approaches. She contributed to the research project "Large Sustainable Establishments" and is currently involved in several projects, focusing on gender and inclusion in STEM sectors, entrepreneurship education and entrepreneurship in the New Space Economy.

**Diana López Molina** has a PhD in Economics, Business and Law, University of Jaén - Spain. Master in Cultural Management with mention in Heritage, by the University of Barcelona - Spain. Professor at the University of Cuenca. Her main lines of research focus on destination management, tourism development, stakeholders and social network analysis. Author and co-author of several articles published in some of the main international journals.

**Pratap Chandra Mandal** is an Assistant Professor (Marketing) at Indian Institute of Management, Shillong, India. He has completed graduate degree from the reputed Indian Institute of Technology, Kharagpur (IIT Kharagpur), India (Bachelor of Technology in Mechanical Engineering), post-graduate degree from Vinod Gupta School of Management, IIT Kharagpur (Masters in Business Adminstration), PhD (Marketing) from Vinod Gupta School of Management, IIT Kharagpur. His research concerns customer relationship management, customer satisfaction, services marketing, marketing intelligence, and qualitative methods in management. He is the editor-in-chief of two international journals and is on the editorial board of journals like Journal of Global Marketing. Pratap has won several prestigious scholarships and awards throughout his academic career.

**Rogelio Martínez Cárdenas**, Ph.D. in Sciences, Full-Time Research Professor, Department of Organizational Studies, Los Altos University Center, University of Guadalajara. Mexico. He is also a Member of the National System of Researchers (SNI) level I,Member of the Scientific Committee of PRERICO (the ICOMOS International Scientific Committee on Places of Religion and Ritual), Member of the Scientific Committee on Cultural Tourism of ICOMOS, Member of the Mexican Academy of Tourism Research. Mexico, Member of the Network of Researchers and Research Centers in Tourism (RICIT), Member of the Network of Researchers of the Religious Phenomenon in Mexico.

**Jaime José Orts Cardador** is a PhD candidate from the University of Cordoba. Lecturer in Marketing of the University of Sevilla (Spain) and Researcher of the Research Group "Quantitative Methods in Economics, Finance and Business". He has a Degree in Business Administration and Law and a Master in Advocacy and Business Advisory from the University of Cordoba. His main lines of research are the relationship between tourism and ethnocentrism, new technology, sustainability and co-creation. He has publish articles on various prestigious journals, such as Journal of Tourism Futures,

Geojournal of Tourism and Geosites or Family Consumer Sciences Research Journal. Indeed, he has attended numerous international congress.

**Francisco Partida Hoy**, Ph.D. in Sciences and Humanities for Interdisciplinary Development, Full-Time Research Professor, Department of Organizational Studies, Los Altos University Center, University of Guadalajara. Mexico. He is also a Member of the National System of Researchers of Mexico (SNI-C). He is a member of the International Research Network in Interdisciplinary Social Sciences.

**Jesús Claudio Pérez Gálvez** is an Associate Professor in the Department of Applied Economics at the University of Córdoba (Spain). He has a Doctoral Degree in Economics (PhD). He has written more than 50 articles that have been published in different academic journals related to tourism such as Current Issues in Tourism, Tourism Culture & Communication, Journal of Heritage Tourism, Journal of Outdoor Recreation and Tourism, or Sustainable Cities and Society. He is also an author of 6 books' chapters and 2 books in prestigious publishers. Similarly, he has been a principal researcher of 2 projects that have been supported by public and private organisations, and as a researcher he has participated in 10 projects. His main lines of research are tourism economics and culture sectors. He is the director of the research group "Quantitative Methods in Economics, Finance and Business" (SEJ-670) and a researcher of "the Ibero-American Network of Research in Economics and Tourism Management (REDEGETUR)". He has conducted different research stays in European countries and Latin America.

**Juan Ignacio Pulido-Fernández**, Ph.D. in Economics, is Full Professor of Applied Economics (Tourism Economics) in the Department of Economics and Head of the Laboratory of Analysis and Innovation in Tourism (LAInnTUR) at the University of Jaén (Spain). His main research interests focus on tourism economics, destination management, sustainability of tourism, tourism impacts, and social network analysis. He has published a number of articles in some of the leading international peer-reviewed journals (Tourism Management, Journal of Sustainable Tourism, Journal of Travel Research, International Journal of Tourism Research, Current Issues in Tourism, Journal of Destination Marketing & Management, Tourism Economics, Tourism Review, etc.) and several books, conference papers, and book chapters of well-known publishers such as Elsevier, Routledge, Edward Elgar, CABI, Emerald, Springer, etc. He has received several international research awards for his contribution to research in the field of tourism economics.

**Lombuso Shabalala** is a lecturer in Tourism Management with an experience in conducting research with local communities living adjacent to protected areas, associated adherence to traditional protocols and com-munity engagement and involvement. Her PhD examined perspectives on the role of cultural heritage tourism in community development in South Africa, using the Mapungubwe World Cultural Heritage Site as a case study. The focus was on how local communities and heritage custodians' can benefit from cultural heritage tourism in heritage sites, as it remains a concern, including the realisation of social and economic development in its true sense. The research required her to establish relationships with the National Park/heritage site management authority, the 06 descendants' groups led by traditional leaders and local people from different background in order to gain a deep understanding of the research problem and other related dynamics. Dr Shabalala joined University of Mpumalanga (UMP) in 2017 as a New Generation of Academics Programme (nGAP) lecturer in Tourism and Heritage, second cohort. She made history by becoming the first nGAP scholar at UMP to successfully complete the programme and graduate with a PhD. Her Doctor of Philosophy Degree was conferred by Wits University on the 14th of December 2020 under the Faculty of Science in the School of Geography, Archaeology & Environmental Studies. She graduated for her PGDip in the faculty of Education & a Master's degree and BTech Degree at University of Johannesburg in the School of Tourism & Hospitality.Her tertiary education started at Tshwane University of Technology, where she achieved a Diploma in Tourism Management. She also holds a Certificate in Entrepreneurship from Wits Business School. In her previous life, she worked as a travel consultant, Customer Service Agent for SA Airlink, Personal Assist to Heads of School, Events Organiser, Faculty Committee Coordinator, Work Integrated Learning Coordinator and Postgraduate administrator, just to name a few. She also facilitated Hospitality Service Excellence Module in the Department of Hospitality study pro-gram. In addition, she developed and facilitate a first-year tourism module in the Bachelor of Arts pro-gramme. Currently, she is full-time employed by the University of South Africa, in the Tourism Unit facilitating Cultural Tourism module. Her research areas of interest include tourism in a broader context, cultural heritage tourism, Tourism development, community engagement and development and events.

**Anna Sörensson** is Associate Professor in Business Administration at Mid Sweden University in Östersund, Sweden and at Inland Norway University in Rena, Norway. Anna Sörensson got her PhD in International marketing from Åbo Akademi University in Åbo, Finland. Her research focuses mainly on sustainability, value creation, tourism, entrepreneurship and large-scale industrial parks. She has published numerous articles, book chapters as well as books. She is research leader for several projects around regional development in semi-rural areas and industrial parks. She is currently engaged in various research initiatives within a Nordic network, focusing on the role of business networks and ecosystems.

**Bruno Barbosa Sousa** is Coordinating Professor of Marketing at Polytechnic Institute of Cávado and Ave (IPCA), Portugal and PhD in Marketing and Strategy in Universidade do Minho, Portugal. Head of Masters Program - Tourism Management and Marketing Tourism (IPCA); CiTUR – Center for Tourism Research, Development and Innovation and UNIAG research member. He has published in the Journal of Enterprising Communities, Tourism Management Perspectives, Current Issues in Tourism, Journal of Organizational Change Management, World Review of Entrepreneurship, Management and Sust. Development, among others.

**Desislava Stoilova** joined the Faculty of Economics at the South-West University "Neofit Rilski", Bulgaria as an assistant professor after graduating in 1999. In 2006 she obtained PhD in Finance with a thesis in the field of financial decentralization and intergovernmental fiscal relations. Since 2010, Desislava Stoilova has been an associate professor at the South-West University "Neofit Rilski". She teaches corporate finance and public finance and is involved in various research projects. Desislava Stoilova is the author of more than 90 publications designed to promote the application of effective methods and tools for financial management in the public and private sectors.

**Alexandru Tăbu că** is a member of higher education faculty since 2001, with teaching and research activities at bachelor and master levels, within the fields of "Computer Science" and "Economic Informatics". He authored over over 40 academic and research papers and books, participated in 13 national level R&D projects and 4 international ones as member/partner coordinator or project manager, participated as member/chair/president in over 21 international conferences, is member of the editorial board of the “Revista de Informatică Aplicată în Management” and the current Editor-in-Chief of the “Journal of Information Systems & Operations Management”. His expertise is focused on high-level programming languages (especially Java), development of web applications, databases management, computer networks, artificial intelligence, 3D modelling and printing, protection and security of electronic data. He also has an extensive expertise in the field of management, with activities and management roles within the private sector, both commercial and NGOs, as well as in the educational and research fields, serving in positions of specialized programs coordinator, project manager, expert consultant, IT director or Chief Information Officer with different entities. He is a graduate of the School of Computer Science for Business Management of the Romanian-American University, graduate of the School of Cybernetics, Statistics and Informatics of the University of Economic Studies of Bucharest, doctor of the University of Economic Studies and a graduate of postdoctoral studies at the Institute of World Economy of the Romanian Academy. Fluent in English and French, he has actively coordinated numerous technological, development and research/education projects with multiple international partners. He was IT Director of the Romanian-American between 2001 and 2020, coordinating IT&C resources management, infrastructure planning and development, IT&C applications development; IT&C security, surveillance, and electronic devices acquisitions/management. Alexandru became Dean of the School of Computer Science for Business Management at the Romanian-American University in 2020. Member of professional associations/organizations: IAKM – International Association for Knowledge Management IETI – International Engineering and Technology Institute CSTA – Computer Science Teacher Association World Academy of Science, Engineering and Technology Fields of interest/research: Cyber security Web applications development Computer Science applied in economics and management Artificial Intelligence Gathering, analyzing and storing electronic data 3D printing and modelling RPA Hardware robots and drones.

**Marco Tregua** is a PhD in Business Science since 2012 and he is an Associate Professor in International Management at the University of Naples Federico II and an Adjunct Professor at the University L'Orientale (Naples). His main research interests include service research, smart innovation, and sustainability management. He co-authored articles in Journal of Service Theory and Practice, International Journal of Management Reviews, and Journal of Business Ethics, among others. He authored various books on management and he took part to international conferences, as well as organized tracks in some of these conferences. He is reviewer for various international journals - including, Technological Forecasting and Social Change, AMS Review, and Journal of Business & Industrial Marketing. Is also Associate Editor at Journal of Knowledge Economy and Springer - Business and Economics.

# Index

## A



## B



## C



## D



## E



## G

## H



## I



## L



## O



## P



## R



## S



## T

## U



## V



## W

www.ingramcontent.com/pod-product-compliance
Lightning Source LLC
LaVergne TN
LVHW062115300926
849161LV00010B/2462